Mechanics of Corrugated and Composite Materials

Mechanics of Corrugated and Composite Materials

Editors

Tomasz Garbowski
Tomasz Gajewski
Jakub Krzysztof Grabski

MDPI • Basel • Beijing • Wuhan • Barcelona • Belgrade • Manchester • Tokyo • Cluj • Tianjin

Editors

Tomasz Garbowski
Department of Biosystems
Engineering
Poznan University of Life
Sciences
Poznan
Poland

Tomasz Gajewski
Institute of Structural
Analysis
Poznan University of
Technology
Poznan
Poland

Jakub Krzysztof Grabski
Institute of Applied
Mechanics
Poznan University of
Technology
Poznan
Poland

Editorial Office
MDPI
St. Alban-Anlage 66
4052 Basel, Switzerland

This is a reprint of articles from the Special Issue published online in the open access journal *Materials* (ISSN 1996-1944) (available at: www.mdpi.com/journal/materials/special_issues/Corrugated_Composite_Materials).

For citation purposes, cite each article independently as indicated on the article page online and as indicated below:

LastName, A.A.; LastName, B.B.; LastName, C.C. Article Title. *Journal Name* **Year**, *Volume Number*, Page Range.

ISBN 978-3-0365-4314-7 (Hbk)
ISBN 978-3-0365-4313-0 (PDF)

© 2022 by the authors. Articles in this book are Open Access and distributed under the Creative Commons Attribution (CC BY) license, which allows users to download, copy and build upon published articles, as long as the author and publisher are properly credited, which ensures maximum dissemination and a wider impact of our publications.

The book as a whole is distributed by MDPI under the terms and conditions of the Creative Commons license CC BY-NC-ND.

Contents

About the Editors vii

Preface to "Mechanics of Corrugated and Composite Materials" ix

Tomasz Garbowski
Mechanics of Corrugated and Composite Materials
Reprinted from: *Materials* **2022**, *15*, 1837, doi:10.3390/ma15051837 1

Anna Kobaszyńska-Twardowska, Jedrzej Łukasiewicz and Piotr W. Sielicki
Risk Management Model for Unmanned Aerial Vehicles during Flight Operations
Reprinted from: *Materials* **2022**, *15*, 2448, doi:10.3390/ma15072448 5

Adam Wosatko
Survey of Localizing Gradient Damage in Static and Dynamic Tension of Concrete
Reprinted from: *Materials* **2022**, *15*, 1875, doi:10.3390/ma15051875 19

Piotr W. Sielicki, James Keith Clutter, Wojciech Sumelka, Tomasz Gajewski, Michał Malendowski and Piotr Peksa et al.
Identification of Aluminium Powder Properties for Modelling Free Air Explosions
Reprinted from: *Materials* **2022**, *15*, 1294, doi:10.3390/ma15041294 53

Jacobs Somnic and Bruce W. Jo
Status and Challenges in Homogenization Methods for Lattice Materials
Reprinted from: *Materials* **2022**, *15*, 605, doi:10.3390/ma15020605 67

Michał Słonina, Dorota Dziurka, Marta Molińska-Glura and Jerzy Smardzewski
Influence of Impregnation with Modified Starch of a Paper Core on Bending of Wood-Based Honeycomb Panels in Changing Climatic Conditions
Reprinted from: *Materials* **2022**, *15*, 395, doi:10.3390/ma15010395 89

Marcin Chybiński and Łukasz Polus
Mechanical Behaviour of Aluminium-Timber Composite Connections with Screws and Toothed Plates
Reprinted from: *Materials* **2021**, *15*, 68, doi:10.3390/ma15010068 113

Berta Suarez, Luisa M. Muneta, Gregorio Romero and Juan D. Sanz-Bobi
Efficient Design of Thin Wall Seating Made of a Single Piece of Heavy-Duty Corrugated Cardboard
Reprinted from: *Materials* **2021**, *14*, 6645, doi:10.3390/ma14216645 133

Saewhan Kim, Laszlo Horvath, Jennifer D. Russell and Jonghun Park
Investigation of the Effect of Pallet Top-Deck Stiffness on Corrugated Box Compression Strength as a Function of Multiple Unit Load Design Variables
Reprinted from: *Materials* **2021**, *14*, 6613, doi:10.3390/ma14216613 165

Tomasz Garbowski, Anna Knitter-Piatkowska and Aleksander Marek
New Edge Crush Test Configuration Enhanced with Full-Field Strain Measurements
Reprinted from: *Materials* **2021**, *14*, 5768, doi:10.3390/ma14195768 181

Damian Mrówczyński, Tomasz Garbowski and Anna Knitter-Piatkowska
Estimation of the Compressive Strength of Corrugated Board Boxes with Shifted Creases on the Flaps
Reprinted from: *Materials* **2021**, *14*, 5181, doi:10.3390/ma14185181 199

Zbigniew Pozorski, Jolanta Pozorska, Ireneusz Kreja and Łukasz Smakosz
On Wrinkling in Sandwich Panels with an Orthotropic Core
Reprinted from: *Materials* **2021**, *14*, 5043, doi:10.3390/ma14175043 217

Tomasz Garbowski, Anna Knitter-Piatkowska and Damian Mrówczyński
Numerical Homogenization of Multi-Layered Corrugated Cardboard with Creasing or Perforation
Reprinted from: *Materials* **2021**, *14*, 3786, doi:10.3390/ma14143786 235

Łukasz Smakosz, Ireneusz Kreja and Zbigniew Pozorski
Edgewise Compressive Behavior of Composite Structural Insulated Panels with Magnesium Oxide Board Facings
Reprinted from: *Materials* **2021**, *14*, 3030, doi:10.3390/ma14113030 255

Tomasz Garbowski, Jakub Krzysztof Grabski and Aleksander Marek
Full-Field Measurements in the Edge Crush Test of a Corrugated Board—Analytical and Numerical Predictive Models
Reprinted from: *Materials* **2021**, *14*, 2840, doi:10.3390/ma14112840 277

Tomasz Garbowski and Tomasz Gajewski
Determination of Transverse Shear Stiffness of Sandwich Panels with a Corrugated Core by Numerical Homogenization
Reprinted from: *Materials* **2021**, *14*, 1976, doi:10.3390/ma14081976 293

About the Editors

Tomasz Garbowski

Tomasz Garbowski, Ph.D., Eng., is currently working as an associate professor at the Faculty of Environmental and Mechanical Engineering at the Poznan University of Life Sciences. In 2010, he obtained a doctorate at the Politecnico di Milano at the Faculty of Mechanical Engineering. In 2020, he obtained a postdoctoral degree at the Poznań University of Technology at the Faculty of Civil and Transport Engineering. Prof. Dr. Tomasz Garbowski is an expert in the field of engineering structures, and he has over 20 years of experience in numerical modeling and optimization of various structures. At the same time, following the path of science and technology, he managed (1) to develop advanced, theoretical computational techniques and algorithms for estimating the compressive strength of various structures and (2) to design/patent several laboratory devices. In his professional career, he was associated with the Poznan University of Technology, Lund University and Politecnico di Milano. He shared his knowledge and experience at over 50 national and international conferences. He is also the author/co-author of over 50 publications in international journals.

Tomasz Gajewski

Tomasz Gajewski, Ph.D., Eng., works at the Poznan University of Technology as an assistant professor in the Institute of Structural Analysis. In 2011, he graduated from this university in the field of construction, specializing in structural engineering. In 2018, he defended his doctorate at Poznan University of Technology in biomechanics. His doctoral dissertation won the competition in computational mechanics for doctoral dissertations announced by the Polish Society of Computer Methods in Mechanics. He has presented at many scientific conferences in the field of applied mechanics and mechanics of materials. He is a co-author of nearly 30 peer-reviewed articles published in prestigious journals, including the {International Journal of Solids and Structures} and the {International Journal of Impact Engineering}. He is a member of the Polish Society of Computer Methods in Mechanics and the International Association of Protective Structures. His professional interests are related to applied computational mechanics; numerical methods; and nonlinear mechanics of materials, including composites.

Jakub Krzysztof Grabski

Jakub Krzysztof Grabski, Ph.D., Eng., is employed as an assistant professor at the Institute of Applied Mechanics, Poznan University of Technology, Poznań, Poland. He holds a Ph.D. in mechanical engineering, awarded in 2016. His research interests include computational mechanics, corrugated cardboard, fluid mechanics, heat transfer, bioengineering, meshless methods and inverse problems. He has published more than 25 papers in peer-reviewed journals and around 20 conference papers. Among the awards he has won, one can distinguish the Scholarship of the Minister of Science and Higher Education (Poland) for outstanding young scientists 2020 and START 2018—stipend for young researchers below 30 from the Foundation for Polish Science. Furthermore, he is a member of the Polish Society of Theoretical and Applied Mechanics and the Polish Association for Computational Mechanics.

Preface to "Mechanics of Corrugated and Composite Materials"

One of the challenges in research by modern engineers is the acquisition of new materials for the creation of various constructions in order to improve their properties, including mechanical ones. One possible way to achieve this goal is through composite materials. Moreover, the use of such materials in various real constructions leads to material, cost, energy and environmental savings, e.g. by reducing the weight of the products, significant reductions in fuel consumption, exhaust emissions and costs during transport can be achieved. Therefore, composite materials are of great practical importance, as seen in various applications in the automotive and aerospace industries, building construction and many other fields.

Composite materials are inhomogeneous materials consisting of at least two various materials of different properties. Considering the construction of the composites, one can distinguish some typical examples, e.g., fibrous composites, when one component of the composite is made of fibers and the other is called a matrix. Another kinds of composite materials are sandwich or layered plates, in which their components are arranged in layers. Both of them have a wide range of applications in various engineering fields. On the other hand, there are multiple methods for analyzing the mechanical properties of these composites, including experimental, analytical or numerical studies. Corrugated cardboard, commonly used in the packaging industry, is a special type of corrugated material. In the case of corrugated cardboard boxes, the key is to obtain a durable and stable structure with a relatively low weight.

Another important issue is the modeling of structures made of composite or corrugated materials. Their specific design and heterogeneity make it very expensive to build a complete model while maintaining all the details and is thus also very time-consuming. Therefore, both the material of individual components (layers) and the cross-sectional geometry are usually a priori homogenized to simplify and speed up the calculations. The simplification should not, however, distort the results that would be obtained using the full model. Therefore, the selection of an appropriate homogenization method is often a key issue when analyzing structures made of corrugated or composite materials.

This Special Issue is devoted to the mechanics of composite materials, particularly corrugated materials, e.g., corrugated cardboard or multilayer boards with a soft core. In addition, the articles published in this Special Issue of *Materials* present different approaches to the research and application of various computational methods and the homogenization of selected composite materials.

Finally, we take this opportunity to express our most profound appreciation to the MDPI Book staff; the editorial team of *Materials*, especially Ms. Daisy Liu, the managing editor of this Special Issue; all of the authors; and all of the professional reviewers.

Tomasz Garbowski, Tomasz Gajewski, and Jakub Krzysztof Grabski
Editors

Editorial

Mechanics of Corrugated and Composite Materials

Tomasz Garbowski

Department of Biosystems Engineering, Faculty of Environmental and Mechanical Engineering, Poznan University of Life Sciences, Wojska Polskiego 50, 60-627 Poznan, Poland; tomasz.garbowski@up.poznan.pl

Citation: Garbowski, T. Mechanics of Corrugated and Composite Materials. *Materials* 2022, 15, 1837. https://doi.org/10.3390/ma15051837

Received: 21 February 2022
Accepted: 26 February 2022
Published: 1 March 2022

Publisher's Note: MDPI stays neutral with regard to jurisdictional claims in published maps and institutional affiliations.

Copyright: © 2022 by the author. Licensee MDPI, Basel, Switzerland. This article is an open access article distributed under the terms and conditions of the Creative Commons Attribution (CC BY) license (https://creativecommons.org/licenses/by/4.0/).

The main aim of this Special Issue in Materials was to collect interesting and innovative works on the mechanics of corrugated and composite materials. Corrugated core materials are increasingly used as structural materials or load-bearing elements in a variety of lightweight engineering structures. Due to the specific composition of the composite layers of corrugated materials, the ratio of their load capacity to the weight of sections is much higher than in the case of traditional solid sections. In addition, the geometries of corrugated structures proposed by scientists from around the world are constantly modified to improve their mechanical properties. Composite materials, due to their unique design properties, can be used in many areas to solve difficult problems where traditional materials often fail.

In this Special Issue, the most interesting research papers on various aspects of this broad research field have been collected. From theoretical issues related to the influence of transversal shear on the parameters of corrugated cardboard, to experimental and numerical analysis of an aluminum structure protecting against the effects of an explosion. By enabling scientists and engineers to present the latest knowledge on advances in theoretical, experimental and computational approaches for corrugated and composite materials, it was possible to present a very comprehensive set of research papers.

In research work [1], the authors were focused on the numerical homogenization of plates with a periodic core. The periodicity of the soft core in this case was related to the sinusoidal shape of the middle layer of the multilayer structure made of cardboard. In these types of plates, the transversal shear has a very large influence on their mechanics. A traditional assumption based on the Kirchhoff–Love theory fails and the Reissner–Mindlin theory must be used. The authors presented an extension of the existing homogenization method based on the elastic equilibrium of the strain energy by including the effects related to transversal shear. This method uses the principles of finite element modeling; however, it does not require any formal numerical analysis. The heart of this approach is the matrix linking the effective strains with displacements in the outer nodes of the representative volumetric element (RVE), and the stiffness matrix of the entire RVE condensed to these nodes.

In article [2], the authors were focused on the mechanics of corrugated cardboard. The aim of the work was to derive simplified predictive models to identify the total stiffness and compressive strength of corrugated board samples. The authors used a non-contact method of measuring deformation on the sample surface, based on virtual optical strain gauges, thus eliminating the unreliable measurement of displacement in the standard edge crush test. Video extensometry was used to collect measurements from the outer surfaces of the sample on both sides. As a representative example in this study, an unsymmetrical five-layer sample with two corrugated layers was used. Reliable determination of the stiffness of multilayer structures made of thin panels is not an easy task because buckling of the panels quickly occurs in this type of section and must be taken into account in the calculations. The authors proposed a very effective analytical model for determining the compressive strength of corrugated board based on video extensometric measurements and taking into account preliminary buckling.

The edge compression response was also analyzed in paper [3], which investigated a composite structural insulating panel (CSIP) with magnesium oxide plate facings. The authors studied a novel multifunctional sandwich panel introduced into residential construction as part of wall, floor and roof assemblies. The study was conducted to build a computational tool for the reliable prediction of CSIP failure modes subjected to various axial loads, both concentric and eccentric. The paper proposed an advanced numerical model (based on the finite element method), which takes into account geometric and material nonlinearities, and also takes into account the effect of bimodularity of the material. Additionally, the model was verified by means of laboratory tests on small-scale CSIP samples with three different slenderness ratios and full-size panels loaded with three different eccentricity values.

Numerical homogenization was also used in [4]. Since homogenization allows for a significant simplification of the computational models [1] and, at the same time, for a very accurate representation of complex plate cross-sections [1], the application of such techniques to the corrugated cardboard packaging becomes a very urgent task. As soon as the homogenized models begin to take into account the creases, cuts and other local effects of the plates, this technique begins to take on a very practical character. The authors used a very practical application of homogenization (already presented in work [1]) extended by also modeling cases containing all local effects resulting from production and processing. The presented approach can be successfully used to model the smear degradation in a finite element or to define the deterioration of stiffnesses on the crease or perforation line.

On the other hand, article [5] presented the important issue of thin facing wrinkling in sandwich panels with a soft core. The local loss of stability in thin facings obviously reduces the load-bearing capacity of the composite panels. Therefore, it is very important to correctly define under what conditions and for what loads this effect is activated in real structures. The paper compares the classic solutions to the problem of facing instability based on an eluted homogeneous and isotropic half-space (i.e., the soft core of the plate). The paper also discusses the use of an orthotropic core, in line with the classic solution of an isotropic core.

Corrugated board was analyzed again in [6]. The authors focused on the load-bearing capacity of corrugated cardboard packaging in a specific configuration of packaging flaps. The raised problem is particularly important in the corrugated board packaging industry, where more and more advanced numerical tools are used to design and estimate the load capacity of its products. Therefore, numerical analyses are becoming a common standard in this branch of production. Because the experimental results showed a significant reduction in the static load-bearing capacity of the package in the case of shifted flap creases, the study investigated the impact of the specific flap configuration on the strength of the box. An updated analytical and numerical approach was used to predict package strength with different flap offsets. The results obtained by the model presented in this paper were also verified with satisfactory compliance with the experimental data.

Paper [7] presented an issue that was partially discussed already in previous works in this series, namely plate edge crushing [2,3] and the use of optical extensometers [2] to measure displacements and deformations on the external surfaces of the tested samples. As is known in the plate edge crush tests, the biggest obstacle is obtaining a reliable measurement of displacements and deformations in the sample. Therefore, the use of video extensometry allowed the authors to develop a method that not only allows the reliable measurement of displacements, but also the identification of the full orthotropic stiffness matrix of the material. This was achieved through the innovative use of two samples: (a) traditional and cut across the wave direction of the corrugated core, and (b) cut at an angle of $45°$. The obtained results were finally compared with the results obtained in the homogenization procedure [1,4] of the corrugated board cross-section.

Corrugated cardboard was also analyzed in two further studies [8,9]. In work [8], the authors focused their attention on the palletization of corrugated cardboard packaging, while in [9], on a rather unusual corrugated cardboard product, i.e., furniture. The first article examined the effect of the stiffness of the top deck of the pallet on the compressive strength of a corrugated board box as a function of the initial thickness of the top deck, the wood grade of the pallet, the size of the box and the grade of the cardboard. The second article focused on optimizing the stool structure by removing material zones in places where the fewest stresses occur. Interestingly, the work [9] also used homogenization methods similar to those presented in [1,4]. The presented results demonstrate the utility of homogenization techniques as an aid in the design process of whole structures made of corrugated cardboard.

A slightly different issue was presented in [10], where the authors focused on the construction of connections in a composite beam made of aluminum and wood. The load capacity, the type of failure and the load slip reaction of reinforced and unreinforced screw connections were examined. It has also been proven that the tested stiffness and strength of connections can be practically used for the correct design and numerical modeling of aluminum–wooden composite beams with reinforced bolted connections.

The topic related to the mechanics of paper and cardboard also appeared in [11], where the authors presented the effect of impregnation of the paper core with acetylated starch on the mechanical properties and energy absorbed in the three-point bending test of wood-based honeycomb panels, under changing temperature and relative air humidity conditions. The paper presented the results of extensive research on materials, various combinations of coatings, core cell geometry and different qualities of cardboard. The results of the experiment and their statistical analysis showed a significant relationship between the impregnation of paper with modified starch and its mechanical properties. In general, this observation obviously allows for the optimization of furniture boards and their further lightweighting.

Selected homogenization methods used for corrugated core materials presented in previous studies [1,4,9] have been systematically summarized in [12]. The homogenization methods presented in this work refer to materials with a lattice core, but their use for materials with a corrugated core is also possible. In both cases, structures made of plates containing structural cores are both light and very stiff. Without the use of homogenization, only conventional methodologies remain based on numerical approaches such as FEA (finite element analysis) and high-performance computational tools, including ANSYS and ABAQUS. However, they require a high computational power in each case of modeling complex core geometries. That is why it is so important to correctly apply the appropriate homogenization method to simplify the model and speed up the calculations, while maintaining the maximum fidelity of the simplified model in relation to the real model.

Last but not least, article [13] in our Special Issue presented the method of modeling the combustion of a popular material—aluminum. The authors conducted a study of aluminum powder in order to isolate the aluminum combustion process and determine an adequate representation of this process. The charges of various masses were investigated, determining the size of the cloud and previously unpublished results of the component ratio in the Al and air mixture. The obtained results of the numerical analysis as well as those obtained from the experimental tests were in good agreement.

To summarize, the problems related to the mechanics of corrugated and composite materials discussed in this Special Issue do not exhaust the topic but are only a small part of this broad topic. All the presented works follow the trend of modern scientific research on materials with a soft core (corrugated, lattice, etc.) and composites, as well as the practical use of homogenization techniques of structures made of these materials.

Funding: This research received no external funding.

Acknowledgments: The guest editors would first like to thank the in-house editor for her inexhaustible diligence and constant support in the creation of this Special Issue. We would like to express our gratitude to all the authors who contributed to the creation of the Special Issue through their valuable scientific research, as well as to the reviewers whose constructive comments and thoughtful suggestions made the quality of the presented works of the highest level.

Conflicts of Interest: The author declares no conflict of interest.

References

1. Garbowski, T.; Gajewski, T. Determination of Transverse Shear Stiffness of Sandwich Panels with a Corrugated Core by Numerical Homogenization. *Materials* **2021**, *14*, 1976. [CrossRef] [PubMed]
2. Garbowski, T.; Grabski, J.K.; Marek, A. Full-Field Measurements in the Edge Crush Test of a Corrugated Board—Analytical and Numerical Predictive Models. *Materials* **2021**, *14*, 2840. [CrossRef] [PubMed]
3. Smakosz, Ł.; Kreja, I.; Pozorski, Z. Edgewise Compressive Behavior of Composite Structural Insulated Panels with Magnesium Oxide Board Facings. *Materials* **2021**, *14*, 3030. [CrossRef] [PubMed]
4. Garbowski, T.; Knitter-Piątkowska, A.; Mrówczyński, D. Numerical Homogenization of Multi-Layered Corrugated Cardboard with Creasing or Perforation. *Materials* **2021**, *14*, 3786. [CrossRef] [PubMed]
5. Pozorski, Z.; Pozorska, J.; Kreja, I.; Smakosz, Ł. On Wrinkling in Sandwich Panels with an Orthotropic Core. *Materials* **2021**, *14*, 5043. [CrossRef] [PubMed]
6. Mrówczyński, D.; Garbowski, T.; Knitter-Piątkowska, A. Estimation of the Compressive Strength of Corrugated Board Boxes with Shifted Creases on the Flaps. *Materials* **2021**, *14*, 5181. [CrossRef] [PubMed]
7. Garbowski, T.; Knitter-Piątkowska, A.; Marek, A. New Edge Crush Test Configuration Enhanced with Full-Field Strain Measurements. *Materials* **2021**, *14*, 5768. [CrossRef] [PubMed]
8. Kim, S.; Horvath, L.; Russell, J.D.; Park, J. Investigation of the Effect of Pallet Top-Deck Stiffness on Corrugated Box Compression Strength as a Function of Multiple Unit Load Design Variables. *Materials* **2021**, *14*, 6613. [CrossRef] [PubMed]
9. Suarez, B.; Muneta, L.M.; Romero, G.; Sanz-Bobi, J.D. Efficient Design of Thin Wall Seating Made of a Single Piece of Heavy-Duty Corrugated Cardboard. *Materials* **2021**, *14*, 6645. [CrossRef] [PubMed]
10. Chybiński, M.; Polus, Ł. Mechanical Behaviour of Aluminium-Timber Composite Connections with Screws and Toothed Plates. *Materials* **2022**, *15*, 68. [CrossRef] [PubMed]
11. Słonina, M.; Dziurka, D.; Molińska-Glura, M.; Smardzewski, J. Influence of Impregnation with Modified Starch of a Paper Core on Bending of Wood-Based Honeycomb Panels in Changing Climatic Conditions. *Materials* **2022**, *15*, 395. [CrossRef] [PubMed]
12. Somnic, J.; Jo, B.W. Status and Challenges in Homogenization Methods for Lattice Materials. *Materials* **2022**, *15*, 605. [CrossRef] [PubMed]
13. Sielicki, P.W.; Clutter, J.K.; Sumelka, W.; Gajewski, T.; Malendowski, M.; Peksa, P.; Studziński, R. Identification of Aluminium Powder Properties for Modelling Free Air Explosions. *Materials* **2022**, *15*, 1294. [CrossRef] [PubMed]

Article

Risk Management Model for Unmanned Aerial Vehicles during Flight Operations

Anna Kobaszyńska-Twardowska *, Jędrzej Łukasiewicz and Piotr W. Sielicki

Faculty of Civil and Transport Engineering, Poznań University of Technology, Piotrowo 3, 60-965 Poznań, Poland; jedrzej.lukasiewicz@put.poznan.pl (J.Ł.); piotr.sielicki@put.poznan.pl (P.W.S.)
* Correspondence: anna.kobaszynska-twardowska@put.poznan.pl

Abstract: Risk management and uncertainty models are practised in all branches of transport. Although unmanned aerial vehicles (UAVs) constitute a branch of the industry rather than transport as a whole, their development is oriented toward increasingly more serious applications involving the transport of goods and people. The constantly growing number of operations employing UAVs requires not only identification of hazard sources or risk assessment recommended by the applicable regulations, but also comprehensive risk management. In order to develop a systematic approach to risk management for air operations of UAVs, the classic risk management method can be used. This work proposes a novel multi-criteria risk model that may serve as the basis for further activities aimed at developing a risk management method for this domain. The model was based on six criteria and validated using a virtual route to risk assessment and valuation.

Keywords: air operation safety; flying risk; risk management; unmanned aerial vehicles

1. Introduction

Due to their characteristics, the use of UAVs is increasingly common in industry, agriculture, construction, photography, and many other areas of human activity [1–5]. The use of UAVs in the energy production industry is also becoming more and more common. UAVs can be used, for example, to measure the amount of coal extracted in opencast mines, to study the composition of smoke emitted by power plants, and to monitor the technical condition of electricity transmission lines. In this context, the UAV is a platform for transporting the measuring device. Such a device can be an RGB camera, LIDAR, or an air quality measuring device.

An example environment that includes selected threads during use of UAVs is shown in Figure 1.

Figure 1. Application of UAVs and selected threads for consideration.

Every transport system functions in conditions of uncertainty that threaten the accomplishment of its objectives related to infrastructure and transport organisation. Risk management is aimed at identifying events that may affect the accomplishment process [5]. Risk management has been practised in an unofficial manner for a very long time; events such as transportation, industrial, and economic disasters contributed to its systematisation, and then risks started to be dealt with in an organised and consistent manner in different areas of human activity [6]. This has led to the development and application of various methods, techniques, procedures, and tools classified under a common name: 'risk management' [7]. Many studies have examined risk management in chemical plants, nuclear power plants, and transport systems; this reflects that these areas generate a considerable number of hazards [7]. Generating hazards in various systems is one of the reasons why safety and risk management procedures were developed by entities involved in process execution in transport systems. Risk management models in transport systems can be found in studies [6–17], among others. Risk management should be treated as one of the tools of safety management systems [16]. Every entity managing elements of a transport system should also provide traffic safety management, ensuring observation and assessment of the number of accidents, casualties, and persons injured in accidents. Moreover, such entities should provide the possibility of completing a transport operation with the lowest risk possible. The path to such a state of safety leads to the development and skilful application of risk management methods [18–20]. Unmanned aerial vehicles (UAVs), i.e., multirotors, planes, and helicopters, are devices that—due to their functional characteristics—are used on an increasingly wide scale in different areas of human activity. Potential uses of UVAs were presented in [21–23].

The growing number of air operations that use UAVs entails a growing number of adverse events involving such vehicles. For this reason, work is underway to increase safety levels whilst operating UVAs. In study [24], the authors suggested a methodology for computing the probability of impact on 3D infrastructures, such as buildings, in the event of a UAV failure during flight. The generation of impact probability maps on the infrastructures is based on Monte Carlo simulations involving a dynamic model of a fixed-wing UAV. In another study, we find an integrated risk assessment method that considers probability and severity models of a UAV impacting people and vehicles on the ground. By introducing the gravity model, density of population and traffic are estimated on a finer scale, which enables more accurate risk assessment. The 3D risk-based path planning problem is first formulated as a special minimum-cost flow problem [25]. Study [26] proposes a framework for computing the risk of collision with an obstacle based on a UAV's predicted trajectory, proximity to static and dynamic obstacles, sub-system state-of-health, and external wind conditions. The problem of safety in UAV operation was described in works [27–30], among others. In addition to scientific studies, there are also legal provisions that apply to UAVs, which are presented below.

The purpose of the article is to present a component of risk management for UAV flights, multi-criteria proposal, and a risk model developed based on a generalised risk model in the context of the applicable regulations.

2. Flight Categories and Assumed Risk Level

Within the European Union, flights of each UAV type take place based on the following EU regulations:

- Commission Delegated Regulation (EU) 2019/945 [31],
- Commission Delegated Regulation (EU) 2020/1058 [32],
- Commission Implementing Regulation (EU) 2019/947 [33].

These regulations define UAV classes and stipulate the rules and procedures related to the operation of these aircraft. According to [31,32], we distinguish seven UAV classes (C0–C6), depending on their equipment, weight, and forward speed in level flight. The categories on which the manner of risk management depends are [34]:

1. OPEN,
2. SPECIFIC,
3. CERTIFIED.

Air operations in the OPEN category may be conducted with an aircraft with maximum take-off mass (MTOM)—understood as the sum of the platform mass and the load mass—of less than 25 kg. The flight takes place within the visual line of sight (VLOS) and within 120 m from the closest point of the surface of the earth. The task of the remote pilot is to keep a safe distance from people [33].

The OPEN category is a non-significant or widely acceptable risk area that does not require risk-mitigating actions [33]. This is due to the low take-off mass, which does not exceed 250 g and 4 kg for subcategories A1 and A2, respectively. The low take-off mass generates low kinetic energy (e.g., for A1, $E_K = 1/2\ mv^2$) during an adverse event such as the UAV striking a person's head. Moreover, in subcategory A2, flights may take place at a distance of 30 m from uninvolved persons or, in the case of low-speed-mode flights, at a distance of 5 m from them. Subcategory A3, which is also part of the OPEN category, is characterised by high take-off mass, but the pilot must conduct air operations over an area where it can reasonably be expected that, under normal circumstances, no uninvolved persons will be endangered, and at a distance of at least 150 m from residential, commercial, industrial, or recreational areas. According to the applicable regulations, the operator is not required to perform a risk assessment in this category of flights [33].

In the case of the SPECIFIC category, the risk related to the performance of the flight is tolerable, i.e., the transport aircraft may be operated, but under certain conditions [33]. This means that an authorisation is required for the performance of such flights, which must take place in accordance with the restrictions included in the operational authorisation or in the standard scenario defined by the legislative body. Flights may take place in compliance with other rules, provided that the UAV holds a light UAS operator certificate (LUC) with appropriate privileges. Authorisation to execute a mission can be obtained from the competent aviation authority in the given country [31]. In Poland, this authority is the Civil Aviation Authority. There are three ways of obtaining an operational authorisation.

The first consists in the pilot making a declaration that they will conduct flights in compliance with the principles of conducting flights stipulated in the so-called standard scenarios. It is assumed that if the pilot conducts the flight in compliance with the principles defined in the standard scenario, the risk related to the performance of the flight is acceptable. Currently, two standard scenarios have been formulated within the European Union. Additionally, in Poland, so-called "national standard scenarios" apply, which are valid for flights conducted in VLOS and BVLOS (beyond visual line of sight), for aircraft masses of up to 4 kg and 25 kg, and for the following UAV types: multirotors, planes, or helicopters. The remote pilot has a total of eight scenarios, i.e., eight different variants of conducting the flight, at their disposal.

The second method of obtaining the operational authorisation is to obtain the appropriate certificate (in the case of the EU, an LUC). The certificate is granted to the operator—understood to be a natural or legal person operating an aircraft—after they pass an inspection by the competent aviation authority in the given country. The certificate authorises the operator to make independent decisions about conducting a flight based on risk assessment.

The third way of obtaining the authorisation, in the case of executing flight missions in a manner not described in the standard scenarios, is to submit a request to the competent aviation authority to issue the authorisation, along with the terms of conducting the flight based on a risk assessment performed independently by the operator. The currently recommended risk assessment method is that developed by the Joint Authorities for Rulemaking of Unmanned Systems (JARUS). The method is called the Specific Operations Risk Assessment (SORA) [34]. It is a very complex and time-consuming process that also requires access to a broad spectrum of technical information to which only the unmanned platform manufacturer has access.

The SORA method is a multi-stage method UAV flight risk assessment method. This assessment requires, inter alia: description of the concept of the operation (CONOPS), in

which the drone operator, preparing for the mission, must describe all the details related to the flight, such as:
- List of UAVs used for the planned operation,
- Competences of the personnel involved in the operation,
- List of names of pilots and support staff,
- Procedures that will be applied in performing the mission,
- Indication of health requirements, which must be met by the personnel performing the mission,
- Declaration of the type of operation, including the purpose, method of performing the operation, restrictions due to environmental or legal conditions, scope of the operation (VLOS or BVLOS), indication of the area over which the operation will be performed together with the population density assessment, description of the so-called risk buffers, and description of the measures taken to ensure safety during the operation,
- Description of the aircraft technical data such as: aircraft size, mass, on-board equipment in the subsystem ensuring flight safety, limitations due to communication range or weather conditions, resistance to precipitation, conditions of minimum visibility, and conditions related to ambient temperature,
- Information regarding to the method of controlling UAV, including the method of controlling the ship and technical parameters of the Ground Control Station,
- Indication of the communication methods with air traffic control,
- Indication of the ways of avoiding collisions with other aircraft, including description of the systems used to achieve this, such as for example ADS-B,
- Description of the ground equipment and description of the fallback procedures.

The second step is to determine the intrinsic Ground Risk Class (GRC). This coefficient is determined on the basis of the assessment of the characteristic dimensions of the aircraft, such as its size, mass, and kinetic energy of potential collision with the ground. The next step is to define the so-called Final GRC of the impact hazard on the ground. In some cases, the GRC value, determined in step 2, may be so high that the resulting safety objectives to be achieved are too demanding for the operator. Therefore, to lower the GRC, one can either change the CONOPS or implement mitigation strategies. Consideration of measures, methods, and features of the system and mission that can positively affect the final GRC value can reduce the actual GRC value. For the reduction of GRC, for example, a parachute system can be used. The fourth step of the SORA assessment is the Determination of the Initial Air Risk Class (ARC). The airborne risk class depends on the determination of the chance of a collision with a manned aircraft. There are four classes, which can be distinguished from one with no risk of collision to one where the probability of collision is high. Another step in the SORA analysis is the application of measures at the strategic level and the definition of the end-risk ARC. Someone must use this step if the risk assessed in step 4th is too high. At this point, strategies, procedures, and constraints are applied to reduce the likelihood of a potential collision before the UAV takes off. The sixth step in the SORA analysis is the definition of the Tactical Mitigation Performance Requirement (TMPR) or the definition of Robustness Levels. In order to minimize the risk of an airborne collision with another aircraft, it is possible to apply tactical measures to reduce this risk. This stage defines the goals to be achieved at different levels of solidity so that a potential meeting in the air does not end in a collision. The seventh step is to organize the Final Specific Assurance and Integrity Levels (SAIL). The SAIL parameter consolidates the GRC risk with the ARC risk and allows to define the requirements for the operation. SAIL is a measure of the level of control over the security of a mission. SAIL is a requirement for a specific concept of operation. SAIL represents the level of confidence in the control of operations. The eighth step of the SORA assessment is the identification of safety objectives at the operational level; the so called Operational Safety Objectives (OSO). This step uses SAIL to assess the safety barriers and to determine their robustness. There are four grades of quality: optional, low robustness, medium robustness, and high robustness. The next step is to address the risk of losing control of the operation, resulting in the violation of adjacent areas on the ground and in the adjacent airspace. These areas may vary according to the different phases of flight. Accurately defining the adjacent area is the job of the operator. The adjacent area is assessed on the basis of whether the failure of the UAV could lead to the collapse of the UAV outside the operational area, assessment of the UAV systems in terms of their reliable maintenance of the UAV in the area of operation, or other threats, the activation of which may lead to the UAV's escape outside the operational area. Once the assessments have been made in accordance with the procedure outlined above, the analysis document must be reviewed by the aviation authority, who can authorize the air operation. Regardless of the fact that this method is recommended by the Polish airspace authorities, the described level of complication of the SORA method and the evaluation model proposed by the authors described in the paper clearly show that the method proposed in the work is easier, does not require the assessment of so many parameters, and is much less time-consuming, which in the case of frequent unmanned missions is extremely important for the operator of aviation.

Article 11 of Regulation 2019/947 presents the procedure for risk assessment and allows for the development of a new, different operational risk assessment model. That model must include the following elements [33]:

- Description of the characteristics of the planned air operation,
- Description of the proposed adequate operational safety measures,
- Identification of the risks of operation on the ground and in the air,
- Risk-mitigating measures.

Flights in the CERTIFIED category occur with the use of UAVs certified based on Article 40 of Commission Delegated Regulation (EU) 2019/945. This category includes flights over assemblies of people, flights by UAVs designed for transporting people, and flights for transporting dangerous goods.

Regardless of the flight category, the risk level should be monitored. Control of the assessment area reduces the likelihood of the occurrence of adverse events (events which may lead to losses), but also facilitates rapid response if such an event does indeed occur. This is why the authors propose a risk model that makes it possible to assess the risk level for each type of flight.

In just the same manner as any other user of a transport system, a UAV operator should assess their physical and mental state before each air operation, and should also check and identify obstacles as well as potential sources of radio signal interference. Moreover, they should ensure an adequate safety level at the take-off and landing sites, including a reserve landing site. Therefore, from the point of view of safety engineering, the operator is responsible for assessing the risk [35]. The principles of the integrated risk management method based on the classical approach integrate two phases:

- Risk assessment, and,
- Responding to risk.

3. A New Risk Assessment Model

The nature of the organization and the goal it wants to achieve are factors that determine the choice of a risk management method. Within the framework of the classic risk management method, which the authors modelled, their components can be distinguished. There are two components in the risk assessment phase:

- Risk analysis,
- Risk evaluation.

The first component—risk analysis—is the systematic use of all available information in the indicated area of analysis, in order to:

- Identify threats—this is a process of systematic procedure to identify threats, which, as a result of their activation, may cause losses in the indicated area of analysis,
- Estimate and prioritize the risks identified in the analysis area—defining the value of the risk measure and assigning it to one of the risk levels of the model used.

As part of the risk assessment phase, the UAV operator should analyse the risk by characterizing the area and identifying potential hazard sources [33]. Next, they should assess the level of risk for the air operation by selecting the appropriate model and measures. The choice of the risk models and measures depends on the degree of complexity, detail, and the amount of information required and used [35–39]. In transport systems, the selection of the method depends on a number of factors, the scope of the process to be executed (e.g., transportation, infrastructure management, and maintenance), the availability of information on possible adverse events, and the experience of the people performing the assessment. An air operation must be preceded by an analysis of potential hazards that could lead to an air accident. There are five sources of potential hazards that, if activated, may cause a loss of control over the UAV, which may result in a UAV striking a person or object on the ground, or even another flying an unmanned or manned aircraft [39]. The five categories of hazard sources, as well as their respective contributing factors, are:

(1) Human error (i.e., human factors in aviation). This problem has been known and studied since the Second World War. Contributors to human error include:
   (a) Communication errors that could lead to a flight team not having full situational awareness;
   (b) Routine errors resulting from long-term aviation practice combined with loss of awareness of existing hazards, caused by frequently repeated activities;
   (c) Inappropriate or insufficient training of personnel;
   (d) Distraction resulting from disruption, confusion, or chaos, etc.;
   (e) Lack of team cooperation due to the lack of a sense of community purpose or communication style;
   (f) Fatigue caused by excessive working hours;
   (g) Lack of an appropriate tool to perform the task, i.e., inadequate aircraft to perform the planned mission;
   (h) Pressure from supervisors to fly in inappropriate conditions;
   (i) Insufficient assertiveness to refuse to perform a potentially hazardous task;
   (j) Stress caused by inadequate preparation for flight;
   (k) Carelessness, incorrect assessment of the situation, or incorrect assessment of the possible consequences of an air accident; and
(2) Failure to comply with procedures.
(3) UAS failure. Each aircraft is subject to pre-flight inspection in accordance with the procedures. However, each aircraft, as a technical facility, may fail during flight. The consequence of a failure in flight is almost always the fall of the craft to the ground.
(4) The appearance of another manned or unmanned aircraft on a collision course. Another aircraft may appear in the airspace in which flight operations are performed. An unexpected event may lead to errors in piloting and, consequently, to the fall of the aircraft.
(5) Rapid deterioration of weather conditions during the flight.
(6) Deterioration in the performance of systems used in steering or navigation, such as GPS. Solar activity is a source of high-intensity electromagnetic radiation emissions. The radiation emitted towards the Earth is usually absorbed by the atmosphere. Therefore, this radiation does not pose a threat to the operation of electronic systems used on board aircraft. However, if an electromagnetic pulse is too intense to be absorbed by the atmosphere, it will reach the Earth and may disrupt the operation of electronic systems. The consequence would be the loss of the ability to read the position of the aircraft from the navigation system, which may lead to an air accident. Electronic systems' performance may also deteriorate as a result of flying in the vicinity of devices emitting electromagnetic radiation. Such devices include BTS stations used in mobile telephony and high-voltage lines.

The schematic diagram of the risk analysis and assessment using the developed model is presented in Figure 2.

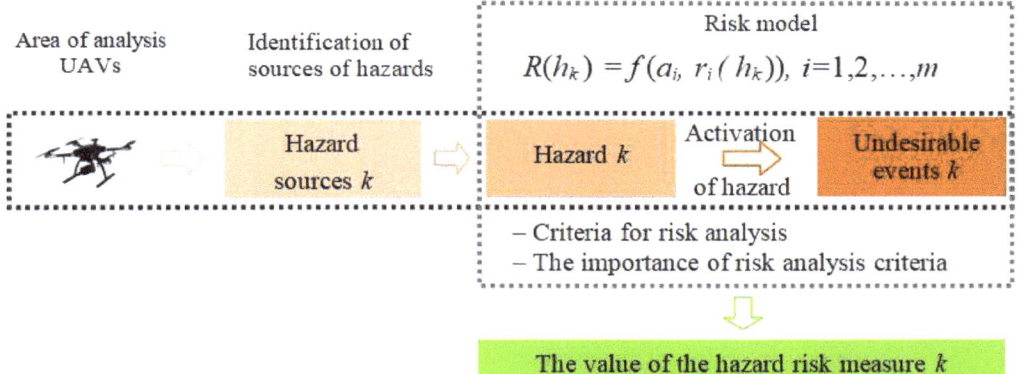

Figure 2. Place of the model and risk measures on the basis of [20].

In managing the risk of threats, there are detailed procedures, models, and risk measures dedicated to the areas of transport: road, rail, air, water, and urban. Currently, there is no model dedicated to the UAV transport system for risk assessment. Filling the research gap, an original risk assessment model for UVAs was proposed.

When developing the models and measures of hazard risks identified within the assessment areas, a generalised risk model presented in [36,37] may be adopted.

Based on the generalised model presented in [38], for the assessment area of UAV flights in built-up areas, authors have developed the model for assessing risk levels. For the model, the set of hazards has the form (for this model, hazards are marked as $h_1, h_2 \ldots h_n$):

$$H_{UAV} = \{h_1, h_2, \ldots, h_n\} \quad (1)$$

The risk model for each hazard from set H_{UAV} is a function of components $r_i(h_k)$ ($i = 1, 2,\ldots, m, k = 1, 2,\ldots, n$). Decisions are made based on the assessment according to 6 criteria K_i ($i = 1, 2, \ldots, 6$) and the measures of significance a_i ($i = 1, 2,\ldots, 6$) of these risk assessment criteria comprising the following set:

$$A = \{a_1, a_2, \ldots, a_6\} \quad (2)$$

The importance measure for each criterion was defined with values from 1–6. In the risk model for UAV flights in a built-up area, 6 criteria with the following names and meanings were assumed:

K1: safety level criterion *SL*. The most important criterion $a_1 = 6$. The measure of risk component $r_1(h_k)$ according to this criterion is determined depending on the value of the safety level indicator (*SL*):

- Low when $SL \leq 4 \times 10^{-4}$,
- Medium when $4 \times 10^{-4} < SL < 2 \times 10^{-2}$,
- High when $SL \geq 2 \times 10^{-2}$.

The safety level indicator is expressed as follows:

$$SL = L_I / L_H \quad (3)$$

where:

SL—safety level indicator for UAV flights conducted in a built-up area,
L_I—number of recorded incidents, and,
L_H—number of flight hours logged.

The value of the *SL* indicator was determined based on analyses of the frequency of adverse events recorded by the entity performing the flight operations. The values of the

SL indicator were presented in Table 1. In the analysis, the assumed annual flying time logged was 2688 h. The values included in the table were proposed based on the experience gained during remote pilot training conducted at the Poznań University of Technology.

Table 1. Safety level indicators.

Frequency	SL
1/1	1
1/8	0.125
1/56	0.018
1/224	0.0045
1/2688	0.0004

Source: Authors' own elaboration.

K2: loss occurrence reach criterion. Criterion of importance measure $a_2 = 5$. The criterion takes into consideration the type of material losses that may be caused by hazard activation. The losses concern the following subareas: infrastructure (subarea 1), natural environment (subarea 2), and people (subarea 3). According to this criterion, the measure of risk component $r_2(h_k)$ is determined by the following principle:

- Low when the losses occurred in only one of the subareas,
- Medium when the losses occurred in two subareas, and,
- High when the losses occurred in all subareas.

K3: material loss criterion for material losses resulting from incidents involving UAVs. According to this criterion, the measure of risk component $r_3(h_k)$ depends on the extent of material losses:

- Low when the losses do not exceed USD 2500,
- Medium when the material value of the losses exceeds USD 2500, but does not exceed USD 125,000, and,
- High when the value of material losses exceeds USD 125,000.

The values provided are based on the subjective assessment of the authors of the model. Measure of importance for this criterion was assumed at the level of $a_3 = 4$.

K4: loss criterion based on the type of incident. Importance measure $a_4 = 3$. The measure of risk component $r_4(h_k)$ depends on the object with which the UAV collided:

- Low when UAV collides with another unmanned or manned aerial vehicle during flight,
- Medium when UAV collides with an obstacle on the ground, and,
- High when UAV collides with a person on the ground.

K5: hazard activation history criterion. Criterion of importance measure ($a_5 = 2$). It is assumed that if a hazard was activated once, it is likely that it will be activated again. The measure of hazard activation $r_5(h_k)$ is determined depending on hazard activation within a year preceding the assessment:

- Low when the event was recorded no more than 5 times,
- Medium when the event occurred no more than 10 times, and,
- High when the event occurred more than 10 times.

K6: hazard activation potential criterion. The criterion depends on the UAV type, competency certificates held, and flight location. The measure of risk component $r_6(h_k)$ for this criterion is determined based on three elements (K6.1, K6.2, K6.3) characterising the flights performed.

Element K6.1—UAV type. This element of risk component $r_6(h_k)$ indicates the potential for hazard activation depending on the UAV type (weight):

- Low when the UAV weight does not exceed 5 kg,
- Average when the UAV weight ranges between 5 and 25 kg, and,
- High when the UAV weight exceeds 25 kg.

Element *K6.2*—competency certificates. This element of risk component $r_6(h_k)$ makes it possible to make the hazard activation potential dependent on the operator's qualifications according to the following principle:
- Low if the operator holds a certificate with additional privileges,
- Average if the operator holds a certificate with basic privileges, and,
- High if the operator has no privileges.

In compliance with the provisions of the law, each remote pilot conducting a UAV flight is required to have formal qualifications and privileges for flights in the given category.

Element *K6.3*—distance from buildings. The measure of this element of risk component $r_6(h_k)$ makes it possible to make the hazard activation potential dependent on the building density within the area where the flights are conducted:
- Low when there are no buildings within a 100-m radius,
- Average when there are buildings within a 30-m radius, and,
- High when there are buildings within a radius less than 30 m.

The measure of risk component $r_6(z_k)$ is determined in accordance with the following principle:
- Low when a maximum of one element of criterion *K6* was rated as average,
- Medium when a maximum of two elements of criterion *K6* were rated as average, and,
- High when more than one element of criterion *K6* was rated as high.

Importance criterion $a_6 = 1$.

The measures of risk component $r_i(h_k)$ for each of the six risk model criteria for UAV flights assume the levels from set:

$$\Omega = \{\text{low, medium, high}\} \tag{4}$$

The elements of set Ω (Formula (4)) of the measures of risk components are assigned a set of risk measure values. Therefore, the result of risk calculation for each hazard from set Z_{UAV} (Formula (1)), according to criterion K_i ($i = 1, 2..., 6$) is the level of risk for component $r_i(z_k)$ from the set of risk measure values. The function enabling estimation of the total risk measure taking into consideration the results of risk calculation according to the six criteria and significance measures of risk assessment criteria assumes the following form:

$$R_{UAV} = \sum_{i=1}^{6} a_i \times r_i \tag{5}$$

The risk measures were selected subjectively following the principle of a starting wetness more important than the probability of their occurrence.

The next step should be risk evaluation, i.e., checking (by evaluation and by comparison) to which risk category (class) the estimated risk belongs (i.e., acceptable, tolerable, or unacceptable) [16].

The values of risk measures were determined, assuming an equal division for the adopted maximum and minimum.

The proposed risk acceptability classification for UAV operations was developed on the basis of the data from Table 2:
- Acceptable risk: no need to take actions to reduce the risk, but the control by the UAV operator should be below 49,
- Tolerable risk: the occurrence of personal or economic losses is medium or unlikely (the level of risk should be monitored); risk level is in the range of 49–78, and,
- Unacceptable risk: area where flight should not be allowed under any circumstances; risk level above 78.

The presented risk tolerability limits constitute only a proposal developed as a result of the work performed. Nevertheless, they can be shifted depending on the area in which BSP operations are performed and their nature.

Table 2. Classification of risk acceptability in UAV operations.

Criterion	Qualitative Measure	Quantitative Measure	Criterion Importance Measure	Risk Component Value	Total Level
z_n—hazard when all measures of threat activation are low (minimum risk level)					
K1	low	1	6	6	
K2	low	1	5	5	
K3	low	1	4	4	21
K4	low	1	3	3	
K5	low	1	2	2	
K6	low	1	1	1	
z_m—hazard when all measures of threat activation are high (maximum risk level)					
K1	high	5	6	30	
K2	high	5	5	25	
K3	high	5	4	20	105
K4	high	5	3	15	
K5	high	5	2	10	
K6	high	5	1	5	

Source: Authors' own elaboration.

4. Results

The possibilities of using the model for the analysis areas related to drone operations located within Poznań were indicated. In order to show an example of an analysis using the model described in the work, a route between real points located in the Polish city of Poznań was proposed (Figure 3). The task that has been programmed before take-off on the drone's computer is to take a photo at the locations indicated by the pilot. The purpose of taking pictures is to control the number of people in places popular among tourists. Such a control may be performed by the police, who need to know where to send patrols to maintain law and order. The flight occurs in conditions where there is no terrorist threat and in a situation where the state is not involved in an armed conflict. The drone does not carry any dangerous cargo, and the only useful cargo that has been mounted on the platform is a camera. The UAV will return to the place of take-off and land after completing the task. The UAV's task will be to take photos in the places indicated by the pilot.

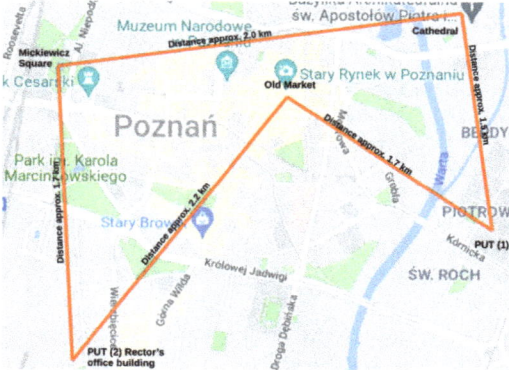

Figure 3. Flight route in Poznań [40].

Assumptions:
1. The flight takes place at a fixed altitude above the rooftops of city buildings.
2. The cruising speed is 30 km/h, (8.3 m/s).
3. The ambient temperature is 24 degrees Celsius, the wind speed is 0 km/h.
4. LiPo battery works for 20 min.

Calculations: S = V × t, therefore we have about 9960 m for the cruise.
Route:

1. The flight begins in the parking lot of the Poznań University of Technology (PUT); the destination is the Old Market Square. Distance approx. 1.7 km.

    Threat sources:
    - Students,
    - PUT service personnel,
    - People passing on the street,
    - Cars,
    - Trees,
    - Cables disconnected in space,
    - Chimney on Grobla Street,
    - Buildings along the flight route,
    - Antennas on buildings.

2. Lowering the flight on Old Market Square to take a photo.
3. A flight from the Old Market Square to another location among the buildings of the PUT. Distance about 2.2 km.

    Threat sources:
    - People,
    - Buildings,
    - Trees,
    - Antennas on roofs,
    - The tower of the Church of Mary Queen in Wilda, approx. 45 m high,
    - Rector's office building, approx. 40 m high,

4. Lowering the flight over the PUT parking lot in order to take a photo.
5. Flight from the car park in front of the PUT to the Imperial Castle on Św. Marcin street. Distance approx. 1.7 km.

    Threat sources:
    - People,
    - Buildings,
    - Trees,
    - Antennas on roofs.

6. Lowering the flight over Mickiewicz Square in order to take a photo.
7. Flight from Mickiewicz Square to the Cathedral. Distance approx. 2.0 km.

    Threat sources:
    - People,
    - Buildings,
    - Trees,
    - Antennas on roofs,
    - Okrąglak building,
    - Przemysl Castle.

8. Lowering the flight over the Cathedral in order to take a photo.
9. Flight from the Cathedral to the place of the drone take-off and landing. Distance 1.5 km.

    Sources of threats:
    - People,
    - Trees,
    - Cars.

The flight takes place at an altitude of 90 m above ground level. Lowering the altitude to take a photo means flight at an altitude of 20 m above ground level.

Risk assessments of threats identified on the flight route in Poznań have been achieved by following the principles of the risk model for UVAs, good engineering practice, and the knowledge of the authors. Table 3 shows risk assessment results for two selected threats.

Table 3. Summary of the results of the risk assessment of selected threats generated during the flight in Poznań.

Criterion	Qualitative Measure	Quantitative Measure	Measure of Criterion Importance	Risk Component Value	Total Level	Risk
	z_1—possibility of hitting a car parked on the premises of PUT					
K1	low	1	6	6		
K2	low	1	5	5		
K3	low	1	4	4	35	acceptable
K4	medium	3	3	9		
K5	medium	3	2	6		
K6	high	5	1	5		
	z_2—possibility of loss of health in the event of a UVA impact					
K1	low	1	6	6		
K2	low	1	5	5		
K3	medium	3	4	12	49	tolerable
K4	high	5	3	15		
K5	medium	3	2	6		
K6	high	5	1	5		

Source: Authors' own elaboration.

5. Conclusions

The risk model indicates the algorithms and parameters of risk assessment and evaluation procedures. The original model is based on six criteria analysis with the possibility of taking into account the validity risk components obtained on the basis of each of the analysis criterion.

Meeting social expectations related to the operation of unmanned aerial vehicles largely depends on the effectiveness of risk management processes for hazards generated in this area of human activity. Currently, UAVs take off, fly up, and automatically cover their routes along the set flight paths. In order to operate without collisions, it is necessary not only to conduct a risk analysis, but also to introduce comprehensive risk management procedures—as in the case of all modes of transport—and the most important of these is to indicate the method or model of risk assessment.

Regulations recommend taking actions aimed at risk assessment. The methods developed for the purposes of such analysis for unmanned flights are far from sufficient.

The risk model presented in the paper is part of the risk management process. Risk estimation is preceded by the selection of the risk model and risk measurement model of threats identified in these analysed areas. The paper proposes a six-criteria risk model for unmanned aerial vehicles, which allows for the presentation of risk in a measurable manner. The criteria relate, inter alia, to the number of losses that may occur during the process being conducted in the human–technology–environment system, the probability of adverse events, and the history. Measures of criteria validity from 1–6 were adopted. For the criteria mentioned, qualitative measures of risk analysis were defined as low, medium, and high, which can be replaced by quantitative risk measures; for example, 1, 3, and 5 for this model. An exemplary UAV flight route in Poznań was developed and the risk for selected identified threats was estimated.

Author Contributions: Conceptualization, A.K.-T. and J.Ł.; methodology, A.K.-T.; software, A.K.-T.; validation, J.Ł., A.K.-T. and P.W.S.; formal analysis, A.K.-T.; investigation, A.K.-T.; resources, A.K.-T.; data curation, J.Ł.; writing—original draft preparation, A.K.-T.; writing—review and editing, J.Ł.; visualization, J.Ł.; supervision, P.W.S.; project administration, P.W.S.; funding acquisition, P.W.S. All authors have read and agreed to the published version of the manuscript.

Funding: This research was funded by the National Centre for Research and Development Poland under the grant DOB-BIO10/01/02/2019 within the framework of the Defence and Security Programme.

Institutional Review Board Statement: Not applicable.

Informed Consent Statement: Not applicable.

Data Availability Statement: Not applicable.

Conflicts of Interest: The authors declare no conflict of interest.

References

1. Alexis, K.; Nikolakopoulos, G.; Tzes, A.; Dritsas, L. Coordination of helicopter UAVs for aerial forest-fire surveillance. In *Applications of Intelligent Control to Engineering Systems*; Valavanis, K.P., Ed.; Springer: Dordrecht, The Netherlands, 2009; pp. 169–193.
2. Goodarzi, F.A.; Lee, D.; Lee, T. Geometric control of a quadrotor UAV transporting a payload connected via flexible cable. *Int. J. Control Autom. Syst.* **2015**, *13*, 1486–1498. [CrossRef]
3. Elmokadem, T. Distributed coverage control of quadrotor multi-UAV systems for precision agriculture. *IFAC-PapersOnLine* **2019**, *52*, 251–256. [CrossRef]
4. Rodríguez-Mata, A.E.; Flores, G.; Martínez-Vásquez, A.H.; Mora-Felix, Z.D.; Castro-Linares, R.; Amabilis-Sosa, L.E. Discontinuous high-gain observer in a robust control UAV quadrotor: Real-time application for watershed monitoring. *Math. Probl. Eng.* **2018**, *2*, 1–10. [CrossRef]
5. Zieniuk, K. Traffic safety at rail crossroads. In Proceedings of the 2nd Polish Technical Conference, Warsaw, Poland, 7–8 September 2016. (In Polish)
6. Jamroz, K.; Chruzik, K.; Gucma, L.; Kadziński, A.; Skorupski, J.; Szymanek, A. Analiza możliwości integracji metod zarządzania ryzykiem podrozdział 7.3. In *Integrated Transport Safety System, Vol 2, Conditions of the Development of Integration of Transport Safety Systems*; Krystek, R., Ed.; WKŁ: Warszawa, Polska, 2009; pp. 280–307. (In Polish)
7. Szymanek, A. *Theory and Methodology of Risk Management in Traffic*; Publishing hause Politechniki Radomskiej: Radom, Poland, 2012. (In Polish)
8. Grisaro, H.Y.; Turygan, S.; Sielicki, W.P. Concrete Slab Damage and Hazard from Close-In Detonation of Weaponized Commercial Unmanned Aerial Vehicles. *J. Struct. Eng.* **2021**, *147*, 04021190. [CrossRef]
9. Jamroz, K. *Risk Management Method in Road Engineering*; Publishing hause Politechniki Gdańskiej: Gdańsk, Poland, 2011. (In Polish)
10. Bonneson, J.; Mccoy, P. Effect of Median Treatment on Urban Arterial Safety: An Accident Prediction Model. Transportation Research Record. *J. Transp. Res. Board* **1997**, *158*, 27–36. [CrossRef]
11. Bureika, G.; Gaidamauska, E.; Kupinas, J.; Bogdevičius, M.; Steišūnas, S. Modelling the assessment of traffic risk at level crossings of Lithuanian railways. *Transport* **2016**, *32*, 282–290. [CrossRef]
12. Ford, G.; Heneker, D. Australian Level Crossing Assessment Model. In Proceedings of the Presentation to the International Rail Safety Conference, Perth, Australia, 24–27 October 2004.
13. Kadziński, A.; Kobaszyńska-Twardowska, A.; Gill, A. The Concept of Method and Models for Risk Management of Hazards Generated at Railway Crossings. In Proceedings of the International Conference Transport Means, Juodkrante, Lithuania, 5–7 October 2016; pp. 297–302.
14. Lovegrove, G.R.; Sayed, T. Macro-level collision prediction models for evaluating neighbourhood traffic safety. *Can. J. Civ. Eng.* **2006**, *33*, 609–621. [CrossRef]
15. Skorupski, J. Methods of risk management in air traffic control. In *Selected Problems of Controlling Flying Objects*; Gruszecki, J., Ed.; Oficyna. Publishing hause Politechniki Rzeszowskiej: Rzeszów, Poland, 2011; pp. 135–144.
16. Skorupski, J. *Quantitative Methods of Air Traffic Incident Analysis*; Oficyna Wydawnicza Politechniki Warszawskiej: Warszawa, Poland, 2018. (In Polish)
17. Jamroz, K.; Chruzik, K.; Gucma, L.; Kadziński, A.; Skorupski, J.; Szymanek, A. The concept of the method of risk management in transport. In *The Integrated System of Transport Safety, Vol 3, Conditions for the Development of Transport Safety Systems Integration*; Krystek, R., Ed.; WKŁ: Warszawa, Poland, 2010; Chapter 4.3; pp. 133–151. (In Polish)
18. Chi, C.-F.; Sigmund, D.; Astardi, M. Classification Scheme for Root Cause and Failure Modes and Effects Analysis (FMEA) of Passenger Vehicle Recalls. *Reliab. Eng. Syst. Saf.* **2020**, *200*, 1–10. [CrossRef]
19. Pauer, G.; Török, A. Introducing a novel safety assessment method through the example of a reduced complexity binary integer autonomous transport model. *Reliab. Eng. Syst. Saf.* **2022**, *217*, 1–15. [CrossRef]
20. Kadziński, A.; Gill, A. The concept of implementation of the Trans-Risk method to risk management in tram transport. *Logistyka* **2011**, *3*, 1053–1064. (In Polish)
21. Aliyari, M.; Behooz, A.; Zewdu Ayele, Y. Hazards identification and risk assessment for UAV-assisted bridge inspections. *Struct. Infrastruct. Eng.* **2021**, *18*, 412–428. [CrossRef]
22. Arravind, R.; Manjunath, J.; Midhunesh, E.; Tamilselvan, D. Seed Dropping UAV: Design of Seed Dropping UAV in Afforestation. *Int. Adv. Res. J. Sci. Eng. Technol.* **2021**, *8*, 490–494. [CrossRef]
23. Kobaszyńska-Twardowska, A.; Łukasiewicz, J. *Monitoring State on Railway and Road Journeys with the Use of Unmanned Aircraft, Education in Safety and Defence*; Scheffs, W., Jaszczur, W., Kamiński, P., Eds.; Kaliskie Towarzystwo Przyjaciół Nauk: Kalisz, Poland, 2020. (In Polish)

24. Levasseur, B.; Bertrand, S. Impact Probability Maps Computation and Risk Analysis for 3D Ground Infrastructures due to UAV Operations. In Proceedings of the 2021 International Conference on Unmanned Aircraft Systems at Athens, Athens, Greece, 15–18 June 2021.
25. Pang, B.; Hu, X.; Dai, W.; Low, K.H. Third Party Risk Modelling and Assessment for Safe UAV Path Planning in Metropolitan. *arxiv* **2021**, arXiv:2107.01834.
26. Banerjee, P.; Gorospe, G. Risk Assessment of Obstacle Collision for UAVs Under Off-nominal Conditions. In Proceedings of the Annual Conference of the PHM Society, Nashville, TN, USA, 28 September–1 October 2020; Volume 12. [CrossRef]
27. Jiang, N.; Wang, K.; Peng, X.; Yu, X.; Wang, Q.; Xing, J.; Li, G.; Zhao, J.; Guo, G.; Han, Z. Anti-UAV: A Large Multi-Modal Benchmark for UAV Tracking. *arxiv* **2021**, arXiv:2101.08466.
28. Bigazzi, L.; Basso, M.; Boni, E.; Innocenti, G.; Pieraccini, M. A Multilevel Architecture for Autonomous UAVs. *Drones* **2021**, *5*, 55. [CrossRef]
29. Lopez, B.; Munoz, J.; Quevedo, F.; Monje, C.A.; Garrido, S.; Moreno, E.L. Path Planning and Collision Risk Management Strategy for Multi-UVA Systems in 3D Environments. *Drones* **2021**, *21*, 4414. [CrossRef]
30. Prygies, J. The UAVs Threat to Airport Security: Risk Analysis and Mitigation. *J. Airl. Airpt. Manag.* **2019**, *9*, 63–96. [CrossRef]
31. Commission Delegated Regulation (EU) 2019/945 of 12 March 2019 on Unmanned Aircraft Systems and on Third-Country Operators of Unmanned Aircraft Systems. Available online: https://eur-lex.europa.eu/legal-content/EN/TXT/?uri=CELEX: 32019R0945 (accessed on 10 January 2022).
32. Commission Delegated Regulation (EU) 2020/1058 of 27 April 2020 Amending Delegated Regulation (EU) 2019/945 as Regards the Introduction of Two New Unmanned Aircraft Systems Classes. Available online: https://eur-lex.europa.eu/legal-content/EN/TXT/?uri=CELEX%3A32020R1058 (accessed on 10 January 2022).
33. Commission Implementing Regulation (EU) 2019/947 of 24 May 2019 on the Rules and Procedures for the Operation of Unmanned Aircraft. Available online: https://eur-lex.europa.eu/legal-content/EN/TXT/?uri=CELEX%3A32019R0947 (accessed on 10 January 2022).
34. Sora-Jarus. Available online: http://jarus-rpas.org/sites/jarus-rpas.org/files/jar_doc_06_jarus_sora_v2.0.pdf (accessed on 5 May 2021).
35. Szopa, T. *Reliability and Safety*; Publishing haus Politechniki Warszawskiej: Warszawa, Poland, 2009. (In Polish)
36. Chruzik, K. *Safety Engineering in Transportation*; Publishing hause Politechniki Śląskiej: Gliwice, Poland, 2016. (In Polish)
37. Sitarz, M.; Chruzik, K.; Wachnik, A. Integrated safety management in rail transport. *Integr. Manag. Syst. Saf. Eng.* **2012**, *19*, 49–51. (In Polish)
38. Kadziński, A. *Study of Selected Aspects of the Reliability of Systems and Facilities for Rail Vehicles*; Poznan University of Technology: Poznan, Poland, 2013. (In Polish)
39. ULC Seminar on: Safety of UAV Flights, Warsaw. 2018, *in press*.
40. Available online: www.googlemaps.pl (accessed on 20 September 2021).

Article

Survey of Localizing Gradient Damage in Static and Dynamic Tension of Concrete

Adam Wosatko

Faculty of Civil Engineering, Cracow University of Technology, Warszawska 24, 31-155 Cracow, Poland; adam.wosatko@pk.edu.pl; Tel.: +48-12-628-2561

Abstract: The continuum damage model should be regularized to ensure mesh-insensitive results in simulations of strain localization, e.g., for concrete cracking under tension. The paper confronts the conventional gradient damage model with its upgrade including a variable internal length scale. In these models, the Helmholtz free energy depends additionally on an averaged strain measure and its gradient. In the formulation for dynamics the equations of motion are discretized simultaneously with an averaging equation. If gradient regularization is employed with a constant internal length parameter, then an artificially expanded damage zone can occur in the strain softening analysis. This broadening effect can be inhibited by a gradient activity function. The localizing character of the gradient activity has physical motivation—the nonlocal interactions in the fracture zone are reduced with the damage growth. The internal length can decrease exponentially or as a cosine function. After presentation of the theory, including the free energy definition, the finite element analyses of three different examples connected with tensile cracking in concrete are discussed: static tension of a double-edge-notched specimen, dynamic direct tension for a configuration without or with a reinforcing bar and tension of an L-shaped specimen under static and dynamic loading.

Keywords: localizing gradient damage; gradient activity function; tension; concrete cracking; impact load; dynamics; finite element method

1. Introduction

Continuum damage mechanics in the most basic version [1] introduces the idea of scalar damage measure reducing the elastic stiffness. A modelling of softening in quasi-brittle materials such as concrete without any regularization leads to results dependent on the introduced discretization. The (initial) boundary value problem—(I)BVP becomes ill-posed when the onset of strain localization occurs in the analysis, cf. [2]. In the finite element method (FEM) a simulation of cracking in concrete is represented by the localization zone limited to a band of one-element width; hence, the density of finite element (FE) mesh erroneously decides about the numerical solution. This deficiency can be partly overcome if the FE size is connected with a certain width derived from the fracture energy, see [3,4]. A regularization should be taken into account in proper modelling of composites, especially of quasi-brittle materials as concrete. There are many concepts to make the concrete model regularized, but in this paper a higher-order theory including a gradient term is employed, according to the fundamentals given in [5].

The scalar damage model with a gradient enhancement was first proposed in [6]. Based on [7,8], the Helmholtz free energy for the damage model with the presence of averaged strain measure is shown in the paper. In the formulation for dynamics an extra averaging equation is added to the equation of motion. The gradient damage model after discretization has independent interpolations of the displacement and averaged strain fields. The gradient activity related to the internal length scale influences the zone of nonlocal interactions, i.e., the width of the crack band is not governed by the density of the FE mesh. It is proved that this model in the implicit version for static as well as dynamic

problems (i.e., for wave propagation problems) is truly nonlocal (see [9]). A wide overview of gradient-enhanced and other nonlocal models for concrete is performed in [10,11].

When the internal length scale in the conventional gradient damage model (CGD) is assumed to be constant as, e.g., in [6,12], then the issue of an artificially expanded damage zone can occur. In fact, the intensity of averaging is the same during the whole localization process and it induces nonlocal mapping of the active damage zone into its enlarged neighbourhood. This shortcoming of the CGD model was first observed by Geers [13,14]. Gradient models can be upgraded by the so-called over-nonlocal formulation presented, e.g., in [15,16]. This approach comes from [17] and it is applied over the years in integral nonlocal models (see, e.g., [18–20]). A linear combination of local and nonlocal state variable (e.g., equivalent strain measure) is used and, moreover, its proportion may change during the loading history, cf. [21,22]. Another upgrade is suggested in [23], where the internal length scale is not represented by a scalar variable, but using a second order tensor as a function of principal stresses at a material point. The idea is known from the CGD model, where in two dimensions the region of averaging determined by a circle transforms into an area specified by an ellipse oriented according to the principal stresses. When the directions of nonlocality are distinguished that way, the modelling of the localization zone becomes anisotropic. Some modification of this approach is the so-called smoothing gradient damage model, where the averaging region depends additionally on a coefficient related to the equivalent strain and smoothly decreasing interaction [24,25].

The constant value of the internal length scale can be replaced by a function of gradient activity. It was first proposed in [13,14], where apart from the averaging equation, one more extra continuity equation for damage or gradient activity variable was introduced. It means that the formulation includes three fields and additional degrees of freedom are present in the finite element. The third field is interpolated to stabilize the iteration process during the computations. This approach can be called the transient gradient damage model (TGD) and it can be modified according to [26]. The gradient activity function is shifted to the denominator in the averaging equation and because of that two primary fields are preserved in the FE interpolation. In [26], the gradient activity increases with the equivalent strain. Another concept is the so-called localizing gradient damage model (LGD) originated in [27,28], where the damage zone is controlled through a reduction of the gradient activity and at the same time the averaging region. An overview of different damage formulations with constant or variable internal lengths, based on the benchmark of one-dimensional tensile bar, is shown in [29]. A comparison and generalization of TGD and LGD models is widely discussed in [30]. Based on [27,31], Figure 1 depicts the idea of a change of the interaction domain in the specimen under uniaxial tension. It is seen that the averaging region narrows when diffuse microcracks progress to the formation of a macrocrack. The decreasing function of gradient activity seems to be more physical, i.e., the influence of nonlocality should be reduced together with the increase of damage.

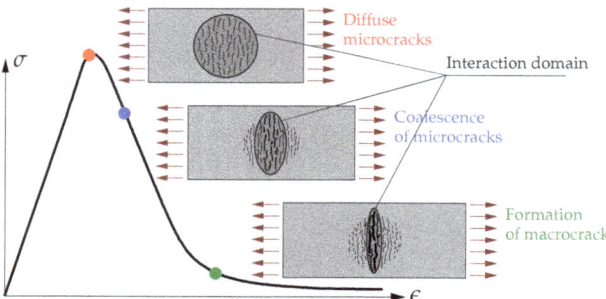

Figure 1. Idea of localizing interaction domain for microcracks in tensile specimen.

The averaging equation given in [27,28] has a different form from the one commonly known and written originally in [6]. The gradient operator is also applied to the function of evolving length scale, not only to the averaged strain. The LGD model has been intensively explored in recent years. Extensive research of this model is presented in [31], also in the context of verification using different examples, not only for concrete, but also for other composite materials. As shown in [32], the model is able to reproduce the size effect. The Ottosen equivalent strain measure as an alternative loading function [33] can be applied in the LGD model to simulate properly a mixed-mode concrete cracking. A so-called micro inertia effect can be considered in the formulation to analyze cracking in dynamic problems (see [34,35]). Moreover, the LGD model can be used in an advanced multi-field analysis [36], where the mechanical problem is coupled to water transport and thermal problems. Different methods of mesh adaptation for this model are suggested in [37].

In this paper, a formulation for dynamics, but without the micro inertia effect, is taken into account. The results for the CGD and LGD models are confronted. Both of them are implemented by the author in the FEAP package [38]. When the LGD model is used, two different functions can decide about the decrease of the gradient activity. The first one has the exponential character and it is known from [27,28], while the second one changes according to the cosine function.

In the paper, the finite element (FE) analysis focuses on the modelling of the cracking phenomenon in concrete for tension tests. Based on the experiments of uniaxial tension for different composite materials, not only the tensile strength can be estimated, but also the fracture energy when the post-peak response is observed. Direct tension can be experimentally investigated using symmetric specimens with two rectangular (see, e.g., [39]) or triangular (see, e.g., [40]) notches as well as dog-bone shaped specimens (see, e.g., [41]). Typically, specimens in the experiments are gripped on opposite flat sides and pulled on one or both sides. Mode I fracture is obtained. It is also possible to examine concrete cracking using large-scale specimens as for example in [42]. However, it is known that the size effect can be validated using direct tension tests, cf. [41]. Another type of a experimental test is compact tension of a composite specimen, e.g., [14,43]. The first benchmark in the current paper is a double-edge-notched specimen under direct static tension according to [39]. In addition, based on the numerical analysis presented in [44], a study of the LGD model is performed for a dynamic direct tension test of plain and reinforced concrete bar. A slightly different investigation refers to fracture in an L-shaped concrete specimen. The final example presented in this paper for the CGD and LGD models is based on the experiment in [45]. A similar experimental study of L-specimen under different loading rates is shown in [46]. The induced tension in the L-shaped specimen is still direct, but the character of failure can evolve from mode I to mixed mode. Next, a separate group are indirect tests. The splitting test was carried out experimentally and reported by many researchers (see, e.g., [47–49]). The compression between the platens activates a perpendicular tension in the middle of the cylinder, hence primary and secondary cracks are generated. This experiment is able to provide the tensile strength for quasi-brittle materials. The split in the concrete cylinder under a static as well as an impact loading can be reproduced using different regularized models, cf. [44,50–53]. The tensile strength is also determined for notched or unnotched beams under three-point bending. The size effect for such beams has been examined in many papers (see, e.g., [54–57]). Quite a broad overview of experimental and numerical tension tests is described in [58].

The content of the paper is as follows. After introduction, Section 2 describes the theory connected with the gradient damage model, in sequence: consequences of postulating a gradient-dependent free energy, the formulation with its discretization and juxtaposition of functions employed in the computations. Section 3 shows three examples: static uniaxial tension of a notched bar, dynamic tension of an unnotched bar without and with reinforcement and finally static and dynamic tension of the L-shaped configuration. Sections 4 and 5 summarize the work and the results presented in the paper.

2. Fundamentals of Implemented Model

2.1. Thermodynamic Analysis

The description of the theory starts by defining an internal variable $\bar{e}$ which is related to deformation and will turn out to be an averaged (nonlocal) strain measure. It is postulated that the Helmholtz free energy depends on this variable and its gradient as follows, cf. [7,8,27,28,59]:

$$\Psi(\epsilon, \bar{e}, \nabla\bar{e}, \omega) = \Psi_1(\epsilon, \omega) + \Psi_2(\epsilon, \bar{e}) + \Psi_3(\nabla\bar{e}) \tag{1}$$

Absolute tensor notation is used in this subsection. The individual components on the right side of this equation are defined as:

$$\Psi_1(\epsilon, \omega) = \frac{1}{2}(1-\omega)\,\epsilon : \mathbb{D}^e : \epsilon, \quad \Psi_2(\epsilon, \bar{e}) = \frac{1}{2}H\,(\tilde{e}-\bar{e})^2, \quad \Psi_3(\nabla\bar{e}) = \frac{1}{2}A\,\nabla\bar{e}\cdot\nabla\bar{e} \tag{2}$$

where ϵ is the strain tensor, $\omega \in [0,1]$ is the scalar damage parameter, $\mathbb{D}^e$ is the fourth order tensor of elastic stiffness, $\tilde{e}(\epsilon)$ is an equivalent strain measure, H is a constant and A is proportional to the square of an internal length scale. In [8,59] an alternative form of the free energy is written in terms of damage and its gradient. A more complex form of the Helmholtz free energy can be postulated for a coupled gradient damage-plasticity model [60].

For a nonlocal continuum formulation the use of the global form of the Clausius–Duhem dissipation inequality for isothermal processes is needed:

$$\dot{\mathscr{D}} = \int_{\mathcal{B}} (\sigma : \dot{\epsilon} - \dot{\Psi})\,\mathrm{d}V \geq 0 \tag{3}$$

where $\dot{\mathscr{D}}$ denotes the time rate of dissipation and σ is the stress tensor. It is defined for a certain domain $\mathcal{B}$, occupied by the material body. Next, the time derivative of Ψ is calculated:

$$\dot{\Psi} = \frac{\partial\Psi}{\partial\epsilon}:\dot{\epsilon} + \frac{\partial\Psi}{\partial\bar{e}}:\dot{\bar{e}} + \frac{\partial\Psi}{\partial\nabla\bar{e}}\cdot\nabla\dot{\bar{e}} + \frac{\partial\Psi}{\partial\omega}:\dot{\omega} \tag{4}$$

and further:

$$\frac{\partial\Psi}{\partial\epsilon} = (1-\omega)\,\mathbb{D}^e : \epsilon + H\,(\tilde{e}-\bar{e})\,s, \qquad s = \frac{\partial\tilde{e}}{\partial\epsilon} \tag{5}$$

$$\frac{\partial\Psi}{\partial\bar{e}} = -H\,(\tilde{e}-\bar{e}), \qquad \frac{\partial\Psi}{\partial\nabla\bar{e}} = A\nabla\bar{e}, \qquad \frac{\partial\Psi}{\partial\omega} = -\frac{1}{2}\epsilon:\mathbb{D}^e:\epsilon = -Y \tag{6}$$

where Y is the damage energy release rate. Substituting Equation (4) into inequality (3) gives:

$$\dot{\mathscr{D}} = \int_{\mathcal{B}} \left[(\sigma - \frac{\partial\Psi}{\partial\epsilon}):\dot{\epsilon} - \frac{\partial\Psi}{\partial\bar{e}}:\dot{\bar{e}} - \frac{\partial\Psi}{\partial\nabla\bar{e}}\cdot\nabla\dot{\bar{e}} - \frac{\partial\Psi}{\partial\omega}\dot{\omega}\right]\mathrm{d}V \geq 0 \tag{7}$$

The first term provides the definition of stress:

$$\sigma = \frac{\partial\Psi}{\partial\epsilon} = (1-\omega)\,\mathbb{D}^e : \epsilon + H\,(\tilde{e}-\bar{e})\,s \tag{8}$$

and, to retrieve the classical form of σ, it has to be assumed that the second component of the above definition is very small in comparison with the first one. This is obvious for elasticity ($H \ll E$, E is Young's modulus) and doubtful close to failure when $\omega \to 1$, but this term is consequently neglected. Upon substitution of Equations (6) and (8) into inequality (7) it reads:

$$\dot{\mathscr{D}} = \int_{\mathcal{B}} [H\,(\tilde{e}-\bar{e})\,\dot{\bar{e}} - A\nabla\bar{e}\cdot\nabla\dot{\bar{e}} + Y\,\dot{\omega}]\,\mathrm{d}V \geq 0 \tag{9}$$

Next, the second term is integrated by parts:

$$\int_{\mathcal{B}} -A\nabla\bar{\epsilon}\cdot\nabla\dot{\bar{\epsilon}}\,\mathrm{d}V = \int_{\mathcal{B}} \nabla(A\nabla\bar{\epsilon})\dot{\bar{\epsilon}}\,\mathrm{d}V - \int_{\partial\mathcal{B}} A\nabla\bar{\epsilon}\cdot\mathcal{N}\dot{\bar{\epsilon}}\,\mathrm{d}S \qquad (10)$$

where $\mathcal{N}$ is the normal to the domain surface $\partial\mathcal{B}$. As noted in [7] the formulation is in fact nonlocal already in the elastic state, since if it is assumed there is no damage growth (i.e., $\dot{\omega} = 0$) and the dissipation must be equal to zero, then:

$$\dot{\mathscr{D}} = \int_{\mathcal{B}} \left[H\left(\tilde{\epsilon} - \bar{\epsilon}\right) + \nabla(A\nabla\bar{\epsilon}) \right] \dot{\bar{\epsilon}}\,\mathrm{d}V - \int_{\partial\mathcal{B}} A\nabla\bar{\epsilon}\cdot\mathcal{N}\dot{\bar{\epsilon}}\,\mathrm{d}S = 0 \qquad (11)$$

The sufficient conditions for Equation (11) to hold are the following equations:

$$H\left(\tilde{\epsilon} - \bar{\epsilon}\right) + \nabla(A\nabla\bar{\epsilon}) = 0 \quad \text{in } V \qquad (12)$$

$$\nabla\bar{\epsilon}\cdot\mathcal{N} = 0 \quad \text{on } S \qquad (13)$$

Assuming $H > 0$ all terms in Equation (12) can be divided by H. Therefore, a gradient scaling factor $\varphi = A/H$ can be introduced to obtain the averaging equation for the CGD model in the following form:

$$\bar{\epsilon} - \nabla(\varphi\nabla\bar{\epsilon}) = \tilde{\epsilon} \qquad (14)$$

When damage grows (i.e., $\dot{\omega} > 0$), the dissipation is:

$$\dot{\mathscr{D}} = \int_{\mathcal{B}} Y\dot{\omega}\,\mathrm{d}V > 0 \qquad (15)$$

which proves the second law of thermodynamics is satisfied. It is also pointed out that in [35,61] an interpretation of the model as a special case of two-scale micromorphic gradient-enhanced continuum is provided, where Equation (14) couples macro- and micromorphic variables.

Next, the case when the gradient activity function depends on damage is taken into account, i.e., $A = A(\omega)$. The Helmholtz free energy becomes:

$$\Psi(\epsilon, \bar{\epsilon}, \nabla\bar{\epsilon}, \omega) = \Psi_1 + \Psi_2 + \frac{1}{2} A(\omega)\nabla\bar{\epsilon}\cdot\nabla\bar{\epsilon} \qquad (16)$$

so that:

$$\frac{\partial\Psi}{\partial\omega} = \frac{\partial\Psi_1}{\partial\omega} + \frac{1}{2}\frac{\mathrm{d}A}{\mathrm{d}\omega}\|\nabla\bar{\epsilon}\|^2 \qquad (17)$$

and the gradient norm now influences the dissipation:

$$\dot{\mathscr{D}} = \int_{\mathcal{B}} \left(Y - \frac{1}{2}\frac{\mathrm{d}A}{\mathrm{d}\omega}\|\nabla\bar{\epsilon}\|^2\right)\dot{\omega}\,\mathrm{d}V > 0 \qquad (18)$$

This inequality is satisfied provided that:

$$\frac{\mathrm{d}A}{\mathrm{d}\omega} \leq \frac{2Y}{\|\nabla\bar{\epsilon}\|^2} \qquad (19)$$

The averaging equation for the LGD model is as follows:

$$\bar{\epsilon} - \nabla(\varphi(\omega)\nabla\bar{\epsilon}) = \tilde{\epsilon} \qquad (20)$$

while Equation (13) holds.

In the conventional gradient-enhanced damage model one assumes the loading function which satisfies:

$$F = \bar{\epsilon} - \kappa^{\mathrm{d}} \leq 0, \qquad \dot{\kappa}^{\mathrm{d}} \geq 0, \qquad F\dot{\kappa}^{\mathrm{d}} = 0 \qquad (21)$$

where $\kappa^{\mathrm{d}} = \max(\kappa_{\mathrm{o}}, \bar{\epsilon})$ and κ_{o} is the damage threshold. Damage ω is a function of the history variable κ^{d} and hence for the active process ω is a function of $\bar{\epsilon}$. Then the Helmholtz free energy depends only on ϵ, $\bar{\epsilon}$ and $\nabla \bar{\epsilon}$ and one can derive:

$$\frac{\partial \Psi}{\partial \bar{\epsilon}} = -Y \frac{\mathrm{d}\omega}{\mathrm{d}\bar{\epsilon}} - H(\tilde{\epsilon} - \bar{\epsilon}) + \frac{1}{2} \frac{\mathrm{d}A}{\mathrm{d}\omega} \frac{\mathrm{d}\omega}{\mathrm{d}\bar{\epsilon}} \|\nabla \bar{\epsilon}\|^2 \tag{22}$$

and express the dissipation as:

$$\dot{\mathscr{D}} = \int_{\mathcal{B}} (Y - \frac{1}{2} \frac{\mathrm{d}A}{\mathrm{d}\omega} \|\nabla \bar{\epsilon}\|^2) \frac{\mathrm{d}\omega}{\mathrm{d}\bar{\epsilon}} \dot{\bar{\epsilon}} \, \mathrm{d}V > 0 \tag{23}$$

which is equivalent to Equation (18).

Following [8], the potential energy functional for dynamic problems can be written as a difference between the potentials of internal and external forces:

$$\Pi = \Pi_{\mathrm{int}} - \Pi_{\mathrm{ext}} = \int_{\mathcal{B}} \Psi \, \mathrm{d}V + \int_{\mathcal{B}} \boldsymbol{u} \cdot \rho \ddot{\boldsymbol{u}} \, \mathrm{d}V - \int_{\mathcal{B}} \boldsymbol{u} \cdot \boldsymbol{b} \, \mathrm{d}V - \int_{\partial \mathcal{B}} \boldsymbol{u} \cdot \boldsymbol{t} \, \mathrm{d}S \tag{24}$$

where $\boldsymbol{u}$ is the displacement vector, $\boldsymbol{b}$ is the body force vector, $\rho \ddot{\boldsymbol{u}}$ defines inertia forces with the density ρ and the acceleration vector $\ddot{\boldsymbol{u}}$, $\boldsymbol{t}$ is the traction vector on boundary $\partial \mathcal{B}$. Minimization of the above functional leads to the weak form of the equation of motion:

$$\int_{\mathcal{B}} \delta \boldsymbol{\epsilon} : \frac{\partial \Psi}{\partial \boldsymbol{\epsilon}} \, \mathrm{d}V + \int_{\mathcal{B}} \delta \boldsymbol{u} \cdot \rho \ddot{\boldsymbol{u}} \, \mathrm{d}V = \int_{\mathcal{B}} \delta \boldsymbol{u} \cdot \boldsymbol{b} \, \mathrm{d}V + \int_{\partial \mathcal{B}} \delta \boldsymbol{u} \cdot \boldsymbol{t} \, \mathrm{d}S \quad \forall \, \delta \boldsymbol{u} \tag{25}$$

On the other hand, the weak form of the averaging Equation (20) can be obtained by multiplication of this equation by a variation of the averaged strain $\delta \bar{\epsilon}$ and integration over domain $\mathcal{B}$. Next, integration by parts according to Green's formula is applied to the gradient term:

$$\int_{\mathcal{B}} \delta \bar{\epsilon} [\nabla (\varphi \nabla \bar{\epsilon})] \, \mathrm{d}V = - \int_{\mathcal{B}} \nabla \delta \bar{\epsilon} \cdot \varphi \nabla \bar{\epsilon} \, \mathrm{d}V + \int_{\partial \mathcal{B}} \delta \bar{\epsilon} \, \varphi \nabla \bar{\epsilon} \cdot \mathcal{N} \, \mathrm{d}S \tag{26}$$

Knowing that the homogeneous natural boundary condition (13) holds, the weak form of the averaging equation is:

$$\int_{\mathcal{B}} \delta \bar{\epsilon} \, \bar{\epsilon} \, \mathrm{d}V + \int_{\mathcal{B}} \nabla \delta \bar{\epsilon} \cdot \varphi \nabla \bar{\epsilon} \, \mathrm{d}V = \int_{\mathcal{B}} \delta \bar{\epsilon} \, \tilde{\epsilon} \, \mathrm{d}V \quad \forall \, \delta \bar{\epsilon} \tag{27}$$

Notice that Equation (27) has the same nature regardless of whether the gradient activity is constant or is a function of ω. Equations (25) and (27) are the starting point for interpolation and linearization.

2.2. System of Matrix Equations

Henceforth, Voigt's notation (also called matrix-vector notation) is used. The formulation for the LGD model has two primary fields, hence independent interpolations of displacements $\boldsymbol{u}$ and of the averaged strain measure $\bar{\epsilon}$ are introduced:

$$\boldsymbol{u} = \boldsymbol{N} \boldsymbol{a} \quad \text{and} \quad \bar{\epsilon} = \boldsymbol{h}^{\mathrm{T}} \boldsymbol{e} \tag{28}$$

where $\boldsymbol{N}$ and $\boldsymbol{h}$ contain appropriate shape functions. Small strains are assumed for the (I)BVP. The secondary fields $\boldsymbol{\epsilon}$ and $\nabla \bar{\epsilon}$ can be computed as:

$$\boldsymbol{\epsilon} = \boldsymbol{B} \boldsymbol{a} \quad \text{and} \quad \nabla \bar{\epsilon} = \boldsymbol{g}^{\mathrm{T}} \boldsymbol{e} \tag{29}$$

where $\boldsymbol{B} = \boldsymbol{L} \boldsymbol{N}$ and $\boldsymbol{g}^{\mathrm{T}} = \nabla \boldsymbol{h}^{\mathrm{T}}$. Matrix $\boldsymbol{L}$ consists of differential operators. The corresponding variations are also interpolated, respectively. Equations (25) and (27) in a discretized form are as follows:

$$\delta \boldsymbol{a}^\mathrm{T} \int_\mathcal{B} \boldsymbol{B}^\mathrm{T} \boldsymbol{\sigma}\, \mathrm{d}V + \delta \boldsymbol{a}^\mathrm{T} \int_\mathcal{B} \boldsymbol{N}^\mathrm{T} \rho \boldsymbol{N}\, \ddot{\boldsymbol{a}}\, \mathrm{d}V = \delta \boldsymbol{a}^\mathrm{T} \int_\mathcal{B} \boldsymbol{N}^\mathrm{T} \boldsymbol{b}\, \mathrm{d}V + \delta \boldsymbol{a}^\mathrm{T} \int_{\partial \mathcal{B}} \boldsymbol{N}^\mathrm{T} \boldsymbol{t}\, \mathrm{d}S \qquad (30)$$

$$\delta e \int_\mathcal{B} \boldsymbol{h}\, \boldsymbol{h}^\mathrm{T} e\, \mathrm{d}V + \delta e \int_\mathcal{B} \boldsymbol{g}\, \varphi\, \boldsymbol{g}^\mathrm{T} e\, \mathrm{d}V = \delta e \int_\mathcal{B} \boldsymbol{h}\, \tilde{\epsilon}\, \mathrm{d}V \qquad (31)$$

Tractions and body forces do not depend on deformation.

The IBVP is linearized and equilibrium has to be achieved at each time step. The detailed derivation for the LGD model can be found in [30]. It finally leads to the following system of the matrix equations for dynamic problems:

$$\begin{bmatrix} \boldsymbol{M}_{aa} & 0 \\ 0 & 0 \end{bmatrix} \begin{bmatrix} \ddot{\boldsymbol{a}}^{t+\Delta t} \\ \ddot{\boldsymbol{e}}^{t+\Delta t} \end{bmatrix} + \begin{bmatrix} \boldsymbol{K}_{aa} & \boldsymbol{K}_{ae} \\ \boldsymbol{K}_{ea} & \boldsymbol{K}_{ee} + \boldsymbol{K}_{ee}^{\mathrm{LGD}} \end{bmatrix} \begin{bmatrix} \Delta \boldsymbol{a} \\ \Delta \boldsymbol{e} \end{bmatrix} = \begin{bmatrix} \boldsymbol{f}_{\mathrm{ext}}^{t+\Delta t} - \boldsymbol{f}_{\mathrm{int}}^{t} \\ \boldsymbol{f}_{\epsilon}^{t} - \boldsymbol{f}_{e}^{t} \end{bmatrix} \qquad (32)$$

The incremental nodal displacements $\Delta \boldsymbol{a}$ and the incremental averaged strain $\Delta \boldsymbol{e}$ are solved for in each time step. Equilibrium is retrieved after iterations in subsequent time steps. The consistent mass matrix is determined in a standard way:

$$\boldsymbol{M}_{aa} = \int_\mathcal{B} \boldsymbol{N}^\mathrm{T} \rho \boldsymbol{N}\, \mathrm{d}V \qquad (33)$$

Obviously, this matrix is not taken into consideration for static problems. The submatrices given in Equation (32) are defined as follows:

$$\boldsymbol{K}_{aa} = \int_\mathcal{B} \boldsymbol{B}^\mathrm{T} (1-\omega)\, \boldsymbol{D}\, \boldsymbol{B}\, \mathrm{d}V, \qquad \boldsymbol{K}_{ae} = -\int_\mathcal{B} \mathcal{G}\, \boldsymbol{B}^\mathrm{T}\, \boldsymbol{D}\, \boldsymbol{\epsilon}\, \boldsymbol{h}^\mathrm{T}\, \mathrm{d}V \qquad (34)$$

$$\boldsymbol{K}_{ea} = -\int_\mathcal{B} \boldsymbol{h}\, \boldsymbol{s}^\mathrm{T} \boldsymbol{B}\, \mathrm{d}V, \qquad \boldsymbol{K}_{ee} = \int_\mathcal{B} \left(\boldsymbol{h}\, \boldsymbol{h}^\mathrm{T} + \varphi\, \boldsymbol{g}\, \boldsymbol{g}^\mathrm{T} \right) \mathrm{d}V \qquad (35)$$

$$\boldsymbol{K}_{ee}^{\mathrm{LGD}} = \int_\mathcal{B} \boldsymbol{g}\, \boldsymbol{g}^\mathrm{T} \boldsymbol{e}\, \varphi_{,\omega}\, \mathcal{G}\, \boldsymbol{h}^\mathrm{T}\, \mathrm{d}V \qquad (36)$$

where $\boldsymbol{D}$ is the elastic stiffness matrix. Additionally, the following notation has been introduced:

$$\mathcal{G} = \frac{\partial \omega}{\partial \kappa^\mathrm{d}} \frac{\partial \kappa^\mathrm{d}}{\partial \bar{\epsilon}} \qquad \text{and} \qquad \varphi_{,\omega} = \frac{\partial \varphi}{\partial \omega} \qquad (37)$$

It should be noted that $\boldsymbol{K}_{ee}^{\mathrm{LGD}}$ does not exist for the CGD model (where φ is constant). The subvectors on the right-hand side in Equation (32) are defined below, the subscript t is skipped:

$$\boldsymbol{f}_{\mathrm{ext}}^{t+\Delta t} = \int_\mathcal{B} \boldsymbol{N}^\mathrm{T} \boldsymbol{b}^{t+\Delta t}\, \mathrm{d}V + \int_{\partial \mathcal{B}} \boldsymbol{N}^\mathrm{T} \boldsymbol{t}^{t+\Delta t}\, \mathrm{d}S, \qquad \boldsymbol{f}_{\mathrm{int}} = \int_\mathcal{B} \boldsymbol{B}^\mathrm{T} \boldsymbol{\sigma}\, \mathrm{d}V \qquad (38)$$

$$\boldsymbol{f}_{\epsilon} = \int_\mathcal{B} \boldsymbol{h}\, \tilde{\epsilon}\, \mathrm{d}V, \qquad \boldsymbol{f}_e = \boldsymbol{K}_{ee}\, \boldsymbol{e} \qquad (39)$$

2.3. Applied Functions

In the computations included in the paper, the equivalent strain measure is determined by the modified von Mises definition [62]:

$$\tilde{\epsilon}(\boldsymbol{\epsilon}) = \frac{(k-1)I_1^\epsilon}{2k(1-2\nu)} + \frac{1}{2k}\sqrt{\left(\frac{(k-1)I_1^\epsilon}{1-2\nu}\right)^2 + \frac{12k J_2^\epsilon}{(1+\nu)^2}} \qquad (40)$$

where $k = f_c/f_t$ is the ratio of uniaxial compressive and tensile strengths, ν is Poisson's ratio, I_1^ϵ and J_2^ϵ are the strain tensor invariants.

In the literature, there are different functions representing the damage growth (see, e.g., [13]). According to the experiment [39] uniaxial softening for tension in concrete can be approximated by an exponential function. The damage history parameter κ^d, after exceeding the threshold κ_o, causes damage ω to grow asymptotically to 1 [12,63]:

$$\omega(\kappa^d) = 1 - \frac{\kappa_o}{\kappa^d}\left(1 - \alpha + \alpha e^{-\eta(\kappa^d - \kappa_o)}\right) \tag{41}$$

where the parameters η and α are respectively associated with material ductility and residual stress which tends to $(1-\alpha)E\kappa_o$ (in one dimension). Hence, the latter parameter prevents the complete loss of material stiffness for $\alpha < 1$ and makes the numerical response more stable. The former one is related to fracture energy G_f of concrete.

The third recalled function decides about the gradient activity. Function $\varphi = \varphi(\omega)$ is able to change the averaging region during the damage process. When the CGD model [6] is considered, then the gradient activity remains constant:

$$\varphi_0 = c_{max} > 0 \tag{42}$$

The parameter c_{max} is related to the internal length scale l as shown in [64], i.e., $c_{max} = 0.5\, l^2$. When the LGD model [27,28] is taken into account, the gradient activity is reduced together with the damage growth:

$$\varphi_1(\omega) = c_{max}\frac{(1-R)\exp(-n\,\omega) + R - \exp(-n)}{1 - \exp(-n)} \tag{43}$$

where c_{max} is still the half of maximum internal length scale squared, R is the residual level of interaction between microprocesses within the localization band and n is the power which changes the intensity of the gradient activity. The character of this function is localizing, because the gradient activity can only decrease. The derivative of function φ_1 equals:

$$\frac{\partial \varphi_1}{\partial \omega} = c_{max}\frac{(R-1)\,n\,\exp(-n\,\omega)}{1 - \exp(-n)} \tag{44}$$

In this paper, an alternative definition of the gradient activity function is also used. The relation $\varphi = \varphi(\omega)$ and its corresponding derivative can be determined by cosine and sine functions:

$$\varphi_2(\omega) = c_{max}\left[0.5\left(\cos(\pi\omega^n) + 1\right)(1-R) + R\right] \tag{45}$$

$$\frac{\partial \varphi_2}{\partial \omega} = 0.5\,\pi\,c_{max}\,n\,(R-1)\,\omega^{(n-1)}\,\sin(\pi\omega^n) \tag{46}$$

The character of function φ_2 is also decreasing. Functions $\varphi_1(\omega)$ and $\varphi_2(\omega)$ as well as their derivatives are depicted in Figure 2. Values $c_{max} = 8.0$ mm^2 and $R = 0.01$ refer to first computed benchmark, discussed in the next section. The function φ_1 is compared for two cases of the intensity parameter, i.e., $n = 1.0$ or $n = 5.0$, while for φ_2 this is $n = 1.0$. It is seen for all cases that non-increasing functions φ corresponds to derivatives $\partial \varphi / \partial \omega$ which are negative or zero at most. More details on gradient activity functions can be found in [30].

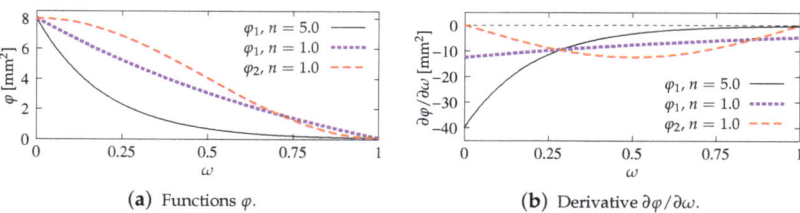

Figure 2. Gradient activity functions with different intensity n, $c_{max} = 8.0$ mm^2, $R = 0.01$.

3. Numerical Examples of Direct Tension

3.1. Static Tensile Cracking on Double-Edge-Notched Specimen

The first example is connected with the experiment presented in [39] for specimens with different dimensions, subjected to direct tension. In [65], the gradient plasticity model was verified using this test to show the size effect and different responses for configurations of direct tension without or with admissible rotation of the free edge. The CGD model was analyzed in [12,66], where the results for symmetric and asymmetric behaviour are obtained and the size effect is demonstrated.

In this paper, only a symmetric response is simulated for one selected set of dimensions. Attention is focused on the mesh-objectivity study and highlighting the difference between results for CGD and LGD models. The plain lightweight concrete bar is notched on both longer edges. The length of the specimen is $L = 250$ mm, the height is $H = 60$ mm, the thickness is $T = 50$ mm. Plane stress conditions are assumed. In the numerical analysis the specimen is set horizontally, see Figure 3. Suitable boundary conditions constrain the displacements on the left, while a uniform static load acts on the right. The total elongation is measured at point E, but indirect displacement control is monitored at point C. The red points, which are adjacent to this point in one line, are linked to have the same horizontal displacement. In other words, all marked points on the right of the zone of mesh densification control the symmetric deformation of the specimen. In the computations four meshes (named A–D) with eight-noded finite elements (FEs) are employed with double densification in the middle, as depicted in Figure 3 for mesh B. Quadratic interpolation of displacements a and linear interpolation of averaged strain e together with 2×2 Gauss integration is applied in FEs. Mesh A includes 2401 nodes and 536 FEs, mesh B—7113 nodes and 1976 FEs, mesh C—13,199 nodes and 3816 FEs and mesh D—24,321 nodes and 7328 FEs. The elasticity data of the concrete model are: Young's modulus $E = 18{,}000$ MPa, Poisson's ratio $\nu = 0.2$. The modified von Mises definition of the equivalent strain in Equation (40) is applied with the ratio $k = 10$. The tensile strength is initially established as $f_t = 3.4$ MPa, but actually the threshold κ_o is adjusted to the maximum stress from the experiment [39] with the corresponding value captured for mesh B. In a similar way the values of parameters α and η defined in Equation (41) are fitted to reproduce the experimental diagram as close as possible. All computed cases for this benchmark are listed in Table 1. The maximum value for the gradient activity function is adopted as $c_{\max} = 8.0$ mm^2. This is the constant internal length parameter for the CGD model. The LGD model is used with the minimum level of gradient interaction $R = 0.01$. The results for this model are compared considering functions φ_1 (with $n = 1.0$ or $n = 5.0$) and φ_2 ($n = 1.0$). These functions are depicted in Figure 2a.

Table 1. Computational cases for static tension test on double-edge-notched specimen (in order of appearance in figures).

Acronym	Model	Type of φ	Mesh	$\kappa_o \times 10^{-4}$	α	η	n
CGD-A	CGD	φ_0	A	1.845	0.96	720	
CGD-B	CGD	φ_0	B	1.845	0.96	720	
CGD-C	CGD	φ_0	C	1.845	0.96	720	
CGD-D	CGD	φ_0	D	1.845	0.96	720	
LGD-A	LGD	φ_1	A	1.975	0.95	90	5.0
LGD-B	LGD	φ_1	B	1.975	0.95	90	5.0
LGD-C	LGD	φ_1	C	1.975	0.95	90	5.0
LGD-D	LGD	φ_1	D	1.975	0.95	90	5.0
LGD-n1-A	LGD	φ_1	A	1.835	0.95	100	1.0
LGD-n1-B	LGD	φ_1	B	1.835	0.95	100	1.0
LGD-n1-C	LGD	φ_1	C	1.835	0.95	100	1.0
LGD-n1-D	LGD	φ_1	D	1.835	0.95	100	1.0
LGD-c-A	LGD	φ_2	A	1.805	0.95	90	1.0
LGD-c-B	LGD	φ_2	B	1.805	0.95	90	1.0
LGD-c-C	LGD	φ_2	C	1.805	0.95	90	1.0
LGD-c-D	LGD	φ_2	D	1.805	0.95	90	1.0

Figures 4 and 5 show the results for the CGD model. In Figure 4a, the diagrams of total force at the right edge versus total bar elongation measured at point E are compared for all meshes; hence, the global response is inspected. A so-called ligament stress versus average strain is plotted in Figure 4b. The concept of the ligament stress can be introduced as follows:

$$\sigma_{\text{lig}} = \frac{F}{B_{\text{lig}} T} \tag{47}$$

where F is the force and B_{lig} is the ligament width, i.e., the width of the bar minus the depths of both notches. The average strain is the average extension of the measurement length over L_m. The measurement base L_m (see Figure 3) is in accordance with the experiment. The placement of extensometers is distinguished by the red points. The average extension is calculated as a difference between the mean of horizontal displacements on the right (in one line with point C) and the mean of horizontal displacements observed analogically on the left. Therefore, Figure 4b presents the diagrams of nominal values. It is clearly seen that mesh-objective results are obtained. The equilibrium paths depicted in both figures overlap, however the softening branch for the coarsest mesh A marginally deviates in the middle of the descent. Figure 5 illustrates contour plots of average strain measure $\bar{\epsilon}$ and damage ω prepared for the final stage of the loading. The range of view is limited to the area in the vicinity of the notches. There are presented the results for only the two utmost cases CGD-A and CGD-D, i.e., for the coarsest mesh A and for the finest mesh D. It is confirmed that the solution is insensitive to the adopted mesh. The localization zone appears between the notches as expected. Nevertheless, a shortcoming is noticeable. The distribution of active damage in Figure 5c,d in comparison to the distribution of averaged strain in Figure 5a,b widens excessively sideways in the ligament area.

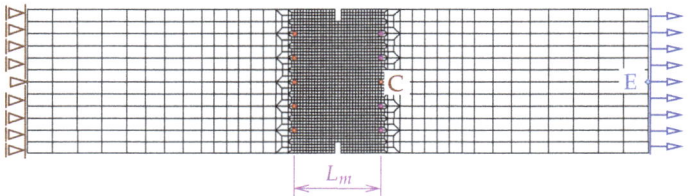

Figure 3. Configuration of static tension test together with mesh B, indirect displacement control at point C, elongation measured at point E.

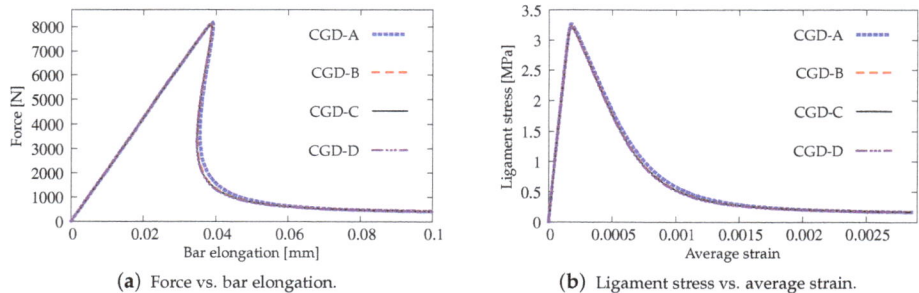

(**a**) Force vs. bar elongation.

(**b**) Ligament stress vs. average strain.

Figure 4. Static tension test, diagrams for CGD model, mesh-sensitivity study.

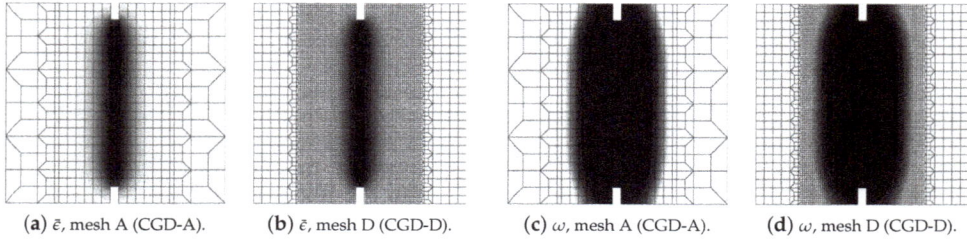

(**a**) $\bar{\epsilon}$, mesh A (CGD-A).

(**b**) $\bar{\epsilon}$, mesh D (CGD-D).

(**c**) ω, mesh A (CGD-A).

(**d**) ω, mesh D (CGD-D).

Figure 5. Static tension test, CGD model, distribution of averaged strain $\bar{\epsilon}$ and damage ω for two utmost cases.

Next, the results for the LGD model are presented. Figure 6 shows diagrams analogical to those presented in Figure 4, but here the LGD model with exponential function φ_1 and intensity $n = 5.0$ is used. Both subfigures, with force-bar elongation diagrams as well as with ligament stress-average strain diagrams, indicate that this model seems to be mesh-dependent. The load-carrying capacity for mesh A is clearly larger than for the other three. However, together with an increasing density of the mesh, differences between subsequent diagrams vanish and finally the solutions for meshes C and D almost overlap, cf. cases LGD-C and LGD-D in Figure 6. Furthermore, in this test the snapback effect is observed and it is stronger for the solution obtained for the LGD model than for the CGD model, cf. Figures 4a and 6a. Figure 7 depicts diagrams where for function φ_1 the intensity parameter is five times smaller, i.e., $n = 1.0$. There are cases from LGD-n1-A to LGD-n1-D. It is visible in Figure 7a that the snapback is delayed if $n = 1.0$. Just after the peak the equilibrium paths run down, but forward and only then backward. The convergence of solutions for subsequent denser and denser meshes has the same character as for the case when the power $n = 5.0$.

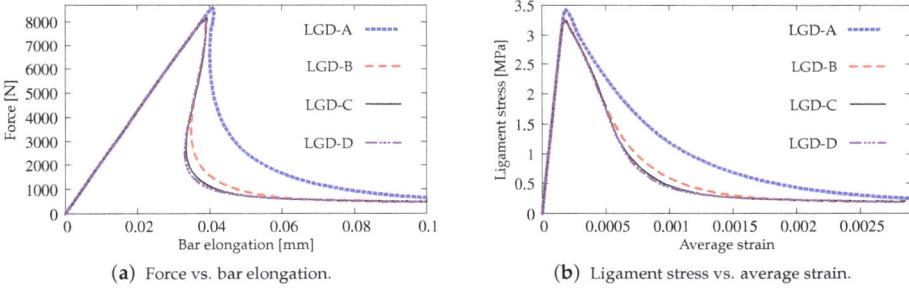

Figure 6. Static tension test, diagrams for LGD model using function φ_1 with $n = 5.0$, mesh-sensitivity study.

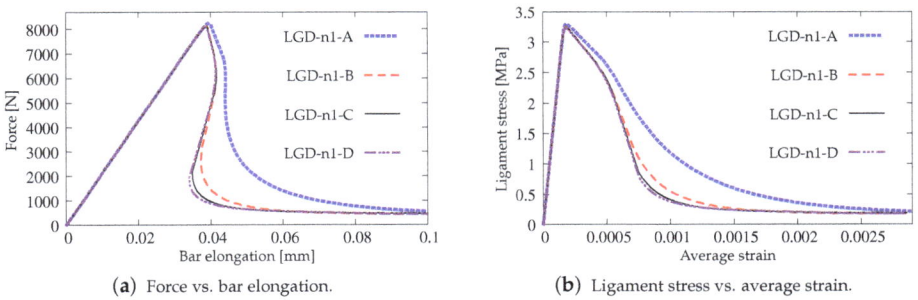

Figure 7. Static tension test, diagrams for LGD model using function φ_1 with $n = 1.0$, mesh-sensitivity study.

The contour plots in Figures 8–10 illustrate the results for the LGD model with function φ_1, but the distributions of damage ω in Figures 9 and 10 differ if the intensity parameter $n = 5.0$ or 1.0, analogically to the diagrams presented above. It is common that the crack is initiated near the notch. It should be noticed that the width of the notch has the width of one FE for mesh A and next it is divided into two (mesh B), three (C) or four (D) FEs along the notch width. The active localization zone for the averaged strain measure $\bar{\varepsilon}$ in the case of the CGD model (see Figure 5a,b), is smeared and insensitive to the size of the notch. In reality, the shape and the size of the notch can influence the initiation point of the crack (see, e.g., experimental results in [39,40]). Moreover, due to the presence of the notches and the fact that concrete exhibits softening in the tension regime, the snapback effect is possible in this test. The solution for the LGD model is influenced by the division of the notch width.

Cracking starts in the left corners for mesh A (case LGD-A) (see Figure 8a). It should be recalled that the left edge of the specimen is constrained in the analysis. For mesh B (case LGD-B) as shown in Figure 8b, the dominant averaged strain runs along the symmetry axis between the notches. For meshes C and D (cases LGD-C and LGD-D) cracking is observed along the nearest line adjacent to the symmetry axis. Hence, the solutions for meshes C and D seem to optimal in terms of energy release during the cracking process and can be recognized as mesh-objective. Of course, it can be questioned that the response depends on the division of the notch width; however, the solutions for meshes C and D are very similar. Despite the fact that the distributions of averaged strain measure $\bar{\varepsilon}$ look almost the same for the LGD model with $n = 5.0$ or 1.0, the distributions of damage ω are different, see Figure 8 and then Figures 9 and 10. It is noticed that the responses for $n = 1.0$ and meshes C and D (cases LGD-n1-C and LGD-n1-D) are almost identical, analogically to the solution with $n = 5.0$ for meshes C and D. However, for smaller intensity $n = 1.0$ the distribution of active damage ω is evidently wider than for $n = 5.0$. On the other hand, it is clear that the damage zone is not spuriously broadened as for the CGD model; hence, the solution for the LGD model with φ_1 and the power $n = 1.0$ is acceptable.

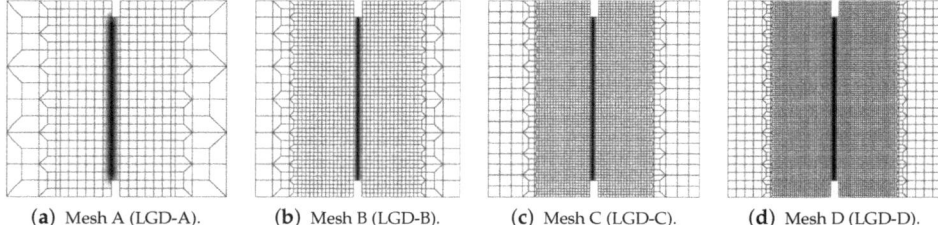

(a) Mesh A (LGD-A). (b) Mesh B (LGD-B). (c) Mesh C (LGD-C). (d) Mesh D (LGD-D).

Figure 8. Static tension test, LGD model using function φ_1 with $n = 5.0$, distribution of averaged strain $\bar{\varepsilon}$, mesh-sensitivity study.

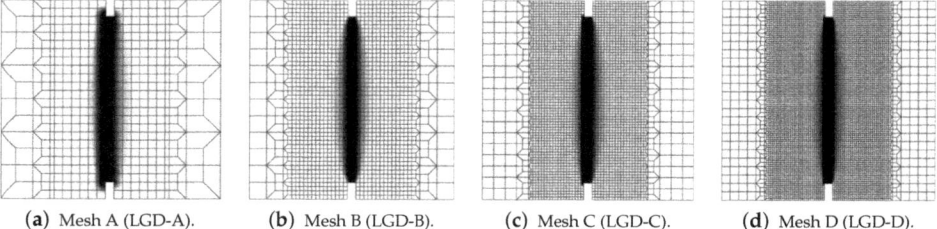

(a) Mesh A (LGD-A). (b) Mesh B (LGD-B). (c) Mesh C (LGD-C). (d) Mesh D (LGD-D).

Figure 9. Static tension test, LGD model using function φ_1 with $n = 5.0$, distribution of damage ω, mesh-sensitivity study.

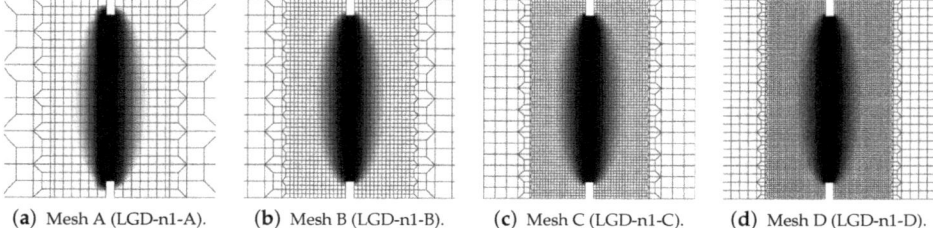

(a) Mesh A (LGD-n1-A). (b) Mesh B (LGD-n1-B). (c) Mesh C (LGD-n1-C). (d) Mesh D (LGD-n1-D).

Figure 10. Static tension test, LGD model using function φ_1 with $n = 1.0$, distribution of damage ω, mesh-sensitivity study.

The results for the LGD model when the gradient activity decreases according to the cosine function φ_2 are presented separately. Again, Figure 11 depicts the force-bar elongation diagrams on the left and the ligament stress-average strain diagrams on the right. The character of all equilibrium paths is similar to the case when for the LGD model function φ_1 with $n = 1.0$ is taken into account. Again, together with increasing densification of meshes, subsequent responses converge to a mesh-objective solution. Similarly, damage distributions in Figure 12 for meshes A (case LGD-c-A) and B (case LGD-c-B) differ from those obtained for meshes C and D (cases LGD-c-C and LGD-c-D). The character of the localization zone for ω when the cosine function φ_2 is used in the LGD model is more diffusive for smaller damage values, but finally, for the largest values of damage ($\omega \to 1.0$), it reminds the distribution obtained for the exponential function φ_1 and $n = 5.0$. Based on these results it can be stated that function φ_2 can be applied in the LGD model.

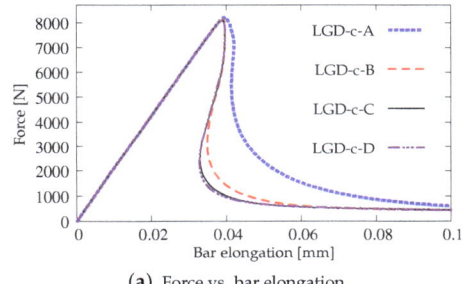

(a) Force vs. bar elongation.

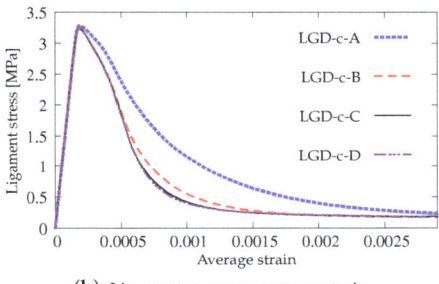

(b) Ligament stress vs. average strain.

Figure 11. Static tension test, diagrams for LGD model using function φ_2, mesh-sensitivity study.

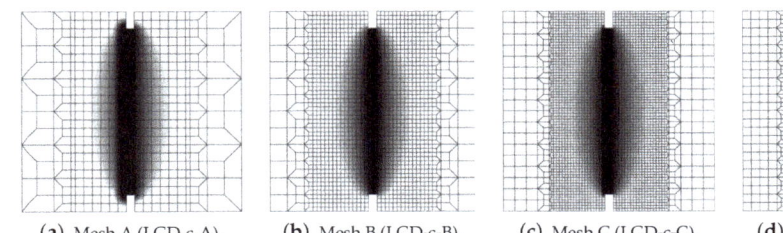

(a) Mesh A (LGD-c-A). (b) Mesh B (LGD-c-B). (c) Mesh C (LGD-c-C). (d) Mesh D (LGD-c-D).

Figure 12. Static tension test, LGD model using function φ_2, distribution of damage ω, mesh-sensitivity study.

Moreover, in this test the response for the LGD model with function φ_2 is more stable during the iteration process. Figure 13 shows a comparison of the diagrams obtained for the total force versus the elongation at the point E, which are zoomed when the peak is attained during the loading process. When the gradient activity strongly decreases as for function φ_1 with the intensity parameter $n = 5.0$, an instability in the computations for the onset of the strain localization is clearly seen. This undiserable effect is overcome for φ_1 and $n = 1.0$ as shown in Figure 13b and for φ_2 as shown in Figure 13c. In Figure 14, the distributions of the gradient activity functions φ_1 and φ_2 are illustrated for mesh C. The scale of the values is reversed, so the black colour denotes the smallest values of function φ, which correspond to the weakest nonlocal interaction. These distributions reflect the active damage zones. The range of the gradient activity is the widest for function φ_1 with milder intensity $n = 1.0$. The distribution of the gradient activity for function φ_2 (with the cosine) is slightly thinner. Based on this observation and taking into account the possible issue of instability for φ_1 with $n = 5.0$ as indicated by the diagrams in Figure 13a, the choice of function φ_2 can be an effective alternative and a reasonable compromise when the LGD model is used.

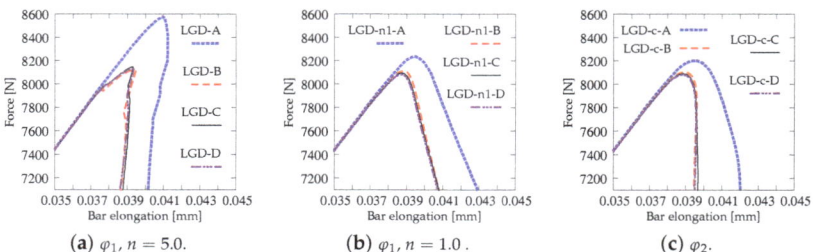

Figure 13. Static tension test, different options for LGD model, diagrams of force vs. bar elongation zoomed near peak.

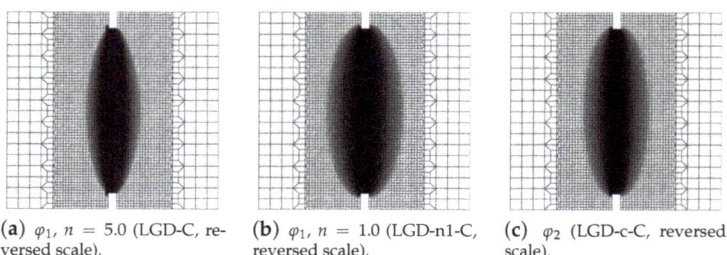

(**a**) φ_1, $n = 5.0$ (LGD-C, reversed scale).
(**b**) φ_1, $n = 1.0$ (LGD-n1-C, reversed scale).
(**c**) φ_2 (LGD-c-C, reversed scale).

Figure 14. Static tension test, mesh C, distribution of gradient activity function for LGD model.

Figure 15 presents a comparison between the applied models and with reference to the experiment [39]. The average displacement given on the horizontal axis is actually the average extension measured over the base L_m shown in Figure 3 between marked red points and it is consistent with the measurement performed in the experiment [39]. The results in Figure 15a for mesh B and in Figure 15b for mesh C do not differ substantially, but the ones for mesh C exhibit a slightly more brittle response. Only the equilibrium paths for cases LGD-n1-B and LGD-n1-C, i.e., when the intensity parameter n equals 1.0, diverge from the others. In subsequent analyses, this case is no longer considered.

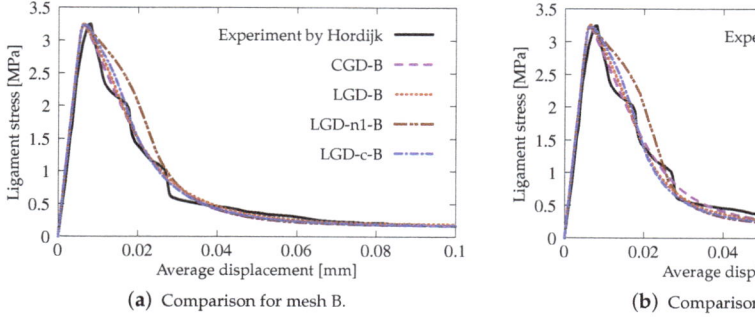

(**a**) Comparison for mesh B.
(**b**) Comparison for mesh C.

Figure 15. Static tension test, comparison with experiment [39], ligament stress vs average displacement, diagrams for meshes B and C.

Summarizing the above considerations, the LGD model is more sensitive to the discretization than the CGD model. In this example, the solution for subsequent meshes approaches the final mesh-objective result. Hence, a sufficiently dense mesh should be employed in the computations. The intensity parameter n for exponential function φ_1, which decides about the rate of gradient activity for the internal length scale, should be larger than 1.0 (see also [30,31]).

3.2. Direct Tension Test under Impact Loading
3.2.1. General Data

The second example concerns a dynamic analysis of tensile wave propagation in a concrete specimen without or with reinforcement. The results of an analogical test, but only for one discretization, were presented in [44]. There were compared two regularized models: Hoffman viscoplasticity and conventional gradient damage (CGD). A similar confrontation—gradient plasticity versus gradient damage, however using only a plain concrete bar, has been carried out in [67]. In this subsection the results obtained for the LGD model are shown for both options: plain and reinforced concrete (RC). The presentation of diagrams for the CGD model is given as a reference solution.

The configuration of the test is illustrated in Figure 16a. This bar is supported along both symmetry axes and normal traction on both (left and right) edges is applied. The load is time-dependent according to a linear-constant function which is drawn in Figure 16b. The traction intensity $p_i = 2.4$ MPa becomes constant for time $t_i = 3 \times 10^{-5}$ s $= 30$ μs. Each time step equals 1 μs. Plane stress conditions with the thickness $T = 50$ mm are assumed again. The length of the specimen is $L = 240$ mm, the height is $H = 56$ mm. This test is just to compare dynamic responses of the models; hence, L and H are adjusted to FE meshes. However, they are similar to the previous example, but the concrete bar is unnotched. Three meshes are applied. Mesh A has 2811 nodes, 960 FEs for RC configuration and the square FE size equals 4 mm. Mesh B has 10,659 nodes, 3600 FEs for RC configuration and the square FE size is 2 mm. Mesh C has 41,475 nodes, 13,920 FEs for RC configuration and the square FE size equals 1 mm. Mesh B with eight-noded FEs (and the same interpolation as previously) is depicted in Figure 16a. When reinforced concrete is taken into account, the rebar is discretized by truss elements located along the horizontal axis.

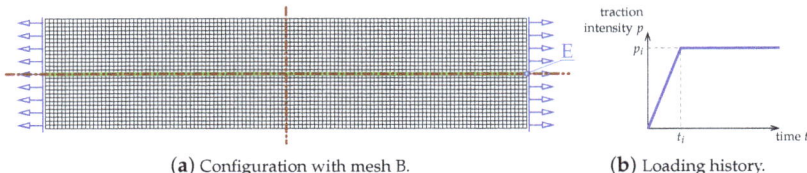

(**a**) Configuration with mesh B.   (**b**) Loading history.

Figure 16. Dynamic direct tension test—definition of specimen and loading history.

The material data for concrete are: Young's modulus $E = 18{,}000$ MPa, Poisson's ratio $\nu = 0.0$ and density $\rho = 2320$ kg/m^3. Exponential damage growth function given in Equation (41) is applied with threshold $\kappa_o = 1.8889 \times 10^{-4}$ (which corresponds to $f_t = 3.4$ MPa) and parameter $\alpha = 0.99$ to keep a small residual stress. Other parameters are juxtaposed in Table 2. The first column provides acronyms for the cases where plain concrete is considered in the analysis. The second column informs about acronyms for the analyses of RC models. A blank field means that only the case without reinforcement is analyzed. The equivalent strain measure is determined by the modified von Mises definition—Equation (40), $k = 10$. In the computations two or three different values of $c_{\max}$ (connected with the maximum internal length scale) are compared. Both gradient activity functions are examined as well. The data for the steel reinforcement are: $E = 200{,}000$ MPa, $\nu = 0.0$, $\rho = 7800$ kg/m^3 and the yield strength is $f_y = 355$ MPa for the perfect plasticity model. Cross section $A_r = 28$ mm^2 indicates that the reinforcement ratio is 1%. In the case of RC, full bond between the concrete matrix and the reinforcement is adopted.

Table 2. Computational cases for dynamic direct tension test.

Plain Concrete	Reinforced Concrete	Model	Type of φ	Mesh	c_{max} [mm^2]	η	R	n
dc-CGD-C-8	rc-CGD-C-8	CGD	φ_0	C	8.0	400		
dc-LGD-A-2	rc-LGD-A-2	LGD	φ_1	A	2.0	180	0.04	5.0
dc-LGD-B-2	rc-LGD-B-2	LGD	φ_1	B	2.0	180	0.04	5.0
dc-LGD-C-2	rc-LGD-C-2	LGD	φ_1	C	2.0	180	0.04	5.0
dc-LGD-A-8	rc-LGD-A-8	LGD	φ_1	A	8.0	180	0.04	5.0
dc-LGD-B-8	rc-LGD-B-8	LGD	φ_1	B	8.0	180	0.04	5.0
dc-LGD-C-8	rc-LGD-C-8	LGD	φ_1	C	8.0	180	0.04	5.0
dc-LGD-A-32		LGD	φ_1	A	32.0	180	0.04	5.0
dc-LGD-B-32		LGD	φ_1	B	32.0	180	0.04	5.0
dc-LGD-C-32		LGD	φ_1	C	32.0	180	0.04	5.0
dc-LGD-C-8-R01		LGD	φ_1	C	8.0	180	0.01	5.0
dc-LGD-C-8-R16		LGD	φ_1	C	8.0	180	0.16	5.0
dc-LGD-C-8-e400		LGD	φ_1	C	8.0	400	0.04	5.0
dc-LGDc-A-2	rc-LGDc-A-2	LGD	φ_2	A	2.0	180	0.04	1.0
dc-LGDc-B-2	rc-LGDc-B-2	LGD	φ_2	B	2.0	180	0.04	1.0
dc-LGDc-C-2	rc-LGDc-C-2	LGD	φ_2	C	2.0	180	0.04	1.0
dc-LGDc-A-8	rc-LGDc-A-8	LGD	φ_2	A	8.0	180	0.04	1.0
dc-LGDc-B-8	rc-LGDc-B-8	LGD	φ_2	B	8.0	180	0.04	1.0
dc-LGDc-C-8	rc-LGDc-C-8	LGD	φ_2	C	8.0	180	0.04	1.0

3.2.2. Results for Plain Concrete

A survey of the test results commences with the comparison of CGD and LGD models based on the diagrams shown in Figure 17. The details for cases dc-CGD-C-8, dc-LGD-C-8 and dc-LGDc-C-8 are listed in Table 2. The parameters for them are selected to fit the elongation-time diagrams. In particular, this concerns parameter η. It is known, based on the comparison of CGD and LGD models for statics in [27,30] as well as in the previous benchmark, that the value of parameter η specifying the rate of damage growth should be much smaller for the LGD model than for the CGD model. This rule is also valid in the dynamic analysis, hence here $\eta = 400$ for the CGD model corresponds to $\eta = 180$ for the LGD model. The elongation history is monitored at point E, so the horizontal displacement is observed as a function of time. The diagrams in Figure 17 intersect each other.

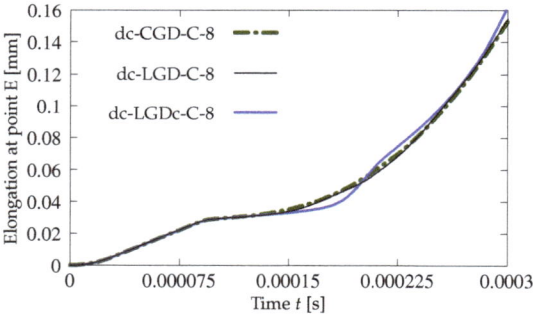

Figure 17. Dynamic tension test, plain concrete, mesh C, $l = 4$ mm or $c_{max} = 8$ mm^2, comparison of models for elongation history.

Figure 18 juxtaposes time-elongation diagrams for all cases solved for the dynamic direct tension test using the LGD model and exponential gradient activity function φ_1 (see Equation (43). It is noticed that the elongation at point E goes to infinity for all cases. It is also seen in Figure 18a,b that the results depend on the mesh, however for larger c_{max} the difference between the solutions for mesh B (case dc-LGD-B-8) and C (dc-LGD-C-8) is smaller than for $c_{max} = 2$ mm^2. It should be explained here that the assumed value of the maximum internal length scale influences in the whole change of the gradient activity function. For example when $c_{max} = 2$ mm^2, then value of φ_1 ranges to $R \times c_{max} = 0.04 \times 2$ mm$^2 = 0.08$ mm^2 corresponding to the minimum level of nonlocal interaction, but when $c_{max} = 8$ mm^2, then φ_1 approaches $R \times c_{max} = 0.32$ mm^2. Hence for $c_{max} = 32$ mm^2 ($R \times c_{max} = 1.28$ mm^2) the time-elongation diagrams are very close to each other (see Figure 18c). It is observed that together with the increase of c_{max} and simultaneously with more influential gradient activity function φ_1 in the LGD model, the diagrams get nearest to one another, but the same level of the elongation at point E is attained slower. The parameter R connected with the residual level of averaging decides about the elongation rate as shown in Figure 18d. Assuming the same $c_{max} = 8$ mm^2, the same mesh C and different values of R which is equal to 0.01 for case dc-LGD-C-8-R01, 0.04 for case dc-LGD-C-8 and 0.16 for dc-LGD-C-8-R16, the differences between the paths are significant. Additionally, the diagram for case dc-LGD-C-8-e400 is drawn in Figure 18d, where the parameter η equals 400 for the LGD model, exactly as the one introduced for the CGD model. The comparison presented here confirms that η should be smaller, otherwise the elongation goes to infinity the fastest of all the cases considered in this section.

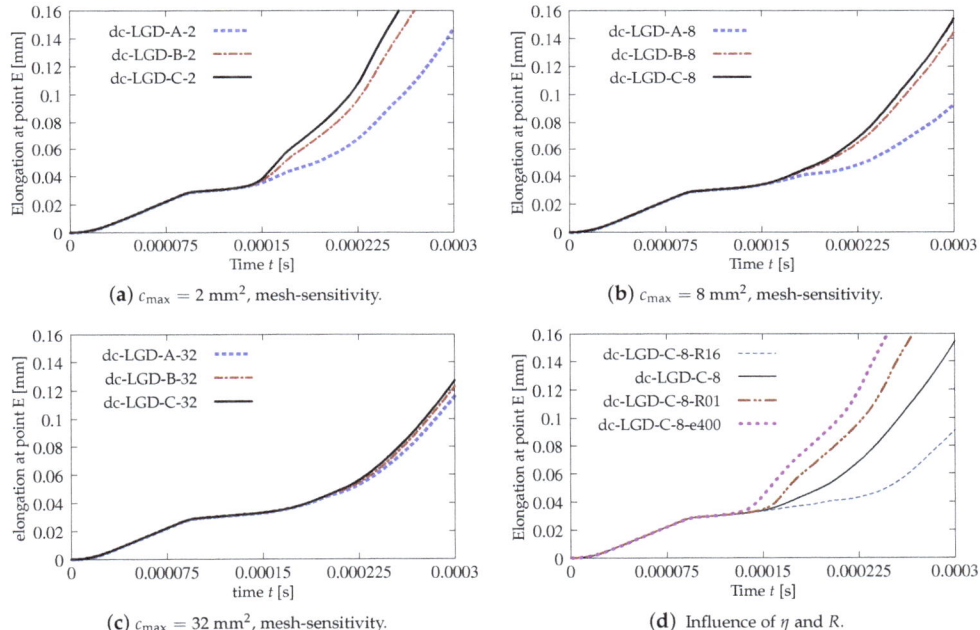

Figure 18. Dynamic tension test, plain concrete, elongation history for LGD model using function φ_1.

Figures 19–23 display contour plots for the LGD model using function φ_1. All next contour plots in this subsection are zoomed on the same central part of the bar which is subjected to impact on the edges. Such impact loading causes formation of two waves which propagate from the sides to the center, then superpose and if only the elastic limit is exceeded for the stress, the wave stops which involves strain localization. In that case one damage zone in the middle is expected. That result is compatible with the analytical solution for the bar with strain softening, cf. [68]. Damage distributions in Figure 19 are made for cases with $c_{max} = 2$ mm^2, subsequently for meshes A (dc-LGD-A-2), B (dc-LGD-B-2) and C (dc-LGD-C-2). The obtained responses are different. Not only two, but even three standing waves corresponding to localization zones occur (case dc-LGD-C-2 for mesh C); hence, this response results from an artificial numerical effect and the FEM analysis is mesh-dependent. When c_{max} is increased to 8 mm^2, then one central zone of localization is anticipated based on the results for the CGD model shown in [44], but still two damage zones appear. The case of mesh A (dc-LGD-A-8) deviates from those of meshes B (dc-LGD-B-8) and C (dc-LGD-C-8). Figure 20 depicts the distribution of averaged strain measure $\bar{\epsilon}$

and Figure 21 shows damage ω at time instant $t = 0.0003$ s. It is visible that the localization zones for mesh A are closer than for meshes B and C. In addition, it can also be noticed that the relation between $\bar{\epsilon}$ and ω is consistent with the results presented in Section 3.1—please confront Figure 8 with Figure 9 and then Figure 20 with Figure 21. The results become fully mesh-independent of the discretization for the case with $c_{max} = 32$ mm^2 (see Figure 22). One standing wave is present in the middle of the bar for each mesh (cases dc-LGD-A-32, dc-LGD-B-32 and dc-LGD-C-32). Moreover, the width of the active damage zone is quite narrow, despite the fact that $c_{max} = 32$ mm^2 is introduced. This value would rather be perceived as too large and causing too broad damage zone in the case of the CGD model with $l = 8$ mm. Therefore, the gradient activity function can significantly reduce the width of the damage zone. Figure 23 includes the contour plots for the additional cases of the analysis of the direct dynamic tension test for plain concrete. It is confirmed that the parameter R, responsible for final nonlocal interaction, truly influences the results for the LGD model. The following cases can be investigated in a sequence: dc-LGD-C-8-R01 with $R = 0.01$ in Figure 23b, dc-LGD-C-8 with $R = 0.04$ in Figure 21c and dc-LGD-C-8-R16 with $R = 0.16$ in Figure 23c. The same mesh C and $c_{max} = 8$ mm^2 are considered. For $R = 0.01$ and 0.04 two spurious localization zones appear. For $R = 0.16$ one proper zone occurs due to the presence of the standing wave in the centre of the specimen, similar to the case with $c_{max} = 32$ mm^2 and $R = 0.04$. However, the distribution of active damage ω for $R = 0.16$ has a more diffusive character. The above remarks coincide with the description of the elongation-time diagrams discussed in the previous paragraph, cf. Figure 18d. The contour plot of damage ω in Figure 23a for case dc-LGD-C-8-e400 with $\eta = 400$ for the LGD model again exhibits two zones. The value of parameter η cannot be the same as for the CGD model. Generally, the response for the LGD model is more brittle.

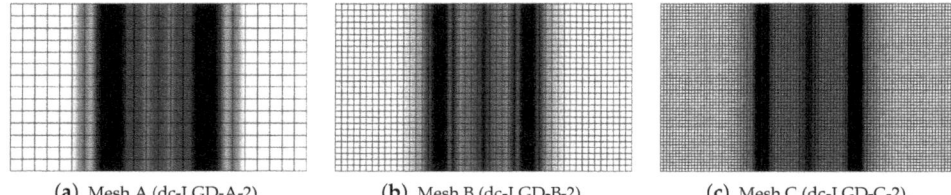

(a) Mesh A (dc-LGD-A-2). (b) Mesh B (dc-LGD-B-2). (c) Mesh C (dc-LGD-C-2).

Figure 19. Dynamic tension test, plain concrete, LGD model using function φ_1 with $c_{max} = 2$ mm^2, distribution of damage ω at $t = 0.0003$ s, mesh-sensitivity study.

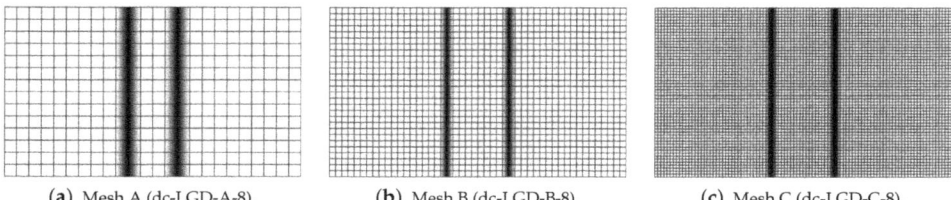

(a) Mesh A (dc-LGD-A-8). (b) Mesh B (dc-LGD-B-8). (c) Mesh C (dc-LGD-C-8).

Figure 20. Dynamic tension test, plain concrete, LGD model using function φ_1 with $c_{max} = 8$ mm^2, distribution of averaged strain $\bar{\epsilon}$ at $t = 0.0003$ s, mesh-sensitivity study.

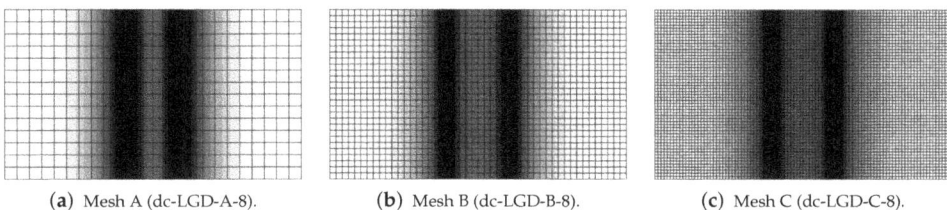

(a) Mesh A (dc-LGD-A-8). (b) Mesh B (dc-LGD-B-8). (c) Mesh C (dc-LGD-C-8).

Figure 21. Dynamic tension test, plain concrete, LGD model using function φ_1 with $c_{max} = 8$ mm^2, distribution of damage ω at $t = 0.0003$ s, mesh-sensitivity study.

(a) Mesh A (dc-LGD-A-32). (b) Mesh B (dc-LGD-B-32). (c) Mesh C (dc-LGD-C-32).

Figure 22. Dynamic tension test, plain concrete, LGD model using function φ_1 with $c_{max} = 32$ mm^2, distribution of damage ω at $t = 0.0003$ s, mesh-sensitivity study.

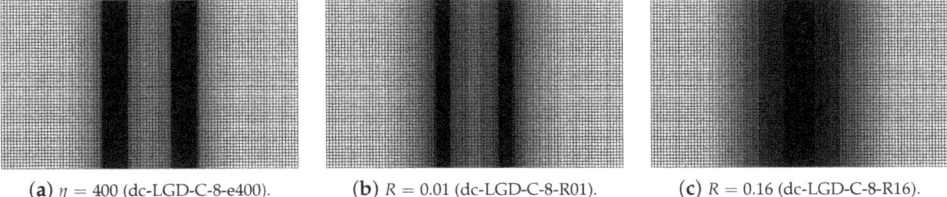

(a) $\eta = 400$ (dc-LGD-C-8-e400). (b) $R = 0.01$ (dc-LGD-C-8-R01). (c) $R = 0.16$ (dc-LGD-C-8-R16).

Figure 23. Dynamic tension test, plain concrete, LGD model using function φ_1 with $c_{max} = 8$ mm^2, mesh C, distribution of damage ω at $t = 0.0003$ s, influence of parameters η or R.

The last paragraph in this subsection describes results for the LGD model, but function φ_2 for variable gradient activity is introduced. This function decreases according to cosine as defined in Equation (45). Figure 24 shows the elongation at point E as the function of time. The diagrams in Figure 24a for $c_{max} = 2$ mm^2 (cases dc-LGDc-A-2, dc-LGDc-B-2 and dc-LGDc-C-2) starting from time $t \approx 0.00017$ diverge in a slightly different directions, while the diagrams in Figure 24b for $c_{max} = 8$ mm^2 (cases dc-LGDc-A-8, dc-LGDc-B-8 and dc-LGDc-C-8) are near to one another and only the elongation rate for mesh A is a bit smaller. It indicates that mesh-objective results can already be obtained for $c_{max} = 8$ mm^2 when function φ_2 is employed for the LGD model. Damage distributions for $c_{max} = 2$ mm^2, i.e., for dc-LGDc-A-2, dc-LGDc-B-2 and dc-LGDc-C-2 shown in Figure 25, although quite narrow damage bands are formed, are different and the width of these bands is also distinctive for each mesh. On the other hand, the increase of c_{max} to 8 mm^2 provides very similar damage distributions as illustrated in Figure 26. One active damage zone in the middle is clearly visible. In the contrast to function φ_1 it can be concluded that the application of φ_2 in the LGD model allows one to obtain results independent of the discretization even for a smaller value of maximum internal length parameter c_{max}.

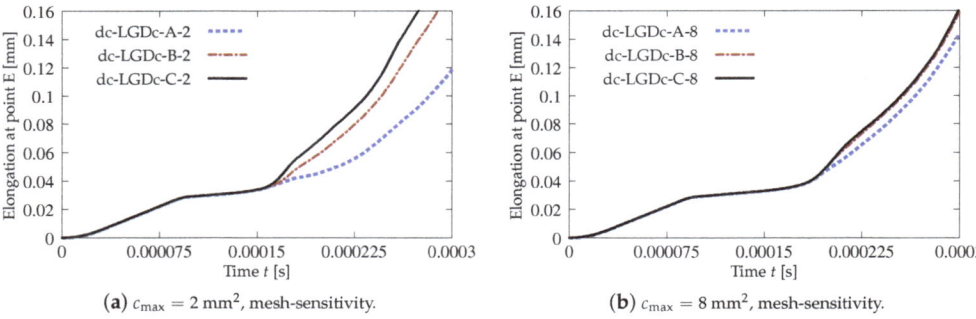

(**a**) $c_{max} = 2$ mm^2, mesh-sensitivity.

(**b**) $c_{max} = 8$ mm^2, mesh-sensitivity.

Figure 24. Dynamic tension test, plain concrete, elongation history for LGD model using function φ_2.

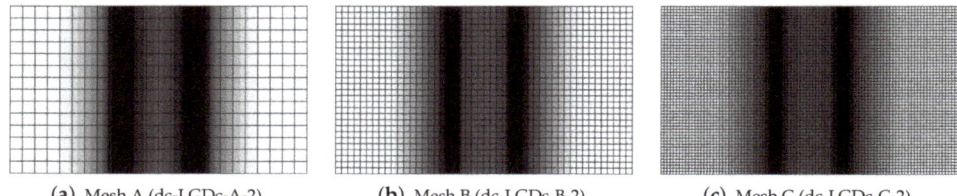

(**a**) Mesh A (dc-LGDc-A-2).

(**b**) Mesh B (dc-LGDc-B-2).

(**c**) Mesh C (dc-LGDc-C-2).

Figure 25. Dynamic tension test, plain concrete, LGD model using function φ_2 with $c_{max} = 2$ mm^2, distribution of damage ω at $t = 0.0003$ s, mesh-sensitivity study.

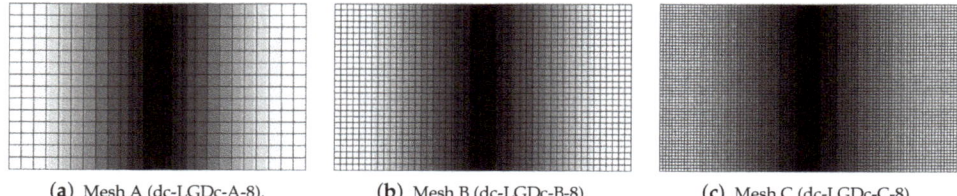

(**a**) Mesh A (dc-LGDc-A-8).

(**b**) Mesh B (dc-LGDc-B-8).

(**c**) Mesh C (dc-LGDc-C-8).

Figure 26. Dynamic tension test, plain concrete, LGD model using function φ_2 with $c_{max} = 8$ mm^2, distribution of damage ω at $t = 0.0003$ s, mesh-sensitivity study.

3.2.3. Results for Reinforced Concrete

In this subsection the results for the RC configuration subjected to dynamic tension are presented. The solution for the LGD model with function φ_1 defined in Equation (43) is illustrated in Figures 27–29. The elongation-time diagrams given in Figure 27 show that the presence of the rebar precludes a progress to infinite displacements. Each curve oscillates around some value of elongation. However, the diagrams for $c_{max} = 2$ mm^2 in Figure 27a are different for each mesh. The denser the mesh is, the smaller amplitude is observed. Contour plots in Figure 28 for damage ω at the final time instant $t = 0.0006$ s depict the localization zones placed near the centre analogically to the distributions when plain concrete specimen is considered, cf. the case with φ_1 and $c_{max} = 8$ mm^2 (Figure 21) or with φ_2 and $c_{max} = 2$ mm^2 (Figure 25). In the subsequent plots of Figure 28 these vertical zones slightly move away from each other. In addition, the presence of the rebar along the horizontal symmetry is seen, where damage does not activate. Actually, the most active damage is present away from the reinforcing bar. This solution is possible when full bond between the steel rebar and the concrete matrix is assumed. However, composite structures of such type can also be modelled with a representation of bond-slip by so-called interface elements, which leads to generation of many localization zones in the vicinity of the reinforcement, see, e.g., [69,70]. Moreover, it is possible to employ an interface zone called an interphase as in [71,72]. It is formed by a layer (or more layers) of FEs with non-zero thickness and represents a transition between the concrete matrix and the reinforcement as weaker concrete. The simplifying assumption of full bond as in the current computations is more suitable for modelling of RC structures with ribbed bars. The diagrams in Figure 27b for the cases with $c_{max} = 8$ mm^2 almost overlap and curves oscillate around 0.019 mm. When the maximum internal length c_{max} is increased, then the strain localization starts from the centre points of the horizontal edges. It is observed for the distributions of damage ω in Figure 29. These cases are analogical to the results for plain concrete when φ_1 and $c_{max} = 32$ mm^2 (Figure 22) or φ_2 and $c_{max} = 8$ mm^2 (Figure 26) are assumed. The damage zones given in Figure 29 are quite narrow. Hence, it is shown for the RC bar under the impact loading that the LGD model with the gradient activity represented by function φ_1 is able to ensure the mesh-objective solution together with a proper (not too wide) distribution of active damage.

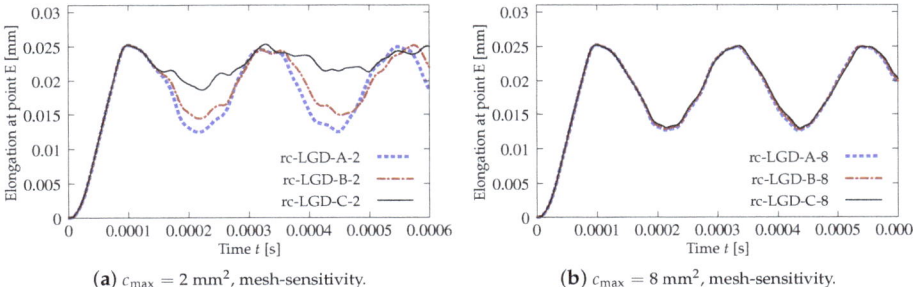

Figure 27. Dynamic tension test, reinforced concrete, elongation history for LGD model using function φ_1.

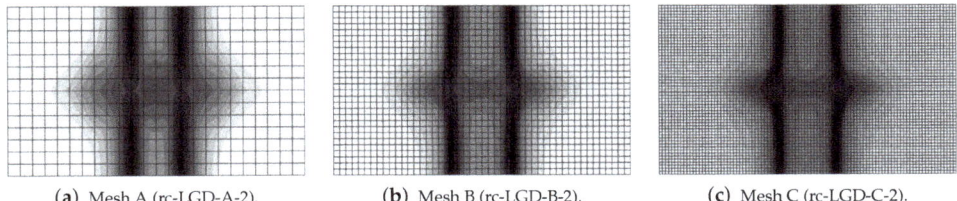

Figure 28. Dynamic tension test, reinforced concrete, LGD model using function φ_1 with $c_{max} = 2$ mm^2, distribution of damage ω at $t = 0.0006$ s, mesh-sensitivity study.

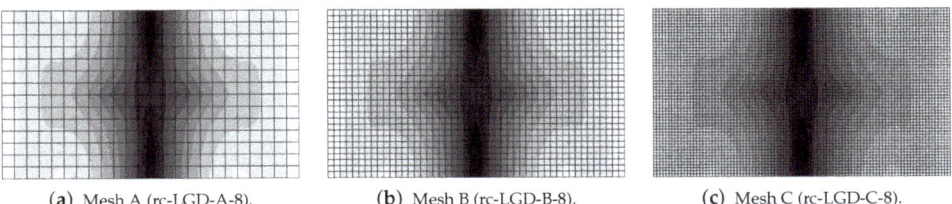

Figure 29. Dynamic tension test, reinforced concrete, LGD model using function φ_1 with $c_{max} = 8$ mm^2, distribution of damage ω at $t = 0.0006$ s, mesh-sensitivity study.

All previous results described in Sections 3.1 and 3.2.2 for the LGD model with application of function φ_2 defined in Equation (45) constituted a reasonable alternative for the gradient activity determined by φ_1. The results for the case with φ_2 and $c_{max} = 2$ mm^2 seem to deny this possibility. The elongation history at point E, shown in Figure 30a, strongly differs for the following meshes. In case rc-LGDc-A-2 for coarse mesh A, after the initial extension, the response oscillates around 0.02 mm. In cases rc-LGDc-B-2 for medium mesh B and rc-LGDc-C-2 for fine mesh C this horizontal displacement runs to infinity, but for the latter case the elongation is more rapid. Differences are also clearly visible for the contour plots in Figure 31. The distribution of damage ω for rc-LGDc-A-2 in Figure 31a is as expected and its character is similar to the one presented for rc-LGD-A-8 in Figure 29a. Active damage develops from the centre points of both horizontal edges. The damage plots for the next meshes, i.e., for cases rc-LGDc-B-2 and rc-LGDc-C-2 depicted in Figure 31b,c, exhibit that the solution is sensitive to the adopted discretization. Damage grows also along the reinforcing bar, which seems to be an undesirable consequence of the full bond assumption. This issue vanishes if larger $c_{max} = 8$ mm^2 is introduced. The diagrams in Figure 30b are the same for each mesh, the reinforcement in the specimen inhibits the displacements going to infinity. The contour plots for damage ω in Figure 32 are almost the same for each mesh, as well. The zones of active damage are wider than for the case with function φ_1 and $c_{max} = 8$ mm^2 (cf. Figure 29), but the solution with φ_2 is still satisfactory. Figure 33 compares the time-elongation diagrams for the CGD and LGD models. The case rc-LGDc-C-8 differs slightly from the others. However, all the diagrams have a similar character—amplitudes have a comparable range, maximum values of elongation are visible at close time instants and the horizontal displacement at point E does not go to infinity.

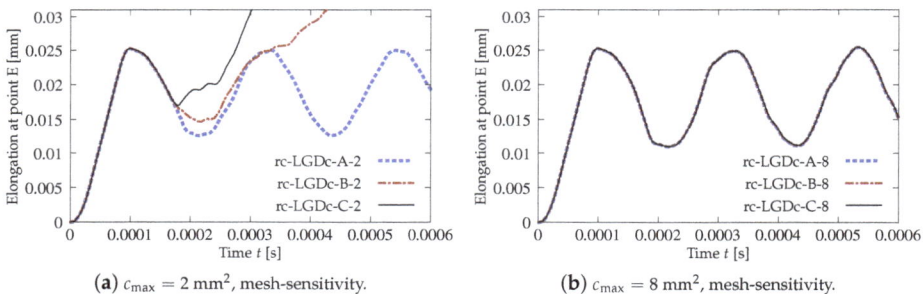

Figure 30. Dynamic tension test, reinforced concrete, elongation history for LGD model using function φ_2.

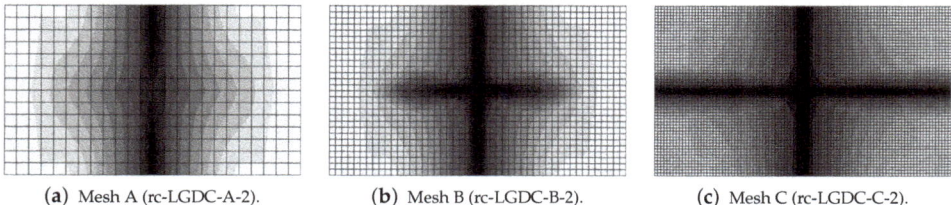

Figure 31. Dynamic tension test, reinforced concrete, LGD model using function φ_2 with $c_{max} = 2$ mm^2, distribution of damage ω at $t = 0.0006$ s, mesh-sensitivity study.

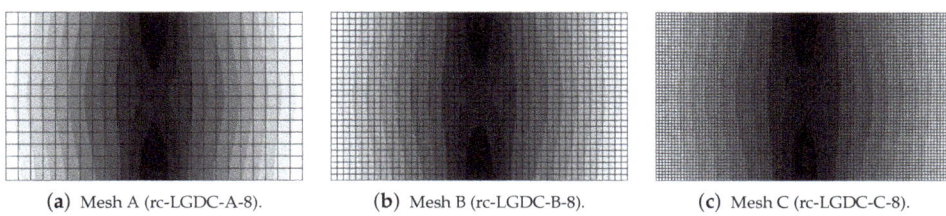

(**a**) Mesh A (rc-LGDC-A-8). (**b**) Mesh B (rc-LGDC-B-8). (**c**) Mesh C (rc-LGDC-C-8).

Figure 32. Dynamic tension test, reinforced concrete, LGD model using function φ_2 with $c_{max} = 8$ mm^2, distribution of damage ω at $t = 0.0006$ s, mesh-sensitivity study.

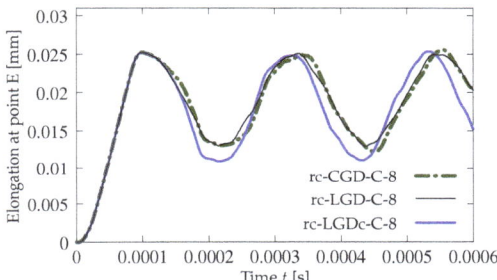

Figure 33. Dynamic tension test, reinforced concrete, comparison of models for elongation history, mesh C, $l = 4$ mm or $c_{max} = 8$ mm^2.

3.3. L-Shaped Specimen under Static and Dynamic Tensile Cracking

The third example is based on the experiment described in [45]. An L-shaped concrete specimen with a fixed lower edge is subjected to tensile cracking from a corner by a vertical load originating from a pull-up clamp. In [45] this structural member is investigated also with different combinations of steel reinforcing bars or orthogonal grids, but the numerical analysis presented below focuses only on plain concrete. The response of the L-specimen can be influenced by different loading rates as shown in [73] for the numerical study with the microplane model for concrete. Furthermore, dynamic fracture of the L-shaped concrete specimen is meticulously reported in [46], where authors' experimental tests are compared with the numerical study. The gradient-enhanced damage model linked with the microplane damage model is verified in [74] by means of a static analysis for the L-specimen. This test for statics is analyzed using the LGD model, see [31,37]. In the current paper, the numerical analysis is carried out for statics as well as for dynamics and the results for the CGD and LGD models are confronted.

Figure 34 presents the L-shaped specimen together with the illustration of the fixed edge and the place where the loading is applied. The geometry of the L-specimen is determined by the characteristic size $D = 250$ mm. The area of crack pattern for the experiment performed in [45] for plain concrete configuration is also depicted in Figure 34. In the computations three meshes are employed. The basic mesh A shown in Figure 34 is homogeneous and square FEs have the side of 5 mm. The number of eight-noded elements is 7500, the number of nodes is 23,604. The next mesh B has 16,875 square eight-noded FEs with the side of $3\frac{1}{3}$ mm for each element, 52,279 nodes and is also uniform. The third mesh C is structural and divided into some regions with rectangular and square FEs. The number of elements is 13,218. The number of nodes is 41,796. However, the region with expected cracking is most densely discretized by FEs with the element size equal to 2.5 mm. For the static analysis the Newton–Raphson method with the arc length control is used. For dynamics the standard Newmark algorithm is applied. The dynamic loading is enforced according to a linear function, but different rates are considered. The list of examined cases is given in Table 3. The loading with average rate is 10 times slower than for the case with the fast rate and 5 times faster than for the case with the slow rate.

Table 3. Cases of loading rates for L-shaped specimen.

Loading Rate	Time Step [μs]	Number of Steps	Final Time t_{fin} [μs]	Final Intensity p_{fin} [MPa]	Slope p_{fin}/t_{fin} [MPa/s]
fast	4.0	150	600.0	24.0	40,000.0
average	5.0	300	1500.0	6.0	4000.0
slow	10.0	366	3660.0	2.928	800.0

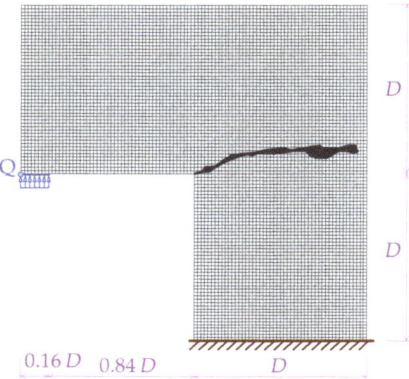

Figure 34. Configuration of L-shaped specimen together with mesh A and area of crack pattern for experiment with static loading performed in [45].

The elastic constants are the same for CGD and LGD models: Young's modulus $E = 25{,}850$ MPa and Poisson's ratio $\nu = 0.18$. When dynamics is analyzed the density ρ equals 2400 kg/m^3. The plane stress configuration with thickness $T = 100$ mm is assumed. The damage threshold $\kappa_o = 1.0445 \times 10^{-4}$ corresponds to tensile strength $f_t = 2.7$ MPa. Exponential softening law given in Equation (41) is employed with $\alpha = 0.96$ and $\eta = 400$ for the CGD model or with $\alpha = 0.95$ and $\eta = 112.5$ for the LGD model. The equivalent strain measure is introduced for both models by the modified von Mises definition (40) with $k = 11.4815$, which reflects to compressive strength $f_c = 31.0$ MPa. The constant internal length parameter c_{max} is equal to 12.5 mm^2 for the CGD model. The LGD model is applied with c_{max} as the half of maximum internal length scale squared. Two options are considered: the gradient activity is determined by function φ_1 defined in Equation (43) with $R = 0.01$ and $n = 5.0$ or function φ_2 defined in Equation (45) with the same R and $n = 1.0$, cf. Figure 2.

Figure 35 shows the diagrams for the load sketched in blue in Figure 34 versus the vertical displacement measured at point Q. The equilibrium paths for the CGD model in Figure 35a almost coincide and are consistent with the experimental result. It is confirmed in Figure 36, where the zones of active damage have the same shape for each mesh and coincide with the region of cracking illustrated in Figure 34. Excessive broadening of the damage zone occurs as shown in Section 3.1 for the results of the CGD model. Again, it is demonstrated that the LGD model is able to overcome this problem. Figure 37 presents analogical contour plots for damage distributions when the LGD model is used with function φ_1. The width of the damage zone is much narrower in the comparison to corresponding plots for the CGD model. On the other hand, a ragged area of damage occurs in a part of the localized zone starting from the corner. It is visible especially for coarse mesh A, see Figure 37a. This effect is connected with too coarse discretization for the LGD model, despite the fact that 7500 FEs is used. The LGD model demands really refined meshes in the computations, see also [27,30,31]. The problem of the zone with a non-smooth edge vanishes together with a denser mesh, cf. Figure 37b for mesh B and Figure 37c for mesh C. Moreover, the ragged areas in the damage distributions are less distinct when the LGD model with the gradient activity using the cosine function φ_2 is taken into account (see Figure 38). The zone of active damage for mesh C in Figure 38c has fully smooth shape and this solution resembles the cracked area from the experiment, cf. Figure 34. The load-displacement diagrams for the LGD model are depicted in Figure 35b for function φ_1 and in Figure 35c for function φ_2. They are in the limit of the gray region obtained for the experiment [45], but vary for the solutions obtained for subsequent meshes. The difference between meshes B and C is smaller for both the functions φ_1 and φ_2. It can be assumed that the density of mesh B is enough to achieve a quite objective solution. As shown for the first example in Section 3.1 the LGD model provides the results independent of the discretization.

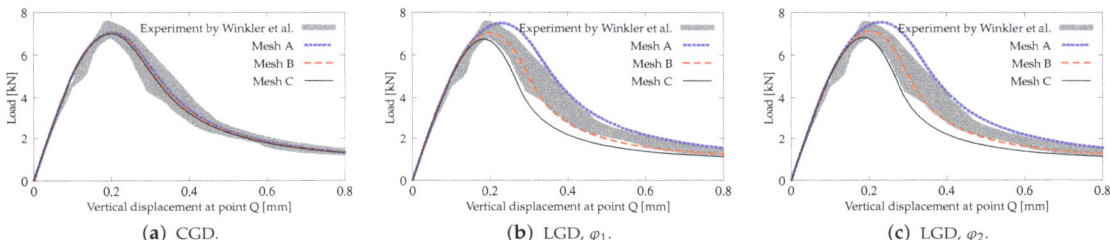

(a) CGD. **(b)** LGD, φ_1. **(c)** LGD, φ_2.

Figure 35. L-shaped test, statics, diagrams of load vs vertical displacement at point Q, mesh-sensitivity study.

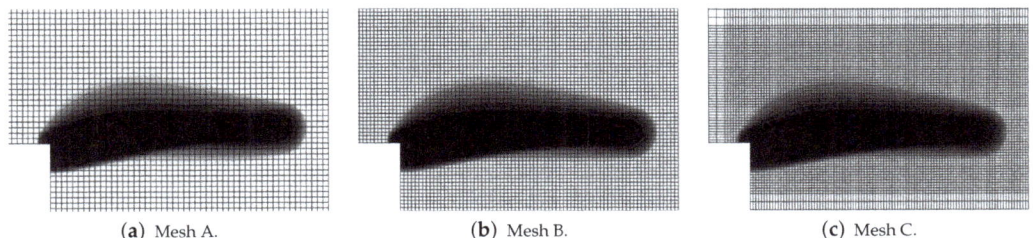

(a) Mesh A. **(b)** Mesh B. **(c)** Mesh C.

Figure 36. L-shaped test, statics, CGD model, distribution of damage ω, mesh-sensitivity study.

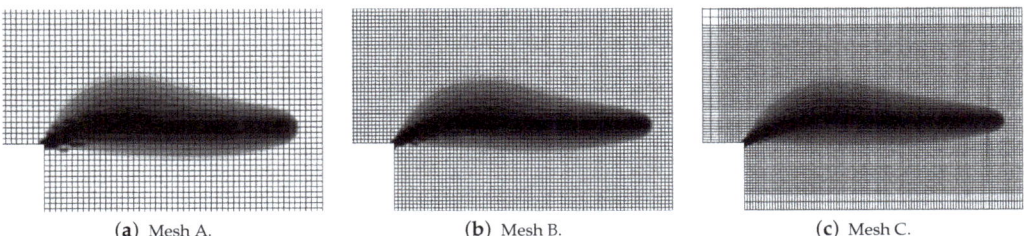

(a) Mesh A. **(b)** Mesh B. **(c)** Mesh C.

Figure 37. L-shaped test, statics, LGD model using function φ_1, distribution of damage ω, mesh-sensitivity study.

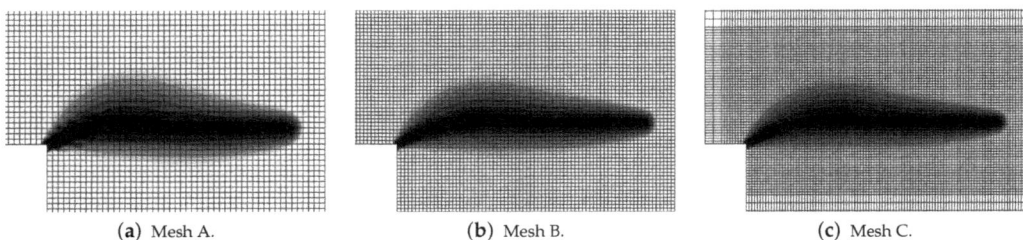

Figure 38. L-shaped test, statics, LGD model using function φ_2, distribution of damage ω, mesh-sensitivity study.

The last part of this section is devoted to the analysis of the L-specimen subjected to the dynamic loading which grows linearly. The attention is focused on the comparison of the models, not the mesh-sensitivity study, hence only mesh B is selected in the computations. The material data for the CGD and LGD models are the same as for statics. Three cases with different rates (fast, average and slow) of the loading are analyzed, according to Table 3. The diagrams of vertical displacement or velocity or acceleration at point Q versus time for these three rates are depicted in Figure 39. It is shown that they correspond to one another for all the applied models and vary with the loading rate. In Figure 39a the displacement around 0.6 mm is attained for time of about 0.5 ms for the fast rate, approximately 1.3 ms for the average rate and close to 3.6 ms for the slow rate. The acceleration can be confronted the velocity, see Figure 39b,c. It is noticed that amplitudes of the acceleration are largest for the fast rate and the maximum value achieved are over 1.5×10^7 mm/s^2. They are strongly reduced to around 2.0×10^6 mm/s^2 for the average rate and finally the acceleration becomes very small for the slow rate. Figures 40–42 show corresponding damage distributions. It is visible in Figure 40 that if the fast rate is investigated the damage zone is directed almost vertically, independently of the used model. Analogically, for the average rate damage develops diagonally for each model (see Figure 41). When the slow rate is taken into account, the damage growth in Figure 42 has a similar direction to those obtained for static computations, but at the end it goes up. The change of the fracture direction from extending upwards for the fast rate to propagating horizontally for the slow rate is also observed for the computations discussed in [46,73]. It is seen for the CGD model that the damage zone is the widest, regardless of the loading rate. For the LGD model this zone is much narrower, however the ragged areas still occur. This problem is reduced if function φ_2 is employed (see, e.g., Figure 41c). For cases with fast or average rates of the loading it can be distinguished that the distribution of the active damage expands and forms an elliptic area perpendicularly to the initial direction of the damage zone. It is probably connected with a transformation of mode I to mixed mode for strain localization. Moreover, branching in cracking of the concrete L-specimen investigated in the experiment can be simulated as shown in [46]. Here, the gradient-enhanced model in both implemented versions (CGD and LGD) is not able to reproduce the branching effect. This effect requires a recognition of the crack tip and for instance an extra projection method for the strain tensor [75].

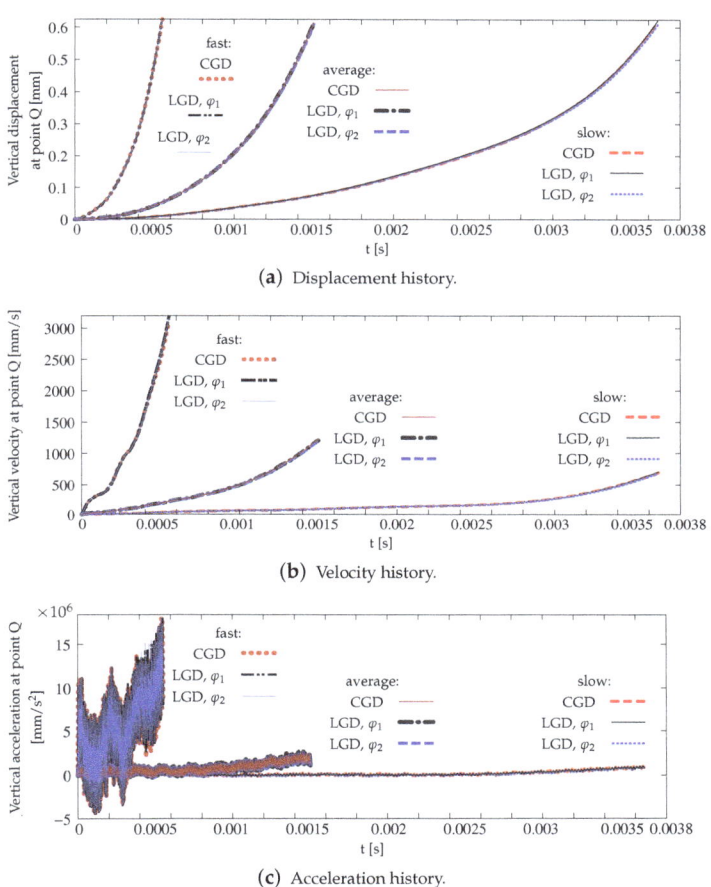

(a) Displacement history.

(b) Velocity history.

(c) Acceleration history.

Figure 39. L-shaped test, dynamics, response histories, comparison of models and different rates of loading.

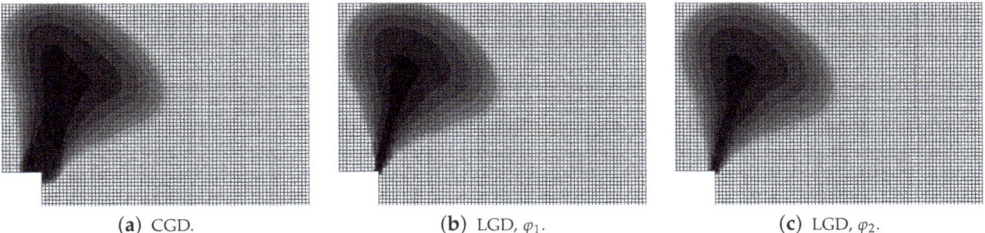

(a) CGD.   (b) LGD, φ_1.   (c) LGD, φ_2.

Figure 40. L-shaped test, dynamics, fast rate of loading, distribution of damage ω for available models.

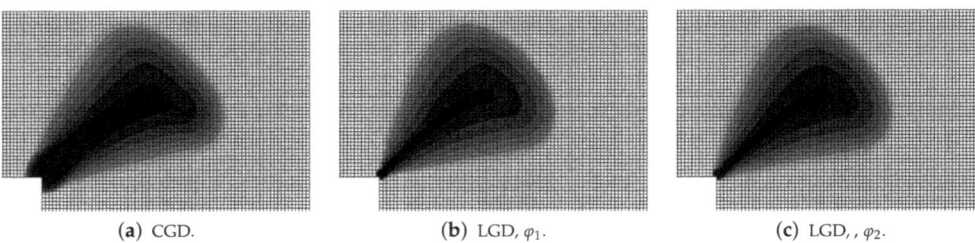

(a) CGD. (b) LGD, φ_1. (c) LGD, , φ_2.

Figure 41. L-shaped test, dynamics, average rate of loading, distribution of damage ω for available models.

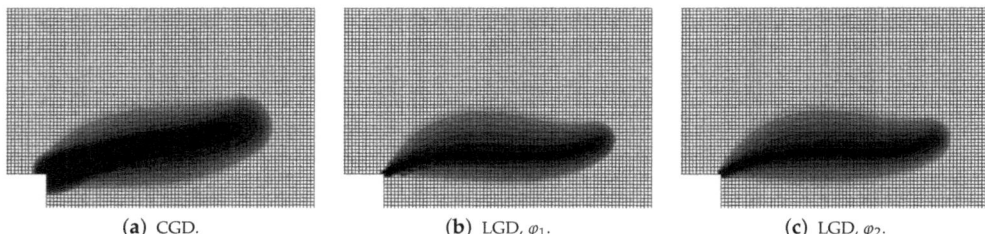

(a) CGD. (b) LGD, φ_1. (c) LGD, φ_2.

Figure 42. L-shaped test, dynamics, slow rate of loading, distribution of damage ω for available models.

4. Discussion

In the paper, the localizing gradient damage model (LGD) is examined in the reference to standard version of this model, called the conventional gradient damage model (CGD). The range of the study is limited to the analysis of tension tests. The results of simulations are widely discussed in Section 3. A summary of performed computations is presented in Table 4. The first part of the table shows that both versions of this nonlocal model (CGD and LGD) are considered, but the dynamic direct tension test is carried out using only the LGD model. Two different functions of the gradient activity are employed in this model. The considered specimens are subjected to static or dynamic tension. The results for double-edge-notched test are compared with the experiment performed in [39]. The second numerical test with dynamic direct tension caused by impact loading is carried out for the configuration without or with reinforcement and it is a continuation of the research published in [44]. The last example concerns tension in the L-shaped specimen, for which static or dynamic problem is solved. Computations for statics are based on the experiment presented in [45] and they are comparable with those presented in [31,74]. The results for dynamics have a rather similar character to those shown in [46]. In the analysis, three or four meshes are used in order to demonstrate a reliable mesh-sensitivity study. The same type of eight-noded FE with Serendipity shape functions for nodal displacements a and bilinear Lagrange shape functions for nodal averaged strains e as well as 2×2 Gauss integration is applied in all the computations. More details of discretization are included in Table 4 or in the description of the model for each example. Conclusions resulting from the survey described in Section 3 are listed below.

Table 4. Summary of computed examples.

Section	Section 3.1	Section 3.2		Section 3.3	
Concrete models	CGD, LGD	LGD		CGD, LGD	
Gradient activity	$\varphi_0, \varphi_1, \varphi_2$	φ_1, φ_2		$\varphi_0, \varphi_1, \varphi_2$	
Specimen	double-edge-notched	unnotched		L-shaped	
Concrete	plain	plain	reinforced	plain	
Analysis	statics	dynamics		statics	dynamics
Increment procedure	indirect displacement control	standard Newmark		arc length control	standard Newmark
Loading	static	impact, linear-constant		static	dynamic, linear
Number of meshes	4	3		3	
Mesh type	densified near the notches	uniform		uniform or structural	uniform
Shape of FEs	square, rectangular, trapezoidal	square		square, rectangular	square
Minimum size of FE	0.625 mm	1 mm		2.5 mm	$3\tfrac{1}{3}$ mm

5. Conclusions

The paper contains the study of the localizing gradient damage model (LGD). The model [27,28] is compared with its precursor [6], i.e., the conventional gradient damage model (CGD). Both models are able to simulate cracking in quasi-brittle composite materials, in particular concrete. When the CGD model is used, a spuriously widening zone of damage occurs in simulations. This problem is overcome by means of the LGD model. The theory presentation starts from the definition of the Helmholtz free energy which depends on the strain tensor, averaged strain measure and its gradient. The averaging equation with constant or variable gradient activity is derived from this definition, cf. [7,8]. The formulation of the LGD model leads to the linearization and discretization of the (I)BVP. For dynamics the mass matrix is additionally defined, but the two-field formulation known from the CGD model holds. Both the models are implemented in the FEAP package [38]. The gradient activity in the LGD model has a localizing character, because the nonlocal interaction domain shrinks with the damage growth (see Figure 1). The gradient activity function is assumed to decrease exponentially as in [27,28] or according to a cosine function as proposed in Equation (45).

When the gradient activity function has the exponential character, then the power n called here the intensity parameter can affect the localizing process of nonlocal averaging significantly. In the computations usually $n = 5.0$ is introduced, but as shown in the example of the double-edge-notched bar it can lead to convergence disturbance at the onset of strain localization, see Figure 13a. A smaller value $n = 1.0$ causes the gradient activity to decrease slower, but then the damage zone becomes wider. In most computational cases the exponential function φ_1 with $n = 5.0$ provides mesh-objective results with an appropriately narrow zone of active damage.

However, the gradient activity function φ_2 can be an alternative to φ_1. The localization zone is then more smeared for smaller damage values, but it is similar to the distribution obtained for φ_1 for damage values approaching 1.0. The convergence disturbance vanishes. Generally, function φ_2 provides correct results in the modelling of concrete cracking using the LGD model, unless a small value of c_{max} defined as the maximum internal length scale squared is applied. For instance, poor results are obtained for $c_{max} = 2$ mm^2 in the direct dynamic tension test for the reinforced concrete (RC) configuration (see Figures 30a and 31).

The application of the LGD model removes the issue of artificially broadening damage zone, but the results become more dependent on the discretization. In the paper static and dynamic tension of concrete is analyzed. Based on the results for all discussed examples, it is realized that only a reasonably refined mesh can assure a fully mesh-objective solution. As demonstrated for the L-specimen test, a problem of ragged areas in the damage distribution can occur for too coarse meshes, but it disappears upon mesh densification.

The double-edge-notched test of static tensile cracking should be computed with an extra care to keep the symmetry and proper convergence. In the dynamic direct tension test for plain concrete one zone of active damage related to a standing wave in the center is expected. The selection of values for the model parameters influences the correctness of the dynamic response. The parameter c_{max} and even more the parameter R associated with the residual interaction cannot be too small, because then two or more localization zones can appear. In the dynamic analysis of the L-shaped specimen, the change of direction of the damage growth zone is reproduced depending on different rates of loading, analogically to [46,73]. However, branching in concrete cracking cannot be simulated using the LGD model in this version, so in this respect it requires a further enhancement in the future.

Summarizing, the LGD model guarantees mesh-objective solution with a correct zone of active damage for static and dynamic problems, and performs better than the CGD model, but it calls for a careful selection of the values of its parameters and requires the use of denser meshes.

Funding: Full open access to the paper is supported by the Faculty of Civil Engineering at the Cracow University of Technology.

Institutional Review Board Statement: Not applicable.

Informed Consent Statement: Not applicable.

Data Availability Statement: Not applicable.

Acknowledgments: Constructive discussions with Jerzy Pamin and the help of Roman Putanowicz in FEAP installation are gratefully acknowledged. All computations were performed on server Krakus at Cracow University of Technology courtesy of Witold Cecot.

Conflicts of Interest: The author declares no conflict of interest.

Abbreviations

The following abbreviations are used in this manuscript:

CGD	conventional gradient damage
FE	finite element
FEM	finite element method
FEs	finite elements
(I)BVP	(initial) boundary value problem
LGD	localizing gradient damage
RC	reinforced concrete
TGD	transient gradient damage

References

1. Kachanov, L.M. Time of rupture process under creep conditions. *Izd. Akad. Nauk SSSR Otd. Tekh. Nauk* **1958**, *8*, 26–31. (In Russian)
2. Rudnicki, J.W.; Rice, J.R. Conditions for the localization of deformation in pressure-sensitive dilatant materials. *J. Mech. Phys. Solids* **1975**, *23*, 371–394. [CrossRef]
3. Pietruszczak, S.; Mróz, Z. Finite element analysis of deformation of strain-softening materials. *Int. J. Numer. Meth. Eng.* **1981**, *17*, 327–334. [CrossRef]
4. Bažant, Z.P.; Oh, B. Crack band theory for fracture of concrete. *RILEM Mater. Struct.* **1983**, *16*, 155–177. [CrossRef]
5. Aifantis, E.C. On the microstructural origin of certain inelastic models. *J. Eng. Mater. Technol.* **1984**, *106*, 326–330. [CrossRef]
6. Peerlings, R.H.J.; de Borst, R.; Brekelmans, W.A.M.; de Vree, J.H.P. Gradient-enhanced damage for quasi-brittle materials. *Int. J. Numer. Meth. Eng.* **1996**, *39*, 3391–3403. [CrossRef]
7. Peerlings, R.H.J.; Massart, T.J.; Geers, M.G.D. A thermodynamically motivated implicit gradient damage framework and its application to brick masonry cracking. *Comput. Methods Appl. Mech. Eng.* **2004**, *193*, 3403–3417. [CrossRef]
8. Dimitrijević, B.J.; Hackl, K. A method for gradient enhancement of continuum damage models. *Tech. Mech.* **2008**, *28*, 43–52.
9. Peerlings, R.H.J.; Geers, M.G.D.; de Borst, R.; Brekelmans, W.A.M. A critical comparison of nonlocal and gradient-enhanced softening continua. *Int. J. Solids Struct.* **2001**, *38*, 7723–7746. [CrossRef]

10. Park, T.; Ahmed, B.; Voyiadjis, G.Z. A review of continuum damage and plasticity in concrete: Part I—Theoretical framework. *Int. J. Damage Mech.* **2021**, 10567895211068174. [CrossRef]
11. Park, T.; Ahmed, B.; Voyiadjis, G.Z. A review of continuum damage and plasticity in concrete: Part II—Numerical framework. *Int. J. Damage Mech.* **2021**, 10567895211063227. [CrossRef]
12. Peerlings, R.H.J.; de Borst, R.; Brekelmans, W.A.M.; Geers, M.G.D. Gradient-enhanced damage modelling of concrete fracture. *Mech. Cohes.-Frict. Mater.* **1998**, *3*, 323–342. [CrossRef]
13. Geers, M.G.D. Experimental Analysis and Computational Modelling of Damage and Fracture. Ph.D. Dissertation, Eindhoven University of Technology, Eindhoven, The Netherlands, 1997. [CrossRef]
14. Geers, M.G.D.; de Borst, R.; Brekelmans, W.A.M.; Peerlings, R.H.J. Strain-based transient-gradient damage model for failure analyses. *Comput. Methods Appl. Mech. Eng.* **1998**, *160*, 133–153. [CrossRef]
15. Di Luzio, G.; Bažant, Z.P. Spectral analysis of localization in nonlocal and over-nonlocal materials with softening plasticity or damage. *Int. J. Solids Struct.* **2005**, *42*, 6071–6100. [CrossRef]
16. Poh, L.H.; Swaddiwudhipong, S. Gradient-enhanced softening material models. *Int. J. Plast.* **2009**, *25*, 2094–2121. [CrossRef]
17. Brinkgreve, R.B.J. Geomaterial Models and Numerical Analysis of Softening. Ph.D. Dissertation, Delft University of Technology, Delft, The Netherlands, 1994.
18. Bobiński, J.; Tejchman, J. Modelling of strain localization in quasi-brittle materials with nonlocal continuum models. In Proceedings of the EURO-C 2006 Conference, Mayrhofen, Austria, 27–30 March 2006; Taylor & Francis: London, UK; Leiden, The Netherlands, 2006; pp. 301–307.
19. Grassl, P.; Jirásek, M. Plastic model with non-local damage applied to concrete. *Int. J. Num. Anal. Meth. Geomech.* **2006**, *30*, 71–90. [CrossRef]
20. Jirásek, M.; Desmorat, R. Localization analysis of nonlocal models with damage-dependent nonlocal interaction. *Int. J. Solids Struct.* **2019**, *174–175*, 1–17. [CrossRef]
21. Bui, Q.V. Initiation of damage with implicit gradient-enhanced damage models. *Int. J. Solids Struct.* **2010**, *47*, 2425–2435. [CrossRef]
22. Nguyen, G.D. A damage model with evolving nonlocal interactions. *Int. J. Solids Struct.* **2011**, *48*, 1544–1559. [CrossRef]
23. Vandoren, B.; Simone, A. Modeling and simulation of quasi-brittle failure with continuous anisotropic stress-based gradient-enhanced damage models. *Comput. Methods Appl. Mech. Eng.* **2018**, *332*, 644–685. [CrossRef]
24. Nguyen, T.H.A.; Bui, T.Q.; Hirose, S. Smoothing gradient damage model with evolving anisotropic nonlocal interactions tailored to low-order finite elements. *Comput. Methods Appl. Mech. Eng.* **2018**, *328*, 498–541. [CrossRef]
25. Vuong, C.D.; Bui, T.Q.; Hirose, S. Enhancement of the smoothing gradient damage model with alternative equivalent strain estimation for localization failure. *Eng. Fract. Mech.* **2021**, *258*, 108057. [CrossRef]
26. Saroukhani, S.; Vafadari, R.; Simone, A. A simplified implementation of a gradient-enhanced damage model with transient length scale effects. *Comput. Mech.* **2013**, *51*, 899–909. [CrossRef]
27. Poh, L.H.; Sun, G. Localizing gradient damage model with decreasing interaction. *Int. J. Numer. Meth. Eng.* **2017**, *110*, 503–522. [CrossRef]
28. Sun, G. Localizing Gradient Damage Models for the Fracture of Quasi-Brittle Materials. Ph.D. Dissertation, National University of Singapore, Singapore, 2017.
29. Jirásek, M. Regularized continuum damage formulations acting as localization limiters. In Proceedings of the Conference on Computational Modelling of Concrete and Concrete Structures (EURO-C 2018), Bad Hofgastein, Austria, 26 February–1 March 2018; CRC Press/Balkema: London, UK, 2018; pp. 25–41.
30. Wosatko, A. Comparison of evolving gradient damage formulations with different activity functions. *Arch. Appl. Mech.* **2021**, *91*, 597–627. [CrossRef]
31. Sarkar, S.; Singh, I.; Mishra, B.; Shedbale, A.; Poh, L. A comparative study and ABAQUS implementation of conventional and localizing gradient enhanced damage models. *Finite Elem. Anal. Des.* **2019**, *160*, 1–31. [CrossRef]
32. Zhang, Y.; Shedbale, A.S.; Gan, Y.; Moon, J.; Poh, L.H. Size effect analysis of quasi-brittle fracture with localizing gradient damage model. *Int. J. Damage Mech.* **2021**, *30*, 1012–1035. [CrossRef]
33. Shedbale, A.S.; Sun, G.; Poh, L.H. A localizing gradient enhanced isotropic damage model with Ottosen equivalent strain for the mixed-mode fracture of concrete. *Int. J. Mech. Sci.* **2021**, *199*, 106410. [CrossRef]
34. Wang, Z.; Poh, L.H. A homogenized localizing gradient damage model with micro inertia effect. *J. Mech. Phys. Solids* **2018**, *116*, 370–390. [CrossRef]
35. Wang, Z.; Shedbale, A.S.; Kumar, S.; Poh, L.H. Localizing gradient damage model with micro intertia effect for dynamic fracture. *Comput. Methods Appl. Mech. Eng.* **2019**, *355*, 492–512. [CrossRef]
36. Tong, T.; Hua, G.; Liu, Z.; Liu, X.; Xu, T. Localizing gradient damage model coupled to extended microprestress-solidification theory for long-term nonlinear time-dependent behaviors of concrete structures. *Mech. Mater.* **2021**, *154*, 103713. [CrossRef]
37. Sarkar, S.; Singh, I.; Mishra, B. Adaptive mesh refinement schemes for the localizing gradient damage method based on biquadratic-bilinear coupled-field elements. *Eng. Fract. Mech.* **2020**, *223*, 106790. [CrossRef]
38. Taylor, R. *FEAP—A Finite Element Analysis Program, Version 7.4, User Manual*; University of California at Berkeley: Berkeley, CA, USA, 2001.

39. Hordijk, D.A. Local Approach to Fatigue of Concrete. Ph.D. Dissertation, Delft University of Technology, Delft, The Netherlands, 1991.
40. Rhee, I.; Lee, J.S.; Roh, Y.S. Fracture parameters of cement mortar with different structural dimensions under the direct tension test. *Materials* **2019**, *12*, 1850. [CrossRef] [PubMed]
41. van Mier, J.G.M.; van Vliet, M.R.A. Experimental investigation of size effect in concrete and sandstone under uniaxial tension. *Eng. Fract. Mech.* **2000**, *65*, 165–188. [CrossRef]
42. Lee, S.K.; Woo, S.K.; Song, Y.C. Softening response properties of plain concrete by large-scale direct tension test. *Mag. Concr. Res.* **2008**, *60*, 33–40. [CrossRef]
43. Ožbolt, J.; Bošnjak, J.; Sola, E. Dynamic fracture of concrete compact tension specimen: Experimental and numerical study. *Int. J. Solids Struct.* **2013**, *50*, 4270–4278. [CrossRef]
44. Wosatko, A.; Winnicki, A.; Pamin, J. Simulations of concrete response to impact loading using two regularized models. *Comput. Assist. Methods Eng. Sci.* **2020**, *27*, 27–60. [CrossRef]
45. Winkler, B.; Hofstetter, G.; Niederwanger, G. Experimental verification of a constitutive model for concrete cracking. *Proc. Inst. Mech. Eng. Part L J. Mater. Des. Appl.* **2001**, *215*, 75–86. [CrossRef]
46. Ožbolt, J.; Bede, N.; Sharma, A.; Mayer, U. Dynamic fracture of concrete L-specimen: Experimental and numerical study. *Eng. Fract. Mech.* **2015**, *148*, 27–41. [CrossRef]
47. Carneiro, F.L.L.B.; Barcellos, A. Tensile strength of concretes. *RILEM Bull.* **1953**, *13*, 97–123.
48. Rocco, C.; Guinea, G.V.; Planas, J.; Elices, M. Mechanisms of Rupture in Splitting Tests. *ACI Mater. J.* **1999**, *96*, 52–60. [CrossRef]
49. Suchorzewski, J.; Tejchman, J.; Nitka, M. Experimental and numerical investigations of concrete behaviour at meso-level during quasi-static splitting tension. *Theor. Appl. Fract. Mech.* **2018**, *96*, 720–739. [CrossRef]
50. Ruiz, G.; Ortiz, M.; Pandolfi, A. Three-dimensional finite-element simulation of the dynamic Brazilian tests on concrete cylinders. *Int. J. Numer. Meth. Eng.* **2000**, *48*, 963–994. [CrossRef]
51. Winnicki, A.; Pearce, C.J.; Bićanić, N. Viscoplastic Hoffman consistency model for concrete. *Comput. Struct.* **2001**, *79*, 7–19. [CrossRef]
52. Wosatko, A.; Pamin, J.; Winnicki, A. Numerical analysis of Brazilian split test on concrete cylinder. *Comput. Concr.* **2011**, *8*, 243–278. [CrossRef]
53. Chodkowski, P.; Bobiński, J.; Tejchman, J. Limits of enhanced of macro- and meso-scale continuum models for studying size effect in concrete under tension. *Eur. J. Environ. Civ. Eng.* **2021**, 1–22. [CrossRef]
54. Le Bellégo, C.; Dubé, J.F.; Pijaudier-Cabot, G.; Gérard, B. Calibration of nonlocal damage model from size effect tests. *Eur. J. Mech. A/Solids* **2003**, *22*, 33–46. [CrossRef]
55. Grégoire, D.; Rojas-Solano, L.B.; Pijaudier-Cabot, G. Failure and size effect for notched and unnotched concrete beams. *Int. J. Num. Anal. Meth. Geomech.* **2013**, *37*, 1434–1452. [CrossRef]
56. Hoover, C.G.; Bažant, Z.P.; Vorel, J.; Wendner, R.; Hubler, M.H. Comprehensive concrete fracture tests: Description and results. *Eng. Fract. Mech.* **2013**, *114*, 92–103. [CrossRef]
57. Syroka-Korol, E.; Tejchman, J.; Mróz, Z. FE investigations of the effect of fluctuating local tensile strength on coupled energetic-statistical size effect in concrete beams. *Eng. Struct.* **2015**, *103*, 239–259. [CrossRef]
58. van Mier, J.G.M.; van Vliet, M.R.A. Uniaxial tension test for the determination of fracture parameters of concrete: State of the art. *Eng. Fract. Mech.* **2002**, *69*, 235–247. [CrossRef]
59. Liebe, T.; Steinmann, P.; Benallal, A. Theoretical and computational aspects of a thermodynamically consistent framework for geometrically linear gradient damage. *Comput. Methods Appl. Mech. Eng.* **2001**, *190*, 6555–6576. [CrossRef]
60. Dimitrijević, B.J.; Hackl, K. A regularization framework for damage-plasticity models via gradient enhancement of the free energy. *Int. J. Numer. Methods Biomed. Eng.* **2011**, *27*, 1199–1210. [CrossRef]
61. Forest, S. Micromorphic approach for gradient elasticity, viscoplasticity, and damage. *ASCE J. Eng. Mech.* **2009**, *135*, 117–131. [CrossRef]
62. de Vree, J.H.P.; Brekelmans, W.A.M.; van Gils, M.A.J. Comparison of nonlocal approaches in continuum damage mechanics. *Comput. Struct.* **1995**, *55*, 581–588. [CrossRef]
63. Mazars, J.; Pijaudier-Cabot, G. Continuum damage theory—Application to concrete. *ASCE J. Eng. Mech.* **1989**, *115*, 345–365. [CrossRef]
64. Askes, H.; Pamin, J.; de Borst, R. Dispersion analysis and element-free Galerkin solutions of second- and fourth-order gradient-enhanced damage models. *Int. J. Numer. Meth. Eng.* **2000**, *49*, 811–832. [CrossRef]
65. de Borst, R.; Pamin, J. Gradient plasticity in numerical simulation of concrete cracking. *Eur. J. Mech. A/Solids* **1996**, *15*, 295–320.
66. Gutiérrez, M.A.; de Borst, R. Deterministic and stochastic analysis of size effects and damage evolution in quasi-brittle materials. *Arch. Appl. Mech.* **1999**, *69*, 655–676. [CrossRef]
67. Pamin, J. Gradient plasticity and damage models: A short comparison. *Comput. Mater. Sci.* **2005**, *32*, 472–479. [CrossRef]
68. Bažant, Z.P.; Belytschko, T. Wave propagation in a strain-softening bar: Exact solution. *ASCE J. Eng. Mech.* **1985**, *111*, 381–389. [CrossRef]
69. Pamin, J.; de Borst, R. Simulation of crack spacing using a reinforced concrete model with an internal length parameter. *Arch. Appl. Mech.* **1998**, *68*, 613–625. [CrossRef]

70. Marzec, I.; Tejchman, J.; Mróz, Z. Numerical analysis of size effect in RC beams scaled along height or length using elasto-plastic-damage model enhanced by non-local softening. *Finite Elem. Anal. Des.* **2019**, *157*, 1–20. [CrossRef]
71. Ferrara, L. A Contribution to the Modelling of Mixed Mode Fracture and Shear Transfer in Plain and Reinforced Concrete. Ph.D. Dissertation, Politechnico di Milano, Milan, Italy, 1998.
72. di Prisco, M.; Ferrara, L.; Meftah, F.; Pamin, J.; de Borst, R.; Mazars, J.; Reynouard, J.M. Mixed mode fracture in plain and reinforced concrete: Some results on benchmark tests. *Int. J. Fract.* **2000**, *103*, 127–148.:1007613001402. [CrossRef]
73. Ožbolt, J.; Sharma, A. Numerical simulation of dynamic fracture of concrete through uniaxial tension and L-specimen. *Eng. Fract. Mech.* **2012**, *85*, 88–102. [CrossRef]
74. Zreid, I.; Kaliske, M. Regularization of microplane damage models using an implicit gradient enhancement. *Int. J. Solids Struct.* **2014**, *51*, 3480–3489. [CrossRef]
75. Li, T.; Marigo, J.J.; Guilbaud, D.; Potapov, S. Gradient damage modeling of brittle fracture in an explicit dynamics context. *Int. J. Numer. Meth. Eng.* **2016**, *108*, 1381–1405. [CrossRef]

Article

Identification of Aluminium Powder Properties for Modelling Free Air Explosions

Piotr W. Sielicki [1], James Keith Clutter [2], Wojciech Sumelka [1], Tomasz Gajewski [1,*], Michał Malendowski [1], Piotr Peksa [1] and Robert Studziński [1]

[1] Faculty of Civil and Transport Engineering, Poznan University of Technology, Maria Sklodowska-Curie Street 5, 60-965 Poznan, Poland; piotr.sielicki@put.edu.pl (P.W.S.); wojciech.sumelka@put.poznan.pl (W.S.); michal.malendowski@put.poznan.pl (M.M.); piotr.peksa@put.poznan.pl (P.P.); robert.studzinski@put.poznan.pl (R.S.)
[2] SciRisq, Inc., 448 W. 19th St., #210, Houston, TX 77008, USA; keith.clutter@scirisq.com
* Correspondence: tomasz.gajewski@put.poznan.pl

Abstract: Aluminium is a component in many energetic formulations. Therefore, its combustion is one of the main thermochemical processes that govern the output from the energetics. Modelling aluminium combustion is a challenging task because the process is highly complex and difficult to measure. Here, tests of aluminium powder were conducted in an effort to isolate the burning of the aluminium and to determine an adequate representation of this process. Charges of 100 g and 500 g were tested, and the size of the Al/air cloud and the ratio of components in the Al/air mixture were determined, which has not been published previously. This information was used to assess the validity of the assumption that the detonation of the mixture was representative of the event. Parameters for the Jones–Wilkins–Lee equation of state for the explosive mixture and detonation products were defined. Simulations of the tests were performed, and the results were consistent with the field test data, indicating that detonation occurred when there was a mixture of 70–75% Al and 25–30% air by mass.

Keywords: aluminium powder; detonation; explosive; combustion; oxidation; equation of state

1. Introduction

The composition of an explosive is a key factor in its efficiency. Most standard military explosives and those used in research operations are condensed explosives, such as trinitrotoluene (TNT) and Plastic Explosive No. 4 (PE4). These substances are ideal for contact explosions due to their brisance and high-intensity shock wave propagation. Furthermore, they can be altered in different ways to change their explosive performances. One common alteration is the addition of various components, such as aluminium (Al) powder [1–3].

The addition of aluminium changes the energy release process and the overall output of an explosive at the microscopic level. Additionally, the ignition and combustion properties of an explosive can be modified, as shown by Liu et al. [4], by coating it with nanosized aluminium particles. Oxidation plays a crucial role in the combustion of aluminium. Gang et al. investigated the combustion and oxidation of Al nanoparticles at the atomistic level [5]. Depending on the amount of O_2 and the temperature, oxidation can be grouped into three categories: mild, chain-like growth oxidation; moderate oxidation; and microexplosion-accelerated oxidation. The microexplosion-accelerated oxidation mechanism was investigated deeply by Gang et al. The burning of separated Al droplets in air was studied by Karasev et al. [6], as well as the mechanisms involved in alumina aggregate formation.

However, the microscopic level is not the only level of interest in terms of energy release processes; the combustion of aluminium nanoparticles has also been investigated at

the macroscopic level. For instance, Lewis et al. [7] studied hexahydro-1,3,5-trinitro-1,3,5-triazine (RDX) explosives with three types of aluminium nanoparticles. They showed that the addition of the nanoparticles can change the fireball temperature from 340 K to 4500 K. Gordon et al. [8] also studied the fireball of aluminised RDX, in addition to its shock wave energy. The authors reported that the shock energy is greater if aluminium is added to the high explosive rather than to the liner. Other studies of aluminised high explosives were conducted by Peuker et al. [9] and Carney et al. [10], in which optical methods were used. In the current study, the afterburn phase was analysed.

The contribution of Al combustion to the afterburn phase of aluminised explosives has been represented in various studies [11] using the Jones–Wilkins–Lee (JWL)–Miller model [12]. This model alters the energy term in the JWL equation such that it has the form

$$P = A\left(1 - \frac{\omega}{R_1 V}\right) e^{-R_1 V} + B\left(1 - \frac{\omega}{R_2 V}\right) e^{-R_2 V} + \frac{\omega(E + \lambda Q)}{V}, \quad (1)$$

where Q is the additional heat released by the aluminium particle combustion, and λ is the progression variable indicating the degree to which the particle has reacted. The degree of reaction equation is given by

$$\frac{d\lambda}{dt} = a(1 - \lambda)^m P^n, \quad (2)$$

where a depends on the particle size, and m and n are reaction rate constants. This model represents the gradual addition of energy seen in the afterburn phase rather than the sudden release of energy observed in the aluminium powder explosives. Here, the rate of gasification, which is associated with the combustion rate equation, is relevant.

Other models have been introduced that also replicate the afterburn energy release due to Al combustion, but they assume that the reaction is proportional to the gasification of the particles [13]. This process is explicitly represented by the change in the diameter of the particles, which can be expressed as

$$\frac{d}{dt}\left[\frac{4}{3}\pi \left(\frac{D}{2}\right)^3 \rho\right] = 4\pi \left(\frac{D}{2}\right)^2 \dot{m}_v, \quad (3)$$

which simplifies to

$$D = D_0 - \frac{2\dot{m}_v}{\rho} t, \quad (4)$$

where D is the particle diameter, D_0 is the initial particle diameter, and $\dot{m}_v$ is the gasification rate of the condensed material, which can be expressed as

$$\dot{m}_v = \frac{\sqrt{3}}{2\pi r^3} \sqrt{kTm} e^{-E_v/RT}, \quad (5)$$

where r is the radius of the molecule, m is the mass of each molecule, k is the Boltzmann constant (1.38×10^{-23} J/K), T is the temperature, E_v is the gasification enthalpy, and R is the gas constant (8.314 J/mol·K).

The afterburn combustion of Al can be used to redefine the degree of reaction, as follows

$$\lambda = 1 - \left(1 - \frac{2\dot{m}_v t}{\rho_{Al} D_0}\right)^3, \quad (6)$$

where $\dot{m}_v$ is the gasification rate, t is time, ρ_{Al} is density of aluminum, and D_0 is initial diameter.

Another group of models address the gasification of the Al particles using an empirical quasi-steady law [14]. The particle radius (r_p) rate is

$$\frac{dr_p}{dt} = -\frac{r_p}{t_b}\left(1 + 0.276\sqrt{Re}\right), \quad (7)$$

where Re is the Reynolds number, which is based on the relative velocity between the gas and the particle, and t_b is the burning time based on

$$t_b = K(D_0)^2, \tag{8}$$

where K is an empirical constant. According to the literature, K is typically set equal to 4×10^6 s/m^2. The mass transfer from the solid to gaseous state is

$$\frac{dm_p}{dt} = -\frac{d}{dt}\left(\frac{4}{3}\pi \rho_p r_p^3\right), \tag{9}$$

where the subscript p denotes the particle properties.

In the current study, the temperature of ignition depends on the state of the Al particles. If an oxide coating is present and is not cracked through some sort of physical process, then the melting point of Al_2O_3 would determine ignition. This melting point is approximately 2050 K. If the oxide layer is cracked, then the ignition temperature would be determined by the melting point of Al, which is approximately 950 K.

The temperature of the particles will depend on the heat feedback from the gas phase to the condensed phase. An investigation of aluminised explosives [15] has shown that the feedback can be represented using Fourier's law

$$q_c = \alpha_g \left(\frac{1}{r}\right)\left(\frac{dT}{dt}\right)_s, \tag{10}$$

where α_g is the thermal conductivity, r is the burning rate, and s denotes the gradient at the surface.

Hence, an understanding of the energy released during aluminium combustion is key to optimising the design of energetic systems and would allow the quantification of aluminium's effect on structures. In this paper, aluminium powder was analysed at the macroscopic level; this approach enables the straightforward development of online (fast) tools that can predict the behaviour of aluminium powder explosives. The current objective was to develop an adequate representation of Al combustion to provide loading predictions for use in the analysis of the interaction between munitions and structures. From this point of view, the robust modelling of such explosives is no trivial task.

Equations of state (EOS) are a key concept in modelling this class of energetics. Various EOS approaches are found in the literature. They have been proposed for aluminised explosive products [16], along with more popular approaches, such as the JWL formula [17–19]. The JWL approach is well known and has the broadest application; thus, it was adopted in the current study. Here, the expansion process of the detonation products from the composite energetics was determined to be crucial. This expansion process affects the prediction of the pressure loading at a particular distance, which is an essential characteristic in determining the effect of the explosive.

This paper analysed the combustion of Al, as this critical process affects the energy outputs of aluminised explosives. The oxidiser that was used in the tests varied according to the specifics of the energetics. In most explosives, the oxidiser is obtained from the products of the organic reaction that forms CO, CO_2, and H_2O. It has been shown that Al combustion is determined by the concentrations of CO_2 and H_2O [20]. Therefore, Al combustion often occurs before any ambient oxidiser is introduced to the Al. Here, pure Al was used to ensure that the oxidation process was related to the mixing of Al powder with ambient air. This provided insights into the combustion of Al, even when the oxidiser originated from typical detonation products.

In this study, a series of range detonation tests with pure aluminium powder mixtures were performed, which has not been published previously. The mass of the charges varied from 0.1 to 0.5 kg. The primary goal of the tests was to measure the pressure–time histories, and these results were replicated using modelling tools. Seven tests were performed, and full data recordings were obtained at standoff distances of approximately 1 and 2 m. The tests were replicated using a modelling tool that incorporated the effects of Al combustion. The EOS and reaction parameters were first defined using thermodynamic codes and analytical tools. Subsequently, as described in the final part of this paper, these values were altered to match the test results.

The paper is structured as follows. In Section 2, the test details, computational assumptions, and an explosive governing equation are presented. Section 3 identifies the explosive parameters for the 100 g charge and presents their validation for the 500 g charge. Section 4 presents the conclusions of the study.

2. Materials and Methods

2.1. Field Test Measurements

In this section, data from the field tests for the 100 g and 500 g aluminium powder charge detonation are described. The experiments were conducted so as to represent a free air blast. Data from the 100 g detonation were used to determine the aluminium modelling parameters. The tests were performed using 6 μm of Al powder with an estimated density of 2.2 to 2.7 g/cc. The aluminium powder is shown in Figure 1a. Photographs from the test site are presented in Figure 1b,c, including a snapshot of the explosion (Figure 1b) and an overview of the explosion area (framed by wooden poles), along with the high-speed camera (Figure 1c). Figure 1d presents details of the explosive devices' mounting scheme. The aluminium powder was hung in a foil bag attached to a string and was located 100 cm from the ground (L) directly between two wooden poles that were 200 cm high (H). The distance between the poles was 500 cm (W). Blast pressure pencil probes were placed at heights of 100 cm (b) and 200 cm (a) from the charge.

Seven detonations were conducted during the field tests. In the first two detonations, the aluminium powder charge mass was 100 g; in the next two, the charge mass was 200 g, and in the last three, the charge mass was 500 g. The data from the second 200 g detonation were rejected. In this case, during aluminium combustion, the foil bag was damaged, and the powder poured out of the bag. Thus, the data could not be considered for further analysis. Because the 200 g case was not represented by two detonations, this charge mass was not taken into account in the subsequent analyses.

(a)   (b)

Figure 1. *Cont.*

(c)

(d)

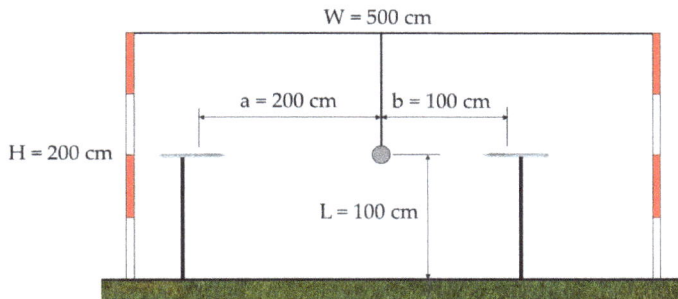

Figure 1. Test set up: (**a**) example of tested mixture of aluminium powder; (**b**) snapshot of the explosion; (**c**) overview of the explosion area; and (**d**) explosive devices' mounting scheme.

The pressure–time histories from all tests were measured at 1 and 2 m from the explosive simultaneously. Two ICP® blast pressure pencil probes were used simultaneously to acquire the data—these are the same probes that were used in [21]. The maximum pressure limit for these sensors is 345 kPa. The results are shown in Figures 2 and 3. All measurements are presented, including those that were rejected (i.e., pressure histories no. 3 (200 g) and no. 4 (labelled as Err, i.e., error)).

The detonations were filmed with a high-speed camera to obtain deeper insights into the reaction process to ensure adequate modelling assumptions. In these types of experiments, a high-speed camera is typically used to assess the deformation due to the blast wave [22] and determine the speed of projectiles and fragments, e.g., [23,24]. In our tests, the high-speed camera was used to estimate the volume of the mixed powder. Figure 4 shows sample images captured immediately after detonation. The time after ignition is shown next to the sequence of images. Powder burning at the time of ignition and thereafter can be observed.

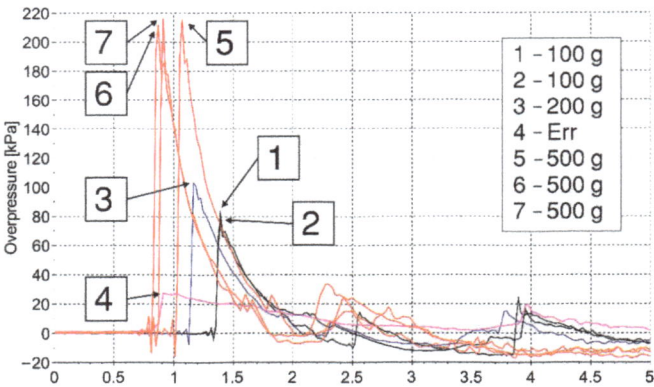

Figure 2. Overpressure measurements at 1 m.

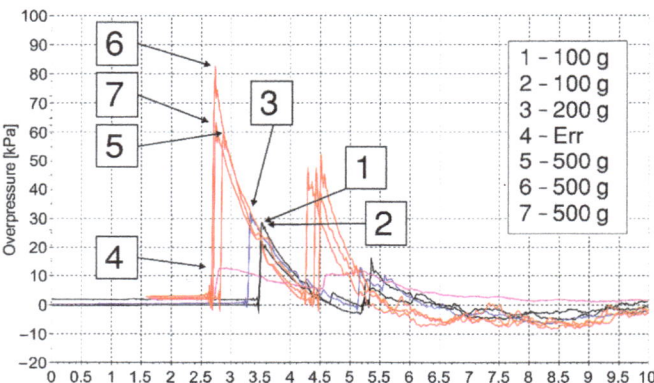

Figure 3. Overpressure measurements at 2 m.

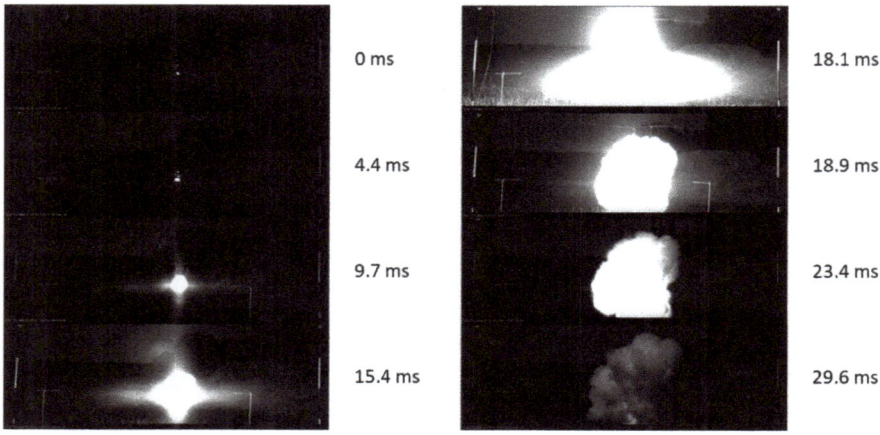

Figure 4. Sequence of images from the 100 g test. The time presented refers to the time after ignition.

If a spherical charge is assumed and the Al density is 2.7 g/cc, the volume of the initial charge would be 37.04 cc, and the charge would have a diameter of 2.07 cm. Notably, there was an apparent spike in output at the 18.1 ms mark. The Al/air cloud at the 18.1 ms mark had a diameter of approximately 41.4 cm and a volume of 37.15 cc. This resulted in an Al density of 2.69×10^{-3} g/cc. Taking the air to be at atmospheric pressure, the volume of powder and air would contain a mixture of 56% Al and 44% air considering masses. This information was used to derive an adequate representation of the explosion process.

The overall pattern for the 500 g tests was similar to that of the 100 g tests. For the 500 g charge, the "explosion" (rapid release of energy) appeared to occur between 2.3 and 5.8 ms after ignition. The diameter of the Al/air cloud at that time varied from 40 to 54 cm. Figure 5 shows an image taken after the "explosion" of the 500 g Al charge. More burning particles of Al were expelled outward after the "explosion" (white arrows) of the 500 g charge compared to that of the 100 g charge, suggesting that the 500 g charge was less effective than the 100 g charge. The analysis of the 500 g test data allowed an adequate representation of the Al combustion to be determined.

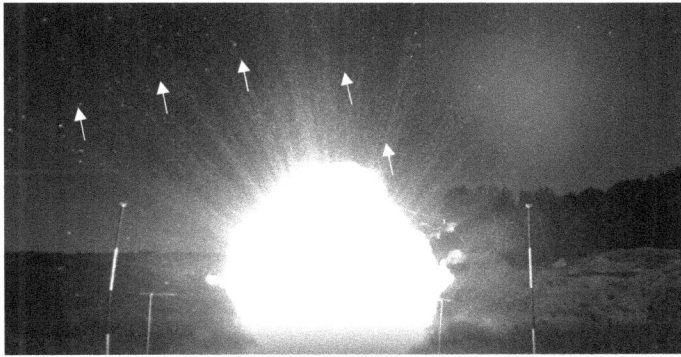

Figure 5. Image of the 500 g test (Test 7), in which burning Al particles (white arrows) were expelled.

2.2. Numerical Modelling Assumptions

The computational model that was developed to simulate the energetics used a Cartesian Adaptive Mesh (CAM) framework; this model simulates scenarios involving a blast, explosion, and release of materials (thus, CAMBER). CAMBER is an object-oriented framework that utilises a variety of material models and reaction laws. The mesh adaptation was used to resolve structures under severe deformation, and the code maps out the locations of gradients in properties [25]. In CAMBER, a finite-volume formulation is used. Various flux calculation schemes have been assessed and proven to be useful in multi-material flows [26]. The advection upstream splitting method (AUSM+) scheme was selected for its simplicity and robustness [27]; high spatial order is achieved via a monotonic upstream-centred scheme for conservation law (MUSCL) extrapolation with limiters. Given the small time steps required to resolve the evolving flow field, explicit time integration was used. The code can be applied in 2D, 2D-axisymmetric, or 3D modes.

2.3. Governing Equation for Explosions

The objective of this study was to formulate an approach to simulate explosions involving aluminium. The energetics used in the present research were for pure aluminium, so the reaction causing the energy release was as follows

$$4Al + 3O \rightarrow 2Al_2O_3. \tag{11}$$

Hence, if Al is part of the explosive composition, the oxidation could arise from the CO_2 and H_2O in the detonation product. In this case, the oxidiser was the O_2 in the air.

There was clearly burning Al prior to the "explosion" at 18.1 ms (see Figure 4), but at this time point, there was a sudden release of energy. It can be assumed that until this time point, the percentage of Al burned was negligible. Furthermore, the assumption was made that the explosive cloud was 56% Al and 44% air by mass (as described in Section 2.1).

A thermochemical analysis was performed as a first estimate; it was assumed that the reaction was essentially the detonation. The Chapman–Jouguet (CJ) conditions are listed in Table 1. A JWL EOS of the following form

$$P = A\left(1 - \frac{\omega}{R_1 V}\right)e^{-R_1 V} + B\left(1 - \frac{\omega}{R_2 V}\right)e^{-R_2 V} + \frac{\omega E}{V}, \tag{12}$$

was used for the explosive material and detonation products. The parameters used are listed in Table 2. The JWL parameters were defined for the Al/air mixture based on the behaviour of such mixtures under shock loading. The rate of the reaction was derived from the detonation velocity.

Table 1. Detonation conditions assumed in the computational thermochemical code for the Al/air explosion.

P (GPa)	UCJ (km/s)	V (cc/g)	T (K)	C (km/s)	γ
0.002	1.166	192.557	3108.4	0.602	0.954

Table 2. JWL parameters assumed in the computational thermochemical code for the detonation products.

Material	ρ_0 (g/cc)	A (GPa)	B (GPa)	R_1	R_2	ω	E_0 (kJ/cc)
explosive	2.68	1.43×10^{-1}	-5.6×10^{-4}	21.875	0.33	0.3507	0
detonation products	2.68	2.86×10^{-2}	2.8×10^{-3}	7.0	0.50	0.3507	2.4×10^{-3} *

* This value was adjusted to 2.7×10^{-3} after initial simulations of the 100 g case to better match the test data.

3. Identification and Validation

3.1. Identification—Simulation of 100 g Tests

The parameters defined in Section 2 were used to simulate the 100 g tests and identify a set of explosive parameters. The initial condition was that there was a 37.04 cc Al/air cloud. Figure 6 shows the sequence of images from the simulation. The contour maps for the concentration of reacting mixture (Al/air), the reaction products, the density, and the pressure are shown at four selected time points. The time noted is relative to $t = 0$ for the tests. Figure 7 shows a comparison between the test data for the pressure–time histories recorded during the simulation at the 1 and 2 m locations.

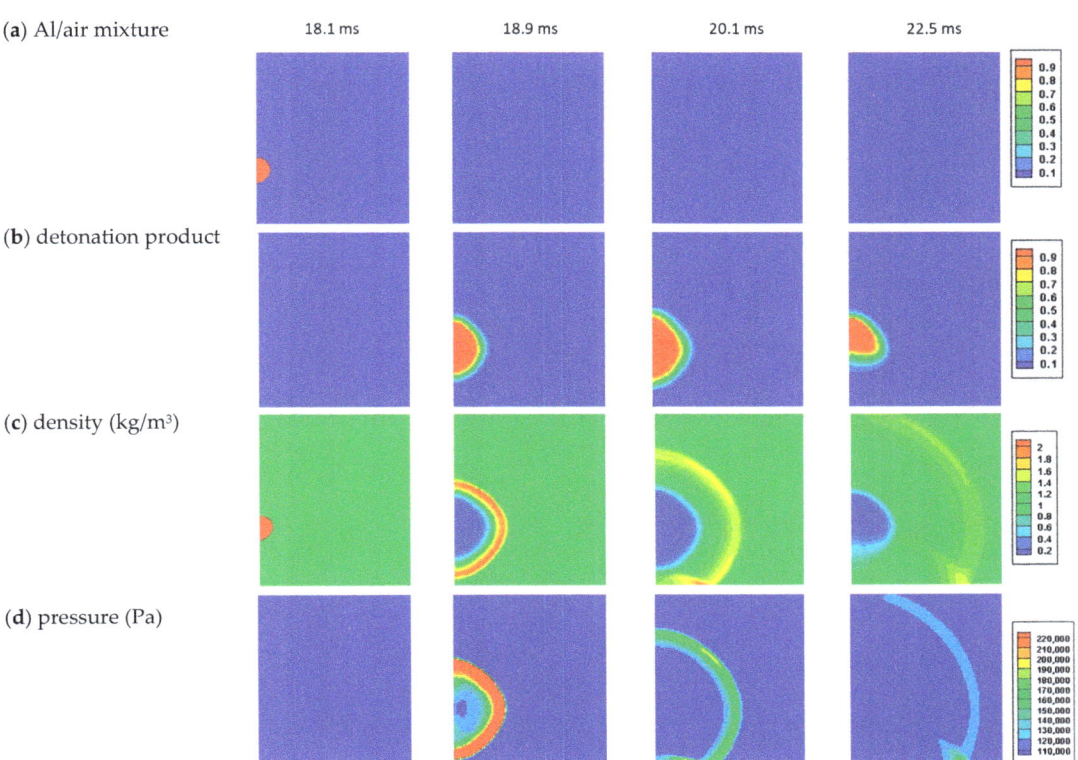

Figure 6. Sequence of images from the 100 g test simulation: (**a**) Al/air mixture concentration; (**b**) detonation product concentration; (**c**) density; and (**d**) pressure are shown at four time points.

The initial pulses in pressure at both locations were similar to the test data in both magnitude and duration. The secondary pulses due to ground reflection were somewhat lower in magnitude and were delayed compared to the test data. This difference could be due to slight differences in the heights. There was an intermediate pulse in one of the 1 m test recordings. While the cause of this pulse was not clear, it was not seen in the simulation results.

These results suggest that the predominant release of energy from the combustion of the Al/air cloud can be represented as a sudden event, or, as we label it here, the "explosion". It appears that the combustion event was essentially a mixing-controlled process. The explosion did not occur until the mass of Al powder expanded to the point where there was sufficient oxidation. Based on the size of the cloud at the time of the explosion and the mass of the Al powder, the cloud distribution was approximately 70% Al and 30% air by mass, providing an oxidiser-to-fuel mole ratio (moles O/moles Al) of 0.17, far below the stoichiometric ratio for the reaction in Equation (1).

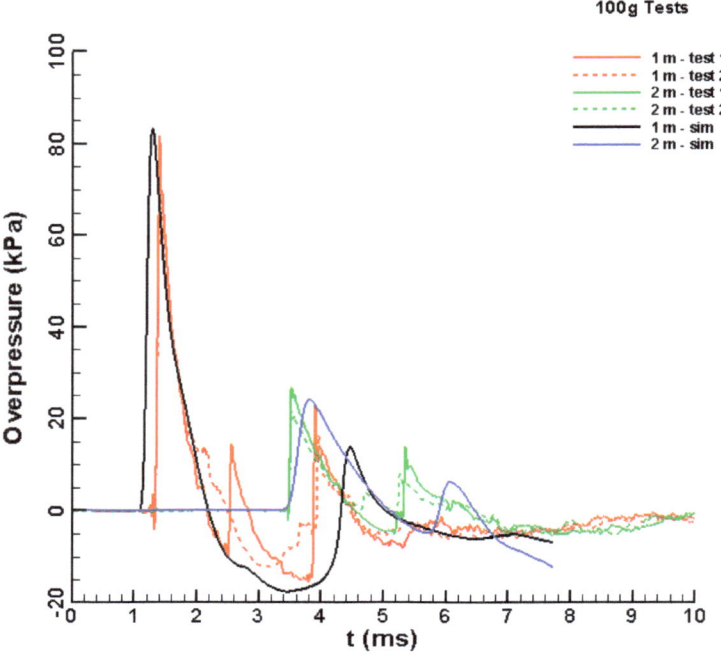

Figure 7. Comparisons between the test data and simulated values for the pressure versus time history at the 1- and 2 m locations for the 100 g charge.

3.2. Validation—Simulation of the 500 g Tests

The 500 g tests were simulated in the validation stage. The same modelling parameters were used in terms of EOS and the rate of reaction. First, the test imagery was used to estimate the size of the spherical Al/air cloud at the point at which there was a noticeable sudden release of energy (i.e., the "explosion"). Three videos were reviewed, and the time of the explosion varied from approximately 3 to 6 ms. The size of the cloud was estimated to be approximately 52 cm in diameter. This diameter would result in a cloud composed of 84% Al and 16% air by mass. Although the fuel-to-oxidiser ratio changed slightly from the 100 g case, the same parameters used in that case were applied. The pressure–time histories predicted at the 1 and 2 m locations are shown in Figure 8. At both locations, the peak simulated pressures were lower than the peak measured pressures.

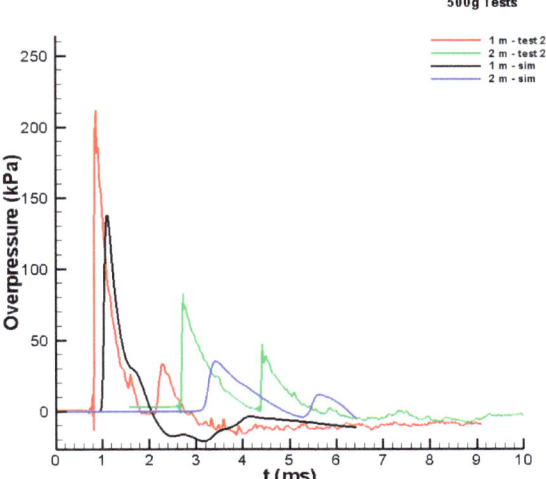

Figure 8. Comparison between test data and simulated values for the pressure versus time history for the 500 g Al/air cloud with a 52 cm diameter.

Because the cloud estimated from the video produced a lower output, several cloud sizes were applied until a good match between the measured and simulated pressure–time histories was achieved. Figure 9 shows the results when the diameter of the Al/air cloud was assumed to be 63 cm. The comparison is moderately good, wherein the peaks at the 2 m location are slightly lower than those in the test data. Using the assumed size of the cloud and the mass of Al, the cloud was found to be 75% Al and 25% air by mass. This result was similar to the ratio found for the 100 g results. The study presented shows that combining the experimental and advanced numerical approaches creates the ability to obtain the synergic effect for better understanding the physical phenomena, similar to [28].

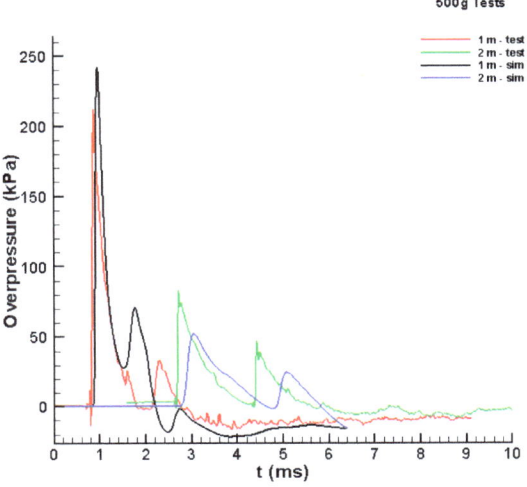

Figure 9. Comparison between test data and simulated values for the pressure versus time history for the 500 g Al/air cloud with a 63 cm diameter.

4. Conclusions

Combustion is the key process in many energetic systems. In this paper, the combustion of Al was investigated using a series of tests and simulations, which has not been published previously in the literature. Here, the Al was isolated and allowed to react with just oxygen in ambient air; the oxidation arose from the detonation products. The results of the 100 g and 500 g Al charges indicated that the sudden explosions occurred when a mixture of 70–75% Al and 30–25% air, by mass, was obtained.

Among others, the novelty of the paper is that the output from the explosions was replicated using the JWL state equation for the product and assuming detonation of the mixture. The detonation was modelled using a prescriptive method that set the burn rate based on the detonation velocity. The delay from the initiation of the event until the time of the explosion is currently under investigation. Further studies will aim to determine whether this delay is related to the time required for the gasification of the Al or the event is a mixing-controlled process.

Author Contributions: Conceptualisation, J.K.C. and P.W.S.; methodology, J.K.C. and P.W.S.; software, P.W.S.; validation, J.K.C., R.S., W.S. and P.W.S.; formal analysis, J.K.C., R.S., W.S., T.G. and P.W.S.; investigation, J.K.C. and P.W.S.; resources, M.M. and T.G.; data curation, M.M. and T.G.; writing—original draft preparation, J.K.C., P.W.S. and T.G.; writing—review and editing, P.W.S., R.S., T.G., M.M., W.S. and P.P.; visualisation, T.G., M.M. and P.P.; supervision, W.S., T.G. and P.W.S.; project administration, P.W.S. and T.G.; funding acquisition, P.W.S., W.S. and P.P. All authors have read and agreed to the published version of the manuscript.

Funding: This research was funded by the National Centre for Research and Development Poland under the grant DOB-BIO10/01/02/2019 within the framework of the Defence and Security Programme.

Data Availability Statement: The data presented in this study are available on request from the corresponding author.

Conflicts of Interest: The authors declare no conflict of interest. The funders had no role in the design of the study; in the collection, analyses, or interpretation of data; in the writing of the manuscript; or in the decision to publish the results.

References

1. Xiang, D.; Rong, J.; He, X.; Feng, Z. Underwater Explosion Performance of RDX/AP-Based Aluminized Explosives. *Central Eur. J. Energetic Mater.* **2017**, *14*, 60–76. [CrossRef]
2. Rubio, M.A.; Rubio, M.A.; Gunduz, I.E.; Gunduz, I.E.; Groven, L.J.; Groven, L.J.; Sippel, T.R.; Sippel, T.R.; Han, C.W.; Han, C.W.; et al. Microexplosions and ignition dynamics in engineered aluminum/polymer fuel particles. *Combust. Flame* **2017**, *176*, 162–171. [CrossRef]
3. Nie, H.-Q.; Chan, H.Y.; Pisharath, S.; Hng, H.H. Combustion characteristic and aging behavior of bimetal thermite powders. *Def. Technol.* **2020**, *17*, 755–762. [CrossRef]
4. Liu, P.; Liu, J.; Wang, M. Ignition and combustion of nano-sized aluminum particles: A reactive molecular dynamics study. *Combust. Flame* **2019**, *201*, 276–289. [CrossRef]
5. Gang, L.; Niu, L.; Hao, W.; Liu, Y.; Zhang, C. Atomistic insight into the microexplosion-accelerated oxidation process of molten aluminum nanoparticles. *Combust. Flame* **2020**, *214*, 238–250. [CrossRef]
6. Karasev, V.V.; Onischuk, A.A.; Glotov, O.G.; Baklanov, A.M.; Maryasov, A.G.; Zarko, V.E.; Panfilov, V.N.; Levykin, A.I.; Sabel-feld, K.K. Formation of charged aggregates of Al_2O_3 nanoparticles by combustion of aluminum droplets in air. *Combust. Flame* **2004**, *138*, 40–54. [CrossRef]
7. Lewis, W.K.; Rumchik, C.G.; Smith, M.J.; Fernando, K.A.S.; Crouse, C.A.; Spowart, J.E.; Guliants, E.A.; Bunker, C.E. Comparison of post-detonation combustion in explosives incorporating aluminum nanoparticles: Influence of the passivation layer. *J. Appl. Phys.* **2013**, *113*, 044907. [CrossRef]
8. Gordon, J.M.; Gross, K.C.; Perram, G.P. Fireball and shock wave dynamics in the detonation of aluminized novel munitions. *Combust. Explos. Shock Waves* **2013**, *49*, 450–462. [CrossRef]
9. Peuker, J.M.; Lynch, P.; Krier, H.; Glumac, N. Optical depth measurements of fireballs from aluminized high explosives. *Opt. Lasers Eng.* **2009**, *47*, 1009–1015. [CrossRef]
10. Carney, J.R.; Miller, J.S.; Gump, J.C.; Pangilinan, G.I. Time-resolved optical measurements of the post-detonation combustion of aluminized explosives. *Rev. Sci. Instrum.* **2006**, *77*, 063103. [CrossRef]

11. Togashi, F.; Baum, J.D.; Soto, O.A.; Löhner, R.; Zhang, F. Numerical simulation of TNT-Al explosives in explosion chamber. In Proceedings of the Seventh International Conference on Computational Fluid Dynamics (ICCFD7), Big Island, HI, USA, 9–13 July 2012.
12. Miller, P.J. A Reactive Flow Model with Coupled Reaction Kinetics for Detonation and Combustion in Non-Ideal Explosives. *MRS Proc.* **1995**, *418*, 413. [CrossRef]
13. Liu, Y.; Wang, H.; Bai, F.; Huang, F.; Hussain, T. A New Equation of State for Detonation Products of RDX-Based Aluminized Explosives. *Propellants Explos. Pyrotech.* **2019**, *44*, 1293–1301. [CrossRef]
14. Balakrishnan, K.; Menon, S. On the Role of Ambient Reactive Particles in the Mixing and Afterburn behind Explosive Blast Waves. *Combust. Sci. Technol.* **2010**, *182*, 186–214. [CrossRef]
15. Xiao, L.-Q.; Fan, X.-Z.; Li, J.-Z.; Qin, Z.; Fu, X.-L.; Pang, W.-Q.; Wang, Y. Effect of Al content and particle size on the combustion of HMX-CMDB propellant. *Combust. Flame* **2020**, *214*, 80–89. [CrossRef]
16. Yue, J.-Z.; Duan, Z.-P.; Zhang, Z.-Y.; Ou, Z.-C. Research on Equation of State For Detonation Products of Aluminized Explosive. *J. Energetic Mater.* **2017**, *35*, 1–9. [CrossRef]
17. Baranowski, P.; Kucewicz, M.; Gieleta, R.; Stankiewicz, M.; Konarzewski, M.; Bogusz, P.; Pytlik, M.; Małachowski, J. Fracture and fragmentation of dolomite rock using the JH-2 constitutive model: Parameter determination, experiments and simulations. *Int. J. Impact Eng.* **2020**, *140*, 103543. [CrossRef]
18. Sielicki, P.W.; Łodygowski, T. Masonry wall behaviour under explosive loading. *Eng. Fail. Anal.* **2019**, *104*, 274–291. [CrossRef]
19. Baranowski, P.; Małachowski, J.; Mazurkiewicz, Ł. Local blast wave interaction with tire structure. *Def. Technol.* **2020**, *16*, 520–529. [CrossRef]
20. Yu, V.; Frolov, P.; Pokhil, P.F.; Logachev, V.S. Ignition and combustion of powdered aluminum in high-temperature gaseous media and in a composition of heterogeneous condensed systems. *Combust. Explos. Shock Waves* **1972**, *8*, 168–187.
21. Gajewski, T.; Sielicki, P.W. Experimental study of blast loading behind a building corner. *Shock Waves* **2020**, *30*, 385–394. [CrossRef]
22. Warnstedt, P.; Gebbeken, N. Innovative protection of urban areas–Experimental research on the blast mitigating potential of hedges. *Landsc. Urban Plan.* **2020**, *202*, 103876. [CrossRef]
23. Sielicki, P.W.; Pludra, A.; Przybylski, M. Experimental measurement of the bullet trajectory after perforation of a chambered window. *Int. J. Appl. Glass Sci.* **2019**, *10*, 441–448. [CrossRef]
24. Sielicki, P.W.; Ślosarczyk, A.; Szulc, D. Concrete slab fragmentation after bullet impact: An experimental study. *Int. J. Prot. Struct.* **2019**, *10*, 380–389. [CrossRef]
25. Clutter, J.K. Application of Computational Modeling for Explosive Hazard Assessments. *Int. J. Prot. Struct.* **2013**, *4*, 293–314. [CrossRef]
26. Luo, H.; Baum, J.D.; Löhner, R. On the computation of multi-material flows using ALE formulation. *J. Comput. Phys.* **2004**, *194*, 304–328. [CrossRef]
27. Liou, M.-S. Progress towards an improved CFD method-AUSM+. In Proceedings of the 12th Computational Fluid Dynamics Conference, San Diego, CA, USA, 19–22 June 1995. [CrossRef]
28. Maier, G.; Bolzon, G.; Buljak, V.; Garbowski, T.; Miller, B. *Synergistic Combinations of Computational Methods and Ex-Periments for Structural Diagnosis, Computer Methods in Mechanic*; Kuczma, M., Wilmanski, K., Eds.; Springer: Berlin/Heidelberg, Germany, 2010; pp. 453–476.

Review

Status and Challenges in Homogenization Methods for Lattice Materials

Jacobs Somnic and Bruce W. Jo *

Advanced Dynamics, Mechatronics and Collaborative Robotics (ADAMS) Laboratory, Department of Mechanical Engineering, State University of New York (SUNY), Incheon 21985, Korea; jacobs.somnic@stonybrook.edu
* Correspondence: bruce.jo@stonybrook.edu

Abstract: Lattice structures have shown great potential in that mechanical properties are customizable without changing the material itself. Lattice materials could be light and highly stiff as well. With this flexibility of designing structures without raw material processing, lattice structures have been widely used in various applications such as smart and functional structures in aerospace and computational mechanics. Conventional methodologies for understanding behaviors of lattice materials take numerical approaches such as FEA (finite element analysis) and high-fidelity computational tools including ANSYS and ABAQUS. However, they demand a high computational load in each geometry run. Among many other methodologies, homogenization is another numerical approach but that enables to model behaviors of bulk lattice materials by analyzing either a small portion of them using numerical regression for rapid processing. In this paper, we provide a comprehensive survey of representative homogenization methodologies and their status and challenges in lattice materials with their fundamentals.

Keywords: homogenization method; lattice materials; periodic cellular materials; multiscale mechanics

1. Introduction

Lattice material is a cellular material consisting of a periodic network of structural elements such as rods or beams. This network of lattices exists over a wide spectrum of scale from the nanoscale to macroscale and has been applied in a wide area of applications. In the nanoscale spectrum, most of the CNT (Carbon Nano Tube) based sensors are made using lattice materials [1] as shown in Figure 1a. Micro-lattices material is being developed intensively as it offers high energy absorption capability [2,3]. On a macroscale, due to its high stiffness and lightweight properties, lattice materials are widely used in aerospace applications [4–8].

Lattice structures or materials could be also classified into several parameters, namely, geometry, deformation properties, and rigidity. These determine a proper approach for understanding dynamics of lattice accurately extend to design. Geometry-based classification is widely received in mathematics and solid-state physics and especially in 2-D, two main categories are considered: regular and semi-regular [9]. Representatives of each group are illustrated in Figure 1. Sub-sequentially, three types exist under the regular lattice, namely, square lattice, triangular lattice, and hexagonal lattice. In semi-regular lattices, unit cells are tessellated Later, eight semi-regular lattices are introduced in this paper for more details [9].

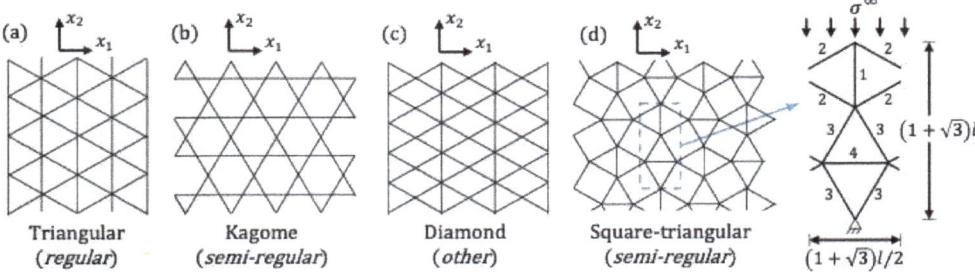

Figure 1. Examples of different lattice topologies: (**a**) triangular; (**b**) Kagome; (**c**) diamond; (**d**) snub square [10].

In engineering applications, spatially periodic patterns of lattices can be viewed as a material or a structure depending on its length scale. When the deformation is at a much larger length scale than the individual beam length, such a network of a lattice is defined as "lattice material". Figure 2 shows such an example of lattice materials. On the other hand, if the length scale between deformation and the individual beam is the same, then it is viewed as a "lattice structure". Asymptotic Theory might be a more suitable approach when we are dealing with lattice materials [11]. Meanwhile, modeling the beam individually is a better approach for lattice structure. This paper will more focus on lattice materials rather than structure as it is more relevant to the homogenization method.

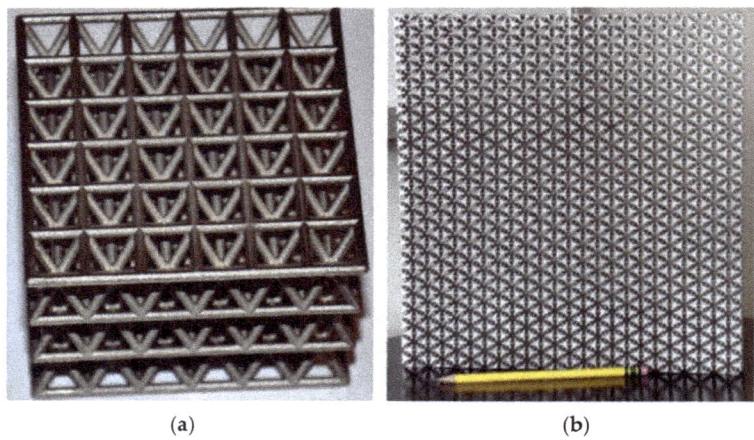

Figure 2. Lattice materials formed by network of beams; (**a**) ultralight Nano-metal truss hybrid lattice; (**b**) penta-mode lattice [12].

The other key parameter that determines a suitable approach for understanding lattices is relative density. The relative density is defined as the density ratio of lattice material to the solid material ($\bar{\rho} = \rho^*/\rho_s$) and has a pivotal role in determining the elastostatic behavior of a lattice. Figure 3 shows the relationship between relative density and relative modulus. Slope 1 depicted in Figure 3 is for stretch-dominated lattice and slope 2 is for bending-dominated lattice. As it can be seen, honeycombs, one of the commonly used cores for sandwich panels, are extraordinarily efficient. Physically, relative density depicts the porosity of lattice material. A low value of relative density indicates high porosity, meanwhile, a high value of that indicates low porosity. For instance, $\bar{\rho} = 1$ means zero porosity as the density of the lattice is the same as one of the solid or bulk. Therefore, it is crucial to employ a proper homogenization model or approach according to the value of relative density. For the low value of relative density, e.g., $\bar{\rho} < 0.3$, applying Euler–Bernoulli beam or Timoshenko beam elements to model the cell-wall deformation will give an accurate result [13–16]. Furthermore, Micro-polar theory [17], Bloch Wave Analysis and Cauchy–Born hypothesis [18] might be employed for such cases as well. For a high value of relative density, the Asymptotic Homogenization method will give a better and more accurate result [11].

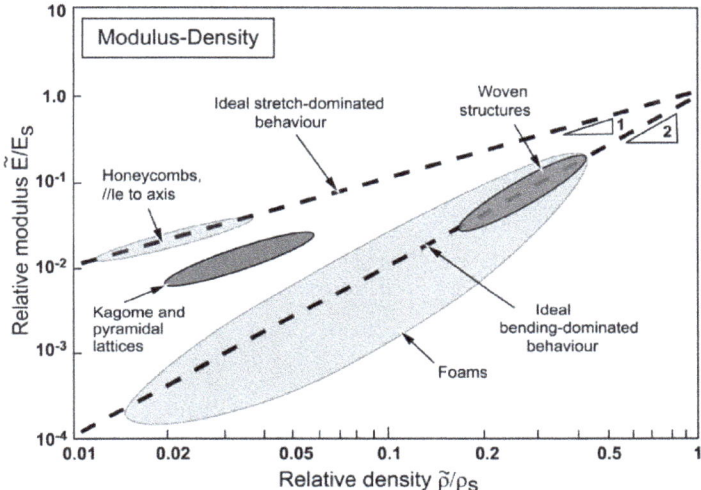

Figure 3. Relative modulus plotted against relative density on logarithmic scales for cellular structure [19].

Lattices can also be categorized into stretching-dominated or bending-dominated based on their rigidity [19]. Some representatives of both categories are shown in Figure 4. A bending-dominated lattice reacts to external loads by cell-wall bending due to its low nodal connectivity at the cell vertices. This results in a microscopic bending-dominated failure mode, where the cell elements collapse by bending stresses [18]. On the other hand, stretching-dominated lattices predominantly behave by stretching due to the high value of nodal connectivity at the cell vertices. For the same porosity or relative density, stretching-dominated lattices are stronger and have higher stiffness than bending-dominated lattices. Gibson and Ashby [20] performed structural analysis and found that the stiffness and the strength of lattice materials scale up with the value of relative density. The strength and stiffness of stretching-dominated lattice scale up linearly by its relative density ($\bar{\rho}$), whereas the strength and stiffness of bending-dominated lattice are scaled up, respectively, by $\bar{\rho}^2$ and $\bar{\rho}^{1.5}$. For example, at $\bar{\rho} = 0.01$, the stretching-dominated lattice is far more superior than the bending-dominated lattice as it is 100 times stiffer and 10 times stronger.

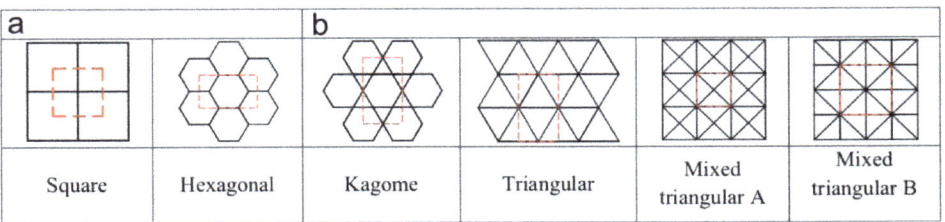

Figure 4. (**a**) Bending dominated lattices (**b**) Stretching dominated lattices [11].

2. Background

For a periodic network of lattices to be considered as material, the characteristic length of its cells needs to be at least one or two orders of magnitude below the medium's overall length scale. Hence, microscale study is vital to understand the full behavior of the structure at the global scale, which is the basic principle of the homogenization method. Numerous analytical and numerical methods have been constructed to determine the mechanical behavior of cellular materials [11,13,14,17,18,21–25]. All of these methods are based on various fields of physics and mathematics ranging from asymptotic theory [11], elasticity theory [13] to micro-polar theory [17]. Moreover, experimental work has been done as well [13,26,27] though it is limited in design complexity due to manufacturability in the process. However, recent advances in 3D manufacturing techniques such as 3D printing has significantly improved the production of lattice materials in terms of accuracy with various kind of solid materials. Nowadays the manufacturing process of lattice structure can be conducted at a very fine scale and with lower overall cost [28–31]. This advancement allows lattice materials to be more experimented on and be tested against existing numerical and analytical models [26,32].

The analytical works to analyze and develop a method to obtain mechanical behaviors and properties of cellular materials have been pioneered by several people; Gibson et al. [13], Masters et al. [16], Wang et al. [14], and Christensen [33]. They derived an analytical closed-form formula of mechanical properties of lattice materials for several shapes and geometry. Their method is based on one common ground assumption, which is that the cell behaves as Euler–Bernoulli beams. They obtain the mechanical properties by solving deformation and equilibrium problems for a single cell, which generates some limitations to the application of the analytical method. It could only be applied to a cell with a simple topology with small strains and no extreme change in geometry. Furthermore, it only works in lattice structures with small relative density value ($\bar{\rho} = 0.3$).

In terms of computational works, several different approaches have been developed. Asymptotic Homogenization (AH) has been extensively employed to obtain the mechanical properties of lattice materials [11,34,35]. AH has been proven and validated to be an effective homogenization method through comparisons with other methods and experimental verification [8]. As it does not have limits in the value of relative density. However, its major shortcoming is the computational cost. It is more expensive than other common approaches, especially when the problem contains a large number of variables [11,36]. Recently, a variational AH of beam-like square lattice structures has been discussed [34] and they explain and result when the microscale of the structure is in the finest scale, i.e., $\epsilon \to 0$. Another computational approach is a matrix-based multiscale method introduced by Vigliotti et al. [24,37]. They performed a linear multiscale analysis and FEA (finite element analysis) on a stretching and bending-dominated lattice [37]. Furthermore, they have applied a method to develop a non-linear model for lattice materials [24].

Some homogenization approaches introduced here come from micro-polar theory [17,38–40] and solid-state physics [18,41]. The micro-polar theory introduces a microscopic rotation in addition to translational deformations. The micro-polar elastic constants of the stiffness matrix can be found through either analysis of the unit cell [17] or an energy approach [40]. From solid-state physics, the combination of Bloch's theorem and the Cauchy–Born hypothesis has been applied to analyze mechanical behavior of planar lattices [18,41].

Recently, Machine Learning has been adopted to study lattice materials [36,42–45]. Koeppe et al. [36] have used a neural network on a set of simulation data to learn a parameterized mechanical model of a lattice structure with particular geometry. Mian et al. [42] obtained an elastic material model for lattice structure using both FEA (finite element analysis) and NN (Neural Network) approaches. These studies have produced results that are in good agreement with both experiment and simulation with a significant increase in computational time and prove that the data-driven method is an effective and efficient as well as reliable and accurate approach. In addition, Machine learning has been used to simulate anisotropic elastic-plastic behavior of cellular structure [45] and deep learning for topology optimization for lattice materials [44]. As machine learning and AI are developing in a rapid trend, data-driven methods are a rising prominent approach and worth looking into in the future of homogenization problems.

As has been briefly summarized above, many varieties of homogenization methods exist to analyze the behavior of lattice materials. All the methods mentioned came from various areas of discipline such as elasticity, solid-state physics, and even computer science. This implies the applications of lattice materials are substantial in many areas of science and engineering disciplines. The objective of this paper is to thoroughly review all the existing method that is relevant according to the author's knowledge and interest. Its foundation, methodology, strength, and limitation will be discussed comprehensively here in a concise form. The final goal that this paper wants to achieve is for the reader to be able to carefully select their homogenization method based on its characteristic so that it could be applied optimally to each particular research.

3. Homogenization Methods

The fundamentals of the homogenization method are the properties of the heterogeneous material could be obtained from the analysis of a small portion of it [12]. The limited portion of the entire heterogeneous material is defined as Representative Volume Element (RVE). To obtain the effective properties, the *RVE* should include the main microstructural characteristic of the heterogonous material and expand to the global medium when uniform strain or stress is applied as boundary condition [12,46,47]. This avoids extensive full-scale simulations. Furthermore, it is noted that this method could be applied only if the homogeneities exist at least a couple of orders of magnitude below the characteristic length of the effective medium.

The concept of homogenization of lattice materials is illustrated in Figure 5 where the *RVE* is applied to a square unit cell. A body Ω with a periodic lattice structure subjected to a traction t at the traction boundary Γ_t, a displacement d at the displacement boundary Γ_d, and a body force f is substituted by a homogenized body $\overline{\Omega}$. The mechanical properties of *RVE* should be determined in such a way that the macroscopic behavior of Ω and $\overline{\Omega}$ are equivalent [12]. Below is a detailed explanation of representative homogenization methods.

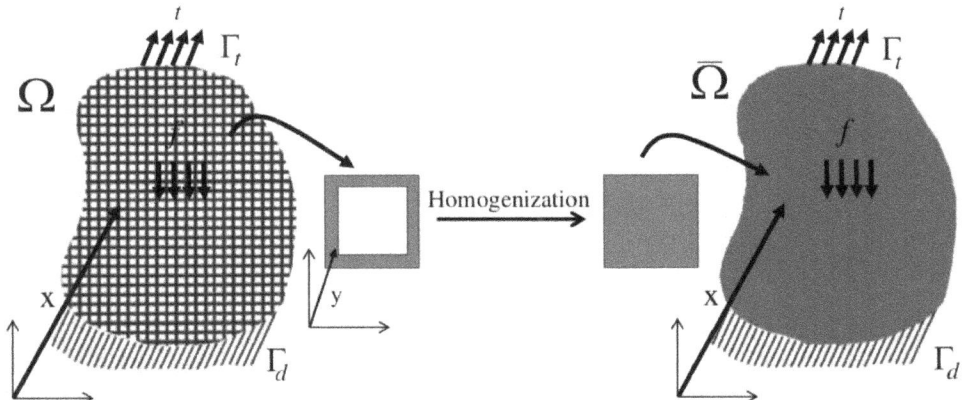

Figure 5. Homogenization concept of a cellular material [12].

3.1. Beam Theory Approach

The Beam Theory approach is also known as the force-based approach [12]. It is employed to model cell-wall deformation just for a unit cell. Then it assumes that the field quantity obtained from the unit cell is uniform over the *RVE*. Over the years, analytical closed-form formula of the mechanical properties of lattice materials for different shapes and geometry has been derived [13,14,16]. Christensen [33] also gives a thorough survey on this approach.

Gibson and Ashby are pioneers in the analysis of cellular materials, in particular of honeycomb shapes [13]. They analyzed the honeycomb shape by employing beam theory on a single unit cell as illustrated in Figure 6. They derived a closed-form solution of mechanical properties for honeycomb shape material and tested their formulation against experimental measurement under two different directional forces as depicted in Figure 6a,b. Masters and Evans [16] took it a step further where they included three mechanisms in their model, namely, flexure, stretching and hinging. They obtained a more general analytical expression for the mechanical properties. Wang and Mcdowell [14] investigated honeycomb structures with seven different cell types. They evaluated in-plane shear properties which had not been considered in most previous research.

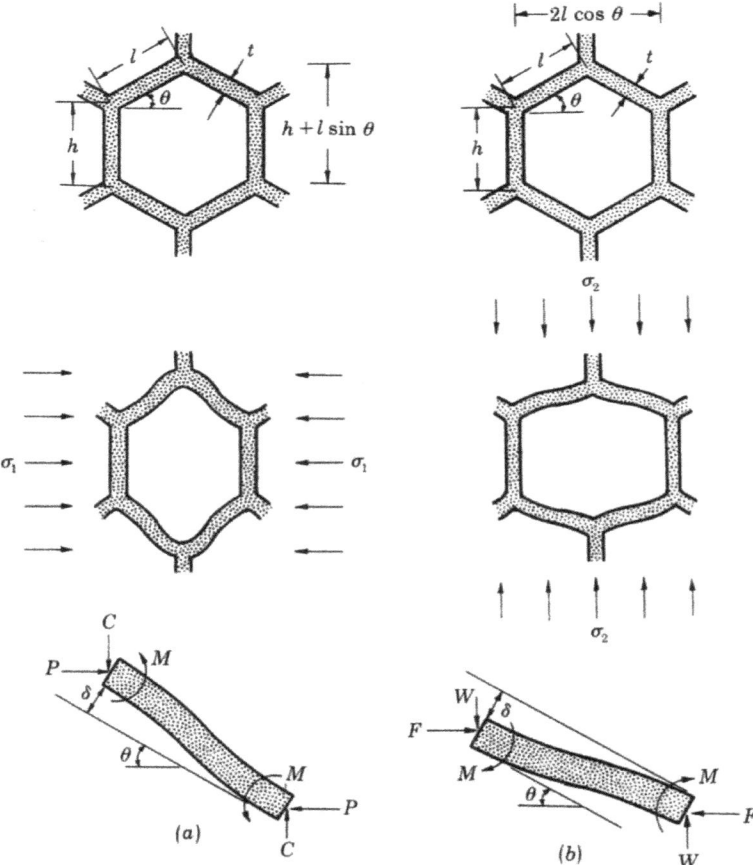

Figure 6. Beam theory analysis on honeycomb structure [13]. (a) and (b) represents structures under two different directional forces.

Different treatments are expected for a different type of unit cell. For bending dominated lattice, the cell walls are treated as beams. Standard beam theory is employed here to calculate effective stiffness. In this case, the *linear-elastic* behavior is predominantly caused by the bending of the cell walls and edges, with minor contributions from shear and axial deformation. For stretching dominated lattice, the cell walls are treated as trusses/columns where the structure is capable of sustaining residual stresses that make equilibrium equations are insufficient to determine the state of internal forces on the cell walls. Additionally, compatibility equations should be used to find the effective elastic properties of the lattice. If the residual stress is assumed zero, then simple truss analysis suffices.

The main advantage of this approach is that the obtained mechanical properties are closed-form analytical formulas and they are useful to generate a chart. Assuming cell wall as a beam limits the applications of this method as follows: First, this formulation can be applied to only cases with low relative density ($\bar{\rho} < 0.3$). Second, this approach cannot be used where geometrical nonlinearities are introduced or when the geometry of a unit cell has a complex topology as Euler's beam formulation assume strains are small enough that large deformation does not occur.

3.2. Strain Energy Equivalence: Surface Average Approach and Volume Average Approach

Strain energy equivalence based method employs a direct application of the *RVE* concept. In this method, the performance of the macroscopic medium are determined solely by the mechanical behavior of its *RVE*. The averages of particular mechanical properties with respect to either the surface of the volume have to be equal in order to obtain the equivalence condition of effective medium and its *RVE* [48]. The constitutive equation for the effective medium and its corresponding *RVE* needs to be calculated in such a way that the condition for equivalence of both volume elements is satisfied.

The first approach for this method is the surface average approach. This approach uses the application of either stress or strain distributions to the surface of the *RVE* [12]. Hence, stress distribution in the *RVE* in assumed to be equivalent to a stress distribution in the volume element consisting of the effective medium if

$$\int_{\Gamma^i_{RVE}} T_i d\Gamma_{RVE} = \int_{\Gamma^i_{RVE}} T_i^* d\Gamma_{RVE} \tag{1}$$

holds, where T_i^* is the traction vector on the surface of the *RVE* and Γ^i_{RVE} is a certain part of its boundary as the part which is orientated parallel to one of the coordinate planes. The second equivalence condition is between the strain tensor generated in the effective medium and its *RVE*, which can be expressed as

$$\overline{\epsilon_{ij}} = \overline{\epsilon_{ij}^*} \tag{2}$$

Furthermore, for a volume element of general shape, the mesoscopic strain can be expressed by

$$\bar{\epsilon} = \frac{1}{2}\frac{1}{V} \int_{\Gamma_{RVE}} (u_i n_j + u_j n_i) \, d\Gamma_{RVE} \tag{3}$$

wre V denotes the volume of the *RVE* and n_i are the components of the normal vector on Γ_{RVE}. Equations (2) and (3) states that the surface integral of the quantity $(u_i n_j + u_j n_i)$ has to be equal for both volume elements.

Surface average approach has a certain limitation. For more complex geometry, such as those that are nonorthotropic, the surface average method gives errors in the prediction of the effective strain energy. This error is due to stress couples that are acting at the intersections of the cell walls and the surfaces of the *RVE*. In order to avoid this problem, a volume average approach can be used. The volume average approach is based on the assumption that the mechanical behavior of the microscopic scale in the *RVE* and the macroscopic medium can be considered equivalent if the *RVE* strain energy is equal to the effective medium. This can be expressed as

$$\overline{w} = \frac{1}{V} \int_{\Omega_{RVE}} w \, d\Omega_{RVE} = \frac{1}{V} \int_{\Omega_{RVE}} w^* \, d\Omega_{RVE} = \overline{w^*} \tag{4}$$

where w denotes the strain energy density distribution and Ω_{RVE} is the area of the RVE. Thus, the strain equivalence condition can be written as

$$\overline{\epsilon_{ij}} = \frac{1}{V}\int_{\Omega_{RVE}} \epsilon_{ij}\, d\Omega_{RVE} = \frac{1}{V}\int_{\Omega_{RVE}} \epsilon_{ij}^{*}\, d\Omega_{RVE} = \overline{\epsilon_{ij}^{*}} \quad (5)$$

Strain energy equivalence method has been commonly used in any kind of cellular structure such as sand which has a corrugated structure [48–52]. The advantage of this method is that it is directly based on the basic laws of continuum mechanics and the conservation of energy and of. Furthermore, there is no limitation in using this method in respect of geometries of the cellular structure and cell topology.

3.3. Micropolar Theory

Classical continuum theory is not suitable when discontinuities or high strain gradients are observed in the domain such as crack tips or notches. Micropolar theory, also known as Cosserat theory, is a generalization of classical continuum theory developed by E. and F. Cosserat [53] and Eringen [54]. The micropolar theory introduces a microscopic rotation in addition to translational deformations and its key assumption is both displacement and rotations of a point are independent kinematic properties. In lattice material, this means joint displacement and joint rotation contribute to the total joint displacement.

In the linear micropolar elasticity theory, the kinematic relations can be written as

$$\epsilon_{ij} = u_{j,i} - e_{kij}\phi_k \quad (6)$$

$$k_{ij} = \phi_{j,i} \quad (7)$$

where $u_{j,i}$ is the displacement gradient, ϵ_{ij} is the strain tensor, ϕ_k is the microrotation, k_{ij} is the curvature strain tensor, and $\phi_{j,i}$ is the microrotation gradient. The generalized strain vector of a micropolar medium can be expressed as follows:

$$\epsilon = [\epsilon_{11}\ \epsilon_{22}\ \epsilon_{12}\ \epsilon_{21}\ k_{13}\ k_{23}]^T = [u_{1,1}\ u_{2,2}\ u_{2,1} - \phi\ u_{1,2} + \phi\ \phi_{3,1}\ \phi_{3,2}]^T \quad (8)$$

The generalized stress vector is given by

$$\sigma = [\sigma_{11}\ \sigma_{22}\ \sigma_{12}\ \sigma_{21}\ m_{13}\ m_{23}]^T \quad (9)$$

where m_{13} and m_{23} are the couple stresses in the x and y planes. The 2D constitutive relations for anisotropic micropolar solids can be written as:

$$\sigma = \overline{C}\epsilon \quad (10)$$

where $\overline{C}$ is the 6×6 matrix of the constitutive law coefficients for a micropolar medium.

In order to characterize a cellular material as a micropolar continuum, the coefficients of the constitutive equations, $\overline{C}$, must be obtained. The micropolar elastic constants of the stiffness matrix can be determined through either structural analysis of the unit cell [17] or an energy approach [40]. The analysis of the unit cell can be done using the beam theory approach to obtain the general deformation state of the RVE, which is a unit cell in this case. The effective stresses and strains over the RVE can be computed using constitutive equations. On the other hand, for the energy approach, the stresses of the cell can be obtained by obtaining the derivation of the strain energy density concerning the strain vector.

Micropolar theory combined with beam theory approach or energy approach has several limitations (1) It could only be applied to unit cells with a certain shape that contains a single joint at the center or the unit cell, and (2) the newly introduced micropolar variable acts as an additional degree of freedom. Hence, an additional step is required to solve the governing equations.

3.4. Solid-State Physics Approach: Bloch's Theorem and Cauchy Born Hypothesis

Due to its similarity, the concept of solid-state physics can be adapted into solid mechanics to investigate the characteristics of lattice materials. The lattice, in solid-state physics, is defined as an infinitely periodic arrangement of points. When periods of the unit cell are perfectly stacked in two or three dimensions, the space is considered to be tessellated. The bases are the mathematical formulation for the physical quantities that are repeated in every cell translation [18]. In continuum mechanics, a lattice material can be described using the above definition.

Bloch wave analysis and the Cauchy–Born hypothesis, in particular, are methods for solid-state physics that can be adapted into solid mechanics to investigate the behavior of lattice materials [18,55]. Bloch's theorem was originally developed to describe the transport of electron particles within the crystal structure of a solid [56]. Then the Bloch's theorem can be applied to analyze the propagation of a wave function over to an infinite lattice structure. On the other hand, the Cauchy–Born hypothesis [41] analyzes a macroscopic mechanism that is induced by an applied strain [12] and states that the infinitesimal displacement field of a periodic lattice is made up of two parts, namely, the deformation obtained by a macroscopic strain field and the periodic displacement field of the unit cell. Bloch's theorem is used to define the propagation of a wave function over the infinite lattice structure. The idea is that the nodal deformation function $d(p_i, \omega) \in C^2$ is written as a wave function in the form of

$$d(p, \omega) = d(j_i + \vec{R}, \omega) = d(j_l, \omega) e^{2\pi i \omega \vec{R}} \quad \forall l \in \{1, 2, \ldots, J\} \tag{11}$$

where ω is the translational vector, p is the position vector for the joints, J is the number of independent nodes within the unit cell, $p_i = j_i + \vec{R}$ is the position vector of any node throughout the lattice and $\vec{R}$ is the Bravais cell vector of any unit cell through the entire lattice. For bar deformation functions, the generalized bar deformation vectors $e(q_m, \omega) \in C^2$ can be written as a wave function of the form:

$$e(q_m, \omega) = e(b_m + \vec{R}, \omega) = e(b_m, \omega) e^{2\pi i \omega \vec{R}} \quad \forall m \in \{1, 2, \ldots, B\} \tag{12}$$

where B is the number of independent bars within the unit cell and $q_m = b_m + \vec{R}$ is the position vector of any bar throughout the lattice. Periodic boundary conditions needs to be applied over the unit cell to simplify the forms of the kinematic and equilibrium matrices for both bars and joints [57,58].

Bloch's theorem defines the deformation mechanism corresponding to periodic joint displacement fields. The Cauchy–Born hypothesis is needed to analyze the macroscopic strain field generated by periodic condition [59,60]. From the definition of the Cauchy–Born hypothesis [61], the infinitesimal displacement field of a periodic joint in a lattice structure can be expressed as:

$$d(j_l + \vec{R}, \vec{\epsilon}) = d(j, \vec{\epsilon} = 0) + \vec{\epsilon} \cdot \vec{R} \tag{13}$$

where $d(j_l + \vec{R}, \vec{\epsilon})$ is the periodic displacement field of joint j_l. Assume that the periodic joints described by the position vectors j_l and $j_l + \vec{R}$, are the two periodic joints i and j within a lattice structure, then Equation (13) can be written as:

$$\begin{bmatrix} u_i \\ v_i \end{bmatrix} = \begin{bmatrix} u_j \\ v_j \end{bmatrix} + \begin{bmatrix} \epsilon_{11} & \frac{1}{2}\epsilon_{12} \\ \frac{1}{2}\epsilon_{21} & \epsilon_{22} \end{bmatrix} \begin{bmatrix} x_i - x_j \\ y_l - y_j \end{bmatrix} \tag{14}$$

where u and v are the joint displacement components in the x and y directions, respectively, and joint i is the independent joint. Notice that the formulation above is written in terms of engineering strain. Equation (14) can be expressed as well as:

$$\begin{bmatrix} u_i \\ v_i \end{bmatrix} = \begin{bmatrix} u_j \\ v_j \end{bmatrix} + \begin{bmatrix} (x_i - x_j) & 0 & \frac{1}{2}(y_i - y_j) \\ 0 & (y_i - y_j) & \frac{1}{2}(x_i - x_j) \end{bmatrix} \begin{bmatrix} \epsilon_{11} \\ \epsilon_{22} \\ \epsilon_{21} \end{bmatrix} \quad (15)$$

or in the shorter term:

$$d_i = d_j + E\bar{\epsilon} \quad (16)$$

Equation (16) is the kinematic boundary condition of the Cauchy–Born hypothesis. Applying this boundary condition to the unit cell joint displacement vector, d, results in:

$$d = T_d \tilde{d} + E\bar{\epsilon} \quad (17)$$

Substituting Equation (17) into the kinematic system of the unit cell results in:

$$B\{T_d \tilde{d} + \tilde{E}\bar{\epsilon}\} = e \quad (18)$$

Equations (17) and (18) describe the application of the Cauchy–Born kinematic boundary condition to the continuum kinematic system of the lattice microstructure to express the relation between the microscopic displacements and a macroscopic strain field. The Cauchy–Born hypothesis cannot be applied to the kinematic compatibility relation of the unit cell without resorting to the Dummy node scheme [18]. This procedure, along with a more detailed derivation of this method, has been extensively discussed in previous literature [18,59–61] and will not be discussed here. This approach has been developed by assuming cell walls as beam elements. Hence, similar to the elasticity theory approach, these assumptions limit its application to low relative densities ($\rho < 0.3$).

3.5. Asymptotic Homogenization Approach

Analytical solutions have shown some limitations in the applications of more general cases. Hence, one of the well-developed theories, with a sound mathematical foundation, that has been successfully used to predict mechanical properties in porous materials [35] is the Asymptotic Homogenization (AH) theory. This method has been validated with experimental results and proven to be a reliable and accurate method among them [62]. Arabnejad et al. performed extensive work on using AH to obtain mechanical properties of the lattice structure [11].

The pivot assumption of AH is that each physical quantity depends on two different scales: one on the macroscopic level x, and the other on the microscopic level, $y = x/\epsilon$ where ϵ is a ratio between RVE size and the size of the macroscopic medium means that stress/strain will vary faster by $1/\epsilon$. AH also assumes that field quantities change smoothly at the macroscopic level and have periodic condition at the microscale. Based on AH, each mechanical variable, such as the displacement field, u, can be expanded into power series concerning to ϵ:

$$u^\epsilon = u_0(x,y) + \epsilon u_1(x,y) + \epsilon^2 u_2(x,y) + \cdots \quad (19)$$

u_1 and u_2 are perturbations in the displacement field due to the microstructure and u_0 is the average value of the displacement field depend only on the macroscopic scale [35]. Take the derivative of the power series we get

$$\frac{du}{dx} = \epsilon(u) = \frac{1}{2}\left(\nabla u_0^T + \nabla u_0\right)_x + \frac{1}{2}\left(\nabla u_1^T + \nabla u_1\right)_y + O(\epsilon) \quad (20)$$

$$\epsilon(u) = \{\bar{\epsilon}(u)\} + \{\epsilon^*(u)\} \quad (21)$$

where $\bar{\epsilon}(u)$ is the macroscopic strain and $\epsilon^*(u)$ is the fluctuating strain at the microscopic level. Note that the terms of $O(\epsilon)$ and higher are neglected. Substitute the above equation into the weak form of equilibrium equation for a cellular body Ω^ϵ:

$$\int_{\Omega^\epsilon} C_{ijkl}\left(\epsilon_{ij}^0(v) + \epsilon_{ij}^1(v)\right)(\bar{\epsilon}_{kl}(u) + \epsilon_{kl}^*(u))d\Omega^\epsilon = \int_\Gamma t_i v_i d\Gamma \tag{22}$$

where C_{ijkl} is the effective stiffness tensor of the RVE, $\epsilon_{ij}^0(v)$ and $\epsilon_{ij}^1(v)$ are the macroscopic and microscopic strains, respectively, and t is the traction at the traction boundary Γ_t. The displacement v is selected to be contant on the macroscopic level and vary only on the microscopic level. Hence, this leads to:

$$\int_{\Omega^\epsilon} C_{ijkl}\epsilon_{ij}^1(v)(\bar{\epsilon}_{kl}(u) + \epsilon_{kl}^*(u))d\Omega^\epsilon = 0 \tag{23}$$

Integrating over the RVE volume (V_{RVE}). Equation (23) may be rephrased as:

$$\int_{V_{RVE}} C_{ijkl}\epsilon_{ij}^1(v)\epsilon_{kl}^* dV_{RVE} = -\int_{V_{RVE}} C_{ijkl}\epsilon_{ij}^1(v)\bar{\epsilon}_{kl} dV_{RVE} \tag{24}$$

The equation above represents a local problem defined on the RVE. For a certain applied macroscopic strain, the material can be characterized if the fluctuating strain ϵ^* is known. The periodicity of the strain field is guaranted by applying periodic boundary conditions on the RVE edges; the displacements at opposite sides of the RVE are constrained to be equal [63]. The equation can be discretized and solved via FE analysis. For this objective, the equation needs to be simplified to obtain a relation between the microscopic displacement field and the force vector. This step will not be explained in this article. Instead, a simple example of solving an equation on one-dimensional domain will be illustrated below.

Consider a composite bar consist of two materials that interchange periodically with Young's moduli E_1 and E_2 which is described in Figure 7. Section 1 of the unit cell has material with a modulus E_1 and length $1 - \alpha$. Section 2 of the unit cell has material with modulus E_2 and length α. The RVE on the microstructure of this case is chosen to be of unit length as is the area of the bar. Equation (24) in 1-D can be rewritten as:

$$\int_0^1 E(x,y)\epsilon^*\epsilon(v)dy = \int_0^1 E(x,y)\epsilon(v)dy \tag{25}$$

where $E(x,y)$ is Young's modulus which varies at both the microscopic and macroscopic levels. First, set $E(x,y) = E$ and rewrite Equation (25) as

$$\int_0^1 E(1 - \epsilon^*)\epsilon(v)dy = 0 \tag{26}$$

Applying integration by parts

$$\int_0^1 v\frac{\partial}{\partial y}E(1 - \epsilon^*)dy + E(1 - \epsilon^*)v \ |_{y=0}^{y=1} = 0 \tag{27}$$

The strong form of Equation (27) is

$$\frac{\partial}{\partial y}E(1 - \epsilon^*) = 0 \tag{28}$$

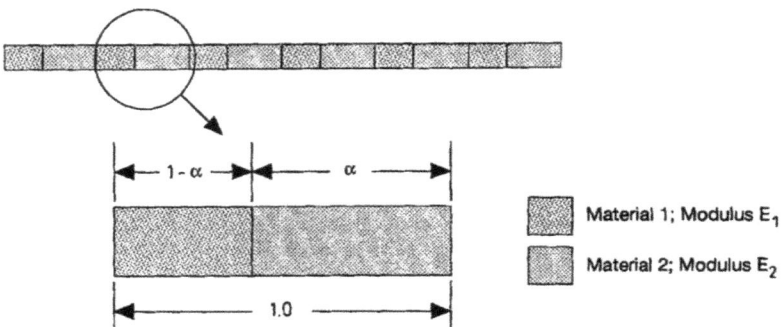

Figure 7. Composite bar used for the one-dimensional analysis [63].

Integrating gives the solution

$$E(1 - \epsilon^*) = c(x) \qquad (29)$$

where $c(x)$ is constant over the microstructure. To determine $c(x)$, the equation is integrated over y

$$\int_0^1 (1 - \epsilon^*) dy = \int_0^1 \frac{c(x)}{E} dy \rightarrow 1 - u^* \big|_0^1 = c(x) \int_0^1 \frac{1}{E} dy. \qquad (30)$$

Since the displacements u^* must be equal at the cell boundaries to ensure periodicity, thus

$$c(x) = \frac{1}{\int_0^1 \frac{1}{E} dy} \qquad (31)$$

Hence, the effective stiffness can be expressed as

$$\overline{E} = \int_0^1 (1 - \epsilon^*) dy = \int_0^1 c(x) \, dy = c(x) = \frac{1}{\int_0^{1-\alpha} \frac{1}{E_1} dy + \int_{1-\alpha}^1 \frac{1}{E_2} dy} \qquad (32)$$

Evaluating the above integral gives us:

$$\overline{E} = \frac{E_1 E_2}{(1 - \alpha) E_2 + \alpha E_1} \qquad (33)$$

Thus, for one-dimensional case, the effective stiffness obtained using AH method and the standard mechanics approach is equal.

The notable advantage of AH is that the stress distribution in microscale can be modeled accurately and thus give us a detailed analysis of the periodic materials. Furthermore, AH has neither limitation on the cell topology nor the range of the relative density which is a substantial gain of this method [11]. The major drawback of the AH method, however, is its computational cost. This can be a high problem if the problem involves complex topology and contains a significant number of variables.

3.6. Multi-Scale Homogenization Method for Lattice Materials

This approach is often called global-local analysis as it involves a two-scale process. This method is originally applied to heterogeneous material in order to create constitutive relationships from the analysis of the *RVE*. This method is developed based on the earlier work done by Eshelby [64] which investigated the mechanics of an ellipsoidal inclusion in an infinite matrix with homogeneous boundary conditions. The *RVE* features are somewhat similar to the ones that Elsheby has studied. It consists of a bounded area of the domain that contains the main microstructural properties of the material and behaves as an infinite medium if boundary conditions are imposed.

In general, this method utilizes a two-scale approach. One is the macroscopic FE model of the homogeneous continuum where boundary conditions are defined by the problem. The other is the microscopic level which numerically investigates the stress-strain relationship where boundary conditions are generated by the macroscopic scale. This approach allows the macroscopic stress to be determined as the gradient of the strain energy density involving the components of the macroscopic gradient. This approach results in a compact matrix formulation for the macroscopic stress as a function of the macroscopic displacement gradient.

The method that is described here is the application multi-scale homogenization method to develop non-linear constitutive models for lattice materials [24]. This homogenization method is done using the principle of work which will be described shortly in this section. The details and derivation of this method can be found in the previous literature by Vigliotti et al. [24,37]. The main procedure for this method is described in Figure 8.

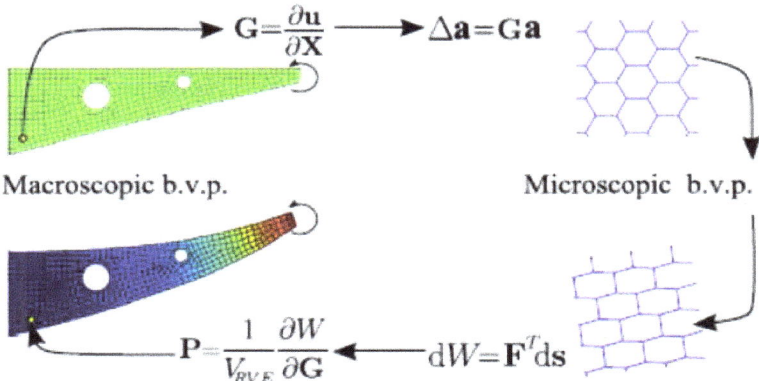

Figure 8. Multiscale scheme [24].

Let s be the vector of the nodal degree freedom of the RVE, the corresponding array of the nodal forces, $F(s)$, can be obtained using FE analysis of the RVE. The distribution of the strain energy, due to macroscopic strain, can be obtained by employing the principle of the virtual work:

$$dW = \int_{V_{RVE}} P_{ij} dG_{ij} dV = F^T ds \qquad (34)$$

where P_{ij} and G_{ij} are the elements of the first Piola-Kirchoff (1PK) stress tensor and the macroscopic displacement, respectively; ds is the variation of the nodal displacements. Assuming that P_{ij} and G_{ij} are constant through out the RVE, the stress tensor can be obtained:

$$P_{ij} = \frac{1}{V_{RVE}} \frac{\partial W}{\partial G_{ij}} = \frac{1}{V_{RVE}} F^T \frac{\partial s}{\partial G_{ij}} \qquad (35)$$

Solving the equation above will introduce the boundary conditions for the microscopic model. Once the microscopic boundary value problem is solved, the components of P as the derivatives of the strain energy density of the lattice concerning G can be determined.

The main advantages of this method are that it accounts for geometrical material nonlinearity as have shown above and this approach has no restrictions in terms of relative density and unit cell shape. This model is capable to capture the local bucking of cell struts under multiple loading conditions and thus can predict the points where bifurcation occurs. However, unlike the AH approach, the choice of the RVE's size might influence the equilibrium equation of the lattice especially in the presence of bifurcations [24]. Hence, a sensitivity analysis should be performed before choosing the size of the *RVE*.

3.7. Machine Learning Approach: Data-Driven Model

In recent years, there has been significant development of homogenization methods using machine learning algorithms [36,42–45]. Machine learning has been proven to be a dependable computational tool and employed in constitutive modeling [65–68]. As described in the previous section, while effective and precise, theoretical and numerical approaches each post major limitation. Theoretical approaches are limited for low relative density, small deformation, and simple geometry. Some of these limitations can be overcome using numerical approaches but these methods, such as FEA or AH, are computationally expensive. An alternative way is to use neural networks to do constitutive modeling based on either experiments or homogenization results as training data. In this section, we will discuss several strategies of implementation of this method that has been developed in recent years.

The fundamental initial phase of using machine learning algorithms, in this case, neural network approaches, is to generate training data. Either experimental data [65,68] or *RVE* simulations can be utilized for training process [45,66,67]. Settgast et al. [45] used the volume average method as their *RVE* simulation method and then used the results as the training data which is shown in Figure 9. The constitutive functions are obtained using neural networks instead of classic material modeling. FNET library is used to implement the neural networks [69]. Their study is limited to small deformation cases for simplicity but their approach can be straightforwardly extended to large deformation case. They can obtain an accurate result with much more efficiency than a direct numerical simulation (DNS) or FEM simulation.

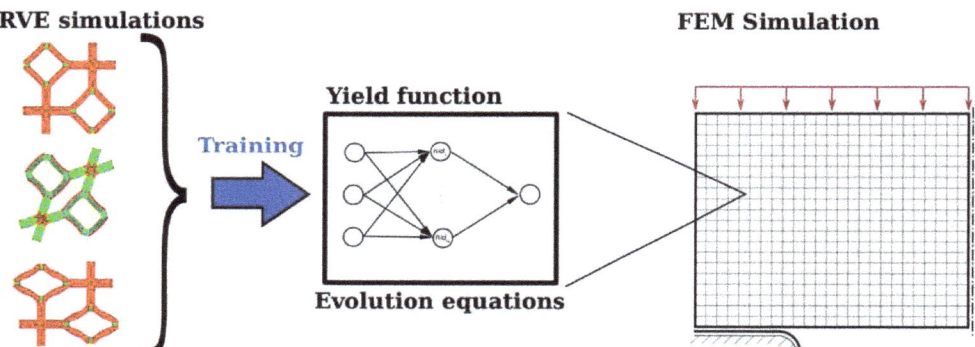

Figure 9. Graphical illustration of machine learning approach by Settgast et al. [45].

The other approach is to use finite element simulation (FEA) as the training data [42]. However, instead of full simulation of finite elements, only several models of lattice materials are simulated using FEA with a significant number of elements to compute the mechanical properties. Mechanical properties and design parameters data are used to train a NN to predict the equivalent properties for various cell sizes and materials with considerably less time than a full FE analysis. The result from this approach is compared with a full FEA simulation and experimental test. Their approach is briefly described in Figure 10. They concluded that the NN model of lattice materials is very accurate, swift, and efficient for use as compared to numerical FEA models. Furthermore, by using this approach a more complicated geometry of lattice can be investigated with significantly less computational time. It was shown that the computational time could be reduced from the order of hours to just order of minutes.

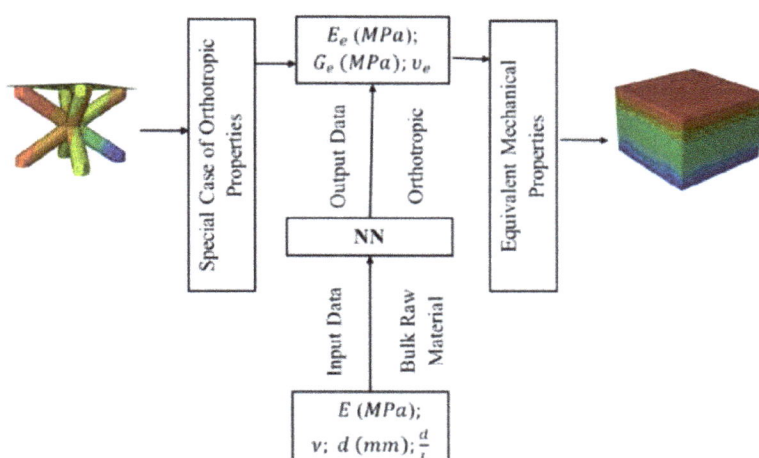

Figure 10. Integration of FEA model to NN model [42].

Another implementation strategy done by Koeppe et al. [36] is to combine experiments and finite element (FE) simulations to obtain training data. Firstly, lattice materials are created and tested under certain loading conditions. The experimental results will be validated against a parameterized FE model. Secondly, the developed FE model is utilized to predict the stresses considering different design variables. Finally, these deformations and design variables are used to train a NN to predict the stresses. This approach results in a significant increase in performance. The computation time for FE simulations is in order of five to ten hours (wall clock time) while the NN approach takes about 0.47 s. The obtained stresses by the neural network are in a good agreement with the FE results.

We try to point out each method's main characteristic, its advantages, and limitation to give a concise comparison for the reader. The summary can be seen in Table 1.

Table 1. Summary of Homogenization Method.

Method	Underlying Theory	Highlights	Limitation
Beam Theory Approach [13,14,16,33]	Apply beam theory analysis on a single cell and assume uniform over the RVE	• Close analytical formula. • Relatively simple and does not need computational power.	• Low relative density value ($\rho < 0.3$). • Simple topology • Small strain and no large deformation.
Strain Energy Equivalence [48–52]	The averages of particular mechanical properties with respect to either the surface of the volume have to be equal in order to obtain the equivalence condition of effective medium and its RVE	• Close analytical formula • No restriction in terms of cell topology and its geometric symmetry	• Small strain and no large deformation
Micropolar Theory [17,38–40]	Introduce a new variable, microscopic rotation, in addition to translational deformations and assume that both displacements and rotations of a point are independent kinematic quantities	• Close analytical formula • It does not need computational power	• It needs to be combined with the beam theory approach or energy approach • Only feasible for unit cells with a certain shape that contains a single joint at the center or the unit cell
Bloch's Theorem and Cauchy–Born Hypothesis [18,55]	• Bloch's theorem is used to study the propagation of a wave function over an infinite lattice structure at a microscopic level. • The Cauchy–Born hypothesis investigate macroscopic mechanisms induced by an applied strain.	• Able to give a description of wave propagation over lattice structure • Able to identify the collapse mechanism subject to macroscopic strain	• Low relative density value ($\rho < 0.3$)
Asymptotic Homogenization (AH) [11,35,62]	• The main idea of AH is that each physical variables consist of two different scales: macroscopic and microscopic level.	• No restriction on the unit cell geometry • Works for all ranges of relative density • Independent from RVE size	• The computational cost is relatively expensive

Table 1. *Cont.*

Method	Underlying Theory	Highlights	Limitation
Multi-Scale Homogenization Method [24,37,64]	This method utilizes a two-scale approach • The macroscopic FE model of the component with certain boundary condition • The microscopic level stress-strain relationship where boundary conditions are imposed by the macroscopic scale	• No restriction on the unit cell geometry • Works for all ranges of relative density • Capable of capturing local bucking of cell walls under multiple loading conditions	• The relatively expensive computational cost • Depends on the RVE size. Hence, an additional convergence analysis needs to be done before using the method
Machine Learning Approach [36,42–45]	Use neural networks to do constitutive modeling based on either experiments or homogenization results as training data	• Significantly low computational cost • No limitation on cell topology and relative density	• Needs to generate a huge amount of data to have an accurate result

4. Conclusions and Future Work

This paper has provided a concise review of several homogenization methods that can be applied to the analysis and design of lattice materials. These methods came from various areas of discipline such as elasticity, solid-state physics, and even computer science. Relative density, cell geometry, lattice category (structure or materials), and cell element assumptions have important roles in the behavior of lattice materials. Hence, it is critical to employ a proper model for the lattice regarding those parameters. A summary of each strength and weakness of each method has been shown in Table 1.

Out of all methods, due to its efficiency and accuracy, there has been a growing interest in the homogenization method using machine learning algorithms recently as it has proven to be a reliable computational tool and has been employed in constitutive modeling. Furthermore, it has been shown in the previous section how the machine learning approaches can overcome some major limitations that are posted by the classical homogenization technique.

Other than increasing efficiency, the recent and future works of homogenization are directed more towards the area of structure optimization. Homogenization coupled with optimization method has proven to increase both the efficiency of the optimization procedure and the overall performance of a lattice structure [70–73]. Stiffness [71], structural compliance [72], structural vibration [70] and energy absorption [73] have been proved to increase quite significantly using a homogenization method in a structural optimization procedure. It can be observed that most of these works use asymptotic homogenization as their method to be combined in the optimization procedure. As mentioned before, machine learning approach has a promising future in terms of its efficiency. Hence, it will be seen in the near future, integrated works of machine learning approach homogenization and optimization algorithm.

Author Contributions: Conceptualization, B.W.J. and J.S.; methodology, J.S. and B.W.J.; software, J.S.; validation, J.S.; formal analysis, J.S.; investigation, J.S. and B.W.J.; data curation, J.S.; writing—original draft preparation, J.S. and B.W.J.; writing—review and editing, J.S. and B.W.J.; visualization, J.S.; supervision, B.W.J.; project administration, B.W.J.; funding acquisition, B.W.J. All authors have read and agreed to the published version of the manuscript.

Funding: This work is sponsored by InnoScience Co., Ltd. (20210901) and supported under the framework of the international cooperation program managed by the National Research Foundation (NRF) of Korea (NSFC 2021K2A9A2A06049018).

Institutional Review Board Statement: Not applicable.

Informed Consent Statement: Not applicable.

Data Availability Statement: All data contained within the article.

Acknowledgments: The authors greatly appreciate National Research Foundation (NRF) of Korea and InnoScience Co., Ltd. for their support.

Conflicts of Interest: The authors declare no conflict of interest.

References

1. Schroeder, V.; Savagatrup, S.; He, M.; Lin, S.; Swager, T.M. Carbon nanotube chemical sensors. *Chem. Rev.* **2019**, *119*, 599–663. [CrossRef] [PubMed]
2. Tancogne-Dejean, T.; Spierings, A.B.; Mohr, D. Additively-manufactured metallic micro-lattice materials for high specific energy absorption under static and dynamic loading. *Acta Mater.* **2016**, *116*, 14–28. [CrossRef]
3. Rashed, M.G.; Ashraf, M.; Mines, R.A.W.; Hazell, P.J. Metallic microlattice materials: A current state of the art on manufacturing, mechanical properties and applications. *Mater. Des.* **2016**, *95*, 518–533. [CrossRef]
4. Bici, M.; Brischetto, S.; Campana, F.; Ferro, C.G.; Seclì, C.; Varetti, S.; Maggiore, P.; Mazza, A. Development of a multifunctional panel for aerospace use through SLM additive manufacturing. *Procedia CIRP* **2018**, *67*, 215–220. [CrossRef]
5. Han, Y.; Wang, P.; Fan, H.; Sun, F.; Chen, L.; Fang, D. Free vibration of CFRC lattice-core sandwich cylinder with attached mass. *Compos. Sci. Technol.* **2015**, *118*, 226–235. [CrossRef]

6. Jenett, B.E.; Calisch, S.E.; Cellucci, D.; Cramer, N.; Gershenfeld, N.A.; Swei, S.; Cheung, K.C. Digital Morphing Wing: Active Wing Shaping Concept Using Composite Lattice-Based Cellular Structures. *Soft Robot.* **2017**, *4*, 33–48. [CrossRef] [PubMed]
7. Li, W.; Sun, F.; Wang, P.; Fan, H.; Fang, D. A novel carbon fiber reinforced lattice truss sandwich cylinder: Fabrication and experiments. *Compos. Part A Appl. Sci. Manuf.* **2016**, *81*, 313–322. [CrossRef]
8. Wei, K.; Peng, Y.; Qu, Z.; Zhou, H.; Pei, Y.; Fang, D. Lightweight composite lattice cylindrical shells with novel character of tailorable thermal expansion. *Int. J. Mech. Sci.* **2018**, *137*, 77–85. [CrossRef]
9. Cundy, H.M. *Mathematical Models*; Oxford University Press: Oxford, UK, 1956.
10. Their, T.; St-Pierre, L. Stiffness and strength of a semi-regular lattice. *Raken. Mek.* **2017**, *50*, 137–140. [CrossRef]
11. Arabnejad, S.; Pasini, D. Mechanical properties of lattice materials via asymptotic homogenization and comparison with alternative homogenization methods. *Int. J. Mech. Sci.* **2013**, *77*, 249–262. [CrossRef]
12. Phani, A.S.; Hussein, M.I. *Dynamics of Lattice Materials*; Wiley Online Library: Hoboken, NJ, USA, 2017.
13. Gibson, L.J.; Ashby, M.F.; Schajer, G.S.; Robertson, C.I. The mechanics of two-dimensional cellular materials. *Proc. R. Soc. London. A Math. Phys. Sci.* **1982**, *382*, 25–42. [CrossRef]
14. Wang, A.-J.; McDowell, D.L. In-Plane Stiffness and Yield Strength of Periodic Metal Honeycombs. *J. Eng. Mater. Technol.* **2004**, *126*, 137–156. [CrossRef]
15. Kelsey, S.; Gellatly, R.; Clark, B. The Shear Modulus of Foil Honeycomb Cores. *Aircr. Eng. Aerosp. Technol.* **1958**, *30*, 294–302. [CrossRef]
16. Masters, I.; Evans, K. Models for the elastic deformation of honeycombs. *Compos. Struct.* **1996**, *35*, 403–422. [CrossRef]
17. Wang, X.L.; Stronge, W.J. Micropolar theory for two–dimensional stresses in elastic honeycomb. *Proc. R. Soc. A Math. Phys. Eng. Sci.* **1999**, *455*, 2091–2116. [CrossRef]
18. Elsayed, M.S.; Pasini, D. Analysis of the elastostatic specific stiffness of 2D stretching-dominated lattice materials. *Mech. Mater.* **2010**, *42*, 709–725. [CrossRef]
19. Ashby, M.F. The properties of foams and lattices. *Philos. Trans. R. Soc. A Math. Phys. Eng. Sci.* **2006**, *364*, 15–30. [CrossRef]
20. Gibson, L.J.; Ashby, M.F. *Cellular Solids: Structure and Properties*; Cambridge University Press: Cambridge, UK, 1999.
21. Gonella, S.; Ruzzene, M. Homogenization and equivalent in-plane properties of two-dimensional periodic lattices. *Int. J. Solids Struct.* **2008**, *45*, 2897–2915. [CrossRef]
22. Rezakhani, R.; Cusatis, G. Generalized mathematical homogenization of the lattice discrete particle model. In Proceedings of the 8th International Conference on Fracture Mechanics of Concrete and Concrete Structures, Toledo, Spain, 10–14 March 2013; pp. 261–271.
23. Tollenaere, H.; Cailleire, D. Continuous Modelling of Lattice Structures by Homogenization. *Dev. Comput. Aided Des. Model. Civ. Eng.* **2009**, *29*, 699–705. [CrossRef]
24. Vigliotti, A.; Deshpande, V.S.; Pasini, D. Non linear constitutive models for lattice materials. *J. Mech. Phys. Solids* **2014**, *64*, 44–60. [CrossRef]
25. Wang, A.-J.; McDowell, D. Yield surfaces of various periodic metal honeycombs at intermediate relative density. *Int. J. Plast.* **2005**, *21*, 285–320. [CrossRef]
26. Park, S.-I.; Rosen, D.W.; Choi, S.-K.; Duty, C.E. Effective Mechanical Properties of Lattice Material Fabricated by Material Extrusion Additive Manufacturing. *Addit. Manuf.* **2014**, *1*, 12–23. [CrossRef]
27. Salehian, A.; Inman, D.J. Dynamic analysis of a lattice structure by homogenization: Experimental validation. *J. Sound Vib.* **2008**, *316*, 180–197. [CrossRef]
28. Du, Y.; Gu, D.; Xi, L.; Dai, D.; Gao, T.; Zhu, J.; Ma, C. Laser additive manufacturing of bio-inspired lattice structure: Forming quality, microstructure and energy absorption behavior. *Mater. Sci. Eng. A* **2020**, *773*, 138857. [CrossRef]
29. Rehme, O.; Emmelmann, C. Rapid manufacturing of lattice structures with selective laser melting. In *Laser-Based Micropackaging*; International Society for Optics and Photonics: San Jose, CA, USA, 2006; Volume 6107, p. 61070K.
30. Tao, W.; Leu, M.C. Design of lattice structure for additive manufacturing. In Proceedings of the 2016 International Symposium on Flexible Automation (ISFA), Cleveland, OH, USA, 1–3 August 2016; pp. 325–332.
31. Tran, H.T.; Chen, Q.; Mohan, J.; To, A.C. A new method for predicting cracking at the interface between solid and lattice support during laser powder bed fusion additive manufacturing. *Addit. Manuf.* **2020**, *32*, 101050. [CrossRef]
32. Cheng, L.; Liang, X.; Belski, E.; Wang, X.; Sietins, J.M.; Ludwick, S.; To, A.C. Natural Frequency Optimization of Variable-Density Additive Manufactured Lattice Structure: Theory and Experimental Validation. *J. Manuf. Sci. Eng.* **2018**, *140*. [CrossRef]
33. Christensen, R. Mechanics of cellular and other low-density materials. *Int. J. Solids Struct.* **2000**, *37*, 93–104. [CrossRef]
34. Barchiesi, E.; Khakalo, S. Variational asymptotic homogenization of beam-like square lattice structures. *Math. Mech. Solids* **2019**, *24*, 3295–3318. [CrossRef]
35. Hassani, B.; Hinton, E. A review of homogenization and topology optimization I—homogenization theory for media with periodic structure. *Comput. Struct.* **1998**, *69*, 707–717. [CrossRef]
36. Koeppe, A.; Padilla, C.A.H.; Voshage, M.; Schleifenbaum, J.H.; Markert, B. Efficient numerical modeling of 3D-printed lattice-cell structures using neural networks. *Manuf. Lett.* **2018**, *15*, 147–150. [CrossRef]
37. Vigliotti, A.; Pasini, D. Linear multiscale analysis and finite element validation of stretching and bending dominated lattice materials. *Mech. Mater.* **2012**, *46*, 57–68. [CrossRef]
38. Askar, A.; Cakmak, A. A structural model of a micropolar continuum. *Int. J. Eng. Sci.* **1968**, *6*, 583–589. [CrossRef]

39. Chen, Y.; Liu, X.N.; Hu, G.K.; Sun, Q.; Zheng, Q.S. Micropolar continuum modelling of bi-dimensional tetrachiral lattices. *Proc. R. Soc. A Math. Phys. Eng. Sci.* **2014**, *470*, 20130734. [CrossRef]
40. Kumar, R.S.; McDowell, D.L. Generalized continuum modeling of 2-D periodic cellular solids. *Int. J. Solids Struct.* **2004**, *41*, 7399–7422. [CrossRef]
41. Chiras, S.; Mumm, D.; Evans, A.; Wicks, N.; Hutchinson, J.; Dharmasena, K.; Wadley, H.; Fichter, S. The structural performance of near-optimized truss core panels. *Int. J. Solids Struct.* **2002**, *39*, 4093–4115. [CrossRef]
42. Alwattar, T.A.; Mian, A. Development of an Elastic Material Model for BCC Lattice Cell Structures Using Finite Element Analysis and Neural Networks Approaches. *J. Compos. Sci.* **2019**, *3*, 33. [CrossRef]
43. Arbabi, H.; Bunder, J.E.; Samaey, G.; Roberts, A.J.; Kevrekidis, I.G. Linking Machine Learning with Multiscale Numerics: Data-Driven Discovery of Homogenized Equations. *JOM* **2020**, *72*, 4444–4457. [CrossRef]
44. Kollmann, H.T.; Abueidda, D.W.; Koric, S.; Guleryuz, E.; Sobh, N.A. Deep learning for topology optimization of 2D metamaterials. *Mater. Des.* **2020**, *196*, 109098. [CrossRef]
45. Settgast, C.; Hütter, G.; Kuna, M.; Abendroth, M. A hybrid approach to simulate the homogenized irreversible elastic–plastic deformations and damage of foams by neural networks. *Int. J. Plast.* **2020**, *126*, 102624. [CrossRef]
46. Yan, J.; Cheng, G.; Liu, S.; Liu, L. Comparison of prediction on effective elastic property and shape optimization of truss material with periodic microstructure. *Int. J. Mech. Sci.* **2006**, *48*, 400–413. [CrossRef]
47. Xia, Z.; Zhou, C.; Yong, Q.; Wang, X. On selection of repeated unit cell model and application of unified periodic boundary conditions in micro-mechanical analysis of composites. *Int. J. Solids Struct.* **2006**, *43*, 266–278. [CrossRef]
48. Hohe, J.R.; Becker, W. Effective stress-strain relations for two-dimensional cellular sandwich cores: Homogenization, material models, and properties. *Appl. Mech. Rev.* **2002**, *55*, 61–87. [CrossRef]
49. Buannic, N.; Cartraud, P.; Quesnel, T. Homogenization of corrugated core sandwich panels. *Compos. Struct.* **2003**, *59*, 299–312. [CrossRef]
50. Hohe, J.; Becker, W. Determination of the elasticity tensor of non-orthotropic cellular sandwich cores. *Tech. Mech.-Eur. J. Eng. Mech.* **1999**, *19*, 259–268.
51. Castaneda, P.P.; Suquet, P. On the effective mechanical behavior of weakly inhomogeneous nonlinear materials. *Eur. J. Mech A Solids* **1995**, *14*, 205–236.
52. Staszak, N.; Garbowski, T.; Szymczak-Graczyk, A. Solid Truss to Shell Numerical Homogenization of Prefabricated Composite Slabs. *Materials* **2021**, *14*, 4120. [CrossRef] [PubMed]
53. Cosserat, E.; Cosserat, F. *Théorie des Corps Déformables*; A. Hermann et fils: Strasbourg, France, 1909.
54. Eringen, A.C. Linear theory of micropolar elasticity. *Theory Micropolar Elast.* **1965**, *15*, 909–923. [CrossRef]
55. Phani, S.; Woodhouse, J.; Fleck, N.A. Wave propagation in two-dimensional periodic lattices. *J. Acoust. Soc. Am.* **2006**, *119*, 1995–2005. [CrossRef]
56. Bloch, F. Über die Quantenmechanik der Elektronen in Kristallgittern. *Eur. Phys. J. A* **1929**, *52*, 555–600. [CrossRef]
57. Langley, R. A Note On The Force Boundary Conditions For Two-Dimensional Periodic Structures With Corner Freedoms. *J. Sound Vib.* **1993**, *167*, 377–381. [CrossRef]
58. Langley, R.; Bardell, N.; Ruivo, H. The response of two-dimensional periodic structures to harmonic point loading: A theoretical and experimental study of a beam grillage. *J. Sound Vib.* **1997**, *207*, 521–535. [CrossRef]
59. Born, M.; Huang, K.; Lax, M. Dynamical Theory of Crystal Lattices. *Am. J. Phys.* **1955**, *23*, 474. [CrossRef]
60. Gurtin, M. *Phase Transformations and Material Instabilities in Solids*; Elsevier: Amsterdam, The Netherlands, 2012.
61. Hutchinson, R.G. *Mechanics of Lattice Materials*; University of Cambridge: Cambridge, UK, 2005.
62. Takano, N.; Ohnishi, Y.; Zako, M.; Nishiyabu, K. Microstructure-based deep-drawing simulation of knitted fabric reinforced thermoplastics by homogenization theory. *Int. J. Solids Struct.* **2001**, *38*, 6333–6356. [CrossRef]
63. Hollister, S.J.; Kikuchi, N. A comparison of homogenization and standard mechanics analyses for periodic porous composites. *Comput. Mech.* **1992**, *10*, 73–95. [CrossRef]
64. Eshelby, J.D. The determination of the elastic field of an ellipsoidal inclusion, and related problems. *Proc. R. Soc. London. Ser. A Math. Phys. Sci.* **1957**, *241*, 376–396. [CrossRef]
65. Al-Haik, M.; Hussaini, M.; Garmestani, H. Prediction of nonlinear viscoelastic behavior of polymeric composites using an artificial neural network. *Int. J. Plast.* **2006**, *22*, 1367–1392. [CrossRef]
66. Fritzen, F.; Fernández, M.; Larsson, F. On-the-Fly Adaptivity for Nonlinear Twoscale Simulations Using Artificial Neural Networks and Reduced Order Modeling. *Front. Mater.* **2019**, *6*, 75. [CrossRef]
67. Le, B.A.; Yvonnet, J.; He, Q. Computational homogenization of nonlinear elastic materials using neural networks. *Int. J. Numer. Methods Eng.* **2015**, *104*, 1061–1084. [CrossRef]
68. Zopf, C.; Kaliske, M. Numerical characterisation of uncured elastomers by a neural network based approach. *Comput. Struct.* **2017**, *182*, 504–525. [CrossRef]
69. Wojciechowski, M. Application of artificial neural network in soil parameter identification for deep excavation numerical model. *Comput. Assist. Methods Eng. Sci.* **2017**, *18*, 303–311.
70. Fan, Z.; Yan, J.; Wallin, M.; Ristinmaa, M.; Niu, B.; Zhao, G. Multiscale eigenfrequency optimization of multimaterial lattice structures based on the asymptotic homogenization method. *Struct. Multidiscip. Optim.* **2019**, *61*, 983–998. [CrossRef]

71. Vlădulescu, F.; Constantinescu, D.M. Lattice structure optimization and homogenization through finite element analyses. *Proc. Inst. Mech. Eng. Part L J. Mater. Des. Appl.* **2020**, *234*, 1490–1502. [CrossRef]
72. Xu, L.; Qian, Z. Topology optimization and de-homogenization of graded lattice structures based on asymptotic homogenization. *Compos. Struct.* **2021**, *277*, 114633. [CrossRef]
73. Zhang, J.; Sato, Y.; Yanagimoto, J. Homogenization-based topology optimization integrated with elastically isotropic lattices for additive manufacturing of ultralight and ultrastiff structures. *CIRP Ann.* **2021**, *70*, 111–114. [CrossRef]

Article

Influence of Impregnation with Modified Starch of a Paper Core on Bending of Wood-Based Honeycomb Panels in Changing Climatic Conditions

Michał Słonina [1,*], Dorota Dziurka [2], Marta Molińska-Glura [3] and Jerzy Smardzewski [1,*]

[1] Department of Furniture Design, Faculty of Forestry and Wood Technology, Poznan University of Life Sciences, Wojska Polskiego 28, 60-637 Poznan, Poland
[2] Department of Mechanical Wood Technology, Faculty of Forestry and Wood Technology, Poznan University of Life Sciences, Wojska Polskiego 28, 60-637 Poznan, Poland; dorota.dziurka@up.poznan.pl
[3] Department of Economics and Forest Technology, Faculty of Forestry and Wood Technology, Poznan University of Life Sciences, Wojska Polskiego 28, 60-637 Poznan, Poland; marta.glura@up.poznan.pl
* Correspondence: michal.slonina@up.poznan.pl (M.S.); jerzy.smardzewski@up.poznan.pl (J.S.); Tel.: +48-61-848-7475 (M.S.); +48-61-848-7425 (J.S.)

Abstract: The main objective of the study was to determine the effect of impregnation of the paper core with acetylated starch on the mechanical properties and absorbed energy in the three-point bending test of wood-based honeycomb panels under varying temperatures and relative air humidity conditions. Nearly six hundred beams in various combinations, three types of facings, three core cells geometries, and two paper thicknesses were tested. The experiment results and their statistical analysis prove a significant relationship between the impregnation of paper with modified starch and mechanical properties. The most effective in absorbing energy, the honeycomb panels, consisted of a core with a wall thickness of 0.25 mm and a particleboard facing.

Keywords: honeycomb panels; starch; impregnation; climatic conditions; strength; stiffness; energy absorption

Citation: Słonina, M.; Dziurka, D.; Molińska-Glura, M.; Smardzewski, J. Influence of Impregnation with Modified Starch of a Paper Core on Bending of Wood-Based Honeycomb Panels in Changing Climatic Conditions. *Materials* **2022**, *15*, 395. https://doi.org/10.3390/ma15010395

Academic Editor: Marco Corradi

Received: 28 November 2021
Accepted: 30 December 2021
Published: 5 January 2022

Publisher's Note: MDPI stays neutral with regard to jurisdictional claims in published maps and institutional affiliations.

Copyright: © 2022 by the authors. Licensee MDPI, Basel, Switzerland. This article is an open access article distributed under the terms and conditions of the Creative Commons Attribution (CC BY) license (https://creativecommons.org/licenses/by/4.0/).

1. Introduction

Production of paper products in 2020 reached the level of 420 million tons. Compared to 1980, this means an increase of 250% [1]. Invariably, for over 2000 years, the paper has been produced mainly from cellulose fibers [2]. It is assumed that the life cycle of cellulose fiber in Europe has an average of 3.5 times its use [3,4], although it is possible up to 6 times. Each cycle of paper reuse reduces its quality [5]. Out of all known paper types, "Kraft liner" is characterized by the best value for money. The quality of the paper means its high mechanical strength to tearing, bending, compression, and resistance to moisture [6]. Kraft liner is made by chemical defibering with at least 80% virgin fibers. It is widely used as a packaging material [7]. In the range of moisture content of the paper from 0% to the fiber saturation point (about 23%), its mechanical properties decrease even by 50% [8–10]. The pulp and paper industry still uses various preservation methods against hygroscopy and shrinking of paper, including impregnation methods. Pohl [11] described the influence of the paper's sizing on the reduction of tensile strength.

This does not mean that waterproof paper cannot be made. However, depending on the chosen path, the process can be more or less complicated and time consuming. The simplest solution is lamination with petroleum-based or aluminum foils. The composite obtained in this way is completely waterproof and has higher mechanical strength, especially for tearing and penetration [12]. Lamination is also an effective barrier against gas penetration. However, it should be remembered that the edges of this paper composite remain hydrophilic. Another solution is to use chemicals while still producing the paper web. Mainly to obtain covalent bonds between cellulose fibers. Urea-formaldehyde (UF), melamine-formaldehyde (MF) and polyamide-epichlorohydrin (PAE) resins are used as an additive to the pulp or preformed paper.

The most commonly used neutral sizing agents are softwood extracts and alkyl ketene dimers (AKD), and alkenyl succinic acid anhydride (ASA) [13,14]. In recent years, efforts have been made to develop environmentally friendly substances that increase the hydrophobic properties of cellulose fibers. We are talking about plant proteins or starch [15,16]. Both cellulose and starch are homoglycans and are the most abundant polysaccharides in nature [17]. Starch is the second most used improver in the pulp and paper industry, right after clay fillers. The usual addition to pulp is in the range of 2–4% [17,18]. Its presence increases the mechanical resistance of the paper to tearing, improves the quality of prints, and most of all increases the resistance to moisture by filling the pores in the cellulose fiber mesh [19]. In 2009, modified starch accounted for 66% of the total volume of starch used against the sizing effect [18]. There are enzymatic, thermal, and chemical modifications [5,20]. In a chemical acetylation process, a hydrogen atom in the hydroxyl (OH) group is replaced by an acetyl group. Starch has three OH groups, so its maximum degree of substitution (DS) is 3. The higher the degree of substitution, the greater the hydrophobicity [21]. However, it should be remembered that the strength of paper precisely increases thanks to the hydrogen bonds between cellulose and starch [15]. As demonstrated by Larotonda et al. [22], acetylation at the DS 1.2–1.7 level provides the best balance between paper strength and resistance to moisture while maintaining the possibility of biodegradability. The production of hydrophobic Kraft liner paper is, therefore, a difficult and complex task. Serious problems are also encountered concerning obtaining water resistance of recycled paper of the "testliner" type. It is recycled, so the cellulose pulp can contain almost all the additives mentioned so far and many more from impurities.

As reported by European and global organizations monitoring the pulp and paper industry, in 2018, more than half of the global paper production was constituted by testliner [1,23]. This paper is mainly used to produce the recycled corrugated panel, both for a sinusoidal core, where its transversal shear properties are significant [24–28], and for facings, where its properties are related to edge crush resistance are important [29–31]. In addition, this paper is used to produce paper fillings (honeycomb cores), used in the production of a three-layer lightweight panel. For the same reasons why recycled paper processing is growing dynamically, the share of light furniture panels in the furniture industry is also growing.

Light wood-based honeycomb panels are widely used in the production of doors [32]. In the 1990s, the technology was adapted to the needs of the furniture industry [33–35]. However, a significant limitation of the widespread use of lightweight panels in the furniture industry is their low stiffness and strength, compared to classic wood materials, such as particleboard, MDF board, or plywood [36–40]. However, these panels are distinguished by an attractive quality factor [41,42]. For this reason, more and more manufacturers of furniture ready for self-assembly (RTA), made of honeycomb panels, dynamically develop the e-commerce market [43–46]. For these products to be safe in terms of construction, research was carried out on the rheology and strength of the constituent materials of light honeycomb sandwich panels under changing climatic conditions [47–50] and the properties of wood-based furniture panels [51–55]. Moreover, research works on methods of securing wood-based honeycomb panels against the destructive effects of variable temperature and air humidity [53,56–59].

Composites based on thin-walled cores are also a sought-after products by the packaging industry to protect valuable loads [60]. Their task is to absorb impact energy [61,62], an indispensable element of the global flow of goods, using diverse and complementary means of transport by land, sea, and air. International transport of goods also means highly different climatic conditions, so it is crucial to properly design thin-walled structures to maintain their ability to absorb energy [63,64] throughout its life cycle. The more energy the composite can absorb, the more effectively it can protect a product against the outside load.

However, the authors' best knowledge shows that the influence of the hydrophobic impregnation of the paper core with modified starch on the mechanical properties of the honeycomb panel has not been investigated so far. Acquiring new knowledge enables learning about the effectiveness of securing furniture elements against the effects of variable high temperature and air humidity. This knowledge will allow the rational design of furniture intended for use in tropical or subtropical climates. It is also justified in the changing demographic structure of the world. By 2050, half of the world's population will live in a tropical climate [65]. Until then, the number of users of honeycomb panel furniture resistant to tropical climatic conditions will increase.

The study aimed to determine the influence of the impregnation of paper with modified starch, the shape and size of the hexagonal core cells obtained from the impregnated paper, and the facing material on the bending of the wood-based lightweight honeycomb panels under changing temperature and relative air humidity conditions.

2. Materials and Methods

2.1. The Shape of Honeycomb Cells

A series of scientific publications [66–68] describes in detail the method of selecting cell geometry and its production processes. On this basis, keeping the previously used determinations, cores with cells geometry C, E, F were selected for the tests (Figure 1). The cores of the cells of type C and E are made of paper testliner having a thickness of 0.15 mm and a weight of 123 g/m^2, and the cores with F cells were made of 0.25 mm thick paper with a grammage of 134 g/m^2. Such a selection of papers was not left to chance. The F-cell paper thickness was determined by static numerical optimization with the Monte-Carlo method [66]. They were assuming that the linear modulus is maximized and the relative cell density is minimized. C and E cores are made of the most used paper in the furniture industry [66,69]. The decision to use cores based on C, E, F cells to create light furniture panels results from a thorough analysis of the elastic constants of individual cores carried out in the publication of Słonina et al. [68]. The exact dimensions of individual types of cells and their relative density are presented in Table 1.

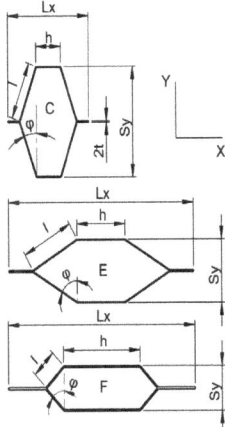

Figure 1. The shape of cells used for research.

Table 1. Characteristics of cells used for tests, where: ρ —relative cell density, S_y —cell width, L_x —cell length, l—length of the free cell wall, h—length of the double cell wall, t—thickness of the cell wall (paper), φ –cell wall inclination angle (Figure 1).

Cell Type	ρ	S_y	L_x	l	h	t	φ
	(–)	(mm)					(°)
C	0.0249	23.28	20.15	12.2	6.0	0.15	20
E	0.0249	13.33	46.48	13.0	12.0	0.15	60
F	0.0585	9.47	46.84	6.3	19.1	0.25	45

The testliner paper was produced by the HM Technology company (HM Technology, Brzozowo, Poland). For cell formation, non-impregnated (N) and impregnated (S) papers were prepared with a 10% aqueous solution of modified acetylated starch (S) (patent number P.430486). Depending on their thickness and impregnation, these papers were marked with the symbols 15N, 25N, 15S, 25S, respectively. The paper [68] presents in detail the method of paper impregnation, forming cells, and obtaining cores. In addition, the results illustrating the elastic properties of paper, which were determined following the PN-EN ISO 1924-2 standard [70], are also presented. For the sake of clarity of this work, Table 2 is summarized by providing the module of linear elasticity MOE (MPa), the module of rupture MOR (MPa) Poisson's ratio, and the maximum breaking force X and Y direction of the material orthotropy, respectively. Table 2 also shows the elastic properties of the materials used to produce the facings of the honeycomb panels. These properties were determined following ISO 13061-6: 2014 [71].

Table 2. Physical and mechanical properties of the materials used (MOE —modulus of linear elasticity, MOR —modulus of rupture, θ –Poisson's ratio, F_{max} —maximal destructive force, X, Y—orthotropy directions, MC—moisture content, SD—standard deviation).

Code	Statistics	Thickness [mm]	MC [%]	Density [kg/m³]	MOE X	MOE Y	MOR X	MOR Y	θ XY	θ YX	F_{max} X	F_{max} Y
					[MPa]				-		[N]	
15N	Mine	0.15	5.72	686	5707	2188	46	16	0.411	0.147	105	36
	SD	0.01	-	-	672	113	1.8	0.30	0.043	0.023	4	0.7
15S	Mine	0.16	7.05	730	5190	2642	49	20	0.308	0.109	110	45
	SD	0.02	-	-	374	102	3.1	0.34	0.033	0.010	7	0.8
25N	Mine	0.25	6.11	745	5372	2153	46	17	0.398	0.160	175	67
	SD	0.02	-	-	200	37	1.8	0.50	0.024	0.017	7	2.0
25S	Mine	0.26	6.67	825	4454	2153	45	17	0.348	0.160	170	67
	SD	0.04	-	-	99	37	1.1	0.50	0.021	0.017	4	2.0
P30	Mine	2.77	6.76	942	4116	3445	14	10	0.161	0.129	1539	1085
	SD	0.02	-	18	276	210	2.3	1.50	0.027	0.026	269	171
H25	Mine	2.41	5.28	965	5496	5183	32	31	0.265	0.257	3080	3030
	SD	0.02	-	19	253	164	2.4	2.00	0.024	0.020	228	187
H20	Mine	1.97	5.55	912	4756	4293	22	23	0.243	0.218	1730	1822
	SD	0.02	-	12	324	295	3.5	1.30	0.030	0.031	279	97

2.2. Honeycomb Manufacturing and Testing

The testliner paper was produced by the HM Technology company (HM Technology, Brzozowo, Polska). Non-impregnated papers were prepared for cell formation. The facing material was selected from wood-based materials that retain the ability to be reused in recycling processes. Thus, a 3.0 mm thick particleboard (P30) covered on one side with melamine paper (Egger, Rion-des-Landes, France) [72], a 2.5 mm thick high-density fiberboard (H25) (IKEA Industry, Orla, Polska) [73], and high-density fiberboard with a thickness of 2.0 mm (H20) (HOMANIT, Karlino, Polska) [74] was used for the tests. On nondecorative surfaces of the same type of facing panel, an adhesive PVAc Woodmax FF12.47 class D2 from Synthos Adhesives (Oswiecim, Poland) was applied in an amount of about 110 g/m². In the next step, along the circuit of bottom facing, a particleboard frame with a thickness of 16.1 mm was created, and a paper core with a thickness of 16.3 mm was placed inside it. Finally, the whole sandwich was closed by the second facing sheet. The assembly process was carried out in an Orma Macchine NPC/DIGIT 6/90 25 × 13 hydraulic press (Bergamo, Italy) for 25 min under a pressure of 0.7 MPa. For each type of impregnated and non-impregnated paper, the cell type and the type of facing six 16 mm thick panels were made with dimensions as shown in Figure 2. A total of 54 panels were manufactured.

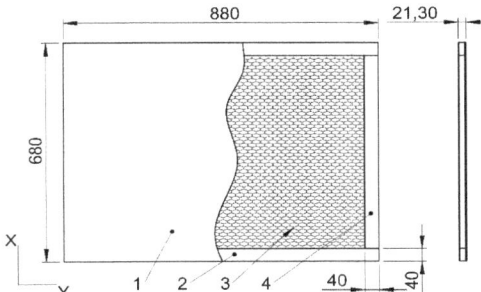

Figure 2. Dimensions and structure of the honeycomb panel sheet: 1—facing, 2—honeycomb core, 3—horizontal stile, 4—vertical stile. Panels thickness equal to 20.3 mm, 21.3 mm, 22.3 mm for H20, H25, P30, respectively.

The panels were seasoned in laboratory conditions until a constant mass of samples was obtained, which proved that they maintained the hygroscopic equilibrium. After this time, the panels were cut into beams 50 mm wide and 20 times their length, plus an allowance of 50 mm. The beams were obtained from the central part of the formed slab so that the samples did not contain stiles. The produced beams were divided into two groups of equal numbers. The first group of beams was stored in dry conditions (D), i.e., in the climate of the production hall at the temperature T = 25 °C and relative air humidity H = 45%, while the second group of beams was stored in a climate similar to tropical (W), i.e., at the temperature T = 28 °C and relative air humidity of H = 85%, until the mass of the samples stabilizes. The selected air temperature and relative humidity complied with EN 318 (2002) requirements and were used as variable factors in the works [68,75,76].

For the selected types of cells (3), the impregnated and non-impregnated paper (2) used, the facings (3), the direction of X, Y orthotropy (2), climatic conditions (2), assuming eight repetitions, in total 576 pieces of beams were prepared for testing (Figure 3). Table 3 presents exemplary determinations for individual types of samples produced. According to the method of marking the beams made of C-type cells, the markings for the remaining E, F-type cells were used, as exemplified in the last row of Table 3.

Figure 3. Examples of beams selected for testing.

Table 3. Method of marking samples prepared for testing (The symbol * indicates the selected cell type, impregnation, facing type, orthotropy direction, climate condition).

Code	Cell Type			Impregnation		Facing Type			Orthotropy Direction		Climate Condition	
	C	E	F	S	N	P30	H25	H20	X	Y	D	W
$CSP_{30}XD$	*			*		*			*		*	
$CSP_{30}XW$	*			*		*			*			*
$CSP_{30}YD$	*			*		*				*	*	
$CSP_{30}YW$	*			*		*				*		*
$CNP_{30}XD$	*				*	*			*		*	
$CNP_{30}XW$	*				*	*			*			*
$CNP_{30}YD$	*				*	*				*	*	
$CNP_{30}YW$	*				*	*				*		*
...												
$ESH_{25}YW$		*		*			*			*		*

Then the beams were subjected to three-point bending (Figure 4) according to the EN 310 [77] standard on the Zwick Z100 testing machine (Zwick GmbH, Ulm, Germany). During the tests, the value of the force was recorded with an accuracy of 2 N and the deflection of the beams in the direction of the force with an accuracy of 0.01 mm. In addition, damage to the beams was recorded using a Samsung SM20E digital camera (SM20E, Samsung, Korea).

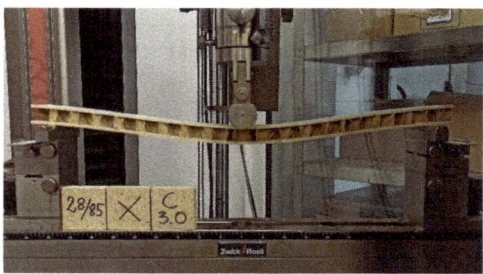

Figure 4. Test stand.

2.3. Mechanical Properties and Energy Absorption

Figure 5 shows an example of a curve expressing the relation of force and deflection for the tested samples. Based on the measured values of the maximum forces causing the sample failure F_{max} (N) modulus of rupture MOR (MPa) was calculated following the EN 310 standard from the dependence:

$$\text{MOR} = \frac{3F_{max}L^3}{2bd^3} \quad (1)$$

where F_{max} is the force at the fracture point (N), L = 20 d is the length of the support span (mm), d is the thickness of the beam (mm), b is the width of the beam (mm).

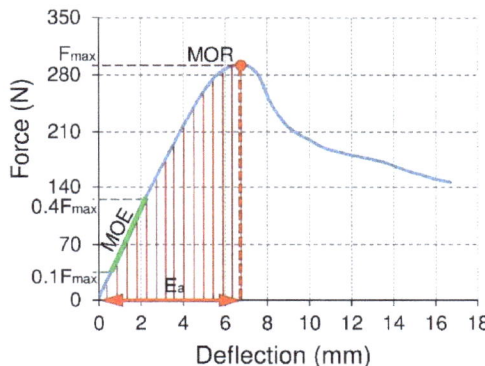

Figure 5. An example of a force-deflection relationship for examined beams made of honeycomb panels (MOR—modulus of rupture, MOE—modulus of elasticity, F_{max}—fracture force, E_a—absorbed energy).

On the other hand, based on the relationship of force and deflection in the rectilinear range, the linear elasticity modulus MOE (MPa) was calculated by the EN 310 standard, from the following equation:

$$\text{MOE} = \frac{(0.4F_{max} - 0.1F_{max})L^3}{48(f_{0.4Fmax} - f_{0.1Fmax})I_s} \quad (2)$$

where $f_{0.4Fmax}$, $f_{0.1Fmax}$ is the beam deflection in mm for a load equal to $0.4F_{max}$, $0.1F_{max}$ (N), $I_s = \frac{bd^3}{12}$ is the moment of inertia (mm^4).

The individual beams were made of thin-walled elements. Therefore, it was concluded that they should be excellent energy-absorbing structures because they can fail with relatively little force. To obtain comparable calculation results, it was decided to count the absorbed energy only to obtain the maximum breaking force of the beam.

By integrating the function expressing the dependence of force on deflection (Figure 5), it is possible to calculate the absorbed energy from the equation [60–64]:

$$E_a = \int_{f1}^{f2} F df \quad (3)$$

where f_1, f_2, is the lower and upper integration limits for the deflection, respectively f. However, due to the inability to determine the exact functions describing the force F deflection relationship f for each tested sample, it was decided to perform graphical integration. For this purpose, the integration interval was divided $< f_1, f_2 >$ into segments

$\Delta f = 0.1$ mm, on which it was assumed that the force F has a constant value. Therefore, the absorbed energy for deflection equal to 10 mm was calculated from the equation:

$$E_a = \sum_{f1=0}^{f2=10} F\Delta f \qquad (4)$$

3. Results and Discussion

The influence of starch impregnation on selected properties of honeycomb panels turned out not to be obvious. Therefore, this part of the work decided to present only the observed quantitative differences. In the other part of the study, a detailed statistical analysis was prepared to show the qualitative relationships and the impact of all selected variable factors on the properties of the tested honeycomb panels.

3.1. Effect of Impregnation on the Panel's Strength

Figures 6–8 illustrate the effects of starch impregnation, type of material, the direction of orthotropy, and climatic conditions on the MOR of honeycomb panel with a core of different cells (C,E,F). The summary shows that the highest MOR (15.3 MPa) was observed among the beams with starch impregnated F-cells for the X orthotropy direction in dry conditions (FSH25XD). Conversely, the lowest MOR (0.9 MPa) occurred in the case of beams with non-impregnated E-type cells for the Y orthotropy direction in tropical conditions (ENH25YW).

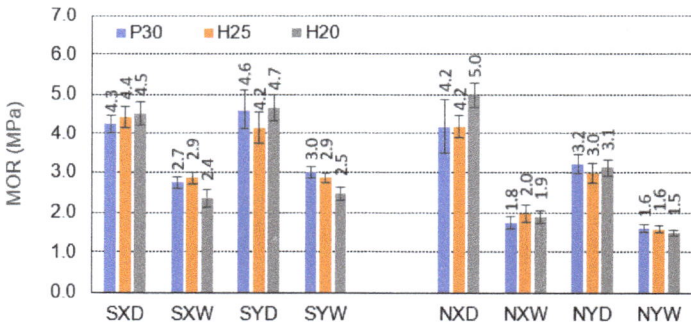

Figure 6. Illustration of the MOR relationship of honeycomb panels with a core of C-cells. Whiskers represent standard deviations.

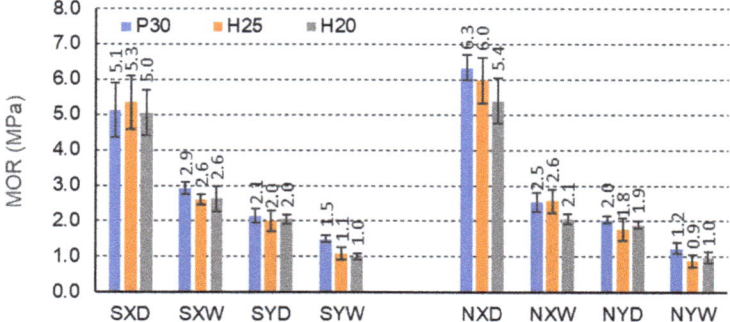

Figure 7. Illustration of the MOR relationship of honeycomb panels with an E-cell core. Whiskers represent standard deviations.

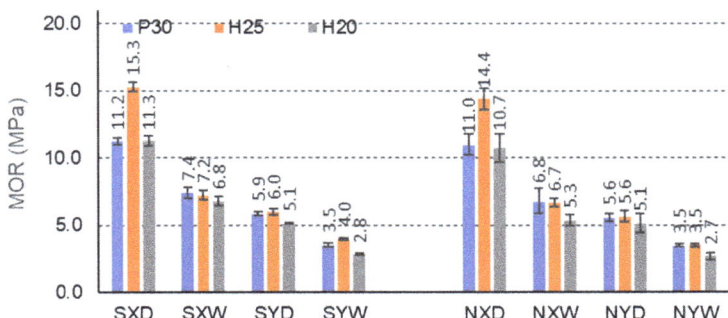

Figure 8. Illustration of the MOR relationship of honeycomb panels with F-type core. Whiskers represent standard deviations.

In the group of beams with C-cells, under all climatic conditions D, W, the starch impregnation improves the MOR of the beams for each case of the facing used and the orthotropy direction (Figure 6). Only CNP30XD beams with P30 facings in dry conditions and the X orthotropy direction show higher strength (5.0 MPa) than the corresponding CSP30XD beams impregnated with starch (4.5 MPa). It should be noted here that the increase in MOR for beams with impregnated cores compared to beams with non-impregnated cores is from 2.3 to 46.7%. For beams with P30, H25, and H20 facings, in dry conditions D and for the direction of orthotropy X, the bending strength increases by 2.3%, 4.5%, and −11.1%, respectively, and in tropical conditions W by 33.3%, 31% and 20.8, respectively. Note that a negative value indicates the opposite tendency to increase—i.e., decrease. For beams with the same facings P30, H25 and H20, in dry conditions D, and for the direction of orthotropy Y, the bending strength increases by 30.4%, 28.6%, and 34.0%, respectively, and in tropical conditions W by 46.7%, 44.8%, and 40.0%, respectively. It is also significant that for C-type cells, there was no clear difference in the strength of the beams in the X and Y orthotropy directions greater by −7.0%, 4.5%, and −4.4% in relation to the strength in the Y direction, and in tropical conditions W by 11.1%, 0.0%, and −4.2%, respectively. For non-impregnated beams, these relationships are significantly different. For beams with P30, H25, and H20 facings, in dry conditions D, the bending strength in the direction of X orthotropy is respectively higher by 23.8%, 28.6%, and 38.0% concerning the strength in the Y direction and tropical conditions W, respectively 11.1%, 20.0%, and 21.1%. Thus, the effect of impregnation on the strength of beams with C-cells is visible, but also on the change of this strength depending on the direction of orthotropy. After impregnation, the influence of the direction of orthotropy on the strength of the beams decreased significantly.

For beams with E-cells, the effect of impregnation is not so pronounced (Figure 7). Beams with P30 facing, not impregnated, in dry conditions D, and the orthotropy direction X (6.3 MPa) show the highest bending strength. In dry conditions D, impregnation with starch significantly reduces the MOR of beams with P30, H25, H20 facings, for the X orthotropy direction, compared to analogous non-impregnated beams by 23.5%, 13.2%, 8.0%, respectively. In tropical conditions, W increases this strength by 13.8%, 0.0%, and 19.2%, respectively. For beams with the same facings P30, H25 and H20, in dry conditions D, and for the direction of orthotropy Y, the bending strength increases by 4.8%, 10.0%, and 5.0%, respectively, and in tropical conditions W, by 20.0%, 18.2%, and 0.0%, respectively. It is also noticeable that clear differences in the strength of the beams in the X and Y orthotropy directions were observed for E-type cells, by 58.8%, 62.3% and 60.0% of the strength in the Y direction, and in tropical conditions by 48.3%, 57.7% and 61.5%, respectively. For non-impregnated beams, these relationships are very similar. For beams with P30, H25, and H20 facings, in dry conditions D, the bending strength in the direction of X orthotropy is, respectively, 68.3%, 70.0%, and 64.8% greater concerning the strength in the Y direction, and in tropical conditions W, respectively 52.0%, 65.4%, and 52.4%. Moreover, in this case, the influence of impregnation on the strength of beams with E-cells is visible. The presented results also illustrate the effect of large and slightly changing orthotropy of the tested beams. It can be assumed that the effect of impregnation on the change of orthotropic properties of the panel is significant.

The F-cell beams also show marked strength differences due to the impregnation of the paper (Figure 8). Beams with H25 facing, impregnated, in dry conditions D, and for the orthotropy direction X (15.3 MPa) show the highest bending strength. Beams with H25 facing, not impregnated, in dry conditions D achieve slightly lower strength for the same direction of orthotropy (14.4 MPa). In dry conditions D, impregnation with starch slightly improves MOR of beams with P30, H25, H20 facings, for the X orthotropy direction, compared to non-impregnated beams by 1.8%, 5.9%, 5.3%, respectively, and in tropical conditions by 8.1%, respectively, 6.9% and 22.1%. Beams with the same facings P30, H25, and H20, in dry conditions D, and for the orthotropy direction Y show greater bending strength by 5.1%, 6.7%, and 0.0%, respectively, and in tropical conditions W by 0.0%, 12.5%, and 3.6%, respectively. As in the case of beams with E-cells, clear differences in the strength of the beams in the X and Y orthotropy directions were observed: 47.3%, 60.8%, and 54.9% of the strength in the Y direction, and in tropical conditions by 52.7%, 44.4%, and 58.8%, respectively. The relations are very similar also for non-impregnated beams. When using P30, H25, and H20 facing, in dry conditions D, the bending strength of the beams in the direction of X orthotropy is greater by 49.1%, 61.1%, and 52.3%, respectively, concerning the strength in the Y direction, and in tropical conditions W, by 48.5%, 47.8%, and 49.1%, respectively. Therefore, it can be concluded that also in this case, the effect of impregnation on the strength of beams with F-cells is visible. Moreover, the test results illustrate the effect of large and slightly changing orthotropy of the tested beams. Hence, it should be concluded that the effect of impregnation on the change of orthotropic properties of the plate with F-cells is significant.

Figure 9 shows deflections of a beam with C-type cells, H25 facings, before and after impregnation (N, S), examined in the direction of the Y-axis in the conditions of dry D and tropical W climate. Under tropical conditions (T = 28 °C/H = 85%, Figure 9b), the beam deflection is much higher compared to beams loaded under dry climate conditions (T = 25 °C/H = 45%, Figure 9a). On the other hand, the beams reduce deflections in dry and tropical conditions after impregnating starch, respectively (Figure 9c,d).

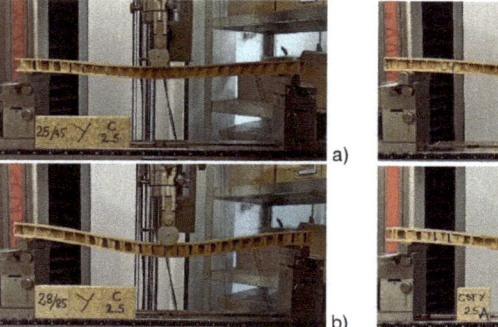
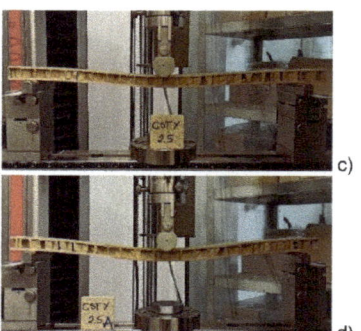

Figure 9. Illustration of the destruction of C-core cell plates: (**a**) CNH25YD beam (**b**) CNH25YW beam (**c**) CSH25YD beam (**d**) CSH25YW beam.

3.2. Effect of Impregnation on the Panel's Stiffness

As shown above, impregnating the core paper with a 10% aqueous acetylated starch water repellant improves the strength of the three-layer furniture panel and its stiffness. This is illustrated in the figures below (Figures 10–12). The average increase in the modulus of linear elasticity MOE for all tested beam combinations is approximately 7%.

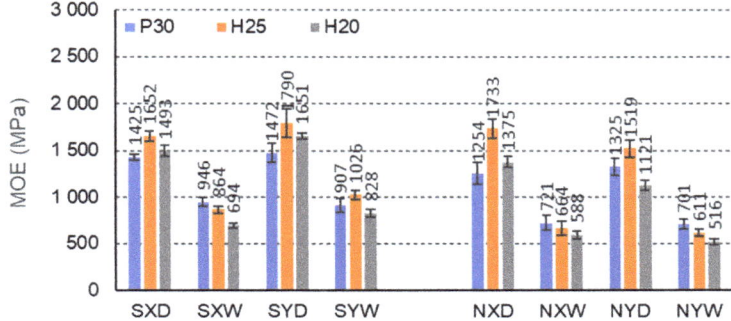

Figure 10. Illustration of the MOE relationship of honeycomb panels with a core of C-cells. Whiskers represent standard deviations.

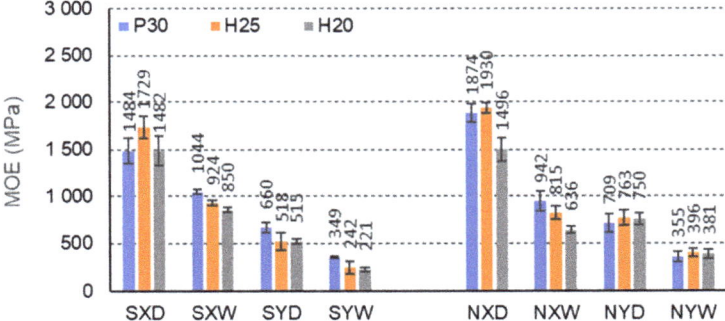

Figure 11. Illustration of the MOE relationship of honeycomb panels with an E-cell core. Whiskers represent standard deviations.

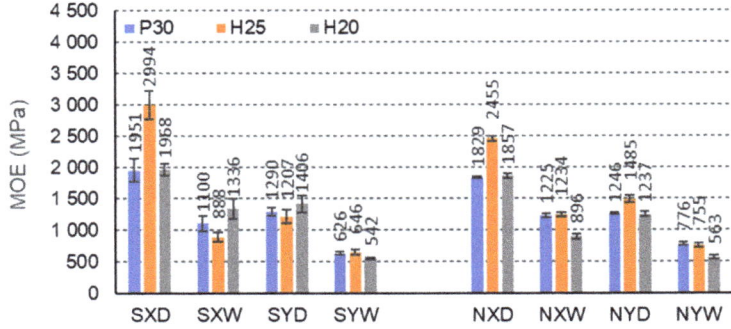

Figure 12. Illustration of the MOE relationship of honeycomb panels with F-type core. Whiskers represent standard deviations.

For C-cell beams, under all climatic conditions, starch impregnation improves the MOE for each case of a facing used and the direction of orthotropy (Figure 10). Only CNH25XD beams with H25 facing in dry conditions and for the X orthotropy direction show a greater modulus of elasticity (1733 MPa) compared to the corresponding beams (CSH25XD) impregnated with starch (1649 MPa). It should be noted that for beams with P30, H25, and H20 facings, in dry conditions D, and for the orthotropy direction X, the MOE increases by 12.0%, −5.1%, and 14.6%, respectively, and in tropical conditions W, respectively by 23.9%, 23.2%, and 15.2%. For beams with the same facings P30, H25 and H20, in dry conditions D, and for the direction of orthotropy Y, the MOE increases by 9.9%, 15.1%, and 32.1%, respectively, and in tropical conditions W by 22.6%, 40.5%, and 37.7%. It is also characteristic that, as in the case of strength changes, no significant difference in linear elasticity modules was observed in the X and Y orthotropy directions for C-type cells. In the orthotropy direction, X is 3.2%, 8.6%, and 10.6% lower concerning the MOE in the Y direction, and in tropical conditions, W is lower by −4.2%, 18.8%, and 19.3%, respectively. Note that a negative value indicates the opposite tendency to decrease, i.e., increase. For non-impregnated beams, these relationships are significantly different. For beams with P30, H25, and H20 facing, in dry conditions D, the MOE in the X orthotropy direction is respectively greater by −5.7%, 12.3%, and 12.1% concerning the MOE in the Y direction, and in tropical conditions W, by 2.6%, 8.0%, and 12.4%, respectively. Thus, the influence of impregnation on the modulus of elasticity of beams with C-cells is visible, but also on the change of this property depending on the direction of orthotropy. After impregnation, the influence of the orthotropy direction on the MOE of the beams changed and diversified. The impregnation of the paper resulted in a weakening of the modulus of linear elasticity of the beams in the direction of the X-axis in favor of increasing the MOE in the direction of the Y-axis. Although the differences are insignificant, they persuade the orthotropic properties of the honeycomb panels.

In the case of beams with E-cells, the effect of impregnation on the modulus of elasticity is also pronounced (Figure 11). The highest MOE is shown for beams with H25 facing, not impregnated, in dry conditions D, and orthotropy direction X (1930 MPa). In dry conditions D, impregnation with starch significantly reduces the MOE of beams with P30, H25, H20 facings for the X orthotropy direction, compared to analogous non-impregnated beams, by 26.2%, 11.7%, 0.9%, respectively. In tropical conditions, W increases this property by 9.7%, 11.7%, and 25.3%, respectively. For beams with the same facings P30, H25 and H20, in dry conditions D, and for the Y orthotropy direction, MOE also decreases by 7.4%, 47.6%, and 45.4%, respectively, and in tropical conditions W, by 2.0%, 63.6%, and 72.7%. It is also noticeable that clear differences in the modulus of elasticity of the beams in the X and Y orthotropy directions were observed for E-type cells, 55.5%, 70.1%, and 65.2% concerning the MOE in the Y direction, and in tropical conditions by 66.6%, 78.3%, and 74.1%, respectively. For non-impregnated beams, these relationships are very similar. For beams with P30, H25, and H20 facings, in dry conditions D, the modulus of elasticity in the X orthotropy direction is respectively higher by 62.1%, 60.5%, and 49.9% concerning the MOE in the Y direction, and in tropical conditions W, by respectively, 62.3% 51.4%, and 40.2%. In this case, a clear influence of impregnation on the modulus of elasticity of beams with E-cells is visible. The presented results also illustrate the effect of large and changing orthotropy of the tested beams. The changes result both from the use of starch as an impregnating agent and the slender shape of the cells. It is clear that in the case of an elongated E-cell with long free walls (l = 13 mm), impregnation weakens the elastic properties of the core in the direction of the X and Y axes, but at the same time reduces the difference between the modulus of elasticity in these directions.

The F-cell beams also show significant strength differences due to the impregnation of the paper (Figure 12). FSH25XD beams show the highest modulus of elasticity with H25 facing, impregnated, in dry conditions D, and for the orthotropy direction X (2994 MPa). FNH25XD beams achieve much lower MOE with H25 facing, not impregnated, in dry conditions D, and for the same direction of orthotropy (2455 MPa). In dry conditions D, impregnation with starch improves the MOE of beams with P30, H25, H20 facings for the X orthotropy direction, compared to non-impregnated beams by 6.2%, 18.0%, 5.4%, respectively, and in tropical conditions W, by respectively −11.3% 12.5%, and 32.9%. Beams with the same facings P30, H25, and H20, in dry conditions D, and for the direction of orthotropy Y also show a higher MOE by 12.0%, −23.0%, and 12.0%, respectively, and in tropical conditions W, lower MOE by respectively, 24.0%, 17.1%, and 3.9%. There were also visible differences in the modulus of elasticity of the beams in the X and Y orthotropy directions to MOE in the Y direction, and tropical conditions W, by 43.1%, 54.3%, and 59.5%, respectively. The relationships are also similar for non-impregnated beams. When using P30, H25, and H20 facing, in dry D conditions, the MOE of the beams in the X direction is higher by 31.9%, 39.5%, and 33.4%, respectively, concerning the MOE in the Y direction, and in tropical conditions W, by 36.6%, respectively, 38.8% and 37.3%. Therefore, it can be concluded that in this case, the effect of the impregnation on the strength of the beams with F-cells is visible. The changes result both from the use of starch as an impregnating agent and the slender shape of the cells. There is a regularity that in the case of an elongated F cell with short free walls (l = 6.3 mm), the impregnation strengthens the elastic properties of the core in the direction of the X-axis. On the other hand, in the direction of the Y-axis, the paper's impregnation contributed to the reduction of the linear elasticity modulus.

3.3. Effect of Impregnation on the Energy Absorption

The more energy the composite can absorb, the more effective it is to protect the protected charge. The research (Figures 13–15) shows that the FNH25XD and FSH25XD beams have the highest energy absorption capacity before and after impregnation E_a = 2474 mJ i E_a = 2823 mJ, respectively.

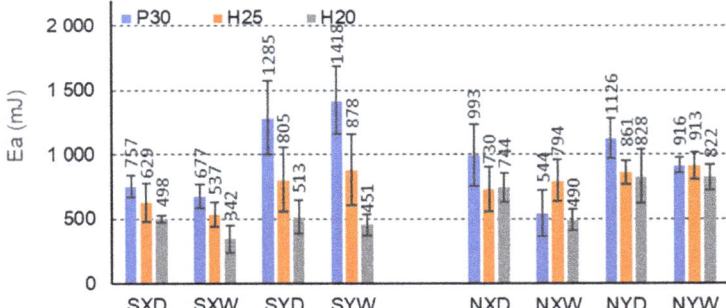

Figure 13. Illustration of the E_a relationship of honeycomb panels with a core of C-cells. Whiskers represent standard deviations.

For beams with C-cells, under all climatic conditions, impregnation with starch significantly reduces the amount of energy absorbed for the case of a facing used and the direction of orthotropy (Figure 13). It should be noted that for beams with P30, H25, and H20 facings, in dry conditions D, and for the orthotropy direction X, the amount of absorbed energy decreases by 31.2%, 16.1%, and 49.4%, respectively, and in tropical conditions W, by −19.5%, 47.7%, and 43.3%. For beams with the same facings P30, H25, and H20, in dry conditions D, and for the direction of orthotropy Y, the amount of energy absorbed also decreases by −12.3%, 6.8%, and 61.4%, respectively, and in tropical conditions W, by −35.5, 3.9% and 82.3%, respectively. However, clear differences in the amount of absorbed energy were observed dependent on the X and Y orthotropy directions, 3.0% concerning the amount of energy absorbed in the Y direction, and in tropical conditions W, respectively 109.8%, 63.5%, and 31.9% lower. For non-impregnated beams, these relationships are significantly more favorable. For beams with P30, H25, and H20 facings, in dry conditions D, the amount of absorbed energy in the X direction is respectively lower by 13.4%, 17.8%, and 11.3% about the amount of energy absorbed in the Y direction, and in tropical conditions W, by 68.2%, 15.0%, and 67.8%, respectively. Thus, the effect of impregnation on the reduction in the amount of absorbed energy of beams with C-type cells is visible, but also on the change of this property depending on the direction of orthotropy. The impregnation of the paper caused a reduction in the ability to absorb energy in the X and Y directions. The differences illustrated are significant and convincing to the honeycomb panels' orthotropic properties in terms of energy absorption.

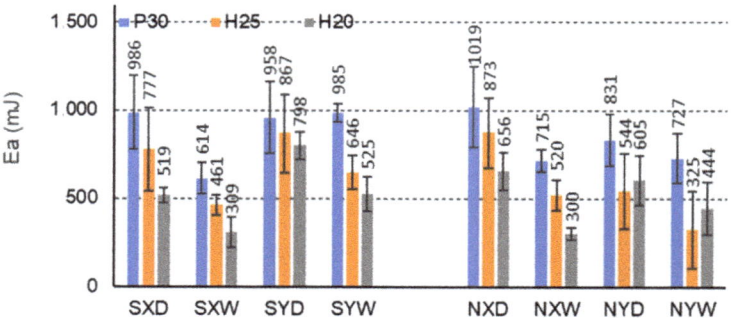

Figure 14. Illustration of the E_a relationship of honeycomb panels with an E-type core. Whiskers represent standard deviations.

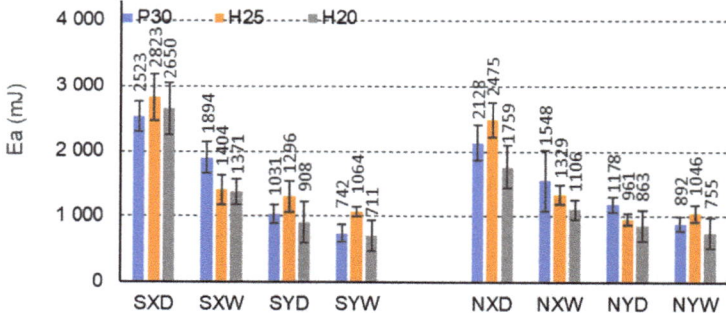

Figure 15. Illustration of the E_a relationship of honeycomb panels with F-type core. Whiskers represent standard deviations.

In the case of beams with E-cells, the effect of impregnation on the amount of energy absorbed is presented in Figure 14. The greatest amount of absorbed energy is shown by beams with P30 facing, not impregnated, in dry conditions D, and for the orthotropy direction X (1019 mJ). In dry conditions D, impregnation with starch significantly reduces the amount of absorbed energy for beams with P30, H25, H20 facings, for the X orthotropy direction, compared to analogous non-impregnated beams by 3.3%, 12.2%, 26.4%, respectively. This property also reduces by 16.5%, 12.8%, and 3.2% in tropical conditions, respectively. For beams with the same facings P30, H25 and H20, in dry conditions D, and for the direction of orthotropy Y, the amount of energy absorbed increases by 13.3%, 37.3%, and 24.2%, respectively, and in tropical conditions W, by 26.1%, 49.8%, and 15.6%. It is also noticeable that for E-type cells, clear differences were observed in the amount of energy absorbed for the beams in the X and Y orthotropy directions; it is, respectively, 2.8%, 11.6%, and 54.1% lower concerning the amount of energy absorbed in the Y direction, and tropical conditions by 60.5%, 40.4%, and 69.9%, respectively. These relationships are different for non-impregnated beams. For beams with P30, H25, and H20 facings, in dry conditions

D, the amount of absorbed energy in the X direction is 18.4%, 37.6%, and 7.6% greater, respectively, concerning the amount of energy absorbed in the Y direction, and in tropical conditions W, by −1.8%, 37.6% and −48.2%, respectively. In this case, a variable influence of impregnation on the amount of absorbed energy is visible for beams with E-cells. The changes result both from the use of starch as an impregnating agent and the slender shape of the cells. The regularity is drawn that in the case of an elongated E cell with long free walls (l = 13 mm), the impregnation weakens the core's ability to absorb energy in the X-axis direction and increases this ability in the Y direction.

F-cell beams also show marked differences in the amount of energy absorbed due to the impregnation of the paper (Figure 15). The highest amount of absorbed energy is shown by FSH25XD beams with H25 facing, impregnated, in dry conditions D, and for the orthotropy direction X (2822 mJ). A much smaller amount of absorbed energy is achieved by FNH25XD beams with H25 facing, not impregnated, in dry conditions D, and for the same direction of orthotropy (2475 mJ). In dry conditions D, impregnation with starch improves the amount of absorbed energy for beams with P30, H25, H20 facings, for the X orthotropy direction, about non-impregnated beams by 15.7%, 12.3%, 33.7%, respectively, and in tropical conditions by W, respectively, by 18.3%, 5.4%, and 19.3%. Beams with the same facing P30, H25, and H20, in dry conditions D, and for the orthotropy Y direction, show a reduction in the amount of absorbed energy by 14.3%, –26.0%, and −4.9%, respectively, and in tropical conditions W, a lower amount of absorbed energy by 20.2%, −1.7% and 6.2%, respectively. There were also clear differences in the energy absorbed for the beams in the X and Y orthotropy directions: 65.8% concerning the amount of energy absorbed in the Y direction, and tropical conditions by 60.9%, 24.2%, and 48.2%, respectively. The relationships are also similar for non-impregnated beams. When using P30, H25, and H20 facing, in dry conditions D, the amount of absorbed energy for the beams in the X orthotropy direction is, respectively, 44.7%, 61.2%, and 50.9% greater than the amount of energy absorbed in the Y direction, and in tropical conditions W, by 42.4%, 21.2% and 31.8%, respectively. Therefore, it can be concluded that in this case, impregnation's effect on the amount of absorbed energy is visible for beams with F-cells. The changes result both from the use of starch as an impregnating agent and also from the slender shape of the cells with short free walls (l = 6.3 mm). The impregnation increases the amount of absorbed energy, especially in the direction of the X-axis. On the other hand, in the direction of the Y-axis, the impregnation of the paper tended to reduce the amount of absorbed energy.

The observations listed above are generally consistent with the current state of knowledge. For example, Pohl [11] showed in his work that an adequately selected impregnating agent increases the strength (MOR) and stiffness (MOE) of light boards with a paper core. On the other hand, the climatic conditions with high air humidity have been repeatedly quoted in the literature [53,54,58] as having a destructive effect on the mechanical properties of furniture boards. Furthermore, the influence of the geometry, wall thickness, and the orientation of the core cells on the stiffness and strength of lightweight three-layer panels is also known as meaningful [42,68,78].

3.4. Statistical Analysis

In order to determine the influence of impregnation and other variable factors on the mechanical properties of the modeled furniture panels, a statistical analysis was performed using the Statistica 13.3 program (StatSoft Polska Sp. z oo, Kraków, Poland).

The statistical model included five factors (starch impregnation, cell type (C, E, F), facing type (H20, H25, P30), climate condition (D, W), orthotropy direction (X, Y)) and three features (MOR, MOE and E_a). Because panels with a paper honeycomb core are characterized by strong orthotropy manifested by significant differences in MOR, MOE and E_a values for the X and Y directions, the data for statistical analysis was divided into two groups. The first group consisted of factors (starch impregnation, cell type, facing type, and climate condition) and three features (MOR, MOE and E_a) for the direction of X orthotropy as well as appropriate factors and features for the direction of Y orthotropy. On this basis, an analysis of the correlation of the analyzed features in individual experiments was prepared. The correlation coefficients presented in Table 4 show that the features (MOR, MOE and E_a) for the X and Y orthotropy directions, respectively, are strongly correlated with each other. Because all the determined correlation coefficients (r) are statistically significant ($p < 0.05$), it was concluded that the further application of the multiple features model to assess the significance of the influence of individual factors on these features could be burdened with some "redundancy". In this situation, it was justified to use a transformation that would allow us to analyze the influence of all factors differentiating the experiment's results on all features simultaneously but avoiding their mutual strong linear correlation. For this purpose, principal components analysis was used [79,80], in which three features of MOR, MOE and E_a were transformed into three principal components (1), (2), (3), which are their linear combinations (Figure 16).

Table 4. The matrix of correlation of features in individual experiments.

Features	MOR		MOE		E_a	
	r		r		r	
	X	Y	X	Y	X	Y
MOR			0.83	0.77	0.92	0.51
MOE	0.83	0.77			0.65	0.34
E_a	0.92	0.51	0.65	0.34		

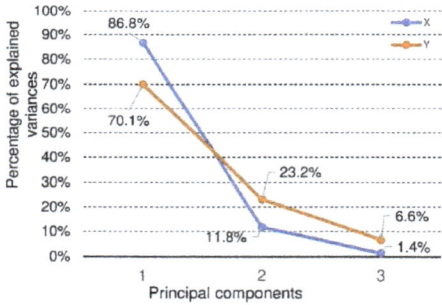

Figure 16. Principal components of feature connected with beams orthotropy in X and Y direction.

Figure 16 shows that for further analysis of the significance of the influence of selected factors on three features (MOR, MOE and E_a) for the direction of X orthotropy, only the first principal component (1) should be left because it explains about 87% of the entire variability in the model. Moreover, in the first component (1), the individual features (MOR, MOE and E_a) are proportionally represented. In the case of the features from the experiment for the direction of the Y orthotropy, the first two principal components (1), (2) should be taken into account because together they explain more than 93% of the entire variability of the model. The contribution of individual features to the main components is presented in Table 5. It is worth noting that in the experiment for the direction of the Y orthotropy in the second principal component (2), the feature E_a plays a fundamental role.

Table 5. Contribution of individual features to the principal components.

Features	X	Y	
	1	1	2
MOR	0.37	0.41	0.03
MOE	0.30	0.36	0.24
E_a	0.33	0.23	0.73

Taking into account the above considerations, the tests of the hypotheses about the significance of differences in mean values for the first principal component (1) in the experiment for the direction of orthotropy X (one-way and multivariate ANOVA) and the significance of differences in mean values for the first and second principal components (1), (2) were started, in the experiment for the direction of orthotropy Y (univariate MANOVA). Table 6 shows that the influence of individual factors on the selected main components (1) and (1), (2) for the directions of orthotropy X and Y, respectively, is statistically significant ($p < 0.05$). The HSD Tukey test was performed on this basis, which indicated statistically significant differences in the results for selected variable factors (Tables 7 and 8).

Table 6. The significance of the influence of individual factors on the principal components for the directions of X and Y orthotropy.

Factors	p	
	X	Y
Cel type	0.000000	0.000000
Facing type	0.016232	0.000000
Climate condition	0.000000	0.000000
Starch impregnation	0.035712	0.000970

Table 7. Summary of statistically homogeneous groups determined on the basis of the HSD Tukey test for selected variable factors in the research for the direction of orthotropy X. (The symbol **** meaning that results are not statistically different).

Variable Factor	Homogeneous Group	
Cel type	a	b
F		****
E	****	
C	****	
Facing type	a	b
H25	****	
P30	****	****
H20		****
Climate condition	a	b
D	****	
W		****
Starch impregnation	a	b
Y	****	
N		****

Table 7 shows that similar mean values of the principal component (1) are obtained for the X orthotropy direction. Therefore, MOR is obtained for E and C cells, and statistically different for an F cell. These differences are clearly visible when comparing Figures 6–15. For example, the average MOR value for CSP30XD, ESP30XD, FSP30XD is 4.3 MPa, 5.1 MPa and 11.2 MPa, respectively. Thus, it can be seen that the mean MOR values for boards with E and C cells are similar, and the differences are statistically insignificant. On the other hand, for the F-type cells, the obtained values are statistically different, which also positively and statistically significantly increases both MOR and MOE. At the same time, it can be seen that each type of cell significantly affects the amount of energy E_a absorbed by the panels.

Further analysis of Table 7 leads to the following observations. Similar mean values of the principal component (1) were obtained for facing type H25 and P30, and statistically different for facing type H20. As an example, we can give the average MOR values for CSP30XW, CSH25XW, CSH20XW, which are equal to 2.7 MPa, 2.9 MPa and 2.4 MPa, respectively, and for ESP30XW, ESH25XW, ESH20XW or FSP30XW, FSH25XW, FSH20XW boards, respectively 2.9 MPa, 2.6 MPa, and 2.6 MPa, 7.4 MPa, 7.2 MPa and 6.8 MPa. Thus, it can be seen that the average MOR values for panels with H25 and P30 facings are similar, and the differences are statistically insignificant. Moreover, these facings have a positive effect on increasing both MOR and MOE compared to the H20 type facings because in this case, the average values of the principal component (1) are statistically different and lower. The comparison of Figures 13–15 also shows that E_a for panels with H25 facing has higher values than panels with P30 and H20 facing.

Table 7 also shows a statistically significant difference in the mean values of the principal component (1) obtained for tropical climatic conditions (W). A similar regularity applies to the lack of impregnation of the core cells with starch (Y). Because, in both cases, the differences are clearly visible in Figures 6–15, it can only be concluded that under dry conditions (D), the MOR values for the cellular plates reach the highest values, similar to the impregnation of paper with starch (S). The beneficial effect of impregnation (S) on the MOR of the tested boards is visible based on the results of tests in dry (D) and tropical (W) conditions. For example, the average MOR value for CSP30XD, ESP30XD, FSP30XD boards is 4.3 MPa, 5.1 MPa, and 11.2 MPa, respectively, and for the boards without impregnation (N), CNP30XD, ENP30XD, FNP30XD, respectively, are 4.2 MPa, 6.3 MPa, and 11.0 MPa. On the other hand, the average MOR value for CSP30XW, ESP30XW, FSP30XW boards is equal to 2.7 MPa, 2.9 MPa, 7.4 MPa, respectively, and for CNP30XW, ENP30XW, FNP30XW boards, 1.8 MPa, 2.5 MPa, and 6.8 MPa, respectively. It can also be seen that the impregnation (Y) of the core cells causes variations in the amount of energy absorbed. Comparison of Figures 13–15 shows that E_a for plates with non-impregnated cells has higher values compared to boards with impregnated cells.

Table 8 shows the statistical significance for the model in a multidirectional classification, therefore taking into account many factors and their interactions. Of course, the values of the first principal component (1) were tested here. It is clear from this table that all factors and their interactions are statistically significant ($p < 0.05$).

Table 9 shows that for the direction of the Y orthotropy, different mean values of the principal components (1), (2) were obtained, thus MOR and the linearly correlated MOE for the selected cell types. For example, the average MOR value for CSP30YD, ESP30YD, FSP30YD is 4.6 MPa, 2.1 MPa, and 5.9 MPa, respectively. The MOE value for the same panels is 1472 MPa, 660 MPa, and 1290 MPa, respectively, and the E_a value is 1285 mJ, 1959 mJ, and 1031 mJ, respectively. Thus, it can be seen that the average values of MOR, MOE, E_a for the plates are different and statistically significant.

Table 8. Statistical significance for the model in the multidirectional classification takes into account the X orthotropy direction.

Factors and Their Interactions	p
Core	0.000000
Facing	0.000000
Conditions	0.000000
Starch	0.000000
Core*Facing	0.000000
Core*Conditions	0.000000
Facing*Conditions	0.000000
Core*Starch	0.000000
Facing*Starch	0.002824
Conditions*Starch	0.009293
Core*Facing*Conditions	0.000000
Core*Facing*Starch	0.000067
Core*Conditions*Starch	0.000000
Facing*Conditions*Starch	0.001572
Core*Facing*Conditions*Starch	0.007842

Table 9. Summary of statistically homogeneous groups determined on the basis of the HSD Tukey test for selected variable factors in the research for the direction of orthotropy Y. (The symbol **** meaning that results are not statistically different).

Variable Factor	Homogeneous Group		
Cel type	a	b	c
E	****		
C		****	
F			****
Facing type	a	b	
H20		****	
H25	****		
P30	****		
Climate condition	a	b	
W	****		
D		****	
Starch impregnation	a	b	
N	****		
Y		****	

Moreover, the analysis of Table 9 leads to further observations that similar mean values of component (1) were obtained for facing type H25 and P30 and statistically different for facing type H20. As an example, we can give the average MOR values for CSP30YW, CSH25YW, CSH20YW which are equal to 3.0 MPa, 2.9 MPa, and 2.5 MPa, respectively, and for ESP30YW, ESH25YW, ESH20YW or FSP30YW, FSH25YW, FSH20YW boards, respectively, 1.5 MPa, 1.1 MPa, 1.0 MPa, 3.5 MPa, 4.0 MPa and 2.8 MPa. Different mean values of the component (2) were obtained for the same facings. For example, for the CSP30YW, CSH25YW, CSH20YW, the MOE is 907 MPa, 1026 MPa, and 828 MPa, respectively, and for the ESP30YW, ESH25YW, ESH20YW or FSP30YW, FSH25YW, FSH20YW plates, it is 349 MPa, 242 MPa, 221 MPa, 626 MPa, 646 MPa, and 542 MPa, respectively. Thus, it can be seen that the average MOR values for panels with H25 and P30 facings are similar, and the differences are statistically insignificant. In addition, these facings have a positive effect on increasing both MOR and MOE compared to H20 facings. The comparison of Figures 13 and 14 also shows that E_a for panels with P30 facing has higher values than panels with H25 and H20 facings.

Table 9 also shows a statistically significant difference in the mean values of the main component (1) obtained for dry climatic conditions (D). A similar pattern applies to the impregnation of core cells with starch (Y). Because, in both cases, the differences are clearly visible in Figures 6–15, it can only be concluded that under dry conditions (D), the MOR and MOE values for the honeycomb boards reach the highest values, similar to the impregnation of paper with starch (S). The beneficial effect of impregnation (S) on the MOR and MOE of the tested boards is visible on the basis of the results of tests in dry (D) and tropical (W) conditions. For example, the average MOR value for the CSP30YD, ESP30YD, FSP30YD boards is 4.6 MPa, 2.1 MPa and 5.9 MPa, respectively, and for the boards without impregnation (N), CNP30YD, ENP30YD, FNP30YD, respectively, are 3.2 MPa, 2.0 MPa, and 5.5 MPa. On the other hand, the average MOR value for the CSP30YW, ESP30YW, FSPand FSP30YW boards equals 3.0 MPa, 1.5 MPa, and 3.5 MPa, respectively, and for CNP30YW, ENP30YW, FNP30YW boards, respectively, 1.6 MPa, 1.2 MPa and 3.5 MPa. The MOE value for the same CSP30YW, ESP30YW, FSP30YW and CNP30YW, ENP30YW, FNP30YW panels is equal to 907 MPa, 349 MPa, 626 MPa, 701 MPa, 355 MPa and 776 MPa, respectively. The comparison of Figures 13 and 14 also shows that E_a for panels with cells impregnated with P30 facings has higher values compared to panels with cells not impregnated with starch.

In order to be able to assess the statistical significance of the factor interactions, only the value of the main component was taken into account in the multidirectional analysis (1). Table 10 shows the statistical significance for the model in the multidirectional classification for the value of only the component (1). It was decided so because, for component (1), we still maintain as much as 70% of the model's variability (Figure 16). This table shows that only the interactions of Conditions*Starch, Core*Facing*Conditions, Core*Conditions*Starch, Core*Facing*Conditions*Starch are not statistically significant.

Table 10. Statistical significance for the model in the multidirectional classification taking into account the direction of the Y orthotropy.

Factors and Their Interactions	p
Core	0.000000
Facing	0.000000
Conditions	0.000000
Starch	0.000000
Core*Facing	0.000000
Core*Conditions	0.000000
Facing*Conditions	0.019208
Core*Starch	0.000000
Facing*Starch	0.014356
Conditions*Starch	0.661232
Core*Facing*Conditions	0.153976
Core*Facing*Starch	0.000074
Core*Conditions*Starch	0.057297
Facing*Conditions*Starch	0.016343
Core*Facing*Conditions*Starch	0.133444

4. Conclusions

The conducted experiments and the analysis of the results made it possible to determine how the variable above-mentioned factors affect the strength of the three-layer honeycomb panels (MOR), the linear elasticity modulus (MOE), and the ability to absorb energy (E_a). The most important conclusions and observations are listed below:

- There is a statistically proven significant relationship between the impregnation of paper with modified starch and the mechanical properties of the produced honeycomb panels with variable cell geometry and various types of facing, under varying temperature and relative air humidity conditions.
- In dry conditions (T = 25 °C/H = 45%), the impregnation increases the flexural strength (MOR) of the honeycomb panels by an average of 18% and the linear elasticity modulus (MOE) by 7%. The average ability to absorb energy after starch impregnation increased by 6%.
- In tropical conditions (T = 28 °C/H = 85%), the impregnation increases the flexural strength of the honeycomb panels by an average of 22% and the modulus of linear elasticity by 14%. The average ability to absorb energy after starch impregnation increased by 6%.
- FSH25YD and FSP30YW lightweight panels show the highest flexural strength in dry and tropical conditions.
- FSH25YD and FSH25YW lightweight panels are the stiffest in dry and tropical conditions.
- The most energy in dry and tropical conditions is absorbed by FSH25YD and FSP30YW lightweight panels, respectively.
- F-shaped cells and H25 facings have the best influence on the mechanical properties of the honeycomb panels.
- F-shaped cells and P30 facings most favorably affect the energy absorption capacity of the honeycomb panels.

Author Contributions: Conceptualization, M.S., D.D., J.S.; methodology, M.S., D.D., J.S.; software, M.S., M.M.-G.; validation, M.S., M.M.-G., J.S.; formal analysis, M.S., J.S.; investigation, M.S., resources, M.S., J.S.; data curation, M.S., D.D.; writing—original draft preparation, M.S., D.D., J.S.; writing—review and editing, D.D., J.S.; visualization, M.S., J.S.; supervision, D.D., J.S.; project administration, M.S., J.S.; funding acquisition, J.S. All authors have read and agreed to the published version of the manuscript.

Funding: This research received no external funding.

Institutional Review Board Statement: Not applicable.

Informed Consent Statement: Not applicable.

Data Availability Statement: The data supporting reported results by the authors can be sent by e-mail.

Conflicts of Interest: The authors declare that they have no known competing financial interest or personal relationships that could have appeared to influence the work reported in this paper.

References

1. BIR Annual Reports. Bureau of International Recycling Paper Division. Available online: https://www.bir.org/publications/annual-reports (accessed on 18 August 2021).
2. Patterson, G. Cellulose before CELL: Historical themes. *Carbohydr. Polym.* **2021**, *252*, 117182. [CrossRef] [PubMed]
3. Ghinea, C.; Elena-Diana, C.; Gavrilescu, M. Life cycle assessment of corrugated board packaging. *Lucr. Științ. Ser. Hortic.* **2017**, *60*, 231–236.
4. ERPC Monitoring Report 2015 | www.cepi.org. Available online: https://www.cepi.org/erpc-monitoring-report-2015/ (accessed on 19 November 2021).
5. Holik, H. *Handbook of Paper and Board*; John Wiley & Sons: Wiley-Vch GmbH & Co. KGaH: Ravensburg, Germany, 2006; ISBN 3527608338.
6. Tipsotnaiyana, N.; Jarupan, L.; Noppakundilograt, S. Enhancement of flexographic print quality on bleached kraft liner using nano-silica from rice husk. *Prog. Org. Coat.* **2015**, *87*, 232–241. [CrossRef]
7. Twede, D.; Selke, S.E.M.; Kamdem, D.-P.; Shires, D.B. *Cartons, Crates, and Corrugated Board: Handbook of Paper and Wood Packaging Technology*; DEStech Publications, Inc.: Lancaster, PA, USA, 2015; ISBN 1605951358.

8. Yeh, K.C.; Considine, J.M.; Suhling, J.C. The influence of moisture content on the nonlinear constitutive behavior of cellulosic materials. In Proceedings of the International Paper Physics Conference, Kona, HI, USA, 22–26 September 1991. Available online: https://www.fpl.fs.fed.us/products/publications/specific_pub.php?posting_id=67813&header_id=p (accessed on 19 November 2021).
9. Niskanen, K. *Mechanics of Paper Products*; de Gruyter: Berlin, Germany, 2011; p. 169. ISBN 978-3-11-025461-7.
10. Kirwan, M.J. *Handbook of Paper and Paperboard*; John Wiley & Sons: Hoboken, NJ, USA, 2013; p. 351; ISBN 9780470670668.
11. Pohl, A. Strengthened corrugated paper honeycomb for application in structural elements. *IBK Ber.* **2009**, *318*, 126–129. [CrossRef]
12. Soroka, W.; Emblem, A.; Emblem, H. *Fundamentals of Packaging Technology*; The Institute of Packaging: Melton Mowbray, UK, 1996; ISBN 0946467005/9780946467006.
13. Ek, M.; Gellerstedt, G.; Henriksso, G. *Pulp and Paper Chemistry and Technology Paper Chemistry and Technology*; de Gruyter: Berlin, Germany, 2009; Volume 3, pp. 275–314. ISBN 9783110213430.
14. Palonen, H.; Stenius, P.; Ström, G. Surfactant behaviour of wood resin components: The solubility of rosin and fatty acid soaps in water and in salt solutions. *Sven. Papp.* **1982**, *85*, R93–R99.
15. Lagus, M. Hydrophobic Surface Sizing of Testliner. Master's Thesis, Faculty of Science and Engineering Åbo Akademi University, Turku, Finland, 2019; pp. 9–11. Available online: https://www.doria.fi/bitstream/handle/10024/168409/lagus_misla.pdf?sequence=2 (accessed on 28 November 2021).
16. Ren, D.; Li, K. Development of wet strength additives from wheat gluten. *Holzforschung* **2005**, *59*, 598–603. [CrossRef]
17. Biermen, J.C. *Handbook of Pulping and Papermaking*; Second, E., Ed.; Academic Press: San Diego, CA, USA, 1996; pp. 171–199; ISBN 978-0-12-097362-0.
18. Maurer, H.W. Starch in the Paper Industry. In *Starch*; Academic Press: Cambridge, MA, USA, 2009; pp. 657–713. [CrossRef]
19. Zeng, H. *Polymer Adhesion, Friction, and Lubrication*; John Wiley & Sons: Hoboken, NJ, USA, 2013; ISBN 1118505131.
20. Gane, P.A.C. Surface Treatment: Sizepress Tradition, Current Development and a Pigmented Chemical Future. In *The Science of Papermaking, 12th Fundamental Research Symposium, Oxford 2001*; Baker, C.F., Ed.; FRC: Manchester, UK, 2018; pp. 1069–1113. [CrossRef]
21. Larotonda, F.D.S.; Matsui, K.S.; Paes, S.S.; Laurindo, J.B. Impregnation of Kraft paper with cassava-starch acetate—Analysis of the tensile strength, water absorption and water vapor permeability. *Starch/Staerke* **2003**, *55*, 504–510. [CrossRef]
22. Larotonda, F.D.S.; Matsui, K.N.; Soldi, V.; Laurindo, J.B. Biodegradable Films Made from Raw and Acetylated Cassava Starch. *Braz. Arch. Biol. Technol.* **2004**, *47*, 477–484. [CrossRef]
23. BIR Global Facts & Figures. Paper and Board Recycling in 2018. Overview of World Statistics. Bureau of International Recycling Paper Division. Available online: https://bir.org/publications/facts-figures/download/723/140/36?method=view (accessed on 20 August 2021).
24. Garbowski, T.; Gajewski, T.; Grabski, J.K. Role of Transverse Shear Modulus in the Performance of Corrugated Materials. *Materials* **2020**, *13*, 3791. [CrossRef]
25. Avilés, F.; Carlsson, L.A.; May-Pat, A. A shear-corrected formulation for the sandwich twist specimen. *Exp. Mech.* **2012**, *52*, 17–23. [CrossRef]
26. Garbowski, T.; Gajewski, T.; Grabski, J.K. Torsional and Transversal Stiffness of Orthotropic Sandwich Panels. *Materials* **2020**, *13*, 5016. [CrossRef] [PubMed]
27. Nordstrand, T.M.; Carlsson, L.A. Evaluation of transverse shear stiffness of structural core sandwich plates. *Compos. Struct.* **1997**, *37*, 145–153. [CrossRef]
28. Garbowski, T.; Gajewski, T. Determination of Transverse Shear Stiffness of Sandwich Panels with a Corrugated Core by Numerical Homogenization. *Materials* **2021**, *14*, 1976. [CrossRef] [PubMed]
29. Garbowski, T.; Grabski, J.K.; Marek, A. Full-Field Measurements in the Edge Crush Test of a Corrugated Board—Analytical and Numerical Predictive Models. *Materials* **2021**, *14*, 2840. [CrossRef]
30. Kmita-Fudalej, G.; Szewczyk, W.; Kołakowski, Z. Calculation of honeycomb paperboard resistance to edge crush test. *Materials* **2020**, *13*, 1706. [CrossRef]
31. Garbowski, T.; Knitter-Piątkowska, A.; Marek, A. New Edge Crush Test Configuration Enhanced with Full-Field Strain Measurements. *Materials* **2021**, *14*, 5768. [CrossRef]
32. Barbu, M.C. Evolution of Lightweight wood composites. *Pro Ligno* **2015**, *11*, 21–26.
33. Bitzer, T. *Honeycomb Technology*; Springer: Dordrecht, The Netherlands, 1997; ISBN 978-94-010-6474-3.
34. Michanickl, A. Development of a new light wood-based panel. In Proceedings of the 5th European Wood-Based Panel Symposium, Hannover, Germany, 4–6 October 2006.
35. Bitzer, T. Honeycomb marine applications. *J. Reinf. Plast. Compos.* **1994**, *13*, 355–360. [CrossRef]
36. Librescu, L.; Hause, T. Recent developments in the modeling and behavior of advanced sandwich constructions: A survey. *Compos. Struct.* **2000**, *48*, 1–17. [CrossRef]
37. Shalbafan, A.; Luedtke, J.; Welling, J.; Thoemen, H. Comparison of foam core materials in innovative lightweight wood-based panels. *Eur. J. Wood Wood Prod.* **2012**, *70*, 287–292. [CrossRef]
38. Smardzewski, J. Elastic properties of cellular wood panels with hexagonal and auxetic cores. *Holzforschung* **2013**, *67*. [CrossRef]

39. Barboutis, I.; Vassiliou, V. Strength Properties of Lightweight Paper Honeycomb Panels for The Furniture. In Proceedings of the International Scientific Conference "10th Anniversary of Engineering Design (Interior and Furniture Design)", Sofia, Bulgaria, 17–18 October 2005.
40. Smardzewski, J.; Jasińska, D. Mathematical models and experimental data for HDF-based sandwich panels with dual corrugated lightweight core. *Holzforschung* **2016**, *71*, 265–273. [CrossRef]
41. Khojasteh-Khosro, S.; Shalbafan, A.; Thoemen, H. Preferences of furniture manufacturers for using lightweight wood-based panels as eco-friendly products. *Eur. J. Wood Wood Prod.* **2020**, *78*, 593–603. [CrossRef]
42. Peliński, K.; Smardzewski, J. Bending behavior of lightweight wood-based sandwich beams with auxetic cellular core. *Polymers* **2020**, *12*, 1723. [CrossRef]
43. Beckers, J.; Weekx, S.; Beutels, P.; Verhetsel, A. COVID-19 and retail: The catalyst for e-commerce in Belgium? *J. Retail. Consum. Serv.* **2021**, *62*, 102645. [CrossRef]
44. Yu, Y.; Wang, Y.; Zhong, R.Y.; Huang, G.Q. E-commerce logistics in supply chain management. *Ind. Manag. Data Syst.* **2017**, *117*, 2263–2286. [CrossRef]
45. Moodley, S. Global market access in the Internet era: South Africa's wood furniture industry. *Internet Res.* **2002**, *12*, 31–42. [CrossRef]
46. Frühwald, A.; Lüdtke, J.; Barbu, M.C.; Thömen, H.; Welling, J. The trend towards lightness: The wood-based panel sector and a new type of lightweight panel. In Proceedings of the 7th International Conference in "Wood Science and Engineering in the Third Millenium"—ICWSE, Brasov, Romania, 4–6 June 2009; pp. 263–269.
47. Bryan, E.L.; Schniewind, A. Strength and rheological properties of particleboard as affected by moisture content and sorption. *For. Prod. J.* **1965**, *144*–148.
48. Dinwoodie, J.M.; Higgins, J.-A.; Paxton, B.H.; Robson, D.J. Creep research on particleboard. *Holz Roh-Werkst.* **1990**, *48*, 5–10. [CrossRef]
49. Seco, J.I.F.-G.; Barra, M.R.D. Long-term deformation of MDF panels under alternating humidity conditions. *Wood Sci. Technol.* **1998**, *32*, 33–41. [CrossRef]
50. Kececi, E.; Asmatulu, R. Effects of moisture ingressions on mechanical properties of honeycomb-structured fiber composites for aerospace applications. *Int. J. Adv. Manuf. Technol.* **2017**, *88*, 459–470. [CrossRef]
51. Chow, P. The deflection of composite furniture panels under constant bending stress. *Deflection Compos. Furnit. Panels Constant Bend. Stress.* **1970**, *11*, 4874–4875.
52. Norvydas, V.; Minelga, D. Strength and stiffness properties of furniture panels covered with different coatings. *Mater. Sci.* **2006**, *12*, 328–332.
53. Smardzewski, J.; Słonina, M.; Maslej, M. Stiffness and failure behaviour of wood based honeycomb sandwich corner joints in different climates. *Compos. Struct.* **2017**, *168*, 153–163. [CrossRef]
54. Smardzewski, J.; Kramski, D. Modelling stiffness of furniture manufactured from honeycomb panels depending on changing climate conditions. *Thin-Walled Struct.* **2019**, *137*, 295–302. [CrossRef]
55. Semple, K.E.; Sam-Brew, S.; Deng, J.; Cote, F.; Yan, N.; Chen, Z.; Smith, G.D. Properties of commercial kraft paper honeycomb furniture stock panels conditioned under 65 and 95 percent relative humidity. *For. Prod. J.* **2015**, *65*, 106–122. [CrossRef]
56. Tankut, N. Effect of various factors on the rigidity of furniture cases. *Afr. J. Biotechnol.* **2009**, *8*, 5265–5270.
57. Bekhta, P.; Ozarkiv, I.; Alavi, S.; Hiziroglu, S. A theoretical expression for drying time of thin lumber. *Bioresour. Technol.* **2006**, *97*, 1572–1577. [CrossRef] [PubMed]
58. Ozarska, B.; Harris, G. Effect of cyclic humidity on creep behaviour of wood-based furniture panels. *Electron. J. Pol. Agric. Univ. Ser. Wood Technol.* **2007**, *10*. Available online: www.ejpau.media.pl/volume10/issue3/abs-11.html (accessed on 18 August 2021).
59. Nilsson, J.; Ormarsson, S.; Johansson, J. Moisture-related distortion and damage of lightweight wood panels—Experimental and numerical study. *J. Indian Acad. Wood Sci.* **2017**, *14*, 99–109. [CrossRef]
60. San Ha, N.; Lu, G. A review of recent research on bio-inspired structures and materials for energy absorption applications. *Compos. Part B Eng.* **2020**, *181*, 107496.
61. Zhang, G.; Wang, B.; Ma, L.; Yiong, J.; Wu, L. Response of sandwich structures with pyramidal truss cores under the compression and impact loading. *Compos. Struct.* **2013**, *100*, 451–463. [CrossRef]
62. Yang, L.; Harrysson, O.; West, H.; Cormier, D. A Comparison of Bending Properties for Cellular Core Sandwich Panels. *Mater. Sci. Appl.* **2013**, *4*, 471–477. [CrossRef]
63. Tao, Y.; Li, W.; Wei, K.; Duan, S.; Wen, W.; Chen, L.; Pei, Y.; Fang, D. Mechanical properties and energy absorption of 3D printed square hierarchical honeycombs under in-plane axial compression. *Compos. Part B Eng.* **2019**, *176*, 107219. [CrossRef]
64. Schneider, C.; Zenkert, D.; Deshpande, V.S.; Kazemahvazi, S. Bending energy absorption of self-reinforced poly(ethylene terephthalate) composite sandwich beams. *Compos. Struct.* **2016**, *140*, 582–589. [CrossRef]
65. About the Centre—JCU Australia. Available online: https://www.jcu.edu.au/cmt/about-the-centre (accessed on 19 August 2021).
66. Peliński, K.; Wojnowska, M.; Maslej, M.; Słonina, M.; Smardzewski, J. Modeling of Density of Periodic Structures Cores of Honeycomb Panels. Research for Furniture Industry. In Proceedings of the XXVIIIth International Conference, Poznań, Poland, 21–22 September 2017; ISBN 9788371608902.
67. Wojnowska, M.; Peliński, K.; Maslej, M.; Słonina, M.; Smardzewski, J. Elastic properties of periodic cores structures of multilayers furniture panels. *J. Adv. Technol. Sci.* **2017**, *6*, 1249–1263.

68. Słonina, M.; Dziurka, D.; Smardzewski, J. Experimental Research and Numerical Analysis of the Elastic Properties of Paper Cell Cores before and after Impregnation. *Materials* **2020**, *13*, 2058. [CrossRef]
69. Sam-Brew, S.; Semple, K.; Smith, G.D. Preliminary Experiments on the Manufacture of Hollow Core Composite Panels. *For. Prod. J.* **2011**, *61*, 381–389. [CrossRef]
70. *ISO 1924-2*; Paper and Board—Determination of Tensile Properties—Part 2: Constant Rate of Elongation Method (20 Mm/Min). ISO: Geneva, Switzerland, 2008.
71. *ISO 13061-6:2014*; Physical and Mechanical Properties of Wood—Test Methods for Small Clear Wood Specimens—Part 6: Determination of Ultimate Tensile Stress Parallel to Grain. Available online: https://www.iso.org/standard/60068.html (accessed on 13 November 2018).
72. EGGER l Mobilier l Agencement Intérieur l Design l Panneaux et Sols. Available online: https://www.egger.com/shop/fr_FR (accessed on 25 August 2021).
73. IKEA Industry Poland—Strona Główna. Available online: https://industry.ikea.pl/ (accessed on 25 August 2021).
74. HOMANIT GmbH & Co. KG. Available online: https://www.homanit.pl/pl/ (accessed on 25 August 2021).
75. Maarof, S.; Jones, P. Thermal comfort factors in hot and humid region: Malaysia. In Proceedings of the International Conference on Smart and Sustainable Built Environments, Delft, The Netherlands, 15–19 June 2009. Available online: http://www.irbnet.de/daten/iconda/CIB14241.pdf (accessed on 18 August 2021).
76. Cheng, V.; Ng, E.; Chan, C.; Givoni, B. Outdoor thermal comfort study in a sub-tropical climate: A longitudinal study based in Hong Kong. *Int. J. Biometeorol.* **2012**, *56*, 43–56. [CrossRef] [PubMed]
77. *EN 310: 1993*; Wood-Based Panels—Determination of Modulus of Elasticity in Bending and of Bending Strength. European Committee for Standardization: Brussels, Belgium, 1993; pp. 1–14.
78. Hao, J.; Wu, Y.; Oporto, G.; Liu, W.; Wang, J. Structural analysis and strength-to-weight optimization of wood-based sandwich composite with honeycomb core under three-point flexural test. *Eur. J. Wood Wood Prod.* **2020**, *78*, 1195–1207. [CrossRef]
79. Jolliffe, I.T.; Cadima, J. Principal component analysis: A review and recent developments. *Philos. Trans. R. Soc. A* **2016**, *374*, 20150202. [CrossRef] [PubMed]
80. Kherif, F.; Latypova, A. Chapter 12—Principal component analysis. In *Machine Learning*; Academic Press: Cambridge, MA, USA, 2020; pp. 209–225; ISBN 9780128157398. [CrossRef]

Article

Mechanical Behaviour of Aluminium-Timber Composite Connections with Screws and Toothed Plates

Marcin Chybiński * and **Łukasz Polus ***

Institute of Building Engineering, Faculty of Civil and Transport Engineering, Poznan University of Technology, Piotrowo 5 Street, 60-965 Poznan, Poland
* Correspondence: marcin.chybinski@put.poznan.pl (M.C.); lukasz.polus@put.poznan.pl (Ł.P.);
Tel.: +48-61-665-2477 (M.C.); +48-61-665-2098 (Ł.P.)

Abstract: This paper presents an investigation of the load-slip behaviour of aluminium-timber composite connections. Toothed plates with bolts are often used for connecting timber structural members with steel structural members. In this paper, toothed plates (C2-50/M10G, C2-50/M12G or C11-50/M12) have been used as reinforcement in aluminium-timber screwed connections for the first time. The push-out test specimens consisted of laminated veneer lumber slabs, aluminium alloy beams, and hexagon head wood screws (10 mm × 80 mm and 12 mm × 80 mm). Of the specimens, 12 additionally had toothed plates as reinforcement, while 8 had no reinforcement. The load carrying-capacity, the mode of failure and the load-slip response of the strengthened and non-strengthened screwed connections were investigated. The use of toothed plate connectors was found to be effective in increasing the strength of aluminium-timber composite connections and ineffective in improving their stiffness. The examined stiffness and strength of the connections can be used in the design and numerical modelling of aluminium-timber composite beams with reinforced screwed connections.

Keywords: aluminium-timber structures; laminated veneer lumber (LVL); toothed plate; screwed connection; shear connection; push-out test

1. Introduction

Currently, great importance is attached to civil engineering solutions being sustainable. The use of timber and engineered wood products in the construction industry reduces the carbon footprint. Growing trees absorb CO_2 from the atmosphere. Furthermore, wood products require less fossil fuels to be produced than other building materials, such as steel [1]. The limitations of sawn timber were overcome after the development of engineered wood products, such as glued-laminated timber, cross-laminated timber and laminated veneer lumber [2]. Recent scientific studies on timber structures can be divided into four groups: material tests (e.g., [3,4]), connections for timber elements (e.g., [5,6]), strengthening of timber elements (e.g., [7–9]), and composite structures with timber structural members.

A composite beam consists of two or more structural elements which are permanently joined [10]. Timber can be combined with non-wood building materials, e.g., with steel [11,12], concrete [13,14], aluminium [15,16] or glass [17,18]. Furthermore, structural elements made of wood-based materials can also be combined with each other [19]. Recently, the experimental behaviour of timber-concrete and steel-timber composite structures has been investigated in a number of studies [20–22]. However, the behaviour of aluminium-timber composite structures has only been studied in a few tests [23–27]. The behaviour of composite elements depends on their connections. In a simply supported composite beam, the slab is designed to resist compression, the girder is designed to resist tension, while shear is transferred through connectors referred to as "shear connectors". There are many types of shear connections used in composite beams with timber elements (see Table 1).

Table 1. Shear connections used in composite beams with timber elements.

Composite Beam	Shear Connection	Example
steel-timber	self-drilling screw [11]	
steel-timber	coach screw [21]	
steel-timber	coach screw [21]	
aluminium-LVL	hexagon head wood screw [25]	
aluminium-LVL	bolt [27]	
LVL-concrete	rectangular notch reinforced with a coach screw [28]	
timber-timber	coach screw [29]	
timber-timber	fully threaded inclined screw [30]	

Screws with hexagonal heads may be used in laterally loaded connections [31]. A large diameter of a hexagonal head wood screw maximises screw resistance against head pull-through. Self-tapping screws are optimised for loading in the axial direction and they can be installed without pre-drilling [32]. The installation of self-tapping screws in cold-formed steel beams is relatively simple. However, when composite beam girders are made of beams with thick flanges, the installation of self-tapping screws requires the use of additional elements to connect the slabs with the girders [33].

The results of experimental tests on aluminium-timber composite beams with screwed connections were presented in [25]. Hexagon head wood screws were used to join an aluminium beam with an LVL slab. The failure mode of the analysed screwed connections was associated with the crushing of the timber, the formation of one plastic hinge within the connector, and the hole ovalisation in the aluminium beam flange. The stiffness and strength of the connection per one connector were relatively low ($k_{0.4}$ = 5.5 kN/mm, P_{ult} = 15.1 kN). For this reason, the authors of this paper proposed to use a toothed plate in the screwed connection. The main goal of this paper was to determine the stiffness and the load-carrying capacity of the screwed connection with the toothed plate.

2. Materials and Methods

2.1. LVL

The material parameters of LVL are presented in Table 2. The engineered wood product was fabricated from Scots pine (*Pinus sylvestris* L.) and Norway spruce (*Picea abies* L. H. Karst) veneers [34].

Table 2. The material parameters of LVL [35].

Material Parameters	Value
Mean value of modulus of elasticity (parallel to grain) $E_{0,mean}$ [MPa]	14,000
Bending strength (flatwise, parallel to grain) $f_{m,0,flat,k}$ [MPa]	50.0
Tension strength (parallel to grain) $f_{t,0,k}$ [MPa]	36.0
Compression strength (parallel to grain) $f_{c,0,k}$ [MPa]	40.0
Mean value of density ρ_{mean} [kg/m^3]	550.0

2.2. Aluminium Alloy

The mechanical properties of the AW-6060 T6 aluminium alloy were determined in a tensile test [36] and are presented in [37] (see Table 3).

Table 3. Mean values of Young's modulus, the 0.2% proof strength and the tensile strength of the AW-6060 T6 aluminium alloy [37].

Parameter	Mean Value
Young's modulus [GPa]	66.4 ± 0.51
0.2% proof strength [MPa]	181.5 ± 1.92
Tensile strength [MPa]	209.8 ± 1.05

2.3. Shear Connectors

Grade 5.8 hot dip galvanised DIN 571 [38] hexagon head wood screws 10 mm × 80 mm and 12 mm × 80 mm were used as shear connectors (see Tables 4 and 5). The mechanical properties of the steel used in the screws were determined experimentally in accordance with [36]. Four round samples were created from 10 mm screws and another four round samples were created from 12 mm screws for the purpose of the tensile tests. The thread was removed in the middle of the screw to obtain a smooth shank and to install the extensometer on the sample (see Figure 1).

Table 4. Mean values, 5%-quantiles and coefficients of variation for the 10 mm screw used in the tests.

Parameter	Mean Value	5%-Quantile	CV [%]
Shank diameter d_0 [mm]	9.43	9.39	0.38
Length L [mm]	85.34	85.07	0.29
Outer thread diameter d_1 [mm]	9.47	9.23	2.41
Inner thread diameter d_2 [mm]	6.95	6.88	0.88
Pitch p [mm]	4.51	4.49	0.48
Thread length L_t [mm]	59.64	59.04	0.96
Shank length L_s [mm]	16.39	16.24	0.86
Head width across flats F [mm]	16.78	16.67	0.61
Head width across corners C [mm]	19.07	18.97	0.51
Head height H [mm]	6.88	6.86	0.24

Table 5. Mean values, 5%-quantiles and coefficients of variation for the 12 mm screw used in the tests.

Parameter	Mean Value	5%-Quantile	CV [%]
Shank diameter d_0 [mm]	11.31	11.29	0.17
Length L [mm]	88.82	88.52	0.33
Outer thread diameter d_1 [mm]	11.62	11.57	0.47
Inner thread diameter d_2 [mm]	8.90	8.89	0.09
Pitch p [mm]	4.81	4.78	0.45
Thread length L_t [mm]	62.13	61.94	0.29
Shank length L_s [mm]	15.63	15.27	2.18
Head width across flats F [mm]	18.66	18.62	0.19
Head width across corners C [mm]	21.22	21.18	0.19
Head height H [mm]	7.89	7.84	0.57

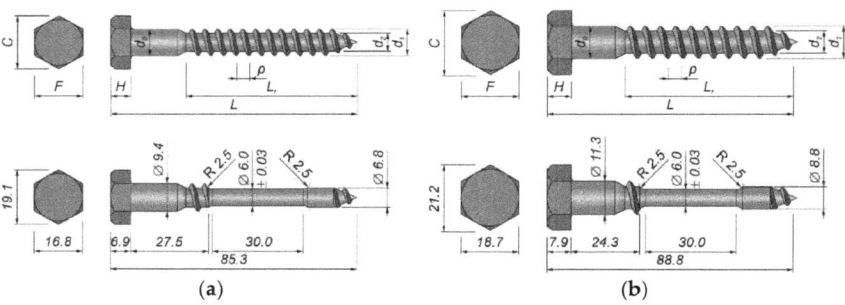

Figure 1. A shear connector: (**a**) 10 mm screw; (**b**) 12 mm screw.

The tensile tests were conducted using an Instron 4483 machine (Instron, High-Wycombe, Buckinghamshire, UK) and an Epsilon 3442-010M-025M-ST extensometer (Epsilon, Jackson, WY, USA) with a 10 mm gauge. The displacement rate was kept constant (0.05 mm/s).

2.4. Toothed Plates

Toothed-plate connectors (C2-50/M10G, C2-50/M12G or C11-50/M12) were used to reinforce the aluminium-timber screwed connections investigated in this paper.

A toothed plate (type C2, Bulldog) is a single-sided connector made from a circular plate. Its edges are cut and bent over to form triangular teeth projecting from one face at 90° to the face (see Figure 2a). Around the screw hole, there is a flange projecting from the same face as the teeth. The dimensions of the toothed plates used in this study are presented in Table 6. They were made from cold rolled uncoated low carbon narrow strips of HC340LA steel (high yield strength steel for cold forming) [39]. The toothed plates were hot dip galvanised (≥45 μm) to protect them from corrosion.

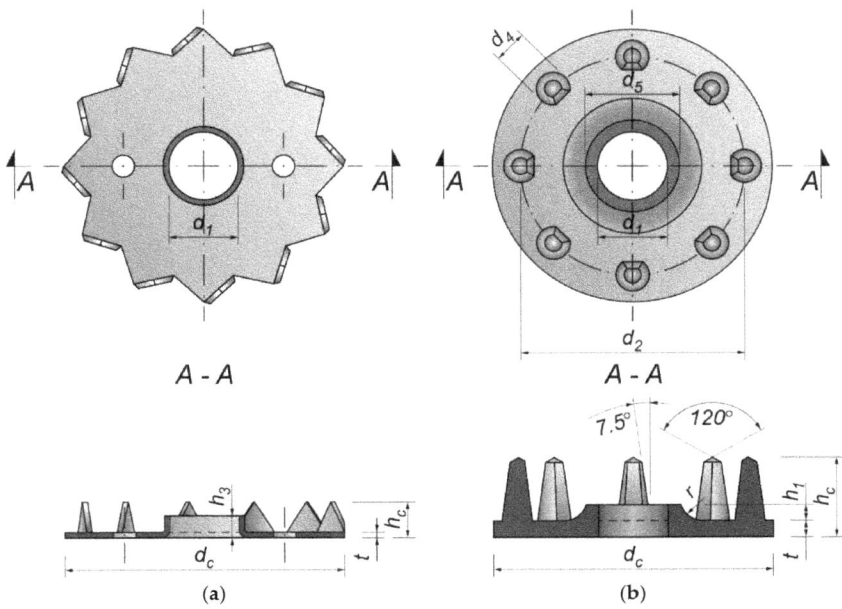

Figure 2. Toothed-plate connectors: (**a**) type C2, Bulldog; (**b**) C11, Geka.

A toothed-plate connector (type C11-50/M12, Geka) is a single-sided connector made from a round plate with spikes on one side of the plate (see Figure 2b). The spikes are equidistant and are arranged in one circle. The toothed plate has a bolt-hole through its centre with a flange around the bolt-hole projecting from the same face as the spikes. The dimensions of the toothed plates used in this study are presented in Table 7. They were made of malleable cast iron EN-GJMB-350-10 (PN-JM 1130) according to EN 1562 [40] and galvanised (Fe/Zn12/C) to protect them from corrosion.

Table 6. Dimensions of C2 (Bulldog) connectors [1,2] [41].

Connector Type	Diameter d_c [mm]	Height h_c [mm]	Thickness Without Zinc-Coating t [mm]	Hole Diameter d_1 [mm]	Flange Height h_3 [mm]	Number of Teeth
C2-50/M10G	50	6.6	1.00	10.4	4.0	12
C2-50/M12G	50	6.6	1.00	12.4	4.0	12

[1] Tolerances: thickness t in accordance with [42,43], other dimensions: ±1.50 mm. [2] Limit deviations for diameter d_1: plus 0.30 mm, minus 0 mm.

Table 7. Dimensions of C11 (Geka) connectors [1] (connector type: C11-50/M12) [41].

Diameter d_c [mm]	Height h_c [mm]	Thickness t [mm]	Diameter of Centre Hole d_1 [mm]	Diameter of Inner Circle d_2 [mm]
50	15	3	12.5	40
Diameter of Spikes at Base d_4 [mm]	Diameter of Flange d_5 [mm]	Radius r [mm]	Height of Flange from Face h_1 [mm]	Number of Spikes
6	17.0	4	3	8

[1] Tolerances on: height h_c, thickness t, radius r and height of flange from face h_1: ±0.50 mm, other dimensions: ±0.80 mm.

2.5. Push-Out Tests

The tests were carried out on twenty models using an Instron 8505 Plus machine (In-stron, High Wycombe, Buckinghamshire, UK). Each experimental model consisted of two timber slabs made of LVL and a beam made of the AW-6060 T6 aluminium alloy (see Figure 3). The LVL slabs were connected with the aluminium beams using four variants of connections. In the first variant, eight hexagon head wood screws (10 × 80 mm^2) without reinforcing toothed plates were used (specimen R10.1–R10.4). In the second variant, eight hexagon head wood screws (10 × 80 mm^2) with reinforcing toothed plates (C2-50/M10G, Bulldog) were used (specimens 10.1–10.4). In the third variant, eight hexagon head wood screws (12 × 80 mm^2) without reinforcing toothed plates were used (specimen R12.1–R12.4). In the four variant, eight hexagon head wood screws (12 × 80 mm^2) with reinforcing toothed plates (C2-50/M12G, Bulldog) were used (specimens 12.1–12.4). In the fifth variant, eight hexagon head wood screws (12 × 80 mm^2) with reinforcing toothed plates (C11-50/M12, Geka) were used (specimens 12.5–12.8).

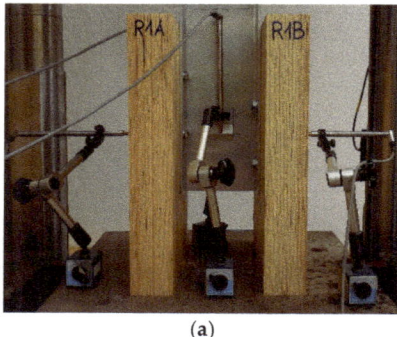
(a)

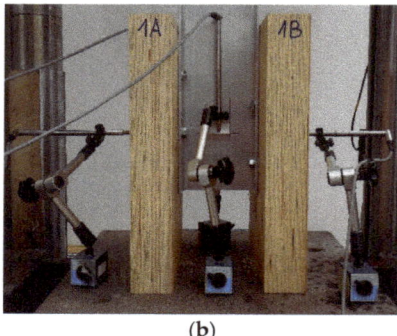
(b)

Figure 3. The tested specimens: (**a**) without reinforcing toothed plates; (**b**) with reinforcing toothed plates.

The holes in the aluminium beams had the same diameter as the screws to reduce the slip between the aluminium beams and the LVL slabs. The pre-drilling diameter in LVL was 7 mm for the 10 mm screw and 8 mm for the 12 mm screw. Pre-drilling started the course of the screw and created pilot holes. Furthermore, the installation of the hexagon head wood screws required less effort. In each specimen, screws were inserted in the face withdrawal direction using a torque wrench (Sandvik Belzer, IZO-I-100, 10–100 Nm). The tread-grain angle was 90°. The torque level was measured during the insertion of the screws using a torque wrench and recorded at the end of the insertion process (35 Nm for 10 mm screw, 50 Nm for 12 mm screw). The toothed plates were pressed into LVL using a hydraulic press and a compressive force equal to 35 kN. The spaces between the screws were 50 mm in the transverse direction and 60 mm in the longitudinal direction. The staggered spacing was used because of the dimensions of the toothed plates. The loading direction was parallel to the LVL grain. Linear variable differential transformers (LVDTs) were used to measure the longitudinal slip between the LVL slabs and the aluminium beam, and the horizontal move of the sample (see Figures 4–6).

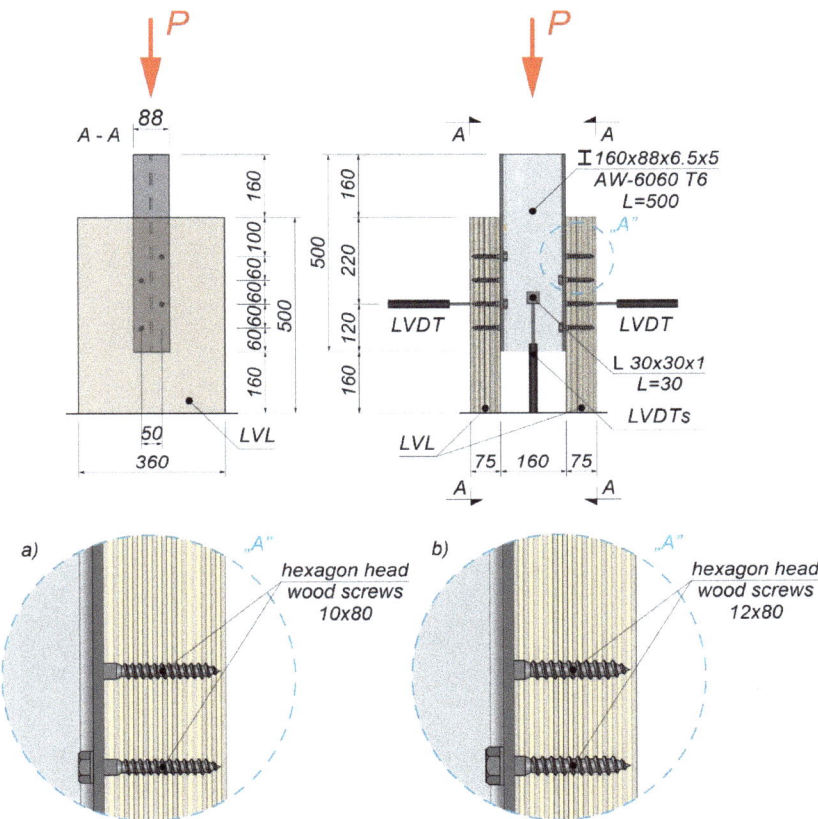

Figure 4. The location of the LVDTs on the specimen without reinforcing toothed plates: (**a**) screws 10 × 80; (**b**) screws 12 × 80.

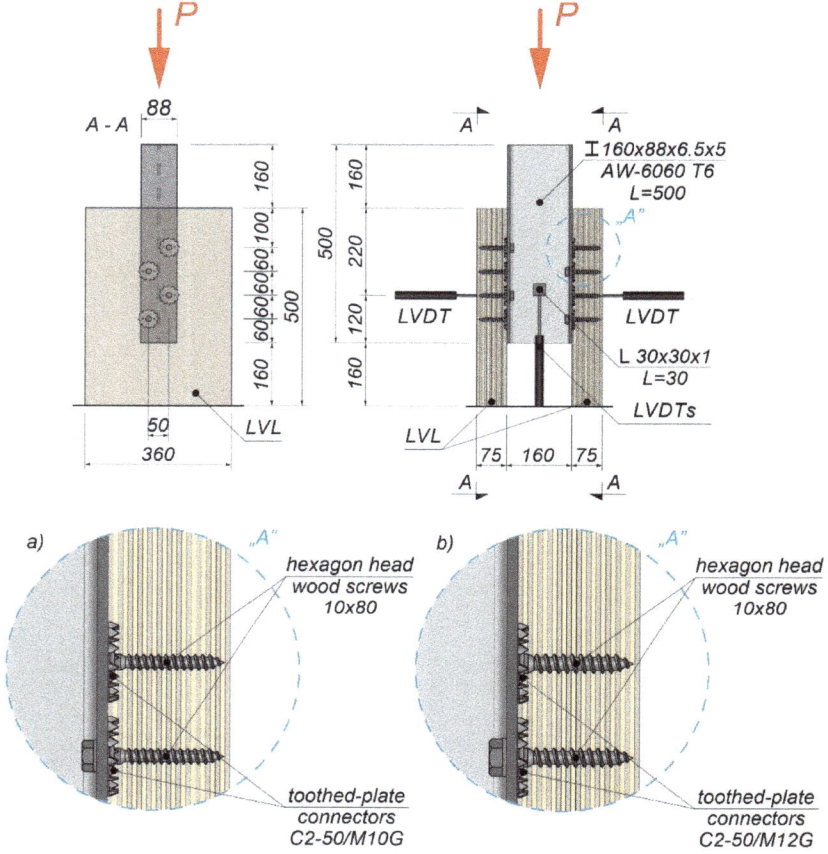

Figure 5. The location of the LVDTs on the specimen with reinforcing toothed plates: (**a**) screws 10 × 80 and toothed-plate connectors (type C2-50/M10G); (**b**) screws 12 × 80 and toothed-plate connectors (type C2-50/M12G, Bulldog).

The push-out tests were performed in line with [44]. In the first part of the test, a load control regime was applied to achieve a regular shape of the load–slip curve and to determine the connection slip modulus for a shear force equal to 40% of F_{max}. In the second part of the test, a constant rate of displacement was used to evaluate the behaviour of the connection once the ultimate load had been achieved. The shear force was first increased from 0 to 40% of F_{est} over two minutes, and it remained at this level for the next 30 seconds. Afterwards the load was reduced from 40% to 10% of F_{est} and kept at this level for additional 30 seconds. Subsequently, the load was increased from 10% to 70% of F_{est}. Up to that point, the push-out tests were performed using a load control regime, and from then on—using a displacement control regime (the piston velocity was 5.0 mm/min). The ultimate load F_{est} = 130.0 kN was calculated based on Equation (8.10e) from Eurocode 5 [45]. The value of F_{est} was modified during the tests taking into account the previous results. The loading procedure was also redefined.

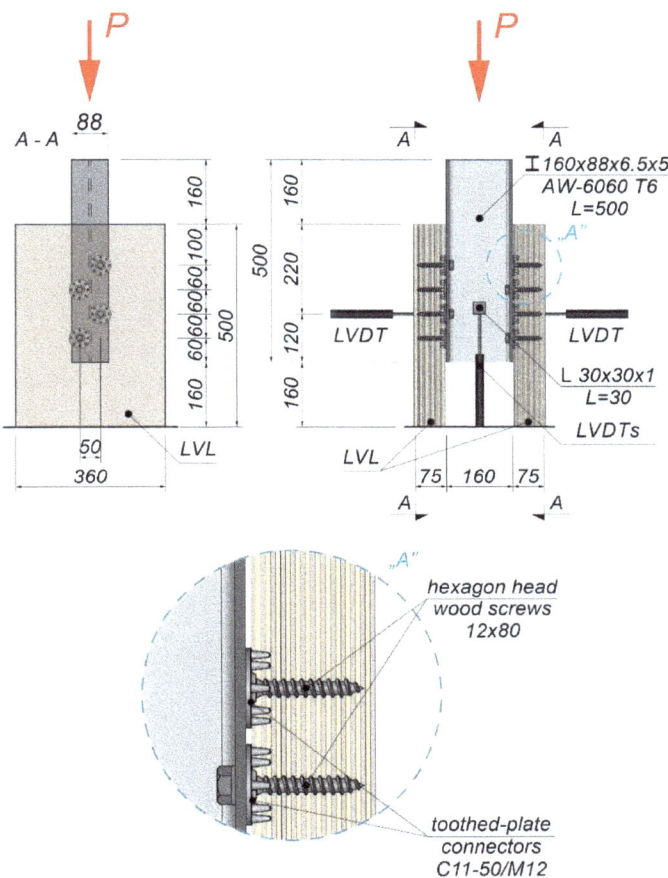

Figure 6. The location of the LVDTs on the specimen with reinforcing toothed plates—screws 12 × 80 and toothed-plate connectors (type C11-50/M12, Geka).

3. Results and Discussion

3.1. The Results of the Tensile Tests of the Steel Used in the Screws

The tensile strength of the steel used in the screws was 553.9 ± 23.6 MPa (4.3%) [46]. The measurement error for the tensile strength of the steel used in the screws was determined using Student's t-distribution with 7 degrees of freedom and a confidence level of 95%.

3.2. The Results of the Push-Out Tests

The results of the push-out tests are presented in Figures 7–9 and in Tables 8–12. The symbols used in Tables 8–12 are as follows: P_{ult}, ultimate load per one connector; s_{ult}, slip corresponding to P_{ult}; $k_{0.4}$ and $k_{0.6}$, slip moduli per one connector. The measurement errors presented in Tables 8–12 were determined using Student's t-distribution with 3 degrees of freedom and a confidence level of 95%.

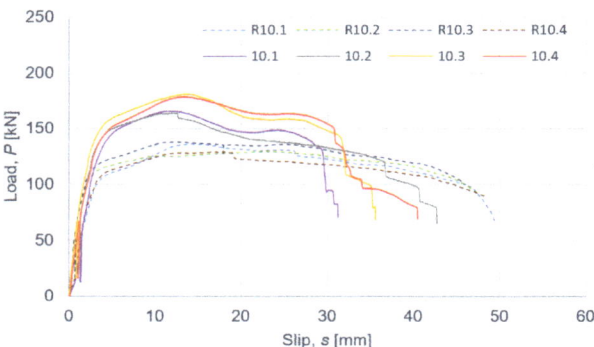

Figure 7. The load–slip curves from the push-out tests of the shear connections with 10 mm screws and with toothed-plate connectors (type C2-50/M10G, Bulldog) in specimens 10.1–10.4 or without toothed-plate connectors in specimens R10.1-R10.4.

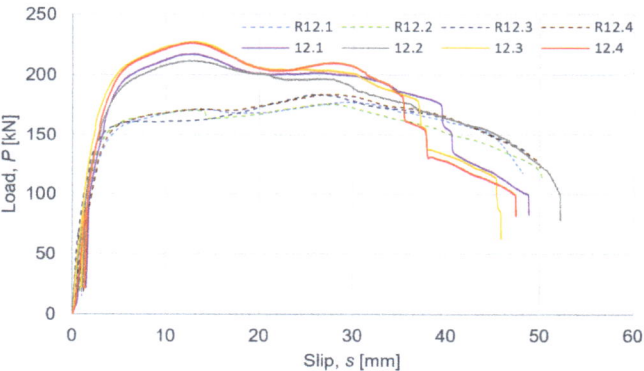

Figure 8. The load–slip curves from the push-out tests of the shear connections with 12 mm screws and with toothed-plate connectors (type C2-50/M12G, Bulldog) in specimens 12.1–12.4 or without toothed-plate connectors in specimens R12.1-R12.4.

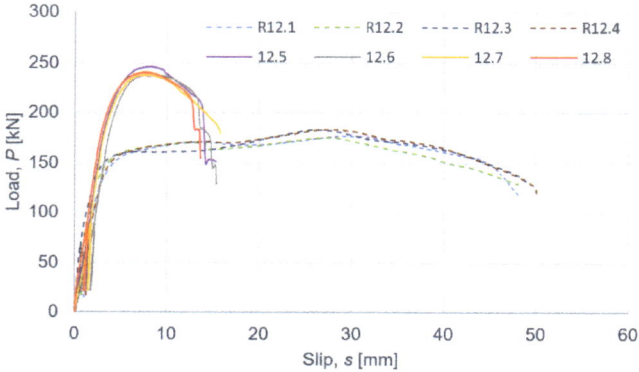

Figure 9. The load–slip curves from the push-out tests of the shear connections with 12 mm screws and with toothed-plate connectors (type C11-50/M12, Geka) in specimens 12.5–12.8 or without toothed-plate connectors in specimens R12.1-R12.4.

Table 8. The results of the push-out tests of the shear connections with 10 mm screws and without toothed-plate connectors (per one connector).

Parameter	Specimen				Mean (R10.1–R10.4)
	R10.1	R10.2	R10.3	R10.4	
P_{ult} [kN]	17.1	16.2	17.3	16.2	16.7 ± 0.9 (5.6%)
s_{ult} [mm]	14.4	23.0	12.4	16.9	16.7 ± 7.3 (43.9%)
$k_{0.4}$ [kN/mm]	4.4	8.6	9.1	4.3	6.6 ± 4.1 (62.8%)
$k_{0.6}$ [kN/mm]	4.2	7.9	7.8	4.7	6.2 ± 3.1 (51.1%)

Table 9. The results of the push-out tests of the shear connections with 10 mm screws and with toothed-plate connectors (type C2-50/M10G, Bulldog) (per one connector).

Parameter	Specimen				Mean (10.1–10.4)
	10.1	10.2	10.3	10.4	
P_{ult} [kN]	20.7	20.5	22.6	22.3	21.5 ± 1.7 (8.0%)
s_{ult} [mm]	11.7	12.3	14.0	13.0	12.8 ± 1.6 (12.3%)
$k_{0.4}$ [kN/mm]	4.8	6.1	8.3	6.5	6.4 ± 2.3 (35.8%)
$k_{0.6}$ [kN/mm]	5.0	6.0	6.9	5.6	5.9 ± 1.3 (21.6%)

Table 10. The results of the push-out tests of the shear connections with 12 mm screws and without toothed-plate connectors (per one connector).

Parameter	Specimen				Mean (R12.1–R12.4)
	R12.1	R12.2	R12.3	R12.4	
P_{ult} [kN]	21.4	21.9	22.9	22.9	22.3 ± 1.2 (5.4%)
s_{ult} [mm]	13.5	27.6	26.3	28.5	24.0 ± 11.2 (46.7%)
$k_{0.4}$ [kN/mm]	6.8	8.9	12.4	5.9	8.5 ± 4.6 (54.1%)
$k_{0.6}$ [kN/mm]	6.0	7.6	9.0	5.8	7.1 ± 2.4 (33.6%)

Table 11. The results of the push-out tests of the shear connections with 12 mm screws and with toothed-plate connectors (type C2-50/M12G, Bulldog) (per one connector).

Parameter	Specimen				Mean (12.1–12.4)
	12.1	12.2	12.3	12.4	
P_{ult} [kN]	27.1	26.4	28.4	28.3	27.6 ± 1.5 (5.6%)
s_{ult} [mm]	12.9	12.5	13.1	12.5	12.8 ± 0.5 (3.7%)
$k_{0.4}$ [kN/mm]	6.2	7.7	9.2	7.0	7.5 ± 2.0 (26.9%)
$k_{0.6}$ [kN/mm]	6.2	7.4	8.5	7.0	7.3 ± 1.5 (20.9%)

Table 12. The results of the push-out tests of the shear connections with 12 mm screws and with toothed-plate connectors (type C11-50/M12, Geka) (per one connector).

Parameter	Specimen				Mean (12.5–12.8)
	12.5	12.6	12.7	12.8	
P_{ult} [kN]	30.8	29.7	29.7	30.0	30.1 ± 0.8 (2.8%)
s_{ult} [mm]	8.0	7.5	8.2	7.6	7.8 ± 0.5 (6.7%)
$k_{0.4}$ [kN/mm]	7.0	5.2	6.5	8.1	6.7 ± 1.9 (28.6%)
$k_{0.6}$ [kN/mm]	7.2	5.8	7.0	8.0	7.0 ± 1.4 (20.7%)

Taking into account the results of the specimens without the reinforcing toothed plates and comparing them with the mean ultimate load and the mean slip modulus of the specimens with the reinforcing toothed plates, the below conclusions were drawn.

The use of toothed-plate connectors in aluminium-timber composite connections can enhance their load-carrying capacity. An enhancement of 28.7% (for 10 mm screws and C2-50/M10G toothed-plate connectors), 23.8% (for 12 mm screws and C2-50/M12G toothed-plate connectors) or 35.0% (for 12 mm screws and C11-50/M12 toothed-plate connectors) was achieved in the respective screwed connections. Upon comparing the slip moduli of the tested connections, it was observed that the use of toothed plate connectors was ineffective in improving the stiffness of the aluminium-timber composite connections.

According to Eurocode 4 [47], a connection is ductile if its characteristic slip capacity is at least 6 mm. All the tested connections had the characteristic slip capacity exceeding 6 mm. However, the screwed connections with the C11-50/M12 toothed-plate connectors (Geka) had a brittle mode of failure—the unthreaded part of the screw was sheared. The screwed connections with the C2-50/M12G toothed-plate connectors (Bulldog) were more ductile than the screwed connections with the C11-50/M12 toothed-plate connectors (Geka) (compare Figures 8 and 9). There was a single shear plane between the toothed-plate connectors and the aluminium beam flange. The stiffness of the Geka toothed-plate connector is higher than the stiffness of the Bulldog toothed-plate connector because the flange height of the former (6 mm) is 1.5 times higher than the flange height of the latter (4 mm), and the flange thickness of the former (2.25 mm) is 2.25 times higher than the thickness of the latter (1 mm). Furthermore, the thickness of the former (3 mm) is 3 times higher than the thickness of the latter (1 mm). In the case of the screwed connections with the C11-50/M12 toothed-plate connectors (Geka), the screws were sheared, whereas in the case of the screwed connections with the C2-50/M12G toothed-plate connectors (Bulldog), the toothed-plate connectors were torn.

The load-carrying capacity of the screwed connections with the C2-50/M12G toothed-plate connectors (Bulldog) (27.6 kN) was 1.09 times lower than the load-carrying capacity of the screwed connections with the C11-50/M12 toothed-plate connectors (Geka) (30.1 kN).

The tested screwed connections with or without Bulldog toothed-plate connectors (C2-50/M10G, C2-50/M12G) showed one distinctive mode of failure presented in Figures 10–13. The authors observed the formation of two plastic hinges within the screw, the crushing of LVL, hole ovalisation in the flange of the aluminium alloy beam, and hole ovalisation in the toothed plate or its tearing. In the specimens where the teeth were strongly connected with the LVL and did not allow for the movement of the toothed plates, the toothed plates were torn (see Figure 11). Some of the screws were sheared near the end of the tests. In Figures 10–14, the symbol l_y was used to present the mean length of the yielded zone in the aluminium flange (measured at the end of the tests). The yielded zone was caused by the bearing of the screw to the hole wall.

The tested screwed connections with Geka toothed-plate connectors (C11-50/M12) showed one distinctive mode of failure presented in Figure 14. The screws were sheared and some of the plate teeth were broken. The authors also observed the crushing of LVL and the hole ovalisation in the flange of the aluminium alloy beam. In the case of Geka toothed-plate connectors, the mean length of the yielded zone in the aluminium flange was shorter than in the Bulldog toothed-plate connectors. The connections with the Geka toothed-plates had a lower slip corresponding to the ultimate load than the connections with the Bulldog toothed-plates.

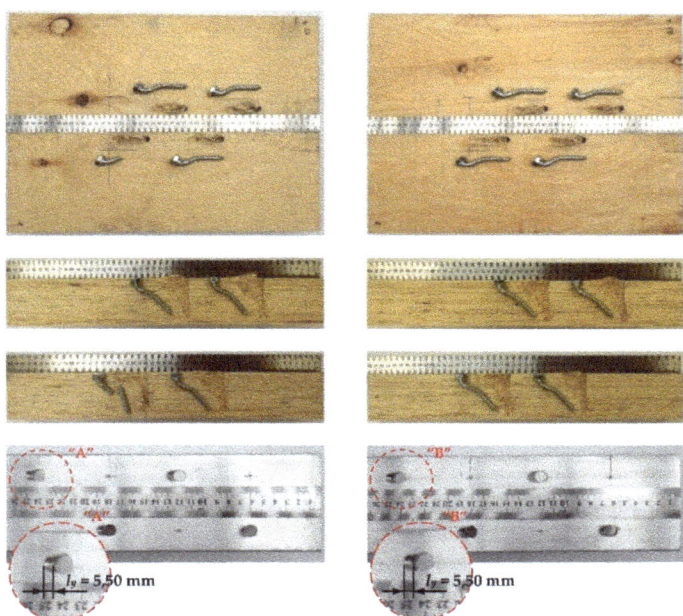

Figure 10. The mode of failure of the aluminium-timber connection with the 10 mm screws and without the reinforcing toothed plates.

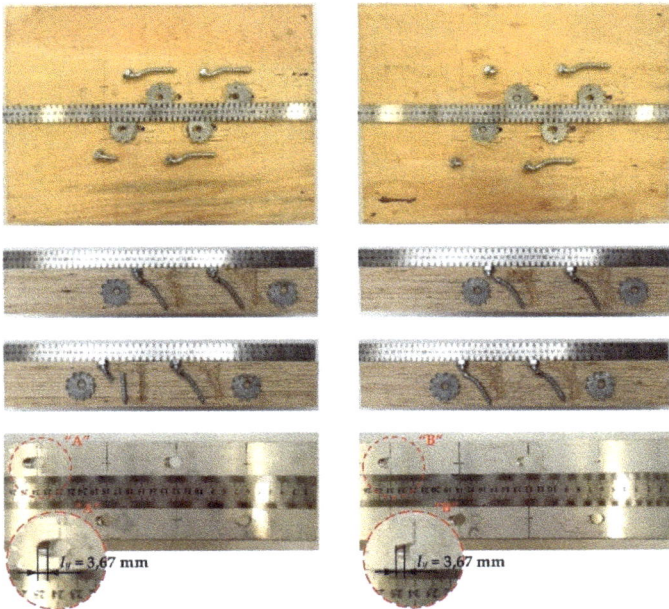

Figure 11. The mode of failure of the aluminium-timber connection with the 10 mm screws and the reinforcing toothed plates (C2-50/M10G, Bulldog).

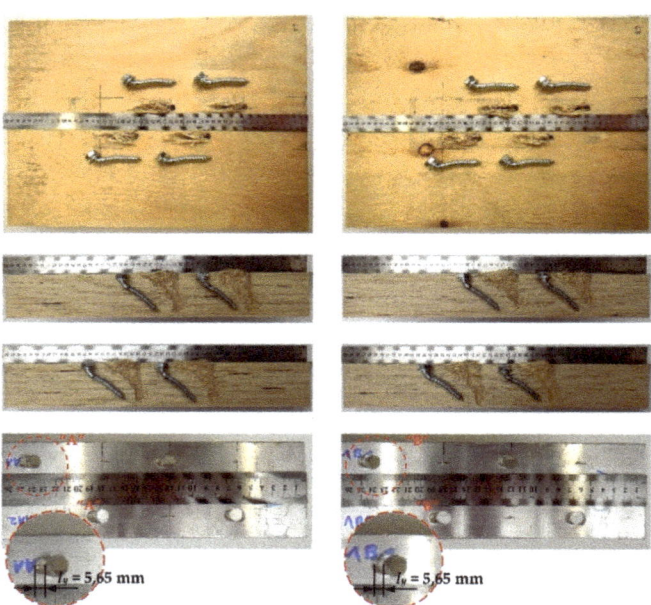

Figure 12. The mode of failure of the aluminium-timber connection with the 12 mm screws and without the reinforcing toothed plates.

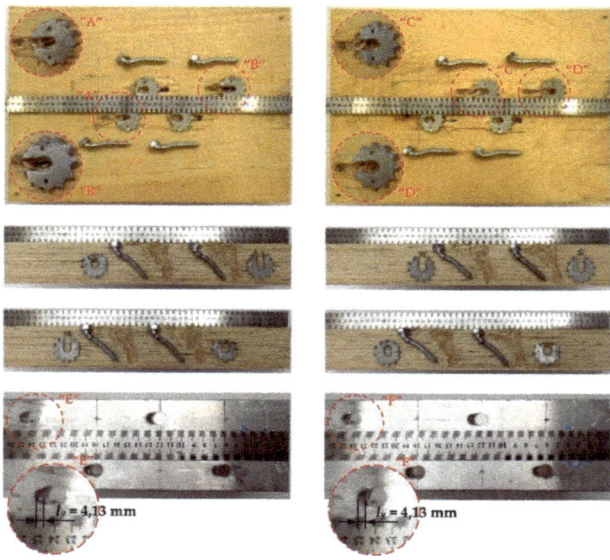

Figure 13. The mode of failure of the aluminium-timber connection with the 12 mm screws and the reinforcing toothed plates (C2-50/M12G, Bulldog).

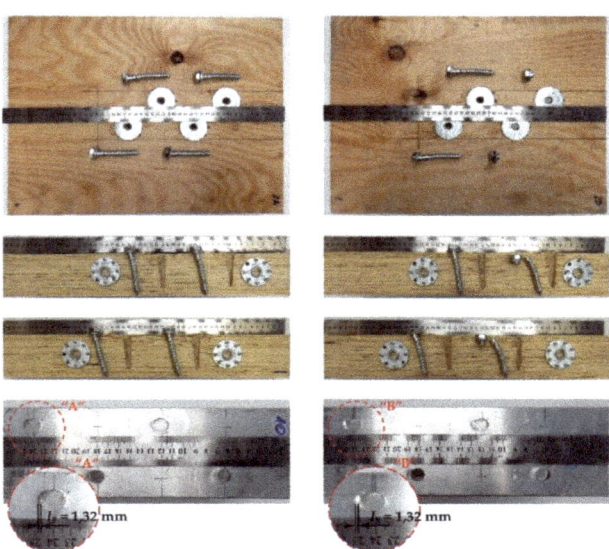

Figure 14. The mode of failure of the aluminium-timber connection with the 12 mm screws and the reinforcing toothed plates (C11-50/M12, Geka).

The failure mode of the tested screwed connections with or without Bulldog toothed-plate connectors is taken into account in Equation (8.10e) presented in [45]:

$$P_{v,Rk} = 2.3\sqrt{M_{y,Rk}f_{h,k}d} + \frac{F_{ax,Rk}}{4} \quad (1)$$

where: $P_{v,Rk}$ is the characteristic load-carrying capacity of the screw in a single shear (13.3 kN for the 9.43 mm screw and 17.5 kN for the 11.31 mm screw) calculated from Equation (1), $f_{h,k}$ is the characteristic embedment strength of the timber (40.8 MPa for the 9.43 mm screw and 40.0 MPa for the 11.31 mm screw) calculated from [45], t is the penetration depth (70.0 mm in this paper), $M_{y,Rk}$ is the characteristic fastener yield moment (54 372 N·mm for the 9.43 mm screw and 87 226 N·mm for the 11.31 mm screw) calculated from [45], $f_{u,k}$ is the characteristic tensile strength of the screw (530.3 MPa—5%-quantile from the tensile tests), and $F_{ax,Rk}$ is the characteristic withdrawal capacity of the fastener (11,011 N for the 9.43 mm screw and 12 059 N for the 11.31 mm screw) calculated from [45].

The mean values of the screw shank diameters (9.43 mm for the 10 mm screw and 11.31 mm for the 12 mm screw) from Tables 3 and 4 were used in the calculations based on Equations (1)–(4).

The characteristic load-carrying capacity of the 9.43 mm screw calculated from Equation (1) (13.3 kN) was 1.29 times lower than the ultimate load per one screw in the screwed connection without the reinforcing toothed plate (17.1 kN) and 1.62 times lower than the ultimate load per one screw in the reinforced screwed connection (21.5 kN). The characteristic load-carrying capacity of the 11.31 mm screw calculated from Equation (1) (17.5 kN) was 1.22 times lower than the ultimate load per one screw in the screwed connection without the reinforcing toothed plate (21.4 kN) and 1.58 times lower than the ultimate load per one screw in the reinforced screwed connection (27.6 kN). The model presented in Eurocode 5 does not take into account the reinforcing toothed plate. For this reason, the values obtained from Equation (1) are similar to the values obtained in the tests of the screwed connections without the reinforcing toothed plates, and lower than the ones from the tests with the reinforcing toothed plates.

The failure mode of the tested screwed connections with Geka toothed-plate connectors (C11-50/M12), i.e., the shearing of the unthreaded part of the screw, is taken into account in the equation presented in Table 3.4 in [48]:

$$P_{v,Rk} = \frac{\alpha_v f_{ub} A}{\gamma_{M2}} \qquad (2)$$

where: $P_{v,Rk}$ is the characteristic load-carrying capacity of the screw in a single shear (26.7 kN for the 11.31 mm screw) calculated from Equation (2), α_v is the coefficient from [48] (0.6), A is the gross cross-section area of the connector, γ_{M2} is the partial safety factor, f_{ub} is the ultimate strength of the steel used in the shear connector.

The characteristic load-carrying capacity of the 11.31 mm screw calculated from Equation (2) (26.7 kN) was 1.03 times lower than the ultimate load per one screw in the screwed connection without the reinforcing toothed plate (27.6 kN) and 1.13 times lower than the ultimate load per one screw in the reinforced screwed connection (30.1 kN). The model presented in Eurocode 5 does not take into account the reinforcing toothed plate. For this reason, the values obtained from Equation (2) are similar to the values obtained in the tests of the screwed connections without the reinforcing toothed plates, and lower than the values from the tests with the reinforcing toothed plates.

Hassanieh et al. [49] presented the formulae that can characterise the load-carrying capacity of the steel-timber screwed connection (per one connector).

$$P_{ult} = (5.95d - 27.2)/2 \qquad (3)$$

where: P_{ult} is the ultimate load per one connector (14.5 kN for the 9.43 mm screw and 20.0 kN for the 11.31 mm screw) calculated from Equation (2), d is the screw diameter.

Steel-timber composite structures are similar to aluminium-timber composite ones. The characteristic load-carrying capacity of the 9.43 mm screw calculated from Equation (3) (14.5 kN) was 1.18 times lower than the ultimate load per one screw in the screwed connection without the reinforcing toothed plate (17.1 kN) and 1.48 times lower than the ultimate load per one screw in the reinforced screwed connection (21.5 kN). The characteristic load-carrying capacity of the 11.31 mm screw calculated from Equation (3) (20.0 kN) was 1.07 times higher than the ultimate load per one screw in the screwed connection without the reinforcing toothed plate (21.4 kN) and 1.38 times lower than the ultimate load per one screw in the reinforced screwed connection (27.6 kN). The model presented by Hassanieh et al. [49] does not take into account the reinforcing toothed plate, neither does the model presented in Eurocode 5. The results of the tests presented in this article show that reinforcing LVL by toothed-plate connectors is effective in increasing the load-carrying capacity of screwed connections. An enhancement of 23.8%, 28.7%, or 35.0% was achieved in the screwed connections with 10 or 12 mm screws, respectively. For this reason, the authors of this paper suggested Equation (3) be modified by adding a coefficient of 1.24, taking into account the lowest value of the enhancements obtained from the tests, to characterise the load-carrying capacity of the aluminium-timber screwed connection reinforced with toothed-plate connectors:

$$P_{ult} = 1.24(5.95d - 27.2)/2 \qquad (4)$$

The characteristic load-carrying capacity of the 9.43 mm screw calculated from Equation (4) (18.0 kN) was 1.19 times lower than the ultimate load per one screw in the reinforced screwed connection (21.5 kN). The characteristic load-carrying capacity of the 11.31 mm screw calculated from Equation (4) (24.9 kN) was 1.11 times lower than the ultimate load per one screw in the screwed connection reinforced by the C2-50/M12G toothed plates (27.6 kN) and 1.21 times lower than the ultimate load per one screw in the screwed connection reinforced by the C11-50/M12 toothed plates (30.1 kN).

In this paper, toothed plates were used as reinforcement. However, LVL can also be reinforced using other steel elements. For example, Hassanieh et al. [49] used reinforcing nail plates. They compared the load-carrying capacity and the stiffness of steel-timber screwed connections with and without nail plates. Hassanieh et al. [49] showed that the use of nail plates increased the stiffness of the connection, e.g., by 22% for 16 mm screws. What is more, reinforcing the LVL slab by nail plates enhanced the load-carrying capacity of the connection, e.g., by 19% for 16 mm screws. They also observed that nail plates had a minor influence on the load-carrying capacity of the steel-timber composite connections loaded in the direction perpendicular to the grain. The influence of the toothed plates (C2-50/M10G, C2-50/M12G, C11-50/M12) used in the tests presented in this article on the load-carrying capacity of the aluminium-timber screwed connections was similar to the impact of the nail plates used by Hassanieh et al. [49] on the load-carrying capacity of the steel-timber screwed connections.

4. Conclusions

In this paper, the load-carrying capacity, stiffness, load-slip response, failure modes and ductility of aluminium-timber screwed connections with and without toothed plates were investigated. Push-out tests with symmetrical configurations were conducted.

Based on the results of the tests, the following conclusions can be drawn. Aluminium-timber screwed connections can be reinforced using toothed plates. Reinforcing LVL by toothed-plate connectors can enhance the load-carrying capacity of screwed connections. Enhancements of 28.7% (for 10 mm screws and C2-50/M10G toothed-plate connectors), 23.8% (for 12 mm screws and C2-50/M12G toothed-plate connectors) or 35.0% (for 12 mm screws and C11-50/M12 toothed-plate connectors) were achieved in the screwed connections. However, the use of toothed plate connectors was found to be ineffective in improving the stiffness of aluminium-timber composite connections.

The authors demonstrated that the existing design rules did not take into account the strengthening effect of toothed plates on the connection load-carrying capacity, and they suggested the use of a coefficient equal to 1.24 to better characterise the load-carrying capacity of aluminium-timber screwed connections reinforced with toothed-plate connectors.

Furthermore, the screwed connections reinforced with toothed plates may be used in aluminium-timber composite beams. The tests presented in this paper make it possible to determine the number of connectors necessary to achieve the required level of composite action. Last, but not least, the obtained load-slip curves for the analysed connections can be used in numerical models of aluminium-timber composite beams, to model connection behaviour using spring elements. This method of connection modelling was used, e.g., in [25,27,30,50,51].

Author Contributions: Conceptualization, M.C. and Ł.P.; methodology, M.C. and Ł.P.; investigation, M.C. and Ł.P.; specimens preparation, M.C. and Ł.P.; writing—original draft preparation, M.C. and Ł.P.; writing—review and editing, M.C. and Ł.P.; visualization, M.C. and Ł.P. All authors have read and agreed to the published version of the manuscript.

Funding: This research was funded by the Polish Ministry of Science and Higher Education under grants 0412/SBAD/0044, 0412/SBAD/0046 and 0412/SBAD/0050.

Institutional Review Board Statement: Not applicable.

Informed Consent Statement: Not applicable.

Data Availability Statement: All data contained within the article.

Acknowledgments: The authors wish to thank STEICO company for the LVL panels.

Conflicts of Interest: The authors declare no conflict of interest.

References

1. Bergman, R.; Puettmann, M.; Taylor, A.; Skog, K.E. The carbon impacts of wood products. *For. Prod. J.* **2014**, *64*, 47. [CrossRef]
2. Porteous, J.; Kermani, A. *Structural Timber Design to Eurocode 5*, 2nd ed.; Wiley-Blackwell: Chichester, UK, 2013.
3. Mirski, R.; Dziurka, D.; Chuda-Kowalska, M.; Wieruszewski, M.; Kawalerczyk, J.; Trociński, A. The usefulness of pine timber (*Pinus sylvestris* L.) for the production of structural elements. Part I: Evaluation of the quality of the pine timber in the bending test. *Materials* **2020**, *13*, 3957. [CrossRef]
4. Witomski, P.; Krajewski, A.; Kozakiewicz, P. Selected mechanical properties of Scots pine wood from antique churches of Central Poland. *Eur. J. Wood Wood Prod.* **2014**, *72*, 293–296. [CrossRef]
5. Brandner, R.; Ringhofer, A.; Grabner, M. Probabilistic models for the withdrawal behavior of single self-tapping screws in the narrow face of cross laminated timber (CLT). *Eur. J. Wood Wood Prod.* **2018**, *76*, 13–30. [CrossRef]
6. Brandner, R.; Ringhofer, A.; Reichinger, T. Performance of axially-loaded self-tapping screws in hardwood: Properties and design. *Eng. Struct.* **2019**, *188*, 677–699. [CrossRef]
7. Bakalarz, M.; Kossakowski, P.; Tworzewski, P. Strengthening of bent LVL beams with near-surface mounted (NSM) FRP reinforcement. *Materials* **2020**, *13*, 2350. [CrossRef]
8. Wdowiak-Postulak, A.; Świt, G. Behavior of glulam beams strengthened in bending with BFRP fabrics. *Civ. Environ. Eng. Rep.* **2021**, *2*, 16. [CrossRef]
9. Kula, K.; Socha, T. Renovation and strengthening of wooden beams with CFRP bands including the rheological effects. *Civ. Environ. Eng. Rep.* **2016**, *22*, 93–102. [CrossRef]
10. Wróblewski, T.; Berczyński, S.; Abramowicz, M. Estimation of the parameters of the discrete model of a steel-concrete composite beam. *Arch. Civ. Mech. Eng.* **2013**, *13*, 209–219. [CrossRef]
11. Kyvelou, P.; Gardner, L.; Nethercot, D.A. Design of composite cold-formed steel flooring systems. *Structures* **2017**, *12*, 242–252. [CrossRef]
12. Chybiński, M.; Polus, Ł.; Szwabiński, W.; Niewiem, P. FE analysis of steel-timber composite beams. In Proceedings of the Computational Technologies in Engineering (TKI'2018): 15th Conference on Computational Technologies in Engineering, Jora Wielka, Poland, 16–19 October 2018; Baranowski, P., Kędzierski, P., Szurgott, A., Eds.; AIP Publishing: Melville, NY, USA, 2019; pp. 020061-1–020061-6. [CrossRef]
13. Łukaszewska, E.; Fragiacomo, M.; Johnsson, H. Laboratory tests and numerical analyses of prefabricated timber-concrete composite floors. *J. Struct. Eng.* **2010**, *136*, 46–55. [CrossRef]
14. Szumigała, M.; Szumigała, E.; Polus, Ł. Laboratory tests of new connectors for timber-concrete composite structures. *Eng. Trans.* **2018**, *66*, 161–173.
15. Szumigała, M.; Chybiński, M.; Polus, Ł. Preliminary analysis of the aluminium-timber composite beams. *Civ. Environ. Eng. Rep.* **2017**, *27*, 131–141.
16. Szumigała, M.; Chybiński, M.; Polus, Ł. Stiffness of composite beams with full shear connection. *IOP Conf. Ser. Mater. Sci. Eng.* **2019**, *471*, 052083. [CrossRef]
17. Furtak, K.; Rodacki, K. Experimental investigations of load-bearing capacity of composite timber-glass I-beams. *Arch. Civ. Mech. Eng.* **2018**, *18*, 956–964. [CrossRef]
18. Kozłowski, M.; Kadela, M.; Hulimka, J. Numerical investigation of structural behavior of timber-glass composite beams. *Procedia Eng.* **2016**, *161*, 78–89. [CrossRef]
19. Bedon, C.; Sciomenta, M.; Fragiacomo, M. Correlation approach for the Push-Out and full-size bending short-term performances of timber-to-timber slabs with Self-Tapping Screws. *Eng. Struct.* **2021**, *238*, 112232. [CrossRef]
20. Łukaszewska, E.; Johnsson, H.; Fragiacomo, M. Performance of connections for prefabricated timber-concrete composite floors. *Mater. Struct.* **2008**, *41*, 1533–1550. [CrossRef]
21. Hassanieh, A.; Valipour, H.R.; Bradford, M.A. Experimental and numerical study of steel-timber composite (STC) beams. *J. Constr. Steel Res.* **2016**, *122*, 367–378. [CrossRef]
22. Vella, N.; Gardner, L.; Buhagiar, S. Analytical modelling of cold-formed steel-to-timber connections with inclined screws. *Eng. Struct.* **2021**, *249*, 113187. [CrossRef]
23. Saleh, S.M.; Jasim, N.A. Structural behavior of timber aluminum composite beams under static loads. *Int. J. Eng. Res. Technol.* **2014**, *3*, 1166–1173.
24. Saleh, S.M.; Jasim, N.A. Structural behavior of timber aluminum composite beams under impact loads. *Int. J. Sci. Eng. Res.* **2014**, *5*, 865–873.
25. Chybiński, M.; Polus, Ł. Theoretical, experimental and numerical study of aluminium-timber composite beams with screwed connections. *Constr. Build. Mater.* **2019**, *226*, 317–330. [CrossRef]
26. Szumigała, M.; Chybiński, M.; Polus, Ł. Composite beams with aluminium girders—A review. In Proceedings of the Modern Trends in Research on Steel, Aluminium and Composite STRUCTURES: XIV International Conference on Metal Structures (ICMS2021), Poznan, Poland, 16–18 June 2021; Giżejowski, M.A., Ed.; Routledge: Leiden, The Netherlands, 2021; pp. 249–255. [CrossRef]
27. Chybiński, M.; Polus, Ł. Experimental and numerical investigations of aluminium-timber composite beams with bolted connections. *Structures* **2021**, *34*, 1942–1960. [CrossRef]

28. Yeoh, D.; Fragiacomo, M.; Deam, B. Experimental behaviour of LVL-concrete composite floor beams at strength limit state. *Eng. Struct.* **2011**, *33*, 2697–2707. [CrossRef]
29. Nie, Y.; Valipour, H.R. Experimental and numerical study of long-term behaviour of timber-timber composite (TTC) connections. *Constr. Build. Mater.* **2021**, *304*, 124672. [CrossRef]
30. Chiniforush, A.A.; Valipour, H.R.; Ataei, A. Timber-timber composite (TTC) connections and beams: An experimental and numerical study. *Constr. Build. Mater.* **2021**, *303*, 124493. [CrossRef]
31. Ringhofer, A. *Axially Loaded Self-Tapping Screws in Solid Timber and Laminated Timber Products*; TU Graz: Graz, Austria, 2017.
32. Ringhofer, A.; Brandner, R.; Schickhofer, G. Withdrawal resistance of self-tapping screws in unidirectional and orthogonal layered timber products. *Mater. Struct.* **2015**, *48*, 1435–1447. [CrossRef]
33. Loss, C.; Piazza, M.; Zandonini, R. Connections for steel-timber hybrid prefabricated buildings. Part I: Experimental tests. *Constr. Build. Mater.* **2016**, *122*, 781–795. [CrossRef]
34. Chybiński, M.; Polus, Ł. Experimental and numerical investigations of laminated veneer lumber panels. *Arch. Civ. Eng.* **2021**, *67*, 351–372. [CrossRef]
35. Komorowski, M. *Manual of Design and Build in the STEICO System, Basic Information, Building Physics, Guidelines*; Forestor Communication: Warsaw, Poland, 2017. (In Polish)
36. European Committee for Standardization. *EN ISO 6892-1, Metallic Materials—Tensile Testing—Part 1: Method of Test at Room Temperature*; European Committee for Standardization: Brussels, Belgium, 2016.
37. Chybiński, M.; Polus, Ł.; Ratajczak, M.; Sielicki, P.W. The evaluation of the fracture surface in the AW-6060 T6 aluminium alloy under a wide range of loads. *Metals* **2019**, *9*, 324. [CrossRef]
38. German Institute for Standardization. *DIN 571:2016-12, Hexagon Head Wood Screws*; German Institute for Standardization: Berlin, Germany, 2016.
39. European Committee for Standardization. *EN 10268, Cold Rolled Steel Flat Products with High Yield Strength for Cold Forming, Technical Delivery Conditions*; European Committee for Standardization: Brussels, Belgium, 2006.
40. European Committee for Standardization. *EN 1562 Founding—Malleable Cast Irons*; European Committee for Standardization: Brussels, Belgium, 2019.
41. European Committee for Standardization. *EN 912, Timber Fasteners, Specifications for Connectors for Timbers*; European Committee for Standardization: Brussels, Belgium, 2011.
42. European Committee for Standardization. *EN 10131, Cold Rolled Uncoated and Zinc or Zinc-Nickel Electrolytically Coated Low Carbon and High Yield Strength Steel Flat Products for Cold Forming—Tolerances on Dimensions and Shape*; European Committee for Standardization: Brussels, Belgium, 2006.
43. European Committee for Standardization. *EN 10140, Cold Rolled Narrow Steel Strip—Tolerances on Dimensions and Shape*; European Committee for Standardization: Brussels, Belgium, 2006.
44. European Committee for Standardization. *EN 26891, Timber Structures—Joints Made with Mechanical Fasteners—General Principles for the Determination of Strength and Deformation Characteristics*; European Committee for Standardization: Brussels, Belgium, 1991.
45. European Committee for Standardization. *EN 1995-1-1, Eurocode 5: Design of Timber Structures—Part 1-1: General—Common Rules and Rules for Buildings*; European Committee for Standardization: Brussels, Belgium, 2004.
46. *Research Report: 100/21/BB.903.0287.05*; The Łukasiewicz Research Network; Metal Forming Institute: Poznań, Poland, 2021.
47. Johnson, R.P. *Designers' Guide to Eurocode 4: Design of Composite Steel and Concrete Structures, EN 1994-1-1*; ICE Publishing: London, UK, 2012.
48. European Committee for Standardization. *EN 1993-1-8, Eurocode 3: Design of Steel Structures—Part 1-8: Design of Joints*; European Committee for Standardization: Brussels, Belgium, 2005.
49. Hassanieh, A.; Valipour, H.R.; Bradford, M.A. Experimental and analytical behaviour of steel-timber composite connections. *Constr. Build. Mater.* **2016**, *118*, 63–75. [CrossRef]
50. Wróblewski, T.; Pełka-Sawenko, A.; Abramowicz, M.; Berczyński, S. Parameter identification of steel-concrete composite beams by finite element method. *Diagnostyka* **2013**, *14*, 43–46.
51. Polus, Ł.; Szumigała, M. Finite element modelling of the connection for timber-concrete composite beams. *IOP Conf. Ser. Mater. Sci. Eng.* **2019**, *471*, 052081. [CrossRef]

Article

Efficient Design of Thin Wall Seating Made of a Single Piece of Heavy-Duty Corrugated Cardboard

Berta Suarez *, Luisa M. Muneta, Gregorio Romero and Juan D. Sanz-Bobi

Mechanical Engineering Department, Escuela Técnica Superior de Ingenieros Industriales, Universidad Politécnica de Madrid, C/José Gutiérrez Abascal, 2, 28006 Madrid, Spain; luisa.mtzmuneta@upm.es (L.M.M.); gregorio.romero@upm.es (G.R.); juandedios.sanz@upm.es (J.D.S.-B.)
* Correspondence: b.suarez@upm.es

Citation: Suarez, B.; Muneta, L.M.; Romero, G.; Sanz-Bobi, J.D. Efficient Design of Thin Wall Seating Made of a Single Piece of Heavy-Duty Corrugated Cardboard. *Materials* **2021**, *14*, 6645. https://doi.org/10.3390/ma14216645

Academic Editors: Tomasz Garbowski, Tomasz Gajewski and Jakub Krzysztof Grabski

Received: 18 September 2021
Accepted: 30 October 2021
Published: 4 November 2021

Publisher's Note: MDPI stays neutral with regard to jurisdictional claims in published maps and institutional affiliations.

Copyright: © 2021 by the authors. Licensee MDPI, Basel, Switzerland. This article is an open access article distributed under the terms and conditions of the Creative Commons Attribution (CC BY) license (https://creativecommons.org/licenses/by/4.0/).

Abstract: Corrugated cardboard has waved cores with small flutes that prevent the use of detailed numerical models of whole structures. Many homogenization methods in the literature overcome this drawback by defining equivalent homogeneous plates with the same mechanical behaviour at a macro-mechanical scale. However, few homogenization works have considered complete structures, focusing mainly on beams or plates. For the first time, this study explores the application of homogenization approaches to larger structures as an aid in their design process. We also considered triple-wall boards rather than single- and double-wall configurations commonly addressed in the literature. To this end, we adapted the homogenization methods proposed by Talbi and Duong to analyze thin-walled stools made of triple-wall corrugated cardboard. Using a progressive design process, we performed an efficient stool design by removing material zones with lower stresses, with 35% less material, 35% lower vertical deflections, and 66% lower stresses than the initial design. Unlike other corrugated cardboard stools, this design comprises just one folded piece instead of three, thus saving storage space. These results demonstrate the utility of homogenization techniques as an aid in the design process of whole structures made of corrugated cardboard. Further research will consider buckling analysis.

Keywords: composite sandwich structures; thin-walled structures; anisotropic material; corrugated core; homogenization approach; first-order shear deformation theory; FSDT; FEM simulation; finite element analysis; design process

1. Introduction

Finite element analysis (FEA) greatly facilitates the design process of many products, avoiding the construction of failed prototypes. Concerning products made of corrugated cardboard, this advantage is not so evident since it is inexpensive and easy to handle, so that prototypes have low economic and time costs. In this paper, the authors aim to show that FEA can also be very useful when designing products made with this material. The main advantage is not to avoid prototyping, but to guide the design stages towards more efficient solutions. Likewise, it could help to choose the most suitable type of cardboard for each product, avoiding the need to gather an extensive assortment of materials to test different prototypes.

In this work, we applied FEA to a piece of furniture made of corrugated cardboard to achieve a more efficient design. To define the material properties, we adapted the homogenization methods proposed by Talbi [1] and Duong [2], as described in Section 2.3.

Conventional furniture designs often rely on traditional knowledge in handicraft manufacturing. Moreover, their structural elements are often intentionally oversized. However, FEA becomes an essential tool when dealing with unconventional furniture made of thin-wall structural elements. In [3–9], we can find some studies on the FEA of wood furniture. Other previous research studies also considered other materials, such as laminated bamboo [10], honeycomb cardboard [11], corrugated cardboard [12] or fibre-reinforced concrete [13].

1.1. Corrugated Cardboard

Corrugated cardboard is a material for everyday use, light, economical and sustainable. In addition to packaging, it can have other uses, such as construction and indoor furniture [14–16]. Its high strength-to-weight ratio makes it ideal for furniture manufacturing, though a careful design is needed to ensure rigidity.

It presents a sandwich structure with small waves in the intermediate layers (Figure 1), called fluting. Flutings are glued to flat sheets of paper, called liners, with a water-resistant starch-based adhesive [17]. Liners support bending loads, and flutings support transverse shear, helping to stabilize the former by resisting out-of-plane deformations [18,19]. In this way, the mechanical properties of liners and flutings are efficiently combined [20], providing a higher stiffness-to-weight ratio than an equivalent solid panel made of any of the individual constituent materials [21]. Liners are usually made of softwood kraft pulp to provide strength, with grammages ranging from 125 to 440 g/m^2, while flutings have lower grammages, from 80 to 180 g/m^2 [15,17,20]. Boards can present various wall configurations: single-sided, with only one fluting and one liner, and single-, double- and triple-wall (Figure 1), with the strength increasing with the number of plies.

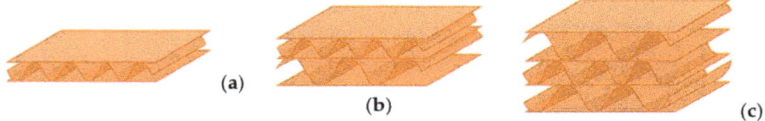

Figure 1. Board styles: (**a**) single-wall; (**b**) double-wall; (**c**) triple-wall. Reprinted with permission from ref. [12]. Copyright 2021 Elsevier.

Flutings are classified by their height and the number of flutes per unit length. Table 1 shows the most common flute types, designated as A, B, C, E or F, the C flute being the most commonly used for boxes. There are other less common flute types, such as D, with a height of 2 mm; G, thinner than 0.55 mm; K, thicker than 5.0 mm; and even a thinner flute, called O [15,22]. These letters were assigned according to their introduction into the market, having no relation to their size [17]. Larger flutes provide greater vertical strength and cushioning, while smaller flutes enhance graphic capabilities and structural integrity.

Table 1. Common flute types [15,23]. Reprinted with permission from ref. [12]. Copyright 2021 Elsevier.

Designation	Picture	Height (in)	Height (mm)	Flutes/m	Pitch (mm)	Take-Up Factor
A flute		1/4″	4.8	108 ± 10	8.0–9.5	≈1.50
B flute		1/8″	3.2	154 ± 10	5.5–6.5	≈1.40
C flute		11/64″	4.0	128 ± 10	6.8–7.9	≈1.45
E flute		1/16″	1.6	295 ± 13	3.0–3.5	≈1.25
F flute		1/32″	0.8	420 ± 13	1.9–2.6	≈1.25

In paperboard manufacture, cellulose fibres tend to align in the flow direction, called machine direction (MD) [15]. The perpendicular direction on the paperboard surface is called cross direction (CD). Corrugated cardboard has the same manufacture direction that paperboard [24], MD being perpendicular to the principal axes of the corrugations and CD parallel to them (Figure 2). Then, both paper and corrugated cardboard are orthotropic materials, with better mechanical properties in MD than in CD [15,25].

Figure 2. Machine direction (MD), cross direction (CD) and through-thickness direction (ZD). Reprinted with permission from ref. [12]. Copyright 2021 Elsevier.

Being a low-cost, lightweight, and environmentally friendly material, the use of corrugated cardboard for packaging has steadily increased in the past decade [19,26]. The global production of packaging paper and board increased from 193 to 256 million tons between 2008 and 2018 [27]. This effect was also influenced by the growth of online commerce [28]. In 2020, the global demand for containerboard was 69 million tons, 40% of the global demand for paper [29]. In 2018, the recycling rate for paper and cardboard packaging in the EU was 83% [30] of waste material. Waste cardboard can be used in its original form, but it can also be used in new composite materials [28].

Due to its great strength-to-weight ratio, excellent burst strength and resistance to crushing, corrugated cardboard is also suitable for furniture manufacture. However, a careful design is needed to ensure rigidity [31]. Thus, a good understanding of its mechanical behaviour is required to use it in an optimum way. Many previous studies have focused on the properties of corrugated cardboard and how the external environment affects its performance [20,32–36]. The mechanical properties of various types of liners and flutings in MD and CD can be found in [1,17,24,25,33,37–49].

1.2. Thin-Wall Furniture

Based on its thickness, we can classify the structural elements of furniture as ultrathin, below 10 mm; thin, from 10 to 15 mm; standard, from 16 to 19 mm; thick, from 20 to 40 mm; and ultra-thick, above 40 mm [50]. Thin-wall furniture, made of thin or ultrathin structural materials, is a current trend in furniture design [51]. It is usually made of wood composite panels, such as plywood, particleboard, or medium-density fibreboard (MDF), which can be laminated with other materials [50]. Due to its light weight, it can be considered a good alternative for trade shows and conventions. It can even be a suitable option for students or professionals with upward mobility, who will probably move often.

When dealing with the design of thin-wall furniture, a structural calculation is of particular relevance [50]. In addition to the strength requirements imposed on the materials, a second challenge lies in the joints between different panels [28,51]. Thin-walled structures can also exhibit buckling and warping problems, extensively studied in the scientific literature. Some analytical, numerical, and experimental studies on the buckling analysis of thin-wall beams can be found in [52,53]. Other studies on the buckling of corrugated cardboard structures can be found in [37,44,46,54,55].

In this work, our objective was to design a thin-wall furniture piece made of a different material, such as heavy-duty corrugated cardboard, whose sandwich structure could provide the required strength. Compared to wood composites, it has the advantage of being foldable. Thus, it requires fewer joints. Being low-cost and easy to transport and mount, in addition to the applications mentioned above, it can also be considered to meet the needs for accommodation in improvised shelters for emergencies [56].

Corrugated Cardboard Furniture

Corrugated cardboard furniture is usually made of pieces that could be flat-packed and assembled at home, using folds, slots and tabs. In the early 1960s, Peter Murdoch designed the Spotty chair [57], a flat-pack disposable chair that could be assembled simply by folding it in shape. In the early 1970s, Craig Hodgetts, Robert Mangurian, and Keith Godard designed Punch-Out [31], a low-cost furniture line made of heavy-duty corrugated cardboard, with flat pieces that even children could assemble to form their own tables and chairs. Today, many specialized companies [58–69] offer a great variety of corrugated cardboard furniture (such as chairs, armchairs, tables, shelves, beds, standing desks or podiums) [70], to be used at home, the office or trade shows. Many freelance designers also present their designs of corrugated cardboard furniture in design and architectural social media platforms or blogs [71–73].

As evidence of the growing interest in this type of furniture, the Japanese bedding company Airweave [74] provided 18,000 and 8000 high-resistance cardboard beds for Olympians and Paralympians at the 2020 Tokyo Olympics [75,76]. They were conceived as a recycling initiative and were intended to be converted into other paper products. They will be reused for COVID-19 patients in a temporary medical facility in Osaka [77].

Another use of waste corrugated cardboard, as part of lightweight multi-layered panels with alternating plies of corrugated cardboard and veneer, was examined in [28]. Their study, considering different types of end corner joints between rigid panels, confirmed the suitability of this material for furniture and interior applications.

1.3. Homogenization Techniques

Different approaches can be used to analyze the strength of corrugated cardboard products: experimental [78]; analytical [79,80]; analytical-numerical [81–83] or purely numerical [33,84–86]. Due to the small size of the fluting, numerical methods are inadequate to analyze any structure made with this material on a micromechanical scale. Instead, we may use homogenization approaches. They allow considering its sandwich structure as a homogeneous plate [87,88], providing almost as accurate responses for homogenized models as for real structures [89].

Some homogenization techniques use analytic methods to obtain the engineering constants of the equivalent material [48,90–93]. Others apply the classical laminate theory (CLT) or the first-order shear deformation theory (FSDT) [1,2,45,94,95] to obtain the stiffness matrix of an equivalent plate [1,2,19,45,96–99]. Others use FEA of a representative volume element (RVE) to find an equivalent homogeneous plate [43,100–104].

Most homogenization studies centre on isolated flutings or single-wall corrugated boards, though some of them also consider double-walled corrugated panels [41,94,98,105–107]. Moreover, most of the existing literature on corrugated cardboard models focuses on homogenization methods, with few practical applications in actual designs.

1.4. Scope of the Study

This work aims to apply FEA for the structural calculation of corrugated cardboard furniture as an aid in its design process. As an example, we chose a stool made of this material to show the effectiveness of this method. This paper shows the process we followed to design the stool, performing a structural calculation of each intermediate design to assess its validity. In a future study, we also intend to consider a buckling analysis of the different design stages. However, this is beyond the scope of this work.

2. Materials and Methods

2.1. Design Stages

As a starting point, we based the first design on the geometry of a commercial stool, the so-called Kenno Stool [108,109] (Figure 3), designed by the Finnish designer Heikki Ruoho [110,111]. We chose this model for its simplicity. It comprises three pieces assembled perpendicularly, forming a closed structure that can be used as either a stool or a low table. It has a trapezoidal shape, resting on the ground, indistinctly, either on the wide or narrow part of the trapezoid. It has two vertical sidewalls with a vertical groove in the middle of their upper side. They are placed parallel to each other and covered by a third piece, whose ends fit into the groove of the former pieces.

Figure 3. 1st design with: (**a**) bottom discontinuity; (**b**) top discontinuity.

We slightly increased its dimensions, since the original stool was conceived for children. We also replaced the original honeycomb cardboard with heavy-duty triple-wall corrugated cardboard [112–115], with which we obtained excellent results in a previous study of cardboard seating [12]. A 1970s child's chair design from the hplusf design lab was made with this material. It was called Punch-out [116] and was temporarily exhibited at the MoMA [117]. Today, some contemporary furniture manufacturers, such as Chairigami (USA) [118] or Konno Konpou (Japan) [119], also use this material.

We applied FEA to this design, using a homogenization approach to characterize the mechanical properties of corrugated cardboard. In Section 2.3 and Appendix A, we present a thorough description of the homogenization technique used in this work.

From the numerical analysis performed, we obtained the deflections and stresses of this stool under some applied loads, according to the European Standards EN 1728 [120] and EN 12520 [121], both applicable to seating designs.

We then modified this design by removing both side panels. Therefore, the second design consisted of a single piece that the final user could fold for storage (Figure 4).

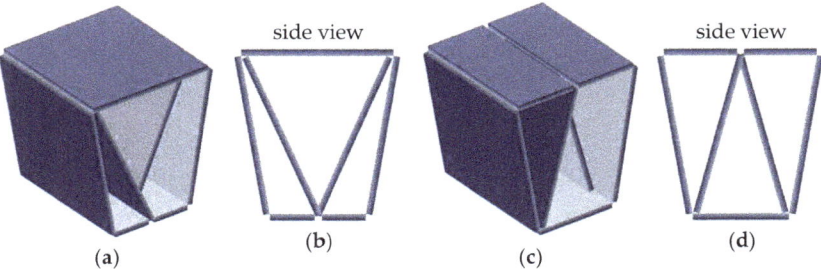

Figure 4. 2nd design with: (**a**,**b**) bottom discontinuity; (**c**,**d**) top discontinuity.

We lengthened the ends of the cardboard panel towards the opposite face and crossed them to ensure the structural strength of the stool. To maintain the total width of the top/bottom face, we placed the crossing point near it. We also reduced the width of one end to insert it into a slot made at the opposite end. The stool should also have two grooves on the top/bottom surface for inserting both ends, preventing them from moving. We also analyzed this design under the same load conditions.

To achieve more significant savings in material and storage space, we even opened the stool downward by removing the lower face (Figure 5). We now crossed both ends at an intermediate height inside the stool. However, it could rest only on the edges that limit the open surface, having a single possible position, unlike the previous designs.

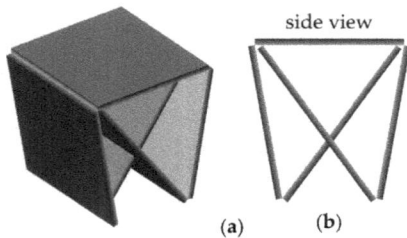

Figure 5. 3rd design: (**a**) perspective view; (**b**) front view.

Next, we modified the design by cutting both ends of the stool directly from the front and rear walls, opening a hole in those walls and folding the cut material inward (Figure 6a). This design saves even more material and storage space, since its ends could be placed inside the cut walls again. The angle formed between the front/rear wall and the seating surface should be the same as the angle between the ends and the seating surface, since both pieces should have the same length. During preliminary simulations, high longitudinal displacements were found at the bottom edges. Hence, we closed it on the bottom side by extending the front/rear walls to the bottom (Figure 6b) and connecting them.

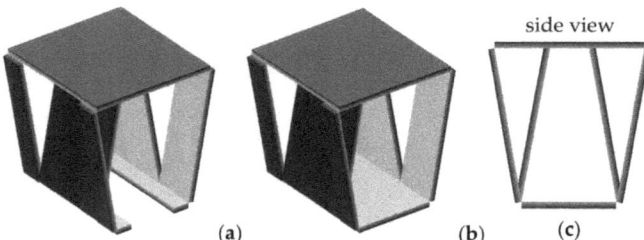

Figure 6. 4th design: (**a**) preliminary open design; (**b**) final closed design; (**c**) side view.

Taking into account the orthotropic behaviour of corrugated cardboard, we analyzed each design for two material orientations: orientation I, with MD (x-axis) parallel to the folding lines, supposed to provide higher bending stiffness, and orientation II, with CD (y-axis) parallel to the folding lines, supposed to ease the folding process. We also considered two different body orientations: the wide part of the trapezium facing up and down.

The results thus obtained clearly show the utility of FEA, even for products made of an inexpensive and easy-to-handle material such as corrugated cardboard.

2.2. Finite Element Models

To develop the FE models of the stool designs, we used commercial software that includes a specific module for the structural analysis of composite materials.

We modelled the stool as a layered linear elastic shell. To do so, we combined the shell elements with a layered linear elastic material suitable for orthotropic laminates. In this way, the program applied the FSDT formulation internally. As input data, we introduced the stiffness matrices of the inner liners, the outer liners, and the fluting, together with the thickness and material model of each layer of the sandwich panel. We also used solid elements to model the loading pad used to apply loads on the seating surface.

We defined the contact conditions between intersecting panels using a mapped mesh defined so that two intersecting panels share the shell nodes lying on their intersection line. To define the contact between the solid elements of the loading pad and the shell elements of the stool panels, we used a multiphysics coupling provided by the commercial software; specifically, we used a solid-thin structure connection for this purpose.

Finally, we performed a static analysis with each model.

In the following sections, we define the FE model in more detail.

2.2.1. Geometry

All the designs considered had a seating surface 380 mm long and 400 mm wide and a height of 400 mm (Figure 7).

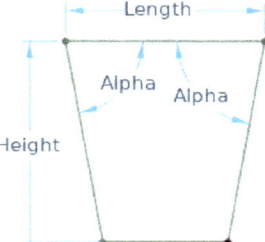

Figure 7. Model main dimensions.

We built finite element (FE) models of all stool designs using homogenized shells with a mapped mesh (Figure 8) made up of square elements approximately 5 mm long. The number of boundary elements used in the models shown in Figure 8 ranges from 1704 for model (f) to 3810 for model (b).

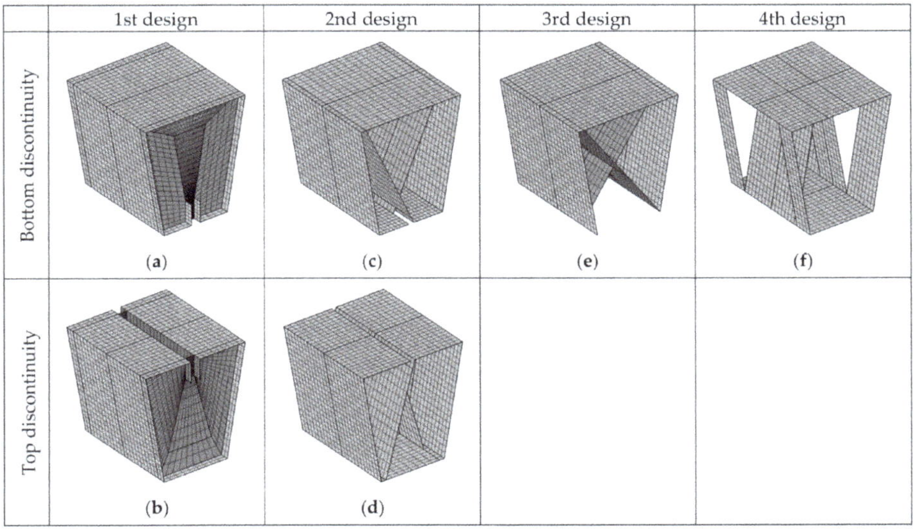

Figure 8. Mapped meshes: (**a**,**b**) 1st design with bottom/top discontinuity; (**c**,**d**) 2nd design with bottom/top discontinuity; (**e**) 3rd design; (**f**) 4th design.

The angle α between the top and front/rear panels was modified from 70° to 90°, with a 5° step, preserving the length of the seating surface. We considered the fourth design with α = 90° just for comparison, since it could rotate around the edges formed by the top and front/rear panels, thus being unstable. Figure 9 gathers the geometry variations for the fourth design to show where the board ends intersect the seating surface.

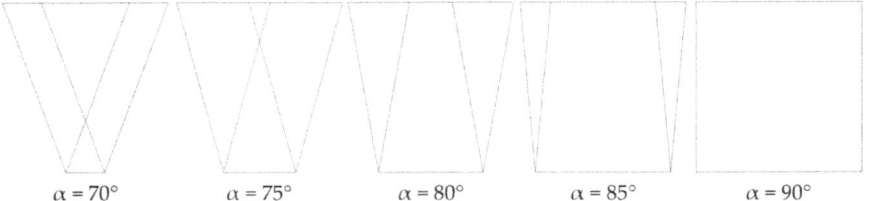

Figure 9. Geometry variations for the 4th design.

2.2.2. Material

The material considered for all designs was a heavy-duty triple-wall A-flute corrugated cardboard. Its homogenized properties were defined in the FE model using a layered material with seven layers: 1 and 7 are outer liners, 3 and 5 inner liners, and 2, 4, and 6 flutings (Figure 10). For each layer, we introduced either the liner thickness or the fluting height, together with its homogenized stiffness matrix, previously computed as described in Appendix A.

Figure 10. Layered material.

We used the engineering constants of the constituent materials reported in [45] to compute the stiffness matrices, since they have high elastic moduli and would provide high bending stiffness. Table 2 shows the engineering constants, E_i, G_{ij}, and ν_{ij}. They are given in the lamina reference frame, with the 2-axis parallel to the CD, and the 1-axis parallel to the MD.

Table 2. Material properties: elastic moduli, E_i, shear moduli, G_{ij}, and Poisson ratios, ν_{ij}. Reprinted with permission from ref. [12]. Copyright 2021 Elsevier.

Parameter	Unit	Heavy Duty		
		Outer Liner	Inner Liner	Fluting
E_1	MPa	8250	8180	4500
E_2	MPa	2900	3120	4500
E_3	MPa	2900	3120	3000
G_{23}	MPa	70	70	35
G_{13}	MPa	7	7	3.5
G_{12}	MPa	1890	1950	1500
ν_{12}	-	0.43	0.43	0.40
ν_{13}	-	0.01	0.01	0.01
ν_{23}	-	0.01	0.01	0.01
t	mm	0.75	0.40	0.25
h	mm	-	-	4.8
P	mm	-	-	8.5

To model the height and period of the fluting, we took the values indicated in the Tri-Wall Pak patent [114] for A flutes. We also took the thicknesses stated in [114] for the liners. For the fluting, we considered the grammage of 150 g/m^2 specified in [113], corresponding to a thickness of 0.25 mm. Table 2 also shows the thickness of the liners and fluting, t, and the height, h, and period, P, of the fluting, all taken from the references mentioned above.

We also considered two orientations: I, with MD (red x-axis) parallel to the folding lines, and II, with CD (green y-axis) parallel to the folding lines (Figure 11).

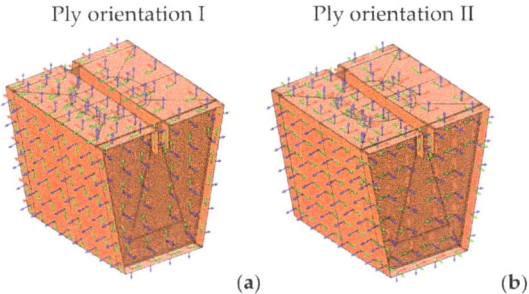

Figure 11. 1st design with top discontinuity (red: MD; green: CD). Ply orientation: (**a**) I; (**b**) II.

2.2.3. Loads and Constraints

We applied the load distribution defined in the Eurocode EN 1728 [120], using a cylindrical loading pad, placed 175 mm from the front edge of the seat and centred on the width of the seating surface (Figure 12).

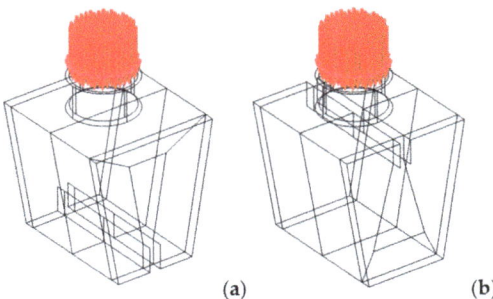

Figure 12. Loads applied to the 1st design with bottom (**a**) and top (**b**) discontinuity.

We modelled the pad as a solid steel cylinder with 180 mm diameter, covered with a 10 mm layer of polyurethane foam, using a free tetrahedral mesh. We applied a vertical force of 1300 N, according to Eurocode EN 12520 [121], for domestic seats. It was uniformly distributed on the upper surface of the cylinder and transmitted to the shell through a multiphysics coupling.

We applied simply supported boundary conditions at the lower edges of the folded panels (Figure 13). We restricted the three displacements of the lower front edge, but only the lateral, y, and vertical, z, displacements of the lower back edge (shown in blue).

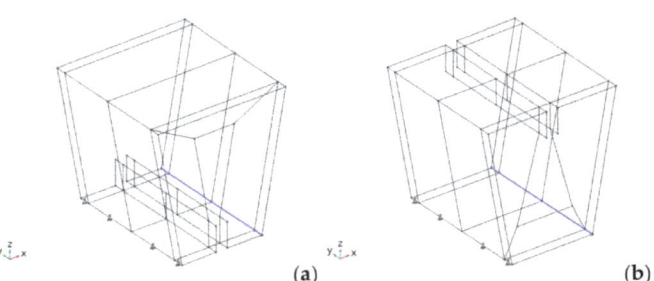

Figure 13. Boundary conditions applied to the 1st design with bottom (**a**) and top (**b**) discontinuity.

2.3. Homogenization Approach

In this study, we applied a homogenization approach based on the first-order shear deformation theory (FSDT). It is an evolution of our previous work [12], which was in turn based on previous research by Talbi [1] and Duong [2].

The stiffness matrix of any lamina of a laminate can be easily formulated in the lamina reference frame, 123. However, to use a common reference system, we need to express the stiffness matrices of all laminas in the global laminate reference frame, xyz. This process is straightforward for liners, since they are flat, but not for flutings. Due to their waved shape, the material parameters for each section differ from the laminate reference frame, xyz, to the lamina reference frame, 123, in which they are known [87] (see Figure 14). Thus, we need to change the reference system of the stiffness matrix of the flutings.

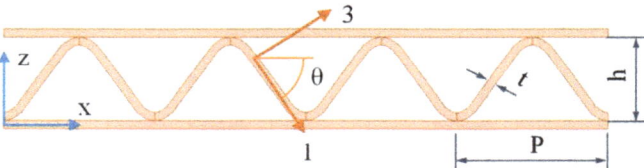

Figure 14. Corrugated lamina showing the laminate, xyz, and lamina, 123, reference frames. Reprinted with permission from ref. [12]. Copyright 2021 Elsevier.

Berthelot [55] applied a similar method to composite materials by rotating around the z-axis, normal to the laminate. For corrugated materials, however, the rotation has to be performed around the y-axis, or CD. Talbi [1] and Duong [2] performed this change of reference system to formulate their homogenization methods for single- and double-wall corrugated cardboard panels, respectively. Once the stiffness matrix of the fluting was transformed, they applied the FSDT to simplify the constitutive equations. Then, they integrated the stresses through the whole laminate thickness to get the internal forces, N and T, and the bending moments, M. After the integration, the z coordinate disappeared from the formulation, reducing the problem's dimensionality from 3D to 2D. Then, they performed a second integration along the MD over a fluting period to obtain the average values. In this way, they expressed the generalized constitutive law as follows.

$$\begin{bmatrix} N \\ M \\ T \end{bmatrix} = \begin{bmatrix} A & B & 0 \\ B & D & 0 \\ 0 & 0 & H \end{bmatrix} \cdot \begin{bmatrix} \varepsilon_m \\ \kappa \\ \gamma_s \end{bmatrix} \quad (1)$$

ε_m is the membrane strain vector, κ the curvature vector, and γ_s the transverse shear strain vector. A is the extensional stiffness matrix, D the bending stiffness matrix, B the bending-extension coupling stiffness matrix and H the transverse shear stiffness matrix. These matrices can be used to model a homogenized shell. For small structures, such as beams or plates, FE analysis can be performed analytically. However, when dealing with larger structures, an FE code is needed. Some FE packages include the FSDT formulation and directly work with the A, B, D, and H matrices. If it is not included, we can use the expressions found in the literature for the engineering constants of the homogenized shell as functions of these matrices [19,122].

In a previous work [12], we also applied this homogenization method. We computed the A, B, D, and H matrices outside the FE model and introduced them into the FE model. However, no additional information concerning the thickness and number of laminas was needed to perform the analysis. Since the FE model had no information to undo the homogenization after the simulation, the results of the analyses were averaged over the laminate thickness, and we needed to post-process them.

In this work, we used a different approach to avoid this post-processing, thus facilitating the graphical representation of the simulation results. As before, we changed the reference system to express the stiffness matrices of the corrugated layers in the laminate reference frame. Unlike before, this time, we directly introduced these matrices into the FE model. However, since they depend on the x-coordinate, they need to be processed before being introduced into the FE model. Thus, we performed a similar integration to that made by Talbi and Duong, but not on the A, B, D, and H matrices, but on the stiffness matrix of the corrugated layers. To do so, we first averaged each matrix through the z-coordinate and then over the x-direction, or MD (see Appendix A).

We then introduced the stiffness matrix of each layer into the FE model. We used a specialized module for composite materials that includes a layered linear elastic material model, which internally performs a second homogenization through the thickness of the whole laminate. It is based on the FSDT, like the methods of Talbi and Duong. This time, the total number of laminas and their respective thickness had to be introduced into the FE model. Then, it had the necessary information to undo the homogenization after the simulations. In this way, the results directly show different stress fields for each lamina, instead of just an average value, with no further post-processing.

The main drawback of this method is that it cannot be performed with basic FE packages but only with specific modules for composite materials. In return, we could simplify the calculation of the stiffness matrices while increasing the precision of the results of the FE analysis. Unlike before, any change in the number of sandwich layers or their thickness can be made directly inside the FE model, keeping the same stiffness matrices. Only when we want to change the geometry of the corrugated layers, we would need to recalculate their stiffness matrices outside the FE model. Using an FE module specialized in composite materials, this methodology also allows one to change the orientation of the corrugated panel and even to consider different orientations for individual layers inside the panel. If desired, it is also possible to perform delamination studies.

3. Results and Discussion
3.1. Homogenized Material Properties

Table 3 gathers the nonzero elements of the stiffness matrices computed for each layer of the corrugated board in the laminate reference frame, using Voigt notation. The fluting has lower values than the liners, since it is mainly void.

Table 3. Elements of the stiffness matrix for each layer, in Voigt notation.

Q_{ij}	Unit	Outer Liner	Inner Liner	Fluting
Q_{11}	[MPa]	8824.2	8801.4	146.2
Q_{12}	[MPa]	1334.2	1444	59.807
Q_{13}	[MPa]	44.361	48.01	145.44
Q_{22}	[MPa]	3102	3357.2	361.6
Q_{23}	[MPa]	35.71	39.08	59.755
Q_{33}	[MPa]	2900.5	3120.6	146.14
Q_{44}	[MPa]	70	70	4.5198
Q_{55}	[MPa]	7	7	0.90365
Q_{66}	[MPa]	1890	1950	5.9147

3.2. Parametric Study for $\alpha = 70°$ to $90°$

For the four stool designs, we performed a parametric variation of α, from 70° to 90°, with a step of 5°. The influence of α found in the vertical deflections for the first, second, and third designs is very low. Similarly, its influence on the longitudinal deflections is also low for the first design. Figure 15 shows the longitudinal deflections for the second and third designs. For the second design, they decrease with increasing α, while for the third design, they increase with increasing α.

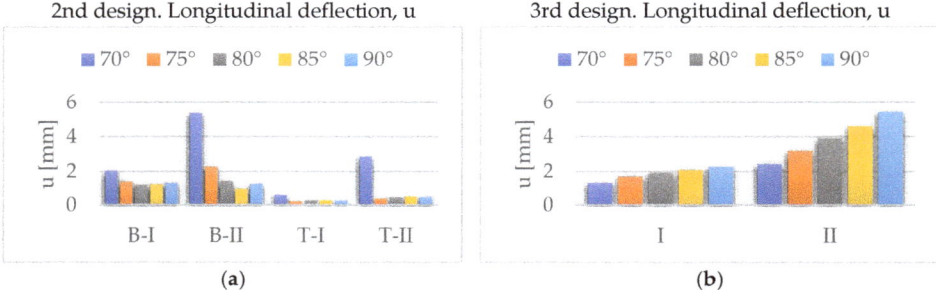

Figure 15. Evolution of maximum longitudinal deflections, u, with α, for designs: (**a**) 2nd; (**b**) 3rd.

Figure 16 shows the vertical and longitudinal deflections found for the fourth design. The former have a minimum for $\alpha = 80°$ and the latter for $\alpha = 75°$. However, since the vertical deflections are better for $\alpha = 80°$, we consider this the best angle.

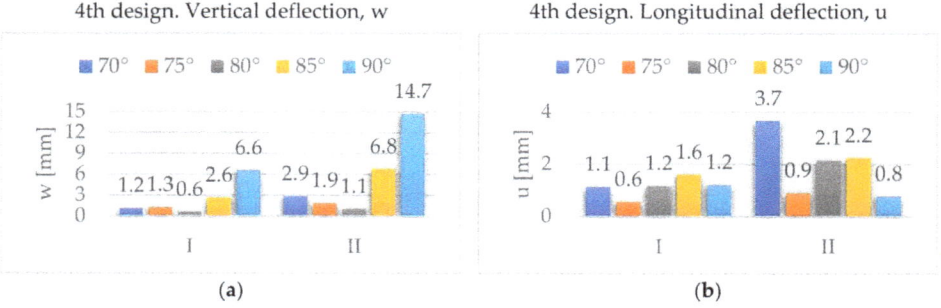

Figure 16. Evolution of maximum deflections with α, for the 4th design: (**a**) w; (**b**) u.

Figure 17 shows the stress distributions σ_{xx} and σ_{yy} in the global reference system for the fourth design. For both orientations, σ_{xx} and σ_{yy} also present a minimum for $\alpha = 80°$.

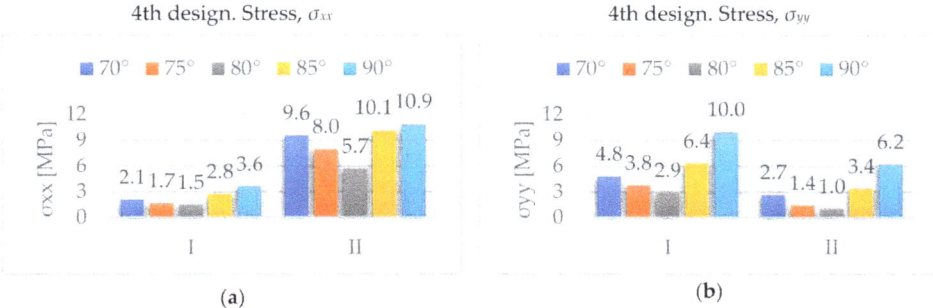

Figure 17. Evolution of maximum stresses [MPa] with α, for the 4th design: (**a**) σ_{xx}; (**b**) σ_{yy}.

3.3. Analysis of Designs with $\alpha = 80°$

3.3.1. First Design for $\alpha = 80°$

This paragraph shows the results obtained for the first design with $\alpha = 80°$ (see Figure 7), considered the best angle from the parametric analysis. Deflections u, v and w, are respectively aligned with the global x-, y- and z-axes (see Figure 13).

Figure 18 shows the vertical deflections, w, for designs with bottom and top discontinuities and both ply orientations.

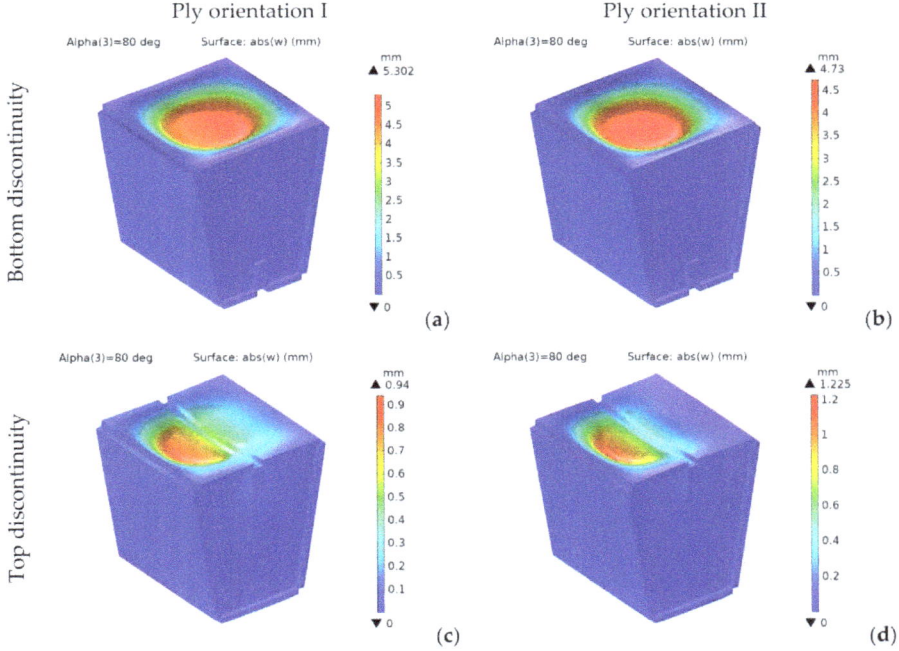

Figure 18. 1st design. Vertical deflection [mm] for bottom (**a,b**) and top (**c,d**) discontinuity.

For the designs with bottom discontinuity, the vertical deflections show a revolution geometry about the vertical axis, with a flat bottom. Their maximum values for top discontinuity are located on the seating surface panel closest to the load application area.

For the designs with bottom discontinuity, they are 11% lower for orientation II. However, for the designs with top discontinuity, they are 23% lower for orientation I, which provides a higher bending stiffness. They are lower for the designs with top discontinuity. They show an 82% reduction for orientation I from bottom to top discontinuity and a 74% reduction for orientation II. We can explain this reduction by the span length of the seating surface, which has a single panel for bottom discontinuity, but is divided into two panels with half the span length for top discontinuity.

For both discontinuities, the longitudinal deflections are lower for orientation II. In any case, the four designs analyzed show small values, below 1 mm.

Since the material is orthotropic, we should not use von Mises stresses. Figures 19 and 20 respectively show the components σ_{xx} and σ_{yy} of the stress tensor in the laminate reference frame.

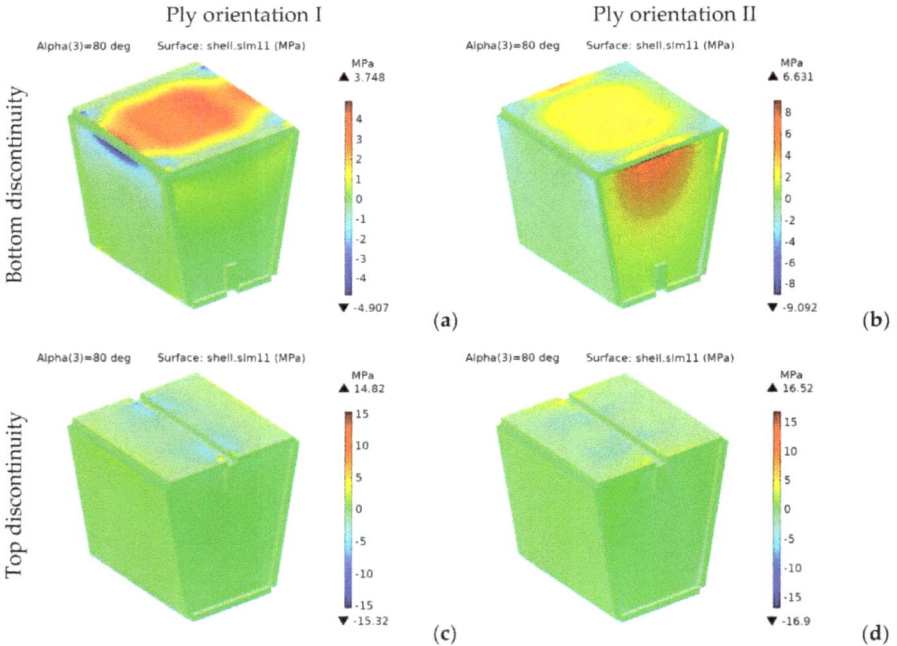

Figure 19. 1st design. Stress σ_{xx} [MPa] for bottom (**a**,**b**) and top (**c**,**d**) discontinuity.

For the designs with bottom discontinuity, σ_{xx} and σ_{yy} are distributed mainly on the seating surface. For orientation I, σ_{yy} is also transmitted to the front and rear panels. On the contrary, for orientation II, σ_{xx} and σ_{yy} are transmitted to the side panels.

For the designs with top discontinuity, the maximum stresses were found on the panels covering the sidewalls, specifically at the vertical ends inserted into the side panels' slots. Figure 21 shows the stress distribution for σ_{xx} and σ_{yy} for the designs with top discontinuity again, but now removing the front panel of the seating surface, thus revealing the stress distribution in such central panels, with the maximum stresses shown in dark red and dark blue.

According to the maximum stress criterion [123], applicable to orthotropic materials, the maximum values of σ_{xx} and σ_{yy} should be lower than the tensile strength of the constituent materials in the MD, $\sigma_{t,MD}$, and in the CD, $\sigma_{t,CD}$, respectively (see Figure 11).

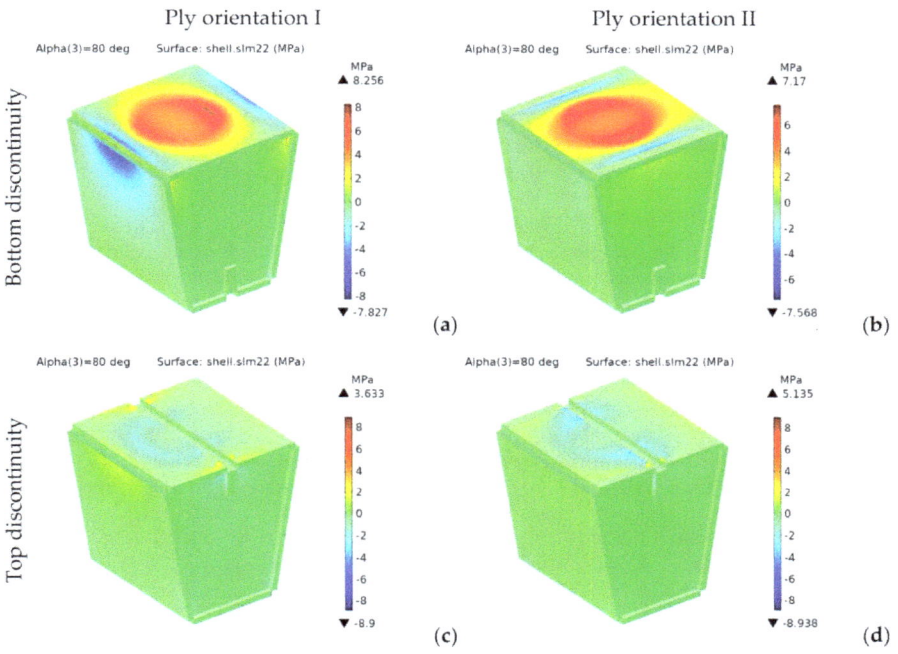

Figure 20. 1st design. Stress σ_{yy} [MPa] for bottom (**a**,**b**) and top (**c**,**d**) discontinuity.

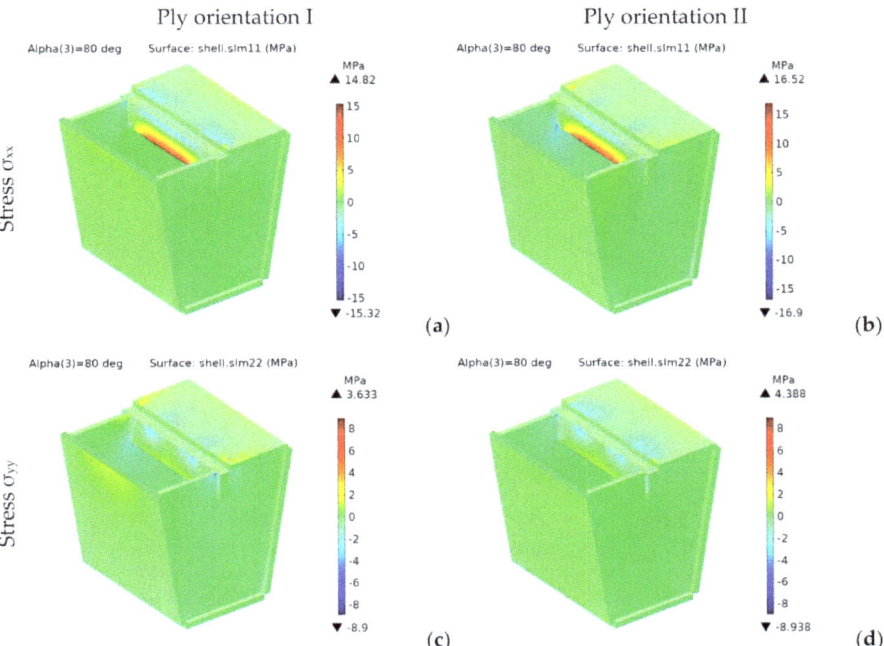

Figure 21. 1st design. Stresses under the seating surface for top discontinuity: (**a**,**b**) σ_{xx} [MPa], (**c**,**d**) σ_{yy} [MPa].

The tensile strength of structural paper can vary from 17 to more than 75 MPa in MD and from 9 to 35 MPa in CD [124]. In this study, we considered as reference values the tensile strengths found in [124] for a base paper with similar elastic moduli that the constituent materials of the analyzed stool: $\sigma_{t,MD}$ = 75.4 MPa in MD and $\sigma_{t,CD}$ = 22.7 MPa in CD. For these limit values, all the configurations analyzed meet the maximum stress criterion. Moreover, even for other materials with tensile strengths quite close to the lower limit of the stress ranges indicated above, the stresses obtained would be above the limit values.

3.3.2. Second Design for $\alpha = 80°$

This paragraph presents the results found for the second design with $\alpha = 80°$. Figure 22 shows the vertical deflections for designs with bottom and top discontinuities and both ply orientations.

For orientation I, the distributions of vertical deflections show a geometry of revolution about the vertical axis, but they have an almost cylindrical shape for orientation II.

They are lower for orientation I and top discontinuity, showing a 92% reduction (from 14.44 to 1.07 mm). The improvement due to orientation is substantially more significant than for the first design, with 57% and 65% reductions for configurations with bottom and top discontinuities, respectively. Regarding the discontinuity location, for the top position, we found 82% and 78% improvements for orientations I and II, respectively.

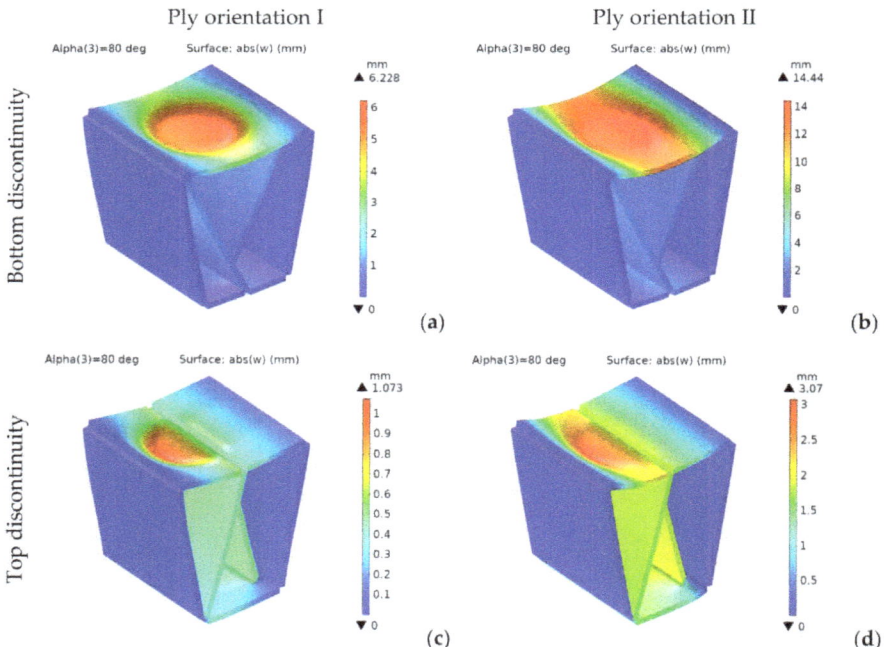

Figure 22. 2nd design. Vertical deflection [mm] for bottom (**a**,**b**) and top (**c**,**d**) discontinuity.

Longitudinal deflections range from 0.3 to 1.4 mm. They are also lower for orientation I and top discontinuity. For both orientations, the highest values are in the middle-upper part of the front inner panel.

Figures 23 and 24, respectively, show the stress distributions σ_{xx} and σ_{yy}.

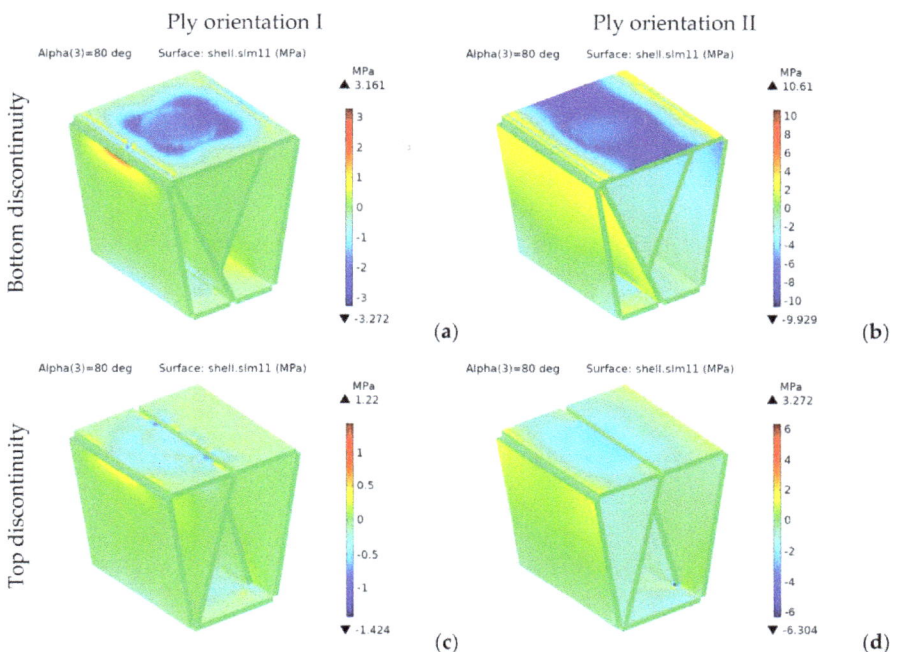

Figure 23. 2nd design. Stress σ_{xx} [MPa] for bottom (**a**,**b**) and top (**c**,**d**) discontinuity.

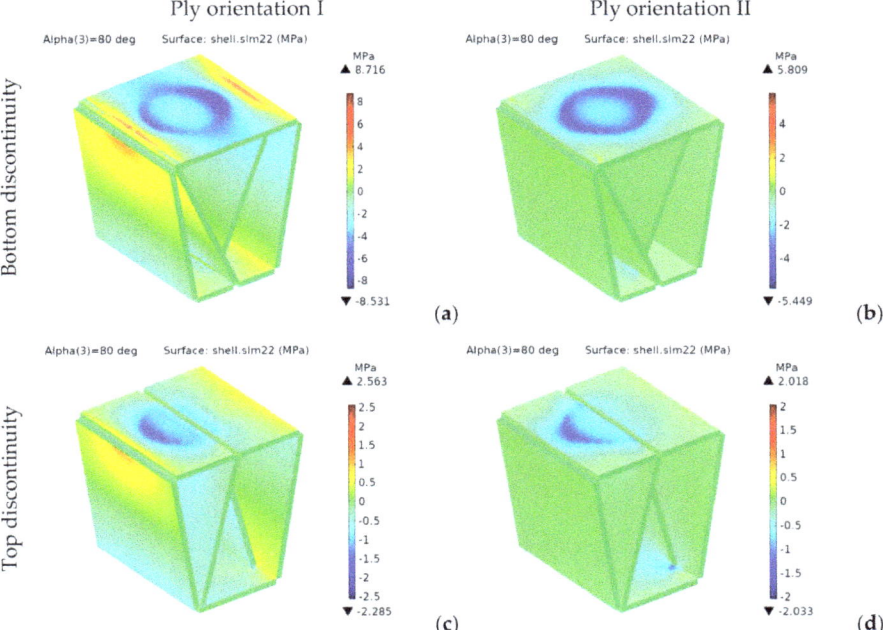

Figure 24. 2nd design. Stress σ_{yy} [MPa] for bottom (**a**,**b**) and top (**c**,**d**) discontinuity.

For the bottom discontinuity, the maximum stresses concentrate in the central area of the seating panel. For orientation I, they are transmitted to the front and rear panels. However, for orientation II they are transmitted to the lateral edges of the seating surface.

Both σ_{xx} and σ_{yy}, are below $\sigma_{t,MD}$ (75.4 MPa) and $\sigma_{t,CD}$ (22.7 MPa), thus complying with the maximum stress criterion. Moreover, they would also be valid for any other structural paper, whose tensile strengths in MD and CD are, respectively, higher than 17 and 9 MPa.

3.3.3. Third Design for $\alpha = 80°$

The stresses and vertical deflections are similar for the third design and the second design with bottom discontinuity. However, the longitudinal displacements are somewhat higher due to the removal of the lower panel. This effect was also shown in preliminary studies for the fourth design, with high longitudinal displacements of the lower rear edge (see Figure 5). Thus, we reintroduced the lower panel in the fourth design, since it prevents relative sliding between the front and rear lower edges.

3.3.4. Fourth Design for $\alpha = 80°$

This paragraph presents the results found for the fourth design with $\alpha = 80°$. Figure 25 shows both the vertical and longitudinal deflections for ply orientation I.

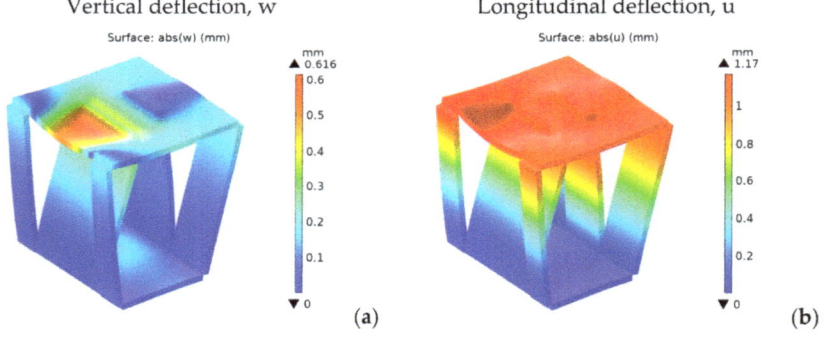

Figure 25. 4th design. Deflections for ply orientation I [mm]: (**a**) vertical, w; (**b**) longitudinal, u.

The trend showing lower vertical deflections for orientation I than for orientation II is maintained. For orientation I, they show an almost trapezoidal shape. For orientation II, they show an almost cylindrical shape placed on the front side of the stool, with its axis oriented from side to side. Maximum vertical and longitudinal deflections for orientation I are 0.6 and 1.2 mm, respectively, these being quite low.

Figure 26 shows the stress distributions σ_{xx} and σ_{yy} in the global reference system.

Besides the seating surface, there are other higher stresses at the intersection of the inner panels with the seating surface and on the folding lines at the lower edge of the front and rear panels, which appear to act as stress concentrators. This effect can be seen as a consequence of using less material. However, the stresses in these zones are quite below the tensile stresses. So, they do not pose any problem, at least from a static point of view.

Both σ_{xx} and σ_{yy} are much lower than $\sigma_{t,MD}$ (75.4 MPa) and $\sigma_{t,CD}$ (22.7 MPa), thus fulfilling the maximum stress criterion. They would also be valid for any other structural paper, whose tensile strengths in MD and CD are, respectively, higher than 17 and 9 MPa.

3.3.5. Comparative Results for $\alpha = 80°$

Figures 27 and 28 show the vertical and longitudinal deflections for all designs.

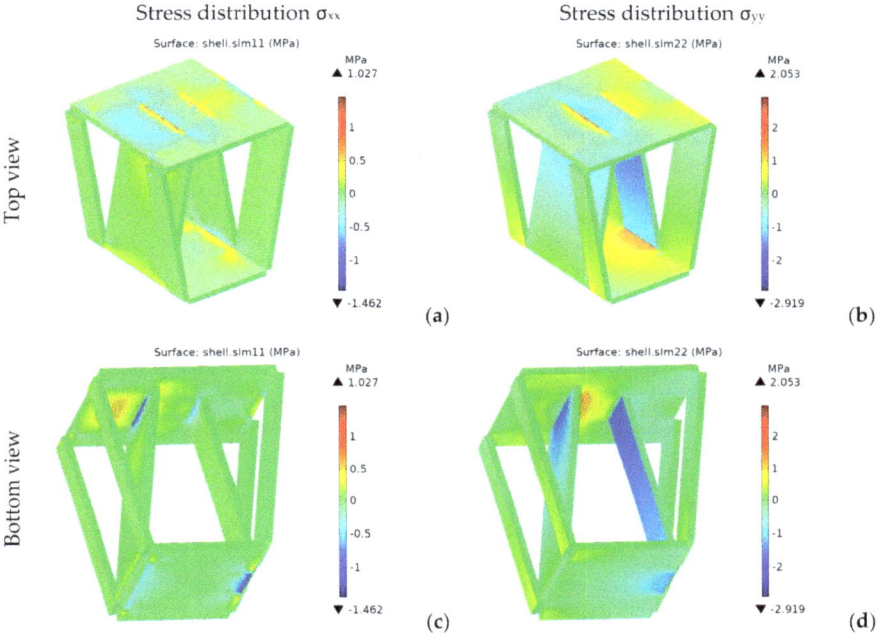

Figure 26. 4th design. Stress for ply orientation I [MPa] (**a**,**c**) σ_{xx}; (**b**,**d**) σ_{yy}.

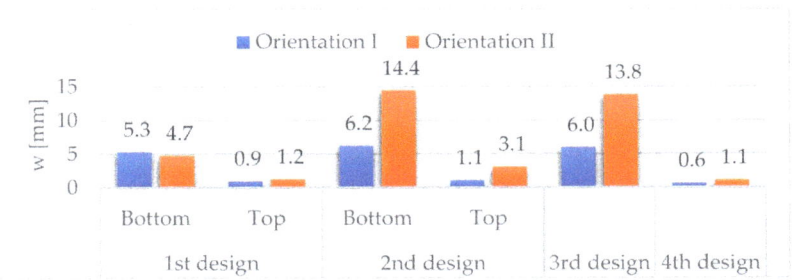

Figure 27. Vertical deflections, w.

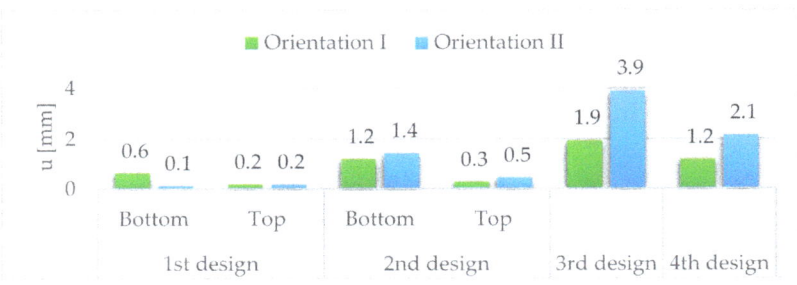

Figure 28. Longitudinal deflections, u.

The vertical deflections for orientation II are higher in the second than in the first design due to the elimination of the side panels. In contrast, for orientation I, they are of the same order of magnitude. In the worst case, the vertical deflections increase 206% (from 4.7 to 14.4 mm), from the first to the second design, while in the most favourable case, they increase by 22% (from 0.9 to 1.1 mm). We can explain this behaviour as the combination of the antagonistic effect of two factors: on the one hand, the negative effect of eliminating the side panels, especially in designs with orientation II, in which the stresses of the seating surface were transmitted to that panel, and on the other hand, the positive effect of introducing a new supporting system, with inner triangular structures. Although this second effect is beneficial for both orientations, it cannot overcome the negative effect of the other factor, especially in designs with orientation II.

For the best configurations of all the designs analyzed, the vertical deflections are lower for the fourth design, being 0.6 and 1.1 mm, respectively, for orientations I and II. Compared to the first design with top discontinuity, with vertical deflections of 0.9 and 1.2 mm, they are reduced by 33% and 8% for orientations I and II, respectively. Compared to the second design with top discontinuity, with deflections of 1.1 and 3.1 mm, they are reduced by 45% and 64%. Compared to the third design, with deflections of 6.0 and 13.8 mm, they are reduced by 90% and 92%. These reductions are lower with respect to the first and second designs because it was not possible to consider any configuration with top discontinuity in the third design.

It is remarkable that after removing a significant amount of material, the vertical deflections for the fourth design are even lower than for the first design with top discontinuity. This effect is due to the high efficiency of the inner panels added when removing the side panels from the first design, since they have a triangular structure, whose effectiveness is well known. Additionally, the results obtained for the fourth design are even better than those found for the second and third designs, which already included the inner panels. This behaviour is due to a better distribution of the intersection lines of the inner panels with the seating surface in the fourth design. The inner panels divide the seating surface into two halves, acting as intermediate supports in the second and third designs. However, they divide it into three zones in the fourth design, acting as two intermediate supports, thus reducing the span and, consequently, the maximum vertical deflections.

The longitudinal deflections are higher for the fourth than for the first and second designs. However, they are kept within reasonable limits of 1.2 mm for orientation I.

Figures 29 and 30 respectively show the stress distributions σ_{xx} and σ_{yy}.

For orientation II, σ_{xx} and σ_{yy} are lower for the fourth design than for any other design. We can see the same trend for orientation I, except for the second design with top discontinuity.

3.4. Summary Results

For the best configurations of each design for $\alpha = 80°$, Table 4 gathers the area, A, the vertical, w, and longitudinal, u, deflections and the stresses along MD, σ_{xx}, and CD, σ_{yy}.

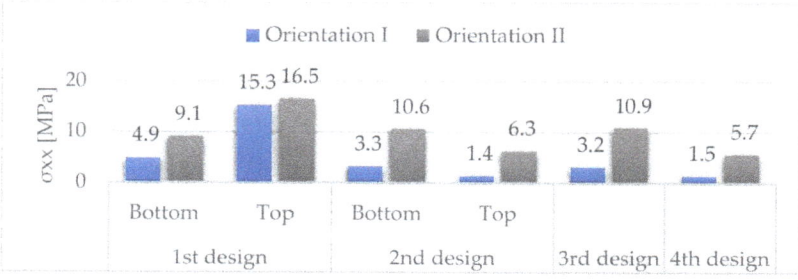

Figure 29. Stresses σ_{xx}.

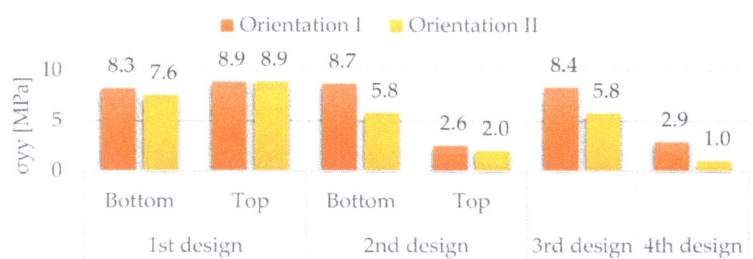

Figure 30. Stresses σ_{yy}.

Table 4. Comparative results for the best configurations found for each design, for $\alpha = 80°$.

Design	Area (m²)	w (mm)	u (mm)	σ_{xx} (MPa)	σ_{yy} (MPa)
1st	0.87	0.9	0.2	15.3	8.9
2nd	0.83	1.1	0.3	1.4	2.6
3rd	0.79	6.0	1.9	3.2	8.4
4th	0.57	0.6	1.2	1.5	2.9

Figure 31 shows the variation of these parameters compared to the best results of the first design, expressed as a percentage of the corresponding value in the first design.

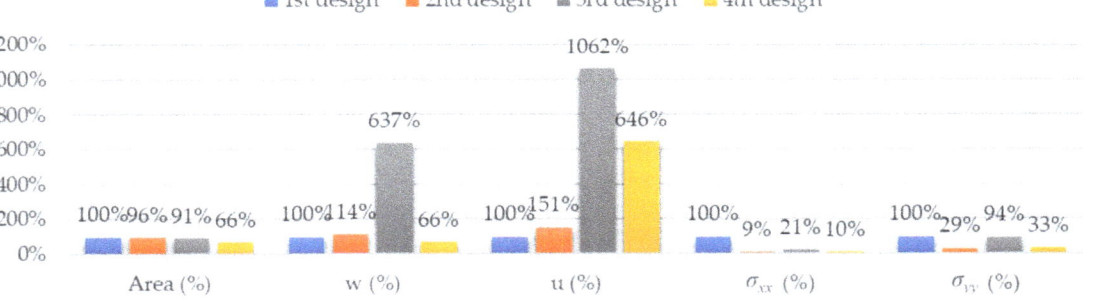

Figure 31. Comparative results for the best configurations found for each design.

In terms of deflections, the best results correspond to the fourth design, with orientation I and $\alpha = 80°$, with maximum vertical and longitudinal deflections of 0.6 and 1.2 mm, respectively. There is a noticeable improvement compared to the first design, from which it evolved, whose best results are maximum vertical and longitudinal deflections of 0.9 and 0.2 mm, respectively. These results lead to a 33% reduction for the vertical deflections, but a 500% increase for the longitudinal deflections. Despite the high increase for the longitudinal deflection, its maximum value is just slightly above 1 mm for the fourth design. Moreover, the fourth design has an area 34% lower than the first design.

We can extract the following conclusions regarding different aspects of the possible configurations of the stool design:

- Ply orientation. The vertical and longitudinal deflections are lower for orientation I, except for the first design, with slightly lower values for orientation I with bottom discontinuity.

- Discontinuity location. The vertical and longitudinal deflections are lower for designs with top discontinuity, because the seating surface is divided into two different panels with half the span of the whole seating surface.
- Bottom panel. We should keep the bottom panel, because it prevents longitudinal sliding between the lower edges of the front and rear panels.
- α angle: In the first three designs, α has little influence on the vertical deflections. However, in the fourth design, the lowest vertical deflections correspond to an intermediate angle of $80°$. The best results correspond to those angles leading to a more uniform distribution of the seating surface. That is, for those designs with the inner panels dividing the seating surface into three zones of equal length, so that none of them tends to present more significant deflections than the others (see Figure 8).

4. Conclusions

4.1. Main Findings

It is known that corrugated cardboard has higher bending stiffness for orientation I. In this work, we quantified this improvement for real applications. For vertical deflections, it ranges from 23% to 65%, finding with the best results for orientation I, except for the first design with bottom discontinuity, with slightly better results for orientation II.

For orientation I, the first design sidewalls show low stresses and can be removed.

As expected, the triangular structures inside the stool improve its static behaviour.

In the first and second designs with top discontinuity, the seating surface is divided into two parts with half the span of the seating surface. This division leads to a more favourable configuration than the corresponding designs with bottom discontinuity.

We should keep the bottom panel, since it prevents any longitudinal sliding between the lower edges of the front and rear panels.

The edges where the inner triangular structure contacts the seating panel act as intermediate supports. The seating surface has two intermediate supports in the fourth design, but only one in the second. Since configurations with more supports are most favourable, the fourth design has better static behaviour than the second and third designs.

4.2. Concluding Remarks

Corrugated cardboard has a great strength-to-weight ratio, excellent burst strength and resistance to crushing, thus being an ideal material for furniture manufacture. However, a careful design is needed to ensure rigidity [31]. This work aimed to apply numerical methods for the structural analysis of corrugated cardboard furniture, as an aid in their design process, to obtain efficient designs with the best resistance-to-cost ratio.

As an example, we chose a stool made of heavy-duty triple-wall A-flute corrugated cardboard. We performed static analyses on various stool designs, with a geometric evolution guided by the stresses found in previous design stages. The selection of this specific type of furniture has no particular relevance, being just a way to show the feasibility and benefits of numerical analysis in the design practice of corrugated cardboard furniture.

To define the mechanical properties of corrugated cardboard, we used a homogenization approach based on the first-order shear deformation theory (FSDT). It is an evolution of our previous work [12], which was in turn based on prior research by Talbi [1] and Duong [2]. Together with [12], a novelty of this work, is applying a homogenization technique to the numerical analysis of whole structures made of corrugated board, thus extending the scope of previous studies, usually limited to beams and plates. Although the analysis of simple structures, such as beams or plates, can be performed analytically, more complex structures, such as those considered in this work, should be studied with numerical techniques, such as FEA. A second novelty is the possibility of analyzing multiple-wall panels of any number of layers, in addition to the single- and double-wall configurations commonly addressed in the literature, also broadening the scope of previous works.

We computed the stiffness matrix of an equivalent homogeneous plate for each fluting, first averaging over the laminate thickness and then along the MD. To model the whole board, we inserted these stiffness matrices of flutings and liners into a FE model, using a layered material model based on the FSDT. Unlike other previous works, this methodology provides a way to easily model multiple-wall boards, since the homogenized matrices are independent of the number of plies of the laminate. In this way, the number of plies and the thickness of the liners can easily be changed inside the FE model.

We then performed a static analysis. The starting design of the stool evolved to three other designs, taking into account the deflections and stresses found in the FEA. Together, we analyzed four different designs under the load conditions defined by the Eurocodes EN 1728 [120] and EN 12520 [121] for seating. The first design, based on the geometry of a commercial stool made of three panels assembled in perpendicular directions, forming a closed structure, was chosen because of its simplicity. We found zones with lower stresses and progressively removed some of them. We also included an inner triangular structure to compensate for removing the side panels from the initial design.

The fourth design has higher strength than the others, showing the lowest vertical deflections and stresses, with reductions of 44% for w, 90% for σ_{xx}, and 67% for σ_{yy} compared to the starting design. It also requires 44% less material, thus reducing material costs. It is also made from a single foldable piece, requiring less storage space and reducing the possibility of losing pieces when stored. Therefore, it is significantly more efficient than the first design, based on its static behaviour, the amount of material needed and the required storage space. However, we do not discuss aesthetic or ergonomic aspects.

As expected, the results of this study demonstrate the utility of homogenization techniques as an aid in the design process of whole structures made of corrugated cardboard. The proposed methodology can be applied to the design process of any other piece of furniture, such as a shelf, a bed, a desk, or any other structural element made of corrugated cardboard. It can help to optimize its design by choosing an optimal geometry for a given material. It can also help to choose the most suitable material for a predefined geometry, by comparing panels with different numbers of walls. In both cases, it would lead to material savings. FE models can also be used to analyze delamination or buckling situations and take corrective actions when needed. These potential situations should be considered in future research. Comparative fatigue analyses would also be interesting [3].

Author Contributions: B.S.: conceptualization, methodology, software, formal analysis, investigation, resources, data curation, writing, writing—review & editing, visualization and supervision. L.M.M.: conceptualization, data curation, writing, writing–review & editing, funding acquisition; J.D.S.-B.: software, formal analysis, investigation, resources, writing. G.R.: methodology, investigation, resources, visualization, writing. All authors have read and agreed to the published version of the manuscript.

Funding: This research received no external funding.

Institutional Review Board Statement: Not applicable.

Informed Consent Statement: Not applicable.

Data Availability Statement: All the raw/processed data required to reproduce these findings were presented in this manuscript.

Conflicts of Interest: The authors declare no conflict of interest.

Appendix A. Homogenized Stiffness Matrix

As shown in (Figure 14), in woven laminas, the 2-axis is parallel to the y-axis. For the 1- and 3-axes, they are tangent and normal to the shape of the flute, respectively.

Flutings have a sinusoidal shape with height h, period P and thickness t (see Figure 14). Thus, in the xyz frame, the geometry of the k-th corrugated layer can be described as follows:

$$z = \frac{h_k - t_k}{2} sin\left(\frac{2\pi}{P_k}x\right). \tag{A1}$$

For the *k-th* corrugated layer, the angle θ_k between the local 1-axis, tangent to the flute, and the global *x*-axis is given by:

$$\theta_k(x) = \operatorname{atan}\left[(h_k - t_k)\frac{\pi}{P_k}\cos\left(\frac{2\pi}{P_k}x\right)\right]. \tag{A2}$$

We can use the angle θ_k to transform the material properties of the constitutive layers from the lamina reference frame to the laminate reference frame. Thus, knowing the material parameters in the reference frame 123, they can be transformed into the reference frame *xyz*. For a rotation angle θ_k around the *y*-axis, the inverse strain transformation, from the reference frame *xyz* to the reference frame 123, can be written as [1,87] (see Appendix B.2):

$$\begin{bmatrix} \varepsilon_{11} \\ \varepsilon_{22} \\ \varepsilon_{33} \\ \gamma_{23} \\ \gamma_{13} \\ \gamma_{12} \end{bmatrix} = \begin{bmatrix} c^2 & 0 & s^2 & 0 & -cs & 0 \\ 0 & 1 & 0 & 0 & 0 & 0 \\ s^2 & 0 & c^2 & 0 & cs & 0 \\ 0 & 0 & 0 & c & 0 & s \\ 2cs & 0 & -2cs & 0 & c^2 - s^2 & 0 \\ 0 & 0 & 0 & -s & 0 & c \end{bmatrix} \cdot \begin{bmatrix} \varepsilon_{xx} \\ \varepsilon_{yy} \\ \varepsilon_{zz} \\ \gamma_{yz} \\ \gamma_{xz} \\ \gamma_{xy} \end{bmatrix}. \tag{A3}$$

where:

$$c = \cos\theta_k; s = \sin\theta_k. \tag{A4}$$

On the other hand, we can write the stress transformation (see Appendix B.3) as follows:

$$\begin{bmatrix} \sigma_{11} \\ \sigma_{22} \\ \sigma_{33} \\ \sigma_{23} \\ \sigma_{13} \\ \sigma_{12} \end{bmatrix} = \begin{bmatrix} c^2 & 0 & s^2 & 0 & -2cs & 0 \\ 0 & 1 & 0 & 0 & 0 & 0 \\ s^2 & 0 & c^2 & 0 & 2cs & 0 \\ 0 & 0 & 0 & c & 0 & s \\ cs & 0 & -cs & 0 & c^2 - s^2 & 0 \\ 0 & 0 & 0 & -s & 0 & c \end{bmatrix} \cdot \begin{bmatrix} \sigma_{xx} \\ \sigma_{yy} \\ \sigma_{zz} \\ \sigma_{yz} \\ \sigma_{xz} \\ \sigma_{xy} \end{bmatrix}. \tag{A5}$$

We can write Equations (A3) and (A5) in compact form as:

$$\varepsilon' = T_\varepsilon \cdot \varepsilon \tag{A6}$$

$$\sigma' = T_\sigma \cdot \sigma, \tag{A7}$$

ε and ε' being the strain vectors in the global and local frames; σ and σ' the stress vectors in the global and local frames; and T_ε and T_σ the strain and stress transformation matrix, respectively.

The constitutive equations in the lamina and laminate reference frames are the following:

$$\varepsilon' = S' \cdot \sigma' \tag{A8}$$

$$\varepsilon = S \cdot \sigma, \tag{A9}$$

S and S' being the compliance matrices in the global and local reference frames, respectively.

Substituting Equations (A6) and (A7) in Equation (A8) and then comparing with Equation (A9), we get:

$$S = T_\varepsilon^{-1} \cdot S' \cdot T_\sigma. \tag{A10}$$

Taking into account that (see Appendix B.3):

$$T_\varepsilon^{-1} = T_\sigma^T \tag{A11}$$

we finally get:

$$S = T_\sigma^T \cdot S' \cdot T_\sigma. \tag{A12}$$

Equation (A12) transforms S' from the lamina reference frame, where material properties are known, to the laminate reference frame, as a function of θ. For orthotropic materials, S' is given by [55]:

$$S' = \begin{bmatrix} \frac{1}{E_1} & -\frac{\nu_{12}}{E_1} & -\frac{\nu_{13}}{E_1} & 0 & 0 & 0 \\ -\frac{\nu_{12}}{E_1} & \frac{1}{E_2} & -\frac{\nu_{23}}{E_2} & 0 & 0 & 0 \\ -\frac{\nu_{13}}{E_1} & -\frac{\nu_{23}}{E_2} & \frac{1}{E_3} & 0 & 0 & 0 \\ 0 & 0 & 0 & \frac{1}{G_{23}} & 0 & 0 \\ 0 & 0 & 0 & 0 & \frac{1}{G_{13}} & 0 \\ 0 & 0 & 0 & 0 & 0 & \frac{1}{G_{12}} \end{bmatrix}. \quad (A13)$$

Using Equations (A12) and (A13), we get the following nonzero elements for S:

$$\begin{aligned}
S_{11} &= \tfrac{c^4}{E_1} + \tfrac{s^4}{E_3} - \tfrac{2c^2s^2\nu_{13}}{E_1} + \tfrac{c^2s^2}{G_{13}};\ S_{12} = -\tfrac{c^2\nu_{12}}{E_1} - \tfrac{s^2\nu_{23}}{E_2}; \\
S_{13} &= -\tfrac{c^4\nu_{13}}{E_1} + \tfrac{c^2s^2}{E_3} + \tfrac{c^2s^2}{E_1} - \tfrac{s^4\nu_{13}}{E_1} - \tfrac{c^2s^2}{G_{13}}; \\
S_{15} &= -\tfrac{2c^3s\nu_{13}}{E_1} + \tfrac{2cs^3}{E_3} - \tfrac{2c^3s}{E_1} + \tfrac{2cs^3\nu_{13}}{E_1} + \tfrac{c^3s}{G_{13}} - \tfrac{cs^3}{G_{13}}; \\
S_{22} &= \tfrac{1}{E_2};\ S_{23} = -\tfrac{c^2\nu_{23}}{E_2} - \tfrac{s^2\nu_{12}}{E_1};\ S_{25} = \tfrac{2cs\nu_{12}}{E_1} - \tfrac{2cs\nu_{23}}{E_2}; \\
S_{33} &= \tfrac{c^4}{E_3} + \tfrac{s^4}{E_1} - \tfrac{2c^2s^2\nu_{13}}{E_1} + \tfrac{c^2s^2}{G_{13}};\ S_{35} = \tfrac{2c^3s}{E_3} - \tfrac{2cs^3\nu_{13}}{E_1} + \tfrac{2c^3s\nu_{13}}{E_1} - \tfrac{2cs^3}{E_1} - \tfrac{c^3s}{G_{13}} + \tfrac{cs^3}{G_{13}}; \\
S_{44} &= \tfrac{c^2}{G_{23}} + \tfrac{s^2}{G_{12}};\ S_{46} = \tfrac{cs}{G_{23}} - \tfrac{cs}{G_{12}}; \\
S_{55} &= \tfrac{c^4}{G_{13}} + \tfrac{s^4}{G_{13}} - \tfrac{2c^2s^2}{G_{13}} + \tfrac{4c^2s^2}{E_1} + \tfrac{8c^2s^2\nu_{13}}{E_1} + \tfrac{4c^2s^2}{E_3}; \\
S_{66} &= \tfrac{c^2}{G_{12}} + \tfrac{s^2}{G_{23}}.
\end{aligned} \quad (A14)$$

After the transformation, we lose the typical structure of the stiffness matrix for orthotropic materials, with the elements of the fourth, fifth, and sixth rows and columns that lie outside its main diagonal equal to zero. The new structure is typical for monoclinic materials, with symmetry around $y = 0$ [125].

In the global reference frame, we can easily obtain the stiffness matrix, Q, by matrix inversion. Thence:

$$Q = S^{-1}. \quad (A15)$$

S_{ij} being functions of θ (through c and s), Q is also a function of θ, which is also a function of x.

For the liners, we can directly compute Q_k from Equations (A13) and (A15). However, for the flutings, we need to average through the z-coordinate, taking into account that the thickness of a corrugated layer, obtained by a vertical cutting, is also a function of θ:

$$t_{zk}(x) = \frac{t_k}{\cos\theta_k(x)} \quad (A16)$$

t_k being the uniform thickness of the fluting layer (see Figure 14). Thus, we can express the averaged stiffness through the layer thickness as:

$$\overline{Q}_{k,z}(x) = \frac{1}{h_k}\int_0^{h_k} Q_k(x)\cdot dz = \frac{1}{h_k}Q_k(x)\int_0^{h_k} dz = \frac{1}{h_k}Q_k(x)\cdot t_{zk}(x) = \frac{Q_k(x)\cdot t_k}{h_k\cdot\cos\theta_k(x)}. \quad (A17)$$

Furthermore, to eliminate the dependence of the stiffness matrix on the x-coordinate, a second homogenization was performed along the x-direction, computing the average values of Q_{ij} over a fluting period [1,2,19,126]. This way, we got a constant value for each matrix element:

$$\overline{Q}_{k,zx} = \frac{1}{P}\int_0^P \overline{Q}_{kz}(x)\cdot dx = \frac{1}{P}\int_0^P \frac{Q_k(x)\cdot t_k}{h_k\cdot\cos\theta_k(x)}\cdot dx = \frac{t_k}{P\cdot h_k}\int_0^P \frac{Q_k(x)}{\cos\theta_k(x)}\cdot dx. \quad (A18)$$

Appendix B. Transformation Matrices

Appendix B.1. Coordinate Transformation of a Generic Vector

The components of a vector $\vec{r}$, in the laminate and lamina reference frames, can be related by:

$$r' = A \cdot r, \qquad (A19)$$

where A is the transformation matrix:

$$A = \begin{bmatrix} c & 0 & -s \\ 0 & 1 & 0 \\ s & 0 & c \end{bmatrix}, \qquad (A20)$$

being $c = \cos\theta$ and $s = \sin\theta$.

The inverse transformation is:

$$r = A^{-1} \cdot r' = A^T \cdot r'. \qquad (A21)$$

From these relationships, the derivatives of x', y' and z' with respect to x, y, and z are:

$$\frac{\delta x'}{\delta x} = c; \; \frac{\delta x'}{\delta z} = -s; \; \frac{\delta y'}{\delta y} = 1; \; \frac{\delta z'}{\delta x} = s; \; \frac{\delta z'}{\delta z} = c; \; \frac{\delta x'}{\delta y} = \frac{\delta y'}{\delta x} = \frac{\delta y'}{\delta z} = \frac{\delta z'}{\delta y} = 0. \qquad (A22)$$

If, instead of a generic vector, we consider the displacement vector with components u, v, w:

$$u = cu' + sw'; \; v = v'; \; w = -su' + cw'. \qquad (A23)$$

From these relationships, the derivatives of u, v, w with respect to x', y', and z' are:

$$\begin{aligned}
\frac{\delta u}{\delta x'} &= c\frac{\delta u'}{\delta x'} + s\frac{\delta w'}{\delta x'}; \; \frac{\delta u}{\delta y'} = c\frac{\delta u'}{\delta y'} + s\frac{\delta w'}{\delta y'}; \; \frac{\delta u}{\delta z'} = c\frac{\delta u'}{\delta z'} + s\frac{\delta w'}{\delta z'}; \\
\frac{\delta v}{\delta x'} &= \frac{\delta v'}{\delta x'}; \; \frac{\delta v}{\delta y'} = \frac{\delta v'}{\delta y'}; \; \frac{\delta v}{\delta z'} = \frac{\delta v'}{\delta z'}; \\
\frac{\delta w}{\delta x'} &= -s\frac{\delta u'}{\delta x'} + c\frac{\delta w'}{\delta x'}; \; \frac{\delta w}{\delta y'} = -s\frac{\delta u'}{\delta y'} + c\frac{\delta w'}{\delta y'}; \; \frac{\delta w}{\delta z'} = -s\frac{\delta u'}{\delta z'} + c\frac{\delta w'}{\delta z'}.
\end{aligned} \qquad (A24)$$

Appendix B.2. Strain Transformations

By definition, the strains in the laminate reference frame, xyz, are given by:

$$\varepsilon_{xx} = \frac{\delta u}{\delta x}; \; \varepsilon_{yy} = \frac{\delta v}{\delta y}; \; \varepsilon_{zz} = \frac{\delta w}{\delta z}; \; \gamma_{yz} = \frac{\delta v}{\delta z} + \frac{\delta w}{\delta y}; \; \gamma_{xz} = \frac{\delta u}{\delta z} + \frac{\delta w}{\delta x}; \; \gamma_{xy} = \frac{\delta u}{\delta y} + \frac{\delta v}{\delta x}. \qquad (A25)$$

In the same way, strains in the lamina reference frame, 123, are given by:

$$\varepsilon_{11} = \frac{\delta u'}{\delta x'}; \; \varepsilon_{22} = \frac{\delta v'}{\delta y'}; \; \varepsilon_{33} = \frac{\delta w'}{\delta z'}; \; \gamma_{23} = \frac{\delta v'}{\delta z'} + \frac{\delta w'}{\delta y'}; \; \gamma_{13} = \frac{\delta u'}{\delta z'} + \frac{\delta w'}{\delta x'}; \; \gamma_{12} = \frac{\delta u'}{\delta y'} + \frac{\delta v'}{\delta x'}. \qquad (A26)$$

Using the chain rule, together with Equation (A22), the strains in the laminate frame can be computed as follows:

$$\varepsilon_{xx} = \frac{\delta u}{\delta x} = \frac{\delta u}{\delta x'}\frac{\delta x'}{\delta x} + \frac{\delta u}{\delta y'}\frac{\delta y'}{\delta x} + \frac{\delta u}{\delta z'}\frac{\delta z'}{\delta x} = \frac{\delta u}{\delta x'}c + \frac{\delta u}{\delta y'}0 + \frac{\delta u}{\delta z'}s = c\frac{\delta u}{\delta x'} + s\frac{\delta u}{\delta z'}. \qquad (A27)$$

Replacing in these expressions the derivatives of Equation (A24), we get:

$$\varepsilon_{xx} = c^2\varepsilon_{11} + cs\gamma_{13} + s^2\varepsilon_{33}. \qquad (A28)$$

Analogously:

$$\varepsilon_{yy} = \varepsilon_{22}; \quad \varepsilon_{zz} = s^2\varepsilon_{11} - cs\gamma_{13} + c^2\varepsilon_{33};$$
$$\gamma_{yz} = c\gamma_{23} - s\gamma_{12}; \quad \gamma_{xz} = (c^2 - s^2)\gamma_{13} + 2cs(\varepsilon_{33} - \varepsilon_{11}); \quad \gamma_{xy} = c\gamma_{12} + s\gamma_{23}. \tag{A29}$$

In matrix form, using the Voigt notation, which gathers the strains in a vector, we can write:

$$\begin{bmatrix} \varepsilon_{xx} \\ \varepsilon_{yy} \\ \varepsilon_{zz} \\ \gamma_{yz} \\ \gamma_{xz} \\ \gamma_{xy} \end{bmatrix} = \begin{bmatrix} c^2 & 0 & s^2 & 0 & cs & 0 \\ 0 & 1 & 0 & 0 & 0 & 0 \\ s^2 & 0 & c^2 & 0 & -cs & 0 \\ 0 & 0 & 0 & c & 0 & -s \\ -2cs & 0 & 2cs & 0 & c^2 - s^2 & 0 \\ 0 & 0 & 0 & s & 0 & c \end{bmatrix} \cdot \begin{bmatrix} \varepsilon_{11} \\ \varepsilon_{22} \\ \varepsilon_{33} \\ \gamma_{23} \\ \gamma_{13} \\ \gamma_{12} \end{bmatrix}. \tag{A30}$$

We obtained the inverse transformation by replacing θ by −θ, that is, sinθ by -sinθ:

$$\begin{bmatrix} \varepsilon_{11} \\ \varepsilon_{22} \\ \varepsilon_{33} \\ \gamma_{23} \\ \gamma_{13} \\ \gamma_{12} \end{bmatrix} = \begin{bmatrix} c^2 & 0 & s^2 & 0 & -cs & 0 \\ 0 & 1 & 0 & 0 & 0 & 0 \\ s^2 & 0 & c^2 & 0 & cs & 0 \\ 0 & 0 & 0 & c & 0 & s \\ 2cs & 0 & -2cs & 0 & c^2 - s^2 & 0 \\ 0 & 0 & 0 & -s & 0 & c \end{bmatrix} \cdot \begin{bmatrix} \varepsilon_{xx} \\ \varepsilon_{yy} \\ \varepsilon_{zz} \\ \gamma_{yz} \\ \gamma_{xz} \\ \gamma_{xy} \end{bmatrix}. \tag{A31}$$

This transformation and its inverse transformation can be written in compact form as follows:

$$\varepsilon' = T_\varepsilon \cdot \varepsilon; \quad \varepsilon = T_\varepsilon^{-1} \cdot \varepsilon', \tag{A32}$$

being T_ε the strain transformation matrix [1,87]:

$$T_\varepsilon = \begin{bmatrix} c^2 & 0 & s^2 & 0 & -cs & 0 \\ 0 & 1 & 0 & 0 & 0 & 0 \\ s^2 & 0 & c^2 & 0 & cs & 0 \\ 0 & 0 & 0 & c & 0 & s \\ 2cs & 0 & -2cs & 0 & c^2 - s^2 & 0 \\ 0 & 0 & 0 & -s & 0 & c \end{bmatrix}; \quad T_\varepsilon^{-1} = \begin{bmatrix} c^2 & 0 & s^2 & 0 & cs & 0 \\ 0 & 1 & 0 & 0 & 0 & 0 \\ s^2 & 0 & c^2 & 0 & -cs & 0 \\ 0 & 0 & 0 & c & 0 & -s \\ -2cs & 0 & 2cs & 0 & c^2 - s^2 & 0 \\ 0 & 0 & 0 & s & 0 & c \end{bmatrix}. \tag{A33}$$

B.3. Stresses Transformations

Cauchy's law [123] gives the components t_1, t_2, t_3 of the stress vector as functions of the stress tensor and the components n_1, n_2, n_3 of the normal vector to the surface. In the lamina reference frame, 123:

$$\begin{bmatrix} t_1 \\ t_2 \\ t_3 \end{bmatrix} = \begin{bmatrix} \sigma_{11} & \sigma_{12} & \sigma_{13} \\ \sigma_{12} & \sigma_{22} & \sigma_{23} \\ \sigma_{13} & \sigma_{23} & \sigma_{33} \end{bmatrix} \cdot \begin{bmatrix} n_1 \\ n_2 \\ n_3 \end{bmatrix}. \tag{A34}$$

In the laminate reference frame, xyz, it can also be written as:

$$\begin{bmatrix} t_x \\ t_y \\ t_z \end{bmatrix} = \begin{bmatrix} \sigma_{xx} & \sigma_{xy} & \sigma_{xz} \\ \sigma_{xy} & \sigma_{yy} & \sigma_{yz} \\ \sigma_{xz} & \sigma_{yz} & \sigma_{zz} \end{bmatrix} \cdot \begin{bmatrix} n_x \\ n_y \\ n_z \end{bmatrix}. \tag{A35}$$

Or, in compact form:

$$t' = \sigma' \cdot n'; \quad t = \sigma \cdot n. \tag{A36}$$

Using Equation (A21) to transform from the local to the global reference frames:

$$A \cdot t = \sigma' \cdot A \cdot n \Rightarrow t = A^{-1} \cdot \sigma' \cdot A \cdot n = A^T \cdot \sigma' \cdot A \cdot n. \tag{A37}$$

Identifying with Equation (A36), we have:

$$\sigma = A^T \cdot \sigma' \cdot A. \tag{A38}$$

Thence, from Equation (A20):

$$\sigma = \begin{bmatrix} \sigma_{xx} & \sigma_{xy} & \sigma_{xz} \\ \sigma_{xy} & \sigma_{yy} & \sigma_{yz} \\ \sigma_{xz} & \sigma_{yz} & \sigma_{zz} \end{bmatrix} = \begin{bmatrix} c & 0 & s \\ 0 & 1 & 0 \\ -s & 0 & c \end{bmatrix} \cdot \begin{bmatrix} \sigma_{11} & \sigma_{12} & \sigma_{13} \\ \sigma_{12} & \sigma_{22} & \sigma_{23} \\ \sigma_{13} & \sigma_{23} & \sigma_{33} \end{bmatrix} \cdot \begin{bmatrix} c & 0 & -s \\ 0 & 1 & 0 \\ s & 0 & c \end{bmatrix}$$

$$= \begin{bmatrix} c^2\sigma_{11} + 2cs\sigma_{13} + s^2\sigma_{33} & c\sigma_{12} + s\sigma_{23} & (c^2 - s^2)\sigma_{13} + cs(\sigma_{33} - \sigma_{11}) \\ c\sigma_{12} + s\sigma_{23} & \sigma_{22} & c\sigma_{23} - s\sigma_{12} \\ (c^2 - s^2)\sigma_{13} + cs(\sigma_{33} - \sigma_{11}) & c\sigma_{23} - s\sigma_{12} & s^2\sigma_{11} + c^2\sigma_{33} - 2cs\sigma_{13} \end{bmatrix}. \tag{A39}$$

Using the Voigt notation again, we can rewrite the above expressions as:

$$\begin{bmatrix} \sigma_{xx} \\ \sigma_{yy} \\ \sigma_{zz} \\ \sigma_{yz} \\ \sigma_{xz} \\ \sigma_{xy} \end{bmatrix} = \begin{bmatrix} c^2 & 0 & s^2 & 0 & 2cs & 0 \\ 0 & 1 & 0 & 0 & 0 & 0 \\ s^2 & 0 & c^2 & 0 & -2cs & 0 \\ 0 & 0 & 0 & c & 0 & -s \\ -cs & 0 & cs & 0 & c^2 - s^2 & 0 \\ 0 & 0 & 0 & s & 0 & c \end{bmatrix} \cdot \begin{bmatrix} \sigma_{11} \\ \sigma_{22} \\ \sigma_{33} \\ \sigma_{23} \\ \sigma_{13} \\ \sigma_{12} \end{bmatrix}. \tag{A40}$$

The inverse transformation is obtained by replacing θ by $-\theta$, that is, substituting $\sin\theta$ by $-\sin\theta$:

$$\begin{bmatrix} \sigma_{11} \\ \sigma_{22} \\ \sigma_{33} \\ \sigma_{23} \\ \sigma_{13} \\ \sigma_{12} \end{bmatrix} = \begin{bmatrix} c^2 & 0 & s^2 & 0 & -2cs & 0 \\ 0 & 1 & 0 & 0 & 0 & 0 \\ s^2 & 0 & c^2 & 0 & 2cs & 0 \\ 0 & 0 & 0 & c & 0 & s \\ cs & 0 & -cs & 0 & c^2 - s^2 & 0 \\ 0 & 0 & 0 & -s & 0 & c \end{bmatrix} \cdot \begin{bmatrix} \sigma_{xx} \\ \sigma_{yy} \\ \sigma_{zz} \\ \sigma_{yz} \\ \sigma_{xz} \\ \sigma_{xy} \end{bmatrix}. \tag{A41}$$

We can write in compact form this transformation and its inverse transformation as follows:

$$\sigma' = T_\sigma \cdot \sigma; \ \sigma = T_\sigma^{-1} \cdot \sigma'. \tag{A42}$$

being T_σ the stress transformation matrix:

$$T_\sigma = \begin{bmatrix} c^2 & 0 & s^2 & 0 & -2cs & 0 \\ 0 & 1 & 0 & 0 & 0 & 0 \\ s^2 & 0 & c^2 & 0 & 2cs & 0 \\ 0 & 0 & 0 & c & 0 & s \\ cs & 0 & -cs & 0 & c^2 - s^2 & 0 \\ 0 & 0 & 0 & -s & 0 & c \end{bmatrix}; \ T_\sigma^{-1} = \begin{bmatrix} c^2 & 0 & s^2 & 0 & 2cs & 0 \\ 0 & 1 & 0 & 0 & 0 & 0 \\ s^2 & 0 & c^2 & 0 & -2cs & 0 \\ 0 & 0 & 0 & c & 0 & -s \\ -cs & 0 & cs & 0 & c^2 - s^2 & 0 \\ 0 & 0 & 0 & s & 0 & c \end{bmatrix}. \tag{A43}$$

As can be seen, the stiffness and strain transformation matrices satisfy the following relations:

$$T_\varepsilon^{-1} = T_\sigma^T \tag{A44}$$

$$T_\sigma^{-1} = T_\varepsilon^T. \tag{A45}$$

References

1. Talbi, N.; Batti, A.; Ayad, R.; Guo, Y. An analytical homogenization model for finite element modelling of corrugated cardboard. *Compos. Struct.* **2009**, *88*, 280–289. [CrossRef]
2. Duong, P.T.M. Modeling and Numerical Simulation for the Double Corrugated Cardboard under Transverse Loading by Homogenization Method. *Int. J. Eng. Sci.* **2017**, *6*, 16–25.
3. Ceylan, E.; Güray, E.; Kasal, A. Structural analyses of wooden chairs by finite element method (FEM) and assessment of the cyclic loading performance in comparison with allowable design loads. *Maderas-Cienc. Tecnol.* **2021**, *23*. [CrossRef]
4. Smardzewski, J.; Gawronski, T. FEM Algorithm for chair optimisation. *Electron. J. Pol. Agric. Univ. Ser. Wood Technol.* **2001**, *4*, 2.

5. Kasal, A. Determination of the strength of various sofa frames with finite element analysis. *Gazi Univ. J. Sci.* **2006**, *19*, 191–203.
6. Hu, W.; Liu, N.; Guan, H. Optimal design of a furniture frame by reducing the volume of wood. *Drewno* **2019**, *62*, 85–97.
7. Gustafsson, S.-I. Optimising ash wood chairs. *Wood Sci. Technol.* **1997**, *31*, 291–301. [CrossRef]
8. Smardzewski, J. Numerical analysis of furniture constructions. *Wood Sci. Technol.* **1998**, *32*, 273–286. [CrossRef]
9. Tankut, N.; Tankut, A.N.; Zor, M. Finite Element Analysis of Wood Materials. *Drv. Ind.* **2014**, *65*, 159–171. [CrossRef]
10. Laemlaksakul, V. Innovative design of laminated bamboo furniture using finite element method. *Int. J. Math. Comput. Simul.* **2008**, *2*, 274–284.
11. Smardzewski, J.; Kramski, D. Modelling stiffness of furniture manufactured from honeycomb panels depending on changing climate conditions. *Thin-Walled Struct.* **2019**, *137*, 295–302. [CrossRef]
12. Suarez, B.; Muneta, M.L.M.; Sanz-Bobi, J.D.; Romero, G. Application of homogenization approaches to the numerical analysis of seating made of multi-wall corrugated cardboard. *Compos. Struct.* **2021**, *262*, 113642. [CrossRef]
13. Baioni, E.; Alessi, R.; Corinaldesi, V.; Lancioni, G.; Rizzini, R. Feasibility Study of a Table Prototype Made of High-Performance Fiber-Reinforced Concrete. *Technologies* **2017**, *5*, 41. [CrossRef]
14. Abdel-Mohsen, M.; Faggal, A.; El-Metwally, Y. Efficiency of Corrugated Cardboard as a Building Material. 2012. Available online: https://www.researchgate.net/publication/351323568 (accessed on 15 September 2021). [CrossRef]
15. Latka, J.F. Paper in architecture: Research by design, engineering and prototyping. *A+ BE Archit. Built Environ.* **2017**, *19*, 1–532.
16. El Damatty, A.; Mikhail, A.; Awad, A. Finite element modeling and analysis of a cardboard shelter. *Thin-Walled Struct.* **2000**, *38*, 145–165. [CrossRef]
17. Zhang, Z.; Qiu, T.; Song, R.; Sun, Y. Nonlinear Finite Element Analysis of the Fluted Corrugated Sheet in the Corrugated Cardboard. *Adv. Mater. Sci. Eng.* **2014**, *2014*, 1–8. [CrossRef]
18. Barbero, E.J. *Finite Element Analysis of Composite Materials Using Abaqus TM*; CRC-Press: Boca Raton, FL, USA, 2013.
19. Aboura, Z.; Talbi, N.; Allaoui, S.; Benzeggagh, M. Elastic behavior of corrugated cardboard: Experiments and modeling. *Compos. Struct.* **2004**, *63*, 53–62. [CrossRef]
20. Twede, D.; Selke, S.; Kamdem, D.; Shires, D. *Cartons, Crates and Corrugated Board: Handbook of Paper and Wood Packaging Technology*; DEStech Publications: Lancaster, PA, USA, 2014.
21. Dayyani, I.; Shaw, A.D.; Flores, E.I.S.; Friswell, M.I. *The Mechanics of Composite Corrugated Structures: A Review with Applications in Morphing Aircraft*; Elsevier: Amsterdam, The Netherlands, 2015; pp. 358–380.
22. Kirwan, M.J. *Handbook of Paper and Paperboard Packaging Technology*, 2nd ed.; John Wiley and Sons: Hoboken, NJ, USA, 2012.
23. Jay Enterprises Limited. Cardboard Thickness and Material. Available online: https://www.jay.co.jp/page/Cardboard_thickness_and_material (accessed on 21 October 2021).
24. Allaoui, S.; Aboura, Z.; Benzeggagh, M.L. Phenomena governing uniaxial tensile behaviour of paper-board and corrugated cardboard. *Compos. Struct.* **2009**, *87*, 80–92. [CrossRef]
25. Luong, V.D.; Abbès, F.; Abbès, B.; Duong, P.T.M.; Nolot, J.-B.; Erre, D.; Guo, Y.-Q. Finite Element Simulation of the Strength of Corrugated Board Boxes Under Impact Dynamics. In Proceedings of the International Conference on Advances in Computational Mechanics, Phu Quoc, Vietnam, 2–4 August 2017; pp. 369–380. [CrossRef]
26. Statista. Production Volume of Paper and Cardboard Worldwide from 2008 to 2018. 2020. Available online: https://www.statista.com/statistics/270314/global-paper-and-cardboard-production/ (accessed on 21 October 2021).
27. Statista. Global Paper Production Volume from 2008 to 2018 by Type. 2020. Available online: https://www.statista.com/statistics/270317/production-volume-of-paper-by-type/ (accessed on 21 October 2021).
28. Jivkov, V.; Simeonova, R.; Antov, P.; Marinova, A.; Petrova, B.; Kristak, L. Structural Application of Light-Weight Panels Made of Waste Cardboard and Beech Veneer. *Materials* **2021**, *14*, 5064. [CrossRef] [PubMed]
29. Statista. Paper Demand Worldwide in 2020, by Type. 2021. Available online: https://www.statista.com/statistics/1089092/global-paper-consumption-by-type/ (accessed on 21 October 2021).
30. Eurostat. Recycling Rate of Packaging Waste by Type of Packaging. 2021. Available online: https://ec.europa.eu/eurostat/databrowser/view/cei_wm020/default/bar?lang=en%2F (accessed on 21 October 2021).
31. Vigna, F. Materiality. Cardboard. Kinder. A Journal Dedicated to Child Design, Past, Present and Future. Available online: http://thekinderjournal.com/003-materiality (accessed on 15 September 2021).
32. Lu, T.; Chen, C.; Zhu, G. Compressive behaviour of corrugated board panels. *J. Compos. Mater.* **2001**, *35*, 2098–2126. [CrossRef]
33. Nordstrand, T. Analysis and testing of corrugated board panels into the post-buckling regime. *Compos. Struct.* **2004**, *63*, 189–199. [CrossRef]
34. Nyman, U.; Gustafsson, P.J. Material and structural failure criterion of corrugated board facings. *Compos. Struct.* **2000**, *50*, 79–83. [CrossRef]
35. Daum, M.; Darby, D.; Batt, G.; Campbell, L. Application of the stress-energy method for generating corrugated board cushion curves. *J. Test. Eval.* **2013**, *41*, 590–601. [CrossRef]
36. Viguié, J.; Dumont, P.; Orgéas, L.; Vacher, P.; Desloges, I.; Mauret, E. Surface stress and strain fields on compressed panels of corrugated board boxes: An experimental analysis by using digital image stereocorrelation. *Compos. Struct.* **2011**, *93*, 2861–2873. [CrossRef]
37. Fadiji, T.; Ambaw, A.; Coetzee, C.J.; Berry, T.M.; Opara, U.L. Application of finite element analysis to predict the mechanical strength of ventilated corrugated paperboard packaging for handling fresh produce. *Biosyst. Eng.* **2018**, *174*, 260–281. [CrossRef]

38. Allaoui, S.; Aboura, Z.; Benzeggagh, M.L. Effects of the environmental conditions on the mechanical behaviour of the corrugated cardboard. *Compos. Sci. Technol.* **2009**, *69*, 104–110. [CrossRef]
39. Patel, P.; Nordstrand, T.; Carlsson, L.A. Local buckling and collapse of corrugated board under biaxial stress. *Compos. Struct.* **1997**, *39*, 93–110. [CrossRef]
40. Allansson, A.; Svärd, B. Stability and Collapse of Corrugated Board: Numerical and Experimental Analysis. Master's Thesis, Lund University, Lund, Sweden, 2001.
41. Park, J.; Kim, G.; Kwon, S.; Chung, S.; Kwon, S.; Choi, W.; Mitsuoka, M.; Inoue, E.; Okayasu, T.; Choe, J. Finite Element Analysis of Corrugated Board under Bending Stress. *J. Fac. Agric. Kyushu Univ.* **2012**, *57*, 181–188. [CrossRef]
42. Fadiji, T.; Berry, T.; Coetzee, C.; Opara, L. Investigating the Mechanical Properties of Paperboard Packaging Material for Handling Fresh Produce Under Different Environmental Conditions: Experimental Analysis and Finite Element Modelling. 2017. Available online: https://scholarworks.rit.edu/japr/vol9/iss2/3 (accessed on 21 October 2021).
43. Daxner, T. Optimum Design of Corrugated Board under Buckling Constraints. In Proceedings of the 7th World Congress on Structural and Multidisciplinary Optimization, Seoul, Korea, 21–25 May 2007.
44. Biancolini, M.; Brutti, C.; Porziani, S. Corrugated board containers design methods. *Int. J. Comput. Mater. Sci. Surf. Eng.* **2010**, *3*, 143–163. [CrossRef]
45. Minh, D.P.T. Analysis and simulation for the double corrugated cardboard plates under bending and in-plane shear force by homogenization method. *Int. J. Mech.* **2017**, *11*, 176–181.
46. Fadiji, T.; Coetzee, C.; Opara, U.L. Compression strength of ventilated corrugated paperboard packages: Numerical modelling, experimental validation and effects of vent geometric design. *Biosyst. Eng.* **2016**, *151*, 231–247. [CrossRef]
47. Isaksson, P.; Krusper, A.; Gradin, P. Shear correction factors for corrugated core structures. *Compos. Struct.* **2007**, *80*, 123–130. [CrossRef]
48. Nordstrand, T.; Carlsson, L.A.; Allen, H.G. Transverse shear stiffness of structural core sandwich. *Compos. Struct.* **1994**, *27*, 317–329. [CrossRef]
49. Kalyankar, N.; Mahakalkar, S.; Giri, J. A Review on Optimization of Corrugated Sheet Box Size for an Industrial Part. *Int. J. Res. Advent Technol. ICATEST* **2015**, 16–19.
50. Jivkov, V.; Elenska-Valchanova, D. Mechanical Properties of Some Thin Furniture Structural Composite Materials. In Proceedings of the 30th International Conference on Wood Science and Technology, Zagreb, Croatia, 12–13 December 2019.
51. Jivkov, V.; Petrova, B. Challenges for furniture design with thin structural materials. In Proceedings of the VI International Furniture Congress, Trabzon, Turkey, 2–4 November 2020.
52. Ruta, G.; Pignataro, M.; Rizzi, N. A direct one-dimensional beam model for the flexural-torsional buckling of thin-walled beams. *J. Mech. Mater. Struct.* **2006**, *1*, 1479–1496. [CrossRef]
53. Piana, G.; Lofrano, E.; Carpinteri, A.; Ruta, G. Effect of local stiffeners and warping constraints on the buckling of symmetric open thin-walled beams with high warping stiffness. *Meccanica* **2021**, *56*, 2083–2102. [CrossRef]
54. Jiménez-Caballero, M.A.; Conde, I.; García, B.; Liarte, R. Design of different types of corrugated board packages using finite element tools. In Proceedings of the SIMULIA Customer Conference, London, UK, 19–21 May 2009.
55. Berthelot, J. *Composite Materials-Mechanical Behavior and Structural Analysis*; Springer: Berlin/Heidelberg, Germany, 1999.
56. Spinillo, C.G.; Fujita, P.T. Do-it-yourself (DIY) furniture for emergency situations: A study on assembling a cardboard bench in Brazil. *Theor. Issues Ergon. Sci.* **2012**, *13*, 121–134. [CrossRef]
57. Cartonlab, La Silla de Cartón. Una Historia de Diseño Sostenible. Available online: https://cartonlab.com/blog/silla-carton/ (accessed on 21 October 2021).
58. Chairigami. Available online: https://www.chairigami.com/ (accessed on 21 October 2021).
59. Quart De Poil. Cardboard. Available online: https://quartdepoil.fr/en/16,cardboard.html (accessed on 21 October 2021).
60. Cartonlab. Available online: https://cartonlab.com/en/ (accessed on 21 October 2021).
61. Kartelier. Available online: https://www.facebook.com/kartelier/about/ (accessed on 21 October 2021).
62. Kartent. Available online: https://shop.kartent.com/en/ (accessed on 21 October 2021).
63. Stange. Available online: https://www.pappmoebelshop.de/home.html (accessed on 21 October 2021).
64. Origami Furniture. Collections. Available online: http://www.origamifurniture.com/collections/?lang=en (accessed on 21 October 2021).
65. Litencarton. Available online: https://www.litencarton.ch/ (accessed on 21 October 2021).
66. Cardboard. Cardboard Furniture and Projects. Available online: http://cardboard.es/portfolio/#productos-de-carton (accessed on 21 October 2021).
67. Cartone Design. Available online: https://cartonedesign.com.br/produtos/ (accessed on 21 October 2021).
68. Igreen. Cool Green Gadgets. Available online: https://www.igreengadgets.com/ (accessed on 21 October 2021).
69. Danbaul x Style. Available online: https://www.danbaul.com/ (accessed on 21 October 2021).
70. Architecture Art Designs. 30 Amazing Cardboard DIY Furniture Ideas. Available online: https://www.architectureartdesigns.com/30-amazing-cardboard-diy-furniture-ideas/ (accessed on 21 October 2021).
71. Behance. Available online: https://www.behance.net/ (accessed on 21 October 2021).
72. Designboom. Available online: https://www.designboom.com/ (accessed on 21 October 2021).
73. Inhabitat. Available online: https://inhabitat.com/ (accessed on 21 October 2021).

74. Airweave. Available online: https://www.airweave.com/ (accessed on 21 October 2021).
75. Gleeson, S. Athletes to Sleep on Recyclable 'Cardboard' Beds during 2020 Olympics in Tokyo. *USA Today Sports*, 2019. Available online: https://eu.usatoday.com/story/sports/olympics/2019/09/24/olympics-2020-athletes-sleep-recyclable-cardboard-beds-tokyo/2429695001/ (accessed on 21 October 2021).
76. Finney, A. Airweave Creates Cardboard Beds and Modular Mattresses for Tokyo 2020 Olympics. 2021. Available online: https://www.dezeen.com/2021/07/11/cardboard-beds-modular-mattresses-airweave-tokyo-2020-olympics/ (accessed on 21 October 2021).
77. Lloyd, O. Tokyo 2020 Cardboard Beds to Be Made Available for COVID-19 Patients in Osaka Inside the Games. 2021. Available online: https://www.insidethegames.biz/articles/1112915/tokyo-2020-cardboard-beds-covid19-osaka (accessed on 21 October 2021).
78. Dimitrov, K.; Heydenrych, M. Relationship between the edgewise compression strength of corrugated board and the compression strength of liner and fluting medium papers. *South. For. J. For. Sci.* **2009**, *71*, 227–233. [CrossRef]
79. Magnucka-Blandzi, E.; Magnucki, K.; Wittenbeck, L. Mathematical modeling of shearing effect for sandwich beams with sinusoidal corrugated cores. *Appl. Math. Model.* **2015**, *39*, 2796–2808. [CrossRef]
80. Magnucka-Blandzi, E.; Magnucki, K. Transverse shear modulus of elasticity for thin-walled corrugated cores of sandwich beams. Theoretical study. *J. Theor. Appl. Mech.* **2014**, *52*, 971–980. [CrossRef]
81. Garbowski, T.; Gajewski, T.; Grabski, J.K. The Role of Buckling in the Estimation of Compressive Strength of Corrugated Cardboard Boxes. *Materials* **2020**, *13*, 4578. [CrossRef]
82. Garbowski, T.; Gajewski, T.; Grabski, J.K. Estimation of the Compressive Strength of Corrugated Card-board Boxes with Various Openings. *Energies* **2020**, *14*, 155. [CrossRef]
83. Garbowski, T.; Gajewski, T.; Grabski, J.K. Estimation of the Compressive Strength of Corrugated Card-board Boxes with Various Perforations. *Energies* **2021**, *14*, 1095. [CrossRef]
84. Garbowski, T.; Gajewski, T.; Grabski, J.K. Role of Transverse Shear Modulus in the Performance of Corrugated Materials. *Materials* **2020**, *13*, 3791. [CrossRef] [PubMed]
85. Nordstrand, T.; Carlsson, L. Evaluation of transverse shear stiffness of structural core sandwich plates. *Compos. Struct.* **1997**, *37*, 145–153. [CrossRef]
86. Luong, V.D.; Bonnin, A.-S.; Abbès, F.; Nolot, J.-B.; Erre, D.; Abbès, B. Finite Element and Experimental Investigation on the Effect of Repetitive Shock in Corrugated Cardboard Packaging. *J. Appl. Comput. Mech.* **2021**, *7*, 820–830.
87. Marek, A.; Garbowski, T. Homogenization of sandwich panels. *Comput. Assist. Methods Eng. Sci.* **2015**, *22*, 39–50.
88. Fadiji, T.; Coetzee, C.; Berry, T.M.; Ambaw, A.; Opara, U.L. The efficacy of finite element analysis (FEA) as a design tool for food packaging: A review. *Biosyst. Eng.* **2018**, *174*, 20–40. [CrossRef]
89. Buannic, N.; Cartraud, P.; Quesnel, T. Homogenization of corrugated core sandwich panels. *Compos. Struct.* **2003**, *59*, 299–312. [CrossRef]
90. Bartolozzi, G.; Orrenius, U.; Pratellesi, A.; Pierini, M. An Equivalent Orthotropic Plate Model for Sinusoidal Core Sandwich Panels in Optimization Processes. In Proceedings of the INTER-NOISE and NOISE-CON Congress and Conference Proceedings, Sorrento, Italy, 16 November 2012; pp. 169–180.
91. Bartolozzi, G.; Pierini, M.; Orrenius, U.; Baldanzini, N. An equivalent material formulation for sinusoidal corrugated cores of structural sandwich panels. *Compos. Struct.* **2013**, *100*, 173–185. [CrossRef]
92. Bartolozzi, G.; Baldanzini, N.; Pierini, M. Equivalent properties for corrugated cores of sandwich structures: A general analytical method. *Compos. Struct.* **2014**, *108*, 736–746. [CrossRef]
93. Shaban, M.; Alibeigloo, A. Three-dimensional elasticity solution for sandwich panels with corrugated cores by using energy method. *Thin-Walled Struct.* **2017**, *119*, 404–411. [CrossRef]
94. Minh, D.P.T.; Khoa, N.N. An analytic homogenization model in traction and bending for orthotropic composite plates with the type of double corrugated cardboard. *Vietnam. J. Mech.* **2016**, *38*, 205–213. [CrossRef]
95. Nguyen-Minh, N.; Tran-Van, N.; Bui-Xuan, T.; Nguyen-Thoi, T. Free vibration analysis of corrugated panels using homogenization methods and a cell-based smoothed Mindlin plate element (CS-MIN3). *Thin-Walled Struct.* **2018**, *124*, 184–201. [CrossRef]
96. Ishikawa, T.; Chou, T.-W. Stiffness and strength behaviour of woven fabric composites. *J. Mater. Sci.* **1982**, *17*, 3211–3220. [CrossRef]
97. Biancolini, M. Evaluation of equivalent stiffness properties of corrugated board. *Compos. Struct.* **2005**, *69*, 322–328. [CrossRef]
98. Duong, P.; Abbès, B.; Djilali, H.A.; Hammou, A.; Makhlouf, M.; Guo, Y. An analytic homogenisation model for shear–torsion coupling problems of double corrugated core sandwich plates. *J. Compos. Mater.* **2012**, *47*, 1327–1341. [CrossRef]
99. Garbowski, T.; Gajewski, T.; Grabski, J.K. Torsional and transversal stiffness of orthotropic sandwich panels. *Materials* **2020**, *13*, 5016. [CrossRef]
100. Sharma, A.; Sankar, B.V.; Haftka, R.T. Homogenization of Plates with Microstructure and Application to Corrugated Core Sandwich Panels. In Proceedings of the 51st AIAA/ASME/ASCE/AHS/ASC Structures, Structural Dynamics and Materials Conference, Orlando, FL, USA, 12–15 April 2010.
101. Atashipour, S.R.; Al-Emrani, M. A realistic model for transverse shear stiffness prediction of composite corrugated-core sandwich elements. *Int. J. Solids Struct.* **2017**, *129*, 1–17. [CrossRef]

102. Heller, D. A Nonlinear Multiscale Finite Element Model for Comb-Like Sandwich Panels. Ph.D. Thesis, Technische Universität Darmstadt, Darmstadt, Germany, 2015.
103. Montemurro, M.; Catapano, A.; Doroszewski, D. A multi-scale approach for the simultaneous shape and material optimisation of sandwich panels with cellular core. *Compos. Part B Eng.* **2016**, *91*, 458–472. [CrossRef]
104. Smardzewski, J.; Jasińska, D. Mathematical models and experimental data for HDF based sandwich panels with dual corrugated lightweight core. *Holzforschung* **2017**, *71*, 265–273. [CrossRef]
105. Hernández-Pérez, A.; Hägglund, R.; Carlsson, L.A.; Avilés, F. Analysis of twist stiffness of single and double-wall corrugated boards. *Compos. Struct.* **2014**, *110*, 7–15. [CrossRef]
106. Garbowski, T.; Knitter-Piątkowska, A.; Mrówczyński, D. Numerical Homogenization of Multi-Layered Corrugated Cardboard with Creasing or Perforation. *Materials* **2021**, *14*, 3786. [CrossRef] [PubMed]
107. Gajewski, T.; Garbowski, T.; Staszak, N.; Kuca, M. Crushing of Double-Walled Corrugated Board and Its Influence on the Load Capacity of Various Boxes. *Energies* **2021**, *14*, 4321. [CrossRef]
108. Philadelphia Museum of Art. "Kenno" Stool. Available online: https://www.philamuseum.org/collections/permanent/325729.html (accessed on 15 September 2021).
109. Archiproducts. Showroom Finland Presents the Novelties for 2013. Available online: https://www.archiproducts.com/es/noticias/showroom-finland-presents-the-novelties-for-2013_31596 (accessed on 15 September 2021).
110. Archilovers. Heikki Ruoho. *Designer*. Available online: https://www.archilovers.com/heikki-ruoho/ (accessed on 15 September 2021).
111. Archilovers. Järvi & Ruoho. *Design Firm*. Available online: https://www.archilovers.com/teams/119359/jarvi-ruoho.html#info (accessed on 15 September 2021).
112. Harta Packaging Industries Sdn Bhd Heavy-Duty Corrugated Board. Available online: https://hartapack.com/home/wp-content/uploads/2019/03/HEAVY-DUTY-CORRUGATED-BOARD-BROCHURE.pdf (accessed on 15 September 2021).
113. Tri-Wall Pack. Tri-Wall Pack. Available online: http://www.tri-wall.co.th/images/column_1272621251/brochuse3.pdf (accessed on 15 September 2021).
114. Anderson, H.R. Triple-Wall Corrugated Board. U.S. Patent 2,985,553, 23 May 1961.
115. ADF Packaging Committee. *Part 15: Packaging Specifications and Classification Systems*; ADF Packaging Committee: Sydney, Australia, 2000.
116. Chairigami. Cardboard Stool. Available online: https://www.chairigami.com/product-page/cardboard-stool (accessed on 15 September 2021).
117. Good Design Award. Cardboard (Tri-Wall) Tables. Available online: https://www.g-mark.org/award/describe/42743?locale=en (accessed on 15 September 2021).
118. Hplusf. PunchOut Furninture. Available online: https://hplusf.com/projects/punch-out-furniture/ (accessed on 15 September 2021).
119. MoMA. A Child's Chair: Delight in Ownership. 2012. Available online: https://www.moma.org/explore/inside_out/2012/07/05/a-childs-chair-delight-in-ownership/ (accessed on 15 September 2021).
120. European Committee for Standardization (CEN). *EN 1728:2013 Furniture—Seating—Test Methods for the Determination of Strength and Durability*; European Committee for Standardization: Brussels, Belgium, 2013.
121. European Committee for Standardization (CEN). *EN 12520:2015—Furniture—Strength, Durability and Safety—Requirements for Domestic Seating*; European Committee for Standardization: Brussels, Belgium, 2015.
122. Garbowski, T.; Marek, A. Homogenization of corrugated boards through inverse analysis. In Proceedings of the 1st International Conference on Engineering and Applied Sciences Optimization, Kos Island, Greece, 4–6 June 2014.
123. Barbero, E.J. *Introduction to Composite Materials Design*; CRC Press: Boca Raton, FL, USA, 2010.
124. Pohl, A. Strengthened Corrugated Paper Honeycomb for Application in Structural Elements. Ph.D. Thesis, ETH Zurich, Zurich, Germany, 2009.
125. Jones, R. *Mechanics of Composite Materials*; Taylor & Francis: Abingdon, UK, 1998.
126. Marek, A. Homogenization Techniques and Constitutive Modeling of Sandwich Panels. Master's Thesis, Poznań University of Technology, Poznań, Poland, 2014.

Article

Investigation of the Effect of Pallet Top-Deck Stiffness on Corrugated Box Compression Strength as a Function of Multiple Unit Load Design Variables

Saewhan Kim [1], Laszlo Horvath [1,*], Jennifer D. Russell [1] and Jonghun Park [2]

1 Department of Sustainable Biomaterials, Virginia Polytechnic Institute and State University, 1650 Research Center Drive, Blacksburg, VA 24061, USA; seabed94@vt.edu (S.K.); jdrussell@vt.edu (J.D.R.)
2 School of Graphic Communications Management, Ryerson University, 125 Bond Street, Toronto, ON M5B 2K3, Canada; jaypark@ryerson.ca
* Correspondence: lhorvat@vt.edu; Tel.: +1-540-231-7673

Citation: Kim, S.; Horvath, L.; Russell, J.D.; Park, J. Investigation of the Effect of Pallet Top-Deck Stiffness on Corrugated Box Compression Strength as a Function of Multiple Unit Load Design Variables. *Materials* **2021**, *14*, 6613. https://doi.org/10.3390/ma14216613

Academic Editor: Tomasz Garbowski

Received: 4 October 2021
Accepted: 30 October 2021
Published: 3 November 2021

Publisher's Note: MDPI stays neutral with regard to jurisdictional claims in published maps and institutional affiliations.

Copyright: © 2021 by the authors. Licensee MDPI, Basel, Switzerland. This article is an open access article distributed under the terms and conditions of the Creative Commons Attribution (CC BY) license (https:// creativecommons.org/licenses/by/ 4.0/).

Abstract: Unit loads consisting of a pallet, packages, and a product securement system are the dominant way of shipping products across the United States. The most common packaging types used in unit loads are corrugated boxes. Due to the great stresses created during unit load stacking, accurately predicting the compression strength of corrugated boxes is critical to preventing unit load failure. Although many variables affect the compression strength of corrugated boxes, recently, it was found that changing the pallet's top deck stiffness can significantly affect compression strength. However, there is still a lack of understanding of how these different factors influence this phenomenon. This study investigated the effect of pallet's top-deck stiffness on corrugated box compression strength as a function of initial top deck thickness, pallet wood species, box size, and board grade. The amount of increase in top deck thickness needed to lower the board grade of corrugated boxes by one level from the initial unit load scenario was determined using PDS™. The benefits of increasing top deck thickness diminish as the initial top deck thickness increases due to less severe pallet deflection from the start. The benefits were more pronounced as higher board grade boxes were initially used, and as smaller-sized boxes were used due to the heavier weights of these unit loads. Therefore, supposing that a company uses lower stiffness pallets or heavy corrugated boxes for their unit loads, this study suggests that they will find more opportunities to optimize their unit loads by increasing their pallet's top deck thickness.

Keywords: corrugated box; compression strength; pallet; unit load; unit load optimization

1. Introduction

Historically, the distribution packaging industry has adapted the method of unitizing single, multiple, or bulk products on a solid platform to make the handling, storing, and transporting of these products easier [1]. This arrangement is called a unit load. In today's supply chains, 80% of products are moved in unit load form [2]. The most common base platform for unit loads is a pallet. Pallets can be made of different materials such as wood, plastic, paper, or metal. Among these materials, wood is by far the most commonly used to manufacture pallets. Wood is the material of choice for over 90% of companies that use pallets in their supply chains in the United States [3]. Furthermore, approximately 804 million new and recycled wood pallets were manufactured in 2016 [4]. Just as wood pallets have become one of the essential elements of a unit load, corrugated boxes also play a crucial role. Corrugated boxes are the most used primary and secondary packaging; in fact, 72% of unit loads are built using corrugated boxes [3].

When designing a unit load, accurately predicting corrugated box compression strength is crucial to avoid package failure from the vertical compression forces during distribution and storage. Therefore, numerous studies have investigated the factors that affect the compression strength of corrugated boxes, including material properties [5–10], manufacturing methods [6,11–16], environmental condition factors [6,8,12,17], and the palletization factor [18–26].

Wood pallet characteristics, such as pallet gaps and pallet overhang, have been included among the main palletization factors that affect box compression strength. In relatively recent years, researchers have endeavored to correlate pallet top-deck stiffness to corrugated box compression strength. Baker [19] and Phanthanousy [24] examined the relationships between the differences in stress concentrations and box compression strength. However, their studies were inconclusive. Phanthanousy found that the stiffness of the pallet's top deck has no notable effect on box compression strength when the wood pallet is designed with deck board gaps.

Meanwhile, Baker [19] found that pallet top-deck stiffness significantly affects box compression strength when the wood pallet is designed with no deck board gaps. Their studies only evaluated situations in which all corners of the boxes were symmetrically supported. However, in many cases, the top deck board of a wood pallet deforms by the weight of the top load and creates asymmetric support conditions for the loaded products. Baker [19] highlighted that asymmetrically supported corrugated boxes are a prevalent condition in most unit loads, and his research found that asymmetric support can decrease corrugated box compression strength by as much as 15%.

In 2020, Quesenberry et al. [25] further investigated the effect of wood pallet top-deck stiffness on corrugated box compression strength when box corners are asymmetrically supported. They concluded that a stiffer top deck board could increase the compression strength of asymmetrically supported corrugated boxes up to 37% when the unit loads are double-stacked on the floor [25]. They also discovered that the effect of pallet top-deck stiffness on box compression strength could be utilized to lower the cost of a unit load by decreasing the required board grade of corrugated boxes and increasing the pallet's top deck thickness. However, the experimental design utilized by Quesenberry only focused on a limited number of variables. Furthermore, the pallet design utilized for his experimental unit load consisted of a single wood species and singular moisture content.

Additionally, the corrugated boxes were made of a single board grade, two flute sizes, and two box sizes. In practice, many wood species with varying moisture content are available for pallet manufacturing; meanwhile, corrugated boxes are produced in multiple board grades and sizes. Nevertheless, there is an absence of studies investigating how these variations may change the effect of top deck stiffness on corrugated box compression strength.

Therefore, the objective of this current paper is to investigate the effect of pallet top-deck stiffness on the compression strength of asymmetrically supported corrugated boxes as a function of currently under-studied variables, including initial top deck thickness, pallet wood species, box size, and board grade.

2. Materials and Methods

This study consisted of two main sections: validation of the analytical pallet design software and unit load scenario analysis.

2.1. Software Validation

The commercially available pallet design software Pallet Design System™ (PDS™) v. 6.2, created by NWPCA (National Wooden Pallet & Container Association, Alexandria, VA, USA) was utilized to replace numerous physical experiments in this study. The box performance data predicted by PDS™ and that Quesenberry et al. [25] found were compared to confirm that the software reproduced the results from the experiment.

2.1.1. Corrugated Box Description for Validation

The same designs of corrugated boxes used by Quesenberry et al. [25] were used to build the unit load model in PDS™ for predictive software validation. Specified parameters from Quesenberry et al. [25] included: Regular Slotted Container (RSC) style with two different external dimensions (length × width × height) 406.4 mm × 247.7 mm × 254 mm and 609.6 mm × 247.7 mm × 254 mm. Unit loads were built with four layers of boxes, and the configuration of boxes was either 3 boxes × 4 boxes (length × width) or 2 boxes × 4 boxes. Both sizes of boxes were built with nominal 0.57 kg/mm Edge Crush Test (ECT) value B-flute and C-flute corrugated board.

2.1.2. Pallet Description for Validation

Quesenberry et al. [25] simulated a 1219.2 mm × 1016 mm GMA™ (Grocery Manufacturers Association) style pallet by using a custom-built, quarter-section pallet for testing purposes. For software validation, a full-sized 1219.2 mm × 1016 mm stringer class, double face, non-reversible, partial four-way, unidirectional bottom, flush, GMA™ style pallet was modeled in PDS™ (see Figure 1). The pallet consisted of three stringers, seven top deck boards, five bottom deck boards, and two fasteners per joint. The stringers were 1219.2 mm long, 31.8 mm wide, and 88.9 mm high. The top and bottom deck boards were 1016 mm long and 88.9 mm wide. The four top deck board thicknesses studied were: 9.5 mm, 12.7 mm, 15.9 mm, and 19.1 mm. All top deck boards were equally spaced 99.6 mm apart. Lead bottom deck boards were spaced 292.1 mm away from the interior bottom deck boards, and the interior bottom deck boards were spaced 95.3 mm apart. Number 1 & better (premium & better), kiln-dried, Spruce–Pine–Fir (SPF) lumber was used for all pallet components.

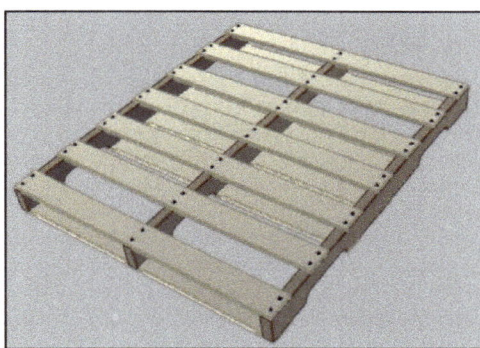

Figure 1. Picture of GMA pallet used for software validation (image generated using PDS™).

2.1.3. Comparison of Box Load Factor and Box Compression Strength Factor

During software validation, the box load factors computed by PDS™ and the box compression strength factor derived from the thesis of Quesenberry [27] were compared. The box load factor is the ratio of the weights on worst loaded box edges to the load if it were evenly distributed. Meanwhile, the box compression strength factor is a new term developed by the authors and is defined as the ratio of the box compression strength when box corners are symmetrically supported on rigid supports to the box compression strength when its corners are asymmetrically supported on an actual pallet. Both the box load factor and the box compression strength factor ultimately provide information about the compression performance of the corrugated box.

Process of Computing Box Load Factor

Box load factors were computed using PDS™ following the steps described below.
Step 1: Built a unit load in PDS™ using boxes and pallets previously described in Sections 2.1.1 and 2.1.2.
Step 2: Set the top deck board thickness to the lowest level (9.5 mm).

Step 3: Set the weight in the box to the load that will just fail the boxes (box safety factor of one) when the support condition is a single floor stack.
Step 4: Report current box load factor when support condition is single floor stack.
Step 5: Increased the top deck board thickness to the following levels (12.7 mm, 15.9 mm, and 19.1 mm).
Step 6: Repeat *steps 3* and *4* for each level of top deck board thickness.
Step 7: Repeat the process for two flute sizes (B and C flute) and two box sizes.

Process of Calculating Box Compression Strength Factor

The box compression strength factor from Quesenberry's study was calculated using Equation (1):

$$CSF = \frac{SCS_{avg}}{ACS_{avg}} \quad (1)$$

where:

CSF = Box compression strength factor.
SCS_{avg} = Average box compression strength when box corners are symmetrically supported on a rigid platform.
ACS_{avg} = Average box compression strength when box corners are asymmetrically supported on the actual pallet.
The unit load scenarios used to calculate the box compression strength factors were varied by two flute sizes, two box sizes, and four thickness levels.

Statistical Analysis

The independent *t*-test was conducted to see whether the difference between box load factors from PDS™ and box compression strength factors from the experiment were statistically significant or not. To confirm the normality assumption of the independent *t*-test, we also ran the Shapiro–Wilk test for each group separately. The similarities between the box performance data from PDS™ and the experiment were also assessed using the Pearson correlation coefficient. The Pearson correlation coefficient is a way to investigate linear dependence between two variables. The measured correlation coefficient (r) ranges between −1 and +1. When the r-value is −1, it indicates a strong negative correlation, while +1 indicates a strong positive correlation, and 0 means no relation. Both statistical analyses were conducted at a significance level of 0.05. The analyses were done using SAS JMP Pro 15® software (SAS Enterprises, Raleigh, NC, USA).

2.2. Unit Load Scenario Analysis

The concept of a unit load cost optimization method that allows for corrugated boxes with decreased board grades by increasing the pallet's top deck thickness was adopted from Quesenberry et al. [25] to modify each unit load scenario. In other words, the analysis was done by determining how much the top deck thickness needed to increase to lower the corrugated board grade by one level from the initial unit load scenario's specific deck board thickness and board grade. A total of 234 unit load scenarios were designed with varying factors for investigation.

2.2.1. Corrugated Box Description for Unit Load Scenario Analysis

Three sizes of RSC-style corrugated boxes were investigated to explore the effect of different box sizes. Three box sizes were chosen that would cover the entire top surface of the 1219.2 mm × 1016 mm pallet and create asymmetrically supported corners. The external dimensions were 203.2 mm × 304.8 mm × 254 mm (small box), 406.4 mm × 254 mm × 254 mm (medium box), and 609.6 mm × 337.8 mm × 254 mm (large box). The boxes were organized in 4 × 5, 3 × 4, and 2 × 3 arrays for small, medium, and large boxes, respectively. Four layers of boxes were used for each unit load. Unit load configurations using the different box sizes are depicted in Figure 2. The boxes were built with two different flute sizes: single-wall C-flute and double-wall BC-flute. The

C-flute and BC-flute corrugated boards were made of commonly manufactured board grades for each flute size. C-flute boards were modeled with nominal 0.52 kg/mm., 0.57 kg/mm, 0.71 kg/mm, and 0.79 kg/mm ECT. BC-flute boards were modeled with nominal 0.86 kg/mm, 0.91 kg/mm, 1.09 kg/mm, and 1.27 kg/mm ECT.

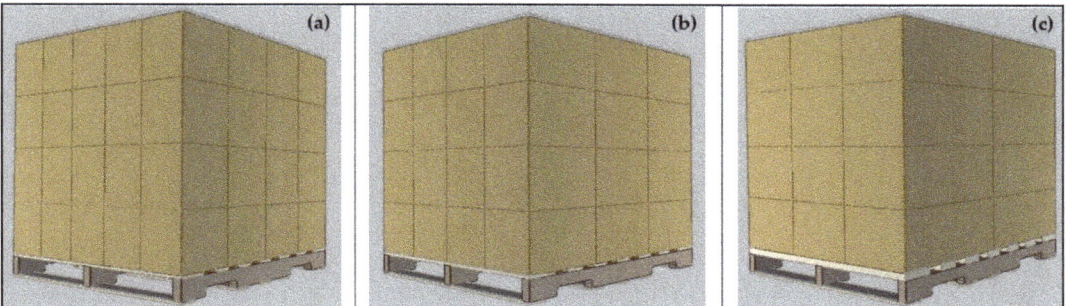

Figure 2. Image of investigated unit load configurations (image generated using PDS™). (**a**) Unit load with small boxes, (**b**) unit load with medium boxes, and (**c**) unit load with large boxes.

2.2.2. Pallet Description for Unit Load Scenario Analysis

For the unit load scenario analysis, the most common size of GMA™ style wood pallet was used. The 1219.2 mm × 1016 mm GMA™ style stringer class wooden pallet is the most commonly used pallet design in North America [28,29]. The specifications were 1219.2 mm × 1016 mm, stringer class, double face, non-reversible, partial four-way, unidirectional bottom, flush, GMA™ style pallet (see Figure 3). The pallet design had three stringers, two lead top deck boards, five interior top deck boards, five bottom deck boards, two fasteners per joint on the interior top deck boards and for all bottom deck board connections, and three fasteners per joint on the lead top deck boards. The pallet design utilized for the unit load scenario analysis (Figure 3) had 50.8 mm wider lead top deck boards than the pallet design used for the software validation process (Figure 1). The spacing between top deck boards has also changed accordingly. The stringers were 1219.2 mm long, 31.8 mm wide, and 88.9 mm high. The interior top deck boards and bottom deck boards were 1016 mm long and 88.9 mm wide. The lead top deck boards were 1016 mm long and 139.7 mm wide. The bottom deck boards were 9.5 mm thick. All top deck boards were spaced 82.6 mm apart. The lead bottom deck boards were spaced 292.1 mm apart from interior bottom deck boards, and interior bottom deck boards were spaced 95.3 mm apart from each other. Number 1 & better (premium & better) grade lumber was used for all pallet components.

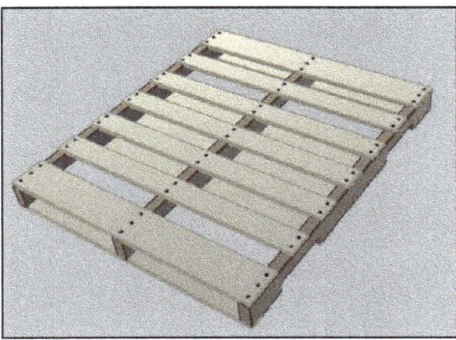

Figure 3. Picture of GMA pallet used for analysis (image generated using PDS™).

Initial top deck thicknesses were varied by four levels to explore which changes in deck board thicknesses would be required to reduce by one level the initial board grade specified for the corrugated boxes. The investigated initial top deck thickness levels were 9.5 mm, 12.7 mm, 15.9 mm, and 19.1 mm. However, unit load scenarios built with kiln-dried southern yellow pine (KD SYP) pallets were designed with 11.1 mm top deck boards, and this thickness was increased to 17.5 mm for the optimized design. This limitation was due to the availability of raw material sizes; only the 11.1 mm and 17.5 mm dimensions could be manufactured effectively.

Wood species used for pallet construction were also varied. The wood species commonly used for pallet construction in the southeastern United States were selected. Selected wood materials were: green, high-density hardwood (Grn HD HW); green, low-density hardwood (Grn LD HW); green, southern yellow pine (Grn SYP); and kiln-dried, southern yellow pine (KD SYP). Green lumber contained 25% or greater moisture content, and kiln-dried lumber had a maximum of 19% moisture content.

2.2.3. Variable Factors

Several factors of the unit load were varied to identify the characteristics that could change the effect of the pallet's top deck board stiffness on box compression strength. The factors evaluated were initial top deck board thickness, pallet wood species, box size, and corrugated board grade. The variable factors that relate to pallets are listed in Table 1, and Table 2 contains the variable factors relating to the boxes.

Table 1. Summary table of variable factors related to pallets.

Pallet wood species	Green high-density hardwood Green low-density hardwood Green southern yellow pine Kiln-dried southern yellow pine
Initial top deck thickness for green lumber	9.5 mm 12.7 mm 15.9 mm 19.1 mm
Fixed range for KD SYP lumber thickness	11.1 mm to 17.5 mm

Table 2. Summary table of variable factors related to corrugated boxes.

Box Size (mm)	Flute Size	ECT Range (kg/mm)
Small (203.2 × 304.8 × 254)	C	0.57 to 0.52 0.71 to 0.57 0.79 to 0.71
Medium (406.4 × 254 × 254)		
Large (609.6 × 337.8 × 254)	BC	0.91 to 0.86 1.09 to 0.91 1.27 to 1.09

2.2.4. Analysis Method

Measurement of Top Deck Thickness Increase

The unit load cost optimization method adopted from Quesenberry et al. [25] was investigated by varying the factors introduced in Section 2.2.3. The change in top deck thickness required to reduce by one level the corrugated board grade used, without downgrading box performance, was measured. This analysis was done with the unit load in the double floor stacked condition. A box safety factor of 3 was selected for the unit load design to comply with the requirements of the ISTA 3E testing standard [30].

Required steps in the analysis were as follows:

Step 1: Construct the unit load in PDS™.

Step 2: Set pallet material as one of the listed wood species (i.e., green high-density hardwood).
Step 3: Set the top deck board as the lowest initial top deck board thickness (9.5 mm). In the case of KD SYP, always set the initial top deck thickness as 11.1 mm.
Step 4: Set corrugated boxes as the higher ECT values in the selected range of board grade (i.e., Choose 0.57 kg/mm if the range was decreasing from 0.57 kg/mm to 0.52 kg/mm).
Step 5: Determine the weight of the box that works to create a box safety factor of three for the double floor stacking condition.
Step 6: Create a new unit load with the corrugated boxes made of lower ECT value from the selected range of corrugated board grade and apply the weight determined in *step 5* (i.e., Select 0.52 kg/mm if the range was 0.57 kg/mm to 0.52 kg/mm).
Step 7: Continuously increase the top deck thickness by 1.6 mm until the unit load again reaches the safety factor of three for safe operation. In the case of KD SYP, always increase the top deck thickness to 17.5 mm.
Step 8: Report the total increase in the top deck board thickness required to achieve the required safety factor of three.
Step 9: Repeat *step 1* to *step 8* after changing the pallet wood species.
Step 10: Repeat from *step 1* to *step 9* after increasing the initial top deck stiffness level.
Step 11: Repeat from *step 1* to *step 10* after changing the range of board grade (i.e., changing from a range of 0.57–0.52 kg/mm to a range of 0.71—0.57 kg/mm).
Step 12: Repeat from *step 1* to *step 11* after changing the size of corrugated boxes (i.e., changing from a small to a medium size box).

Unit Load Scenario Classification System

The amount that the top deck thickness increased was categorized as one of three grades to make it easier to identify which scenarios had smaller or larger increases in top deck thickness: less than 12.7 mm (grade 1), 12.7 mm to 25.4 mm (grade 2), and beyond 25.4 mm increase (grade 3). For better visualization, a color-coding system was also applied; green for grade 1, yellow for grade 2, and red for grade 3. Grade 1 scenarios were considered as cases with high potential to apply the unit load optimization process. Grade 2 scenarios were considered cases that may be possible to apply the optimization method depending on the manufacturer's circumstances. Because pallets made of deck boards thicker than 25.4 mm are unprecedented; grade 3 scenarios were considered unrealistic unit load designs.

3. Results and Discussion

3.1. Software Validation Results

Measurement of the box load factors and box compression strength factors on varied top deck thicknesses, box sizes, and flute sizes are presented in Table 3. The comparison of box load factors and box compression strength factors is plotted in Figure 4. It was observed that PDS™ tends to overestimate the effect of top deck stiffness when compared to the experiment results. However, the independent t-test showed that the difference between PDS™ and the experiment was not statistically significant ($t_{(25)} = -0.85$, p-value = 0.40). The Shapiro-Wilk test confirmed that the normality assumptions were met (PDS: $W = 0.927$, p-value = 0.216; Quesenberry: $W = 0.919$, p-value = 0.160). Furthermore, the Pearson correlation coefficient revealed a strong positive correlation, $r = 0.911$ (p-value < 0.0001), between box load factors from PDS™ and box compression strength factors from experiment results. In other words, the PDS™ and Quesenberry's [27] experiments had a similar pattern.

Table 3. Summary table of box load and compression strength factors.

Topdeck Thickness (mm)	Box Load and Compression Strength Factor							
	Small C-Flute Box		Large C-Flute Box		Small B-Flute Box		Large B-Flute Box	
	PDS	Experiment	PDS	Experiment	PDS	Experiment	PDS	Experiment
9.5	1.366	1.362	1.332	1.363	1.375	1.513	1.360	1.334
12.7	1.268	1.145	1.225	1.152	1.307	1.320	1.258	1.172
15.9	1.187	1.090	1.153	1.116	1.222	1.298	1.179	1.117
19.1	1.136	1.005	1.109	1.075	1.165	1.105	1.129	1.022

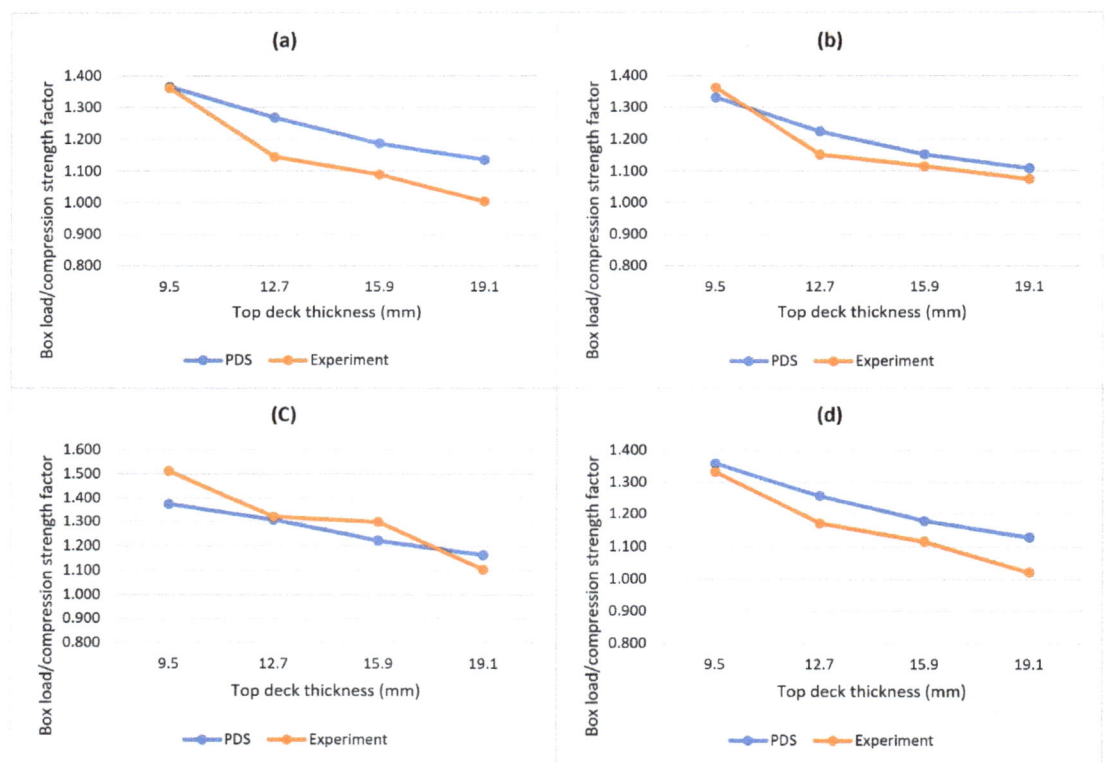

Figure 4. Comparison of box load factors and box compression strength factors of each type of boxes in response to pallet top-deck thickness. (**a**) Small C-flute box scenarios, (**b**) shows large C-flute box scenarios, (**c**) shows small B-flute box scenarios, and (**d**) shows large B-flute box scenarios.

3.2. Unit Load Scenario Analysis Results

Tables 4 and 5 report the amount of top deck board thickness increase required to reduce the corrugated board grade by one level as a function of starting top deck thickness, wood species, initial board grade, and box sizes for the unit loads consisting of C-flute boxes and BC-flute boxes, respectively. A streamlined grading system has been applied, as described in Section 2.2.4, for better visualization and identification of the level of top deck thickness increase. The top deck thickness increase for grade 3 scenarios was reported as N/A (not applicable) because adding an extra inch of thickness to a pallet deck board is highly cost-prohibitive.

Table 4. The amount of top deck board thickness required to optimize unit loads consisting of C-flute boxes.

	C-Flute		Amount of Top Deck Thickness Increase (mm)								
			0.57–0.52 kg/mm ECT			0.71–0.57 kg/mm ECT			0.79–0.71 kg/mm ECT		
		Initial Top Deck Thickness (mm)	Grn HD HW	Grn LD HW	Grn SYP	Grn HD HW	Grn LD HW	Grn SYP	Grn HD HW	Grn LD HW	Grn SYP
C-Flute	Small	9.5	3.2	3.2	3.2	8	6.4	8	3.2	3.2	3.2
		12.7	4.8	4.8	6.4	N/A	N/A	N/A	4.8	3.2	4.8
		15.9	15.9	9.5	N/A	N/A	N/A	N/A	9.5	6.4	9.5
		19.1	N/A	N/A	N/A	N/A	N/A	N/A	N/A	N/A	N/A
	Medium	9.5	4.8	4.8	4.8	22.2	22.2	12.7	3.2	3.2	3.2
		12.7	12.7	8	8	N/A	N/A	N/A	8	6.4	4.8
		15.9	N/A	N/A	N/A	N/A	N/A	N/A	N/A	N/A	15.9
		19.1	N/A	N/A	N/A	N/A	N/A	N/A	N/A	N/A	N/A
	Large	9.5	8	9.5	9.5	N/A	N/A	N/A	9.5	11.1	11.1
		12.7	N/A	19.1	19.1	N/A	N/A	N/A	12.7	12.7	12.7
		15.9	N/A	N/A	N/A	N/A	N/A	N/A	N/A	N/A	N/A
		19.1	N/A	N/A	N/A	N/A	N/A	N/A	N/A	N/A	N/A

Grade 1: less than 12.7 mm (green), Grade 2: 12.7 mm to 25.4 mm (yellow), Grade 3: beyond 25.4 mm increase (red). Note: Grn HD HW: green high-density hardwood, Grn LD HW: green low-density hardwood, Grn SYP: green southern yellow pine.

Table 5. The amount of top deck board thickness required to optimize unit loads consisting of BC-flute boxes.

			Amount of Top Deck Thickness Increase (mm)								
			0.91–0.86 kg/mm ECT			1.09–0.91 kg/mm ECT			1.27–1.09 kg/mm ECT		
		Initial Top Deck Thickness (mm)	Grn HD HW	Grn LD HW	Grn SYP	Grn HD HW	Grn LD HW	Grn SYP	Grn HD HW	Grn LD HW	Grn SYP
BC-Flute	Small	9.5	1.6	1.6	1.6	4.8	4.8	4.8	4.8	4.8	4.8
		12.7	3.2	1.6	1.6	19.1	6.4	6.4	8	6.4	6.4
		15.9	3.2	3.2	3.2	N/A	N/A	N/A	N/A	N/A	15.9
		19.1	12.7	3.2	6.4	N/A	N/A	N/A	N/A	N/A	N/A
	Medium	9.5	3.2	3.2	1.6	8	6.4	6.4	6.4	6.4	6.4
		12.7	3.2	3.2	3.2	N/A	19.1	19.1	12.7	9.5	8
		15.9	6.4	4.8	4.8	N/A	N/A	N/A	N/A	N/A	N/A
		19.1	N/A	12.7	12.7	N/A	N/A	N/A	N/A	N/A	N/A
	Large	9.5	6.4	9.5	8	N/A	N/A	N/A	N/A	N/A	N/A
		12.7	6.4	6.4	6.4	N/A	N/A	N/A	N/A	N/A	N/A
		15.9	9.5	9.5	9.5	N/A	N/A	N/A	N/A	N/A	N/A
		19.1	N/A	N/A	N/A	N/A	N/A	N/A	N/A	N/A	N/A

Grade 1: less than 12.7 mm (green), Grade 2: 12.7 mm to 25.4 mm (yellow), Grade 3: beyond 25.4 mm increase (red). Note: Grn HD HW: green high-density hardwood, Grn LD HW: green low-density hardwood, Grn SYP: green southern yellow pine.

Tables 6 and 7 present the KD SYP scenarios' amount of top deck board thickness increase required to reduce the corrugated board grade by one level as a function of the different factors for the unit loads built using C-flute and BC-flute boxes, respectively.

Table 6. The amount of top deck board thickness required to optimize unit loads consisting of KD SYP pallet and C-flute boxes.

		Initial Top Deck Thickness (mm)	Amount of Top Deck Thickness Increase (mm)		
			0.79–0.71 kg/mm ECT	0.71–0.57 kg/mm ECT	0.57–0.52 kg/mm ECT
			Kiln-Dried Southern Yellow Pine		
C-Flute	Small	11.1	17.5	N/A	17.5
	Medium		N/A	N/A	N/A
	Large		N/A	N/A	N/A

Note: The deckboard thickness sizes available for kiln-dried southern yellow pine (KD SYP) were limited because the available raw material size only allows the cost-effective production of 11.1 mm and 17.5 mm deckboard thicknesses.

Table 7. The amount of top deck board thickness required to optimize unit loads consisting of KD SYP pallet and BC-flute boxes.

		Initial Top Deck Thickness (mm)	Amount of Top Deck Thickness Increase (mm)		
			0.91–0.86 kg/mm ECT	1.09–0.91 kg/mm ECT	1.27–1.09 kg/mm ECT
			Kiln-Dried Southern Yellow Pine		
BC-Flute	Small	11.1	N/A	N/A	17.5
	Medium		N/A	N/A	17.5
	Large		N/A	N/A	17.5

Note: The deckboard thickness sizes available for kiln-dried southern yellow pine (KD SYP) were limited because the available raw material size only allows the cost-effective production of 11.1 mm and 17.5 mm deckboard thicknesses.

To investigate how different factors such as the initial top deck board thickness, pallet wood species, box size, and board grade effect the feasibility of optimizing the strength of the corrugated boxes by changing the stiffness of the pallets, researchers looked at the changes in the proportions of different grade scenarios in response to each variable factor.

Figure 5 shows how the proportions of various grade scenarios changed when different initial top deck thicknesses were used for the pallet design. As the initial top deck thickness increased, there was a significant reduction in the proportion of grade 1 scenarios. These are the scenarios where it is highly feasible to reduce the corrugated board grade with a reasonable amount of top deck thickness change. The proportion of grade 1 scenarios started from 78% with 9.5 mm initial top deck thickness and decreased to 50%, 24%, and 4% when the initial top deck thickness was 12.7 mm, 15.9 mm, and 19.1 mm, respectively. Correlatingly, the ratio of grade 3 scenarios was almost inversely proportional to the ratio of grade 1 scenarios as the initial top deck thickness increased. The proportion of grade 3 increased from 17% to 31%, 70%, and 91% when the initial top deck thickness was 9.5 mm, 12.7 mm, 15.9 mm, and 19.1 mm, respectively. Unlike other grade scenarios, no consistent trend was found in the proportion of grade 2 scenarios.

Figure 6 shows the changes in the proportions of the various unit load scenario grades when different wood species were used to build the pallets. The percent of different grade levels were similar for the scenarios using green low-density hardwood and green SYP with around 40% grade 1, 10% grade 2, and 50% grade 3. KD SYP scenarios behaved differently than the other wood species scenarios. They had a much lower number of feasible scenarios than the others. Grade 1 scenarios of KD SYP accounted for only 28%, while grade 1 scenarios of green lumber accounted for between 35–40%. The reduction of feasible scenarios might be attributable to the high stiffness of the KD SYP species. A highly stiff top deck will not bend enough to make a difference in board grade when top deck thickness changes. In addition, the results could have been affected by the limited availability of various KD SYP thicknesses. KD SYP lumber required a larger jump in top deck thicknesses than the 1.59 mm increases used with green species.

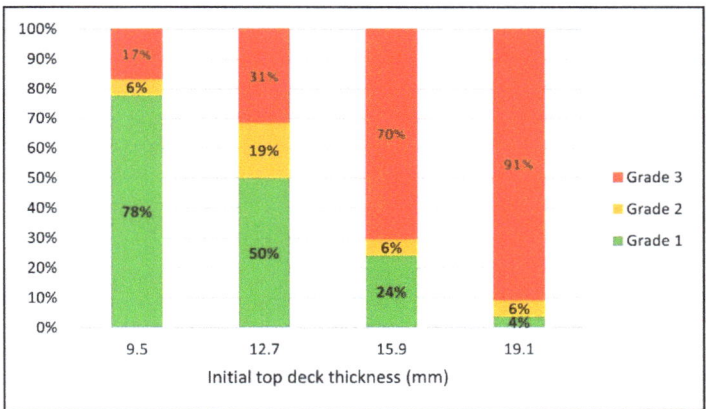

Figure 5. Changes in the proportions of the different grade scenarios in response to the initial top deck thickness for green wood scenarios.

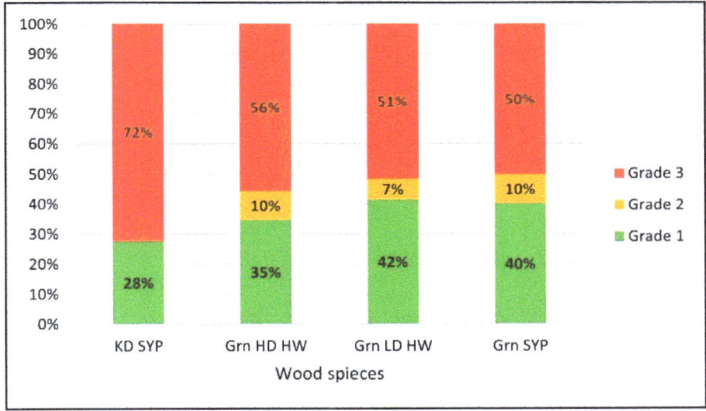

Figure 6. Changes in the proportions of the different grade scenarios in response to the pallet wood species. Note: KD SYP: kiln-dried southern yellow pine, Grn HD HW: green high-density hardwood, Grn LD HW: green low-density hardwood, Grn SYP: green southern yellow pine.

Furthermore, the proportion of the grade 1 scenarios for Grn HD HW was slightly lower (35%) than the other green lumber scenarios (40–42%). Since Grn HD HW does not have a limit on the level of top deck thickness increase, this could provide further evidence that the stiffness of the material affects the feasibility of the design scenario. Overall, the results indicate that the feasibility of using increased deck board thickness to lower the corrugated boxboard grade decreases when species with higher material stiffness are initially used to construct the pallets.

Similar trends in the proportional changes of different unit load scenario grades were observed from the initial top deck thickness effect and the pallet wood species effect. Both results indicated a significant reduction in the potential to decrease board grade by increasing top deck stiffness when the pallet was initially designed with stiffer pallet wood material. In other words, this unit load optimization method is more effective when the unit load is initially designed using lower stiffness pallets.

Figure 7 displays changes in the proportions of different grade scenarios as a function of the range of board grade reduction. It was discovered that for the scenarios where the ECT change is greater between the consecutive board grade levels, the proportion of grade 1 scenarios decreases, and the ratio of grade 3 considerably increases. The ratio of grade 1 scenarios ranged between 41% and 82% for the cases with 0.05 kg/mm to 0.08 kg/mm ECT reduction. On the other hand, the proportion of grade 1 scenarios ranged only between 8% and 28% when it required 0.14 kg/mm to 0.18 kg/mm ECT value reduction. These results also show that the higher the initial board grade is, the more opportunities there are to reduce the board material with minor changes to top deck thickness. For instance, the proportion of grade 1 scenarios significantly increased from 41% to 49% and 82% when the board grade reduction range was 0.57–0.52 kg/mm, 0.79–0.71 kg/mm, and 0.91–0.86 kg/mm ECT, respectively. In this analysis, higher board grade also meant that the boxes supported more weight than lower board grade boxes. It indicates that the effect was more prominent for scenarios that had greater unit load weight because having more weight in the boxes causes more bending to the deck boards, which increases stress concentrations on the boxes.

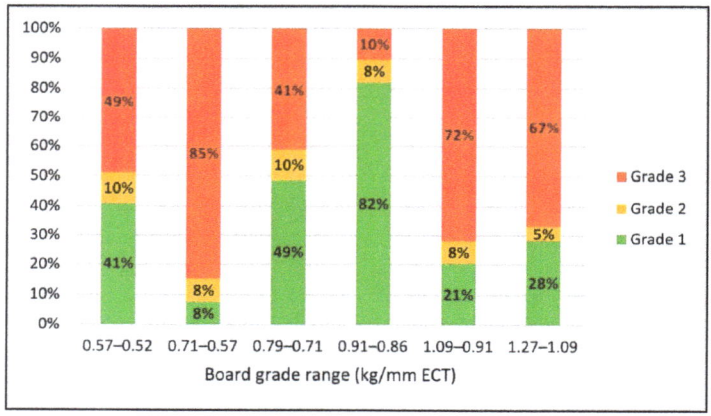

Figure 7. Changes in the proportions of the different grade scenarios in response to the range of board grade reduction.

Figure 8 shows changes in the proportions of various unit load scenario grades for the three different box sizes. The proportion of the grade 1 scenarios decreased from 57% to 39% and 21% and the proportion of the grade 3 scenario increased from 38% to 47% and 72% as package size increased from small to medium to large boxes. There was no consistent trend with the proportion of grade 2 scenarios. The results indicated that the feasibility is greater to reduce the corrugated board grade by increasing the thickness of top deck boards for unit loads consisting of small-sized boxes rather than larger ones. Similar to the board grade effect, this trend could be explained by weight differences per unit load. Although each small box held a lighter weight than the medium and large boxes in this analysis, the small box scenarios contained much heavier weight as a whole unit load than the scenarios with larger-sized boxes because these unit loads required more of the small boxes to create the same size load.

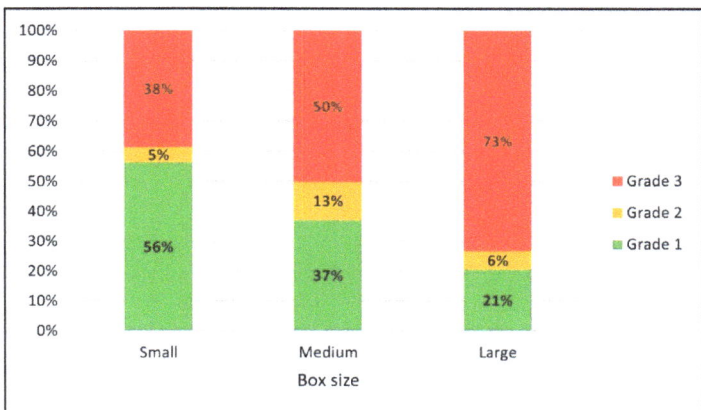

Figure 8. Changes in the proportions of the different grade scenarios in response to the box sizes.

Overall, it was found that all investigated variable factors had an observable influence on the feasibility of using an increase in pallet top-deck stiffness to lower the board grade of the corrugated boxes. Unit load scenarios to which it was more feasible to apply the unit load cost optimization method were observed as the initial unit load was designed with less stiff pallet top-deck boards; either thinner top deck boards or lower density wood species. For box-related variables, unit loads of smaller-sized boxes, unit loads with a smaller range of board grade reduction, and unit loads with higher initial board grades all created more favorable situations on which to apply the unit load optimization method due to the heavier weight of these unit loads.

4. Limitations and Assumptions

1. Only a standard GMA™ style, stringer class, wooden pallet design was investigated in the study.
2. PDS can only run analysis up to 38.1 mm top deck board thickness, so the scenarios requiring top deck boards thicker than 38.1 mm were not simulated. Therefore, the color grading system was applied to show the comparison between these different scenarios.
3. Due to the functional limitations of PDS™ regarding top deck thickness increases, the correlation between pallet stiffness (kg/mm top deck deflection) and the amount of wood material that needed to be added was not investigated.

5. Conclusions

The key findings of this study were as follows:

- The benefits of increasing a pallet's top deck thickness to reduce the corrugated board grade diminish as the initial stiffness of the pallet increases.
- There were more opportunities to optimize unit load designs when the ECT values between the different board grade levels were lower.
- There were more possibilities of decreasing board grade when the initial board grade was higher, and/or when the box size was smaller, mostly due to the heavier weight of these unit loads, which caused greater pallet bending. Pallets made of Kiln-Dried Southern Yellow Pine are less likely to be able to be optimized using the investigated methods because of the limited deck board thicknesses that can be cost-effectively manufactured from the available raw materials.

Therefore, this study suggests that companies that use low stiffness pallets or have unit loads of heavy boxes could have more opportunities to optimize their unit loads by increasing the top deck thickness of their pallets.

The study also revealed that changing the top deck board stiffness cannot be done without considering the effects of other factors such as initial top deck board thickness, pallet wood species, box size, and board grade. Therefore, the unit load optimization process that reduces corrugated board grade by increasing top deck stiffness needs to be a holistic process.

The next phase of the project will focus on investigating whether the increase in pallet top-deck stiffness and the resulting reduction in corrugated boxboard grade can create an environmentally beneficial scenario.

Author Contributions: S.K. and L.H. developed the research methodology, S.K. conducted the modeling and the analysis, S.K. developed the original draft, L.H., J.P. and J.D.R. reviewed and edited the paper, L.H. finalized the paper. This research project was conducted under the supervision of L.H. All authors have read and agreed to the published version of the manuscript.

Funding: This research was funded by the Industrial Affiliate Program of the Center for Packaging and Unit Load Design at Virginia Tech.

Institutional Review Board Statement: Not applicable.

Informed Consent Statement: Not applicable.

Data Availability Statement: The data presented in this study are available on request from the corresponding author.

Acknowledgments: The PDS™ software package used for the data analysis provided by the National Wooden Pallet and Container Association.

Conflicts of Interest: The authors declare no conflict of interest.

References

1. White, M.S.; Hamner, P. Pallets Move the World: The Case for Developing System-Based Designs for Unit Loads. *For. Prod. J.* **2005**, *55*, 3.
2. Raballand, G.; Aldaz-Carroll, E. How Do Differing Standards Increase Trade Costs? The Case of Pallets. *World Econ.* **2007**, *30*, 685–702. [CrossRef]
3. McCrea, B. Annual Pallet Report: 2020's Market Evaluation. Available online: https://www.mmh.com/article/annual_pallet_report_2020s_market_evaluation (accessed on 12 June 2021).
4. Gerber, N.; Horvath, L.; Araman, P.; Gething, B. Investigation of New and Recovered Wood Shipping Platforms in the United States. *BioResources* **2020**, *15*, 2818–2838. [CrossRef]
5. Almanza, B.A.; Cooksey, K.; Cooksey, R.C.; Jaffe, W.F. Effect of Reprocessed Material on Selected Physical Characteristics of Corrugated Shipping Cartons Used in Foodservice Operations. *Foodserv. Res. Int.* **1993**, *7*, 177–183. [CrossRef]
6. Kellicutt, K.Q.; Landt, E.F. *Basic Design Data for Use of Fiberboard in Shipping Containers*; USDA Forest Service: Madison, WI, USA, 1958.
7. McKee, R.C.; Gander, J.W.; Wachuta, J.R. Compression Strength Formula for Corrugated Boxes. *Paperboard Packag.* **1963**, *48*, 149–159.
8. Frank, B. Corrugated Box Compression—A Literature Survey. *Packag. Technol. Sci.* **2014**, *27*, 105–128. [CrossRef]
9. Popil, R.E.; Schaepe, M.K.; Haj-Ali, R.; Wei, B.S.; Choi, J. Adhesive Level Effect on Corrugated Board Strength–Experiment and FE Modeling. In *2007 International Progress in Paper Physics Seminar*; Paper Physics International Committee: Oxford, OH, USA, 2006; pp. 1–6.
10. Kawanishi, K. Estimation of the Compression Strength of Corrugated Fibreboard Boxes and Its Application to Box Design Using a Personal Computer. *Packag. Technol. Sci.* **1989**, *2*, 29–39. [CrossRef]
11. Singh, J.; Attema, A.; Olsen, E.; Vorst, K. Effect of Manufacturer's Joint Fastening Corrugated Fiberboard Boxes. *J. Appl. Packag. Res.* **2009**, *3*, 233–247.
12. Frank, B. Box Compression Analysis of World-Wide Data Spanning 46 Years. *Wood Fiber Sci.* **2006**, *38*, 399–416.
13. Han, B.J.; Park, J.M. Finite Element Analysis of Vent/Hand Hole and Science. *Packag. Technol. Sci.* **2007**, 39–47. [CrossRef]
14. Jinkarn, T.; Boonchu, P.; Bao-Ban, S. Effect of Carrying Slots on the Compressive Strength of Corrugated Board Panels. *Kasetsart J. Nat. Sci.* **2006**, *40*, 154–161.
15. Kwak, W. Analysis of Compression Strength of Corrugated Shipping Containers with Different Designed Hand Holes. Master's Thesis, Rochester Institute of Technology, Rochester, NY, USA, June 2010.
16. Surber, R.; Catlin, A. Estimating the Effects of Interiors on Corrugated Box Stacking Strength. *Packag. Technol.* **1982**, *28*, 15–23.
17. Whitsitt, W.J.; McKee, R.C. *Effect of Relative Humidity and Temperature on Stacking Performance*; Institute of Paper Chemistry: Appleton, WI, USA, 1972.

18. DiSalvo, M.H. Interactive Effects of Palletizing Factors on Fiberboard Strength. Master's Thesis, San Jose State University, San Jose, CA, USA, August 1999.
19. Baker, M. Effect of Pallet Deckboard Stiffness on Corrugated Box Compression Strength. Ph.D. Thesis, Virginia Polytechnic Institute and State University, Virginia, VA, USA, February 2016.
20. Kellicut, K.Q. *Effect of Contents and Load Bearing Surface on Compressive Strength and Stacking Life of Corrugated Containers*; Technical Association of the Pulp and Paper Industry: Peachtree Corners, GA, USA, 1963.
21. Singh, S.P.; Singh, J.; Saha, K. Effect of Palletized Box Offset on Compression Strength of Unitized and Stacked Empty Corrugated Fiberboard Boxes. *J. Appl. Packag. Res.* **2011**, *5*, 157–167.
22. Godshall, W.D. *Effects of Vertical Dynamic Loading on Corrugated Fiberboard Containers*; USDA Forest Service: Madison, WI, USA, 1968.
23. Marcondes, J.A. Effect of Load History on the Performance of Corrugated Fibreboard Boxes. *Packag. Technol. Sci.* **1992**, *5*, 179–187. [CrossRef]
24. Phanthanousy, S. The Effect of the Stiffness of Unit Load Components on Pallet Deflection and Box Compression Strength. Master's Thesis, Virginia Polytechnic Institute and State University, Blacksburg, VA, USA, May 2017.
25. Quesenberry, C.; Horvath, L.; Bouldin, J.; White, M.S. The Effect of Pallet Top Deck Stiffness on the Compression Strength of Asymmetrically Supported Corrugated Boxes. *Packag. Technol. Sci.* **2020**, *33*, 547–558. [CrossRef]
26. Yoo, J. Modeling Compressive Stress Distributions at the Interface between a Pallet Deck and Distribution Packaging. Ph.D. Thesis, Virginia Polytechnic Institute and State University, Blacksburg, VA, USA, September 2011.
27. Quesenberry, C. The Effect of Pallet Top Deck Stiffness on the Compression Strength of Asymmetrically Supported Corrugated Boxes. Master's Thesis, Virginia Polytechnic Institute and State University, Blacksburg, VA, USA, December 2019.
28. Bejune, J.J. Wood Use Trends in the Pallet and Container Industry: 1992–1999. Master's Thesis, Virginia Polytechnic Institute and State University, Blacksburg, VA, USA, May 2001.
29. Clarke, J.W.; White, M.S.; Araman, P.A. Comparative Performance of New, Repaired, and Remanufactured 48- By 40-Inch GMA-Style Wood Pallets. *For. Prod. J.* **2005**, *55*, 83–88.
30. ISTA 3E. *Similar Packaged-Products in Unitized Loads for Truckload Shipment*; International Safe Transit Association: East Lansing, MI, USA, 2017.

Article

New Edge Crush Test Configuration Enhanced with Full-Field Strain Measurements

Tomasz Garbowski [1], Anna Knitter-Piątkowska [2,*] and Aleksander Marek [3]

1 Department of Biosystems Engineering, Poznan University of Life Sciences, Wojska Polskiego 50, 60-627 Poznań, Poland; tomasz.garbowski@up.poznan.pl
2 Institute of Structural Analysis, Poznan University of Technology, Piotrowo 5, 60-965 Poznań, Poland
3 Faculty of Engineering and Physical Sciences, University of Southampton, Highfield SO17 1BJ, UK; a.marek@soton.ac.uk
* Correspondence: anna.knitter-piatkowska@put.poznan.pl

Abstract: The standard edge crush test (ECT) allows the determination of the crushing strength of the corrugated cardboard. Unfortunately, this test cannot be used to estimate the compressive stiffness, which is an equally important parameter. This is because any attempt to determine this parameter using current lab equipment quickly ends in a fiasco. The biggest obstacle is obtaining a reliable measurement of displacements and strains in the corrugated cardboard sample. In this paper, we present a method that not only allows for the reliable identification of the stiffness in the loaded direction of orthotropy in the corrugated board sample, but also the full orthotropic material stiffness matrix. The proposed method uses two samples: (a) traditional, cut crosswise to the wave direction of the corrugated core, and (b) cut at an angle of 45°. Additionally, in both cases, an optical system with digital image correlation (DIC) was used to measure the displacements and strains on the outer surfaces of samples. The use of a non-contact measuring system allowed us to avoid using the measurement of displacements from the crosshead, which is burdened with a large error. Apart from the new experimental configuration, the article also proposes a simple algorithm to quickly characterize all sought stiffness parameters. The obtained results are finally compared with the results obtained in the homogenization procedure of the cross-section of the corrugated board. The results were consistent in both cases.

Keywords: corrugated cardboard; edge crush test; orthotropic elasticity; digital image correlation; compressive stiffness

Citation: Garbowski, T.; Knitter-Piątkowska, A.; Marek, A. New Edge Crush Test Configuration Enhanced with Full-Field Strain Measurements. *Materials* **2021**, *14*, 5768. https://doi.org/10.3390/ma14195768

Academic Editor: Aniello Riccio

Received: 31 August 2021
Accepted: 29 September 2021
Published: 2 October 2021

Publisher's Note: MDPI stays neutral with regard to jurisdictional claims in published maps and institutional affiliations.

Copyright: © 2021 by the authors. Licensee MDPI, Basel, Switzerland. This article is an open access article distributed under the terms and conditions of the Creative Commons Attribution (CC BY) license (https://creativecommons.org/licenses/by/4.0/).

1. Introduction

The increasing consumer demands and absorptive power of the merchant market in today's world, resulting in the need to pack, store and securely ship more and more various goods, in addition to growing ecological awareness, have led to the increasing interest of manufacturers in cardboard packaging. This fact, in turn, has triggered the inevitable, continuous, and intensive development of numerous corrugated cardboard testing techniques over the last decades.

Assessing the load-bearing capacity of corrugated cardboard products is crucial for their proper design, production final usage, and re-use processes. It is important to emphasize here that corrugated cardboard comprises a few layers, and thus can be called a sandwich structure. Its mechanical properties are directly related to two characteristic in-plane directions of orthotropy, i.e., a machine direction (MD) that is perpendicular to the main axis of the fluting and parallel to the paperboard fiber alignment, and a cross direction (CD), which is parallel to the fluting.

Numerous approaches to sandwich element strength determination, including for corrugated cardboard, can be found in the literature. Analytical methods, starting already in the 1950s, were presented, e.g., in [1–5], whereas numerical methods can be found in [6–11], and analytical-numerical techniques in [12–16]. Analytical calculations of the edge crush resistance of cellular paperboard, both in MD and CD, based on the paperboard's geometric parameters and the mechanical properties of the materials used for its production, was discussed by Kmita-Fudalej et al. [17]. Park et al. [18] investigated the edgewise compression behavior of corrugated paperboard while applying the finite element method (FEM) as well as experimental analysis, i.e., load vs. displacement plots, edge crush tests (ECT) and failure mechanisms. In recent years, methods of artificial intelligence, including artificial neural networks, have become widespread to predict the strength of composite materials, e.g., sandwich structures as presented by Wong et al. [19].

While executing numerical simulations in examining corrugated cardboard, the comprehensive knowledge of each layer's material properties is necessary. By reason of the anisotropy of the paper-based materials, this is a demanding task. In such a case a good solution is to implement a method called homogenization. This approach efficiently allows us to simplify multi-layer models into single-layered model, described by the effective properties of the composite [9,10,20]. The application of this technique has the benefits of significant savings in computation time while maintaining the accuracy of the results. Hohe [21] presented the strain energy approach as being applicable to sandwich panels for homogenization and proposed an equivalence of a representative element of the heterogeneous and homogenized elements for this purpose.

Another option, in addition to analytical or numerical analysis, for the estimation of corrugated board strength is to carry out measurements from an experiment. Physical testing is very common in the paper industry, and a number of typical tests have been developed to unify the process of the characterization of corrugated cardboard mechanical properties. The aforementioned ECT is used to evaluate the compressive strength, the load during this examination is applied perpendicularly to the axis of the flutes. In the bending test (BNT), four-point bending is executed, two supports are at the bottom of the cardboard whereas two equal forces act on the sample from the opposite side. The shear stiffness test (SST) involves twisting the cardboard cross-section by applying a pair of forces to opposite corners while the other two remain supported. In the torsional stiffness test (TST) the cardboard sample is twisted in both directions. The box compressive test (BCT) is conducted to examine the load bearing capacity of the whole cardboard box [12–14,22]. The bursting and humidity tests should also be mentioned here.

Since ECT is standardized, four different methods have been described, i.e., the edge-clamping method [23], the neck-down method [24], the rectangular test specimen method [24–26] and the edge-reinforced method [27,28]. One of the major characteristics which differentiates these tests is the shape of the samples. To assemble the measurements from the outer surfaces of the specimen during the examination, video extensometry can be employed. Such a procedure is based on the measurement of the relative distances between pairs of points traced across images captured at different load values [15]. This is a method comparable to, yet simpler than digital image correlation (DIC) which, as full-field non-contact optical measurement method, is gaining more popularity in the field of experimental mechanics since it ensures very high accuracy of data acquisition. Hägglund et al. applied DIC while examining thickness changes during the ECT of damaged and undamaged panels made of corrugated paperboard [29]. The implementation of DIC for the investigation of the strain and stress fields of paperboard panels subjected to BCT and analysis of their post-buckling behavior was discussed by Viguié et al. in [30–32]. A distortional hardening plasticity model for paperboard was presented by Borgqvist et al. [33], who introduced a yield surface characterized by multiple hardening variables attained from simple uniaxial tests. The comparison between the results acquired from the model and the experimental results received while using DIC were demonstrated as well. Combined compression and bending tests of paperboards and laminates for liquid containers while applying DIC were executed by Cocchetti et al. [34,35], who identified the material parameters of anisotropic elastic-plastic material models of foils. For this purpose, inverse analysis was employed while processing the results received from both the experiment and the numerical FEM simulations. DIC and the virtual fields method (VFM) for the recognition of general anisotropy parameters of a filter paper and a paperboard have been discussed by Considine [36]. Åslund et al. applied the detailed FEM for the investigation of the corrugated sandwich panel failure mechanism while performing the ECT and compared the results with the measurements obtained with the use of DIC [37]. Zappa et al. studied the inflation of the paperboard composites which are used in the packaging of beverages while applying DIC [38]. Paperboard boxes with ventilation holes subjected to a compression load were investigated using DIC by Fadiji et al. [39].

It should be pointed out that in a large part of the above-mentioned studies, 3-ply corrugated cardboard specimens were tested. In this study, 5-ply double-wall corrugated cardboard samples were examined. While performing ECT, an optical system with digital image correlation (DIC) is used to determine the displacements on the outer surface of the specimen. The proposed method uses two types of samples, i.e., traditional, cut crosswise to the direction of the wave direction of the corrugated core, and a novel procedure involving a cut at an angle of 45°. Such an approach not only allows for the reliable identification of the stiffness in one direction of orthotropy, but also for the measurement of the full material stiffness matrix, i.e., 4 independent parameters. The obtained results were verified by the results acquired in the homogenization procedure of the cross-section of the corrugated board. As proven, in both cases, the outcomes were very consistent.

2. Materials and Methods

2.1. Corrugated Cardboard

In the current study, a 5-ply corrugated cardboard marked as EB-650 was used. The top liner is made of white, coated, recycled cardboard TLWC with a grammage of 140 g/m^2. The cross-section has two corrugated layers: (a) low flute (E wave) and (b) high flute (B wave). Both the wavy layers and the flat layer between them, forming the mid liner, are made of lightweight WB cardboard, also recycled, with a grammage of 100 g/m^2. As a bottom liner, again the white recycled test liner with a grammage of 120 g/m^2 is used. The geometry of the cross-section of the corrugated board and the configuration of the respective layers are shown in Figure 1, where 5 samples are placed one on top of the other.

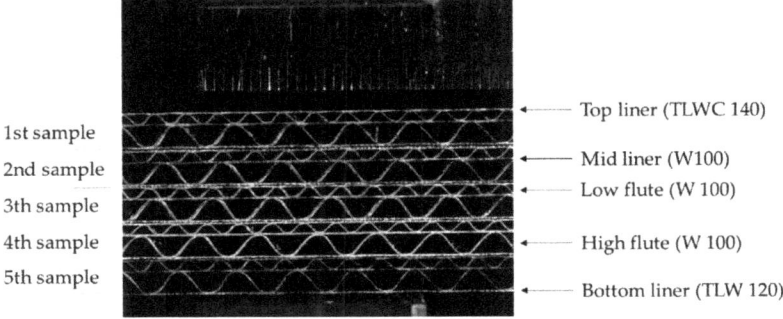

Figure 1. Visualization of 5 samples (stacked on top of each other) of the analyzed corrugated cardboard.

Table 1 presents the geometrical parameters of both wavy layers (flutes). The second and third columns of Table 1 shows the wave period (pitch) and the wave amplitude (height), respectively. The take-up ratio, which defines the ratio of the length of the non-fluted corrugated medium to the length of the fluted web, is specified in the last column of Table 1.

Table 1. The geometrical features of both corrugated layers of EB-650.

Wave (Flute)	Pitch (mm)	Height (mm)	Take-Up Ratio (–)
E	3.50	1.18	1.242
B	6.48	2.5	1.315

Paperboard, which is a main component of corrugated board, is made of cellulose fibers. The orientation of fibers is not random, but rather results from the production process, which causes that their vast majority is arranged along the web, called the machine direction (MD). The second direction, perpendicular to the MD, is called the cross direction (CD). Paperboard is both stronger and stiffer along the fiber direction.

In general, materials whose mechanical properties depend on fiber orientation are called orthotropic materials. As a component of corrugated cardboard is paper, it is also able to be considered as an orthotropic material. The orientation of the fibers, shown in Figure 2, makes the corrugated board stronger along the direction of the wave. Thus, the corrugated layers compensate (through the take-up factor) for the weaker mechanical properties of the board in CD.

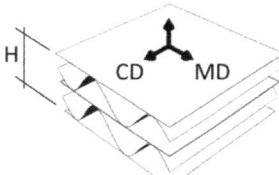

Figure 2. Material orientation in the corrugated board.

Table 2 presents the material properties of the individual layers of the corrugated board. The compressive strength in CD, SCT_{CD}, is measured while using the short-span compression test according to DIN EN ISO 3037 [26]. The compressive strength of the combined corrugated board in CD, ECT_{CD}, specified by the producer–Aquila Września–is 7.6 kN/m (±10%), while the total thickness of the EB-650, H is 4.3 mm (±0.2 mm).

Table 2. Mechanical properties of individual layers of 5EB650C3.

Layer Name	Thickness (μm)	E_{MD} (kN/m)	E_{CD} (kN/m)	SCT_{CD} (kN/m)
TLWC 140	180	725	323	2.32
W 100	160	886	328	1.76
TLW 120	170	907	313	1.81

2.2. The Edge Crush Test

The edge crush test (ECT) is a standard test to assess the compressive strength of corrugated board. The test is performed according to FEFCO DIN EN ISO 3037 [25,26], where a 100 mm long and 25 mm high specimen (see Figure 3a,b) is loaded between two rigid plates along its height (see Figure 4a). In order to preserve the parallelism of the cut edges of the sample, it should be cut on a special device, e.g., a FEMat CUT device [22] (see Figure 4b), where the samples are pneumatically cut with one-sided ground blades. All ECT tests were performed under controlled and standard air conditions, i.e., 23 °C and 50% relative humidity.

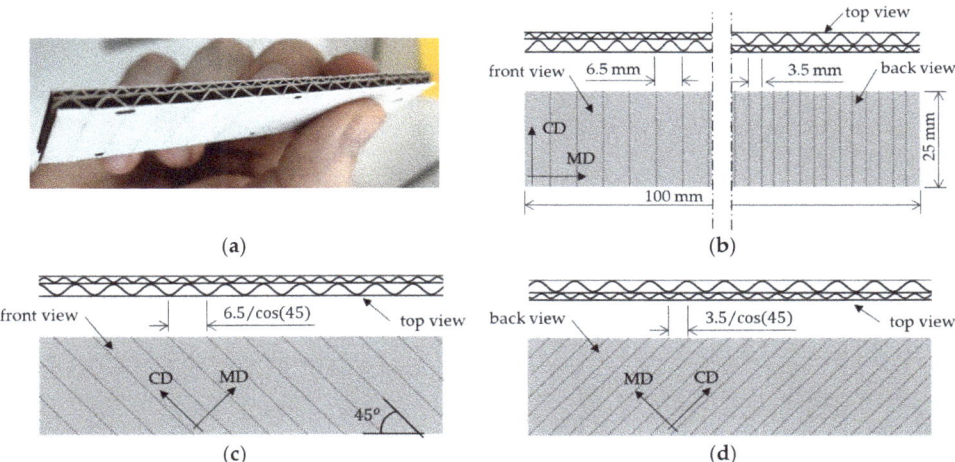

Figure 3. The sample for the standard and new edge crush test: (**a**) standard sample view; (**b**) standard ECT sample–front, back and top view; (**c**) new ECT sample–front and top view; (**d**) new ECT sample–back and top view.

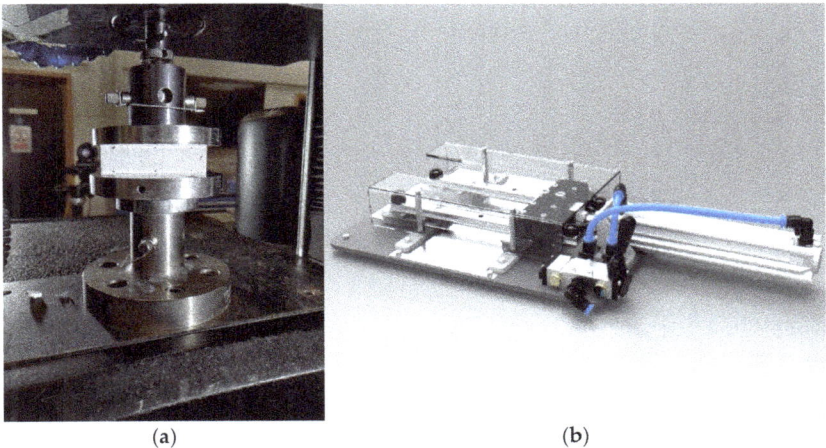

Figure 4. Edge crush test: (**a**) Universal Testing Machine (Instron 5569); (**b**) FEMAT lab device.

As already mentioned above, the typical ECT is only used to determine the compressive strength of the corrugated board in CD. Here, the new ECT test setup was also used to determine all of the elastic orthotropic properties of the in-plane tension/compression behavior of corrugated cardboard. For this purpose, beside the traditional method, we also tested samples cut at an angle of 45° to the wave direction (see Figure 3c,d). Since the measurement in standard testing machines is considerably affected by the clearance and susceptibility on the crosshead, non-contact optical techniques are required to credibly measure displacements (deformations or strains).

Additionally, measurement without direct contact does not affect the measurement itself. In contact measurements (e.g., traditional extensometers), noise is introduced into the measurement, which may distort the actual measured values.

2.3. Optical Measurements of Sample Deformation

In this study, as mentioned, the specimen was tested while using optical displacement and strain measurements, i.e., virtual extensometry and digital image correlation (DIC). Two cameras (the stereo DIC setup) were employed to track the deformation on the front faces to account for the out-of-plane bending produced by the non-symmetrical section, and single a camera was employed on the back faces for standard optical extensometry, per the test setup shown in Figure 5a. Each of the two faces of the specimen were printed with the speckle pattern for both optical methods, i.e., DIC and video extensometry. Here, three models of deformation measurements were used, namely:

- Crosshead from the machine.
- Stereo (2.5D) DIC on the front (see Figure 5b) plus extensometry on the back.
- Extensometry on the front and back.

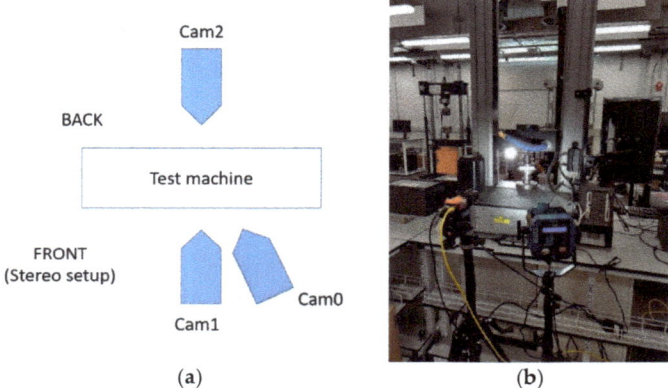

Figure 5. Setup of the optical measurements: (**a**) configuration of cameras on the front and back face; (**b**) cameras recording the front face.

The specimen was sandwiched between two platens and aligned using 3D printed L-brackets. Two 5 MPx cameras (Manta G504-b, Allied Vision, Stadtroda, Germany) were used to record greyscale images during the test, see Figure 5. The video extensometry was performed using the MatchID DIC platform (v. 2020.2.0, MatchID, Ghent, Belgium). The cameras were calibrated while applying the MatchID calibration plate (MatchID, Ghent, Belgium) to acquire the pixel (px) to mm conversion rate of ~50 µm/px. The specimen was manually preloaded with a very small load (15 N) to ensure that both edges of the specimen were touching the loading plates. Then, the measured load cell and the displacement were zeroed, and the L-brackets supporting the sample were removed. The load and the crosshead displacement were synchronized with the cameras. The accuracy of the measurement was estimated using a set of 25 static images (without any movement); the standard deviation of the measured elongation was evaluated to be 4 µm, which can be considered the level of uncertainty. The optical displacements were averaged for each face and compared against the crosshead displacement.

In total, 5 samples in CD and 5 samples using the 45° direction were tested. Unfortunately, data from one of the samples in the CD experiment were not recorded properly on the PC and were removed from the statistics. The loading rate was set to 5 mm/min (which is different from the standard rate 12.5 mm/min) because the samples failed too quickly for cameras to get enough data.

The following stereo DIC procedures, with camera "Cam1" as the main, were utilized in this research:

- Perform DIC on the sample's face while using images from Cam1 and Cam0; region of interest (ROI) visible in Figure 6b.
- Align the data coordinate system with the specimen material direction, i.e., $11 = MD$, $22 = CD$, $yy = $ vertical (see Figure 6a).
- Calculate strain from the displacements.
- Select a subregion and extract the data; all data in the subregion is averaged giving one value of desired quantities per image, namely: ε_{11}, ε_{22}, ε_{12}, ε_{yy}.
- Shear strains reported as tensor shear strain component ε_{12}, need to be doubled for the engineering component.

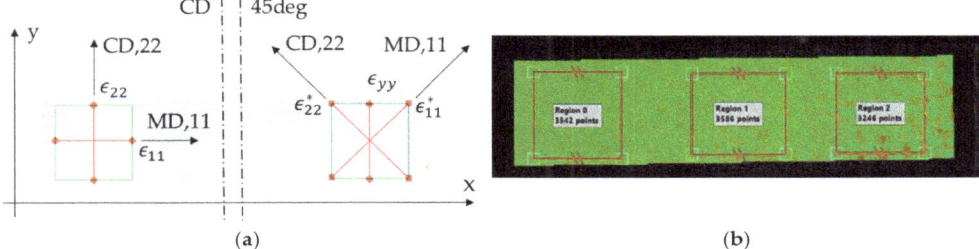

Figure 6. Virtual optical gauges (**a**) sample in CD and in 45°; (**b**) ROI visualization. The * denotes a material orientation in the sample cut in the 45°.

On the other hand, the video extensometry main procedures utilized in this study, were as follows:

- Use a speckle pattern compatible with DIC (pen marks would work equally well, per [15]).
- Only perpendicular cameras were used (front = Cam1, back = Cam2).
- Length of vertical gauges was 350 px (see Figures 6 and 7), while the length of the gauges in the 45° direction were chosen to be 490 px, which is ×1.4 of the vertical gauge (see Figures 6a and 7b).
- The three gauges in their respective directions were averaged to produce a single value of strain, i.e., ε_{11}, ε_{22} and ε_{yy} in the 45° direction tests, or ε_{11} and ε_{22} in the CD tests.
- All membrane strain is the average of the front and back strains. Ideally, it should be obtained from the trapezoidal distribution of the paperboard cross-section under combined compression/bending. Here, it was simply averaged.
- The shear strain can be calculated from the strain gauge rosette (see Figure 7b): $\varepsilon_{12} = \varepsilon_{yy} - 0.5(\varepsilon_{11} + \varepsilon_{22})$.

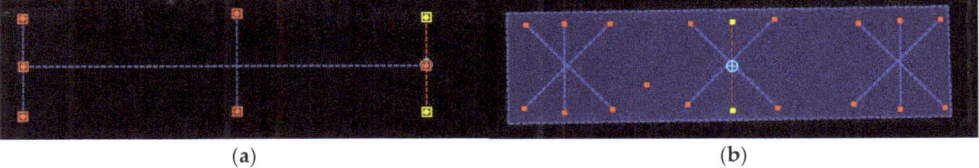

Figure 7. Virtual optical gauges (**a**) sample in CD; (**b**) sample in 45°.

Using the tests for CD, ε_{yy} (in the CD direction) and ε_{xx} (in the MD direction) were measured from each image either by averaging large region from the DIC (see Figure 6b) or by using virtual extensometers: 3 vertical plus 1 horizontal (see Figure 7a). The front and back data were averaged to remove artificial bending data. A similar methodology was used in case of the ECT in a 45° direction. All stiffnesses, e.g., F_{yy} vs. ε_{yy} were calculated from the linear portion of the graphs.

2.4. Proposed Method to Identify Matrix **A**

The identification of matrix **A** is based here on two sets of tests, namely: (a) the standard ECT, in CD and (b) the new ECT in 45° direction. The well-known relation between cross-sectional forces and general strains has the form:

$$\begin{bmatrix} \sigma_{11} \\ \sigma_{22} \\ \sigma_{12} \end{bmatrix} = \begin{bmatrix} A_{11} & A_{12} & 0 \\ A_{12} & A_{22} & 0 \\ 0 & 0 & A_{66} \end{bmatrix} \begin{bmatrix} \varepsilon_{11} \\ \varepsilon_{22} \\ \varepsilon_{12} \end{bmatrix}, \tag{1}$$

where σ_{ij} are the components of the sectional force vector, in [N/mm]; A_{ij} are the stiffness components, in [N/mm]; and ε_{ij} are the membrane (in-plane) strains.

From Equation (1) two sets of equations can be extracted, namely in the CD test:

$$\begin{aligned} A_{12}\varepsilon_{11} + A_{22}\varepsilon_{22} &= \sigma_{22}, \\ A_{11}\varepsilon_{11} + A_{12}\varepsilon_{22} &= 0, \end{aligned} \tag{2}$$

and in the 45° direction test:

$$\begin{aligned} A_{11}\varepsilon_{11} + A_{12}\varepsilon_{22} &= \sigma_{11}^{45} = 0.5\sigma^{45}, \\ A_{12}\varepsilon_{11} + A_{22}\varepsilon_{22} &= \sigma_{22}^{45} = 0.5\sigma^{45}. \end{aligned} \tag{3}$$

By building up a matrix of those equations from two experiments and solving it in the least square sense (se e.g., [40]) the components of matrix $A = [A_{11}, A_{12}, A_{22}]$ can be easily obtained. Component A_{66} can be obtained independently, from the ECT in the 45° direction.

If one uses stresses instead of sectional forces, the following equations can be derived from the test in the CD:

$$\begin{bmatrix} \frac{E_{11}}{1-\nu_{12}\nu_{21}} & \frac{E_{22}\nu_{12}}{1-\nu_{12}\nu_{21}} \\ \frac{E_{11}\nu_{21}}{1-\nu_{12}\nu_{21}} & \frac{E_{22}}{1-\nu_{12}\nu_{21}} \end{bmatrix} \begin{Bmatrix} \varepsilon_{11} \\ \varepsilon_{22} \end{Bmatrix} = \begin{Bmatrix} 0 \\ \sigma_{22} \end{Bmatrix}, \tag{4}$$

and from the test in the 45° direction:

$$\begin{bmatrix} \frac{E_{11}}{1-\nu_{12}\nu_{21}} & \frac{E_{22}\nu_{12}}{1-\nu_{12}\nu_{21}} \\ \frac{E_{11}\nu_{21}}{1-\nu_{12}\nu_{21}} & \frac{E_{22}}{1-\nu_{12}\nu_{21}} \end{bmatrix} \begin{Bmatrix} \varepsilon_{11}^* \\ \varepsilon_{22}^* \end{Bmatrix} = \frac{1}{2}\begin{Bmatrix} \sigma_{45} \\ \sigma_{45} \end{Bmatrix}. \tag{5}$$

From the test in the CD only, just two constitutive components can be computed, namely Poisson's ratio:

$$\nu_{21} = -\frac{\varepsilon_{11}}{\varepsilon_{22}}, \tag{6}$$

and the elastic modulus:

$$E_{22} = \frac{\sigma_{22}}{\varepsilon_{22}}. \tag{7}$$

On the other hand, from both the CD and 45° tests, all orthotropic stiffness coefficients can be obtained, namely elastic stiffness in MD:

$$E_{11} = -\frac{\sigma_{22}\sigma_{45}}{\varepsilon_{11}\sigma_{45} - 2\varepsilon_{11}^*\sigma_{22}}, \tag{8}$$

elastic stiffness in CD:

$$E_{22} = \frac{\sigma_{22}}{\varepsilon_{22}}, \tag{9}$$

Poisson's ratio ν_{12}:

$$\nu_{12} = \frac{\varepsilon_{11}\sigma_{45}}{\varepsilon_{11}\sigma_{45} - 2\varepsilon_{11}^*\sigma_{22}}, \tag{10}$$

Poisson's ratio ν_{21}:

$$\nu_{21} = 1 - \frac{2\varepsilon_{22}^*\sigma_{22}}{\varepsilon_{22}\sigma_{45}}, \tag{11}$$

or using the symmetry principals:

$$\nu_{21} = \nu_{12} \frac{E_{22}}{E_{11}}. \tag{12}$$

The stiffness in the 45° direction can be computed directly from the test in 45° direction:

$$E_{45} = \frac{\sigma_{45}}{\varepsilon_{yy}}, \tag{13}$$

and is used to compute the last missing coefficient, namely the in-plane shear stiffness:

$$G_{12} = \left(\frac{2\nu_{12}}{E_{11}} - \frac{1}{E_{11}} - \frac{1}{E_{22}} + \frac{4}{E_{45}} \right). \tag{14}$$

3. Results
3.1. The ECT Enhanced with Optical Measurement Techniques

First, four tests of the CD are presented. Figure 8 shows the differences in the displacements measured by optical techniques (solid line) and taken from the machine crosshead (dashed line).

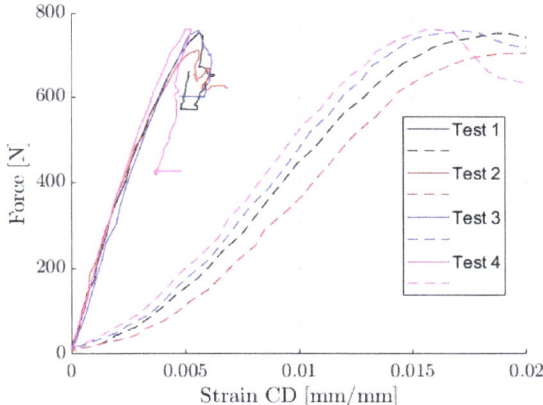

Figure 8. Force-displacement curves. Optical extensometry–solid lines; from machine crosshead–dashed lines.

Table 3 shows the elastic stiffness index, which was computed from the linear part of the curves shown in Figure 8. It should be pointed out that the cross-sectional force is normalized by the sample length ($L = 100$ mm) but not by the sample thickness. This approach complies with the specifications of the corrugated board manufacturers and allows the presentation of results regardless of the sample thickness.

Table 3. Elastic stiffness index in CD computed from the displacement measurement by the optical extensometry and from machine crosshead, as well as the edgewise compression strength in CD.

Test ID	E—Optical (N/mm)	E—Crosshead (N/mm)	ECT (N/mm)
1	1447.45	441.82	−7.548
2	1380.25	536.82	−7.151
4	1531.96	450.66	−7.609
5	1615.12	611.39	−7.640
Mean (N/mm)	1493.70	510.17	−7.487
Std (N/mm)	102.01	79.93	0.227
Cov (%)	6.829	15.668	−3.038

3.2. DIC vs. Extensometry

Then the stereo DIC and the extensometry approach were compared. For this analysis, the selected test in the direction 45° was carefully analyzed. The DIC data in the zones occupied by extensometers were averaged and compared (see Figures 9 and 10).

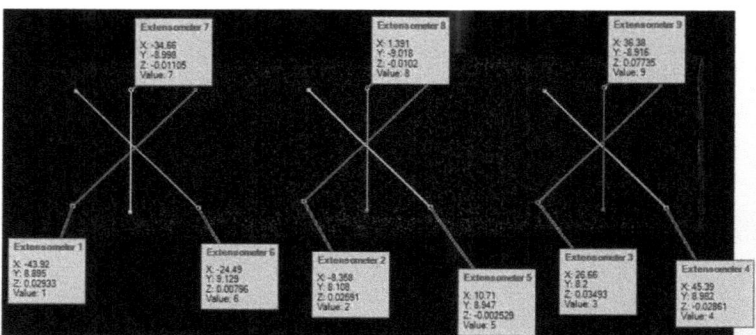

Figure 9. Location of each strain gauge on the sample in the test in the 45° direction.

The results presented in Figure 10 are comparable, but not identical in terms of elasticity, mainly due to a certain inhomogeneity in the deformation caused by the crushing of the edges, which obviously affected the extensometers. However, this can be reduced, e.g., by shortening the gauge length, which appears to be a key a priori choice. The question of how long the extensometers should be is discussed in the next subsection.

It is known that the error in strain measurements comes from error in the measured displacements (here it is constant at ~0.01 px) and the length of the gauge. Although it seems that the longer the gauge, the better, but the longer the gauge, the greater the risk of taking into account the edge effects of the sample, where (especially in the case of unwaxed samples) the largest local deformations (i.e., crushing and wrinkling) are usually concentrated.

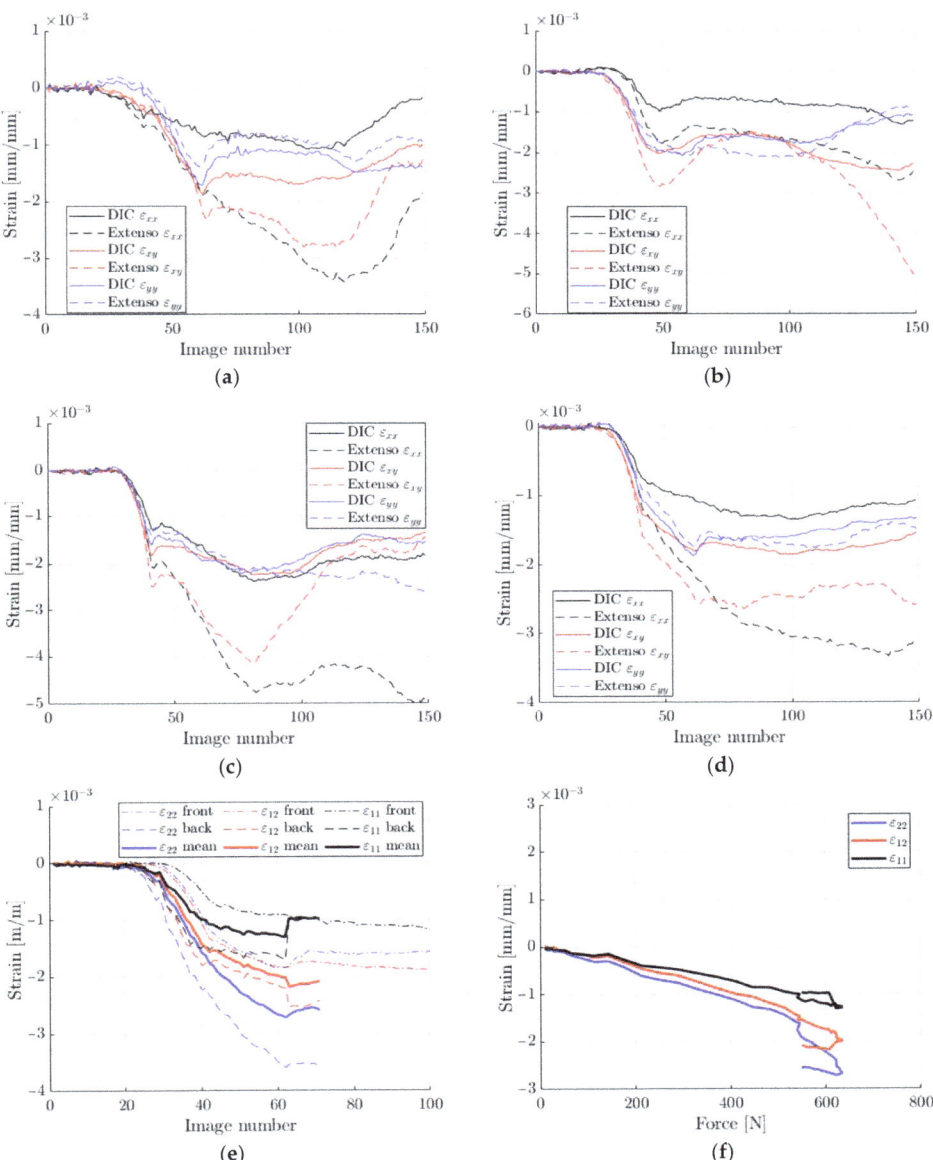

Figure 10. DIC vs. virtual extensometry comparison: (**a**) region 1; (**b**) region 2; (**c**) region 3; (**d**) mean from 3 regions; (**e**) back-to-front average; (**f**) strains resulting from forces.

3.3. Length of Virtual Extensometry

A study on the length of the optical extensometry was performed on the test number 3 data in the CD–full-field data was extracted (i.e., strains and displacements). Virtual extensometers were generated with varied lengths at different horizontal positions and compared against the averaged vertical strains from the DIC. For example, two points were selected in the center of the sample: one at $Y_1 = +10$ mm with respect to the center of the sample height, the other at $Y_2 = -10$ mm and the extensometer strain was calculated from $\varepsilon_{yy} = (v_1 - v_2)/20$.

Three horizontal positions of the virtual strain gauges were considered: (1) left at 25% of the width; (2) mid at 50% and (3) right at 75% of the sample width. They were also averaged. Figure 11 shows the location of the optical strain gauges. The length of each gauge varies from 4 to 20 mm.

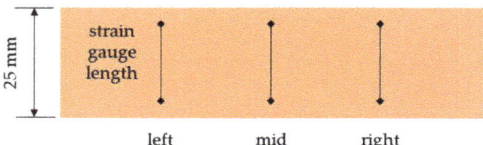

Figure 11. Location of the virtual strain gauges.

Figure 12 shows a comparison of strain calculated while using different lengths of virtual gauges with the DIC measurements.

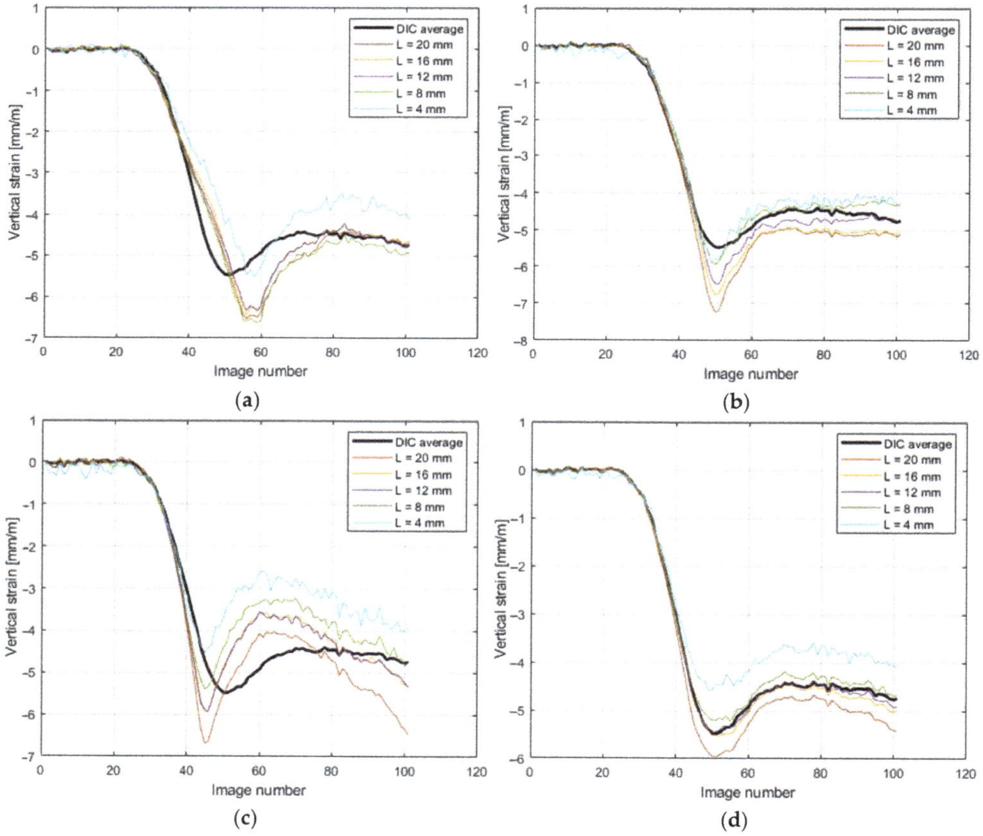

Figure 12. Comparison of strains measured by different lengths of virtual gauges with DIC measurements. (**a**) left set; (**b**) mid set; (**c**) right set; (**d**) averaged.

The main observation was that for the test in the 45° direction, the extensometers should be arranged in a rectangular configuration (15 mm × 15 mm box, with longer gauges on the diagonal) or circular gauges (so as to keep the gauge length of 15 mm).

3.4. Consistency of Tests in 45 Deg Direction

The last issue was to check the data consistency of the new test in the 45° direction. For all the CD tests, the force-strain data was very consistent, but unfortunately this was not the case for the 45° tests. For each recorded level of the force, the measured strain components averaged back-to-front are plotted (see Figure 13). It is visible that the tests can be split into two, more consistent groups (see Figure 14). Group 2 had a stiffer response in the 11 (MD) direction.

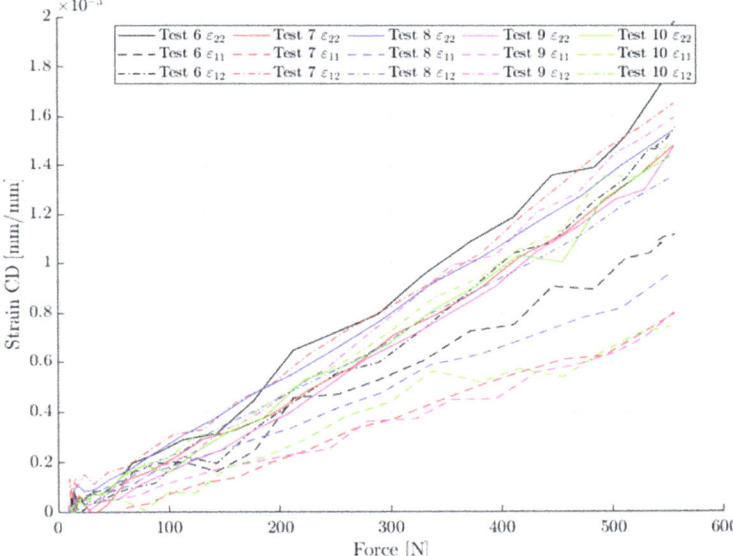

Figure 13. The consistency of the data from tests 6–10.

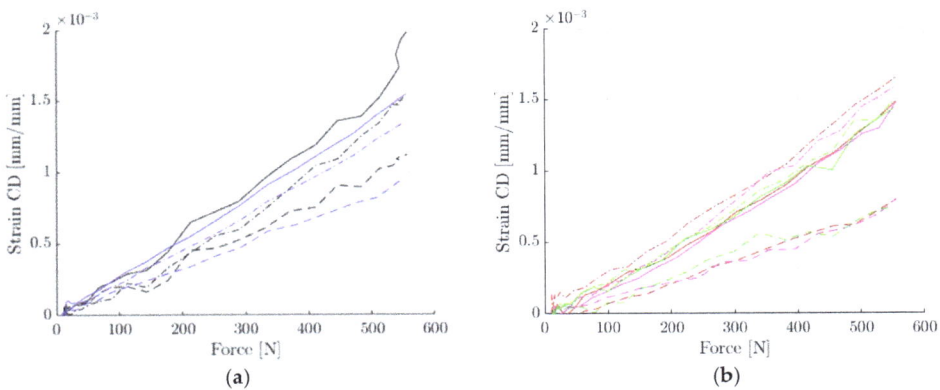

Figure 14. The consistency of data in tests 6–10: (**a**) group 1 (tests 6 and 8); (**b**) group 2 (tests 7, 9 and 10).

The reasons for the difference are not fully clear. One of the observations was that group 1 (i.e., test 6 and 8) had a high flute oriented towards the stereo DIC setup (front face as depicted in Figure 3c). Local buckling on that face is more pronounced and that could have affected the measured strain. However, even when using extensometers instead of full DIC, the trend stayed the same. Group 1 had (accidentally) a different orientation of fluting with respect to the plate than group 2 (Figure 3c,d).

3.5. Full Matrix A Identification

First, by combining tests 2 and 6 and using Equations (2) and (3) with the least square approximation, one can identify the full A matrix (see Table 4).

Table 4. The components of A matrix.

Parameter:	Test 2 and 6	Group 1	Group 2
A_{11} (N/mm)	2581	2583.0	3554.0
A_{12} (N/mm)	158	103.5	158.1
A_{22} (N/mm)	1674 (1500 [1])	1765.0	1792.0
A_{66} (N/mm)	1078	1061.0	946.0

[1] Results obtained directly from test 2 in the CD using Equation (7) or (9).

The Poisson's ratio computed directly from the CD test (see Equation (6)) turned out to be ~0.07, which is much closer to the value cited here: $A_{12}/A_{22} = 0.09$. In all cases, force was normalized by specimen width (100 mm). In the investigation, test number 1 was removed from the data pool due to an artefact point.

Finally, the same procedure as above was used, but with the two separate groups discussed in previous subsection shown in Figure 14. In total, 178 (group 1) and 204 (group 2) points were used here to calculate the in-plane stiffnesses (A_{11}, A_{12}, A_{22}). This separation made it possible to study the effects of positioning unsymmetric samples on the ECT apparatus.

The reconstructed elastic forces from the identified parameters are shown in Figures 15 and 16—multiple lines represent multiple tests. These data show good model fitting.

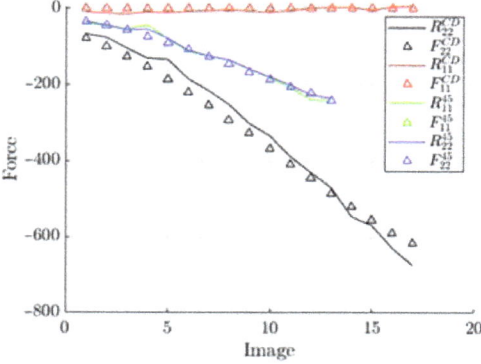

Figure 15. Curves reconstructed from the identified A matrix vs. measured force.

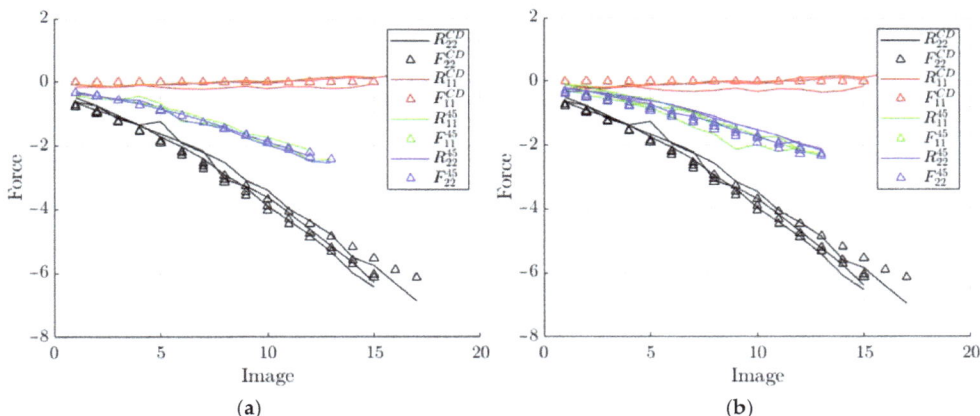

Figure 16. Curves reconstructed from the identified A matrix vs. measured force: (**a**) using tests in group 1; (**b**) using tests in group 2.

4. Discussion

The previous section provides the outcomes of the research, presenting, among others, typical ECT results enriched with digital image correlation and/or optical, virtual extensometry techniques. The results summarized in Table 3 clearly show that the use of the displacements obtained from the machine crosshead introduces an error in the estimation of the stiffness index, underestimating this value almost 3 times. The same observation can also be found in the recent work of Garbowski et al. [15]. The compressive strength given in Table 3 (shown in column 4) is consistent with the value provided by the manufacturer of the corrugated board, namely 7.6 N/mm ±10%.

The comparison of strains obtained from the DIC and while using virtual extensometers is presented in Figure 10. These results were comparable, but not identical. The best fit can be observed for the vertical strain ε_{yy}. Based on the observations regarding the length of the optical extensometer and its influence on the accuracy of the results, 15 mm segments were used for further analyses. This can be observed in Figure 12, where the calculated strains were compared while using DIC and extensometers of different lengths. The main conclusion is that when applying longer gauges, the results are more stable. However, if the optical extensometer is too long (i.e., longer than 15 mm) or too short (i.e., shorter than 8 mm), the differences can be as high as 15%.

The use of extensometers with a length of ~20 mm causes false results due to the proximity of the measuring tip to the crushed edge of the sample (which is 25 mm high). On the other hand, the use of short gauges of ~5 mm is affected by larger noise and causes the measurements to have an error due to buckling from the plane of the sample (see Figure 17b). The moment when the sample buckles is shown in Figure 12d–image number 38 (for a strain gauge 4 mm long). The influence of buckling (which manifests in the form of an out-of-plane deformation) on the measurement of in-plane deformations can be easily eliminated using the stereo DIC procedure. However, if optical extensometry is to be used, a fairly large area where the results obtained with the extensometer match those obtained with the DIC should be in the range of 8–16 mm.

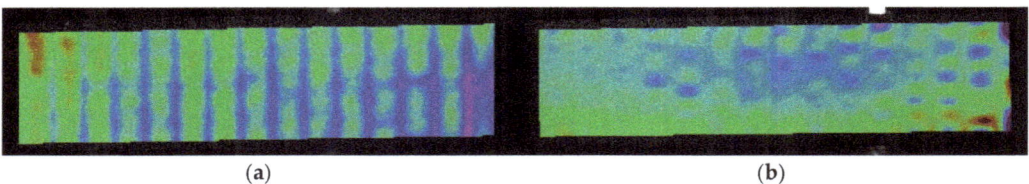

Figure 17. The ECT sample during the CD test: (**a**) sample during the CD test–no buckling; (**b**) sample during the CD test–buckling.

Table 4 shows the identified components of matrix A. The second column shows the results obtained during tests 2 and 6, while columns 3 and 4 show the results obtained while using two different test groups. The groups included samples with a higher flute from the front (on the side of the DIC stereo set) and samples with a lower flute from the front. It is evident that the results for group 2, especially in the case of A_{11} and A_{12}, differed significantly from the results obtained in the first procedure, while considering group 1. This was due to the asymmetric cross-section of the sample and the different level of buckling on the sample side with the higher flute. Out-of-plane deformation related to buckling distorts measurement and therefore introduces noise that distorts the results. Other components of matrix A did not differ more than 10% when using different measurement techniques, which was very promising.

In order to validate the results presented in Table 4, the numerical homogenization procedure (for details see recent works by Garbowski and Gajewski [9] or Garbowski et al. [10]) of the cross-section of corrugated board BE-650 (see Figure 18) was used. The numerical homogenization technique used the geometrical and constitutive parameters presented in Tables 1 and 2. The following results were obtained while employing the homogenization technique: $A_{11} = 2620$ N/mm, $A_{12} = 185$ N/mm, $A_{22} = 1812$ N/mm, $A_{66} = 906$ N/mm. The results are in good agreement, which proves that the use of optical techniques in conjunction with the new setup of the ECT (samples cut at an angle of 45° with respect to the direction of corrugation) can be effective in determining the stiffness of corrugated cardboard.

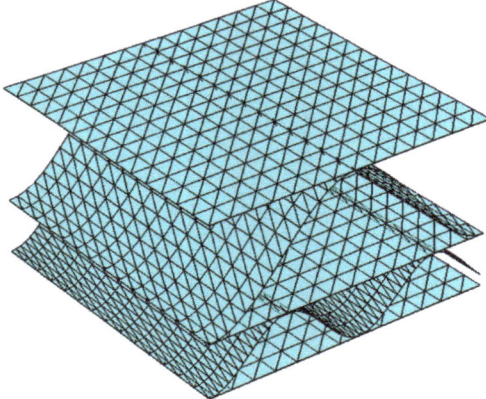

Figure 18. Visualization of the finite element model of corrugated board BE-650.

5. Conclusions

The main conclusion is that stereo DIC and/or optical extensometry techniques can be used to evaluate stiffness in a standard edge crush test. In order to determine all the stiffness coefficients, it is necessary to use an additional, new test specimen cut at an angle of 45° to the direction of the corrugation. By applying the results from the two samples simultaneously and using a least squares minimization approach, all of the stiffness components can be easily identified. The only concern is proper surface selection in unsymmetrical corrugated cardboard samples for stereo DIC measurement, especially in the 45° tests. However, this is easily remedied by using a larger sample set and averaging the results.

Author Contributions: Conceptualization, T.G.; methodology, T.G.; software, T.G. and A.M.; validation, A.M., A.K.-P. and T.G.; formal analysis, A.M. and T.G.; investigation, A.M., A.K.-P. and T.G.; resources, A.M.; data curation, A.M.; writing—original draft preparation, A.K.-P. and T.G.; writing—review and editing, A.K.-P., T.G. and A.M.; visualization, A.M. and T.G.; supervision, T.G.; project administration, T.G.; funding acquisition, A.K.-P. and T.G. All authors have read and agreed to the published version of the manuscript.

Funding: The APC was funded by the Ministry of Science and Higher Education, Poland, the statutory funding at Poznan University of Life Sciences, grant number 506.569.05.00 and the statutory funding at Poznan University of Technology, grant number 0411/SBAD/0004.

Institutional Review Board Statement: Not applicable.

Informed Consent Statement: Not applicable.

Data Availability Statement: The data presented in this study are available on request from the corresponding author.

Acknowledgments: Special thanks to the FEMat Sp. z o. o. company (Poznań, Poland) (www.fematsystems.pl—accessed on 21 July 2021) for providing the laboratory equipment and commercial software.

Conflicts of Interest: The authors declare no conflict of interest.

References

1. Kellicutt, K.; Landt, E. Development of design data for corrugated fibreboard shipping containers. *Tappi J.* **1952**, *35*, 398–402.
2. Maltenfort, G. Compression strength of corrugated containers. *Fibre Contain.* **1956**, *41*, 106–121.
3. McKee, R.C.; Gander, J.W.; Wachuta, J.R. Compression strength formula for corrugated boxes. *Paperboard Packag.* **1963**, *48*, 149–159.
4. Magnucka-Blandzi, E.; Magnucki, K.; Wittenbeck, L. Mathematical modeling of shearing effect for sandwich beams with sinusoidal corrugated cores. *Appl. Math. Model.* **2015**, *39*, 1796–2808. [CrossRef]
5. Magnucka-Blandzi, E.; Magnucki, K. Transverse shear modulus of elasticity for thin-walled corrugated cores of sandwich beams. Theoretical study. *J. Theor. Appl. Mech.* **2014**, *52*, 971–980. [CrossRef]
6. Nordstrand, T.M.; Carlsson, L.A. Evaluation of transverse shear stiffness of structural core sandwich plates. *Comp. Struct.* **1997**, *37*, 145–153. [CrossRef]
7. Garbowski, T.; Gajewski, T.; Grabski, J.K. Role of transverse shear modulus in the performance of corrugated materials. *Materials* **2020**, *13*, 3791. [CrossRef] [PubMed]
8. Garbowski, T.; Gajewski, T.; Grabski, J.K. Torsional and transversal stiffness of orthotropic sandwich panels. *Materials* **2020**, *13*, 5016. [CrossRef] [PubMed]
9. Garbowski, T.; Gajewski, T. Determination of transverse shear stiffness of sandwich panels with a corrugated core by numerical homogenization. *Materials* **2021**, *14*, 1976. [CrossRef] [PubMed]
10. Garbowski, T.; Knitter-Piątkowska, A.; Mrówczyński, D. Numerical homogenization of multi-layered corrugated cardboard with creasing or perforation. *Materials* **2021**, *14*, 3786. [CrossRef]
11. Domaneschi, M.; Perego, U.; Borgqvist, E.; Borsari, R. An industry-oriented strategy for the finite element simulation of paperboard creasing and folding. *Packag. Tech. Sci.* **2017**, *30*, 269–294. [CrossRef]
12. Garbowski, T.; Gajewski, T.; Grabski, J.K. The role of buckling in the estimation of compressive strength of corrugated cardboard boxes. *Materials* **2020**, *13*, 4578. [CrossRef]
13. Garbowski, T.; Gajewski, T.; Grabski, J.K. Estimation of the compressive strength of corrugated cardboard boxes with various openings. *Energies* **2021**, *14*, 155. [CrossRef]
14. Garbowski, T.; Gajewski, T.; Grabski, J.K. Estimation of the compressive strength of corrugated cardboard boxes with various perforations. *Energies* **2021**, *14*, 1095. [CrossRef]
15. Garbowski, T.; Grabski, J.K.; Marek, A. Full-field measurements in the edge crush test of a corrugated board—Analytical and numerical predictive models. *Materials* **2021**, *14*, 2840. [CrossRef] [PubMed]
16. Gajewski, T.; Garbowski, T.; Staszak, N.; Kuca, M. Crushing of double-walled corrugated board and its influence on the load capacity of various boxes. *Energies* **2021**, *14*, 4321. [CrossRef]

17. Kmita-Fudalej, G.; Szewczyk, W.; Kołakowski, Z. Calculation of honeycomb paperboard resistance to edge crush test. *Materials* **2020**, *13*, 1706. [CrossRef] [PubMed]
18. Park, J.; Park, M.; Choi, D.S.; Jung, H.M.; Hwang, S.W. Finite element-based simulation for edgewise compression behavior of corrugated paperboard for packaging of agricultural products. *Appl. Sci.* **2020**, *10*, 6716. [CrossRef]
19. Wong, J.E.; Mustapha, K.B.; Shimizu, Y.; Kamiya, A.; Arumugasamy, S.K. Development of surrogate predictive models for the nonlinear elasto-plastic response of medium density fiberboard-based sandwich structures. *Int. J. Lightweight Mater. Manuf.* **2021**, *4*, 302–314.
20. Marek, A.; Garbowski, T. Homogenization of sandwich panels. *Comput. Assist. Methods Eng. Sci.* **2015**, *22*, 39–50.
21. Hohe, J. A direct homogenization approach for determination of the stiffness matrix for microheterogeneous plates with application to sandwich panels. *Compos. Part. B* **2003**, *34*, 615–626. [CrossRef]
22. FEMat Systems. Available online: http://fematsystems.pl/home_en (accessed on 25 April 2021).
23. TAPPI T 839 om-12. *Edge Compression Test for Strength of Corrugated Fiberboard Using the Clamp Method (Short Column Test)*; TAPPI: Peachtree Corners, GA, USA, 2009.
24. TAPPI T 838 cm-12. *Edge Crush Test Using Neckdown*; TAPPI: Peachtree Corners, GA, USA, 2009.
25. FEFCO NO.8. *Edgewise Crush Resistance of Corrugated Fiberboard*; FEFCO: Brussel, Belgium, 1997.
26. ISO 3037:2013. *Corrugated Fibreboard—Determination of Edgewise Crush Resistance (Unwaxed Edge Method)*; ISO: Geneva, Switzerland, 2013.
27. TAPPI T 811 om-11. *Edgewise Compressive Strength of Corrugated Fibreboard (Short Column Test)*; TAPPI: Peachtree Corners, GA, USA, 2009.
28. ISO 13821:2002. *Corrugated Fibreboard—Determination of Edgewise Crush Resistance—Waxed Edge Method*; ISO: Geneva, Switzerland, 2002.
29. Hägglund, R.; Åslund, P.E.; Carlsson, L.A.; Isaksson, P. Measuring thickness changes of edgewise compression loaded corrugated board panels using digital image correlation. *J. Sandw. Struct. Mater.* **2010**, *14*, 75–94. [CrossRef]
30. Viguié, J.; Dumont, P.J.J.; Vacher, P.; Orgéas, L.; Desloges, I.; Mauret, E. Analysis of the strain and stress field of cardboard box during compression by 3D Digital Image Correlation. *Appl. Mech. Mater.* **2010**, *24–25*, 103–108. [CrossRef]
31. Viguié, J.; Dumont, P.J.J.; Orgéas, L.; Vacher, P.; Desloges, I.; Mauret, E. Surface stress and strain fields on compressed panels of corrugated board boxes. An experimental analysis by using Digital Image Stereocorrelation. *Comp. Struct.* **2011**, *93*, 2861–2873. [CrossRef]
32. Viguié, J.; Dumont, P.J.J. Analytical post-buckling model of corrugated board panels using digital image correlation measurements. *Comp. Struct.* **2013**, *101*, 243–254. [CrossRef]
33. Borgqvist, E.; Lindström, T.; Tryding, J.; Wallin, M.; Ristinmaa, M. Distortional hardening plasticity model for paperboard. *Int. J. Solids Struct.* **2014**, *51*, 2411–2423. [CrossRef]
34. Cocchetti, G.; Mahini, M.R.; Maier, G. Mechanical characterization of foils with compression in their planes. *Mech. Adv. Mater. Struct.* **2014**, *21*, 853–870. [CrossRef]
35. Garbowski, T.; Maier, G.; Novati, G. On calibration of orthotropic elastic-plastic constitutive models for paper foils by biaxial tests and inverse analyses. *Struct. Multidisc. Optim.* **2012**, *46*, 111–128. [CrossRef]
36. Considine, J.M.; Pierron, F.; Turner, K.T.; Vahey, D.W. General anisotropy identification of paperboard with virtual fields method. *Exp. Mech.* **2014**, *54*, 1395–1410. [CrossRef]
37. Åslund, P.E.; Hägglund, R.; Carlsson, L.A.; Isaksson, P. An analysis of strain localization and formation of face wrinkles in edge-wise loaded corrugated sandwich panels using a continuum damage model. *Int. J. Solids Struct.* **2015**, *56–57*, 248–257. [CrossRef]
38. Zappa, E.; Liu, R.; Bolzon, G.; Shahmardani, M. High resolution non-contact measurement techniques for three-dimensional deformation processes of paperboard laminates. *Mater. Today Proc.* **2017**, *4*, 5872–5876. [CrossRef]
39. Fadiji, T.; Coetzee, C.J.; Opara, U.L. Evaluating the displacement field of paperboard packages subjected to compression loading using digital image correlation (DIC). *Food Bioprod. Process.* **2020**, *123*, 60–71. [CrossRef]
40. Maier, G.; Bolzon, G.; Buljak, V.; Garbowski, T.; Miller, B. Synergic Combinations of Computational Methods and Experiments for Structural Diagnoses. In *Computer Methods in Mechanics*; Advanced Structured Materials; Kuczma, M., Wilmanski, K., Eds.; Springer: Berlin/Heidelberg, Germany, 2010; Volume 1, pp. 453–476.

Article

Estimation of the Compressive Strength of Corrugated Board Boxes with Shifted Creases on the Flaps

Damian Mrówczyński [1], Tomasz Garbowski [2] and Anna Knitter-Piątkowska [3,*]

[1] Research and Development Department, Femat Sp. z o.o., Romana Maya 1, 61-371 Poznań, Poland; damian.mrowczynski@fematproject.pl
[2] Department of Biosystems Engineering, Poznan University of Life Sciences, Wojska Polskiego 50, 60-627 Poznań, Poland; tomasz.garbowski@up.poznan.pl
[3] Institute of Structural Analysis, Poznan University of Technology, Piotrowo 5, 60-965 Poznań, Poland
* Correspondence: anna.knitter-piatkowska@put.poznan.pl

Abstract: In the modern world, all manufacturers strive for the optimal design of their products. This general trend is recently also observed in the corrugated board packaging industry. Colorful prints on displays, perforations in shelf-ready-packaging and various types of ventilation holes in trays, although extremely important for ergonomic or functional reasons, weaken the strength of the box. To meet the requirements of customers and recipients, packaging manufacturers outdo each other with new ideas for the construction of their products. Often the aesthetic qualities of the product become more important than the attention to maintaining the standards of the load capacity of the packaging (which, apart from their attention-grabbing functions, are also intended to protect transported products). A particular flaps design (both top and bottom) and its influence on the strength of the box are investigated in this study. An updated analytical–numerical approach is used here to predict the strength of packaging with various flap offsets. Experimental results indicated a significant decrease in the static load-bearing capacity of packaging in the case of shifted flap creases. The simulation model proposed in our previous work has been modified and updated to take into account this effect. The results obtained by the model presented in this paper are in satisfactory agreement with the experimental data.

Keywords: corrugated board; box strength estimation; packaging flaps; crease line shifting

Citation: Mrówczyński, D.; Garbowski, T.; Knitter-Piątkowska, A. Estimation of the Compressive Strength of Corrugated Board Boxes with Shifted Creases on the Flaps. *Materials* **2021**, *14*, 5181. https://doi.org/10.3390/ma14185181

Academic Editor: Dimitrios Tzetzis

Received: 29 July 2021
Accepted: 6 September 2021
Published: 9 September 2021

Publisher's Note: MDPI stays neutral with regard to jurisdictional claims in published maps and institutional affiliations.

Copyright: © 2021 by the authors. Licensee MDPI, Basel, Switzerland. This article is an open access article distributed under the terms and conditions of the Creative Commons Attribution (CC BY) license (https://creativecommons.org/licenses/by/4.0/).

1. Introduction

The relentless increase in consumption all around the contemporary world is reflected in the significant growth in the production of various goods. This, in turn, entails the necessity of their packing, safe storing and transportation to any destination. Due to growing ecological awareness and concern for the environment, the perfect choice is undoubtedly corrugated cardboard boxes. The undeniable facts are that they are recyclable, easy for disposal, ecological, durable under appropriate conditions and easy to store in a flat form after manufacturing. Among their numerous advantages, one cannot fail to mention the easy imprint of brand names on them. This is highly useful in cases of shelf-ready packaging (SRP) or retail-ready packaging (RRP) when, after being transported to the site, the packaged products are placed directly on the shelves. Upon opening the cardboard boxes along the specially designed and made perforations, products are ready to purchase. Such a solution is a huge time-saver for large companies.

In the case of individual recipients of merchandise, especially when shopping online (which nowadays is a significant part of the sales market), a very important factor is the possibility of smoothly returning purchased products if the consumer is not satisfied, for a range of reasons. Retailers that offer reusable packaging to send back purchased goods are very competitive on the market. Again, corrugated cardboard boxes are perfect in such situations. They are easy to open thanks to well thought-out perforations and, after re-sealing with the built-in adhesive strip, are ready to send back. However, it must not be forgotten that the packaging must have sufficient durability to survive the return transport.

Therefore, in view of the above, scientific research while applying analytical as well as numerical methods and/or laboratory tests has been an inherent part of a separate branch of industry, i.e., the production of corrugated cardboard packaging, for many years.

The proper mechanical strength of the paperboard or corrugated cardboard boxes is directly connected with two characteristic in-plane directions of orthotropy. Machine direction (MD) is perpendicular to the main axis of the fluting and parallel to the paperboard fiber alignment, whilst cross direction (CD) is parallel to the fluting. In order to examine the strength of corrugated cardboard boxes, one can perform some fundamental physical tests, i.e., compressive, tensile or bursting strength tests, which, in practical terms, are the most significant. The most prevalent are the box compression test (BCT) and the edge crush test (ECT) for corrugated cardboard.

A significant impact on the load-bearing capacity of packages is undoubtedly the various perforations, openings and flap locations on corrugated cardboard boxes. The first two issues have been meticulously discussed by Garbowski et al. in [1] and [2], respectively. In the present study, the influence of the flap locations on the strength of corrugated cardboard boxes, as another article in a series, is discussed. The conducting of physical experiments usually involves a great deal of time and cost. Therefore, recently, other methods of testing corrugated boxes have emerged to determine their strength by physical testing only.

Alternatively, the compressive strength of boxes can be assessed based on formulae that have been presented in numerous literatures. Their adoption, thanks to their simplicity, results in quick and easy solutions for practical applications. Moreover, no additional experiments are necessary. The parameters that are introduced in these formulae can be systemized into three groups: paper, board and box parameters [3]. In the first group one can specify: the ring crush test (RCT), Concora liner test (CLT), liner type, weights of liner and fluting, corrugation ratio and a constant related to fluting. In the second one: thickness, flexural stiffnesses in MD and CD, ECT and moisture content. Finally, in the third: dimensions and perimeter of the box, applied load ratio, stacking time, buckling ratio and printed ratio. Nearly 70 years ago, the paper (RCT, flute constant) and box (perimeter, box constant) parameters were applied for the prediction of boxes' compressive strength in the formula presented by Kellicutt and Landt [4]. The dependence of critical force on paper parameters (CLT, type of liner) and cardboard box dimensions in the BCT was presented in [5].

Generally applicable in the packaging industry is the procedure proposed by McKee et al. [6], in which the parameters of the paperboard (ECT, flexural stiffnesses) and the box perimeter were introduced. Nevertheless, the provided formula is applicable only for comparatively simple boxes. Throughout the years, many scientists endeavored to broaden the applicability of the McKee's analytical formulae. Allerby et al. [7] modified the constants and exponents in the above-mentioned approach. Schrampfer et al. [8], in turn, amended McKee's approach by extending the possibility of implementing a broader range of cutting methods and equipment. Batelka and Smith [9] enhanced the relationship with the dimensions of the box and Urbanik and Frank [10] introduced the Poisson's ratio as well. The arbitrary chosen constant value as a parameter in the McKee's formula limited its applicability to simple standard boxes. Moreover, Garbowski et al. [1,2,11] examined this approach for more sophisticated cases and modified the McKee's formula. One cannot forget that the compression strength of corrugated paperboard boxes [12] depends on many factors, such as moisture content of the box [13,14], the presence of openings, ventilation holes and perforations [1,2,15], storage time, stacking conditions [16] and numerous others.

An alternative option to compute the strength of the boxes is to implement, the well-known in engineering, finite element method (FEM). It has been involved in a lot of research, including the problems of numerical analysis with regard to the transverse shear stiffness of corrugated cardboards [17–21] as well as buckling and post-buckling phenomena [22]. The method that efficiently allows one to simplify the examined models is homogenization [23–27]. The result of this procedure is one single layer described by the effective properties of the composite, rather than building the layers made out of different materials. The advantage of this approach to the problem is a significant saving of calculation time while maintaining the appropriate accuracy of the results. The approach based on strain energy, applicable to sandwich panels in the issue of homogenization, was presented by Hohe [28]. For this purpose, a representative element of the heterogeneous and homogenized elements was proposed. Another method, using a periodic homogenization technique considered by Buannic et al. [29], allows not only for an equivalent membrane and the pure bending characteristics of period plates but also, in a modified version, includes the transfer of shear effect in the analysis. The FEM was applied by Biancolini [30] for the examination of a micromechanical part of the considered plate. In the aftermath of application, the energy equivalence between the model and the equivalent plate as well as the stiffness properties of the sandwich plate were obtained. In turn, Abbès and Guo [31] analyzed the plate, which was decomposed into two beams in the directions of the plate, which allowed them to find the torsion rigidity of the orthotropic sandwich plates. The method of treating the quasi-static equilibrium of a material subjected to deformation with hardening was proposed in [32]. Therefore, the experimental data obtained in the dynamic case of deformation could be compared with the data calculated for the quasi-static case. The laboratory tests, properly chosen and scheduled, were performed right on the composite. Layered elements, on which effective parameters can be measured directly, are an alternative method for homogenization. This very approach is proposed in the present research.

An operation during which fold and perforation lines are introduced is defined as creasing. One cannot neglect its impact on the load-bearing capacity of corrugated paperboard. Undeniably, those lines reduce the mechanical strength of the manufactured corrugated paperboard boxes, hence the results of extensive research can be found in the literature. The comparison between the experimental and FEM numerical results, performed in order to examine the creasing influence on the local strength of corrugated paperboard, was discussed by Thakkar et al. [33]. The impact of creasing and subsequent folding on the mechanical properties of laminated paperboard has been picked up by Beex and Peerlings [34], who performed physical as well as numerical experiments, whilst Giampieri et al. [35], to acquire the mechanical response of creased paperboard after folding, used a constitutive model. Domaneschi et al. [36] and Awais et al. [37] proposed an essential (from a practical point of view) solution for the packaging industry, basing it on the FEM simulations of paperboard creasing. Experimental, as well as numerical, studies on the influence of the creasing process during press forming on the paperboard mechanical properties were conducted by Leminen et al. [38].

The particular top and bottom flaps design, which is directly related to the flap creases, and their influence on the strength of corrugated cardboard boxes is investigated in this study. An updated analytical–numerical approach is used to predict the strength of the packaging with various flap offsets. Experimental results pointed out a significant decrease in the static load-bearing capacity of packaging in the case of shifted flap creases. The simulation model, proposed in the previous works of the authors [1,11], has been modified and updated to take this effect into account as well. The results obtained during the analysis of the numerical model proposed in the paper are in adequate agreement with the experimental data. This approach by which the prediction of the strength of boxes with offset flaps is analyzed is, to our knowledge, very pioneering and constitutes an innovative contribution to the development of the field related to the prediction of the load capacity of corrugated cardboard packaging.

2. Materials and Methods

2.1. Corrugated Board Packaging with Shifted Flaps

In previous works, the authors analyzed packages with perforations [1] and openings [2]. Here, the focus is on packages with offset flaps. Such packaging is becoming standard in retail-ready packaging that is also used for shipping. The shifting of the crease line (see Figure 1) makes the flaps more adjustable after closing. Unfortunately, the load-bearing capacity of packaging with shifted flaps significantly diminishes.

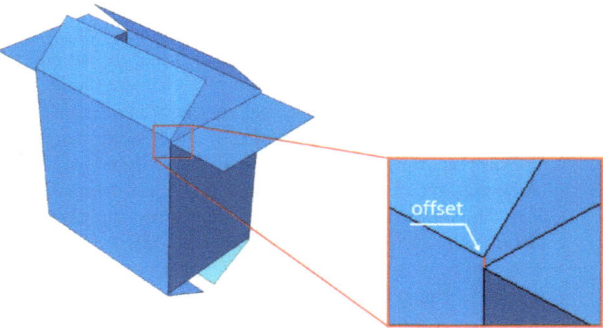

Figure 1. Box with offset flaps.

The drop in box strength results from a certain sequence of loading, in which the edges of the two shifted (elongated) walls of the package are loaded first, while the other two are only loaded after buckling and/or crushing of the first two (see Figure 2).

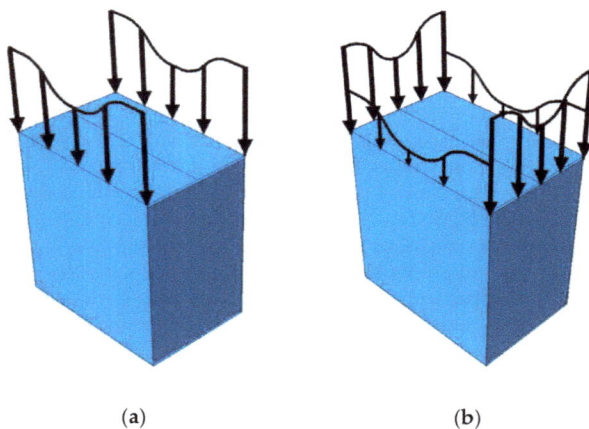

Figure 2. Sequence of loading of the package vertical walls: (**a**) edges loaded in the first step; (**b**) edges loaded in the second step.

In order to derive a simplified calculation algorithm for estimating the strength of boxes with offset flaps, a series of tests was first performed in the laboratory for various boxes made of different corrugated cardboard. All studies were carried out on the BCT press [39] (see Figure 3). In order to be able to perform computer predictions of the packaging load capacity, it is required in the first step to identify the material parameters of the corrugated board, then to select the appropriate material model and finally to build a numerical or analytical model that takes into account the geometry of the analyzed box.

 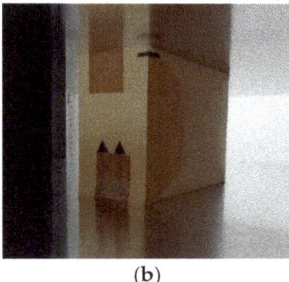

Figure 3. BCT tests: (**a**) BCT press; (**b**) packaging with the shifted offsets on the flaps.

The following sections describe the laboratory testing of corrugated board, the constitutive modeling of corrugated cardboard, a numerical simulation model and a simple analytical algorithm for estimating the load capacity of corrugated cardboard packaging.

2.2. Laboratory Testing of Corrugated Board

Laboratory tests of the corrugated cardboard were performed to determine its stiffness and strength. The four most commonly used tests are: edge crush test, shear stiffness testing, torsional stiffness test and 4-point bending test. The edge crush test (ECT) measures the compressive strength of a corrugated board sample. This test is performed for relatively stocky specimens, so that the failure mechanism is the crushing of the sample, not the loss of stability. The ECT value is often used to determine the load capacity of the corrugated cardboard package in analytical [6], analytical–numerical [1,2,11] or purely numerical [40,41] approaches.

The shear stiffness test (SST) is used to measure the shear stiffness of a sample by applying two equal forces at opposite corners. The measurement of displacements and reaction forces on the supports enables the required stiffness to be calculated. The SST is characterized by a high sensitivity to crushing the sample, resulting in processes such as die-cutting and laminating. The torsional stiffness test (TST) consists of twisting the sample by 10 degrees in both directions and is performed to determine the torsional stiffness. Only the linear part of the bending moment/angle of rotation diagram is being considered for this purpose. The obtained TST values are valid even for highly crushed, broken and flaccid samples.

The bending stiffness test (BNT) is used to determine the bending stiffness in the 4-point bending test. The static scheme of the tested sample allows a constant bending moment and a shear force equal to zero between the internal supports to be obtained, which provides more accurate measurement of the bending stiffness value. On the other hand, the presence of a shear force between internal and external supports makes it possible to take into account the effect of the shear stiffness as well.

2.3. Corrugated Board: Material Model and Constitutive Parameters

Since paperboard is an orthotropic material, many material parameters are needed for its correct mathematical description. Therefore, more laboratory tests should be carried out. In papermaking laboratories one can determine visual, functional and mechanical properties of paperboard or corrugated board. The most popular mechanical tests include, for example: (a) short span compression test (SCT) of paperboard; (b) tensile test of paperboard; (c) resistance to bursting of paperboard or corrugated board; (d) edge crush test (ECT) of corrugated board; (e) flat crush test (FCT) of single walled corrugated board; (f) corrugated board bending stiffness (4-point bending test).

Some of these tests can be directly used for linear elastic material model calibration, namely the plane strain Young's modulus in two perpendicular directions, Kirchhoff's modulus and Poisson's ratio. The modulus of elasticity (i.e., Young's modulus) is a quantity well known to designers and engineers, but less common in paper specifications in the cardboard packaging industry. Traditionally, the stiffness modulus can be determined while performing a uniaxial tensile test of a sample. As paperboard is an orthotropic material, more tests are required to determine all elastic parameters (see Figure 4).

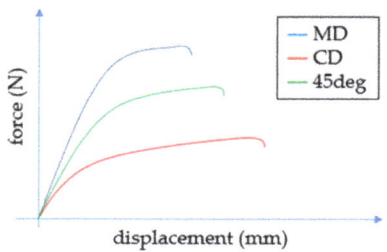

Figure 4. The load–displacement curves in MD, CD and 45 deg.

Determining the elastic parameters is an important step in the box load-bearing capacity estimation procedure, thus the brief introduction to some basic definitions, the constitutive description of the paperboard and the method of calibrating material constants will be presented in the subsequent sections. For orthotropic materials in a plane stress state, the relationship between elastic strains and stresses can be written as:

$$\begin{bmatrix} \varepsilon_{11} \\ \varepsilon_{22} \\ 2\varepsilon_{12} \end{bmatrix} = \begin{bmatrix} 1/E_1 & -\nu_{21}/E_2 & 0 \\ -\nu_{12}/E_1 & 1/E_2 & 0 \\ 0 & 0 & 1/G_{12} \end{bmatrix} \begin{bmatrix} \sigma_{11} \\ \sigma_{22} \\ \sigma_{12} \end{bmatrix}, \qquad (1)$$

where E_1 is Young's modulus in the Machine Direction (MD); E_2 is Young's modulus in the Cross Direction (CD); G_{12} is Kirchhoff's modulus and ν_{12}, ν_{21} are Poisson's coefficients. Due to the symmetry of the material compliance/stiffness matrix, the relationship between the Poisson's coefficients is as follows:

$$\frac{\nu_{12}}{E_1} = \frac{\nu_{21}}{E_2}. \qquad (2)$$

The Hill model [42] can be successfully employed to describe the behavior of the paper in an inelastic phase. Implementation of the Hill model requires the definition of the elastic domain described by the plastic yield function and the description of the material hardening:

$$f(\sigma, \kappa) = \sqrt{a_1 \sigma_{11}^2 + a_2 \sigma_{22}^2 - a_{12} \sigma_{11} \sigma_{22} + 3 a_3 \sigma_{12}^2} - \sigma_0(\kappa) \leq 0, \qquad (3)$$

where $\sqrt{*}$ is an effective stress σ_{eff}, which can be reduced to classical Huber-Mises criterion for isotropic materials if $a_1 = a_2 = a_{12} = a_3 = 1$; $\sigma_0(\kappa)$ is a yield stress function; κ is a hardening parameter, usually related to effective plastic strains; σ_{ij} are the stresses in main orthotropic directions; a_i and a_{12} are called anisotropic parameters, which can be determined from simple tensile tests in the main orthotropic directions:

$$a_1 = \frac{\sigma_0^2}{\sigma_{10}^2}, \quad a_2 = \frac{\sigma_0^2}{\sigma_{20}^2}, \quad a_3 = \frac{\sigma_0^2}{3\sigma_{120}^2}, \qquad (4)$$

where: σ_0 is the initial yield stress in the reference direction; σ_{10} is the yield stress in first direction (e.g., MD); σ_{20} is the yield stress in second direction; σ_{120} is the yield stress in shearing.

The remaining parameter a_{12} can be determined from the equation:

$$a_{12} = a_1 + a_2 + 3a_3 - 4a_{45}, \tag{5}$$

where a_{45} is the anisotropic parameter determined from a tensile test in an angled direction of 45 deg. As for most materials, only the values σ_{10}, σ_{20} and σ_{120} are known, in practical applications for the coefficient a_{12} usually a simplified relationship is assumed, e.g.,:

$$a_{12} = \frac{\sigma_0^2}{\sigma_{10}\sigma_{20}}. \tag{6}$$

It is a known fact that paperboard behaves differently under tension and compression. Therefore, the chosen plasticity criterion (which is symmetric in case of tension and compression) is not appropriate for this type of material. However, for simple strength calculations with a stress state dominated by compression, this model is a sufficient approximation. For the correct analysis of the structure in the complex stress state, one of the more sophisticated constitutive models should be used, e.g., [43–48].

2.4. Numerical Predictive Model

The numerical model of the box was built in the Abaqus Unified FEA software (2020, Dassault Systèmes Simulia Corp., Providence, RI, USA.) [49]. Two types of models had to be created: (i) the non-offset packaging and (ii) the package with flaps offset. In order to simplify the computations and save the computing time, only 1/8 part of the box was modeled instead of the whole packaging (see Figure 5). The material used in the model was linear elastic orthotropic model with Hill plasticity.

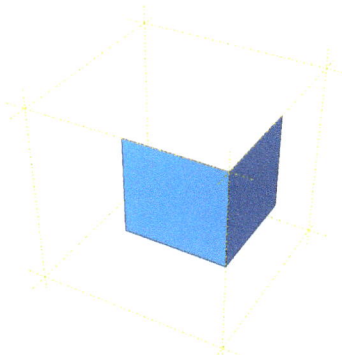

Figure 5. Scheme of the 1/8 part of the package.

To obtain the appropriate behavior of the numerical model, symmetry boundary conditions were defined on each edge (see Figure 6). For the packaging model without offset, only one computation step was defined, in which the displacement was applied on both edges. In the case of the package with offset flaps, in the first step only the offset edge was loaded and in the second step the load was then applied to the non-offset edge. The 4-node quadrilaterals shell elements with full integration, named S4, were used for all computations. For different dimensions of packaging, different values of mesh size were assumed. For example, for the package dimensions 500 × 500 × 500 mm the approximate global size of the element was 12 mm, which ultimately gave 882 elements, 946 nodes and 5676 degrees of freedom. To add the initial deformations (resulting from imperfections) of the box vertical walls, a buckling analysis was performed before the main calculations. The first buckling mode of the model found in this way was later introduced in the next step in the form of scaled imperfections.

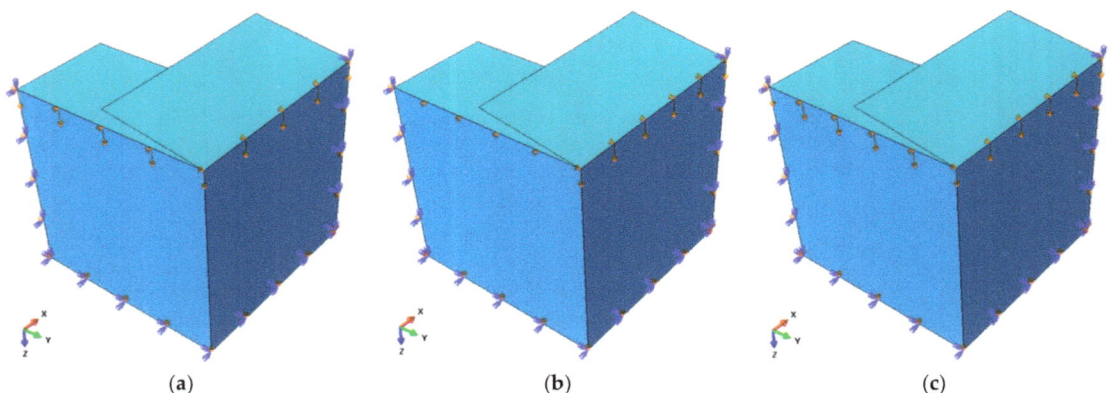

Figure 6. Boundary conditions for the case of: (**a**) the non-offset package; (**b**) the package with offset flaps (first step); (**c**) the package with offset flaps (second step).

2.5. Analytical Predictive Model

The simplified procedure for estimating the compressive strength of a corrugated cardboard box with offset flaps proposed here is based on an analytical model. The algorithm exploits the basic constitutive parameters of a single box wall, namely: ECT_{CD}—compressive strength in CD, $E_{CD} = E_2$—compressive stiffness of corrugated boards in CD and $E_{MD} = E_1$—compressive stiffness of corrugated boards in MD. Since in some cases the instability of a single wall may occur before plasticization, it is also necessary to determine the critical load for an orthotropic rectangular plate, e.g., from the formula [1,2,11]:

$$P_{cr}^i = \frac{\pi^2}{B_i^2} \frac{t_i^3}{12} \sqrt{E_{CD}^i E_{MD}^i} \left(\frac{mB_i}{H} + \frac{H}{mB_i} \right)^2, \qquad (7)$$

where B_i is the width of the i-th panel; t_i is the i-th panel thickness; H is the box height; m is the number of half-waves for which P_{cr}^i reaches the minimum.

The analysis of strength estimation of a box with shifted flaps, as already discussed in the previous section, consists of two stages, in which the higher walls (i.e., the shifted ones) are loaded first (see Figure 2a), while the lower walls are loaded only if preliminary crushing and/or buckling of the first two walls occurs (see Figure 2b). Therefore, the overall load capacity of the packaging is the sum of the load capacity of two pairs of opposite walls of the box, namely:

$$BCT = \alpha BCT_1 + BCT_2, \qquad (8)$$

where

$$BCT_1 = 2kECT^r \left(P_{cr}^1 \right)^{1-r} \gamma_1 \gamma_2 B_1 \qquad (9)$$

is the load capacity of the shifted walls, while

$$BCT_2 = 2kECT^r \left(P_{cr}^2 \right)^{1-r} \gamma_3 \gamma_4 B_2 \qquad (10)$$

is the load capacity of lower walls.

In Equations (9) and (10) k is a certain constant and r is an exponent, $r \in (0,1)$, and γ_i are the reduction coefficients. B_1 and B_2 are base dimensions, which are shown in Figure 7. The α coefficient reduces the value of the first term in Equation (8) due to the initial failure and/or buckling of the walls loaded in the first step (see Figure 8). This factor can be calculated using the formula below:

$$\alpha = 1 - \frac{u_{off} - u_0}{u_{max} - u_0}, \tag{11}$$

where u_{off} is an offset of higher walls; $u_{max} = H$ is assumed to be equal to the height of the box; u_0 is the vertical deformation corresponding to the maximum load. The latter can be calculated from Hooke's law considering the stiffness in the CD direction, E_{CD}; single box wall height, H (see Figure 7); shifted wall width, B_1; board thickness, t; the compressive strength, BCT_1 (see Figure 8). Thus, finally we obtain:

$$u_0 = \frac{BCT_1}{2tB_1 E_{CD}} H. \tag{12}$$

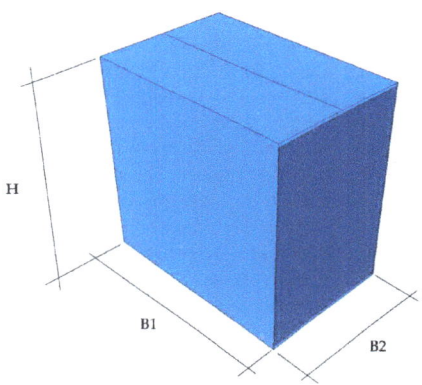

Figure 7. Box dimension symbols.

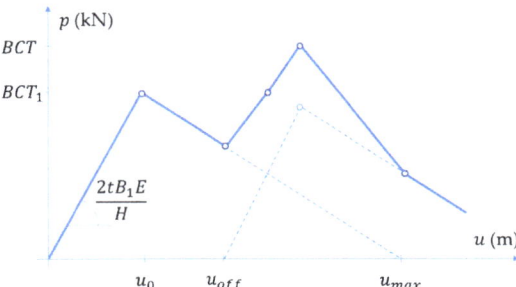

Figure 8. Force-displacement visualization of the proposed method.

The reduction factors γ_i are always less than one and depend on the ratio of the box dimensions and the exponents r_i. The γ_1 factor in Equation (9) reads:

$$\gamma_1 = \min\left[\left(\frac{B_1}{H}\right)^{r_1}, 1\right], \tag{13}$$

while γ_2:

$$\gamma_2 = \min\left[\left(\frac{B_1}{B_2}\right)^{r_2}, 1\right]. \tag{14}$$

Similarly, the coefficient γ_3 in Equation (10) is:

$$\gamma_3 = \min\left[\left(\frac{B_2}{H}\right)^{r_3}, 1\right], \quad (15)$$

while γ_4:

$$\gamma_4 = \min\left[\left(\frac{B_2}{B_1}\right)^{r_4}, 1\right]. \quad (16)$$

All unknown factors in Equations (8)–(10), namely constant k and exponent r, and the four exponents r_i in Equations (13)–(16), can be found by calibration with experimental data. The calibration procedure will be presented in the following section.

2.6. Calibration Procedure

The main goal of this study is to propose a reliable analytical model for the quick estimation of the load capacity of offset packaging. Therefore, the calibration of the coefficients in the analytical equations is particularly important. Unfortunately, the limited number of laboratory results creates a risk that the analytical model will be valid only for a small set. In order to extend the applicability of the proposed model, a calibration procedure consisting of two stages was engaged: (i) in the first step, special attention was paid to the correct mapping of experimental results into a numerical model; (ii) in the second one, the already tuned numerical model was used to generate much larger sets of cases, which were then utilized to identify the sought parameters in the analytical model.

In the first step, the only unknowns are the initial imperfections. Therefore, a very simple strategy is used, in which the numerical model is calibrated with experimental data by appropriate scaling of the initial deformations of the vertical box walls. In the second step, the coefficients in Equations (9) and (10) are identified in the assumed order: first the constant k as well as exponents r and r_1, then r_2 and r_3. In both cases, simple techniques were used to minimize the discrepancy between analytical model prediction and numerical results with the use of the least squares method.

3. Results

3.1. Corrugated Board: Material Testing

In order to correctly determine the properties of the material, it was necessary to examine samples of corrugated board in several typical laboratory tests. For this purpose, a FEMat BSE device (FEMat Sp z o.o., Poznan, Poland) [50] was used. In total, seven different types of corrugated cardboard with a grammage of 350 to 965 g/m^2 were tested. Since cardboard is a very heterogeneous material, at least 10 samples in each test were examined for each grade in order to obtain statistically reliable results. In Table 1, the sample results for the BC-780 grade are summarized. The first column represents a test number, the second column shows the sample thickness and in the third to ninth columns the results obtained from different tests in both orthotropy directions are demonstrated (all test symbols are explained in the previous section).

Figure 9 demonstrates the force-displacement curves from all tests of the corrugated cardboard. Since both shape of the curve and the calculated shear stiffness (SST) in the machine and cross directions are almost identical, only the values in the MD are shown. In Table 2, the mean values of the tests for all seven grades are presented. The first column represents grades that were used in the packaging for which the box compression test was carried out (details will be discussed in the next section). In the second to ninth columns, the measured stiffnesses obtained from the BSE device are shown.

Table 1. Test values for BC-780 corrugated cardboard grade.

Test	THK	ECT	BNT-MD	BNT-CD	SST-MD	SST-CD	TST-MD	TST-CD
1	6.49	10.77	10.79	10.47	2.96	3.05	3.10	1.79
2	6.50	10.66	10.55	9.66	3.02	2.77	3.05	1.74
3	6.49	10.93	10.53	9.20	2.90	2.99	3.08	1.79
4	6.53	11.28	10.31	10.11	2.80	2.86	3.26	1.71
5	6.53	11.15	10.29	11.24	2.95	2.91	3.20	1.70
6	6.52	11.41	11.13	11.94	2.95	2.77	3.31	1.92
7	6.52	11.85	11.06	10.92	2.95	2.77	3.29	1.85
8	6.55	10.82	11.11	11.03	2.96	2.70	3.29	1.90
9	6.53	11.44	10.42	9.05	3.10	2.90	3.45	1.88
10	6.55	11.44	10.74	10.43	3.12	2.87	3.35	1.88

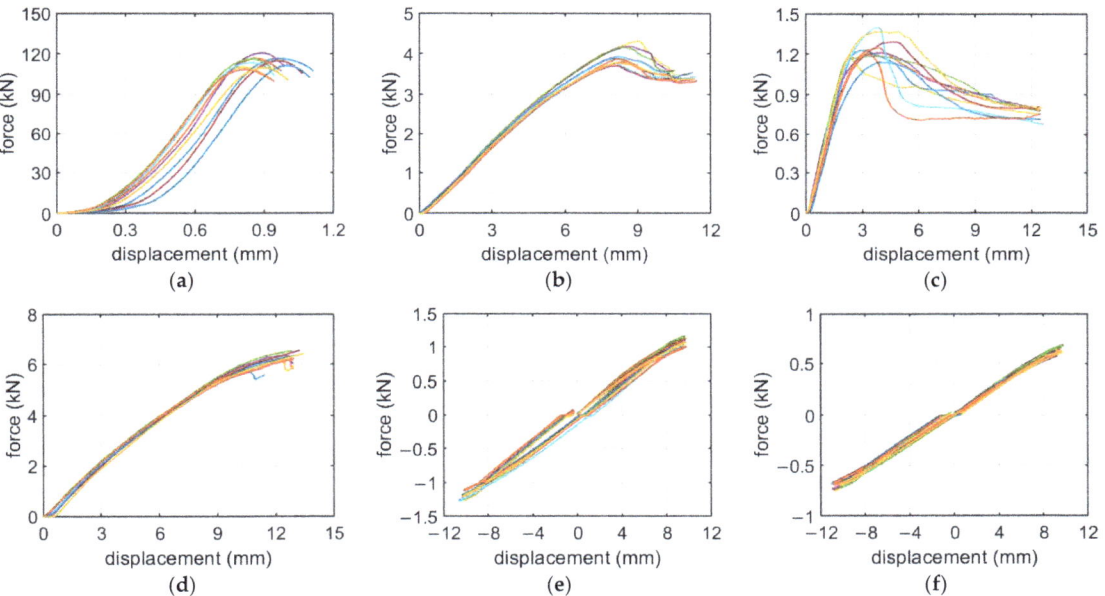

Figure 9. Force-displacement curves for BC-780 corrugated cardboard in various tests: (**a**) ECT; (**b**) BNT–MD; (**c**) BNT–CD; (**d**) SST; (**e**) TST–MD; (**f**) TST–CD.

Table 2. Test values for corrugated cardboard grades.

Grade	THK	ECT	BNT-MD	BNT-CD	SST-MD	SST-CD	TST-MD	TST-CD
E-350	1.49	4.68	0.36	0.80	0.19	0.24	0.18	0.18
E-380	1.59	5.41	0.49	1.16	0.26	0.31	0.23	0.23
B-400	2.80	5.50	1.50	2.94	0.55	0.57	0.60	0.38
EE-585	2.77	9.05	1.46	2.94	0.67	0.71	0.70	0.73
BC-780	6.52	11.18	10.69	10.41	2.97	2.86	3.24	1.82
EB-880	4.42	15.11	6.32	10.70	2.33	2.28	2.47	2.06
EB-965	4.55	13.69	5.68	11.39	2.24	2.26	2.42	1.89

3.2. Box Compression Test (BCT)

In the next step, the load capacity of the packaging was checked. For this purpose, the FEMat BCT-20T20 compact press (FEMat Sp. Z o.o., Poznan, Poland) [38] was exploited (see Figure 3a). A total number of 18 samples of various dimensions and materials were prepared. The analysis was carried out for two types of packaging: without and with an offset. In Table 3, the results obtained with the box compression test are presented. In the first column, corrugated cardboard grades are shown. The second, third and fourth columns show the dimensions of the package (see Figure 7). For offset packaging, the edge of the B_1 dimension is the offset edge. The fifth column represents the value of the load capacity of the package without offset. Columns six and seven are the BCT values for the offset package: the sixth column is the value of the first extreme and the seventh column is the value of the second extreme.

Table 3. Main dimensions and BCT values of various corrugated cardboard packaging.

Name	B_1 (mm)	B_2 (mm)	H (mm)	BCT (N)		
				Without Offset	With Offset 1	With Offset 2
E-350-1	300	200	300	875	566	767
E-350-2	450	100	450	704	454	656
E-380	300	200	300	1003	663	1131
B-400-1	300	200	300	2048	1265	1556
B-400-2	450	100	450	1498	1104	1201
EE-585	300	200	300	2409	1452	1855
BC-780	300	200	200	4995	2989	3817
EB-880	300	200	300	5352	3404	3700
EB-965	300	200	200	4445	3124	3830

In Figure 10, the force-displacement diagrams for boxes with dimensions 300 × 200 × 200 mm, with and without offset, made of BC-780 and EB-965 corrugated cardboard are shown.

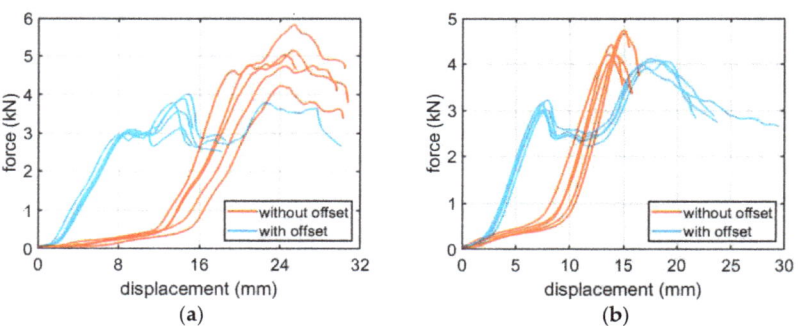

Figure 10. Selected measurements from a BCT press for grades: (**a**) BC-780; (**b**) EB-965.

3.3. Prediction Results of the Numerical Model

Having the geometry of all the tested boxes and the material properties of the corrugated cardboards, it was possible to build numerical models and calibrate the only one remaining component: the initial imperfections. These are especially important in the geometrically nonlinear FE analysis. To introduce preliminary deformations into the model, first a buckling analysis was carried out to find the first preferred buckling mode, which was then introduced as a deformed shape of the load-bearing panels of the box.

The influence of the imperfection size on the load capacity of the box 300 × 200 × 200 mm made of BC-780 is shown in Figure 11.

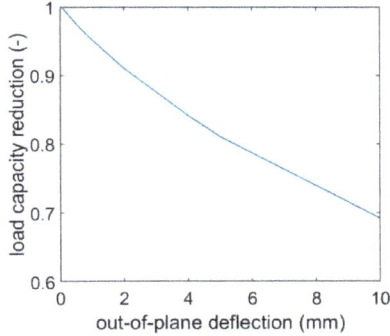

Figure 11. Influence of the imperfections on the load capacity of the BC-780 box.

After a successful calibration procedure, the results obtained with the numerical model are summarized in Table 4, which also shows the differences between the calculated and the measured values of the BCT.

Table 4. Comparison of measured and numerically determined BCT values for various corrugated cardboard packaging.

Name	BCT (N)			
	Measured Values		Numerical Values	
	First Extreme	Second Extreme	First Extreme	Second Extreme
E-350-1	566	767	520	778
E-350-2	454	656	448	648
E-380	663	1131	641	1132
B-400-1	1265	1556	1185	1540
B-400-2	1104	1201	1126	1117
EE-585	1452	1855	1468	1834
BC-780	2989	3817	2993	3690
EB-880	3404	3700	3222	3555
EB-965	3124	3830	3265	3653

3.4. Prediction Results of the Analytical Model

As already discussed, the main step was to calibrate the coefficients in the analytical formulas for the load capacity estimation of corrugated board packaging. For this purpose, synthetically generated results were utilized. Thanks to the use of numerical results, the range of packaging dimensions was much wider, which resulted in a greater number of analyzed cases and therefore made the calibration more reliable.

Table 5 shows all coefficients found in the minimization process used in Equations (9) and (10), while in Figure 12 the discrepancy function in two-dimensional space $[r_3, r_4]$ is shown. It can be seen that in the selected range of parameters r_3 and r_4 there is only one local minimum, which is also the global minimum (see Figure 12).

Table 5. Coefficients values.

k	r	r_1	r_2	r_3	r_4
	0.55	0.50	1.00	—	—
0.75	0.55	—	—	−1.00	0.50

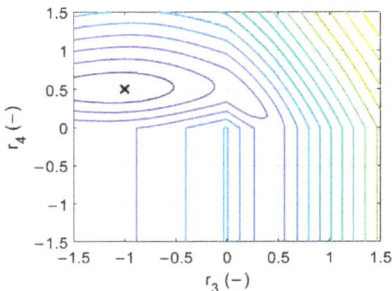

Figure 12. Error function in the sought parameters (r_3 and r_4) space. The location of the optimal value is marked with 'x'.

Figure 13 shows the estimation errors obtained from the analytical model in the calibration procedure for all offset and non-offset boxes. Table 6 presents a comparison of the results obtained from the tuned analytical model with the experimental results.

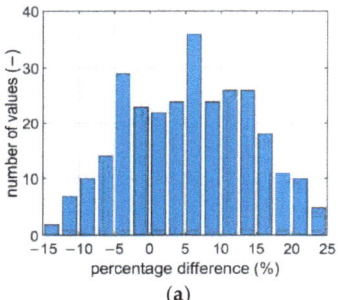
(a)

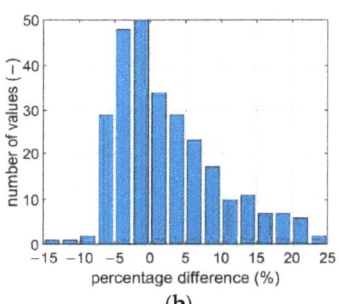
(b)

Figure 13. The prediction error distribution obtained while using the analytical model: (a) first extreme; (b) second extreme.

Table 6. Comparison of measured and analytically determined BCT values for various corrugated cardboard packaging.

Name	BCT (N)			
	Measured Values		Analytical Values	
	First Extreme	Second Extreme	First Extreme	Second Extreme
E-350-1	566	767	553	752
E-350-2	454	656	471	657
E-380	663	1131	709	1135
B-400-1	1265	1556	1171	1642
B-400-2	1104	1201	1197	1323
EE-585	1452	1855	1516	1913
BC-780	2989	3817	2975	3764
EB-880	3404	3700	3360	3854
EB-965	3124	3830	3079	3877

Figures 14 and 15 show the distribution of the prediction error in the design space, which are the main dimensions of the box (L, B, H). It can be seen that the greatest error occurs with boxes that are short and long.

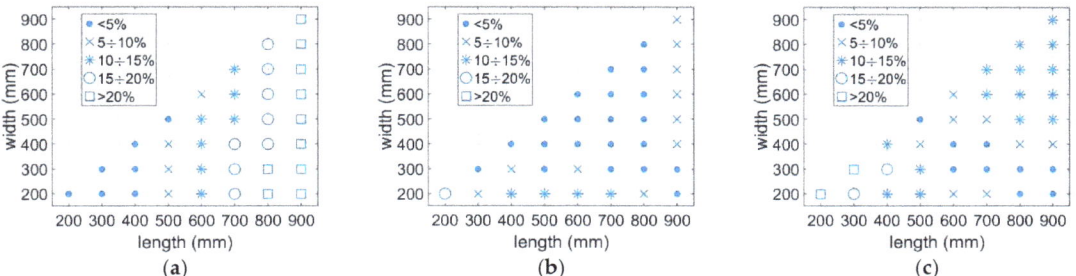

Figure 14. The prediction error distribution obtained using the analytical model for the first extreme: (**a**) H = 200 mm; (**b**) H = 500 mm; (**c**) H = 800 mm.

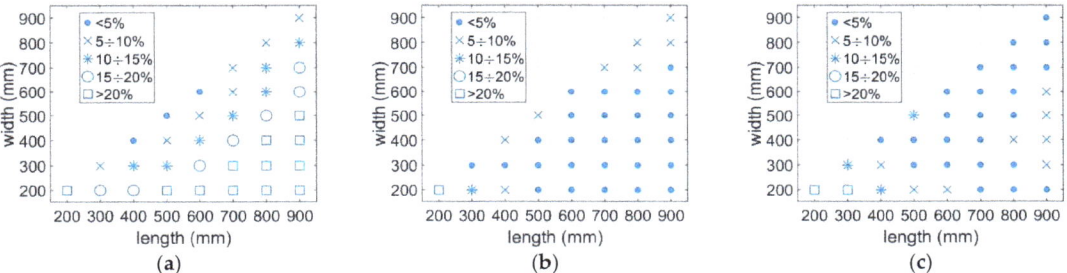

Figure 15. The prediction error distribution obtained using the analytical model for the second extreme: (**a**) H = 200 mm; (**b**) H = 500 mm; (**c**) H = 800 mm.

4. Discussion

Since corrugated board is an orthotropic and non-homogeneous material, a large number of tests were required for the correct characterization of its mechanical parameters. This means that when testing both corrugated cardboard and boxes made of such material, one can expect a large dispersion of test results. This is related to the heterogeneity of the paper itself, as well as the corrugated cardboard, and the inaccuracy of the assemblies of the tested packaging. Thus, the number of tests in the case of boxes should not be less than five, as is the case with testing the corrugated cardboard samples.

Among the many mechanical tests of corrugated board available in the papermaking laboratory, the most important define not only the static edge crush resistance but also the flexural and torsional stiffness of the specimen. In this study, the BSE system [50], which allows the examination of five physical parameters of cardboard (for three of them in both directions of orthotropy), was exploited. Based on the results of all laboratory tests (see Table 1 and Figure 9), homogenized parameters describing the elastic and plastic behavior of the particular corrugated cardboard were obtained.

In order to diversify the set of BCT laboratory results, various corrugated cardboards (a total of seven types) that are used for box production and nine different dimensions of the packaging structure, in two variants (without and with offsets), were tested. The results are presented in Table 3, where among the dimensions of the boxes and the symbols of the corrugated board one can also find the BCT results for two cases: (a) without offsets in column five and (b) with offsets in columns six and seven. The sixth column of Table 3 presents the force value for which two offset walls have been crushed. This is clearly seen in Figure 10: the first peak in the blue result plots. Column seven of Table 3 shows the maximum force value obtained in the BCT test.

Both predictive models take into account the behavior shown in Figure 10, which is characteristic for the offset boxes. The numerical model is loaded sequentially, first on the walls with an offset and then when the displacement of the upper surface exceeds the given offset, the two remaining walls are also loaded. As already mentioned, after calibrating the material model and for the given geometry, the only unknown was the size of the imperfections of the vertical walls. These parameters were in each case adjusted so that the estimates agreed with the laboratory results. The effect of the applied imperfection in a specific case (box EB-780) is shown in Figure 11.

This phenomenon is treated slightly differently in the analytical model, which is based solely on the geometry of the box, its strength in CD and both stiffnesses in MD and CD. In this case, the imperfections are embedded in the predictive model through the critical load term in Equations (9) and (10), while the sequential crushing of the shifted and non-shifted faces is captured by independently determining two values and scaling the maximum force in the first peak by the factor α (see Equation (8)). This allows the degraded resistance of walls with an offset and the resistance of walls without an offset to be taken into account in the second peak. The tuning exponents found by the minimization procedure (shown in Table 5) reached the optimal values of 0.5 or 1.0, while the constant k and exponent r reached values of 0.75 and 0.55, respectively.

The use of data synthetically generated by the calibrated numerical model allowed a much greater accuracy of the tuned parameters in the analytical model to be obtained. This was mainly due to a larger range of results numerically generated for various geometric dimensions of boxes that could not be physically produced and tested in the BCT press. Figure 13 shows the distribution of the prediction error of the load capacity of various corrugated board packages without and with an offset. The largest discrepancies occur for packages with a relatively large proportion of dimensions (see Figures 14 and 15). However, the average error in both cases does not exceed 7%. Overall, the proposed predictive analytical model can capture the first peak in any experimentally tested sample fairly correctly, and the error in most cases is less than 7%. The greatest differences can be observed for samples B-400-1 and B-400-2, where the error was 8% and 9%, respectively. Similar conclusions can be drawn when predicting a second peak. In most cases, the error did not exceed 5%; only for the B-400-2 sample did it reach 9%.

In general, the application of analytical models existing in the literature, e.g., those proposed in [4–10] or even more the recent models presented by Garbowski et al. [1,2,11], does not allow one to predict the strength of boxes with shifted flaps. The reason is that these models do not take into account the sequential crush of the package walls. Particular attention should also be paid to modeling with purely numerical models, because special techniques for sequential loading of the walls with appropriate imperfections should be considered as well. The results presented in Tables 4 and 6 show the precision with which both the numerical model and the proposed analytical model reflect the laboratory results for selected constructions of corrugated cardboard boxes. The results obtained from both models do not differ by more than 10% from the experimental results.

5. Conclusions

This article presents numerical and analytical models for predicting the strength of boxes with displaced flaps. The obtained results are in accordance with the conducted laboratory tests. In both models, the mechanical parameters of the corrugated board obtained from the selected laboratory tests were implemented. Both models are based on a sequential approach for the loading of the vertical walls of a box; the walls with an offset are loaded first, then the walls without an offset. At the moment of loading the walls without offset, the two walls loaded in the first step are already partially damaged. Therefore, this type of packing is characterized by much lower load-bearing capacity than packages with flaps without an offset. Thanks to the methodology presented in this paper and utilization of such predictive tools, it is possible not only to design packaging more consciously, but also to deliver and optimally use the material for their manufacturing, and thus improve the sustainable economy of the production plant.

Author Contributions: Conceptualization, T.G.; methodology, T.G.; software, T.G. and D.M.; validation, D.M., A.K.-P. and T.G.; formal analysis, D.M.; investigation, D.M. and A.K.-P.; resources, D.M.; data curation, D.M.; writing—original draft preparation, A.K.-P., D.M. and T.G.; writing—review and editing, A.K.-P. and T.G.; visualization, D.M.; supervision, T.G.; project administration, T.G.; funding acquisition, A.K.-P. and T.G. All authors have read and agreed to the published version of the manuscript.

Funding: The APC was funded by the Ministry of Science and Higher Education, Poland, the statutory funding at Poznan University of Life Sciences, grant number 506.569.05.00 and the statutory funding at Poznan University of Technology, grant number 0411/SBAD/0004.

Institutional Review Board Statement: Not applicable.

Informed Consent Statement: Not applicable.

Data Availability Statement: The data presented in this study are available on request from the corresponding author.

Acknowledgments: Special thanks to the FEMat Sp. z o. o. company (Poznan, Poland) (www.fematsystems.pl—accessed on 21 July 2021) for providing the commercial software.

Conflicts of Interest: The authors declare no conflict of interest.

References

1. Garbowski, T.; Gajewski, T.; Grabski, J.K. Estimation of the compressive strength of corrugated cardboard boxes with various perforations. *Energies* **2021**, *14*, 1095. [CrossRef]
2. Garbowski, T.; Gajewski, T.; Grabski, J.K. Estimation of the compressive strength of corrugated cardboard boxes with various openings. *Energies* **2021**, *14*, 155. [CrossRef]
3. Sohrabpour, V.; Hellström, D. Models and Software for Corrugated Board and Box Design. In Proceedings of the 18th International Conference on Engineering Design (ICED 11), Copenhagen, Denmark, 15–18 October 2011.
4. Kellicutt, K.; Landt, E. Development of design data for corrugated fiberboard shipping containers. *Tappi J.* **1952**, *35*, 398–402.
5. Maltenfort, G. Compression strength of corrugated containers. *Fibre Contain.* **1956**, *41*, 106–121.
6. McKee, R.C.; Gander, J.W.; Wachuta, J.R. Compression strength formula for corrugated boxes. *Paperboard Packag.* **1963**, *48*, 149–159.
7. Allerby, I.M.; Laing, G.N.; Cardwell, R.D. Compressive strength—From components to corrugated containers. *Appita Conf. Notes* **1985**, 1–11.
8. Schrampfer, K.E.; Whitsitt, W.J.; Baum, G.A. *Combined Board Edge Crush (ECT) Technology*; Institute of Paper Chemistry: Appleton, WI, USA, 1987.
9. Batelka, J.J.; Smith, C.N. *Package Compression Model*; Institute of Paper Science and Technology: Atlanta, GA, USA, 1993.
10. Urbanik, T.J.; Frank, B. Box compression analysis of world-wide data spanning 46 years. *Wood Fiber Sci.* **2006**, *38*, 399–416.
11. Garbowski, T.; Gajewski, T.; Grabski, J.K. The role of buckling in the estimation of compressive strength of corrugated cardboard boxes. *Materials* **2020**, *13*, 4578. [CrossRef] [PubMed]
12. Frank, B. Corrugated box compression—A literature survey. *Packag. Technol. Sci.* **2014**, *27*, 105–128. [CrossRef]
13. Stott, R.A. Compression and stacking strength of corrugated fibreboard containers. *Appita J.* **2017**, *70*, 76–82.
14. Junli, W.; Quancheng, Z. Effect of moisture content of corrugated box on mechanical properties. *J. Lanzhou Jiaotong Univ.* **2006**, *25*, 134–136.
15. Archaviboonyobul, T.; Chaveesuk, R.; Singh, J.; Jinkarn, T. An analysis of the influence of hand hole and ventilation hole design on compressive strength of corrugated fiberboard boxes by an artificial neural network model. *Packag. Technol. Sci.* **2020**, *33*, 171–181. [CrossRef]
16. Zhang, Y.-L.; Chen, J.; Wu, Y.; Sun, J. Analysis of hazard factors of the use of corrugated carton in packaging low-temperature yogurt during logistics. *Procedia Environ. Sci.* **2011**, *10*, 968–973. [CrossRef]
17. Nordstrand, T.; Carlsson, L. Evaluation of transverse shear stiffness of structural core sandwich plates. *Compos. Struct.* **1997**, *37*, 145–153. [CrossRef]
18. Nordstrand, T. Basic Testing and Strength Design of Corrugated Board and Containers. Ph.D. Thesis, Lund University, Lund, Sweden, 2003.
19. Avilés, F.; Carlsson, L.A.; May-Pat, A. A shear-corrected formulation of the sandwich twist specimen. *Exp. Mech.* **2012**, *52*, 17–23. [CrossRef]
20. Garbowski, T.; Gajewski, T.; Grabski, J.K. Role of transverse shear modulus in the performance of corrugated materials. *Materials* **2020**, *13*, 3791. [CrossRef] [PubMed]
21. Garbowski, T.; Gajewski, T.; Grabski, J.K. Torsional and transversal stiffness of orthotropic sandwich panels. *Materials* **2020**, *13*, 5016. [CrossRef] [PubMed]

22. Urbanik, T.J.; Saliklis, E.P. Finite element corroboration of buckling phenomena observed in corrugated boxes. *Wood Fiber Sci.* **2003**, *35*, 322–333.
23. Garbowski, T.; Jarmuszczak, M. Homogenization of corrugated paperboard. Part 1. Analytical homogenization. *Pol. Pap. Rev.* **2014**, *70*, 345–349. (In Polish)
24. Garbowski, T.; Jarmuszczak, M. Homogenization of corrugated paperboard. Part 2. Numerical homogenization. *Pol. Pap. Rev.* **2014**, *70*, 390–394. (In Polish)
25. Garbowski, T.; Marek, A. Homogenization of Corrugated Boards through Inverse Analysis. In Proceedings of the 1st International Conference on Engineering and Applied Sciences Optimization, Kos Island, Greece, 4–6 June 2014; pp. 1751–1766.
26. Marek, A.; Garbowski, T. Homogenization of sandwich panels. *Comput. Assist. Methods Eng. Sci.* **2015**, *22*, 39–50.
27. Garbowski, T.; Gajewski, T. Determination of Transverse Shear Stiffness of Sandwich Panels with a Corrugated Core by Numerical Homogenization. *Materials* **2021**, *14*, 1976. [CrossRef] [PubMed]
28. Hohe, J. A direct homogenization approach for determination of the stiffness matrix for microheterogeneous plates with application to sandwich panels. *Compos. Part B* **2003**, *34*, 615–626. [CrossRef]
29. Buannic, N.; Cartraud, P.; Quesnel, T. Homogenization of corrugated core sandwich panels. *Compos. Struct.* **2003**, *59*, 299–312. [CrossRef]
30. Biancolini, M.E. Evaluation of equivalent stiffness properties of corrugated board. *Compos. Struct.* **2005**, *69*, 322–328. [CrossRef]
31. Abbès, B.; Guo, Y.Q. Analytic homogenization for torsion of orthotropic sandwich plates. *Appl. Compos. Struct.* **2010**, *92*, 699–706. [CrossRef]
32. Ghiță, C.; Pop, N.; Cioban, H. Quasi-Static behavior as a limit process of a dynamical one for an anisotropic hardening material. *Comput. Mater. Sci.* **2012**, *52*, 217–225. [CrossRef]
33. Thakkar, B.K.; Gooren, L.G.J.; Peerlings, R.H.J.; Geers, M.G.D. Experimental and numerical investigation of creasing in corrugated paperboard. *Philos. Mag.* **2008**, *88*, 3299–3310. [CrossRef]
34. Beex, L.A.A.; Peerlings, R.H.J. An experimental and computational study of laminated paperboard creasing and folding. *Int. J. Solids Struct.* **2009**, *46*, 4192–4207. [CrossRef]
35. Giampieri, A.; Perego, U.; Borsari, R. A constitutive model for the mechanical response of the folding of creased paperboard. *Int. J. Solids Struct.* **2011**, *48*, 2275–2287. [CrossRef]
36. Domaneschi, M.; Perego, U.; Borgqvist, E.; Borsari, R. An industry-oriented strategy for the finite element simulation of paperboard creasing and folding. *Packag. Technol. Sci.* **2017**, *30*, 269–294. [CrossRef]
37. Awais, M.; Tanninen, P.; Leppänen, T.; Matthews, S.; Sorvari, J.; Varis, J.; Backfolk, K. A computational and experimental analysis of crease behavior in press forming process. *Procedia Manuf.* **2018**, *17*, 835–842. [CrossRef]
38. Leminen, V.; Tanninen, P.; Pesonen, A.; Varis, J. Effect of mechanical perforation on the press-forming process of paperboard. *Procedia Manuf.* **2019**, *38*, 1402–1408. [CrossRef]
39. FEMat BCT Press. Available online: http://fematsystems.pl/bct_en/ (accessed on 21 July 2021).
40. Garbowski, T.; Jarmuszczak, M. Numerical Strength Estimate of Corrugated Board Packages. Part 1. Theoretical Assumptions in Numerical Modeling of Paperboard Packages. *Pol. Pap. Rev.* **2014**, *70*, 219–222. (In Polish)
41. Garbowski, T.; Jarmuszczak, M. Numerical Strength Estimate of Corrugated Board Packages. Part 2. Experimental tests and numerical analysis of paperboard packages. *Pol. Pap. Rev.* **2014**, *70*, 277–281. (In Polish)
42. Hill, R. A theory of the yielding and plastic flow in anisotropic metals. *Proc. R. Soc. London. Ser. A Math. Phys. Sci.* **1948**, *193*, 281–297. [CrossRef]
43. Hoffman, O. The brittle strength of orthotropic materials. *J. Compos. Mater.* **1967**, *1*, 200–206. [CrossRef]
44. Tsai, S.W.; Wu, E.M. A general theory of strength for anisotropic materials. *J. Compos. Mater.* **1971**, *5*, 58–80. [CrossRef]
45. Xia, Q.S.; Boyce, M.C.; Parks, D.M. A constitutive model for the anisotropic elastic–plastic deformation of paper and paperboard. *Int. J. Solids Struct.* **2002**, *39*, 4053–4071. [CrossRef]
46. Makela, P.; Ostlund, S. Orthotropic elastic–plastic material model for paper materials. *Int. J. Solids Struct.* **2003**, *40*, 5599–5620. [CrossRef]
47. Borgqvist, E.; Lindström, T.; Tryding, J.; Wallin, M.; Ristinmaa, M. Distortional hardening plasticity model for paperboard. *Int. J. Solids Struct.* **2014**, *51*, 2411–2423. [CrossRef]
48. Robertsson, K.; Wallin, M.; Borgqvist, E.; Ristinmaa, M.; Tryding, J. A rate-dependent continuum model for rapid converting of paperboard. *Appl. Math. Model.* **2021**, *99*, 497–513. [CrossRef]
49. Abaqus Unified FEA Software. Available online: https://www.3ds.com/products-services/simulia/products/abaqus (accessed on 21 July 2021).
50. FEMat BSE System. Available online: http://fematsystems.pl/bse-system_en/ (accessed on 21 July 2021).

Article
On Wrinkling in Sandwich Panels with an Orthotropic Core

Zbigniew Pozorski [1,*], Jolanta Pozorska [2], Ireneusz Kreja [3] and Łukasz Smakosz [3]

[1] Institute of Structural Engineering, Faculty of Civil and Transport Engineering, Poznan University of Technology, ul. Piotrowo 5, 60-965 Poznań, Poland
[2] Department of Mathematics, Faculty of Mechanical Engineering and Computer Science, Czestochowa University of Technology, Armii Krajowej 21, 42-201 Częstochowa, Poland; jolanta.pozorska@pcz.pl
[3] Department of Structural Mechanics, Faculty of Civil and Environmental Engineering, Gdańsk University of Technology, ul. Gabriela Narutowicza 11/12, 80-233 Gdańsk, Poland; ikreja@pg.edu.pl (I.K.); lukasz.smakosz@pg.edu.pl (Ł.S.)
* Correspondence: zbigniew.pozorski@put.poznan.pl

Abstract: This paper deals with the local loss of stability (wrinkling) problem of a thin facing of a sandwich panel. Classical solutions to the problem of a facing instability resting on a homogeneous and isotropic substructure (a core) are compared. The relations between strain energy components associated with different forms of core deformations are discussed. Next, a new solution for the orthotropic core is presented in detail, which is consistent with the classic solution for the isotropic core. Selected numerical examples confirm the correctness of the analytical formulas. In the last part, parametric analyses are carried out to illustrate the sensitivity of wrinkling stress to a change in the material parameters of the core. These analyses illustrate the possibility of using the equations derived in the article for the variability of Poisson's ratio from −1 to 1 and for material parameters strongly deviating from isotropy.

Keywords: sandwich panels; local instability; strain energy; wrinkling; orthotropic core

1. Introduction

In a typical sandwich element, the two facings are joined to each other by a relatively thick but deformable core. The deformations and stresses in the sandwich panel are caused by the acting loads (wind, snow, self-weight, live load), but they are also largely due to thermal loads. As a result of these interactions, the facing can be compressed, and because it is connected to a susceptible substructure (a core), it very often experiences local loss of stability (wrinkling).

Wrinkling is undoubtedly one of the most common damage mechanisms of a sandwich element. For this reason, the correct estimation of the stress leading to the loss of facing stability is a key issue that has been undertaken by many researchers using various approaches: analytical, numerical, experimental, or mixed (or some combination of these approaches). Numerical methods allow for solving many complex problems, and the performed experiments allow for the verification of the obtained results. Nevertheless, analytical solutions should also be treated as very valuable, even if they are obtained with significant simplifications. Simple formulas are easy for engineering application and allow for a very quick (and continuous) assessment of the sensitivity of the solution to a change in design parameters.

With full awareness of the new challenges related to the sandwich structures (anisotropy [1], influence of extreme excitations [2], new production technologies [3], and many others), this work is an attempt to take a deeper look at the known classical solutions to the local instability problem [4–6]. The presented solution for an orthotropic core is based on the work of [7], in which sandwich columns under compression were considered, and the solution was presented in the form of hyperbolic functions. It also clearly refers to the classic solution for an isotropic core [6], where a facing and a core were assumed as infinite and the differential equation written for the facing was used.

The above-mentioned classic approaches to the problem of facing instability are constantly being used and extended to more and more complex issues. The analytical model that leads to wrinkling of the orthotropic face layer supported by a transversely isotropic core was presented in [8]. Wrinkling of a composite-facing sandwich panel under biaxial loading was discussed in [9]. Article [10] presents the solution to the symmetrical face sheet wrinkling problem using the energy method. The approach focused on a 3D case of wrinkling of orthotropic face sheets was presented in [11]. The analytical approach to the problem of anisotropic facing instability was presented in the works [12,13]. Wrinkling in sandwich structures with a functionally graded core was discussed in [14]. The papers [15–17] are examples of work on wrinkling, in which the core was modeled using higher-order theories, which allowed, among others, to take into account the influence of the core transverse compressibility.

This paper is divided into three parts. In the first one, we present some relations between the classical solutions to the analyzed problem of wrinkling. We believe that they will shed a slightly different light on known solutions. This applies to the conditions of reaching the critical stress, the influence of the Poisson ratio on the wrinkling stress, and the relationship between strain energy components. In the second part, the solution for the orthotropic core is derived and discussed, and we focus on the interpretation of the solution and the question of the conditions for obtaining it. In the third part, a parametric analysis of the solution for the orthotropic core is presented, illustrating the sensitivity of the solution (especially the wrinkling stress) to a change in some material parameters. In our opinion, this is essential for the optimal design of layered structures. By assuming certain constraints on material parameters, we can specify a solution with the maximum value or the minimum sensitivity.

2. Formulation of the Problem

We are considering a sandwich panel consisting of two thin facings and a thick but deformable core. Due to the bending of the composite panel, considerable compressive stresses may be generated in its facing, resulting in a local loss of stability. The instability has the form of wrinkling. In general, due to the variety of support and load conditions, the problem can be very complex; however, in practical civil engineering problems, a facing is usually compressed unidirectionally [18].

The wrinkling phenomenon may be considered as a compression effect of a thin facing (treated as a beam or plate) supported by a continuous elastic core (Figure 1). The facing in tension is ignored because the deformation of the core quickly disappears as the distance from the compressed facing increases. It is convenient to assume that the compressed facing is infinitely long and the core extends to infinity on one side of the facing. The wrinkling is associated with short waves of buckling of the facing. Figure 1 shows a fragment of the deformed facing supported by the core.

It is assumed that the face layer is in a uniform stress and strain state. The deformations of the facing, which are infinite and periodic, induce strain and stress in the core. Core deformations quickly decay as the variable z increases, and the rate of this decay depends on the assumed displacement field.

The core and facing materials are homogeneous. Suppose the core is isotropic or orthotropic with one of the orthotropic axes coinciding with the direction of the compression. The facing material could be orthotropic if its axes were aligned with the material axes of the core. These are quite strong assumptions, but they give analytical results that are relatively easy to interpret.

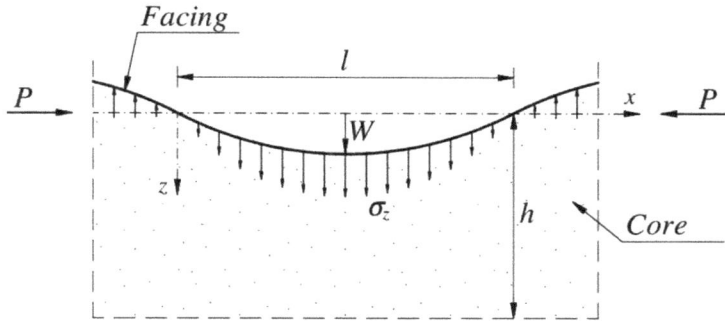

Figure 1. Assumed shape of a wrinkling.

3. Classical Solutions of the Wrinkling Problem

3.1. Energy Method—Linear Decay Function

Following the proposition of Hoff and Mautner [4], the core is affected only in a small zone with depth h (smaller than the thickness of the core). The shape of the face deformation is assumed in the sinusoidal form (Figure 1), and the core deformation field vanishes linearly with coordinate z:

$$w_C = w_F \frac{(h-z)}{h} = W \frac{(h-z)}{h} \sin \frac{\pi x}{l}, \tag{1}$$

where w_C, w_F, and W denote the vertical displacement of the core, face, and the displacement amplitude, respectively. The term l is a half wavelength of the wrinkles. Comparing the sum of strain energy of the core and the facing (per half wavelength) with the external work done by an applied work, the expression on the compressive stress in the facing is obtained:

$$\sigma_x = \frac{E_C l^2}{\pi^2 t_F h} + \frac{h G_C}{3 t_F} + \frac{\pi^2 E_F}{12}\left(\frac{t_F}{l}\right)^2. \tag{2}$$

Symbols E_C and G_C denote the modulus of elasticity and shear modulus of the isotropic core material, respectively. The thickness of the facing is t_F, whereas the modulus of elasticity of the isotropic facing material is E_F.

The minimum value of the compressive stress (2) corresponds to the critical (wrinkling) stress, and it can be found by using derivatives of σ_x with respect to h and l:

$$\sigma_w = \sqrt[3]{\frac{3}{4}} \cdot \sqrt[3]{E_C G_C E_F} \cong 0.909 \cdot \sqrt[3]{E_C G_C E_F}. \tag{3}$$

It is worth noting that reaching the wrinkling stress corresponds to a situation in which each term on the right-hand side of Equation (2) is equal to each other.

3.2. Energy Method—Exponential Decay Function

Plantema [5] assumed the displacement field of the exponential form

$$w_C = w_F e^{-kz} = W e^{-kz} \sin \frac{\pi x}{l}, \tag{4}$$

where $k \geq 0$ is an auxiliary constant (with the unit inverse to the unit of variable z). The use of the strain energy of the core makes it possible to represent the compressive stress of the facing as

$$\sigma_x = \frac{E_C k l^2}{2\pi^2 t_F} + \frac{G_C}{2k t_F} + \frac{\pi^2 E_F}{12}\left(\frac{t_F}{l}\right)^2. \tag{5}$$

The wrinkling stress is obtained from the conditions of zeroing the derivatives of σ_x with respect to k and l. As we can see, a slightly different assumption of the displacement field leads to a different result. First of all, the condition for reaching the extreme (minimum) stress σ_x is different. Again, when the critical stress is reached, each term of Equation (5) has the same value. The wrinkling stresses (3) and (6) are independent of the Poisson ratio of the core material.

$$\sigma_w = \frac{3}{2 \cdot \sqrt[3]{6}} \cdot \sqrt[3]{E_C G_C E_F} \cong 0.825 \cdot \sqrt[3]{E_C G_C E_F} \tag{6}$$

3.3. Differential Equation Method

The solution based on the differential equation method was presented by Allen [6]. Stresses in the elastic isotropic medium can be defined using the Airy stress function $F(x,z)$. The strain compatibility in the x–z plane leads to the bi-harmonic differential equation.

$$\frac{\partial^4 F}{\partial z^4} + 2 \frac{\partial^4 F}{\partial x^2 \partial z^2} + \frac{\partial^4 F}{\partial x^4} = 0. \tag{7}$$

Equation (7) is satisfied by the function

$$F(x,z) = A \sin \frac{\pi x}{l} (1 - Bz) e^{-\frac{\pi z}{l}}, \tag{8}$$

where A and B are constants. Constant B can be found by using the condition that the x-displacements and strains at the surface of the core ($z = 0$) are equal to zero. Constant A can be expressed by the amplitude W of the z-displacement at $z = 0$. By using Allen's method, nearly the entire mechanical field is obtained, which depends on x and z variables. If the state of plane stress is assumed, then displacements u, v, and w, strains ε_x, ε_y, ε_z, and γ_{xz}, and stresses σ_x, σ_y, and τ_{xz} are non-zero.

The equilibrium differential equation for the facing has the form

$$B_F \frac{d^4 w}{dx^4} + P \frac{d^2 w}{dx^2} = \sigma_z, \tag{9}$$

where the stress σ_z is the effect of the interaction between the facing and the core (see Figure 1). The symbol B_F denotes the face bending stiffness per unit width. For the beam theory (as used here), $B_F = E_F t_F^3/12$; in the case of the plate theory, $B_F = E_F t_F^3/12(1 - \nu_F^2)$. Using the function of the facing displacement

$$w = W \sin \frac{\pi x}{l}, \tag{10}$$

and the parameter $m = l/t_F$, the compressive stress in the facing can be expressed as

$$\sigma_x = \frac{\pi^2 E_F}{12 m^2} + \frac{a}{\pi} m = \sigma_1 + \sigma_2, \tag{11}$$

where

$$a = \frac{2 E_C}{(1 + \nu_C) \cdot (3 - \nu_C)} \tag{12}$$

is the material constant. The two terms of the solution for (11) are denoted as σ_1 and σ_2, respectively.

From the condition for the extreme, $d\sigma_x/dm = 0$, we can find $m = \pi \cdot \sqrt[3]{E_F/6a}$ and the minimum critical (wrinkling) stress:

$$\sigma_w = \sqrt[3]{\frac{9}{2(1 + \nu_C) \cdot (3 - \nu_C)^2}} \cdot \sqrt[3]{E_C G_C E_F} = r \cdot \sqrt[3]{E_C G_C E_F}. \tag{13}$$

If we assume the facing stiffness as for the plate, $B_F = E_F t_F^3/12(1-\nu_F^2)$, the modulus E_F should be replaced by $E_F/(1-\nu_F^2)$.

It is interesting that for the minimum value of σ_x (11), the second expression (σ_2) is exactly two times higher than the first (σ_1) [19]. From some literature sources, e.g., [6] p. 159, Figure 8.3, it can be drawn incorrectly that both of these values are equal. The value of the first root (r) depends only on the Poisson ratio of the core material ν_C, but for the typical range of this parameter, the root r reaches the value from 0.780 to 0.794. It is also worth noting that as the Poisson ratio tends to -1, the critical stress would increase to infinity, although this is a rather theoretical situation.

3.4. Comparison of Classical Solutions

3.4.1. Influence of the Poisson Ratio

Let us return first to Allen's solution. The result (13) was obtained for a plane stress state. Assuming a plane strain state, the procedure is analogous; however, the functions of stresses, strains, and displacements are different. Equation (11) is valid, but:

$$a = \frac{2E_C(1-\nu_C)}{(1+\nu_C)\cdot(3-4\nu_C)}, \tag{14}$$

$$\sigma_w = \sqrt[3]{\frac{9(1-\nu_C)^2}{2(1+\nu_C)\cdot(3-4\nu_C)^2}} \cdot \sqrt[3]{E_C G_C E_F} = s \cdot \sqrt[3]{E_C G_C E_F}. \tag{15}$$

Of course, the value of s in (15) is different than r in (13). To compare Allen's solutions in the case of the plane stress and plane strain states, see Figure 2.

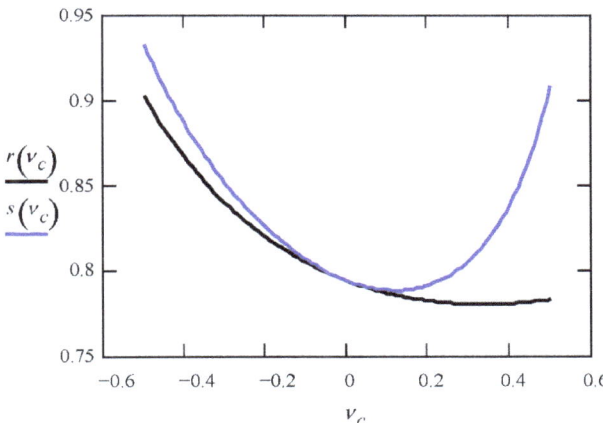

Figure 2. Comparison of Allen's solution in the case of the plane stress (r) and plane strain (s) states.

It should come as no surprise that for $\nu_C = 0$, the coefficients r and s are identical and equal to 0.794. For negative values of ν_C, the coefficients r and s take similar values that are much higher than 0.794. For ν_C tending to -1, the values of r and s, and hence the critical stress values, tend to infinity. In the range of ν_C (-1; $+0.5$), the critical stresses in the plane strain state are higher than in the plane stress state, but the greatest differences between r and s appear for ν_C close to 0.5. This is obvious because in a plane state of stress, the material has the potential to deform in the y-direction (perpendicular to the plane), which facilitates the deformation of the facing. The plane strain condition limits the deformation (in the y-direction) and makes it difficult to buckle the facing. The greater the Poisson ratio, the greater the significance of this effect. For some order, let us remind you that the Poisson ratio of the core material does not affect the critical stresses in the case of the solutions given by Hoff and Mautner (3) and Plantema (6).

3.4.2. Assumptions and Strain Energy Considerations

The Hoff–Mautner and Plantema solutions are based on an energy approach. The assumption of a specific displacement field turns out to be very effective and quickly leads to a solution. However, it is worth noting that in contrast to Allen's solution, the assumed displacement fields ((1) or (4)) result in non-fulfillment of most of the differential equilibrium equations of a solid (mass forces were omitted in Equation (16)):

$$\sigma_{ji,j} = 0. \tag{16}$$

Let us return to the solution presented by Allen [6]. In the case of a plane stress state, constant B is

$$B = -\frac{\pi}{2l}(1 + \nu_C), \tag{17}$$

and the stresses in the core are expressed as the corresponding derivatives of the function $F(x,z)$. By using commonly known physical and geometric relationships, we determine the fields of strain and displacement. Therefore, we can calculate the appropriate components of the strain energy of the core, obtaining, respectively:

$$\frac{1}{2}\int_0^\infty \int_0^l \sigma_x \varepsilon_x dx dz = \frac{1}{16}\frac{A^2}{E_C}\frac{\pi^3}{l^2}(1+\nu_C)\left(1-\nu_C^2\right), \tag{18}$$

$$\frac{1}{2}\int_0^\infty \int_0^l \sigma_z \varepsilon_z dx dz = \frac{1}{16}\frac{A^2}{E_C}\frac{\pi^3}{l^2}(1+\nu_C)\left(13 - 4\nu_C - \nu_C^2\right), \tag{19}$$

$$\frac{1}{2}\int_0^\infty \int_0^l \tau_{xz}\gamma_{xz} dx dz = \frac{1}{16}\frac{A^2}{E_C}\frac{\pi^3}{l^2}(1+\nu_C)\left(10 - 4\nu_C + 2\nu_C^2\right). \tag{20}$$

For $\nu_C = 0$, the ratio of energies expressed in (18)–(20) is 1:13:10. Let us recall that under the condition of loss of stability, the elastic energy in the facing is half of the elastic energy in the core. Commenting on the relations between the energies in the core, we can say that the share of energy (18) resulting from the deformation of the core along the x-direction (ε_x) is small, which can justify the omission of this term in classical energy methods. For the sake of order, we note that the fulfillment of the condition of loss of local stability for each of the previously discussed classical energy methods means that the energy components on the left side of Equations (19) and (20) are equal to each other, and the integral (18) is equal to zero.

An additional point requires clarification. Each of the presented classical methods differs in the final result, but only because of different assumptions and not because of the method itself. For example, this is easily demonstrated by using Allen's mechanical fields for the energy approach. Then, it turns out that the obtained expression for the critical stress is identical to (13).

For an illustration of the assumptions made in Allen's solution, Figure 3 presents the displacement fields $w(x, z)$ (perpendicular to the facing i.e., along the z-axis) and $u(x, z)$ (along the x-axis). The values are given assuming the constant $A = 1$, see (8). The isotropic material of the core $E_C = 4$ MPa, $\nu_C = 0.05$ and a facing with a thickness of $t_F = 0.5$ mm made of an isotropic material $E_F = 210$ GPa were assumed. The range of the x-axis corresponds to $2l = 74$ mm, while the z-coordinates are given in millimeters. In Figure 3a, for $z = 0$, we can see a full sinusoid with an extreme equal to 3.248×10^{-5}, which disappears with increasing z. The amplitude of the sinusoid decreases 10 times for $z = 36$ mm. In Figure 3b, according to the assumption, for $z = 0$, the horizontal displacements are equal to zero. The variability of the function $u(x, z)$ in the x-direction is described by the cosine function, the extreme value of 4.253×10^{-6} is reached for $z = 12$ mm; at a distance of $z = 60$ mm, the function value is 10 times smaller than the extreme. The rapid disappearance of displacements with the increment of the z-coordinate, and the values of $w(x, z)$ being one order greater than $u(x, z)$, are both noteworthy, as they, among other things, justify the omission of longitudinal deformations in classical energy methods.

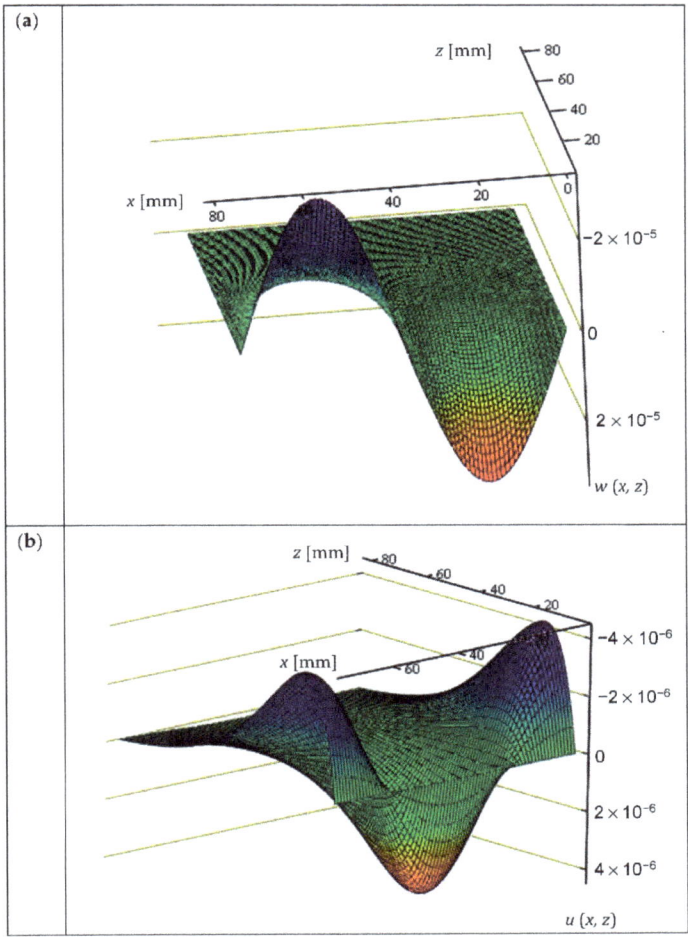

Figure 3. Solution obtained by using the differential equation method: (**a**) vertical displacement $w(x, z)$, (**b**) horizontal displacement $u(x, z)$.

4. Solution for the Orthotropic Core
4.1. Differential Equation

A certain solution to the problem of facing wrinkling resting on an orthotropic elastic substructure and loaded on the edge (in the facing plane) was presented in [7]. A similar approach was used in [8]. The following is a detailed solution, which is an extension of [6], formally based on [7,8], but it differs in some nuances. Efforts were made to present the solution precisely in order to also discuss the conditions for obtaining this solution.

Suppose we have an orthotropic core, in which orthotropic axes coincide with the axes of the element. The facing is compressed uniaxially, and the load direction is according to the material axes of the core. Such a situation is very common in practice [20]. The constitutive relation for the orthotropic core material is:

$$\left\{\begin{array}{c}\varepsilon_x\\ \varepsilon_y\\ \varepsilon_z\\ \varepsilon_{xy}\\ \varepsilon_{xz}\\ \varepsilon_{yz}\end{array}\right\} = \left[\begin{array}{cccccc} 1/E_x & -v_{yx}/E_y & -v_{zx}/E_z & 0 & 0 & 0\\ -v_{xy}/E_x & 1/E_y & -v_{zy}/E_z & 0 & 0 & 0\\ -v_{xz}/E_x & -v_{yz}/E_y & 1/E_z & 0 & 0 & 0\\ 0 & 0 & 0 & 1/2G_{xy} & 0 & 0\\ 0 & 0 & 0 & 0 & 1/2G_{xz} & 0\\ 0 & 0 & 0 & 0 & 0 & 1/2G_{yz}\end{array}\right] \left\{\begin{array}{c}\sigma_x\\ \sigma_y\\ \sigma_z\\ \tau_{xy}\\ \tau_{xz}\\ \tau_{yz}\end{array}\right\}. \quad (21)$$

In the case of a 2D problem, relation (21) can be simplified to:

$$\left.\begin{array}{c}\varepsilon_x = a_{xx}\sigma_x - a_{xz}\sigma_z\\ \varepsilon_z = -a_{xz}\sigma_x + a_{zz}\sigma_z\\ \varepsilon_{xz} = (1/2G_{xz})\tau_{xz}\end{array}\right\}. \quad (22)$$

In the case of plane stress state, material constants a_{xx}, a_{zz}, and a_{xz} are:

$$\left.\begin{array}{c}a_{xx} = 1/E_x\\ a_{zz} = 1/E_z\\ a_{xz} = v_{xz}/E_x\end{array}\right\}, \quad (23)$$

whereas for the plane strain state, we have:

$$\left.\begin{array}{c}a_{xx} = \frac{1-v_{xy}v_{yx}}{E_x}\\ a_{zz} = \frac{1-v_{yz}v_{zy}}{E_z}\\ a_{xz} = \frac{v_{xz}+v_{xy}v_{yz}}{E_x}\end{array}\right\}. \quad (24)$$

The compatibility of strains in the x–z plane requires:

$$\frac{\partial^2\varepsilon_x}{\partial z^2} + \frac{\partial^2\varepsilon_z}{\partial x^2} - 2\frac{\partial^2\varepsilon_{xz}}{\partial x \partial z} = 0. \quad (25)$$

After introducing the Airy stress function $F(x,y)$ such that

$$\sigma_x = \frac{\partial^2 F}{\partial z^2},\ \sigma_z = \frac{\partial^2 F}{\partial x^2},\ \tau_{xz} = -\frac{\partial^2 F}{\partial x \partial z}, \quad (26)$$

condition (25) takes the following form:

$$a_{zz}\frac{\partial^4 F}{\partial x^4} + 2\left(\frac{1}{2G_{xz}} - a_{xz}\right)\frac{\partial^4 F}{\partial x^2 \partial z^2} + a_{xx}\frac{\partial^4 F}{\partial z^4} = 0. \quad (27)$$

By using substitution

$$\eta = \epsilon z = \left(\sqrt[4]{a_{zz}/a_{xx}}\right)z, \quad (28)$$

we obtain

$$\frac{\partial^4 F(x,\eta)}{\partial x^4} + 2\kappa\frac{\partial^4 F(x,\eta)}{\partial x^2 \partial \eta^2} + \frac{\partial^4 F(x,\eta)}{\partial \eta^4} = 0, \quad (29)$$

where κ is a dimensionless quantity and depends only on the material parameters of the core,

$$\kappa = \frac{1}{\sqrt{a_{xx}a_{zz}}}\left(\frac{1}{2G_{xz}} - a_{xz}\right). \quad (30)$$

For an isotropic material, $\kappa = 1$.

4.2. Solution of the Differential Equation

To find a solution of (29), we separate variables:

$$F(x, \eta) = G(x)H(\eta) \tag{31}$$

and assume the sinusoidal form of function G (A_1 is a constant)

$$G(x) = A_1 \sin \frac{\pi x}{l} \tag{32}$$

which leads to

$$\frac{d^4 H}{dx^4} - 2\kappa \left(\frac{\pi}{l}\right)^2 \frac{d^2 H}{d\eta^2} + \left(\frac{\pi}{l}\right)^4 H = 0. \tag{33}$$

By assuming that the function $H(\eta) = e^{\lambda \eta}$ is a general solution of Equation (33), we obtain a solution in the form of a linear combination of this function:

$$H(\eta) = C_1 e^{\lambda_1 \eta} + C_2 e^{\lambda_2 \eta} + C_3 e^{\lambda_3 \eta} + C_4 e^{\lambda_4 \eta}, \tag{34}$$

where

$$\left.\begin{array}{ll} \lambda_1 = +\frac{\pi}{l}\sqrt{\kappa - \sqrt{\kappa^2-1}}, & \lambda_2 = -\frac{\pi}{l}\sqrt{\kappa - \sqrt{\kappa^2-1}} \\ \lambda_3 = +\frac{\pi}{l}\sqrt{\kappa + \sqrt{\kappa^2-1}}, & \lambda_4 = -\frac{\pi}{l}\sqrt{\kappa + \sqrt{\kappa^2-1}} \end{array}\right\}. \tag{35}$$

The positive solutions for λ have to disappear to allow an exponential decrease in the stresses in the thickness direction z. Therefore, $C_1 = 0$, $C_3 = 0$, and

$$F(x, y) = \left[C_2 e^{-\frac{\pi}{l}\sqrt{\kappa - \sqrt{\kappa^2-1}}\epsilon z} + C_4 e^{-\frac{\pi}{l}\sqrt{\kappa + \sqrt{\kappa^2-1}}\epsilon z}\right] A_1 \sin \frac{\pi x}{l} = \\ \left[B_1 e^{-\frac{\pi}{l}\sqrt{\kappa - \sqrt{\kappa^2-1}}\epsilon z} + B_2 e^{-\frac{\pi}{l}\sqrt{\kappa + \sqrt{\kappa^2-1}}\epsilon z}\right] \sin \frac{\pi x}{l}, \tag{36}$$

where $B_1 = C_2 A_1$ and $B_2 = C_4 A_1$ are constants. These constants can be calculated with the following boundary conditions:

$$\varepsilon_x(z=0) = 0, \tag{37}$$

which reflects the observation that the face material is typically much stiffer than the core material, and

$$\sigma_z(z=0) = A \sin \frac{\pi x}{l}, \tag{38}$$

because the stress at the interface in the z-direction is distributed as a sine wave with a certain amplitude A corresponding to the assumed wave deformation. From the assumed boundary conditions, we obtain:

$$\begin{cases} B_1 = -A\left(\frac{l}{\pi}\right)^2 \frac{a_{xz} + a_{xx}\epsilon^2\left(\kappa + \sqrt{\kappa^2-1}\right)}{2a_{xx}\epsilon^2\sqrt{\kappa^2-1}} \\ B_2 = A\left(\frac{l}{\pi}\right)^2 \frac{a_{xz} + a_{xx}\epsilon^2\left(\kappa - \sqrt{\kappa^2-1}\right)}{2a_{xx}\epsilon^2\sqrt{\kappa^2-1}} \end{cases}. \tag{39}$$

It is easy to note that $B_1 + B_2 = -A\left(\frac{l}{\pi}\right)^2$.

The equilibrium differential equation for the facing has the same form as (9). By integrating ε_z (22), we can find the following expression for the facing displacement $w_F = w(z=0)$

$$w(z=0) = \frac{\pi}{l} \sin \frac{\pi x}{l} \left[a_{xz} B_1 \epsilon \sqrt{\kappa - \sqrt{\kappa^2-1}} + a_{xz} B_2 \epsilon \sqrt{\kappa + \sqrt{\kappa^2-1}} + a_{zz} B_1 \frac{1}{\epsilon \sqrt{\kappa - \sqrt{\kappa^2-1}}} + a_{zz} B_2 \frac{1}{\epsilon \sqrt{\kappa + \sqrt{\kappa^2-1}}} \right]. \tag{40}$$

By performing some additional algebraic transformations as suggested by Allen [6], one can arrive at the analogy of (11) with

$$a = \frac{\sqrt{\kappa^2 - 1}}{\sqrt{\kappa + \sqrt{\kappa^2 - 1}} - \sqrt{\kappa - \sqrt{\kappa^2 - 1}}} \frac{2a_{xx}\epsilon}{2a_{xx}a_{xz}\epsilon^2 - a_{xz}^2 + a_{xx}a_{zz}(2\kappa + 1)}. \quad (41)$$

From the condition for the extreme $d\sigma_x/dm = 0$, we have as before

$$m = \pi \cdot \sqrt[3]{\frac{E_F}{6a}} \quad (42)$$

and the minimum critical (wrinkling) stress is obtained (the solution is consistent with (13)):

$$\sigma_w = \frac{3}{2\sqrt[3]{6}} \cdot \sqrt[3]{a^2 E_F}. \quad (43)$$

It is easy to prove that again, $\sigma_2 = 2\sigma_1$ (see also Figure 4).

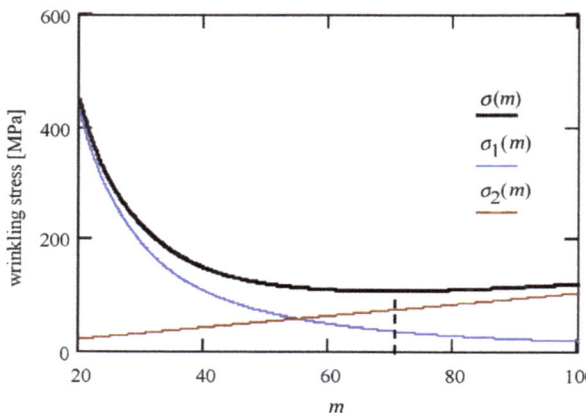

Figure 4. Wrinkling stress as a function of m parameter.

Based on the quick analysis of Equation (41), it can be concluded that for a, which has the nature (and the measurement unit) of the stiffness modulus (of the core), the condition $\kappa > 1$ must be satisfied to reach real values. With smaller values of κ, the roots in Equation (41) are complex numbers. However, it is somewhat surprising that despite the complex roots in (41), the value of a,

$$a = \sqrt{\frac{\kappa + 1}{2}} \frac{2a_{xx}\epsilon}{2a_{xx}a_{xz}\epsilon^2 - a_{xz}^2 + a_{xx}a_{zz}(2\kappa + 1)}, \quad (44)$$

is real if the condition $\kappa > -1$ is satisfied. In order for parameter m to be positive, the denominator in expression (41) must be positive (the nominator is positive). When the denominator in (41) approaches 0^+, a and consequently also σ_w tend to infinity.

Let us take a moment to analyze the value of κ in a plane stress state. According to (30), we have

$$\kappa = \sqrt{E_x E_z} \left(\frac{1}{2G_{xz}} - \frac{\nu_{xz}}{E_x} \right). \quad (45)$$

Modules E_x, E_z, and G_{xz} must be positive. In this situation, if ν_{xz} is negative, then κ will always be positive. If $\nu_{xz} = 0.5$, then κ is positive when $E_x > G_{xz}$; if $\nu_{xz} = 1$, then κ is positive when $E_x > 2G_{xz}$. Let us recall that in the case of orthotropic materials, the condition for the stability of the material behavior is not only the positive values of the E_x, E_z, and G_{xz} modules, but also, among others [21],

$$|\nu_{xz}| < \sqrt{E_x/E_z}. \tag{46}$$

5. Examples
5.1. Analytical Solutions

The first example concerns the facing with a thickness of $t_F = 0.5$ mm made of an isotropic material ($E_F = 210$ GPa) placed on an isotropic core ($E_C = 4$ MPa, $\nu_C = 0.05$; therefore $G_C = E_C/2(1 + \nu_C) = 1.905$ MPa). According to the approach of Hoff–Mautner (3), Plantema (6), and Allen (13), we will obtain the following wrinkling stresses, respectively: $\sigma^{H-M} = 106.32$ MPa, $\sigma^P = 96.49$ MPa, and $\sigma^A = 92.36$ MPa.

Now let us consider the same facing ($t_F = 0.5$ mm $E_F = 210$ GPa) supported by an orthotropic substructure ($E_x = 10$ MPa, $E_z = 4$ MPa, $\nu_{xz} = 0.05$, $G_{xz} = 3$ MPa).

We assume a plane state of stress in the x–z plane and look for the critical stress that will cause the wrinkling of the facing. According to (28), (30), and (41), we will get $\epsilon = 1.257$, $\kappa = 1.022$, and $a = 3.256$ MPa. The wrinkling stress is achieved for $m = 69.336$ (see (42)) and according to (43), $\sigma_w = 107.8$ MPa. Figure 4 shows the dependence of the critical stress (solid line) on the m parameter. The blue and brown lines show both stress components (11).

5.2. Numerical Solutions

Numerical analysis of the instability problems of all kinds of structures is an intriguing and fascinating task, but it is not easy. First of all, it should be realized that numerical models are often much more complex than analytical models. This is due to the fact that commercial software (using, for example, the finite element method) allows for a relatively quick creation of spatial models. However, the problem is that the appropriate model class requires boundary conditions corresponding to this model. Therefore, these conditions are usually different than in the analytical model, which makes it difficult to compare the solutions. This issue was pointed out by numerous researchers [22–24]. This problem also arises when it comes to determining the critical stresses in a thin facing resting on a susceptible substructure.

The numerical analysis of the discussed issue was prepared using ABAQUS, which is a software suite for finite element analysis and computer-aided engineering. The problem was solved using two different classes of numerical models: 2D and 3D. A detailed description of the 3D model is presented below. The results obtained for the 2D model are presented at the end of the subsection.

The three-dimensional model was created in order to fully analyze the phenomenon of loss of stability in conditions close to the plane stress state. Of course, we also tried to make the numerical model as close as possible to the analytical model. The model space is not infinite, but the dimensions have been defined so that the displacements, strains, and stresses at the edge of the model are relatively small; the core body was 1.2 m long and 0.3 m high. The core thickness was 0.05 m, which should provide a freedom of deformation along the y-axis. A facing strip 0.5 mm thick and 0.7 m long rests on such a substructure. The geometry of the system is shown in Figure 5.

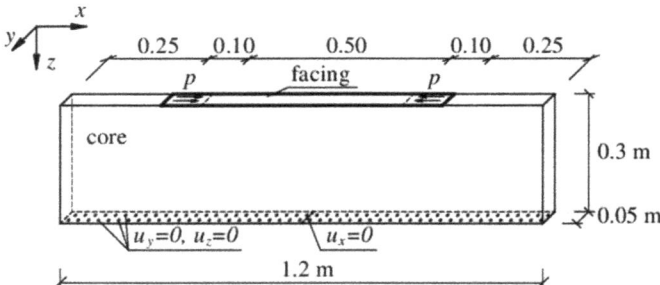

Figure 5. Numerical model of the problem of compression of a thin facing resting on a susceptible substructure.

In order to compress the facing, an area of 0.10 m × 0.05 m was determined on its two ends, to which a uniform pressure p was applied in the x-direction (tangent to the facing, opposite at the two ends). The load application area is distant from the edge of the substructure (0.25 m). The decision was made to apply the load distributed over the surface because the attempt to load the system in the form of a linear load applied to the edge of the facing caused too much local disturbance. As the system had to be supported, after several attempts, it was decided to support the bottom surface of the substructure. The displacement conditions $u_y = 0$, $u_z = 0$ were assumed on the entire bottom surface, and additionally, $u_x = 0$ was assumed in the middle of this surface, which is shown in Figure 5. This support had a small influence on the behavior of the system, while ensuring its necessary stabilization. When trying to limit the displacements on the sides of the substructure, it turned out that these limitations affect the behavior of the system and cause stress disturbances. The attempt to define the boundary conditions identical to those in the analytical model was unsuccessful. The assumption that the horizontal displacement of the facing equals zero made it practically impossible to induce the appropriate stress state in this facing. The description of the model shows that despite all efforts, the numerical model has some deviations from the theoretical model in which the core (substructure) is an infinite elastic half-space.

The material parameters of the 3D numerical model corresponded to the analytical model. The facing material was assumed to be isotropic elastic (E_F = 210 GPa, ν_F = 0.3). In the case of an isotropic core, it was assumed E_C = 4 MPa, ν_C = 0.05. When the case with the orthotropic core was analyzed, its parameters were defined as follows: E_x = 10 MPa, E_y = 10 MPa, E_z = 4 MPa, $\nu_{xy} = \nu_{xz} = \nu_{yz}$ = 0.05, $G_{xy} = G_{xz} = G_{yz}$ = 3 MPa. The 3D model uses C3D8 solid elements (core) and S4 shell elements (facing), in which there is no reduced integration. Interaction between the facing and the core was defined using a TIE connection, which causes the displacements of nodes of one surface to be identical to the displacements of nodes on the other surface. The size of the finite element mesh was constant and equal to 0.01 m. It is worth mentioning that the problem of facing wrinkling is mesh-dependent. The mesh should be dense enough to allow deformation of the core and facing. Thus, the mesh size is dependent on the finite element itself (a shape function) as well as the properties of the facing and core materials. In the case of S4 finite elements (doubly curved general purpose shell, finite membrane strains), it is sufficient if there are two finite elements per half-wavelength l. In our case, the half-wavelength was in the order of 0.035–0.038 m; therefore, the size of the finite elements turned out to be small enough (0.01 m).

Since the phenomenon of face wrinkling is associated with the local deformation of the compressed face, a geometrically nonlinear static analysis and the Riks method were used. Due to the symmetry of the problem, it turned out to be beneficial to introduce into the model's initial imperfections as a linear combination of buckling modes of the structure. The buckling modes were solved independently. The size of the introduced imperfections was very small. The sum of four modes multiplied by 0.00001 was introduced, which meant that the positions of the model nodes were disturbed about 0.025 mm. This means that the amplitude of the imperfection was 5% of the facing thickness.

The load applied to the model could increase to the value of 2000 kPa, which corresponds to a compressive force of 10 kN and a compressive stress in the facing of 400 MPa. Obviously, such a load value was never realized because the facing had previously buckled. The applied load level was determined on the basis of the LPF (Load Proportionality Factor) value.

Another interesting challenge of numerical analysis is the question of recognizing when a structure loses stability and when it does not. Unfortunately, as in real conditions, and unlike in analytical solutions, in a numerical solution, there is usually no unambiguous parameter indicating the state of the system (stable–unstable). Wrinkles in the compressed facing appear very quickly, which is illustrated in Figure 6a (only the facing was presented). A certain determinant of instability may be the appearance of a nonlinear relationship between LPF and arc length factor (Figure 6b), indicating the nonlinear nature of the process [25]. One should also pay attention to the difference between the compressive stress in the facing in the x-direction calculated on the basis of the currently applied force divided by the facing cross-section area and the stress obtained in the FE model that takes into account nonlinear effects, i.e., local deformations. The comparison of these stresses for the first eight load increments is presented in Table 1. The stress values estimated at the FE nodes are much higher due to the effect of the load acting on the distance resulting from the deformation of the facing. Since the material was originally assumed to be perfectly elastic, the stresses in the model can be very high.

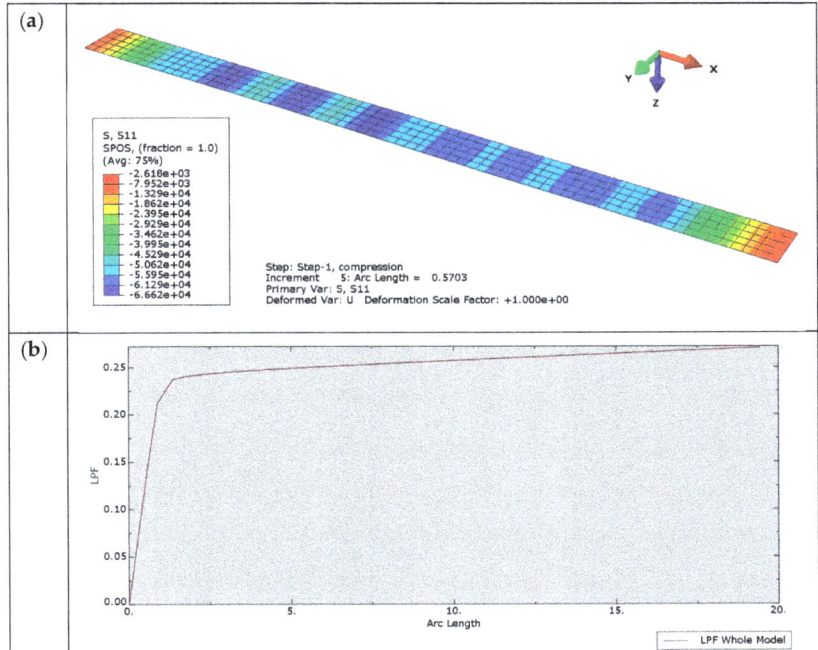

Figure 6. Numerical solution of the compression of the elastic facing resting on the susceptible core: (a) σ_x stress at the top of the facing (fifth load increment) (b) LPF–arc length relation.

Table 1. The comparison of compressive stress in the facing for the load increments of the numerical model.

Load Increment	The Percentage Completion of the Load Step (LPF)	Theoretical Compressive Stress σ_x [MPa]	Extreme Compressive Stress Read in the Model Nodes σ_x [MPa]
1	0.0156	6.24	6.72
2	0.0313	12.52	13.52
3	0.0547	21.88	23.88
4	0.0898	35.92	39.99
5	0.142	56.80	66.62
6	0.213	85.20	129.5
7	0.238	95.20	263.8
8	0.241	96.40	330.4

This situation, which is complex for evaluation, definitely changes after assuming that the facing material is perfectly elastic–plastic. Assuming the yield point $f_y = 270$ MPa (the value is consistent with the characteristics of typical steel sheets used for the production of sandwich panels), in the ninth load increment, for LPF = 0.239, the LPF–arc length diagram breaks down (Figure 7), which corresponds to the theoretical facing compression stress $0.239 \times 400 = 95.6$ MPa.

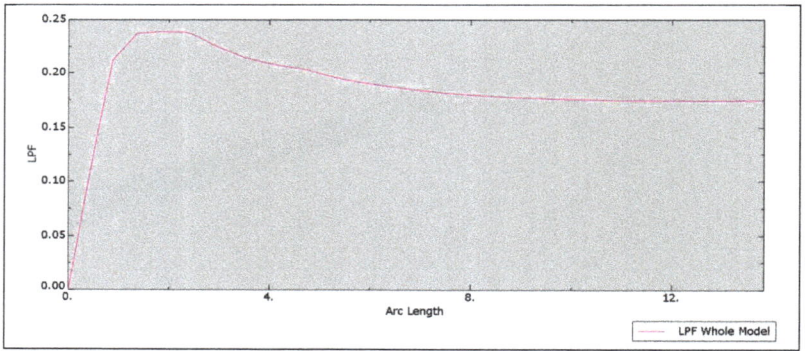

Figure 7. Numerical solution of the compression of the elastic–plastic facing resting on the susceptible core: LPF–arc length relation.

A very similar relationship can be observed in the analysis of the problem with the orthotropic core. A breakdown of the LPF–arc length relationship occurred for LPF = 0.284, which corresponds to the theoretical stress 113.6 MPa. Of course, the stresses in the nodes of the model are different and reach the yield point of the material.

The obtained numerical results (95.6 MPa and 113.6 MPa) are close to the theoretical values (92.36 MPa and 107.8 MPa). Introduction of the yield stress for the facing material facilitates the interpretation of the numerical results. It is also worth paying attention to the fact that for the seventh or eighth load increment (Table 1), the stresses in the core reach the values close to the strength of typical core materials.

A number of numerical analyses were also carried out using the 2D model. The geometry and boundary conditions of this model corresponded to the geometry and boundary conditions of the 3D model. The main difference between the models was that they used plane (not spatial) finite elements: CPS4 for the core and B23 beam elements for the facing. It turned out that the 2D model behaves very similarly to the 3D model. Among other things, there are similar difficulties in interpreting the moment of loss of stability. This situation changes after assuming that the facing material is perfectly elastic–plastic. For the isotropic core, the LPF–arc length relationship is very similar to the relation presented in Figure 7, but the breakdown occurs for LPF = 0.227, which corresponds to the facing compression stress 0.227 × 400 = 90.8 MPa. For the orthotropic core, the extreme LPF value is 0.259, which corresponds to the stress of 103.6 MPa. These values are similar to the analytical results, although they are slightly lower than in the case of the 3D model.

6. Parametric Analysis

Description of the Models

Using the derived formulas, the influence of the material parameters of the orthotropic core on the value of the wrinkling stress was calculated and illustrated (Figure 8). Modulus E_x = 10 MPa was assumed as constant. The modules E_z and G_{xz} are variable. Moreover, each of the graphs corresponds to a different value of the Poisson ratio ν_{xz}, namely −1.0, 0.0, 0.5, and 1.0. For additional illustration of the problem, the graphs of the parameter κ are also presented in Figure 8.

The basic conclusions from the analysis of the graphs are quite obvious and consistent with the case of the isotropic core: the greater the stiffness of the core, the higher the wrinkling stress. It gets more interesting when ν_{xz} = 1, because with large E_z and G_{xz} the parameter κ approaches −1 and the parameter a increases strongly. In the case when ν_{xz} = −1, the parameter κ takes values in the typical range (positive values), but with large values of E_x and G_{xz}, the parameter a (44) reaches much higher values and grows faster than the parameter m drops (42). It should be emphasized that for the presented range of variability, $\kappa > -1$ and a is a positive value.

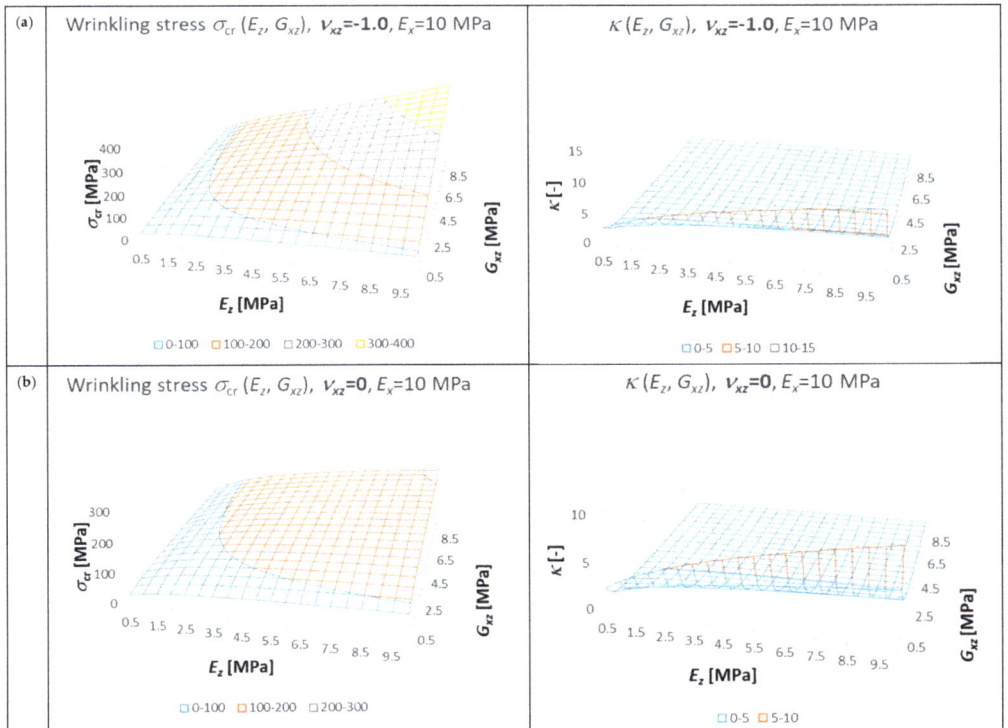

Figure 8. *Cont.*

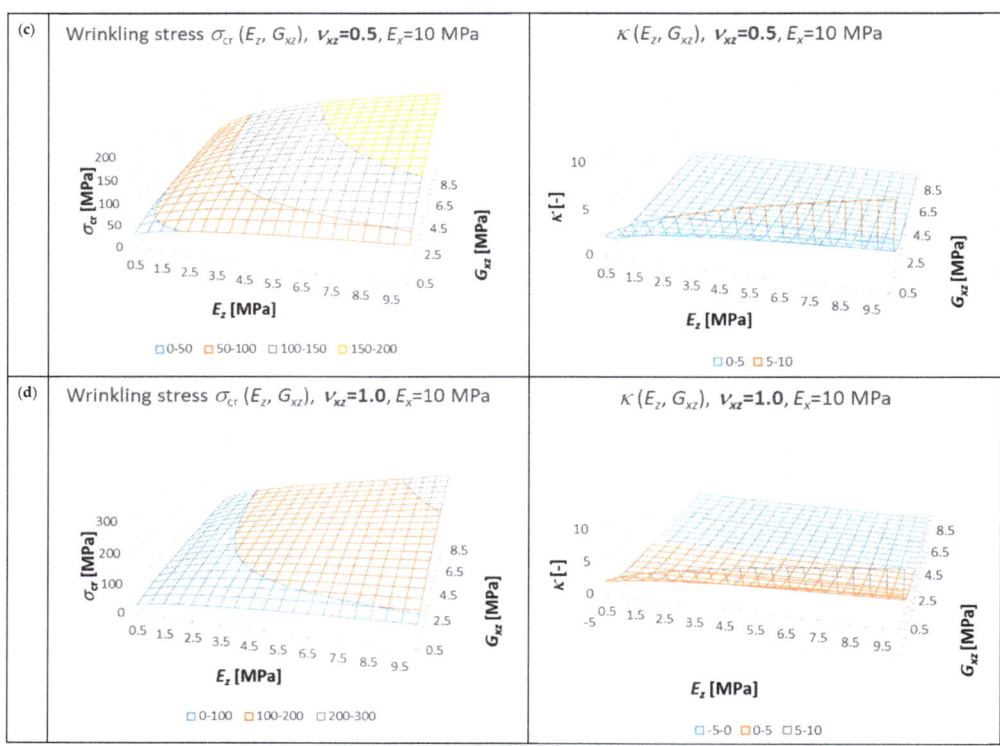

Figure 8. Influence of core material parameters on the value of wrinkling stress and the parameter κ: (**a**) $\nu_{xz} = -1.0$, (**b**) $\nu_{xz} = 0$, (**c**) $\nu_{xz} = 0.5$, (**d**) $\nu_{xz} = 1.0$.

7. Conclusions

The first part of the article contained a short survey of the classical solutions to the problem of instability of a facing resting on a homogeneous and isotropic substructure (core). It was presented how the assumptions concerning the displacement field affect the solution of the problem. Next, the dependence of the solution [6] on the value of the Poisson ratio was presented, and strain energy analyses were carried out to investigate the relationships between the individual components of the deformation energy of the core. In the second part of the paper, the derivation of the formula for the critical stress in the case of uniaxial compression of the thin facing resting on the orthotropic core was presented. The conditions for the existence of the solution were discussed, which in principle are met for a wide range of variability of material parameters. The numerical example confirming the compliance of the selected analytical solution with the numerical one was also presented. The article discussed the applied models in detail and explained the difficulties associated with determining the load and support boundary conditions. The presented numerical model has not been experimentally verified, although a similar model was verified in [19] for a core with the Poisson ratio ranging from 0 to 0.3. The third part of the article presented the results of the parametric analysis, i.e., the effect of changing the material parameters of the orthotropic core on the wrinkling stress. This type of analysis can be of great importance in the optimal design of sandwich systems where local loss of stability plays a significant role. The developed solution can be easily introduced into the optimization procedure.

The presented work confirms that the further development of analytical methods in solving the discussed problem is advisable and important, both from a scientific and engineering point of view. Undoubted benefits also come from the possibility of numerical analysis of the issue under discussion. The applied FE models revealed that due to the local loss of stability, the stresses in the facing locally increase to the yield point, and the stresses in the core reach values similar to the strength of the core material. This means that if we want to accurately understand the stress state in the facing and the core, a relatively simple and attractive analytical approach should be supplemented with a numerical solution.

Author Contributions: Conceptualization, Z.P. and J.P.; methodology, Z.P.; software, Ł.S.; validation, I.K. and Ł.S.; formal analysis, J.P.; investigation, Z.P.; resources, Z.P. and I.K.; data curation, J.P.; writing—original draft preparation, Z.P.; writing—review and editing, I.K. and Ł.S.; visualization, Ł.S.; supervision, I.K.; project administration, Z.P.; funding acquisition, Z.P. and J.P. All authors have read and agreed to the published version of the manuscript.

Funding: This APC was funded by Poznan University of Technology, grant number 0411/SBAD/0004 and Czestochowa University of Technology.

Institutional Review Board Statement: Not applicable.

Informed Consent Statement: Not applicable.

Data Availability Statement: The data presented in this study are available on request from the corresponding author.

Conflicts of Interest: The authors declare no conflict of interest. The funders had no role in the design of the study; in the collection, analyses, or interpretation of data; in the writing of the manuscript, or in the decision to publish the results.

References

1. Vescovini, R.; D'Ottavio, M.; Dozio, L.; Polit, O. Buckling and wrinkling of anisotropic sandwich plates. *Int. J. Eng. Sci.* **2018**, *130*, 136–156. [CrossRef]
2. Studziński, R.; Gajewski, T.; Malendowski, M.; Sumelka, W.; Al-Rifaie, H.; Peksa, P.; Sielicki, P.W. Blast test and failure mechanisms of soft-core sandwich panels for storage halls applications. *Materials* **2021**, *14*, 70. [CrossRef] [PubMed]
3. Zaharia, S.M.; Enescu, L.A.; Pop, M.A. Mechanical performances of lightweight sandwich structures produced by material extrusion-based additive manufacturing. *Polymers* **2020**, *12*, 1740. [CrossRef] [PubMed]
4. Hoff, N.J.; Mautner, S.E. Buckling of Sandwich Type Panels. *J. Aeronaut. Sci.* **1945**, *12*, 285–297. [CrossRef]
5. Plantema, F.J. *Sandwich Construction; the Bending and Buckling of Sandwich Beams, Plates and Shells*; John Wiley & Sons, Inc.: New York, NY, USA, 1966.
6. Allen, H.G. *Analysis and Design of Structural Sandwich Panels*; Pergamon Press: Oxford, UK, 1969.
7. Norris, C.B.; Ericksen, W.S.; March, H.W.; Smith, C.B.; Boller, K.H. *Wrinkling of the Facing of Sandwich Construction Subjected to Edgewise Compression, Report No. 1810*; Forest Products Laboratory: Madison, WI, USA, 1961.
8. Vonach, W.K.; Rammerstorfer, F.G. Wrinkling of thick orthotropic sandwich plates under general loading conditions. *Arch. Appl. Mech.* **2000**, *70*, 338–348. [CrossRef]
9. Birman, V.; Bert, C.W. Wrinkling of composite-facing sandwich panels under biaxial loading. *J. Sandw. Struct. Mater.* **2004**, *6*, 217–237. [CrossRef]
10. Lopatin, A.; Morozov, E. Symmetrical facing wrinkling of composite sandwich panels. *J. Sandw. Struct. Mater.* **2008**, *10*, 475–497. [CrossRef]
11. Koissin, V.; Shipsha, A.; Skvortsov, V. Wrinkling in sandwich panels—An analytical approach. *J. Sandw. Struct. Mater.* **2011**, *13*, 705–730. [CrossRef]
12. Fagerberg, L. The effect of local bending stiffness on wrinkling of sandwich panels. *J. Eng. Marit. Environ.* **2003**, *217*, 111–119. [CrossRef]
13. Fagerberg, L.; Zenkert, D. Effects of anisotropy and multiaxial loading on the wrinkling of sandwich panels. *J. Sandw. Struct. Mater.* **2005**, *7*, 177–194. [CrossRef]
14. Birman, V.; Vo, N. Wrinkling in sandwich structures with a functionally graded core. *J. Appl. Mech.* **2017**, *84*, 021002. [CrossRef]
15. Frostig, Y. On wrinkling of a sandwich panel with a compliant core and self-equilibrated loads. *J. Sandw. Struct.* **2011**, *13*, 663–679. [CrossRef]
16. Hohe, J.; Librescu, L. Recent results on the effect of the transverse core compressibility on the static and dynamic response of sandwich structures. *Composites Part B Eng.* **2008**, *39*, 108–119. [CrossRef]
17. Phan, C.N.; Bailey, N.W.; Kardomateas, G.A.; Battley, M.A. Wrinkling of sandwich wide panels/beams based on the extended high-order sandwich panel theory: Formulation, comparison with elasticity and experiments. *Arch. Appl. Mech.* **2012**, *82*, 1585–1599. [CrossRef]

18. *EN 14509:2013 Self-Supporting Double Skin Metal Faced Insulating Panels—Factory Made Products—Specifications*; British Standards Institution: London, UK, 2013.
19. Pozorski, Z. *Sandwich Panels in Civil Engineerin—Theory, Testing and Design*; Wydawnictwo Politechniki Poznańskiej: Poznań, Poland, 2016.
20. Garbowski, T.; Gajewski, T.; Grabski, J.K. Torsional and transversal stiffness of orthotropic sandwich panels. *Materials* **2020**, *13*, 5016. [CrossRef] [PubMed]
21. Lempriere, B.M. Poisson's Ratio in Orthotropic Materials. *AIAA J.* **1968**, *6*, 2226–2227. [CrossRef]
22. Steeves, C.A.; Fleck, N.A. Collapse mechanisms of sandwich beams with composite faces and a foam core, loaded in three-point bending. Part II: Experimental investigation and numerical modelling. *Int. J. Mech. Sci.* **2004**, *46*, 585–608. [CrossRef]
23. Smakosz, Ł.; Kreja, I.; Pozorski, Z. Flexural behavior of composite structural insulated panels with magnesium oxide board facings. *Arch. Civ. Mech. Eng.* **2020**, *20*, 1–21. [CrossRef]
24. Pozorski, Z.; Wojciechowski, S. The influence of symmetrical boundary conditions on the structural behaviour of sandwich panels subjected to torsion. *Symmetry* **2020**, *12*, 2093. [CrossRef]
25. Riks, E. An incremental approach to the solution of snapping and buckling problems. *Int. J. Solids Struct.* **1979**, *15*, 524–551. [CrossRef]

Article

Numerical Homogenization of Multi-Layered Corrugated Cardboard with Creasing or Perforation

Tomasz Garbowski [1], Anna Knitter-Piątkowska [2,*] and Damian Mrówczyński [3]

[1] Department of Biosystems Engineering, Poznan University of Life Sciences, Wojska Polskiego 50, 60-627 Poznań, Poland; tomasz.garbowski@up.poznan.pl
[2] Institute of Structural Analysis, Poznan University of Technology, Piotrowo 5, 60-965 Poznań, Poland
[3] Research and Development Department, Femat Sp. z o. o., Romana Maya 1, 61-371 Poznań, Poland; damian.mrowczynski@fematproject.pl
* Correspondence: anna.knitter-piatkowska@put.poznan.pl

Abstract: The corrugated board packaging industry is increasingly using advanced numerical tools to design and estimate the load capacity of its products. This is why numerical analyses are becoming a common standard in this branch of manufacturing. Such trends cause either the use of advanced computational models that take into account the full 3D geometry of the flat and wavy layers of corrugated board, or the use of homogenization techniques to simplify the numerical model. The article presents theoretical considerations that extend the numerical homogenization technique already presented in our previous work. The proposed here homogenization procedure also takes into account the creasing and/or perforation of corrugated board (i.e., processes that undoubtedly weaken the stiffness and strength of the corrugated board locally). However, it is not always easy to estimate how exactly these processes affect the bending or torsional stiffness. What is known for sure is that the degradation of stiffness depends, among other things, on the type of cut, its shape, the depth of creasing as well as their position or direction in relation to the corrugation direction. The method proposed here can be successfully applied to model smeared degradation in a finite element or to define degraded interface stiffnesses on a crease line or a perforation line.

Keywords: corrugated cardboard; numerical homogenization; strain energy equivalence; perforation; creasing; flexural stiffness; torsional stiffness

1. Introduction

Colorful boxes and packaging are designed to attract the customers' attention and, as a consequence, to drive the sales of various goods ranging from bulky products, through food, children's toys, cosmetics, and many others. A growing awareness of concern for the natural environment has led many companies to opt for packaging that can be easily recycled or disposed of, biodegradable, and space-saving after manufacturing. A corrugated cardboard undoubtedly has all of these qualities. Moreover, it is easy to print on, for example, the brand name. Corrugated cardboard is easy to shape via creasing along the suitable lines and, furthermore, creating openings, ventilation holes, or perforations does not cause much difficulty. The latter is essential with regard to shelf-ready packaging (SRP) or retail-ready packaging (RRP) when the product, after transportation to the site, is placed on the shelves and after tearing off the flap along the appropriately designed perforation, is ready for sale. Thus, a lot of time is saved, which nowadays leads to significant profits for large companies.

Of course, one cannot only focus on the aesthetic values because the packaging, in fact, plays a much more important role such as securing the goods during storage or safe transport to the destination place. The load-bearing capacity of the corrugated cardboard boxes and the influence of humidity, openings and perforation arrangement, or the location of flaps is under constant investigation. Therefore, scientific research has become an integral part of a distinct branch of industry (i.e., cardboard packages production). Manufacturers of these packaging types strive for effective, economical, and easy-to-use solutions, which results in the continuous, lasting over many years, development of research on cardboard strength while using various analytical, numerical, and experimental methods.

Compressive, tensile, or bursting strength tests are routinely executed to assess the load-bearing capacity of corrugated cardboard boxes. The box compression test (BCT) and the edge crush test (ECT) are the best known. Inextricably related to the mechanical strength of the paperboard or corrugated cardboard boxes are two characteristic in-plane directions of orthotropy (i.e., perpendicular to the main axis of the fluting and parallel to the paperboard fiber alignment—machine direction (MD) as well as parallel to the fluting—cross direction (CD)).

Another option for estimating the compressive strength of the boxes is the application of analytical formulae in which, in general, three groups of parameters such as paper, board, and box parameters are present [1]. Ring crush test (RCT), Concora liner test (CLT), liner type, weights of liner and fluting, corrugation ratio, and a constant related to fluting belong to the first group. Thickness, flexural stiffnesses in MD and CD, ECT, and moisture content are affiliated with the second group whereas dimensions and perimeter of the box, applied load ratio, stacking time, buckling ratio, and printed ratio are in the third one. Already in 1952, Kellicutt and Landt [2] proposed the calculations of box compressive strength while employing the formula with parameters introduced in the paper (RCT, flute constant) and box (perimeter, box constant). In 1956, Maltenfort [3] indicated the relation between the critical force and paper parameters (CLT, type of liner) and cardboard box dimensions in the BCT. In the approach proposed by McKee, Gander, and Wachuta [4] in 1963, the parameters of the paperboard (ECT, flexural stiffnesses) and the box perimeter were applied. Even though this formula is commonly used in the packaging industry due to its simplicity, which leads to quick and easy solutions for practical implementations, it is applicable only to simple standard boxes. Therefore, scientists have been making attempts to extend the implementation of McKee's analytical approach. Allerby et al. [5] modified the constants and exponents, whilst Schrampfer et al. [6] improved McKee's method by expanding the range of cutting methods and equipment. Batelka et al. [7] augmented the relationship by introducing the dimensions of the box and Urbanik et al. [8] included the Poisson's ratio. Further modification of the above-mentioned McKee's formula for solving more complex problems has been proposed by Aviles et al. [9] and later, by Garbowski et al. [10–12].

Over recent decades, meshless and meshfree methods (e.g., the collocation method) have become popular numerical techniques for solving partial differential equations and have been beneficial while considering corrugated cardboard problems. Wang and Qian [13] proposed the meshfree stabilized collocation method (SCM) and introduced the reproducing kernel function as the approximation. Wang et al. [14] employed the meshfree radial basis collocation method (RBCM), which utilizes infinitely continuous radial basis functions (RBFs), as the approximation for the static and dynamic eigenvalue analysis of the thin functionally graded shells (FGSs) with in-plane material inhomogeneity. The buckling analysis of thin FG plates, also with in-plane material inhomogeneity, while applying radial basis collocation method (RBCM) and Hermite radial basis function collocation method (HRBCM) was discussed by Chu et al. [15]. The main advantages of the above-mentioned approaches are high accuracy and exponential convergence.

Unquestionably, many determinants affect the compression strength of the corrugated paperboard boxes [16] including the moisture content of the box [17,18], openings, ventilation holes and perforations [11,12,19], storage time and conditions [20], stacking load [21], or a very significant one—creasing. As a result of such a process, fold and perforation lines are performed and through this, the mechanical strength of the manufactured corrugated paperboard boxes is diminished.

A very effective, commonly applied in engineering, technique to determine the strength of the boxes is the finite element method (FEM). Thakkar et al. [22] compared the experimental and FEM numerical results to investigate the creasing impact on the local strength of corrugated paperboard; Beex and Peerlings [23], in turn, conducted physical and numerical experiments to examine the influence of creasing and subsequent folding on the mechanical properties of the laminated paperboard. A constitutive model was implemented by Giampieri et al. [24] in order to obtain the mechanical response of creased paperboard after folding. FEM simulations of paperboard creasing, which appeared to be significant from a practical standpoint, have been proposed by Domaneschi et al. [25] and Awais et al. [26]. Leminena et al. [27] performed experimental and numerical analyses to examine the influence of the creasing process during the press forming on the paperboard mechanical properties. FEM has also been involved in research raising the issue of numerical analysis in relation to transverse shear stiffness of the corrugated cardboards [28–32] or buckling and post-buckling phenomena [33].

The examined models can be facilitated to one single layer described by the effective properties of the composite instead of building layers composed of different materials. Such a method, called homogenization, has been used extensively over the last years by Garbowski et al. [32,34–37]. A clear advantage of this technique is the significant saving in calculation time while preserving the precision of the results. Hohe [38] proposed a representative element of the heterogeneous and homogenized elements based on strain energy to analyze sandwich panels. A periodic homogenization method presented by Buannic et al. [39] enabled them to obtain an equivalent membrane and pure bending characteristics of period plates and, in a modified version, to incorporate the transfer shear effect in the analysis. Biancolini [40] engaged FEM to study a micromechanical part of the considered plate. Thanks to the energy equivalence between the model and the homogenized plate, the stiffness properties of the sandwich plate were received. Decomposition of the plate into two beams in directions of the plate allowed Abbès and Guo [41] to define the torsion rigidity of the orthotropic sandwich plates. An interesting approach based on empirical observation can also be found in the recent work of Gallo et al. [21]. A multiple scales asymptotic homogenization approach was presented by Ramírez-Torres et al. [42] where the effective properties of hierarchical composites with periodic structure at different length scales has been studied, whereas in [43], the authors used the asymptotic homogenization technique to the equations describing the dynamics of a heterogeneous material with evolving micro-structure, obtaining a set of upscaled, effective equations.

The following article, as the next one in the series, provides theoretical considerations that develop and extend the numerical homogenization technique already presented in the prior works of the authors. The proposed homogenization procedure also takes into consideration the creasing and/or perforation of corrugated board (i.e., processes that evidently weaken the stiffness and strength of the corrugated board locally). However, it is not always easy to estimate how exactly these processes affect the bending or torsional stiffness. The fact is that the decrease in stiffness depends, among others, on the type of cut, its shape, and the depth of creasing as well as their position or direction in relation to the corrugation orientation. The method proposed here can be successfully implemented to model smeared degradation in a finite element or to define degraded interface stiffnesses on a crease line or a notch line.

2. Materials and Methods

2.1. Corrugated Board—Material Definition

Corrugated board, as a fibrous material, is characterized by strong orthotropy. The mechanical properties of its components (i.e., cardboard) depend on the direction of the fibers in the individual layers of the composite. Paper and paperboard are more than twice as stiff in the machine direction (MD) than in the cross direction (CD). This is related to the fibers which, due to the production process, arrange along the MD. In this direction, the material is more resistant to tearing and crushing, although it has lower ductility than in CD (see Figure 1).

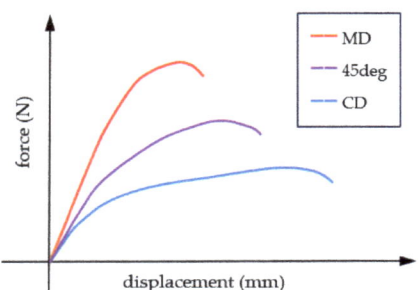

Figure 1. Paperboard mechanical behavior. The stress–strain relationships in different material directions.

The linear elastic orthotropic material can be described by the following stress–strain relationships:

$$\begin{bmatrix} \varepsilon_{11} \\ \varepsilon_{22} \\ 2\varepsilon_{12} \\ 2\varepsilon_{13} \\ 2\varepsilon_{23} \end{bmatrix} = \begin{bmatrix} 1/E_1 & -\nu_{21}/E_2 & 0 & 0 & 0 \\ -\nu_{12}/E_1 & 1/E_2 & 0 & 0 & 0 \\ 0 & 0 & 1/G_{12} & 0 & 0 \\ 0 & 0 & 0 & 1/G_{13} & 0 \\ 0 & 0 & 0 & 0 & 1/G_{23} \end{bmatrix} \begin{bmatrix} \sigma_{11} \\ \sigma_{22} \\ \sigma_{12} \\ \sigma_{13} \\ \sigma_{23} \end{bmatrix} \quad (1)$$

where E_1 is the Young's modulus in the machine direction (MD); E_2 is the Young's modulus in the cross direction (CD); G_{12} is the Kirchhoff's modulus, ν_{12}; ν_{21} is the Poisson's coefficients. Due to the symmetry of the material compliance/stiffness matrix, the relationship between the Poisson's coefficients is as follows:

$$\frac{\nu_{12}}{E_1} = \frac{\nu_{21}}{E_2} \quad (2)$$

The material orientation was always the same in all layers (see Figure 2). This is related to the corrugated board production process in which the paper (for the production of both flat and corrugated layers) is rolled on a corrugator machine from multi-tone bales.

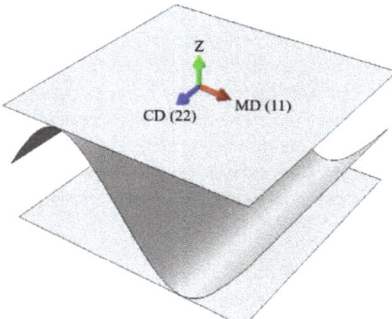

Figure 2. Material orientation.

The paperboard, as already mentioned, was modeled here using classical linear elastic orthotropy (see Equation (1)). The material data were taken from the literature [40,44,45]. All material data are presented in Table 1 (i.e., E_1, E_2, ν_{12}, G_{12}, G_{13} and G_{23}, which represents Young's moduli in both directions, Poisson's ratio, in-plane shear modulus and two transverse shear moduli, respectively).

Table 1. Material data of intact double wall corrugated cardboard used for modeling the paper layers according to orthotropic constitutive relation.

Layers	E_1 (MPa)	E_2 (MPa)	v_{12} (-)	G_{12} (MPa)	G_{13} (MPa)	G_{23} (MPa)
liners	3326	1694	0.34	859	429.5	429.5
fluting	2614	1532	0.32	724	362	362

The thickness of all flat layers (liners) in both single- and double-walled corrugated boards was assumed to be 0.30 mm; for all corrugated layers (flutes) in both models, the thickness was also taken as 0.30 mm.

2.2. Creases and Perforations—Numerical Study

The main goal of this work was to numerically analyze many cases of perforation with possible creasing and its effect on the stiffness reduction of corrugated board. The variants include not only different types of perforation (e.g., 4/4—4 mm cut, 4 mm gap; 2/6—2 mm cut, 6 mm gap; and 6/2—6 mm cut, 2 mm gap), but also different orientations of the cuts in the sample (from 0 to 90 deg. every 15 degrees). All cases are compiled in Table 2 and are shown in Figure 3.

Table 2. Sample symbols.

Perforation Type	Model SW	Model DW
4 mm cut, 4 mm gap	SW-44-Y [1]-xx [2]	DW-44-Y-xx
2 mm cut, 6 mm gap	SW-26-Y-xx	DW-26-Y-xx
6 mm cut, 2 mm gap	SW-62-Y-xx	DW-62-Y-xx

[1] Y means model type and can be: F-flute or C-cut. [2] xx is the cut or crease orientation and can be: 00, 15, 30, 45, 60, 75, or 90.

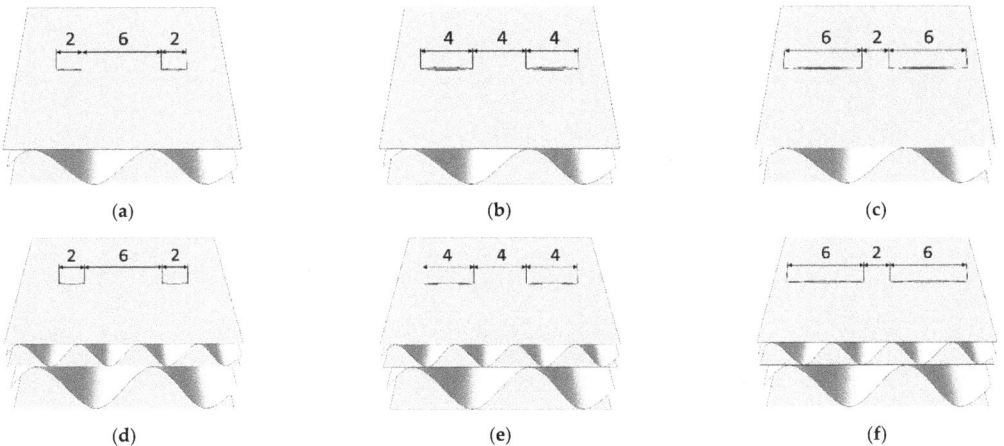

Figure 3. Perforation types: (**a**) Type 2/6—model SW; (**b**) Type 4/4—model SW; (**c**) Type 6/2—model SW; (**d**) Type 2/6—model DW; (**e**) Type 4/4—model DW; (**f**) Type 6/2—model DW.

Two hypothetical corrugated boards were analyzed here, namely single-walled (SW) with 8 mm flute period, 4 mm height and double-walled (DW) with 4 mm flute period, 2 mm flute height (for lower layer) and 8 mm flute period, 4 mm flute height (for higher layer). Figure 4 shows the visualizations of the geometry of both examples.

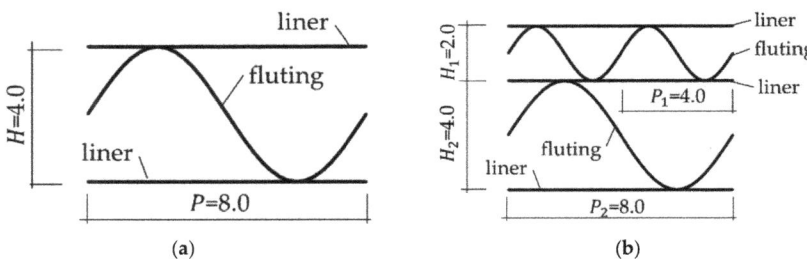

Figure 4. Geometry of the sample: (**a**) single layer; (**b**) double layer.

Both the influence of the flute orientation and the cutting orientation on the decrease in the stiffness of the corrugated board were examined. In case C, the cutting orientation changed to 00, 15, 30, 45, 60, 75, 90 degrees (see Figure 5) while the flute orientation remained constant.

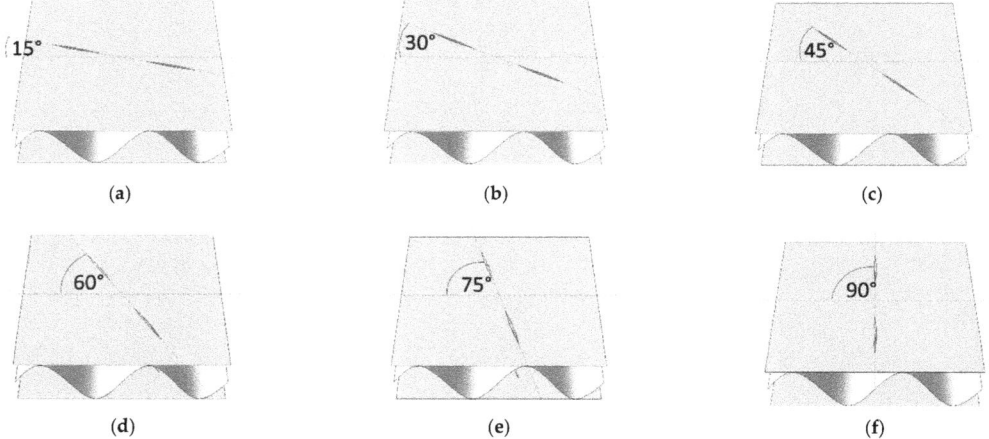

Figure 5. Perforation orientation in sample SW-44-C: (**a**) rotation by 15 degrees; (**b**) rotation by 30 degrees; (**c**) rotation by 45 degrees; (**d**) rotation by 60 degrees; (**e**) rotation by 75 degrees; (**f**) rotation by 90 degrees.

In case F, the flute orientation were changed to 00, 15, 30, 45, 60, 75, 90 degrees (see Figures 6 and 7) while the cut orientation remained constant. All cases are summarized in Table 2.

Both single-walled and double-walled models with perforations of 4/4 mm, 2/6 mm, and 6/2 mm in the variant 00 deg. of cut and flute rotation were crushed by 10, 20, and 30%. This consideration results from the observation of the serial production of packaging in which crushing is an element built into the entire cutting and perforation process. The additional crushing during cutting is the result of using rubber in the area of perforation knives that additionally crush the cross-section. The crushed geometry of both kinds of samples is shown in Figure 8.

All crushed samples were marked with an additional symbol R-xx, where xx means the amount of crush (i.e., 10, 20, or 30). Therefore, for example, a single-walled specimen with a cut/flute rotated by 0 degrees with a cut version of 44 and crushed by 10% has the symbol SW-44-C-00-R-10.

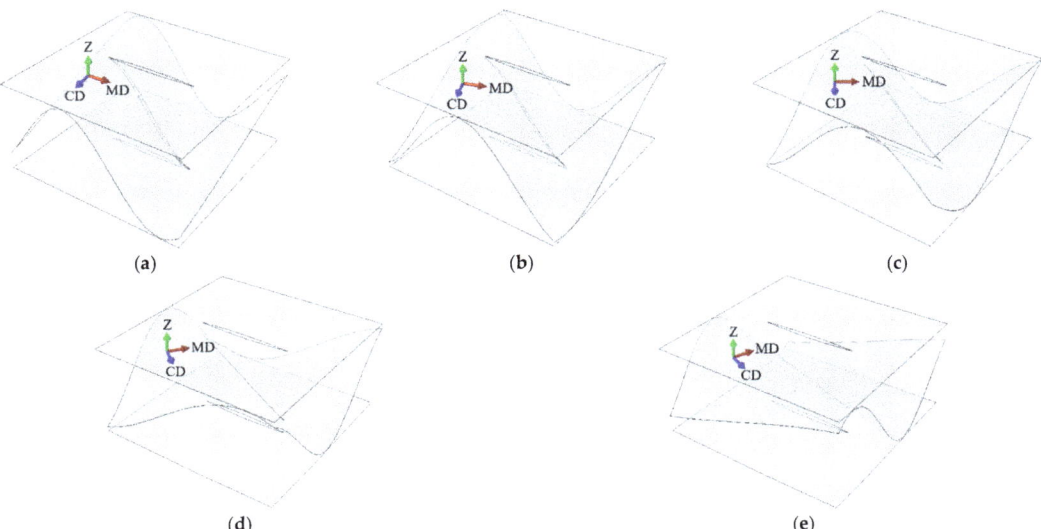

Figure 6. Perforation orientation in sample SW-44-F: (**a**) rotation by 15 degrees; (**b**) rotation by 30 degrees; (**c**) rotation by 45 degrees; (**d**) rotation by 60 degrees; (**e**) rotation by 75 degrees.

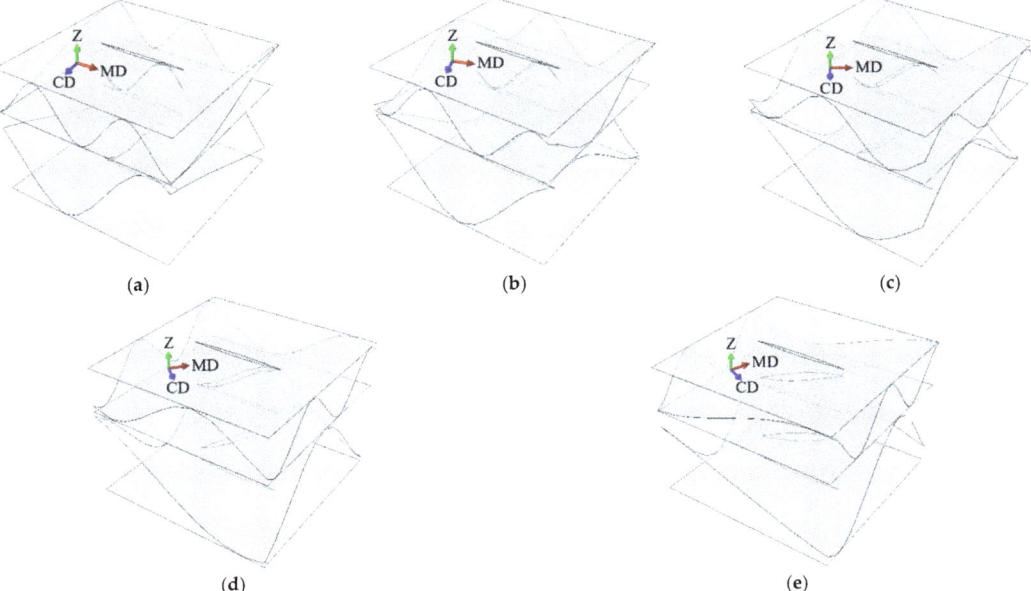

Figure 7. Perforation orientation in sample DW-44-F: (**a**) rotation by 15 degrees; (**b**) rotation by 30 degrees; (**c**) rotation by 45 degrees; (**d**) rotation by 60 degrees; (**e**) rotation by 75 degrees.

Additionally, what was verified during this research was the influence of the position of the cut in the corrugated boards' cross-section along the wave on the stiffness reduction. For this purpose, four additional representative volumetric element (RVE) models were created in two variants of the SW and DW samples, in which the flute was shifted by 1/16 of the period (P) from 1/16 P to 4/16 P (see Figure 9).

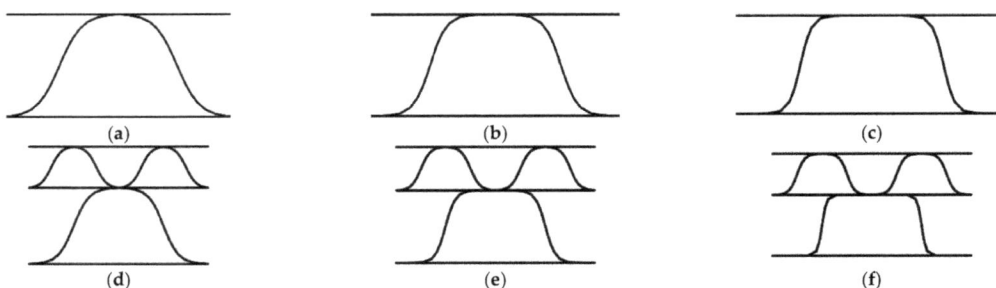

Figure 8. Crushed samples: (**a**–**c**) Single-walled sample crushed by 10%, 20%, and 30%, respectively; (**d**–**f**) Double-walled sample crushed by 10%, 20%, and 30%, respectively.

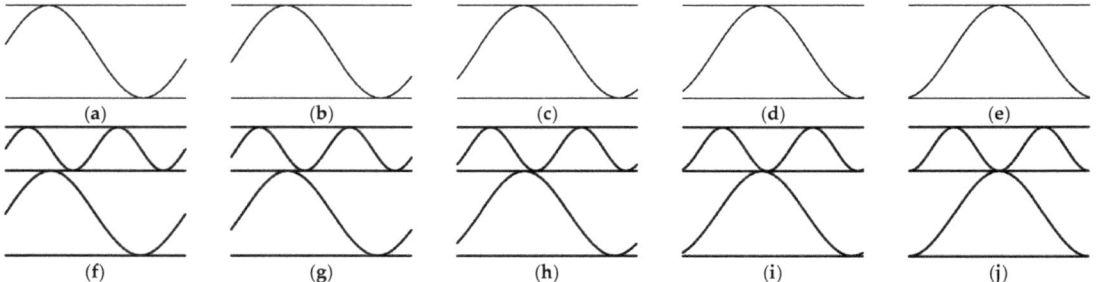

Figure 9. Cross section of the corrugated board along the wave: (**a**) the reference SW sample—no offset; (**b**) SW sample—offset equal to 1/16 P; (**c**) SW sample—offset equal to 2/16 P; (**d**) SW sample—offset equal to 3/16 P; (**e**) SW sample—offset equal to 4/16 P; (**f**) the reference DW sample—no offset; (**g**) DW sample—offset equal to 1/16 P; (**h**) DW sample—offset equal to 2/16 P; (**i**) DW sample—offset equal to 3/16 P; (**j**) DW sample—offset equal to 4/16 P.

2.3. Homogenization Technique

In order to determine the effect of cuts on the stiffness of the corrugated board, the numerical homogenization method was used here. This method, originally proposed by Biancolini [40] and later extended by Garbowski and Gajewski [32], is based on the elastic energy equivalence between the simplified shell model and the full RVE of corrugated cardboard. The RVE is a finite element (FE) representation of a small, periodic section of the full 3D corrugated board structure. The complete derivations of the constitutive model can be found in [32]. In the present study, only the basic assumptions are presented below.

The displacement based on finite element formulation for a linear analysis can be represented by an equation:

$$\mathbf{K}_e \, \mathbf{u}_e = \mathbf{F}_e, \tag{3}$$

where $\mathbf{K}_e$ is a statically condensed global stiffness matrix of the RVE; $\mathbf{u}_e$ is a displacement vector of external nodes; and $\mathbf{F}_e$ is a vector of the nodal forces applied to external nodes. In Figure 10, the FE mesh and mesh nodes are shown.

Static condensation relies on the removal of unknown degrees of freedom (DOF) and then the formulation of the stiffness matrix for a smaller number of degrees of freedom, called the primary unknown or principal DOF. In the analyzed cases, the eliminated degrees of freedom is the internal RVE nodes and the external nodes are the primary unknowns. The statically condensed FE stiffness matrix is computed from the equation:

$$\mathbf{K}_e = \mathbf{K}_{ee} - \mathbf{K}_{ei}\, \mathbf{K}_{ii}^{-1} \mathbf{K}_{ie}, \tag{4}$$

where the stiffness matrix contains four subarrays related to internal (subscript i) and external (subscript e) nodes:

$$\begin{bmatrix} \mathbf{K}_{ee} & \mathbf{K}_{ei} \\ \mathbf{K}_{ie} & \mathbf{K}_{ii} \end{bmatrix} \begin{bmatrix} \mathbf{u}_e \\ \mathbf{u}_i \end{bmatrix} = \begin{bmatrix} \mathbf{F}_e \\ 0 \end{bmatrix}. \tag{5}$$

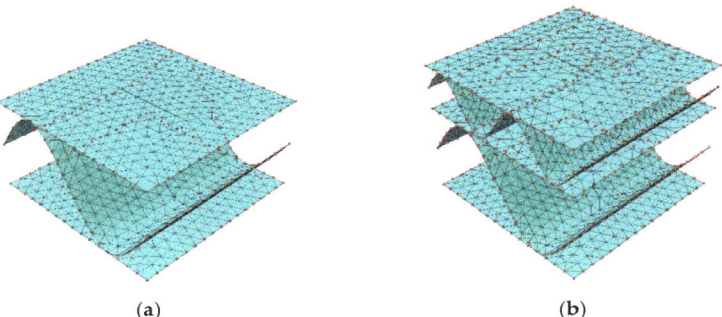

Figure 10. RVE—external (in red color) and internal nodes and finite elements: (**a**) SW model; (**b**) DW model.

Static condensation reduces the total elastic strain energy to the work of external forces on the corresponding displacements. The total elastic strain energy can be calculated from the equation:

$$E = \frac{1}{2} \mathbf{u}_e^T \mathbf{F}_e. \tag{6}$$

The balance of the total energy for the full 3D shell model and the simplified shell model is ensured by an appropriate definition of displacements in the external RVE nodes and by enabling the membrane and bending behavior. More details can be found in Garbowski and Gajewski [32]. The generalized displacements are related to the generalized strains on the RVE edge surfaces, which can be represented by the relationship:

$$\mathbf{u}_i = \mathbf{H}_i \, \epsilon_i, \tag{7}$$

where for a single node ($x_i = x$, $y_i = y$, $z_i = z$) the $\mathbf{H}_i$ matrix adopted for RVE shell model can be determined:

$$\begin{bmatrix} u_x \\ u_y \\ u_z \\ \theta_x \\ \theta_y \end{bmatrix}_i = \begin{bmatrix} x & 0 & y/2 & xz & 0 & yz/2 & z/2 & 0 \\ 0 & y & x/2 & 0 & yz & xz/2 & 0 & z/2 \\ 0 & 0 & 0 & -x^2/2 & -y^2/2 & -xy/2 & x/2 & y/2 \\ 0 & 0 & 0 & 0 & -y & -x/2 & 0 & 0 \\ 0 & 0 & 0 & x & 0 & y/2 & 0 & 0 \end{bmatrix} \begin{bmatrix} \varepsilon_x \\ \varepsilon_y \\ \gamma_{xy} \\ \kappa_x \\ \kappa_y \\ \kappa_{xy} \\ \gamma_{xz} \\ \gamma_{yz} \end{bmatrix}_i \tag{8}$$

While using the definition of the elastic strain energy for a discrete model:

$$E = \frac{1}{2} \mathbf{u}_e^T \mathbf{K} \, \mathbf{u}_e = \frac{1}{2} \epsilon_e^T \mathbf{H}_e^T \mathbf{K} \, \mathbf{H}_e \, \epsilon_e \tag{9}$$

and considering a finite element as subjected to bending, tension, and transverse shear, the elastic internal energy is expressed by:

$$E = \frac{1}{2}\epsilon_e^T \, \mathbf{H}_k \, \epsilon_e \{area\}. \tag{10}$$

For a homogenized composite, the stiffness matrix can be easily determined as:

$$\mathbf{H}_k = \frac{\mathbf{H}_e^T \, \mathbf{K} \, \mathbf{H}_e}{area}. \tag{11}$$

The presented homogenization method is based on replacing the full 3D shell model with a simplified shell model and computing the effective stiffness of the RVE. Such a procedure significantly accelerates the computations and maintains a very high accuracy of the results.

The matrix $\mathbf{H}_k$ is formed by the matrices $\mathbf{A}$, $\mathbf{B}$, $\mathbf{D}$, and $\mathbf{R}$ as follows:

$$\mathbf{H}_k = \begin{bmatrix} \mathbf{A}_{3\times3} & \mathbf{B}_{3\times3} & \\ \mathbf{B}_{3\times3} & \mathbf{D}_{3\times3} & \\ & & \mathbf{R}_{2\times2} \end{bmatrix} \tag{12}$$

where $\mathbf{A}$ represents extensional and shear stiffnesses; $\mathbf{B}$ represents extension-bending coupling stiffnesses; and $\mathbf{D}$ represents bending and torsional stiffnesses, while $\mathbf{R}$ represents transverse shear stiffness.

In general, the stiffness matrix $\mathbf{A}$ is independent of the position of a neutral axis. For the most symmetrical cross sections, all elements of stiffness matrix $\mathbf{B}$ are equal to zero. However, for unsymmetrical sections (i.e., double-walled corrugated board samples) matrix $\mathbf{B}$ is a non-zero, which indicates that there is a coupling between bending/twisting curvatures and extension/shear loads. Traditionally, these couplings have been suppressed for most applications by choosing the position of the neutral axis that minimizes the values of $\mathbf{B}$. Alternatively, uncoupled matrix $\mathbf{D}$ can be computed from the formula:

$$\mathbf{D} = \mathbf{D}_0 - \mathbf{B}\mathbf{A}^{-1}\mathbf{B}, \tag{13}$$

where $\mathbf{D}_0$ represents the original (coupled) bending and torsional stiffnesses.

Within all analyses, the 3-node triangular general-purpose shell elements, named S3, were used for the computations. In every examined case, approximate global size equal to 0.5 mm was assumed. Due to the analysis of different orientations of flutings or cuts in the sample, the number of elements changed. For example, in the case of the SW-44-C-00 sample—2002 elements, 1099 nodes, and 6594 degrees of freedom were obtained, and for the DW-44-C-00 sample—3972 elements, 2074 nodes, and 12,444 degrees of freedom were obtained.

3. Results

3.1. Validation of the Proposed Method

The proposed numerical method was first verified by direct comparison of the obtained results with the existing solutions from the literature. One example concerns an assembled sandwich structure consisting of a corrugated tooth-shaped core enclosed between two sheets. A reference solution is available from Buannic et al. [39]. According to the notation used in the literature, the T2 panel was tested here. The FE models used in this comparison for the T2 sandwich consists of 3-node and 4-node shell elements and are shown in Figure 11. Error estimation was performed and the maximum deviation was less than 2.5%.

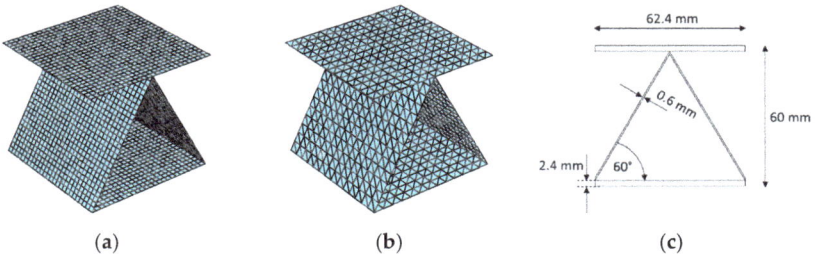

Figure 11. Representative shell elements of saw tooth geometry with quadrilateral mesh (single period): (**a**) model with a fine 4-node mesh; (**b**) model with a coarse 3-node mesh; (**c**) model geometry.

On the basis of the above validation (see Table 3) carried out on two numerical models: (a) model with a fine mesh (see Figure 11a) and (b) model with a coarse mesh (see Figure 11b), it was found that the solution does not depend on the element type and on the size of the finite element. It is important, however, to correctly represent any curvatures, therefore, in the case of sinus-like fluting, at least 16 segments are required to obtain correct results [32].

Table 3. The stiffnesses of representative shell element computed for a different approach of modeling confronted with data from [39] for saw tooth geometry.

Stiffness	Ref. [39]	Corse Model	Fine Model
A_{11}, (N/mm)	$1.108 \cdot 10^6$	$1.118 \cdot 10^6$	$1.118 \cdot 10^6$
A_{22}, (N/mm)	$1.358 \cdot 10^6$	$1.380 \cdot 10^6$	$1.378 \cdot 10^6$
A_{12}, (N/mm)	$3.324 \cdot 10^5$	$3.449 \cdot 10^5$	$3.448 \cdot 10^5$
A_{33}, (N/mm)	$4.168 \cdot 10^5$	$4.115 \cdot 10^5$	$4.115 \cdot 10^5$
D_{11}, (N·mm)	$9.195 \cdot 10^8$	$9.211 \cdot 10^8$	$9.210 \cdot 10^8$
D_{22}, (N·mm)	$9.822 \cdot 10^8$	$9.926 \cdot 10^8$	$9.925 \cdot 10^8$
D_{12}, (N·mm)	$2.758 \cdot 10^8$	$2.777 \cdot 10^8$	$2.777 \cdot 10^8$
D_{33}, (N·mm)	$3.220 \cdot 10^8$	$3.269 \cdot 10^8$	$3.268 \cdot 10^8$
A_{44}, (N/mm)	-	$5.194 \cdot 10^4$	$5.184 \cdot 10^4$
A_{55}, (N/mm)	-	$7.408 \cdot 10^4$	$7.376 \cdot 10^4$

3.2. Detailed Results

This section presents all the results of numerical tests for both single-walled (SW) and double-walled (DW) corrugated board samples. First, Tables 4 and 5 show an example of the $\mathbf{A}_k$ matrix, calculated while using the SW and DW models, respectively (both unperforated).

Table 4. Constitutive stiffness matrix $\mathbf{A}_k$ for the SW model without perforation.

		A & B			B & D			R	
		1	2	3	1	2	3	4	5
A & B	1	2184.4	388.92	0	0	0	0		
	2	388.92	1756.9	0	0	0	0		
	3	0	0	667.81	0	0	0		
B & D	1	0	0	0	8628.2	1506.5	0		
	2	0	0	0	1506.5	5469.3	0		
	3	0	0	0	0	0	2300.2		
R	4							105.08	0
	5							0	130.91

Table 5. Constitutive stiffness matrix A_k for the DW model without perforation.

		A & B			B & D			R	
		1	2	3	1	2	3	4	5
A & B	1	3313.8	593.33	0	1117.1	195.90	0		
	2	593.33	2967.5	0	196.36	1200.6	0		
	3	0	0	1077.8	0	0	409.89		
B & D	1	1117.1	196.36	0	20 619	3620.8	0		
	2	195.90	1200.6	0	3620.8	15 042	0		
	3	0	0.0	409.89	0	0	5934.5		
R	4							233.13	0
	5							0	242.28

Due to the volume limitations of the data that can be presented in all the following tables, only the values from the main diagonals of the A_k matrix are shown. This simplification does not introduce an error in the analyses of the results, mainly because the components $(*)_{12}$ are related to the elements $(*)_{11}$ and $(*)_{22}$ in each matrix. The **B** matrix was also disregarded. However, it has been accounted for using Equation (13) in the **D** matrix, which is presented in all tables below.

Since the DW model is asymmetric, all matrices **A**, **B**, **D**, and **R** are non-zero; in particular, matrix **B** (see Table 5), which combines the bending effects with the membrane stiffness of the plate.

Table 6 shows the selected stiffnesses of all SW models with no perforation and fluting, rotated by an angle of 0 to 90 every 15 degrees. It is worth noting that in the case of models with rotated fluting by 90 degrees SW-0-F-90 and with non-rotating fluting SW-0-F-0, the stiffness values $(*)_{11}$ and $(*)_{22}$ were swapped (the same holds for $(*)_{44}$ and $(*)_{55}$).

Table 6. Selected stiffnesses in SW samples with no perforation and with different flute orientations.

	SW-0-F-00	SW-0-F-15	SW-0-F-30	SW-0-F-45	SW-0-F-60	SW-0-F-75	SW-0-F-90
A_{11} (MPa mm)	2184.4	2127.2	1990.3	1854.2	1774.2	1751.5	1756.9
A_{22} (MPa mm)	1756.9	1751.5	1774.2	1854.2	1990.3	2127.2	2184.4
A_{33} (MPa mm)	667.81	699.26	760.50	792.80	760.50	699.30	667.80
D_{11} (MPa mm^3)	8628.2	8313.5	7480.9	6521.5	5897.3	5575.8	5469.3
D_{22} (MPa mm^3)	5469.3	5575.8	5897.3	6520.4	7480.9	8313.5	8628.2
D_{33} (MPa mm^3)	2300.2	2425.2	2650.1	2755.4	2650.1	2425.2	2300.2
R_{44} (MPa mm)	105.08	108.15	119.80	132.90	127.20	126.20	130.90
R_{55} (MPa mm)	130.91	126.16	127.20	132.80	119.80	108.10	105.10

Table 7 shows the selected stiffnesses of all DW models with no perforation and fluting rotated by an angle of 0 to 90 every 15 degrees (see Figure 7). For the DW-0-F-45 and SW-0F-45 samples, the same values were obtained for all $(*)_{11}$ and $(*)_{22}$ as well as $(*)_{44}$ and $(*)_{55}$, which was expected. This is, of course, due to the symmetry in both the geometrical setup and the material orientation.

Table 7. Selected stiffnesses in DW samples with no perforation and with different flute orientations.

	DW-0-F-00	DW-0-F-15	DW-0-F-30	DW-0-F-45	DW-0-F-60	DW-0-F-75	DW-0-F-90
A_{11} (MPa mm)	3313.8	3250.6	3090.4	2955.2	2912.0	2939.7	2967.5
A_{22} (MPa mm)	2967.5	2939.7	2912.0	2955.3	3090.4	3250.6	3313.8
A_{33} (MPa mm)	1077.8	1127.5	1225.3	1275.9	1225.3	1127.5	1077.8
D_{11} (MPa mm^3)	20,242	19,610	17,980	16,221	15,123	14,662	14,556
D_{22} (MPa mm^3)	14,556	14,662	15,123	16,220	17,980	19,610	20,242
D_{33} (MPa mm^3)	5778.6	6071.8	6634.3	6910.6	6634.3	6071.8	5778.6
R_{44} (MPa mm)	233.13	240.21	246.71	257.56	247.51	242.88	242.28
R_{55} (MPa mm)	242.28	242.88	247.51	257.43	246.71	240.21	233.13

Figure 12 shows the stiffness reduction of thee perforated models (both SW and DW) depending on the perforation rotation angle. The normalization term in each case is the A_k matrix of the corresponding non-perforated sample (i.e., all stiffnesses in the perforated SW models are divided by the corresponding stiffnesses in nonperforated SW model).

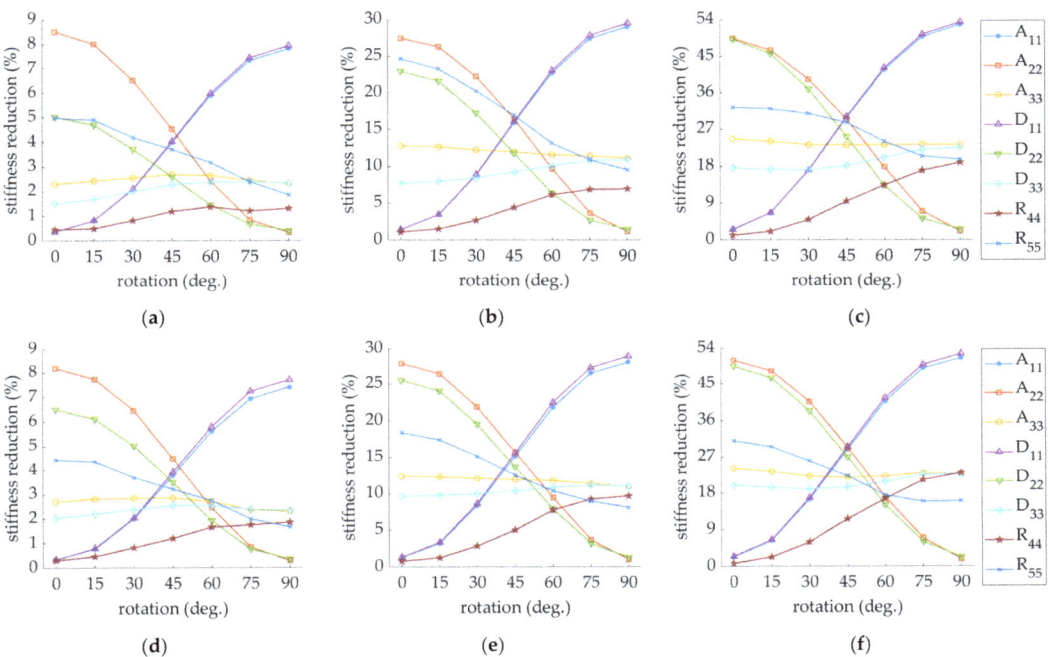

Figure 12. Stiffness degradation in sample: (**a**) SW-26; (**b**) SW-44; (**c**) SW-62; (**d**) DW-26; (**e**) DW-44; (**f**) DW-62.

Tables 8 and 9 summarize the chosen values of stiffness for a selected case of SW sample with fluting rotated by 15 degrees, for four cases of perforation: (i) no perforation; (ii) 2/6 mm (i.e., the normalized cut is 25%); (iii) 4/4 mm (i.e., the normalized cut is 50%); and (iv) 6/2 mm (i.e., the normalized cut is 75%).

Table 8. The selected stiffnesses in SW models for different perforations and flute rotated by 15 degrees.

Stiffness	SW-0-F-15	SW-26-F-15	SW-44-F-15	SW-62-F-15
A_{11} (MPa mm)	2127.2	2116.1	2082.1	2052.3
A_{22} (MPa mm)	1751.6	1609.1	1267.7	885.12
A_{33} (MPa mm)	699.26	681.92	608.30	524.18
D_{11} (MPa mm^3)	8313.4	8276.1	8166.4	8048.5
D_{22} (MPa mm^3)	5575.8	5290.9	4291.8	2877.2
D_{33} (MPa mm^3)	2425.2	2384.5	2216.7	1968.9
R_{44} (MPa mm)	108.15	107.68	106.48	106.77
R_{55} (MPa mm)	126.16	120.04	94.100	83.465

Figure 13 shows the selected values of the stiffness reduction of the SW samples with the flute rotated by 15, 30, 45, 60, and 75 degrees. All stiffnesses were normalized by the A_k matrix of the non-perforated sample with the appropriate fluting orientation (see Figure 6). Figure 14 presents the selected values of the stiffness reduction of the DW samples with the flute rotated by 15, 30, 45, 60, and 75 degrees. All stiffnesses were normalized by the A_k matrix of the non-perforated sample with the appropriate fluting orientation (see Figure 7).

Table 9. Stiffness reduction for both SW and DW samples with flute rotated by 15 degrees for three cases of perforation.

Stiffness Reduction	SW-26-F-15 (%)	SW-44-F-15 (%)	SW-62-F-15 (%)	DW-26-F-15 (%)	DW-44-F-15 (%)	DW-62-F-15 (%)
$1 - A_{11}/A_{11}^*$	0.523	2.121	3.519	0.508	1.903	3.364
$1 - A_{22}/A_{22}^*$	8.133	27.66	49.46	7.852	27.77	50.98
$1 - A_{33}/A_{33}^*$	2.480	13.01	25.04	2.735	12.66	24.50
$1 - D_{11}/D_{11}^*$	0.449	1.769	3.187	0.467	1.786	3.247
$1 - D_{22}/D_{22}^*$	5.110	23.03	48.40	6.377	25.41	49.18
$1 - D_{33}/D_{33}^*$	1.677	8.598	18.81	2.171	10.25	20.88
$1 - R_{44}/R_{44}^*$	0.435	1.545	1.273	−0.349	1.032	1.177
$1 - R_{55}/R_{55}^*$	4.851	25.41	33.84	4.060	18.48	30.95

* denotes the reference value of non-perforated specimen (i.e., SW-0-F-15).

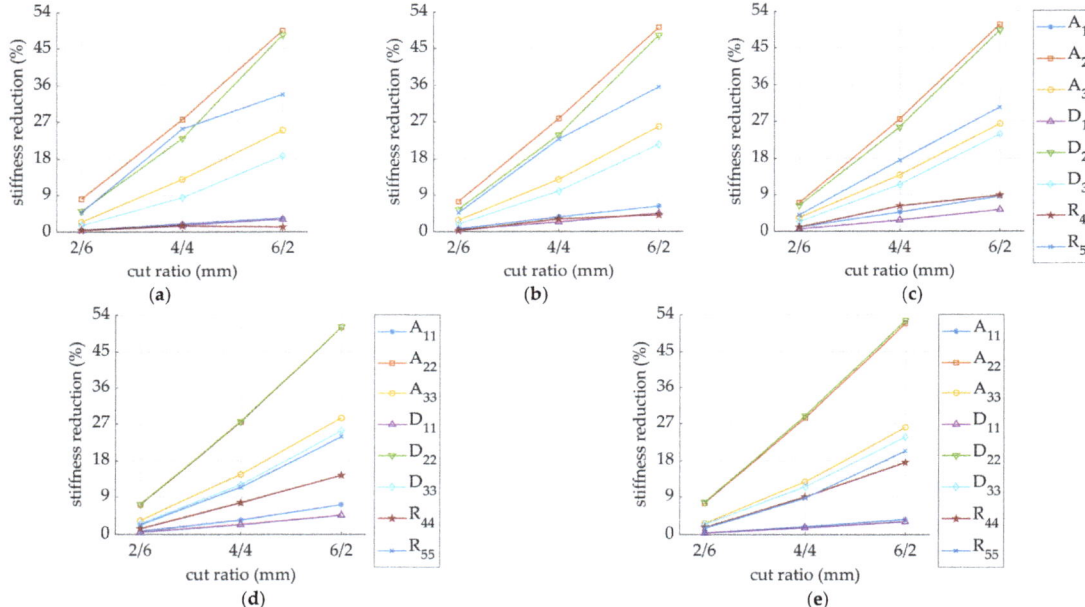

Figure 13. Stiffness degradation in sample SW: (**a**) F-15; (**b**) F-30; (**c**) F-45; (**d**) F-60; (**e**) F-75. Three types of perforations were analyzed (2/6 mm, 4/4 mm, or 6/2 mm).

In the process of cutting corrugated board, perforation may occur in various locations relative to the fluting position, therefore the impact of fluting shift on stiffness changes has also been analyzed. Figure 15 presents the values of the stiffness reduction depending on the location of the cut in relation to the fluting position for the SW and DW samples in three perforation varieties: 2/6 mm, 4/4 mm, and 6/2 mm.

Due to noticed increase of R_{44} and R_{55} stiffnesses (negative stiffness reduction values shown in Figure 15), non-perforated samples were also examined. The values of the stiffness reduction depending on the fluting shift for the SW sample are summarized in Table 10, whereas the values of the stiffness reduction depending on the fluting shift for the DW sample are listed in Table 11.

As the perforation process is inseparable from the crushing process, this effect on the reduction of stiffness has also been tested. The influence of additional crushing of 10, 20, and 30% of the initial height of the corrugated board on the stiffness degradation of SW and DW samples is presented in Figure 16. The comprehensive study of the impact of crushing on single-walled corrugated board is presented in a recent study of Garbowski et al. [44], while for the double-walled structures, see Gajewski et al. [45].

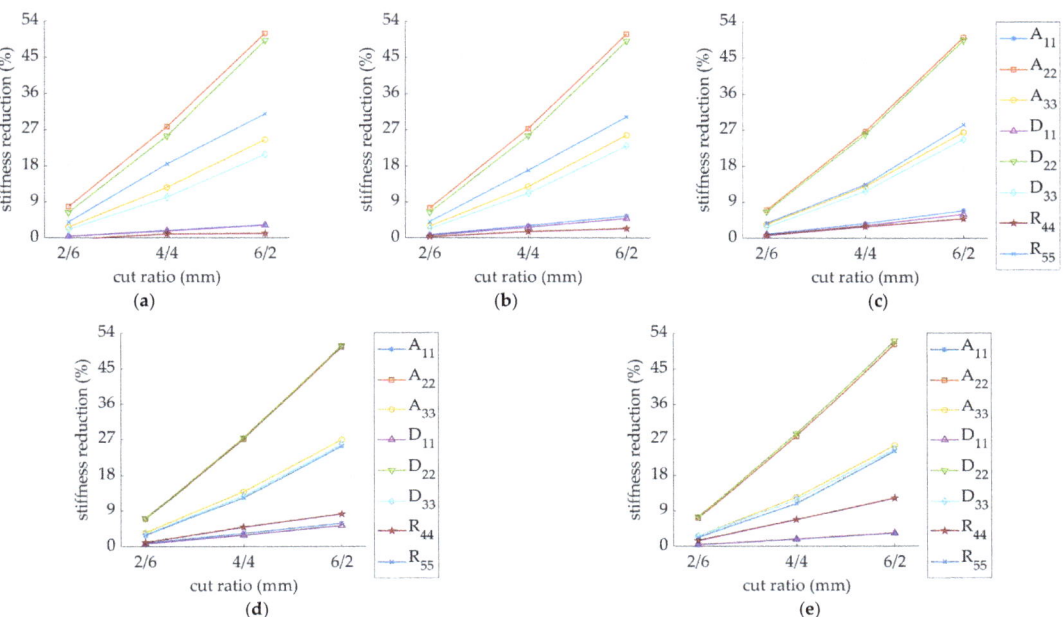

Figure 14. Stiffness degradation in a sample DW: (**a**) F-15; (**b**) F-30; (**c**) F-45; (**d**) F-60; (**e**) F-75. Three types of perforation were analyzed (2/6 mm, 4/4 mm, or 6/2 mm).

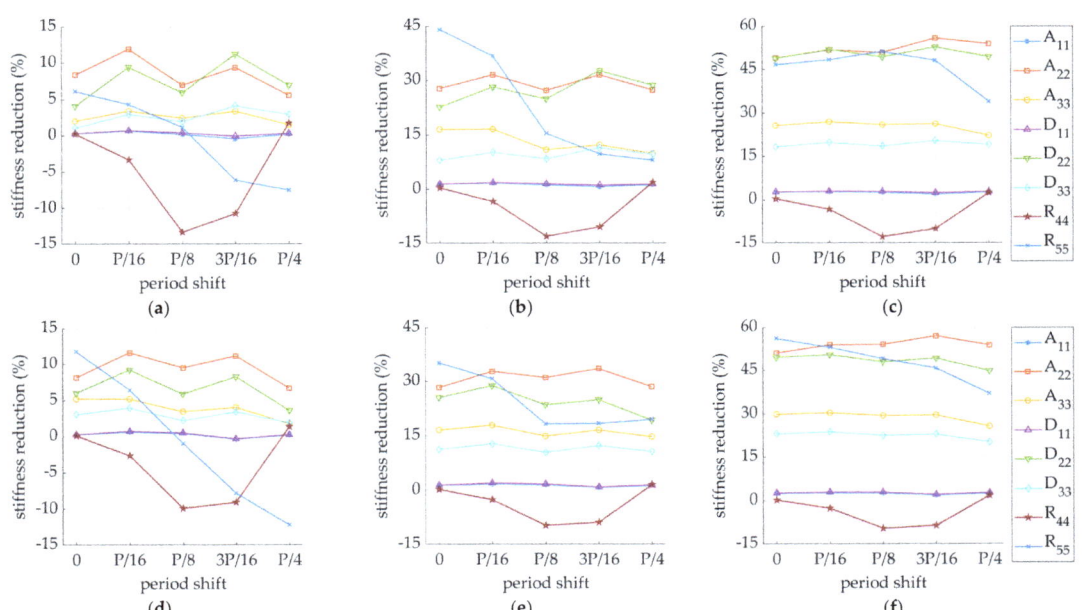

Figure 15. Stiffness degradation in sample C-0: (**a**) SW-26; (**b**) SW-44; (**c**) SW-62; (**d**) DW-26; (**e**) DW-44; (**f**) DW-62.

Table 10. Uncut samples SW. Stiffness reduction in terms of flute offset.

Stiffness Reduction	1/16 P (%)	2/16 P (%)	3/16 P (%)	4/16 P (%)
$1 - A_{11}/A_{11}^*$	−0.023	−0.121	−1.061	−0.055
$1 - A_{22}/A_{22}^*$	−0.018	−0.061	−0.086	−0.003
$1 - A_{33}/A_{33}^*$	−0.035	−0.089	−0.062	0.038
$1 - D_{11}/D_{11}^*$	0.023	0.099	−0.687	0.059
$1 - D_{22}/D_{22}^*$	0.018	0.053	−0.007	0.050
$1 - D_{33}/D_{33}^*$	0.124	0.495	1.102	1.720
$1 - R_{44}/R_{44}^*$	3.533	13.41	10.63	1.771
$1 - R_{55}/R_{55}^*$	1.286	4.036	8.186	8.956

* denotes the reference value of non-shifted flute.

Table 11. Uncut samples DW. Stiffness reduction in terms of flute offset.

Stiffness Reduction	1/16 P (%)	2/16 P (%)	3/16 P (%)	4/16 P (%)
$1 - A_{11}/A_{11}^*$	−0.018	−0.094	−1.052	−0.037
$1 - A_{22}/A_{22}^*$	−0.013	−0.044	−0.075	−0.003
$1 - A_{33}/A_{33}^*$	−0.032	−0.082	−0.056	0.039
$1 - D_{11}/D_{11}^*$	0.012	0.029	−1.048	−0.012
$1 - D_{22}/D_{22}^*$	0.011	0.009	−0.062	0.021
$1 - D_{33}/D_{33}^*$	−0.029	0.110	0.459	0.880
$1 - R_{44}/R_{44}^*$	2.706	9.932	8.977	1.396
$1 - R_{55}/R_{55}^*$	2.378	6.572	11.88	15.28

* denotes the reference value of non-shifted flute.

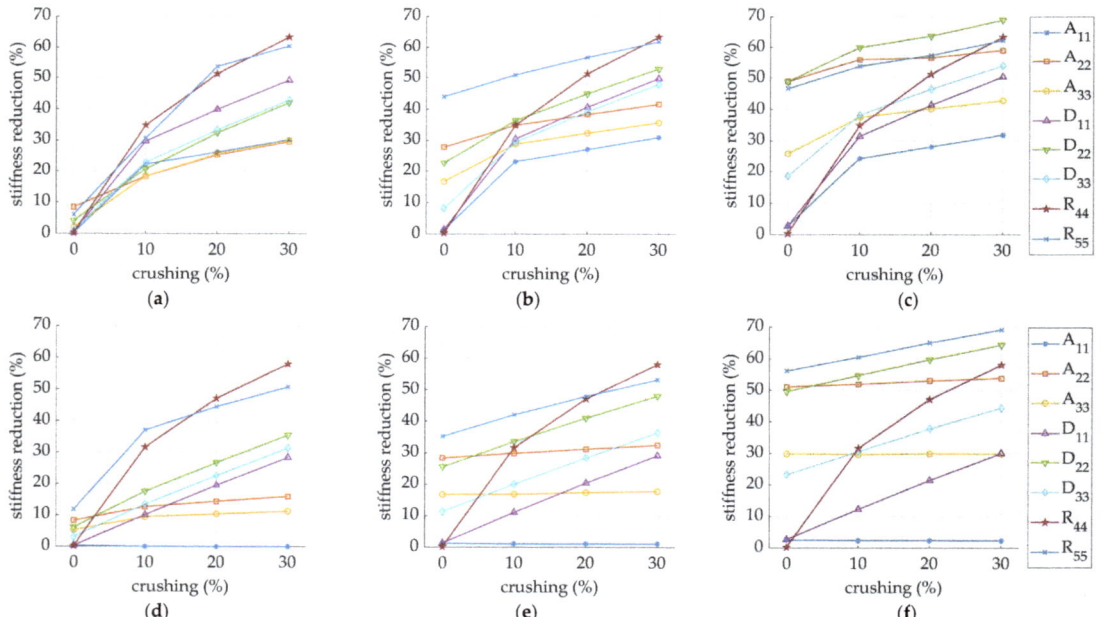

Figure 16. Stiffness degradation in sample: (**a**) SW-26-C-0-R-xx; (**b**) SW-44-C-0-R-xx; (**c**) SW-62-C-0-R-xx; (**d**) DW-26-C-0-R-xx; (**e**) DW-44-C-0-R-xx; (**f**) DW-62-C-0-R-xx. Here xx is a crush level (0%; 10%, 20%, and 30%).

4. Discussion

On the basis of the conducted analyses and the obtained results, it can be concluded that the perforations to a greater or lesser extent affected the stiffness degradation not only in the **A** sub-matrix (responsible for the tensile/compression stiffness) and in the **D** sub-matrix (responsible for bending/torsion stiffness), but also in the **R** sub-matrix (responsible for the transversal shear stiffness).

For samples with different perforation orientations (see Figure 5), the reduction in stiffness was related to the rotation angle of the perforation. In the samples with a rotation angle below 30 degrees, the greatest reduction occurred for matrix elements with indices 22 and 55. If the rotation angle was greater than 60 degrees, mainly matrix elements with indices 11 and 44 were reduced. This rule applied to both types of samples (i.e., SW and DW). When the perforation was rotated by an angle equal to 45 degrees, the matrix elements with indices 11, 22, 44, and 55 were evenly degraded.

For 2/6 mm perforation in model SW (see Figure 12a), the maximum degradation did not exceed 10% and was applied to A_{22} (for perforation rotation angle < 30 degrees) and A_{11}, D_{11} (for perforation rotation angle > 60 degrees). It is worth noting that the decrease in the stiffness D_{22} and R_{55} for the rotation angle of the perforation equal to 0 degrees was relatively high and amounted to 5% for the perforation type 2/6 mm. The remaining stiffnesses degraded less than 3% in this case. A similar observation applied to the DW model (see Figure 12d).

While considering the 4/4 mm type perforation (see Figure 12b), the observations were as follows: reduction of A_{22}, D_{22} was about 25% for a perforation rotation of 0 degrees and about 0% for a 90-degree rotation; R_{55} degraded about 25% when the perforation was rotated by 0 degrees and about 10% when the perforation was rotated by 90 degrees; reduction of A_{33} and D_{33} was about 10% regardless of the perforation rotation angle, while the degradation of A_{11} and D_{11} varied from around 0% to 30% for 0 degrees and 90 degrees, respectively; and the degradation of R_{44} did not exceed 5%. In the DW model (see Figure 12e), a similar decrease could be observed. The reductions R_{44} and R_{55} look slightly different; this is related to a different ratio of the sample height to its dimensions in the plan.

The greatest reductions were observed for the sample with the 6/2 mm perforation type (see Figure 12c,f). This is obviously related to the largest cut-to-gap ratio (which amounts to 75% in this case). In the case of the SW model, both the stiffness reductions A_{11} and D_{11} as well as A_{22} and D_{22} reached a maximum value of slightly more than 50%. The reduction of A_{33}, D_{33}, and R_{55} varied between 15 and 30%. The R_{44} stiffness reduction was approximately 0% for the non-rotated perforation, while for the rotation angle of 90 degrees, it was about 20%. A very similar stiffness degradation could be observed for the DW model (see Figure 12f).

For samples with different fluting orientations (see Figures 13 and 14), the greatest reduction in stiffness always occurred in the direction perpendicular to the perforation (i.e., $(*)_{22}$ and $(*)_{55}$), regardless of material orientation. Both A_{22} and D_{22} stiffnesses had the greatest reductions and amounted to about 50% in the case of 6/2 mm perforation for all fluting orientations. Slightly smaller reductions in stiffness were observed for R_{44}, A_{33}, and D_{33} ranging from 15 to 30% (for 6/2 mm perforation type), depending on the orientation of the fluting. The smallest stiffness reductions were observed for A_{11}, D_{11}, and R_{55}.

When analyzing the stiffness reductions for models with shifted fluting (see Figure 9), even in the case without perforation, slight differences in stiffness could be observed (see Tables 10 and 11) and concerned mainly R_{44} and R_{55}. Small fluctuations were also observed in models with perforation for both cases of SW and DW (see Figure 15), where again, the R_{44} and R_{55} showed the greatest dependence on fluting shift.

By also adding to the model the crushing of fluting (see Figure 8) that accompanies the perforations during the treatment of corrugated board, the degradation for some stiffnesses can increase several times (see Figure 16). The more perforated the model (i.e., 6/2 mm perforation type), the smaller the further reductions in the stiffness A_{22}, D_{22}, and R_{55}.

The remaining stiffnesses were drastically reduced with the increase in the crushing of the cross-section of the corrugated board. It is worth noting that for the DW model, the stiffnesses reduction of A_{11}, A_{22}, and A_{33} did not depend on the amount of crushing.

5. Conclusions

This article presents the comprehensive numerical analyses of the effect of perforation on reducing stiffness while implementing homogenization techniques. The acquired knowledge can be used for numerical modeling, for example, of corrugated cardboard packaging with perforations. Knowing the specific values of the stiffness reduction, it is possible to correctly model the perforation line and thus accurately estimate the load capacity of the packaging. The reduction in individual stiffnesses depends not only on the type of perforation, but also on the orientation of the perforation and the orientation of the fluting, but does not depend on the location of the perforation along the wavelength. Further development of the launched research is planned related to the validation of the proposed model with experimental models while engaging the non-contact displacement measurements [46].

Author Contributions: Conceptualization, T.G.; Methodology, T.G.; Software, T.G.; Validation, T.G. and D.M.; Formal analysis, T.G. and D.M.; Investigation, D.M., T.G. and A.K.-P.; Writing—original draft preparation, A.K.-P., T.G. and D.M.; Writing—review and editing, A.K.-P. and T.G.; Visualization, D.M. and T.G.; Supervision, T.G.; Project administration, T.G.; Funding acquisition, T.G. and A.K.-P. All authors have read and agreed to the published version of the manuscript.

Funding: The APC was funded by the Ministry of Science and Higher Education, Poland, the statutory funding at Poznan University of Life Sciences, grant number 506.569.05.00 and the statutory funding at Poznan University of Technology, grant number 0411/SBAD/0004.

Institutional Review Board Statement: Not applicable.

Informed Consent Statement: Not applicable.

Data Availability Statement: The data presented in this study are available on request from the corresponding author.

Acknowledgments: Special thanks to the FEMat Sp. z o. o. company (Poznań, Poland) (www.fematsystems.pl— accessed on 21 May 2021) for providing the commercial software.

Conflicts of Interest: The authors declare no conflict of interest.

References

1. Sohrabpour, V.; Hellström, D. Models and software for corrugated board and box design. In Proceedings of the 18th International Conference on Engineering Design (ICED 11), Copenhagen, Denmark, 15–18 October 2011.
2. Kellicutt, K.; Landt, E. Development of design data for corrugated fiberboard shipping containers. *Tappi J.* **1952**, *35*, 398–402.
3. Maltenfort, G. Compression strength of corrugated containers. *Fibre Contain.* **1956**, *41*, 106–121.
4. McKee, R.C.; Gander, J.W.; Wachuta, J.R. Compression strength formula for corrugated boxes. *Paperboard Packag.* **1963**, *48*, 149–159.
5. Allerby, I.M.; Laing, G.N.; Cardwell, R.D. Compressive strength—From components to corrugated containers. *Appita Conf. Notes* **1985**, 1–11.
6. Schrampfer, K.E.; Whitsitt, W.J.; Baum, G.A. *Combined Board Edge Crush (ECT) Technology*; Institute of Paper Chemistry: Appleton, WI, USA, 1987.
7. Batelka, J.J.; Smith, C.N. *Package Compression Model*; Institute of Paper Science and Technology: Atlanta, GA, USA, 1993.
8. Urbanik, T.J.; Frank, B. Box compression analysis of world-wide data spanning 46 years. *Wood Fiber Sci.* **2006**, *38*, 399–416.
9. Avilés, F.; Carlsson, L.A.; May-Pat, A. A shear-corrected formulation of the sandwich twist specimen. *Exp. Mech.* **2012**, *52*, 17–23. [CrossRef]
10. Garbowski, T.; Gajewski, T.; Grabski, J.K. The role of buckling in the estimation of compressive strength of corrugated cardboard boxes. *Materials* **2020**, *13*, 4578. [CrossRef]
11. Garbowski, T.; Gajewski, T.; Grabski, J.K. Estimation of the compressive strength of corrugated cardboard boxes with various openings. *Energies* **2021**, *14*, 155. [CrossRef]
12. Garbowski, T.; Gajewski, T.; Grabski, J.K. Estimation of the compressive strength of corrugated cardboard boxes with various perforations. *Energies* **2021**, *14*, 1095. [CrossRef]

13. Wang, L.; Qian, Z. A meshfree stabilized collocation method (SCM) based on reproducing kernel approximation. *Comput. Methods Appl. Mech. Eng.* **2020**, *371*, 113303. [CrossRef]
14. Wang, L.; Liu, Y.; Zhou, Y.; Yang, F. Static and dynamic analysis of thin functionally graded shell with in-plane material inhomogeneity. *Int. J. Mech. Sci.* **2021**, *193*, 106165. [CrossRef]
15. Chu, F.; He, J.; Wang, L.; Zhong, Z. Buckling analysis of functionally graded thin plate with in-plane material inhomogeneity. *Eng. Anal. Bound. Elem.* **2016**, *65*, 112–125. [CrossRef]
16. Frank, B. Corrugated box compression—A literature survey. *Packag. Technol. Sci.* **2014**, *27*, 105–128. [CrossRef]
17. Stott, R.A. Compression and stacking strength of corrugated fibreboard containers. *Appita J.* **2017**, *70*, 76–82.
18. Junli, W.; Quancheng, Z. Effect of moisture content of corrugated box on mechanical properties. *J. Lanzhou Jiaotong Univ.* **2006**, *25*, 134–136.
19. Archaviboonyobul, T.; Chaveesuk, R.; Singh, J.; Jinkarn, T. An analysis of the influence of hand hole and ventilation hole design on compressive strength of corrugated fiberboard boxes by an artificial neural network model. *Packag. Technol. Sci.* **2020**, *33*, 171–181. [CrossRef]
20. Zhang, Y.-L.; Chen, J.; Wu, Y.; Sun, J. Analysis of hazard factors of the use of corrugated carton in packaging low-temperature yogurt during logistics. *Procedia Environ. Sci.* **2011**, *10*, 968–973. [CrossRef]
21. Gallo, J.; Cortés, F.; Alberdi, E.; Goti, A. Mechanical behavior modeling of containers and octabins made of corrugated cardboard subjected to vertical stacking loads. *Materials* **2021**, *14*, 2392. [CrossRef]
22. Thakkar, B.K.; Gooren, L.G.J.; Peerlings, R.H.J.; Geers, M.G.D. Experimental and numerical investigation of creasing in corrugated paperboard. *Philos. Mag.* **2008**, *88*, 3299–3310. [CrossRef]
23. Beex, L.A.A.; Peerlings, R.H.J. An experimental and computational study of laminated paperboard creasing and folding. *Int. J. Solids Struct.* **2009**, *46*, 4192–4207. [CrossRef]
24. Giampieri, A.; Perego, U.; Borsari, R. A constitutive model for the mechanical response of the folding of creased paperboard. *Int. J. Solids Struct.* **2011**, *48*, 2275–2287. [CrossRef]
25. Domaneschi, M.; Perego, U.; Borgqvist, E.; Borsari, R. An industry-oriented strategy for the finite element simulation of paperboard creasing and folding. *Pack. Technol. Sci.* **2017**, *30*, 269–294. [CrossRef]
26. Awais, M.; Tanninen, P.; Leppänen, T.; Matthews, S.; Sorvari, J.; Varis, J.; Backfol, K. A computational and experimental analysis of crease behavior in press forming process. *Procedia Manuf.* **2018**, *17*, 835–842. [CrossRef]
27. Leminena, V.; Tanninena, P.; Pesonena, A.; Varis, J. Effect of mechanical perforation on the press-forming process of paperboard. *Procedia Manuf.* **2019**, *38*, 1402–1408. [CrossRef]
28. Nordstrand, T. Basic Testing and Strength Design of Corrugated Board and Containers. Ph.D. Thesis, Lund University, Lund, Sweden, 2003.
29. Nordstrand, T.; Carlsson, L. Evaluation of transverse shear stiffness of structural core sandwich plates. *Comp. Struct.* **1997**, *37*, 145–153. [CrossRef]
30. Garbowski, T.; Gajewski, T.; Grabski, J.K. Role of transverse shear modulus in the performance of corrugated materials. *Materials* **2020**, *13*, 3791. [CrossRef]
31. Garbowski, T.; Gajewski, T.; Grabski, J.K. Torsional and transversal stiffness of orthotropic sandwich panels. *Materials* **2020**, *13*, 5016. [CrossRef] [PubMed]
32. Garbowski, T.; Gajewski, T. Determination of transverse shear stiffness of sandwich panels with a corrugated core by numerical homogenization. *Materials* **2021**, *14*, 1976. [CrossRef]
33. Urbanik, T.J.; Saliklis, E.P. Finite element corroboration of buckling phenomena observed in corrugated boxes. *Wood Fiber Sci.* **2003**, *35*, 322–333.
34. Garbowski, T.; Jarmuszczak, M. Homogenization of corrugated paperboard. Part 1. Analytical homogenization. *Pol. Pap. Rev.* **2014**, *70*, 345–349. (In Polish)
35. Garbowski, T.; Jarmuszczak, M. Homogenization of corrugated paperboard. Part 2. Numerical homogenization. *Pol. Pap. Rev.* **2014**, *70*, 390–394. (In Polish)
36. Marek, A.; Garbowski, T. Homogenization of sandwich panels. *Comput. Assist. Methods Eng. Sci.* **2015**, *22*, 39–50.
37. Garbowski, T.; Marek, A. Homogenization of corrugated boards through inverse analysis. In Proceedings of the 1st International Conference on Engineering and Applied Sciences Optimization, Kos Island, Greece, 4–6 June 2014; pp. 1751–1766.
38. Hohe, J. A direct homogenization approach for determination of the stiffness matrix for microheterogeneous plates with application to sandwich panels. *Compos. Part B* **2003**, *34*, 615–626. [CrossRef]
39. Buannic, N.; Cartraud, P.; Quesnel, T. Homogenization of corrugated core sandwich panels. *Comp. Struct.* **2003**, *59*, 299–312. [CrossRef]
40. Biancolini, M.E. Evaluation of equivalent stiffness properties of corrugated board. *Comp. Struct.* **2005**, *69*, 322–328. [CrossRef]
41. Abbès, B.; Guo, Y.Q. Analytic homogenization for torsion of orthotropic sandwich plates: Application to corrugated cardboard. *Comp. Struct.* **2010**, *92*, 699–706. [CrossRef]
42. Ramírez-Torres, A.; Penta, R.; Rodríguez-Ramos, R.; Merodio, J.; Sabina, F.J.; Bravo-Castillero, J.; Guinovart-Díaz, R.; Preziosi, L.; Grillo, A. Three scales asymptotic homogenization and its application to layered hierarchical hard tissues. *Int. J. Solids Struct.* **2018**, *130–131*, 190–198. [CrossRef]

43. Ramírez-Torres, A.; Di Stefano, S.; Grillo, A.; Rodríguez-Ramos, R.; Merodio, J.; Penta, R. An asymptotic homogenization approach to the microstructural evolution of heterogeneous media. *Int. J. Non-Lin. Mech.* **2018**, *106*, 245–257. [CrossRef]
44. Garbowski, T.; Gajewski, T.; Mrówczyński, D.; Jędrzejczak, R. Crushing of single-walled corrugated board during converting: Experimental and numerical study. *Energies* **2021**, *14*, 3203. [CrossRef]
45. Gajewski, T.; Garbowski, T.; Staszak, N.; Kuca, M. Crushing of double-walled corrugated board and its influence on the load capacity of various boxes. *Preprints* **2021**, 2021050667. [CrossRef]
46. Garbowski, T.; Grabski, J.K.; Marek, A. Full-field measurements in the edge crush test of a corrugated board—Analytical and numerical predictive models. *Materials* **2021**, *14*, 2840. [CrossRef] [PubMed]

Article

Edgewise Compressive Behavior of Composite Structural Insulated Panels with Magnesium Oxide Board Facings

Łukasz Smakosz [1,*], Ireneusz Kreja [1] and Zbigniew Pozorski [2]

1 Department of Structural Mechanics, Faculty of Civil and Environmental Engineering, Gdańsk University of Technology, ul. Gabriela Narutowicza 11/12, 80-233 Gdańsk, Poland; ireneusz.kreja@pg.edu.pl
2 Institute of Structural Analysis, Faculty of Civil and Transport Engineering, Poznan University of Technology, ul. Piotrowo 5, 60-965 Poznań, Poland; zbigniew.pozorski@put.poznan.pl
* Correspondence: lukasz.smakosz@pg.edu.pl

Abstract: Edgewise compression response of a composite structural insulated panel (CSIP) with magnesium oxide board facings was investigated. The discussed CSIP is a novel multifunctional sandwich panel introduced to the housing industry as a part of the wall, floor, and roof assemblies. The study aims to propose a computational tool for reliable prediction of failure modes of CSIPs subjected to concentric and eccentric axial loads. An advanced numerical model was proposed that includes geometrical and material nonlinearity as well as incorporates the material bimodularity effect to achieve accurate and versatile failure mode prediction capability. Laboratory tests on small-scale CSIP samples of three different slenderness ratios and full-scale panels loaded with three different eccentricity values were carried out, and the test data were compared with numerical results for validation. The finite element (FE) model successfully captured CSIP's inelastic response in uniaxial compression and when flexural action was introduced by eccentric loads or buckling and predicted all failure modes correctly. The comprehensive validation showed that the proposed approach could be considered a robust and versatile aid in CSIP design.

Keywords: composites; sandwich panel; composite structural insulated panel; magnesium oxide board; bimodular material; experimental mechanics; computational mechanics; finite element analysis

1. Introduction

The composite structural insulated panel (CSIP) is a novel product introduced to the housing industry as a part of the wall, floor, and roof assemblies in low-rise buildings. It is a type of multifunctional sandwich panel that combines enveloping, thermoinsulational, and structural roles. Composite materials with low weight to strength ratio and modularized components allow to significantly reduce the time and cost of transport and assembly, making them an attractive alternative to traditional construction materials [1–5]. The CSIP is a developed version of a structural insulated panel (SIP), which uses mainly wood-based facing materials, such as oriented strand board (OSB), that are prone to biological and environmental degradation [6,7]. The use of the right composite facings can solve this problem and, depending on the type of material used, introduce additional advantages.

The subject of the present research is a CSIP with magnesium oxide board (MgO board) facings and an expanded polystyrene (EPS) core, bound together by a polyurethane adhesive (Figure 1). The MgO board is a relatively new cladding material, composed of a magnesia cement mortar matrix and a glass-fiber mesh reinforcement. Such use of the MgO board provides the panel with high strength and stiffness, immunity to biological corrosion, flame retardancy, and environmental sustainability [8–11]. The analyzed CSIP overcomes the disadvantages of a traditional SIP and allows to create more durable and eco-friendly buildings.

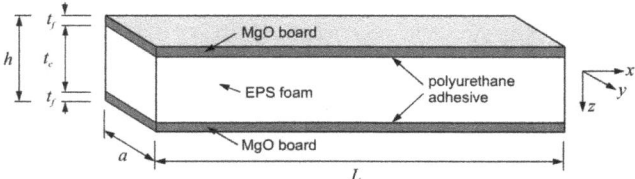

Figure 1. Schematic layout of the analyzed CSIP.

The CSIP under consideration is intended for use as a structural element of walls, which means it has to be suitable for in-plane load transfer. The need for a sufficient thermal insulation and structural strength results in a relatively high total thickness to length ratio. This type of geometry makes it prone to premature initiation of local damage, and the actual failure pattern is difficult to predict at the design stage. Possible failure modes, when subjected to in-plane compression, include yielding of facings, core shear, global buckling, inward local buckling (core crushing), and outward local buckling (delamination) [12]. The prominent difference in facing and core stiffness and the complex nature of their interactions make a prediction of CSIP failure mode a challenging task. Therefore, it is essential to provide a computational tool well-suited for this type of composite.

Several investigations on the subject of sandwich panel behavior under axial loads were carried out in recent years. The compressive behavior of sandwich column samples with carbon/epoxy facings and two types of core material, polyvinyl chloride foam and aluminum honeycomb, was investigated in [13]. Local buckling failure was observed in the soft foam core samples, whereas no wrinkling occurred in the honeycomb sample, due to its high thickness–direction stiffness. Fundamental analytical expressions allowed to predict the wrinkling load when it appeared before the core yield, but the formulas had to be modified to account for the stiffness loss in cases where the core failed first. CSIPs with thermoplastic glass/polypropylene facings and an EPS core were analyzed in [14,15]. The first report [14] concentrates on global buckling failure of small-scale samples caused by concentric and eccentric loads. The authors derive formulae that consider the orthotropic facings and the core shear deformation to predict the elastic buckling load successfully. The second study [15] concerns full-scale CSIPs subjected to eccentric compression. All tested panels failed by local buckling, and an analytical model for critical wrinkling stress was proposed and validated for the elastic range. Furthermore, a 3D continuum FE model with geometric nonlinearity was used for a parametric study, highlighting the possibilities of such an approach in CSIP design. Mechanical behavior of panels with low density polyethylene facings and a lightweight polyethylene foam core under edgewise compression was investigated in [16]. An experimental study on small-scale samples was carried out, utilizing strain and out-of-plain deformation measurements, and multiple cases of localized buckling were captured. A high fidelity 3D continuum FE model accounting for thickness irregularities as well as material and geometrical nonlinearities was created and successfully validated against experimental results. Afterward, the model was used in a parametric study to assess the sensitivity of panel's response to changes in layers' thickness and interface irregularities. An extensive study on the influence of slenderness ratio on the compressive behavior of glass fiber reinforced polymer (GFRP) facings and polyurethane foam core sandwich panels' compressive response was carried out in [17]. The observed failure types were global buckling, wrinkling, GFRP yield, and core shear. The authors correlated the failure modes to the slenderness ratio and proposed analytical expressions for ultimate load prediction in the elastic range. An investigation of axial performance of single sandwich wall panels and panel assemblies jointed with a novel connector system was performed in [18]. The observed failure modes were local buckling of GFRP skins, and global instability resulting from delamination between the core and facings. A linear elastic theoretical study was carried out and the obtained results were in a reasonable agreement with the experimental data. Load-bearing sandwich panels with glass fiber reinforced polymer (GFRP) facings and a foam-web core subjected to edgewise compression were discussed in [19]. Outward local buckling and compressive facing yield failure types were observed, depending on the foam-web layout. Analytical formulae calculating critical local buckling stress, and axial load capacity of the panel were derived and validated in an experimental examination. Elastic range consideration was sufficient in this case as well. One of the few examples of MgO board strength research was presented in [9]. The structural behavior of wall-panels with MgO board facings and a glass fiber reinforced polyurethane foam core was investigated. Full-scale panels with different support assemblies and a panel with a damaged facing were tested in uniaxial compression. The observed failure modes were facing buckling followed by vertical cracking and facing cracking due to shear sliding. It was also observed that the presence of local damage in the board caused cracks propagating from the weakened area and led to a significant reduction of the load-bearing capacity of the panel. Examples of nonlinear FE approach to sandwich panel analysis can be found in [20,21]. Numerical studies of composite response to local loads were performed with consideration of both material and geometrical nonlinearities. Core layers were modeled with continuum solids and facings were treated as structural shells. This approach allowed for a more detailed insight into sandwich layer interactions. A high fidelity method of sandwich panel FE modeling is presented in [22]. Nonlinear material behavior was applied to all components, taking into account the difference in tensile and compressive responses of textile-reinforced cement faces, and high deformability of an extruded polystyrene foam (XPS) core in compression. The numerical approach was validated by comparison of surface strain results in different layers with comprehensive digital image correlation data. Structural behavior of SIPs with OSB facings subjected to concentric and eccentric compression was analyzed in a joint experimental and analytical study in [23]. Full-scale panels with different configurations of slenderness ratio and foam core type were tested, and the observed force-deflection responses were predominately linear until failure. Failure modes consisted of facing crushing at different locations, core shear, core rupture near the interface, and debonding at the adhesive layer. Several design recommendations, along with empirical expressions for SIP's ultimate axial strength, were proposed.

The analyzed CSIP and its components were subjected to various mechanical tests to identify its failure patterns and establish material properties of the MgO board and the EPS core [24,25]. Both core and facing yield were noted before failure initiation, therefore limiting the computational model to the elastic range would be inadequate. Material and geometrical nonlinearities had to be considered. Moreover, it was observed that the structural response and the parameter values depended strongly on the stress state of the materials and that the most notable differences occurred between compression and tension. The observed material bimodularity was incorporated into a preliminary FE model, which significantly improved the simulation results' overall quality. An attempt to use this approach for CSIP edgewise compression analysis was made [26]. The numerical analysis produced qualitatively acceptable results; however, the samples' stiffness and strength were considerably underestimated. Quite recently, a refined description of the bimodular material model was proposed and positively validated [27]. As a result, a notable improvement of similarity between numerical and experimental curves, and accuracy of failure mode prediction was achieved for flexural behavior.

In the current work, the refined bimodular FE approach was used to simulate the behavior of the MgO board CSIP under concentric and eccentric edgewise compression. The validation of the numerical model was accomplished by comparing its outcomes with the results of laboratory tests performed on samples of different geometries and eccentricity values. Both small-scale and full-scale samples were investigated for comprehensive validation. The study aims to propose a robust, versatile computational framework that can be used as a reliable design aid for predicting CSIP failure modes in compression.

2. Materials and Methods

2.1. Experimental Analysis

A series of laboratory edgewise compression tests was executed on a variety of CSIP samples (Table 1). Small-scale CSIP columns of three different heights (L1, L2, L3) were tested under uniaxial compression, and full-scale panels were subjected to compression with three different eccentricity values (e0, e1, e2). The test series aimed to produce a variety of compressive responses and failure modes to provide experimental data for the comprehensive validation of the FE model.

Table 1. CSIP samples' geometry and test setup parameters.

Sample	n	Core Type	t_f mm	t_c mm	a mm	L mm	e mm	Rotation at Supp.	L_e mm	λ
L1	2	EPS15	11	20	100	275	0	Fixed	138	8.7
L2	2	EPS21	11	20	100	645	0	Fixed	323	20.4
L3	1	EPS15	11	20	100	955	0	Free	955	60.4
e0	1	EPS21	11	152	1000	2750	0	Free	3080	37.3
e1	1	EPS21	11	152	1000	2750	27	Free	3080	37.3
e2	1	EPS21	11	152	1000	2750	54	Free	3080	37.3

Note: n = number of tested samples; t_f, t_c, a, L = specimen dimensions (Figure 1); e = eccentricity; L_e = effective length; λ = slenderness ratio.

Small-scale edgewise compression tests were performed based on the procedure given in [28]. The tests were conducted on an Instron 5569 machine (Instron, Buckinghamshire, UK) using displacement control and a continuous recording of cross-head movement, u_x, and reaction force, F_x. CSIP columns' dimensions were assumed with a gradually increasing slenderness in an attempt to produce both facing yield and global buckling failure modes. Since the original panel was too thick to observe buckling behavior in small-scale, all specimens were modified by removing the central portion of the core and using an adhesive to create columns of reduced thickness. This interference in the composite layout did not influence the compressive behavior of the samples in any noticeable way. It was noted that the EPS cores of the source panels had two different densities: 15 kg/m^3 (EPS15) and 21 kg/m^3 (EPS21). Other than that, the cross-section of all samples remained constant, and three different heights were considered (Table 1). In the case of L1 and L2 columns, support profiles with 30 mm high flanges were used (Figure 2a). The flanges were discarded for the L3 column to reduce rotational stiffness and increase slenderness (Figure 2b). A stabilizing layer of mortar was applied in all cases to ensure uniform stress distribution.

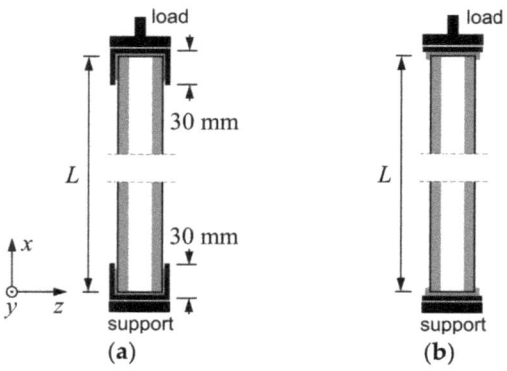

Figure 2. Schematic diagram of small-scale laboratory tests: (**a**) L1 and L2, (**b**) L3.

A full-scale CSIP compression test procedure was developed based on small-scale research and panel application guidelines provided by the producer. The test stand comprised an Instron Labtronic® 8800 structural testing system (Instron, Buckinghamshire, UK) with a NBC Elettronica TA10 load cell (N.B.C. Elettronica Group s.r.l., Delebio, Italy) and a tested panel (LS Tech-Homes S.A., Czechowice-Dziedzice, Poland) mounted horizontally in two steel profiles acting as pin supports (Figure 3). The mounting profiles were designed to warrant sufficient rigidity with 165 mm distance from a panel's edge to the pin, and a 100 mm high flange (Figure 4a). A stabilizing layer was used between the sample and the profiles for uniform stress distribution. The assembly was attached to a steel frame, that allowed for a horizontal movement of the loading profile (Figure 3b) and blocked all translations of the support profile (Figure 3c). The connection between the pin supports and the steel frame allowed to apply loads with a set eccentricity value. Three levels of eccentricity were selected to produce a substantially varied response: 0, $d/6$ (27 mm) and $d/3$ (54 mm), where d is distance between facing centroids, $d = h - t_f$. All tests were performed under displacement control with continuous recording of reaction force, F_x, horizontal displacement, u_x, using cross-head movement and a linear variable differential transformer (LVDT), vertical displacements, u_z, using LVDTs, and facing longitudinal strains, $\varepsilon_{x,f}$, using strain gauges (SG). The measuring devices were LVDTs with a precision of 0.01 mm, and tubular strain gauges with a grid length of 60 mm. Measuring devices' placement is shown in Figure 4b.

Figure 3. Full-scale CSIP test stand: (**a**) overall view, (**b**) loading assembly, (**c**) support assembly [26].

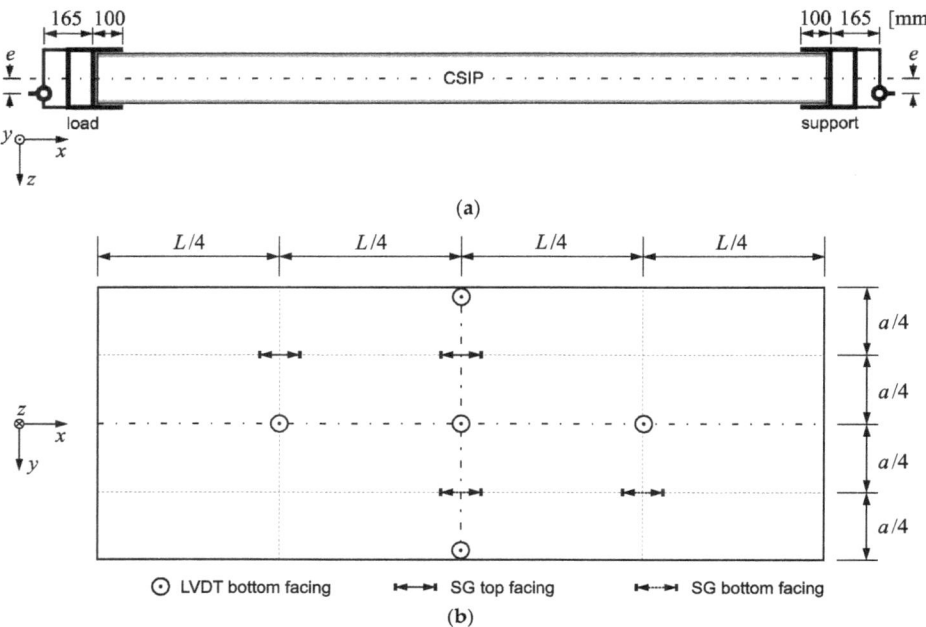

Figure 4. Schematic diagram of full-scale laboratory tests: (**a**) load and support, (**b**) positions of measuring devices.

Information considering the number of tested samples, the EPS core's density, specimen dimensions, and characteristics affecting slenderness is summarized in Table 1. The slenderness ratio was calculated from:

$$\lambda = L_e \sqrt{\frac{A_f}{J_y}} = L_e \sqrt{\frac{2t_f a}{\frac{a}{12}(h^3 - t_c^3)}} = L_e \sqrt{\frac{24 t_f}{h^3 - t_c^3}}, \quad (1)$$

where: L_e—effective length; A_f—cross-sectional area of facings; J_y—moment of inertia of facings; remaining symbols in accordance with Figure 1. The effective length was assumed as: $L_e = L/2$ for specimens with rotational constraints (L1, L2), $L_e = L$ for the L3 sample, and $L_e = L + 2 \times 165$ mm to account for mounting profiles' height for full-scale panels (e0, e1, e2).

2.2. Numerical Analysis

The proposed approach was applied to perform a numerical study, validate the FE model, and assess its viability as a design aid tool. Both small-scale and full-scale tests described in Section 2.1 were reproduced as simulations and the computational results were compared with the test data. In total, six numerical test assemblies were created using ABAQUS software [29] (version 6.11, Dassault Systèmes, Providence, RI, USA). The computations were supplemented by an author's procedure, implemented to account for dependence of material response from stress state [27].

A continuum approach was taken and all simulations were performed in plane stress state. The test samples were discretized using four-node elements with reduced integration and hourglass control. A regular geometry mesh established in a convergence study, consisting of 4 mm × 4 mm elements in the core area and 1 mm × 4 mm in the facings, was used in all cases (Figure 5). Sample dimensions and layer arrangements were adopted in accordance with Table 1. Perfect bonding was assumed between facings and core constituents since no pre-failure delamination was observed in laboratory tests.

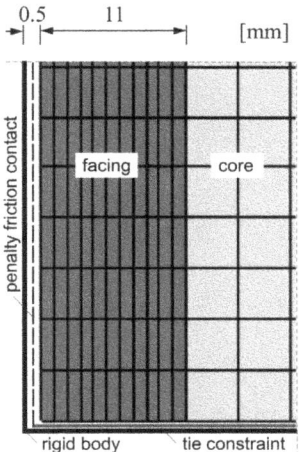

Figure 5. FE mesh section in the support area and rigid body contact interactions.

The loading and support profiles were idealized as linear rigid bodies to ensure indirect load transfer and uniform stress distribution in the analyzed samples. Two types of interactions between a specimen and a rigid body profile were defined: (1) tie constraint at the edge perpendicular to the direction of compression and (2) penalty friction with a 0.1 coefficient on the sides parallel to the direction of compression (Figure 5). Gaps of 0.5 mm between a modeled sample and a rigid profile were created on the edges with the frictional contact to reflect small clearances that were present in laboratory tests. The boundary conditions and loads were prescribed on the rigid profiles' reference points (Figure 6). The profiles' geometries were adjusted to match the experimental support conditions: flanges were used for L1 and L2 specimens (Figure 6a), no flanges were created for the L3 column (Figure 6b), and simplified shapes were generated for full-scale panels (Figure 6c).

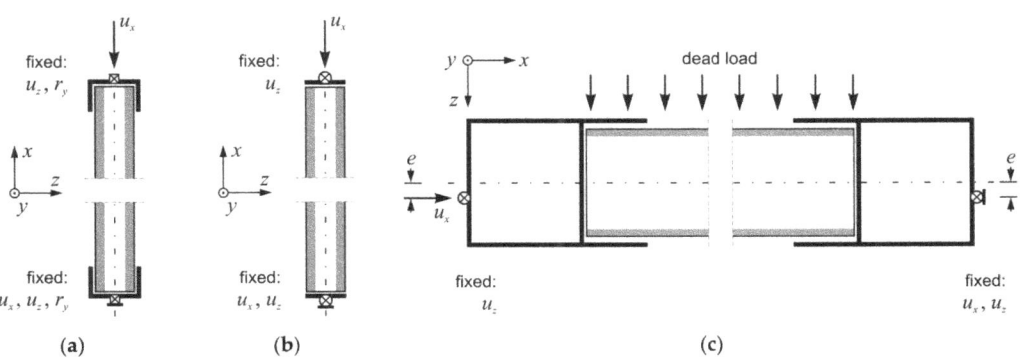

Figure 6. Boundary conditions used in simulations of (**a**) L1, L2, (**b**) L3, (**c**) e0, e1, e2 tests.

The computations were realized as geometrically nonlinear static analysis. Samples were loaded using displacement control in all simulations (Figure 6). In case of full-scale tests dead load was considered additionally, due to horizontal orientation of the specimens (Figure 6c), with mass densities of 1130 kg/m^3 for MgO board and 21 kg/m^3 for EPS [24,25]. Both core and facing constituents were defined with isotropic elastic–plastic material models. An extended Drucker–Prager model with hyperbolic yield criterion, available in the ABAQUS software [29], was applied for both constituents. MgO board property values were characterized by a substantial scatter [24,25] so instead of using averaged values two descriptions representing experimental result boundaries were defined as MgO min and MgO max. A damage initiation criterion defined in ABAQUS [29] in terms of equivalent plastic fracture strain, $\varepsilon^{pl,eq}$, and stress triaxiality factor, η, was used for failure mode prediction. Parameter values defining the material model are presented in Table 2.

Table 2. Material parameter values used in FEA [27].

Material Model	SSV	E MPa	v	σ_{pl} MPa	E_{pl} MPa	β	ψ	p_{t0} MPa	$\varepsilon^{pl,eq}$	η
MgO min	−1	2430	0.18	5.0	1205	25	10	8	1.6×10^{-3}	-3.2×10^{-1}
	1	6325	0.18	4.8	1940	25	10	8	1.4×10^{-3}	3.3×10^{-1}
MgO max	−1	3885	0.18	18.2	1130	25	10	8	3.0×10^{-4}	-3.2×10^{-1}
	1	8845	0.18	6.1	1495	25	10	8	1.3×10^{-3}	3.3×10^{-1}
EPS15	−1	5.0	0.09	0.075	0.14	1	1	0.7	1.0	−1.0
	0	6.1	0.09	0.075	3.45	1	1	0.7	8.3×10^{-3}	-1.5×10^{-2}
	1	7.2	0.09	0.135	4.08	1	1	0.7	8.0×10^{-3}	3.3×10^{-1}
EPS21	−1	6.8	0.12	0.090	0.18	2	2	0.5	1.0	−1.0
	0	9.2	0.12	0.090	5.21	2	2	0.5	1.4×10^{-2}	-1.5×10^{-2}
	1	10.5	0.12	0.160	5.94	2	2	0.5	7.1×10^{-3}	3.3×10^{-1}

Note: E = modulus of elasticity; v = Poisson's ratio; σ_{pl} = yield stress; E_{pl} = modulus of hardening; β = angle of friction; ψ = dilation angle; p_{t0} = initial hydrostatic tension strength; $\varepsilon^{pl,eq}$ = equivalent plastic fracture strain; η = stress triaxiality factor.

Computations were terminated when the damage initiation criterion variable (DICV) reached unity. All experimental samples lost their load-bearing capacity after initial failure, so reaching the criterion fulfillment was sufficient to identify the failure mode, and damage evolution analysis was not performed. A stabilization algorithm with numerical damping factor of 1×10^{-9} was used to prevent convergence issues occurring directly before failure.

An author's procedure was supplemented during computations to account for the material bimodularity effect. The procedure allowed to prescribe material property values in all integration points, depending on their stress states at the beginning of each increment in an automated manner. The algorithm generates a stress state variable (SSV) based on a following set of conditions:

$$\text{SSV} = \begin{cases} -1 & \text{when } \sigma_{max} \leq 0 \\ |\sigma_{max}/\sigma_{min}| - 1 & \text{when } |\sigma_{min}| > |\sigma_{max}| \\ 0 & \text{when } |\sigma_{min}| = |\sigma_{max}| \\ \sigma_{min}/\sigma_{max} + 1 & \text{when } |\sigma_{min}| < |\sigma_{max}| \\ 1 & \text{when } \sigma_{min} \geq 0 \end{cases} \quad (2)$$

where $\sigma_{min} = \min(\sigma_1, \sigma_2, \sigma_3)$, $\sigma_{max} = \max(\sigma_1, \sigma_2, \sigma_3)$, and $\sigma_1, \sigma_2, \sigma_3$ are the principal stress values. SSV generated from (2) describes stress state in any given integration point and can be used with most material models as a field variable, enabling definition of multiple values for a selected parameter. Characteristic states for which parameter values were defined in this finite element analysis (FEA) were SSV = −1 (compression), SSV = 0 (shear), and SSV = 1 (tension). In cases where SSV values fell between the defined characteristic states, parameter values were automatically obtained through linear interpolation. A summary of characteristic SSV values and corresponding material parameter values used in the analysis is shown in Table 2. The majority of presented data were established in course of an experimental investigation, supplemented by a literature study and a parameter identification analysis as an extensive part of previous research [25–27].

3. Results

Experimental data obtained from small- and full-scale compression tests are presented and compared with computational results obtained from the proposed FE model. Four types of results are discussed: (1) SSV distribution maps at failure initiation (only in FEA), (2) failure modes, (3) force–displacement curves and (only in full-scale) force–strain curves, (4) failure stress values.

3.1. Small-Scale Sample Tests

SSV distribution maps are presented in Figure 7. Only the MgO min variant is shown as MgO max outcomes are very similar. Both shorter samples, L1 and L2, were identified as wholly under compression (Figure 7a,b), whereas the highest column, L3, was recognized as under compression before buckling and shifted into a flexural deformation when the buckling occurred (Figure 7c). After the critical load was reached and further vertical displacement was applied, one facing remained nearly entirely under compression, and in the other substantial areas under tension appeared in the center and near the supports. All of the SSV maps depict physically reasonable behavior and exemplify that the author's procedure works as intended.

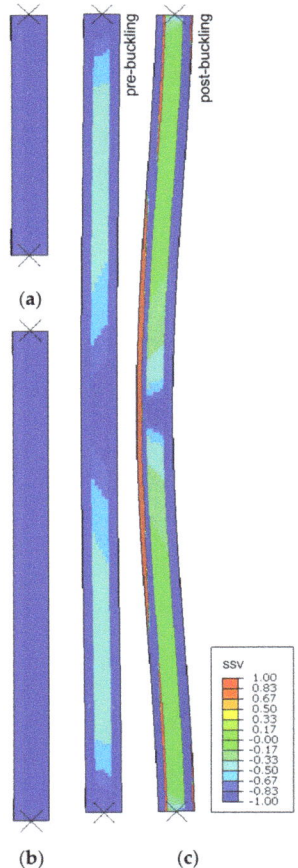

Figure 7. SSV distribution in compression simulations of (**a**) L1, (**b**) L2, and (**c**) L3 samples.

Failure modes are presented as experimental observations and DICV distributions in Figures 8–10. In both shorter samples, L1 and L2, the failure initiated on the edges of the facings, in the contact zone with the support profiles, and in both cases, the computational predictions agree with laboratory test observations (Figures 8 and 9). No flexural deformation occurred in the L1 sample throughout the experiment, neither in laboratory specimens nor in their numerical representation. A post-failure deflection occurred in the L2 sample laboratory test (Figure 9c), but since the FEA's focus was on the failure initiation, this behavior was not investigated further in simulations (Figure 9a,b). The use of the MgO min and MgO max variants did not affect the location of failure initiation points, however, for MgO min, both facings were recognized as under significant strain with DICV values close to 1 across the whole area (Figures 8a and 9a), whereas for MgO max, the peak DICV values appeared only in concentrated areas near the supports (Figures 8b and 9b). A global buckling occurred in the highest column, L3, and failure initiated in its central section (Figure 10). It can be seen that the numerical sample deformed symmetrically (Figure 10a,b), whereas the physical specimen cracked around one-third of its height (Figure 10c). The imperfection of support conditions and sample positioning in the laboratory test was the most probable cause of this difference.

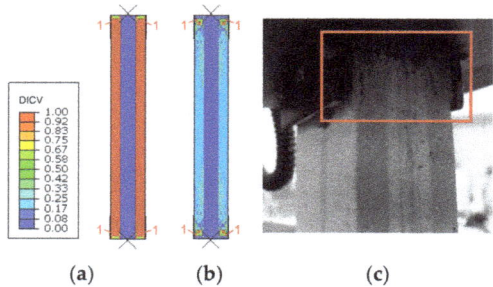

Figure 8. Comparison of failure modes in the L1 sample compression test obtained from FEA (**a**) MgO min, (**b**) MgO max variants, and (**c**) experimental observation.

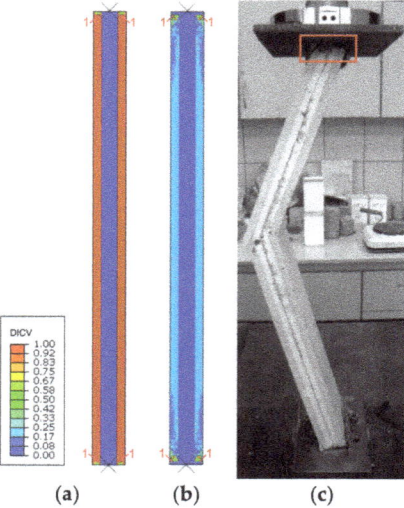

Figure 9. Comparison of failure modes in the L2 sample compression test obtained from FEA (**a**) MgO min, (**b**) MgO max variants, and (**c**) experimental observation.

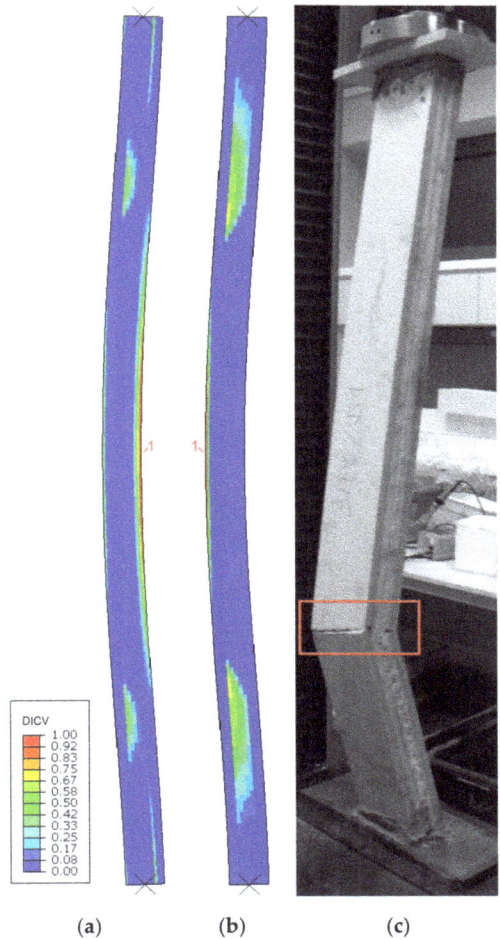

Figure 10. Comparison of failure modes in the L3 sample compression test obtained from FEA (a) MgO min, (b) MgO max variants, and (c) experimental observation.

Force–displacement, $F_x(u_x)$, experimental curves for individual samples, averaged when more than one reading was available, are compared with FE model outcomes for MgO min and MgO max variants in Figure 11. Every computational curve was matched against a corresponding experimental curve by resampling the analyzed datasets in their shared domain and calculating a coefficient of determination, r^2, used here as a measure of curve similarity [30]. The closer the r^2 value is to unity, the stronger the resemblance of the computational curve to the experimental one.

Examination of the L1 sample results shows that the material model variant outcomes encompass the experimental series quite well. The values of r^2, obtained in relation to the averaged curve, range from 0.4 to 0.7 and similarity with individual laboratory specimens is even more pronounced (Figure 11a). The L2 sample FEA plot for the MgO max variant is in very good agreement with the averaged experimental data (r^2 nearing unity) and a nearly exact match with one of the individual specimen results (Figure 11b). In the MgO min case, the plot shape diverges from experimental curves, but the predicted failure load is in a satisfactory agreement with the minimal laboratory reading.

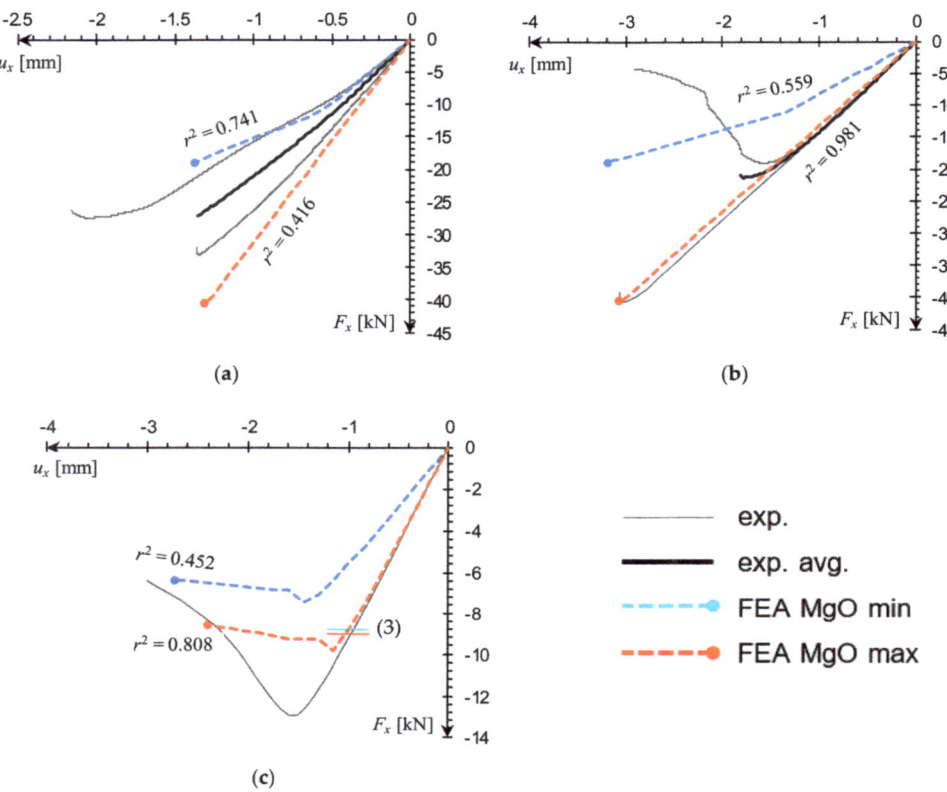

Figure 11. Comparison of small-scale sample compression $F_x(u_x)$ curves obtained from FEA against experimental data for (**a**) L1, (**b**) L2, (**c**) L3.

For the L3 column, the MgO max curve shape is very similar to the experimental plot, while the MgO min prediction is visibly underestimated (Figure 11c). It is worth to note a qualitative difference between plotlines recorded in global buckling, and the ones corresponding to failure by facing edges cracking. In the first case there is a smooth transition from the peak and into the post-critical slope (Figure 11c), while in the latter irregular drops are visible (Figure 11a,b). An equivalent buckling load was additionally estimated using a formula for sandwich columns with core shear effect, derived in [14] and adjusted to assume facing material isotropy:

$$F_x^{eq} = \frac{F_E}{1 + \frac{F_E}{A_s G_c}} = \frac{\pi^2}{L_e^2} \frac{E_f J_y}{\left(1 + \frac{\pi^2}{L_e^2} \frac{E_f J_y}{A_s G_c}\right)}, \quad (3)$$

where: F_E—critical buckling load; $A_s = a(h + t_c)/2$—shear area of the column; G_c—core shear modulus; L_e—effective length; E_f—modulus of elasticity of facings; $J_y = a(h^3 - t_c^3)/12$—moment of inertia of facings about the centroid of the panel. The L3 sample buckling load obtained for parameters listed in Table 2, ranges from 8.8 to 9.1 kN which fits within the numerical prediction (Figure 11c). Computational and analytical results are both significantly lower than the laboratory test reading. Again, this can be explained by the influence of boundary conditions. In both FEA and analytical estimation (3), a free rotation was assumed on both ends, whereas laboratory sample supports had some rotational stiffness.

The result summary is shown in Table 3, with experimental failure stress obtained from (4) assuming $e = 0$.

$$\sigma_{x,f} = \frac{F_x}{2at_f} + \frac{F_x e}{\frac{a}{12}(h^3 - t_c^3)} \frac{h}{2}, \quad (4)$$

Table 3. Summary of small-scale FEA result similarity to experimental data.

Sample	Experimental		FEA			Comparison			Failure Mode Pred.
	F_x^u kN	$\sigma_{x,f}^u$ MPa	Fac. Mat. Variant	F_x^u kN	$\sigma_{x,f}^u$ MPa	δF_x^u %	$\delta\sigma_{x,f}^u$ %	r^2	
L1	−27.08	−14.13	MgO min	−18.93	−9.04	30.1	36.0	0.741	Correct
			MgO max	−40.51	−19.02	49.6	34.6	0.416	Correct
L2	−21.36	−13.71	MgO min	−18.91	−9.05	11.5	34.0	0.559	Correct
			MgO max	−40.49	−19.03	89.5	38.8	0.981	Correct
L3	−12.91 [a]	−5.95 [a]	MgO min	−7.48 [a]	−3.47 [a]	42.3	41.7	0.452	Correct
			MgO max	−9.83 [a]	−4.98 [a]	24.1	16.3	0.808	Correct

[a] Buckling failure.

3.2. Full-Scale CSIP Tests

Dead load influence was additionally considered in the full-scale FEA since the compressed panels were oriented horizontally. Due to CSIPs' low weight, the obtained mid-span vertical deflection was less than 0.9 mm; however, it did play a notable role in the case of concentric compression test simulation. A comparison of numerical results obtained with and without dead load consideration in relation to experimental data is shown in Figure 12. It can be seen that while its influence on horizontal deflection was insignificant (Figure 12a), it caused a qualitative change in the nature of vertical deflection response (Figure 12b).

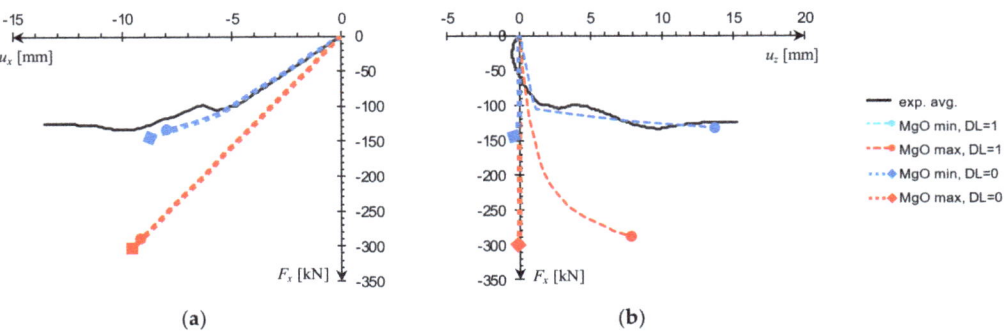

Figure 12. Dead load influence on e0 panel FEA results: (a) $F_x(u_x)$, (b) $F_x(u_z)$ at L/2.

The SSV distribution maps at failure initiation are presented in Figure 13. The facings of the e0 sample ($e = 0$) were identified as being entirely under compression, while substantial portions of the core edged towards shear (Figure 13a). The slight downward deflection of the panel is caused by the consideration of the dead load. The deflection of two remaining CSIPs is directed upwards, due the compressive load placement. There is a noticeable flexural deformation in the e1 sample ($e = 27$ mm). Both facings remain in the state of compression, but large portions of the core are recognized as approaching shear (Figure 13b). In the e2 sample ($e = 54$ mm), the flexural deformation is more pronounced

(Figure 13c). The whole bottom facing is identified as being under compression; however, tension dominates in the central part of the top facing. Portions of the core that are not under uniaxial compression continue to grow and translate into small areas staying under pure shear. The shear stress state progression in the core coincides with changes in each specimen's vertical deflection direction and intensity. It appears to be a consequence of flexural action becoming more pronounced as the eccentricity value increases. The presented results indicate a physically reasonable pattern of dependency between eccentricity value and stress state distribution in the core and facings.

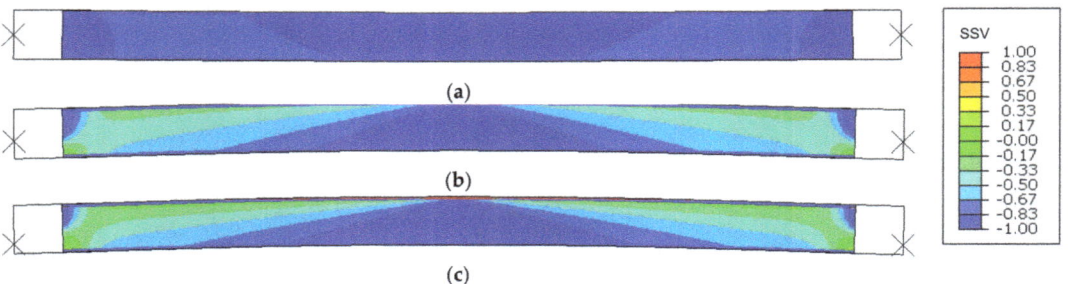

Figure 13. SSV distribution in natural-scale panel compression simulations for (**a**) e0, (**b**) e1, (**c**) e2.

A comparison between failure modes predicted in FEA and those observed in experimental tests is presented in Figures 14–16. It can be seen that the DICV values in the MgO min variants are distributed more evenly across the facing subjected to stronger compression (Figures 14a, 15a and 16a), while the MgO max variants result in maps with distinct peak values concentrated on facing edges, in the contact zone with loading profiles (Figures 14b, 15b and 16b). In all cases, the DICV distribution maps indicate failure initiation on the edge of the facing subjected to higher intensity compressive stress for both facing material variants, which results in failure of the top facing in the $e = 0$ case, and failure of the bottom facing in two remaining cases. All predicted failure locations are in agreement with experimental observations (Figures 14c, 15c and 16c).

Data plots obtained from both experimental and numerical analyses were arranged into three categories: (1) force–displacement, $F_x(u_x)$, (2) force–deflection, $F_x(u_z)$, and (3) force–strain, $F_x(\varepsilon_{x,f})$. Experimental displacements were measured with LVDTs, and experimental strains were obtained as SG readings. Computational curves were compared with corresponding experimental curves (averaged, if available, individual, if not) by calculating the coefficient of determination, r^2, for each pair of the resampled datasets [30]. The experimental test of uniaxial compression ($e = 0$) resulted in a failure load value $F_x^u = 127$ kN, which is unexpectedly low, as the corresponding results of both eccentric load tests were higher. However, the comparison with numerical outcomes showed that this result is actually within the FE model's prediction range (Figure 17a,b). Numerical force–strain curves are very close to the experimental response as well (Figure 17c,d). It is worth to note an appearance of a small loop, clearly visible in all experimental force–strain curves around $F_x = 100$ kN. A possible cause for this might be a material defect in one of the facings leading to localized damage, resulting in a premature drop of the ultimate load, and irregularities in $F_x(\varepsilon_{x,f})$ curves. This occurrence is in line with the results of previous research, which showed that compressive strength of the analyzed MgO board varies significantly from sample to sample [25,26].

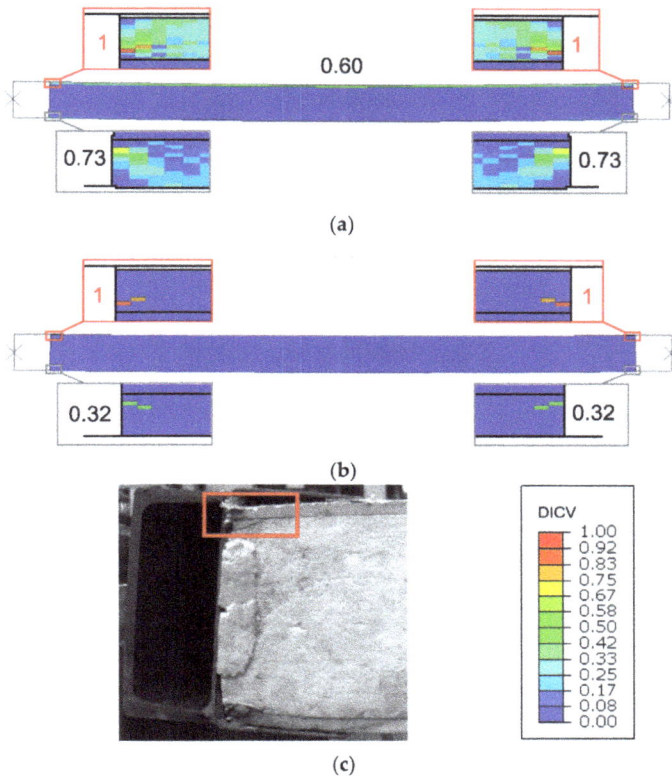

Figure 14. Comparison of failure modes in natural-scale e0 panel compression test; FEA results: (**a**) MgO min, (**b**) MgO max; (**c**) experimental observation.

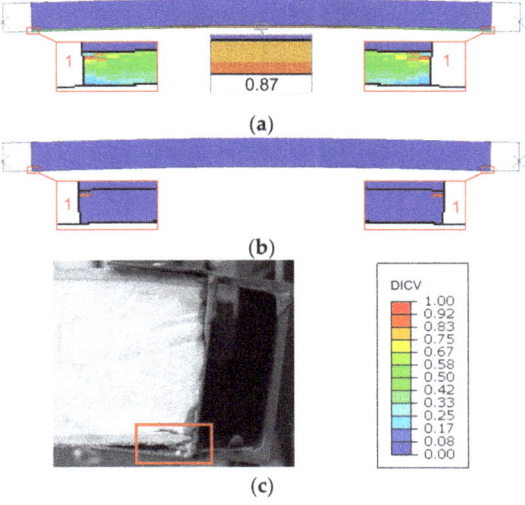

Figure 15. Comparison of failure modes in natural-scale e1 panel compression test; FEA results: (**a**) MgO min, (**b**) MgO max; (**c**) experimental observation.

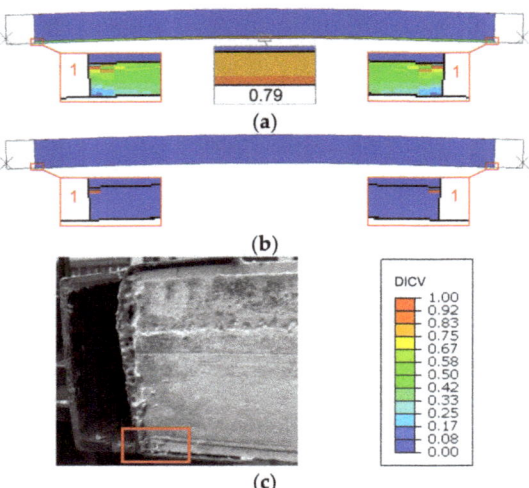

Figure 16. Comparison of failure modes in natural-scale e2 panel compression test; FEA results: (**a**) MgO min, (**b**) MgO max; (**c**) experimental observation.

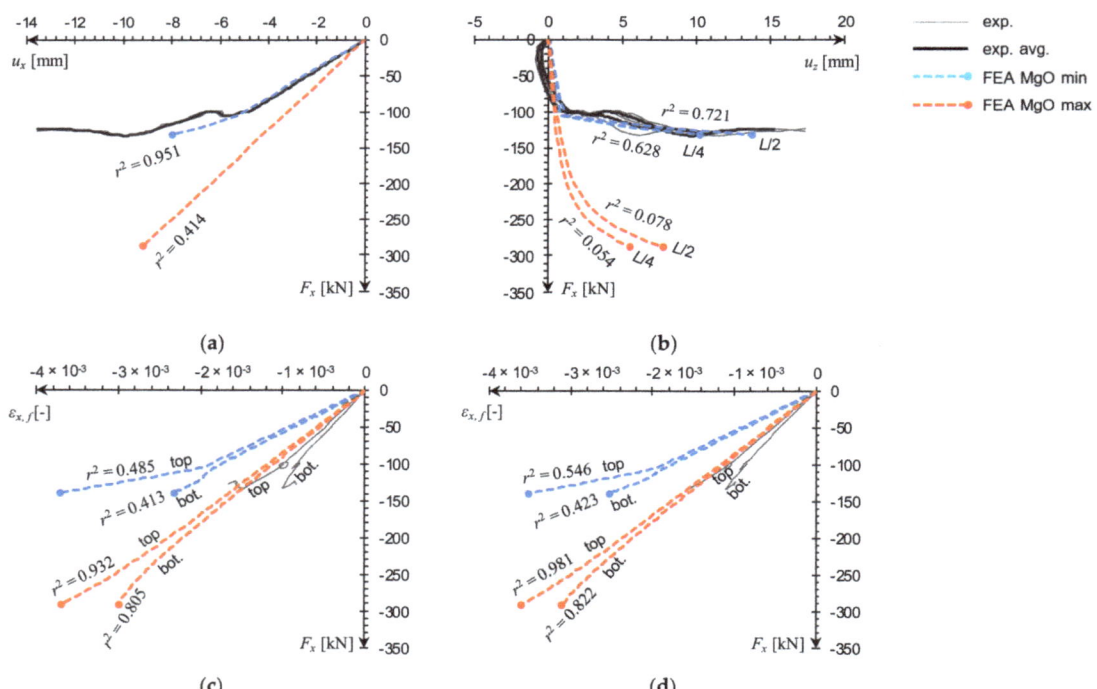

Figure 17. Comparison of natural-scale e0 panel compression test curves obtained from FEA against experimental data: (**a**) $F_x(u_x)$, (**b**) $F_x(u_z)$, (**c**) $F_x(\varepsilon_{x,f})$ at $L/2$, (**d**) $F_x(\varepsilon_{x,f})$ at $L/4$.

The results of both eccentric load tests exhibit a similar level of agreement between numerical and experimental curves. The numerical force–displacement curves place themselves concentrically around the experimental data (Figures 18a and 19a) and force–deflection curves in mid- and quarter-span are close to laboratory measurements for the MgO max outcomes (Figures 18b and 19b). It can be seen that the FE model is able to reproduce the flexural deformation quite well, with deflection in $L/2$ being slightly more accurate than in $L/4$. The distinction between $L/2$ and $L/4$ deflections is quite apparent, unlike the uniaxial load case, in which the difference is barely visible (Figure 17b). Force–strain curves obtained from the MgO max variant are in very good agreement with experimental measurements in the e1 test (Figure 18c,d) and for the bottom facing in the e2 test (Figure 19c). The laboratory measurements at the top facing in the e2 test indicate strain being negative in the initial loading stage, and transitioning into tension for the remainder of the test. Both numerical curves remained mostly in the negative strain range and transformed into tension only near the end of the simulation. This qualitative difference led to very low r^2 values, however, shapes of numerical curves still resemble experimental ones quite well.

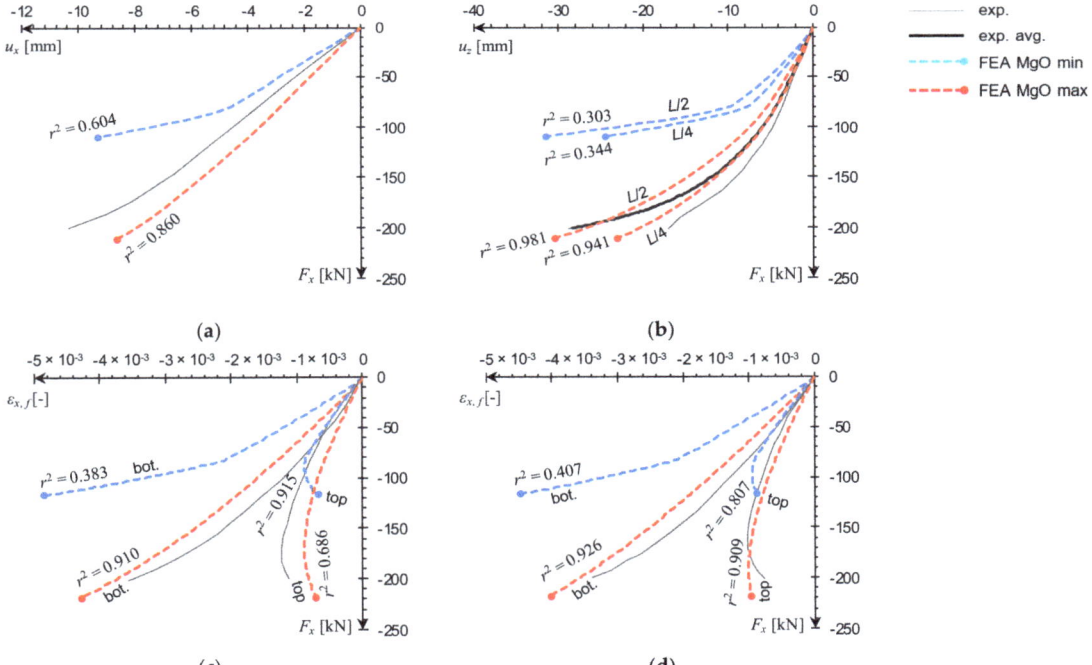

Figure 18. Comparison of natural-scale e1 panel compression test curves obtained from FEA against experimental data: (a) $F_x(u_x)$, (b) $F_x(u_z)$, (c) $F_x(\varepsilon_{x,f})$ at $L/2$, (d) $F_x(\varepsilon_{x,f})$ at $L/4$.

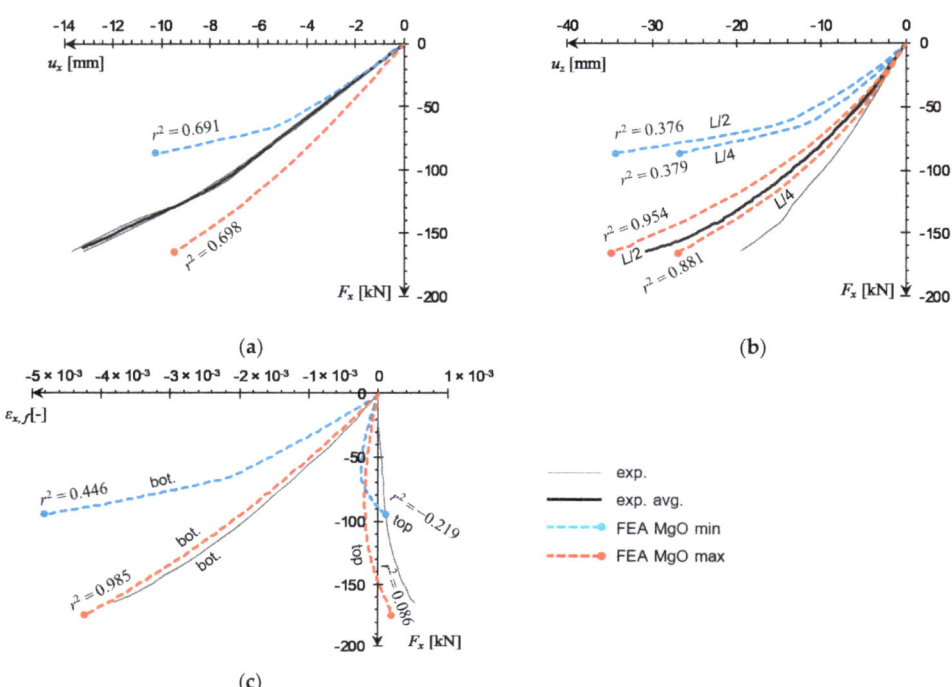

Figure 19. Comparison of natural-scale e2 panel compression test curves obtained from FEA against experimental data: (a) $F_x(u_x)$, (b) $F_x(u_z)$, (c) $F_x(\varepsilon_{x,f})$ at $L/2$.

A summary of FEA and experimental results is presented in Table 4. The experimental failure stress values were obtained from (4). The best overall numerical result accuracy was obtained for MgO min in the e0 panel and MgO max for e1 and e2 specimens.

Table 4. Summary of full-scale test results.

Sample	Experimental		Fac. Mat. Variant	FEA		Comparison		r^2 (-)							Failure Mode Pred.
	F_x^u kN	$\sigma_{x,f}^u$ MPa		F_x^u kN	$\sigma_{x,f}^u$ MPa	δF_x^u %	$\delta \sigma_{x,f}^u$ %	$F_x(u_x)$	$F_x(u_z)$ L/2	$F_x(u_z)$ L/4	$F_x(\varepsilon_{x,f})$ L/2 top	$F(\varepsilon_{x,f})$ L/2 bot	$F_x(\varepsilon_{x,f})$ L/4 top	$F_x(\varepsilon_{x,f})$ L/4 bot	
e0	−133.3	−5.77	MgO min	−133.0	−9.59	0.3	66.2	0.951	0.721	0.628	0.485	0.413	0.546	0.423	Correct
			MgO max	−288.0	−20.66	116.0	258.1	0.414	0.078	0.054	0.932	0.805	0.981	0.822	Correct
e1	−199.8	−12.35	MgO min	−109.1	−9.12	45.4	26.2	0.604	0.303	0.344	0.915	0.383	0.807	0.407	Correct
			MgO max	−211.2	−19.58	5.7	58.5	0.860	0.981	0.941	0.686	0.910	0.909	0.926	Correct
e2	−161.9	−10.10	MgO min	−86.3	−9.12	46.7	9.7	0.691	0.376	0.379	−0.219	0.446	-	-	Correct
			MgO max	−165.3	−19.59	2.1	94.0	0.698	0.954	0.881	0.086	0.985	-	-	Correct

4. Discussion

Experimental tests on samples of varying slenderness and load eccentricity values allowed to obtain a varied response for a comprehensive FE model validation. The low slenderness L1 ($\lambda = 8.7$) and L2 ($\lambda = 20.4$) samples failed by facing crushing without visible transverse deflection occurring before failure initiation. A significant increase of slenderness ($\lambda = 60.4$) in the L3 column caused a global buckling response accompanied by a pronounced flexural deformation leading to facing tensile failure. The full-scale panels' slenderness ($\lambda = 37.3$) was slightly higher than L2 samples' and no form of local or global buckling was observed. In the concentrically loaded e0 panel only a slight deflection caused by the gravitational force was noted; however, the introduction of load eccentricities in e1 ($e = 27$ mm) and e2 ($e = 54$ mm) panels resulted in pronounced transverse deflections.

In the case of the e2 test, positive strain readings were recorded in the middle of the top facing; however, the bottom facing was subjected to intensified compression and the failure initiated on its edge.

The FE model was able to reproduce all of the effects listed above and allowed to reach a better understanding of processes taking place in CSIPs subjected to edgewise compression. The SSV maps, produced as results of the stress state identification, depicted changes taking place in all simulated samples in a physically sound way.

In the low-slenderness concentrically loaded numerical samples (L1, L2, e0) the SSV maps were dominated by values equal or close to -1 throughout the whole analysis. A slight deflection in the e0 specimen was interpreted by the algorithm as a minor shift towards shear in the core, whilst, the reminder of the deformable area was considered as under compression. Material parameter values used in these simulations were heavily centered around SSV = -1 dataset. Introduction of load eccentricity in e1 and e2 cases produced visible changes in SSV maps, signaling an increased variation of material parameter selection and reflecting the intensification of flexural action. The appearance of a region under tension in the upper facing of the e2 panel test simulation was captured on the SSV map as well. All of these simulations resulted in failure located on the facing edges, in complete agreement with laboratory test observations. Failure criteria used in FEA produced very similar ultimate stress values for all facing crushing cases, both small- and full-scale. This shows that compressive failure data obtained from small-scale laboratory tests can be used in a numerical analysis of full-scale CSIPs.

The simulation of the high-slenderness L3 column is the best showcase of the proposed model's capabilities. At the initial stage, the SSV maps recognized the whole specimen as being under compression. When the reaction force reached a critical value both facings remained under compression, but a slight transverse deflection formed, accompanied by an SSV distribution shift towards shear in the core. The critical load values obtained from the model were in very good agreement both with experimental and analytical results. Further vertical displacement intensified the flexural deformation in the post-buckling range and caused a qualitative change in the SSV distribution: one facing remained under compression, substantial areas under tension appeared in the other facing, and most of the core was recognized as under shear. Throughout the whole analysis, material properties in different areas of the sample were assigned based on three different datasets corresponding to SSV = -1, SSV = 0, and SSV = 1. In the post-buckling range, the load-bearing capacity kept decreasing as the transverse deflection increased. At the final stage, failure initiation condition for the MgO board in tension was fulfilled first, resulting in a failure mode consistent with the experimental one.

The results showed that the quality of MgO board is a vital factor for computational accuracy, as it has a direct impact on how the facing material model is defined. The use of MgO min and MgO max descriptions was dictated by a substantial scatter in experimental results and it produced numerical results in form of ranges. It allowed to illustrate that even though the concentrically compressed e0 panel failed at lower load than both e1 and e2 specimens, it was actually within expectations based on small-scale MgO board strength study.

No local buckling or pre-failure delamination were observed in any of the experimental tests. Moreover, such behavior seems unlikely in the CSIP's case, due to the brittle nature of the MgO board damage. Delamination was observed only after facing cracking occurred, and the sample lost its load-bearing capacity. This effect was not in the scope of the present study; however, perfect bonding between layers can be substituted with cohesive contact to track delamination progression if needed.

The presented results showed that the proposed model was able to identify all failure types correctly and capture effects characteristic to compression of various CSIP specimens. Consideration of material bimodularity with the use of author's procedure allowed for accurate modeling of flexural action in case of high-slenderness and eccentrically loaded specimens. It is worth noting that even though the number of samples in each laboratory test was quite limited, the covered spectrum of geometries and loading conditions was wide enough to observe varied responses that were successfully reproduced in numerical simulations. Moreover, the proposed numerical approach was used with the same set of material parameter values to successfully reproduce CSIP failure under flexure [27], which further improves its reliability.

5. Conclusions

Numerical simulations of compression tests on CSIP specimens of varied slenderness, subjected to loads with different eccentricity values, were performed and compared with experimental data. The following conclusions can be drawn, based on the obtained results.

- The proposed stress state dependent numerical approach enables an automatic differentiation of elastic, plastic, and failure properties in the entire specimen throughout the whole analysis. This functionality allows accounting for flexural action caused by load eccentricity and global buckling. The presented SSV maps show that the procedure identifies stress state distribution changes in all CSIP samples in a physically sound manner.
- The numerical model identified all failure modes correctly. It was able to capture the e0 panel's premature failure and global buckling of the L3 column. A high level of curve similarity for both force–displacement and force–strain curves was obtained as well. A few slight differences were noted that can be attributed to the idealization of boundary conditions in FEA.
- The model allows for efficient macroscale calculations and to avoid detailed mesoscale modeling. The author's procedure enhances the capabilities of a homogenized approach in a straightforward manner.
- The availability of comprehensive material property information for different stress states is preferred; however, this approach allows for a simple introduction of additional data once it is obtained from experimental tests.

Based on the successful validation performed in this study, the FE model can be considered feasible for CSIP compression simulations. As the previous research [27] has proven it is suitable for flexural analysis, meaning that it can be applied to different loading conditions. Therefore, the proposed approach can be considered a reliable and robust aid for CSIP design. Moreover, the procedure can be supplemented to 3D problems where the core is discretized with continuum solid elements and the facings with structural shell elements. Further research in this direction is planned to test the approach with different kinds of CSIPs, SIPs, and other sandwich panels.

Author Contributions: Conceptualization, Ł.S., I.K. and Z.P.; methodology, Ł.S. and I.K.; software, Ł.S.; validation, Ł.S. and Z.P.; formal analysis, Ł.S. and I.K.; investigation, Ł.S.; resources, I.K. and Z.P.; data curation, Ł.S.; writing—original draft preparation, Ł.S.; writing—review and editing, I.K. and Z.P.; visualization, Z.P.; supervision, I.K.; project administration, I.K. and Z.P.; funding acquisition, Ł.S. and I.K. All authors have read and agreed to the published version of the manuscript.

Funding: The APC was funded by the Faculty of Civil and Environmental Technology, Gdańsk University of Technology, Poland.

Institutional Review Board Statement: Not applicable.

Informed Consent Statement: Not applicable.

Data Availability Statement: The data presented in this study are available on request from the corresponding author.

Acknowledgments: The authors acknowledge the access to computational software provided by the Centre of Informatics—Tricity Academic Supercomputer & networK (CI TASK) and the financial support by the Innovative Economy Operational Programme [POIG.01.04.00-24-073/09-03].

Conflicts of Interest: The authors declare no conflict of interest. The funders had no role in the design of the study; in the collection, analyses, or interpretation of data; in the writing of the manuscript, or in the decision to publish the results.

References

1. Uddin, N.; Vaidya, A.; Vaidya, U.; Pillay, S. Thermoplastic composite structural insulated panels (CSIPs) for modular panelized construction. In *Developments in Fiber-Reinforced Polymer (FRP) Composites for Civil Engineering*; Elsevier: Amsterdam, The Netherlands, 2013; pp. 302–316, ISBN 9781845691455.
2. Mohamed, M.; Hussein, R.; Abutunis, A.; Huo, Z.; Chandrashekhara, K.; Sneed, L.H. Manufacturing and Evaluation of Polyurethane Composite Structural Insulated Panels. *J. Sandw. Struct. Mater.* **2016**, *18*, 769–789. [CrossRef]
3. Chróścielewski, J.; Miśkiewicz, M.; Pyrzowski, Ł.; Rucka, M.; Sobczyk, B.; Wilde, K. Modal Properties Identification of a Novel Sandwich Footbridge—Comparison of Measured Dynamic Response and FEA. *Compos. Part B Eng.* **2018**, *151*, 245–255. [CrossRef]
4. Sharafi, P.; Nemati, S.; Samali, B.; Ghodrat, M. Development of an Innovative Modular Foam-Filled Panelized System for Rapidly Assembled Postdisaster Housing. *Buildings* **2018**, *8*, 97. [CrossRef]
5. Murčinková, Z.; Živčák, J.; Zajac, J. Experimental Study of Parameters Influencing the Damping of Particulate, Fibre-Reinforced, Hybrid, and Sandwich Composites. *Int. J. Mater. Res.* **2020**, *111*, 688–697. [CrossRef]
6. Kermani, A. Performance of Structural Insulated Panels. *Proc. Inst. Civ. Eng. Struct. Build.* **2006**, *159*, 13–19. [CrossRef]
7. Panjehpour, M. Structural Insulated Panels: State-of-the-Art. *Trends Civ. Eng. Archit.* **2018**, *3*, 336–340. [CrossRef]
8. El-Gammal, M.A.; El-alfy, A.M.H.; Mohamed, N.M. Using Magnesium Oxide Wallboard as an Alternative Building Façade Cladding Material in Modern Cairo Buildings. *J. Appl. Sci. Res.* **2012**, *8*, 2024–2032.
9. Manalo, A. Structural Behaviour of a Prefabricated Composite Wall System Made from Rigid Polyurethane Foam and Magnesium Oxide Board. *Constr. Build. Mater.* **2013**, *41*, 642–653. [CrossRef]
10. Kibert, C.J. *Sustainable Construction: Green Building Design and Delivery*, 3rd ed.; John Wiley & Sons, Inc.: Hoboken, NJ, USA, 2013; ISBN 9780470904459.
11. Choi, I.; Kim, J.; Kim, H.-R. Composite Behavior of Insulated Concrete Sandwich Wall Panels Subjected to Wind Pressure and Suction. *Materials* **2015**, *8*, 1264–1282. [CrossRef]
12. Carlsson, L.A.; Kardomateas, G.A. *Structural and Failure Mechanics of Sandwich Composites*; Solid Mechanics and Its Applications; Springer: Dordrecht, The Netherlands, 2011; Volume 121, ISBN 978-1-4020-3224-0.
13. Gdoutos, E.E.; Daniel, I.M.; Wang, K.-A. Compression Facing Wrinkling of Composite Sandwich Structures. *Mech. Mater.* **2003**, *35*, 511–522. [CrossRef]
14. Mousa, M.A.; Uddin, N. Global Buckling of Composite Structural Insulated Wall Panels. *Mater. Des.* **2011**, *32*, 766–772. [CrossRef]
15. Mousa, M.A.; Uddin, N. Structural Behavior and Modeling of Full-Scale Composite Structural Insulated Wall Panels. *Eng. Struct.* **2012**, *41*, 320–334. [CrossRef]
16. Boccaccio, A.; Casavola, C.; Lamberti, L.; Pappalettere, C. Structural Response of Polyethylene Foam-Based Sandwich Panels Subjected to Edgewise Compression. *Materials* **2013**, *6*, 4545–4564. [CrossRef] [PubMed]
17. Mathieson, H.; Fam, A. Axial Loading Tests and Simplified Modeling of Sandwich Panels with GFRP Skins and Soft Core at Various Slenderness Ratios. *J. Compos. Constr.* **2015**, *19*, 4014040. [CrossRef]
18. Abdolpour, H.; Escusa, G.; Sena-Cruz, J.M.; Valente, I.B.; Barros, J.A.O. Axial Performance of Jointed Sandwich Wall Panels. *J. Compos. Constr.* **2017**, *21*, 4017009. [CrossRef]
19. Wang, L.; Wu, Z.; Liu, W.; Wan, L. Structural Behavior of Load-Bearing Sandwich Wall Panels with GFRP Skin and a Foam-Web Core. *Sci. Eng. Compos. Mater.* **2018**, *25*, 173–188. [CrossRef]
20. Pozorska, J.; Pozorski, Z. Analysis of the Failure Mechanism of the Sandwich Panel at the Supports. *Procedia Eng.* **2017**, *177*, 168–174. [CrossRef]
21. Studziński, R.; Pozorski, Z. Experimental and Numerical Analysis of Sandwich Panels with Hybrid Core. *J. Sandw. Struct. Mater.* **2018**, *20*, 271–286. [CrossRef]
22. Vervloet, J.; Tysmans, T.; El Kadi, M.; De Munck, M.; Kapsalis, P.; Van Itterbeeck, P.; Wastiels, J.; Van Hemelrijck, D. Validation of a Numerical Bending Model for Sandwich Beams with Textile-Reinforced Cement Faces by Means of Digital Image Correlation. *Appl. Sci.* **2019**, *9*, 1253. [CrossRef]
23. Jacques, E.; Makar, J. Behaviour of Structural Insulated Panels (SIPs) Subjected to Short-Term out-of-Plane Transverse Loads. *Can. J. Civ. Eng.* **2019**, *46*, 858–869. [CrossRef]
24. Smakosz, Ł.; Tejchman, J. Evaluation of Strength, Deformability and Failure Mode of Composite Structural Insulated Panels. *Mater. Des.* **2014**, *54*, 1068–1082. [CrossRef]
25. Smakosz, Ł. Experimental and Numerical Analysis of Sandwich Panels with Magnesium-Oxide Board Facings and an Expanded Polystyrene Core. Ph.D. Thesis, Gdańsk University of Technology, Gdańsk, Poland, 2017. (In Polish)
26. Smakosz, Ł.; Kreja, I. Experimental and numerical evaluation of mechanical behaviour of composite structural insulated wall panels under edgewise compression. In *Advances in Mechanics: Theoretical, Computational and Interdisciplinary Issues*; CRC Press: Boca Raton, FL, USA, 2016; pp. 521–524.
27. Smakosz, Ł.; Kreja, I.; Pozorski, Z. Flexural Behavior of Composite Structural Insulated Panels with Magnesium Oxide Board Facings. *Arch. Civ. Mech. Eng.* **2020**, *20*, 105. [CrossRef]

28. ASTM C364/C364M-16. *Standard Test Method for Edgewise Compressive Strength of Sandwich Constructions*; ASTM International: West Conshohocken, PA, USA, 2016.
29. Dassault Systèmes Simulia Corp. *ABAQUS/CAE User's Manual*; Dassault Systèmes: Providence, RI, USA, 2011.
30. Montgomery, D.C.; Runger, G.C. *Applied Statistics and Probability for Engineers*, 3rd ed.; John Wiley & Sons, Inc.: Hoboken, NJ, USA, 2003; ISBN 0-471-20454-4.

Article

Full-Field Measurements in the Edge Crush Test of a Corrugated Board—Analytical and Numerical Predictive Models

Tomasz Garbowski [1], Jakub Krzysztof Grabski [2,*] and Aleksander Marek [3]

[1] Department of Biosystems Engineering, Poznan University of Life Sciences, Wojska Polskiego 50, 60-627 Poznań, Poland; tomasz.garbowski@up.poznan.pl
[2] Institute of Applied Mechanics, Poznan University of Technology, Jana Pawła II 24, 60-965 Poznań, Poland
[3] Faculty of Engineering and Physical Sciences, University of Southampton, Highfield SO171BJ, UK; a.marek@soton.ac.uk
* Correspondence: jakub.grabski@put.poznan.pl

Abstract: This article focuses on the derivation of simplified predictive models for the identification of the overall compressive stiffness and strength of corrugated cardboards. As a representative example an unsymmetrical 5-ply sample (with E and B flute) was used in this study. In order to exclude unreliable displacement measurement in the standard edge crush test, virtual strain gauges were used. Video extensometry was employed to collect measurements from the outer surfaces of the sample on both sides. Additional data allowed real force-displacement curves to be obtained, which were used in the validation procedure. To emulate the experimental results, besides a simple analytical model, a 3D numerical model fully reflecting the geometry of the corrugated board, based on the finite elements method was also built. In both cases good agreement between the experimental results and the analytical and numerical calculations was observed. This proved that the proposed analytical model can be successfully used to determine the overall stiffness and compressive strength of corrugated board, provided that the geometry and properties of all the layers of the board are known. The simple model presented in this work enables quick and reliable design and prototyping of new assemblies without the need to manufacture them.

Keywords: corrugated cardboard; edge crush test; orthotropic elasticity; digital image correlation

Citation: Garbowski, T.; Grabski, J.K.; Marek, A. Full-Field Measurements in the Edge Crush Test of a Corrugated Board—Analytical and Numerical Predictive Models. *Materials* **2021**, *14*, 2840. https://doi.org/10.3390/ma14112840

Academic Editor: Enrique Casarejos

Received: 28 April 2021
Accepted: 21 May 2021
Published: 26 May 2021

Publisher's Note: MDPI stays neutral with regard to jurisdictional claims in published maps and institutional affiliations.

Copyright: © 2021 by the authors. Licensee MDPI, Basel, Switzerland. This article is an open access article distributed under the terms and conditions of the Creative Commons Attribution (CC BY) license (https://creativecommons.org/licenses/by/4.0/).

1. Introduction

Prediction of material strength is an important issue for designing and manufacturing of products made from corrugated paperboard. In the literature, authors have applied many different approaches for strength investigations of corrugated sandwich structures, including paperboard, i.e., analytical [1,2], numerical [3–7], or analytical-numerical [8–10] methods. Recently, Kmita-Fudalej et al. presented an analytical prediction of the strength of honeycomb paperboard based on the mechanical properties of the paper used and the geometrical features of the investigated structure [11]. Park et al. performed numerical simulation using the finite element method (FEM) in order to estimate the strength in the edge crush test (ECT) [12]. Recently, artificial intelligence methods have become popular, e.g., artificial neural networks, for prediction of strength of composite materials, including sandwich structures [13]. An alternative to the numerical prediction of the strength of corrugated board is its experimental measurement.

To perform numerical simulations, detailed knowledge of the material properties of the constituents is required. This is however a challenging task, due to the inherent anisotropy of paper-based materials. As a result, physical testing of corrugated paperboard is much more popular within the industry.

A number of typical tests to characterize mechanical properties of corrugated paperboard have been developed to standardize the process. The compressive strength is investigated by performing the ECT, in which the loading is applied perpendicularly to the axis of the flutes. In the bending test (BNT), four-point bending test is performed, in which there are two supports at the bottom of the paperboard and two equal forces acting on the sample from the opposite side. The shear stiffness test (SST) is carried out by applying a pair of forces on the opposite corners (two others are supported), causing the cross-section of the paperboard to be twisted. The torsional stiffness test (TST) is conducted by twisting a sample in both directions. Other tests of the paperboard are namely bursting and humidity tests. In order to investigate the strength of the whole container made from the corrugated paperboard, the box compressive test (BCT) is carried out [14].

Analytical and numerical predictive models of the strength obtained in the ECT are considered in this paper. The ECT is standardized; there are four different methods of the ECT described in the standards. One of the main features that distinguish these tests is the shape of the specimens. These methods are as follows: edge-clamping method [15], neck-down method [16], rectangular test specimen method [16–18], and edge-reinforced method [19,20]. Here, the rectangular test specimen method with a specimen with dimensions of 100 mm $\times$ 25 mm was used. More details about these standards of the ECT can be found in [21].

As a verification method for the results obtained from analytical and numerical approaches, presented in this study, a video extensometry technique was used, where pairs of points are tracked across images taken at various levels of loading and their relative distance is measured. This is a similar, but simpler approach to digital image correlation (DIC), which is an advanced full-field non-contact optical method of measurement that is recently becoming popular in the area of experimental mechanics, due to its very high accuracy. However, application of those techniques for investigation of the paperboard strength is rather limited in the literature. Hägglund et al. investigated thickness changes during the ECT in the corrugated paperboard using the DIC [22]. The authors examined both damage and undamaged panels. In the series of papers [23–25], Viguié and collaborators employed the DIC technique in order to study the strain and stress fields of paperboard panels during the box compression test. Borgqvist et al. proposed a distortional hardening plasticity model for paperboard [26]. The authors introduced a yield surface described by multiple hardening variables and showed that they can be obtained from simple uniaxial experiments. The results obtained from the model were compared with the results obtained from experiments using DIC. Cocchetti et al. investigated identification of material parameters of anisotropic elastic-plastic material models in the case of foils [27,28]. The authors considered paperboards and laminates for liquid containers. They performed combined compression and bending tests using DIC. On the other hand, numerical simulations using the FEM were used in a direct analysis. The parameters of the model were obtained from an inverse analysis, employing results of the experiment and simulations. Considine used DIC and the virtual fields method (VFM) technique to identify general anisotropy parameters of a filter paper and a paperboard [29]. Åslund and collaborators investigated the failure mechanism of the corrugated sandwich panels during the ECT using the detailed finite element method and compared it with the measurements obtained using DIC [30]. Zappa et al. investigated inflation of the paperboard composites using in beverage packaging using the DIC technique [31]. Recently, Fadiji et al. employed DIC to analyze a paperboard box with ventilation holes under compression loading [32]. In most of the investigations mentioned above, samples of 3-ply corrugated cardboards were examined. In this study, an optical method was employed to verify the analytical and numerical results in the ECT analysis of double-wall corrugated cardboard, i.e., 5-ply corrugated cardboard samples with E and B flutes.

Here, analytical and numerical models are proposed to identify paperboard stiffness and to predict the compressive strength of the corrugated paperboard. Optical extensometry is employed to validate the obtained results. Both the analytical and numerical approaches achieved accurate results.

2. Materials and Methods

2.1. Corrugated Cardboard

In the research, 5-layer corrugated cardboard named 5EB650C3, produced in Aquila Września—the Polish branch of the VPK Group—was used. This grade consists of an external coated layer of a white recycled base liner board with a grammage of 140 g/m². Both corrugated layers (E and B flutes) and the flat layer in between are made from lightweight recycled fluting WB with a grammage of 100 g/m². As an internal layer again the white test liner with a grammage of 120 g/m² was used. The arrangement of individual layers and the geometry of the cardboard cross-section are shown in Figure 1.

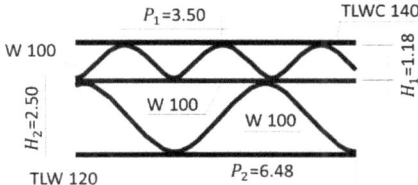

Figure 1. The cross section of 5EB650C3 corrugated board.

The geometrical features of both corrugated layers (flutes) are presented in Table 1. Take-up ratio is defined as the ratio of the length of the non-fluted corrugated medium to the length of the fluted web. For the correct numerical modeling of corrugated layers, a sine-shaped corrugated layer is usually considered. This however is an approximation to the real shape of the flute produced. The theoretical take-up factors can be computed from the formula:

$$\alpha = \frac{1}{P} \int_0^P \sqrt{1 + \left(\pi \frac{H}{P} \cos\left(\frac{2\pi x}{P}\right)\right)^2} \, dx, \qquad (1)$$

where H is the height, P denotes the pitch. Thus, for the E-flute one can obtain $\alpha = 1.239$, and for the B-flute, $\alpha = 1.302$, which are very close to the actual values given in Table 1. The above formula results from a sine-like shape assumption and is equal to the length of the fluting divided by the flute pitch (wave period).

Table 1. The geometrical features of both corrugated layers of 5EB650C3.

Wave (Flute)	Pitch [mm]	Height [mm]	Take-Up Ratio [–]
E	3.50	1.18	1.242
B	6.48	2.5	1.315

Since corrugated cardboard consists of several layers of paperboard, made of cellulose fibers, its mechanical properties depend on the fiber orientation of its components. In paperboard, two main, mutually perpendicular directions can be determined. First, along the fiber orientation, which is called Machine Direction (MD). Material is both stiffer and stronger in this direction. The second is perpendicular to the MD and is called Cross Direction (CD). The paper-forming fibers make the corrugated board also an orthotropic material, in which the MD is along the waves (see Figure 2). The corrugated layers thus compensate through take-up factor for the weaker mechanical performance of the cardboard in the CD.

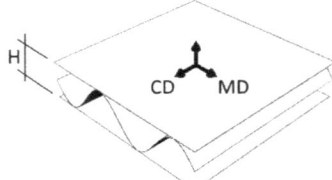

Figure 2. The material orientation in corrugated board.

Specified by the producer, the compressive strength, ECT of the combined corrugated board (5EB650C3) in CD is 7.6 kN/m ($\pm$10%), while its overall thickness H is 4.3 mm ($\pm$0.2 mm).

The material properties of the individual layers are presented in Table 2. The SCT_{CD} value represents a compressive strength in CD from the short-span compression test according to DIN EN ISO 3037 [18].

Table 2. The mechanical properties of individual layers of 5EB650C3.

Layer Name	Thickness [μm]	E_{MD} [kN/m]	E_{CD} [kN/m]	SCT_{CD} [kN/m]
TLWC 140	180	725	323	2.32
W 100	160	886	328	1.76
TLW 120	170	907	313	1.81

2.2. Measurements

A typical test to determine the compressive strength of corrugated board is the ECT (according to the FEFCO standard DIN EN ISO 3037 [17,18]), in which a specimen that is 100 mm long and 25 mm high (see Figure 3) is loaded along its height between two rigid plates (see Figure 4a). The samples should be cut on a special cutter with the use of one-sided ground blades to maintain the parallelism of the cut edges. According to the standard, the air condition should be controlled, and the test should be carried out at 23 °C and 50% relative humidity. All the ECT tests were performed in a controlled environment as standard on an FEMat ECT/FCT laboratory apparatus (FEMat Sp. z o. o., Poznan, Poland) [33], see Figure 4b.

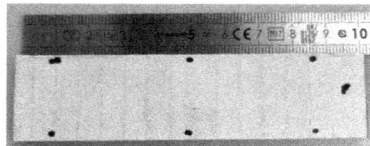

Figure 3. The sample for the edge crush test.

The ECT is used explicitly to determine the compressive strength of the corrugated board in CD. Although most testing machines allow the recording of curves from the entire test, it is not possible to use these curves for a reliable determination of e.g., compression stiffness. The measured displacements do not represent the elastic deformation of the specimen as they are significantly affected by the clearance and susceptibility on the crosshead, local pressure on sample unevenness (edge effects), etc. Therefore, non-contact optical techniques are required to reliably measure displacements (deformations or strains). Additionally a measure without direct contact does not influence the measure. In measurements with contact (e.g., traditional extensometers), noise is introduced into the measurement and thus the actual measured values are distorted.

Figure 4. Edge crush test: (**a**) Universal Testing Machine (Instron 5569); (**b**) FEMAT lab. device.

2.3. Optical Measurements of Sample Deformation

In this study, the specimen was also tested using optical extensometry. Two cameras were used to track the deformation of both faces to account for the out-of-plane bending produced by the non-symmetrical section. The front face is the higher flute, while the back face is the lower flute of the paperboard, see Figure 5a. Each of the two faces of the specimen was marked with three sets of dots in order to enable point tracking. In Figure 5b, one can observe the sets of points on one of these faces. The single set of points, marked in this figure by squares connected by a dotted line, is a virtual extensometer, for which the extension is observed during the test. The video extensometry was performed using MatchID DIC platform (v. 2020.2.0, MatchID, Ghent, Belgium). The specimen was sandwiched between two platens and aligned using 3D printed L-brackets.

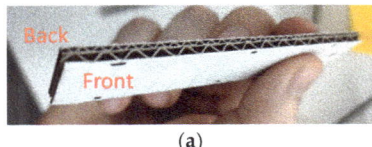
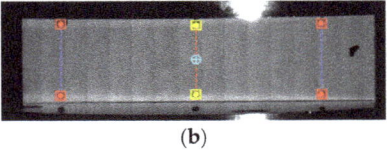

Figure 5. Specimen: (**a**) back and front face of the specimen; (**b**) virtual extensometers on the front face of the specimen.

Two 5 MPix cameras (Manta G504-b, Allied Vision, Allied Vision, Stadtroda, Germany) were used to record grey scale images during the test, see Figure 6. Cameras were calibrated using MatchID calibration plate (MatchID, Ghent, Belgium) to obtain the pixel to mm conversion rate of ~50 µm/pix. The specimen was manually pre-loaded to a very small load (15 N) to make sure both plates were in contact. After that the measured load cell and displacement were zeroed and the supporting L-brackets removed. Once the cameras started recording, the sample was loaded using displacement control at 0.5 mm/min. The load and the crosshead displacement were synchronized with the cameras. The virtual extensometers were used to measure displacement between the marked points. They were placed roughly 2 mm away from the loading edge in order to avoid measuring additional phenomena occurring in the surrounds of the loading edge. The accuracy of the measurement was estimated using a set of 25 static images (without any movement); standard deviation of the measured elongation was e4valuated to be 4 µm, which can be considered the level of uncertainty. Optical displacements were averaged for each face and compared against the crosshead displacement.

(a)

(b)

Figure 6. Setup of the optical measurements: (**a**) camera recording the front face; (**b**) camera recording the back face.

2.4. Predictive Models

Two different models were used to estimate the compressive strength of the corrugated board in the CD: (a) a simplified analytical model and (b) a fully detailed 3D numerical model. The former model is based on an iterative procedure, while the latter model is based on the FEM.

The simplified estimation procedure proposed here consists of a simple analytical model and uses the basic constitutive parameters of the individual i-th layer, namely: SCT_{CD}^i, compressive strength in CD and $\overline{E}_{CD}^i$, stiffness index in CD. As in some cases single layer instability may occur before plasticity activation, the critical load should be calculated from the formula [8–10]:

$$P_{cr}^i = \frac{\pi^2}{b_i^2} \frac{t_i^2}{12} \sqrt{E_{CD}^i E_{MD}^i} \left(\frac{mb_i}{L} + \frac{L}{mb_i} \right)^2, \qquad (2)$$

where, b_i is the width of the separated plate and is related to a pitch or a half-wave length of the flute (see Figure 7); t_i is the i-th board thickness; E_{CD}^i is the stiffness index in CD; E_{MD}^i is the stiffness index in MD; L is the sample height (always equal 25 mm); m is the number of half-waves for which P_{cr}^i reaches the minimum.

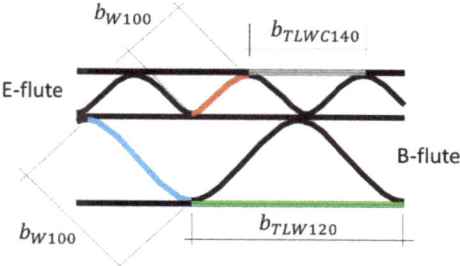

Figure 7. Width of the i-th layer.

The deformation corresponding to the maximum load can be calculated from Hooke's law considering the stiffness in the CD direction, sample height, L, and the compressive strength or critical load, whichever occurs first (see Figure 8). So for the i-th layer the relation takes the form:

$$u_0^i = \frac{p_{max}^i}{E_{CD}^i} L, \qquad (3)$$

where:

$$p_{max}^i = \min\left(SCT_{CD}^i, P_{cr}^i\right). \qquad (4)$$

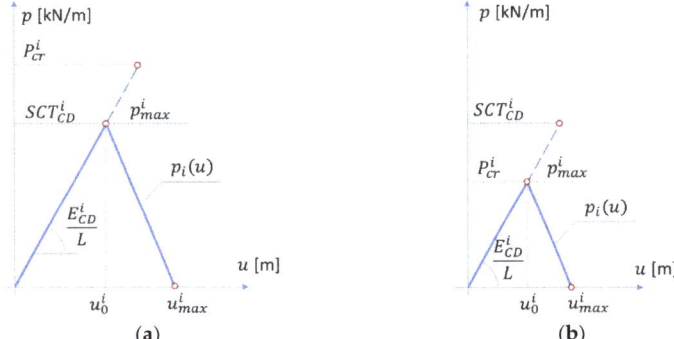

Figure 8. Compressive strength vs. deformation. (**a**) the case where the SCT is lower than the critical load of the i-th layer; (**b**) the case where the critical load is lower than the SCT of the i-th layer.

If it is assumed that the failure once initiated successively progresses over time and, for example, for the value of u_{max}^i, the compression resistance of the i-th layer reaches zero, we obtain a bilinear curve describing the constitutive behavior of a single panel. It was assumed on the basis of experimental observations, that the ultimate deformation equals:

$$u_{max}^i = \frac{3}{2} u_0^i. \qquad (5)$$

Now, the ECT value can be obtained by simple summation over all layers including the take-up ratio. The displacement-dependent formula for ECT is therefore:

$$ECT(u) = \sum_{i=1}^{n} p_i(u)\, \alpha_i, \qquad (6)$$

where α_i is the take-up factor of the corrugated layers calculated by Equation (1) or taken from Table 1.

The second model was built in the Abaqus Unified FEA® [34] software (version 2020, Dassault Systemes SIMULIA Corp., Johnston, IA, USA), which uses a linear elastic orthotropic material model with von Mises plasticity. Shell elements used in the calculations are quadrilaterals with four nodes, named S4, which use the full integration scheme with built-in techniques to prevent locking phenomena. The approximate size of a single element was 1 mm, which gives in total 17,825 elements, 18,668 nodes, and 112,008 degrees of freedom. In order to provide all the required material constants, the empirical equations provided by Baum [35] were used. First the E_{MD}^i and E_{CD}^i stiffness indexes (given in Table 2) were transformed to stiffness coefficients E_1^i and E_2^i, respectively, by the equation:

$$E_1^i = \frac{E_{MD}^i}{t_i}, \quad E_2^i = \frac{E_{CD}^i}{t_i}. \qquad (7)$$

The in-plane shear stiffness can be computed from the empirical formula [35]:

$$G_{12}^i = 0.387\sqrt{E_1^i E_2^i}. \tag{8}$$

The Poisson ratio in the 1–2 plane can be assumed from [35] as:

$$\nu_{12}^i = 0.293\sqrt{\frac{E_1^i}{E_2^i}}. \tag{9}$$

Both transversal stiffnesses were computed using the approximation from [36]:

$$G_{13}^i = \frac{E_1^i}{55}, \quad G_{23}^i = \frac{E_2^i}{35}. \tag{10}$$

The compressive strength can be determined by dividing the SCT value in the CD by the appropriate thickness of a single i-th layer.

$$\sigma_0^i = \frac{SCT_{CD}^i}{t_i}. \tag{11}$$

All the computed values of the constitutive parameters for each layer are summarized in Table 3.

Table 3. The mechanical properties of individual layers of 5EB650C3.

Layer Name	E_1 [MPa]	E_2 [MPa]	ν_{12} [–]	G_{12} [MPa]	G_{13} [MPa]	G_{23} [MPa]
TLW 120	5669	2050	0.176	1319	103	59
W 100	5537	2050	0.209	1112	101	59
TLWC 140	4028	1794	0.196	1040	73	51

3. Results

3.1. Edge Crush Test Results

Here, first the results of the edge crush tests are presented. The dispersion of the obtained results is due to the heterogeneity of the corrugated cardboard samples, including local imperfections, lack of parallelism of the sample edges, local detachment of the corrugated layers, etc. Although the specimen is held by steel blocks during the test to prevent global out-of-plane buckling, local buckling on the outer surfaces of the specimen still could be observed. A slight bend, which is the result of the nonsymmetric cross-section of the sample, also could be observed.

It is worth noting that the elastic stiffness, which could be determined from the linear part of the experimental curves, is not the real stiffness because it includes all the effects of the crossbar compliance and the sample imperfections, especially visible in the initial part of the curves (see Figure 9).

3.2. Optical Measurements Results

Figure 10 presents the results obtained from the video extensometry measurements. In Figure 10a, one can observe the extension in terms of the image number from the virtual extensometers on the front face (on the left side, at the center and on the right side), on the back face (on the left side, at the center and on the right side) and on the crosshead. In Figure 10b, the applied force is shown in terms of the image number. The maximum absolute value of the applied force was approximately 703 N, while the mean value obtained from the ECT measurements was equal to 751 N. However, it should be noted that a pre-load of 15 N was applied and after that the measurements started from zero value. Here, the loading rate (0.5 mm/min) was significantly slower than the typical

10 mm/min due to the limited frame rate of the cameras, which reduces the measured maximum load through relaxation.

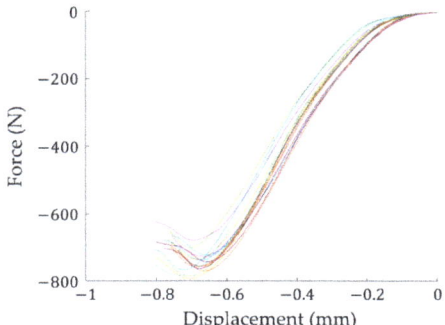

Figure 9. Edge crush test results (on the FEMat ECT/FCT laboratory apparatus).

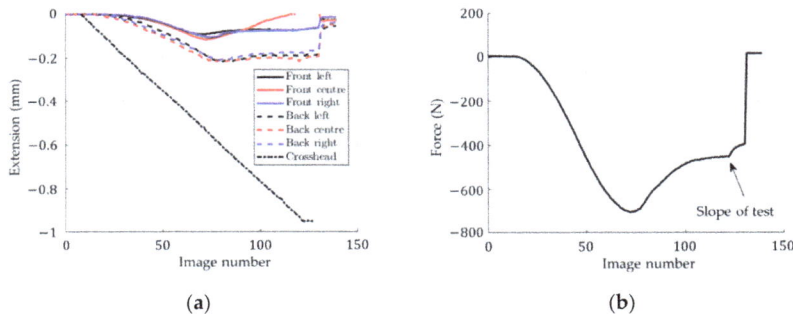

Figure 10. Optical measurements results: (**a**) extension, (**b**) applied force.

3.3. Predictive Analytical Model

In the predictive analytical model, constitutive curves are first constructed based on the specific material parameters of the individual layers (see Table 2), based on Equations (2)–(6). The results of the buckling analysis and other parameters necessary to build the constitutive curves are summarized in Table 4.

Table 4. The mechanical properties of individual layers of 5EB650C3.

Layer Name	b (mm)	L (m)	SCT_{CD} (kN/m)	P_{cr} (kN/m)
TLWC 140	3.50	25	2.32	4.212
W 100 (E)	2.17	25	1.76	9.573
W 100	-	25	1.76	-
W 100 (B)	4.26	25	1.76	2.444
TLW 120	6.48	25	1.81	1.237

Figure 11a shows an example of the eigenmode of the individual separated i-th plate, calculated as simply supported plate loaded along the L dimension. Figure 11b shows all constitutive curves, where the maximum value of the compressive load is equal to SCT_{CD} for the TLWC140 layer and all W100 layers, while for the TLW120 layer it is the critical load value due to the dimension b_i (see Equation (2)), which is the largest in this case.

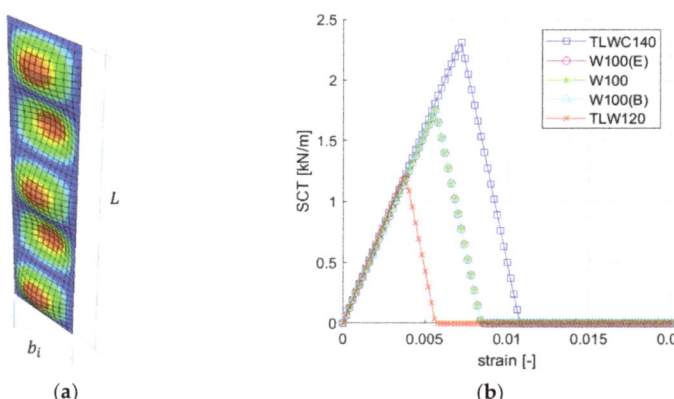

Figure 11. Analytical model: (**a**) Visualization of first buckling mode for the *i*-th layer; (**b**) constitutive relationships for all corrugated board layers.

3.4. Predictive Numerical Model

In order to correctly calculate the compressive strength using the FEM in the simulation of the ECT, two steps of the numerical procedure had to be used, namely: (1) perturbation analysis, where the eigenmode and eigenvector were calculated, and (2) geometric and material nonlinear iterative analysis, in which geometric imperfections are introduced based on the calculated eigenvalues and eigenvectors from the first analysis.

The first perturbation analysis was only to find the initial shape imperfection in the numerical model of the ECT sample, which was later entered as the first scaled eigenvector of the model (see Figure 12) in the Abaqus Unified FEA® software. This imperfect geometry was used in nonlinear analysis where the standard Newton–Raphson algorithm was used to find convergence in the subsequent iterations.

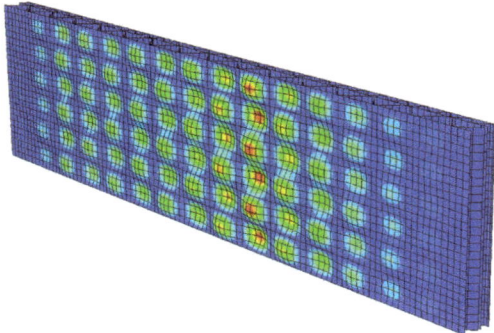

Figure 12. Numerical model. Visualization of the first buckling mode for the whole corrugated board (front view).

The equivalent plastic strains on both sides of the ECT sample model in the last iteration are shown in Figure 13, where the plasticized region is marked in a dark red color.

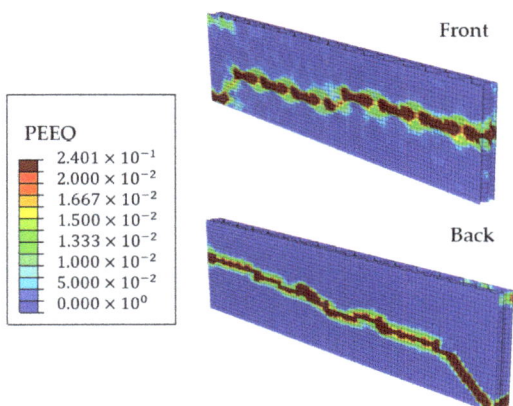

Figure 13. Equivalent plastic strains on both sides of the ECT sample in the last iteration of the nonlinear analysis.

The displacements on both sides of the ECT sample in the last iteration are shown in Figure 14, where the unloaded part of the sample is shown in blue.

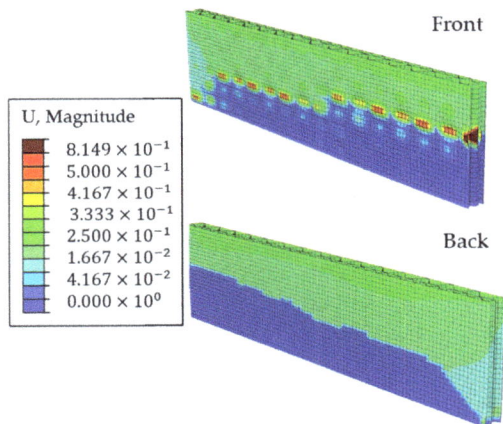

Figure 14. Displacements on both sides of the ECT sample in the last iteration of the nonlinear analysis.

Figures 13 and 14 clearly show that the induced imperfections cause the first-mode buckling deformation of the sample and eventually the sample is damaged at about half its height. Numerical observations confirmed the experimental results, in which the correct failure mode in the ECT is the crush (crease) of the sample between its span, not the crush at the edges.

3.5. Compilation of All Results

Experimental results based on non-contact full-field displacement measurements and crosshead displacement (see Figure 15a) are presented here together with the results from various predictive models. Figure 15b shows the force-displacement curve obtained from a numerical full detailed 3D FE model.

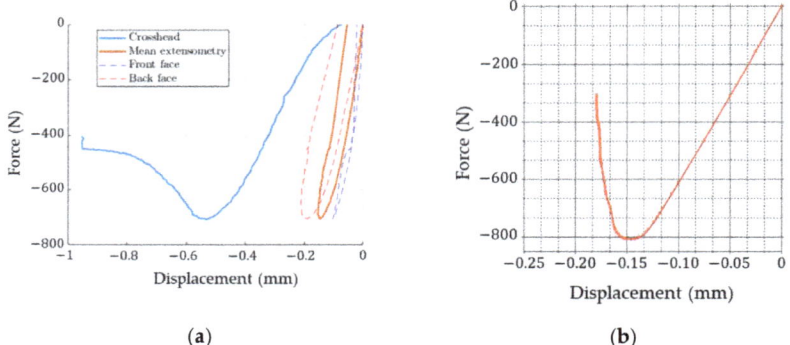

Figure 15. Experimental and numerical results: (**a**) load–displacement curves from experimental studies; (**b**) load–displacement curves from numerical studies.

Figure 16 presents the summary of all results including the lower and upper bound of the analytical solutions. The lower bound can be computed by the formula:

$$P_{min} = \epsilon_{min} \sum_{i=1}^{n} E_{CD}^{i} \alpha_i, \tag{12}$$

where minimal strain, ϵ_{min} equals:

$$\epsilon_{min} = \min\left(\frac{p_{max}^{i}}{E_{CD}^{i}}\right), \tag{13}$$

while the upper bound can be obtained from the equation:

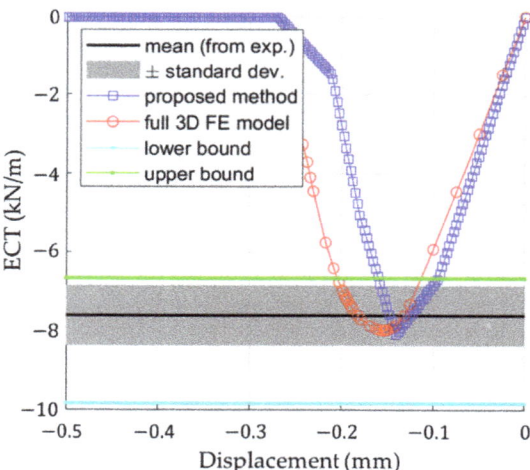

Figure 16. Summary of all results.

Figure 16 also shows the results of the analytical method proposed here, as well as the experimental data (mean value ± one standard deviation) and results from the numerical validation model. Table 5 summarizes all measured and computed stiffnesses and compressive strengths in CD of the corrugated board 5EB650C3.

Table 5. The measured/calculated compressive stiffness and strength in CD of the corrugated board 5EB650C3.

Test/Model	ECT_{CD} (kN/m)	E_{CD} (kN/m)
Producer specification	7.60	-
FEMat—crosshead	7.51	1991
Instron—crosshead	7.03	2142
Instron—opt. extensometry	7.03	6442
Numerical model	7.94	5920
Analytical model	8.08	7063

4. Discussion

The first and main observation (conclusion) to be drawn from this study is that the overall stiffness of a corrugated board sample cannot be determined from a typical ECT. This is clearly seen in Figures 10 and 15a, where the slope of the force-displacement curve (with displacement measurement from the crosshead) gives about a three times less rigid response than when the displacement measurement is based on optical extensometry (Figure 15a). The use of non-contact measurement techniques makes it possible to correctly measure the displacements on the outer surfaces of the sample (excluding the edge areas of the sample and crosshead compliance). Therefore, in order to determine the stiffness of the corrugated board in the CD in the ECT, virtual extensometers are required.

The results summarized in Table 5 show that the analytical and numerical models give very similar values for the compressive stiffness compared to the measurement based on optical extensometry, while the stiffness value calculated from the displacements of the crossbars (on both machines) is three times smaller and cannot be treated as a representative value. The difference between the measured/calculated compressive stiffness does not exceed 10%. The compressive strength measured and calculated using both: (a) the numerical model and (b) the proposed analytical method differs by about 5% from the stated value of 7.6 kN/m. The results obtained with the analytical model are slightly higher than the measured values (stiffness: 9%, compressive strength: 6%). The full 3D FE model gives a slightly higher value of compressive strength (4.5%) and a slightly lower value of compressive stiffness (8%), which may be the result of introduced imperfections.

The second conclusion is that the proposed analytical formula for estimating stiffness and compressive strength appears to be very promising. It has the same accuracy as a full detailed 3D FE model (see Figures 15b and 16) while being easier to implement and much faster to operate. Both analytical and numerical models can easily capture the compressive strength, ECT, and the overall stiffness of the corrugated board in the CD, as evidenced by the experimental results (see Figure 16). It is worth noting that the force-displacement curves from the optical measurement are in good agreement with the curves plotted by the predictive models (the maximum force appears between the displacement range: 0.1–0.2 mm, see Figures 15 and 16).

If one would like to optimize the design of the corrugated board by appropriate selection of solid boards for individual layers, it is enough to raise the basis weight of the weakest layer (in this case the TLW120 layer). By drawing the stress–strain curves of individual layers using Equations (3)–(6), it is easy to determine, which layer is the weakest. Figure 17 shows the constitutive curves of individual layers, taking into account the increase in the grammage of the TLW120 layers by 10% (Figure 17a) and 20% (Figure 17b).

Table 6 summarizes the simulation results where the basis weight of each of the layers was increased by 10 and 20 percent, respectively, and the effect of this change on the estimated edge crush resistance of the cross-section was checked using Equation (6). By far the biggest improvement is noted when the TLW120 layer is changed (strengthened). By increasing the basis weight of this layer by 10%, the ECT increases by 10.64%, and by increasing the basis weight by 20%, the ECT changes by as much as 24.33%.

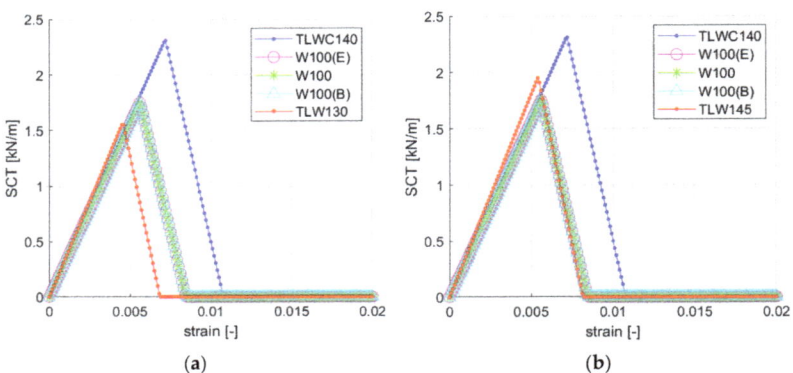

Figure 17. Stress-strain curves: (a) TLW120 exchanged with TLW130; (b) TLW120 exchanged with TLW145.

Table 6. The effect of improving individual corrugated board layers by 10 and 20 percent, respectively, on the changes in the ECT.

Reference		Single Layer Improved by 10%			Single Layer Improved by 20%		
Paperboard Symbol	ECT (kN/m)	Paperboard Symbol	ECT (kN/m)	Diff. (%)	Paperboard Symbol	ECT (kN/m)	Diff. (%)
TLWC 140	8.08	TLWC 155	8.261	2.24	TLWC 170	8.442	4.48
W 100 (E)	8.08	W 110 (E)	8.297	2.69	W 120 (E)	8.515	5.38
W 100	8.08	W 110	8.255	2.17	W 120	8.430	4.33
W 100 (B)	8.08	W 110 (B)	8.310	2.85	W 120 (B)	8.541	5.71
TLW 120	8.08	TLW 130	8.940	10.64	TLW 145	10.046	24.33

5. Conclusions

This paper presents predictive models for the evaluation of compressive strength and stiffness of corrugated board in CD. The models proposed here and the obtained analytical and numerical results were compared with the experimental results. Good agreement in the obtained results was observed. The accuracy achieved with the full 3D FE model was within 95%, while the accuracy of the simplified analytical model was around 94%. Similar results were obtained by Perks et al. [12], who modeled different standards of the ECT test using the finite element method. However, the ECT prediction methods presented here (using both analytical and numerical models) are slightly more accurate than the results obtained by Parks et al. Only the optical measurement allows the correct drawing of load–displacement curves in the edge crush test. The use of crosshead displacement could not be used to calculate the stiffness of the corrugated board. In further research, further investigations on the use of full-field measurement methods (DIC) to estimate more material constants from the edge crush test are planned.

Author Contributions: Conceptualization, T.G.; methodology, T.G.; software, T.G.; formal analysis, T.G.; investigation, T.G. and A.M.; writing—original draft preparation, T.G., J.K.G., and A.M.; writing—review and editing, T.G., J.K.G., and A.M.; visualization, T.G. and A.M.; supervision, T.G. and J.K.G.; project administration, T.G.; funding acquisition, T.G. All authors have read and agreed to the published version of the manuscript.

Funding: The APC was funded by the Ministry of Science and Higher Education, Poland, the statutory funding at Poznan University of Life Sciences, grant number 506.569.05.00.

Institutional Review Board Statement: Not applicable.

Informed Consent Statement: Not applicable.

Data Availability Statement: The data presented in this study are available on request from the corresponding author.

Acknowledgments: Special thanks to the FEMat company (www.fematsystems.pl accessed on 25 April 2021) for providing the laboratory equipment and commercial software. The authors also thank AQUILA VPK Września for providing samples of corrugated cardboard for this study.

Conflicts of Interest: The authors declare no conflict of interest.

References

1. Magnucka-Blandzi, E.; Magnucki, K.; Wittenbeck, L. Mathematical modeling of shearing effect for sandwich beams with sinusoidal corrugated cores. *Appl. Math. Model.* **2015**, *39*, 1796–2808. [CrossRef]
2. Magnucka-Blandzi, E.; Magnucki, K. Transverse shear modulus of elasticity for thin-walled corrugated cores of sandwich beams. Theoretical study. *J. Theor. Appl. Mech.* **2014**, *52*, 971–980. [CrossRef]
3. Nordstrand, T.M.; Carlsson, L.A. Evaluation of transverse shear stiffness of structural core sandwich plates. *Comp. Struct.* **1997**, *37*, 145–153. [CrossRef]
4. Garbowski, T.; Gajewski, T.; Grabski, J.K. Role of transverse shear modulus in the performance of corrugated materials. *Materials* **2020**, *13*, 3791. [CrossRef] [PubMed]
5. Garbowski, T.; Gajewski, T.; Grabski, J.K. Torsional and transversal stiffness of orthotropic sandwich panels. *Materials* **2020**, *13*, 5016. [CrossRef]
6. Garbowski, T.; Gajewski, T. Determination of transverse shear stiffness of sandwich panels with a corrugated core by numerical homogenization. *Materials* **2021**, *14*, 1976. [CrossRef] [PubMed]
7. Domaneschi, M.; Perego, U.; Borgqvist, E.; Borsari, R. An industry-oriented strategy for the finite element simulation of paperboard creasing and folding. *Packag. Tech. Sci.* **2017**, *30*, 269–294. [CrossRef]
8. Garbowski, T.; Gajewski, T.; Grabski, J.K. The role of buckling in the estimation of compressive strength of corrugated cardboard boxes. *Materials* **2020**, *13*, 4578. [CrossRef]
9. Garbowski, T.; Gajewski, T.; Grabski, J.K. Estimation of the compressive strength of corrugated cardboard boxes with various openings. *Energies* **2021**, *14*, 155. [CrossRef]
10. Garbowski, T.; Gajewski, T.; Grabski, J.K. Estimation of the compressive strength of corrugated cardboard boxes with various perforations. *Energies* **2021**, *14*, 1095. [CrossRef]
11. Kmita-Fudalej, G.; Szewczyk, W.; Kołakowski, Z. Calculation of honeycomb paperboard resistance to edge crush test. *Materials* **2020**, *13*, 1706. [CrossRef] [PubMed]
12. Park, J.; Chang, S.; Jung, H.M. Numerical prediction of equivalent mechanical properties of corrugated paperboard by 3D finite element analysis. *Appl. Sci.* **2020**, *10*, 7973. [CrossRef]
13. Wong, J.E.; Mustapha, K.B.; Shimizu, Y.; Kamiya, A.; Arumugasamy, S.K. Development of surrogate predictive models for the nonlinear elasto-plastic response of medium density fibreboard-based sandwich structures. *Int. J. Lightweight Mater. Manuf.* **2021**, *4*, 302–314. [CrossRef]
14. FEMat Systems. Available online: http://fematsystems.pl/home_en (accessed on 25 April 2021).
15. TAPPI T 839 om-12. *Edge Compression Test for Strength of Corrugated Fiberboard Using the Clamp Method (Short Column Test)*; TAPPI: Peachtree Corners, GA, USA, 2009.
16. TAPPI T 838 cm-12. *Edge Crush Test Using Neckdown*; TAPPI: Peachtree Corners, GA, USA, 2009.
17. FEFCO NO.8. *Edgewise Crush Resistance of Corrugated Fiberboard*; FEFCO: Brussel, Belgium, 1997.
18. ISO 3037:2013. *Corrugated Fibreboard—Determination of Edgewise Crush Resistance (Unwaxed Edge Method)*; ISO: Geneva, Switzerland, 2013.
19. TAPPI T 811 om-11. *Edgewise Compressive Strength of Corrugated Fibreboard (Short Column Test)*; TAPPI: Peachtree Corners, GA, USA, 2009.
20. ISO 13821:2002. *Corrugated Fibreboard—Determination of Edgewise Crush Resistance—Waxed Edge Method*; ISO: Geneva, Switzerland, 2002.
21. Park, J.; Park, M.; Choi, D.S.; Jung, H.M.; Hwang, S.W. Finite element-based simulation for edgewise compression behavior of corrugated paperboard for packing of agricultural products. *Appl. Sci.* **2020**, *10*, 6716. [CrossRef]
22. Hägglund, R.; Åslund, P.E.; Carlsson, L.A.; Isaksson, P. Measuring thickness changes of edgewise compression loaded corrugated board panels using digital image correlation. *J. Sandwich Struct. Mater.* **2010**, *14*, 75–94. [CrossRef]
23. Viguié, J.; Dumont, P.J.J.; Vacher, P.; Orgéas, L.; Desloges, I.; Mauret, E. Analysis of the strain and stress field of cardboard box during compression by 3D Digital Image Correlation. *Appl. Mech. Mater.* **2010**, *24–25*, 103–108. [CrossRef]
24. Viguié, J.; Dumont, P.J.J.; Orgéas, L.; Vacher, P.; Desloges, I.; Mauret, E. Surface stress and strain fields on compressed panels of corrugated board boxes. An experimental analysis by using Digital Image Stereocorrelation. *Comp. Struct.* **2011**, *93*, 2861–2873. [CrossRef]
25. Viguié, J.; Dumont, P.J.J. Analytical post-buckling model of corrugated board panels using digital image correlation measurements. *Comp. Struct.* **2013**, *101*, 243–254. [CrossRef]

26. Borgqvist, E.; Lindström, T.; Tryding, J.; Wallin, M.; Ristinmaa, M. Distortional hardening plasticity model for paperboard. *Int. J. Solids Struct.* **2014**, *51*, 2411–2423. [CrossRef]
27. Cocchetti, G.; Mahini, M.R.; Maier, G. Mechanical characterization of foils with compression in their planes. *Mech. Adv. Mater. Struct.* **2014**, *21*, 853–870. [CrossRef]
28. Garbowski, T.; Maier, G.; Novati, G. On calibration of orthotropic elastic-plastic constitutive models for paper foils by biaxial tests and inverse analyses. *Struct. Multidisc. Optim.* **2012**, *46*, 111–128. [CrossRef]
29. Considine, J.M.; Pierron, F.; Turner, K.T.; Vahey, D.W. General anisotropy identification of paperboard with virtual fields method. *Exp. Mech.* **2014**, *54*, 1395–1410. [CrossRef]
30. Åslund, P.E.; Hägglund, R.; Carlsson, L.A.; Isaksson, P. An analysis of strain localization and formation of face wrinkles in edge-wise loaded corrugated sandwich panels using a continuum damage model. *Int. J. Solids Struct.* **2015**, *56–57*, 248–257. [CrossRef]
31. Zappa, E.; Liu, R.; Bolzon, G.; Shahmardani, M. High resolution non-contact measurement techniques for three-dimensional deformation processes of paperboard laminates. *Mater. Today Proc.* **2017**, *4*, 5872–5876. [CrossRef]
32. Fadiji, T.; Coetzee, C.J.; Opara, U.L. Evaluating the displacement field of paperboard packages subjected to compression loading using digital image correlation (DIC). *Food Bioprod. Process.* **2020**, *123*, 60–71. [CrossRef]
33. FEMat Systems. Available online: http://fematsystems.pl/ect_en (accessed on 25 April 2021).
34. Abaqus Unified FEA® Software. Available online: https://www.3ds.com/products-services/simulia/products/abaqus (accessed on 25 April 2021).
35. Baum, G.A.; Brennan, D.C.; Habeger, C.C. Orthotropic elastic constants of paper. *Tappi* **1981**, *64*, 97–101.
36. Mann, R.W.; Baum, G.A.; Habeger, C.C. Determination of all nine orthotropic elastic constants for machine-made paper. *Tappi* **1980**, *63*, 163–166.

Article

Determination of Transverse Shear Stiffness of Sandwich Panels with a Corrugated Core by Numerical Homogenization

Tomasz Garbowski [1] and Tomasz Gajewski [2,*]

[1] Department of Biosystems Engineering, Poznan University of Life Sciences, Wojska Polskiego 50, 60-627 Poznan, Poland; tomasz.garbowski@up.poznan.pl
[2] Institute of Structural Analysis, Poznan University of Technology, Piotrowo 5, 60-965 Poznan, Poland
* Correspondence: tomasz.gajewski@put.poznan.pl

Abstract: Knowing the material properties of individual layers of the corrugated plate structures and the geometry of its cross-section, the effective material parameters of the equivalent plate can be calculated. This can be problematic, especially if the transverse shear stiffness is also necessary for the correct description of the equivalent plate performance. In this work, the method proposed by Biancolini is extended to include the possibility of determining, apart from the tensile and flexural stiffnesses, also the transverse shear stiffness of the homogenized corrugated board. The method is based on the strain energy equivalence between the full numerical 3D model of the corrugated board and its Reissner-Mindlin flat plate representation. Shell finite elements were used in this study to accurately reflect the geometry of the corrugated board. In the method presented here, the finite element method is only used to compose the initial global stiffness matrix, which is then condensed and directly used in the homogenization procedure. The stability of the proposed method was tested for different variants of the selected representative volume elements. The obtained results are consistent with other technique already presented in the literature.

Keywords: corrugated board; numerical homogenization; strain energy equivalence; finite element method; plate stiffness properties; shell structures; transverse shear

Citation: Garbowski, T.; Gajewski, T. Determination of Transverse Shear Stiffness of Sandwich Panels with a Corrugated Core by Numerical Homogenization. *Materials* **2021**, *14*, 1976. https://doi.org/10.3390/ma14081976

Academic Editor: Michele Bacciocchi

Received: 1 April 2021
Accepted: 14 April 2021
Published: 15 April 2021

Publisher's Note: MDPI stays neutral with regard to jurisdictional claims in published maps and institutional affiliations.

Copyright: © 2021 by the authors. Licensee MDPI, Basel, Switzerland. This article is an open access article distributed under the terms and conditions of the Creative Commons Attribution (CC BY) license (https://creativecommons.org/licenses/by/4.0/).

1. Introduction

Corrugated cardboard is widely used as packaging and protective material in almost all industries. Whenever a product is displayed in shop windows, it is often packaged in colorful and branded corrugated cardboard packaging. This becomes a required standard all over the world. The packaging is not only to attract the eye of the customer, but is often the main protection for the product that is transported to warehouses or directly delivered to customers by courier companies. Along with the growth of e-commerce, the amount of packaging that goes to the market also grows. Fortunately, corrugated cardboard is a material that is not only environmentally friendly, but also easily recycled. These features largely contributed to the noticeable growth of the corrugated board packaging market in recent years. As a result of the growing awareness of producers and their customers, ecological products are gaining in popularity and therefore require more attention.

As long as the corrugated board is made of paper and the paper is made of cellulose fibers, which mainly come from trees, we must pay particular attention to the sustainable use of virgin and recycled fibers. The only way to achieve savings in the material used for the production of packaging is to focus the attention on the optimal selection of the composition of raw materials and a thorough strength analysis of corrugated board products. Currently, not only simple transport packages need to be optimized, but also more complex structures, e.g., SRP (shelf ready boxes) or displays. For typical box designs, it is sufficient to estimate the strength of a corrugated cardboard box on the basis of any analytical formula found in the literature; from the simplest and most popular [1] to the more complex [2–7].

McKee and coworkers developed the formula in which a compressive strength in cross direction of corrugated cardboard, its thickness and base dimension of the box is required to provide a simple estimation of the box strength. This approach is only valid for very simple flap boxes and can be used for regular shaped packages without perforation and holes. In the recent years many attempts were made to extend the applicability of simple analytical methods and to improve their accuracy. Allerby and coworkers modified constants and exponents in original McKee formulation which slightly improved its accuracy [2]. Schrampfer et al. extended the applicability of the McKee formula for wider range of boxes [8]. Batelka et al. included all box dimensions in their formula [3], while Urbanik et al. included also inelastic buckling phenomenon [4]. Recently, the numerical-analytical formula was proposed by Garbowski et al. to take into account also holes [6] and perforation [7] in the estimation of the box strength.

The strength of a slender box depends on the compressive strength of the corrugated board, but also on the critical load that its vertical walls must withstand. Therefore many research has been devoted to the phenomenon of corrugated board buckling [9–13]. Since corrugated board is a laminated material with a special fiber orientation, the buckling analysis requires advances models. Both the orthotropic nature of the material and its layered cross-section should be taken into account [14]. Therefore, the finite element method is the most appropriate method to calculate the critical load capacity of panels made of corrugated board. Especially in the case of complex shapes of such panels or in the presence of holes and perforations [6,7] where analytical formulas are difficult to apply.

In recent years, to assess the strength of corrugated cardboard structures, both hybrid methods [4,6,7,15] or purely numerical [16–19] have been increasingly used. A recent review can be found here [20]. Since corrugated cardboard boxes, fruit trays, displays and retail ready boxes are very often complex 3D structures loaded in various ways, the finite element method [21] is most often used for calculations of such structures. Corrugated board has a soft corrugated core, therefore the traditional Kirchhoff–Love plate theory is usually replaced with the Mindlin–Reissner shell theory, which also takes into account the transverse shear in the shell members. This require proper selection of the finite element (FE), which is of key importance for obtaining the correct results of numerical simulation. It is known that both triangular and quadrilateral shell FE suffer from a so-called shear locking. To overcome such limitations, many improvements to the traditional FE have been proposed in the literature, e.g., Bathe and Dvorkin [22,23], where auxiliary shear modes were applied. These modes was first used by MacNeal [24,25] and later extended by Done and Lamain [26] and Onate et al. [27]. This element has been successfully implemented and used in the work by Garbowski et al. [13], in which the authors prove that the mechanical behavior of this element in twisting tests is identical to the analytical predictions.

In case of structures made of corrugated boards very rarely the full multi-layered structure of the cross-section is modeled. Typically, a complex multi-layer cross-section is replaced with a single-layer model that has equivalent properties very similar to those of the full model. Such converting process is called homogenization. The homogenization of composite laminates has been the subject of interest of many researchers for several decades. One of the recent method that uses a strain energy was proposed in 2003 by Hohe [28] for homogenization of sandwich panels with hexagonal honeycomb core. The author uses a strain energy based procedure with assumed mechanical equivalence between a representative volume element (RVE) of a periodic plate and the simplified model, provided that the effective deformation in both models are equal in an average sense. Buanic et al. proposed a periodic homogenization method in which both an equivalent membrane, bending and shearing characteristics of periodic plates can be computed [29]. Biancolini obtained both membrane and bending properties for plates with corrugated core using the strain energy equivalence between the numerical model of RVE and single layered equivalent model [30]. The comparison of different approaches to homogenization of sandwich panels with corrugated boards can be found, e.g., in Garbowski and Jarmuszczak [31,32], and Marek and

Garbowski [33]. The application of inverse analysis to homogenization of corrugated board was presented in the work of Garbowski and Marek [34].

An extension of the homogenization method proposed by Biancolini is presented here. The proposed generalization allows to take into account transverse shear in the process of homogenization of the corrugated cardboard. As already mentioned, transverse shear plays an important role in the mechanical behavior of the corrugated board, therefore many researchers have proposed different methods to calculate the effective transverse shear stiffness of the corrugated board [14,35–38]. This article presents the strain energy equivalence between RVE-base method of the full multi-layer corrugated cardboard FE model and the equivalent single-layer shell model. The proposed approach allows to calculate all properties of tensile, bending and transverse shear stiffnesses, which are extremely important if one would like to properly model the behavior of homogenized sandwich with corrugated cores. The method presented here has promising applications, not only to corrugated cardboards, but also for other types of sandwich or composite structures, including dynamic analysis, e.g., [39,40]. The results obtained by our method were compared with the results from the literature. A satisfactory agreement with the literature data was obtained.

2. Materials and Methods

The homogenization method proposed here is based on the equivalent of the deformation energy between a small part of a periodic multi-layer structure cut from corrugated cardboard and its simplified single-layer counterpart. Given the representative volume element (RVE) of the full detailed corrugated board model on the one hand and the simplified model on the other hand, the effective properties can be calculated, provided that the effective strains in both models are equal in an average sense. For the correct representation of the geometry of the cross-section a finite element models are used here.

Corrugated cardboard is a material made of several layers of paperboard. It consists of alternating flat and corrugated layers. The cellulose fibers in each of these layers are oriented along the waves, see Figure 1. This direction is called the machine direction (MD). The second, in plane direction, perpendicular to the fibers orientation, is called the cross direction (CD). The out of plane direction is the thickness direction.

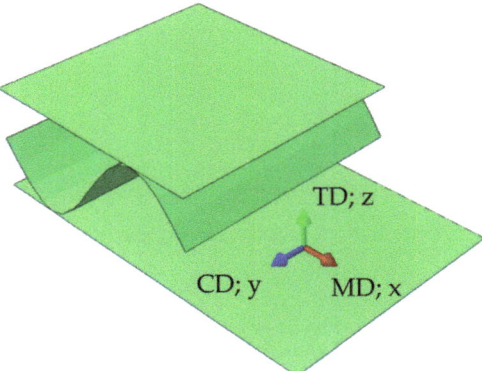

Figure 1. Material orientations.

In order to compute all effective parameters of equivalent single-layered model, first the RVE need to be constructed. Here the single-wall corrugated cardboard is investigated therefore a selected RVE consists of singe period (see Figure 2) of the wavey layer. This selection was made to test the effect of the RVE type on the quality and stability of the calculated effective membrane, bending and transverse shear stiffnesses of the equivalent plate. The most problematic and least stable parameters identified by the homogenization method proposed here turned out to be both transverse shear stiffness in plane 13 (MD-TD) and 23 (CD-TD). Therefore, other RVE types and boundary conditions were also investigated in this study to check the robustness of the proposed approach.

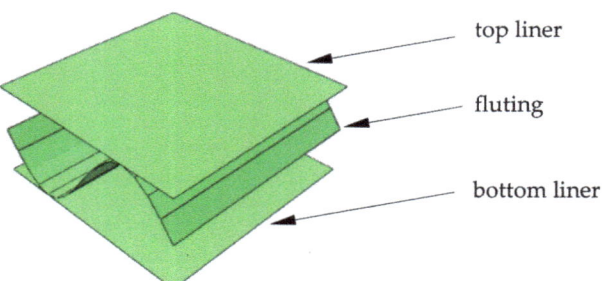

Figure 2. Representative volume element (RVE).

In the traditional displacement based linear formulation of finite element we have:

$$\mathbf{K}_e \, \mathbf{u}_e = \mathbf{F}_e, \tag{1}$$

where $\mathbf{K}_e$ is a statically condensed (through elimination of internal nodes) the global stiffness matrix of the RVE, $\mathbf{u}_e$ is a displacement vector of the external nodes and $\mathbf{F}_e$ is a vector of the nodal force applied to the external nodes. The FE mesh and external nodes are visualized in Figure 3.

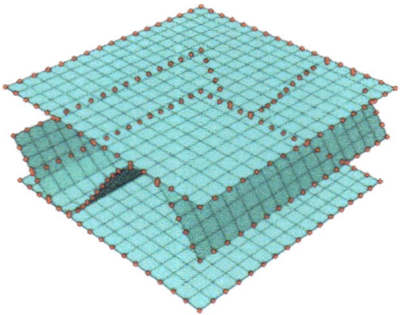

Figure 3. External (in red color) and internal nodes of RVE.

The stiffness matrix condensed to external nodes can be computed by the following equation:

$$\mathbf{K} = \mathbf{K}_{ee} - \mathbf{K}_{ei} \, \mathbf{K}_{ii}^{-1} \mathbf{K}_{ie} \tag{2}$$

where overall stiffness matrix is partitioned into external (subscript e) and internal (subscript i) nodes into four submatrices in the following way:

$$\begin{bmatrix} \mathbf{K}_{ee} & \mathbf{K}_{ei} \\ \mathbf{K}_{ie} & \mathbf{K}_{ii} \end{bmatrix} \begin{bmatrix} \mathbf{u}_e \\ \mathbf{u}_i \end{bmatrix} = \begin{bmatrix} \mathbf{F}_e \\ 0 \end{bmatrix} \tag{3}$$

After static condensation (Equation (2)), the strain energy stored in the system is:

$$E = \frac{1}{2} \mathbf{u}_e^T \, \mathbf{F}_e \tag{4}$$

The energetic equivalence between the FE model of the RVE and the simplified shell model can be established by a proper definition of the displacements and rotations in the external nodes. These general displacements at each boundary node are related to the generalized strains, which for membrane behavior reads:

$$\begin{bmatrix} \varepsilon_x^0 \\ \varepsilon_y^0 \\ \gamma_{xy}^0 \end{bmatrix} = \begin{bmatrix} \partial u_0/\partial x \\ \partial v_0/\partial y \\ \partial u_0/\partial y + \partial v_0/\partial x \end{bmatrix}. \qquad (5)$$

Displacements are related with rotations in the following way:

$$\left\{ \begin{array}{c} u(x,y,z) \\ v(x,y,z) \\ w(x,y,z) \end{array} \right\} = \left\{ \begin{array}{c} -z\,\theta_x(x,y) \\ -z\,\theta_y(x,y) \\ w_0(x,y) \end{array} \right\}, \qquad (6)$$

while rotations according to Kirchhoff–Love assumption are considered as:

$$\left\{ \begin{array}{c} \theta_x \\ \theta_y \end{array} \right\} = \left\{ \begin{array}{c} \partial w/\partial x \\ \partial w/\partial y \end{array} \right\}. \qquad (7)$$

Since in Kirchhoff–Love plate theory the normal remains orthogonal to the middle plane after deformation, we have:

$$\left\{ \begin{array}{c} \partial u/\partial z \\ \partial v/\partial z \end{array} \right\} = \left\{ \begin{array}{c} -\partial w/\partial x \\ -\partial w/\partial y \end{array} \right\}. \qquad (8)$$

The normal strains can be than computed from Equations (6) and (7):

$$\begin{bmatrix} \varepsilon_x \\ \varepsilon_y \\ \gamma_{xy} \end{bmatrix} = \begin{bmatrix} \partial u/\partial x \\ \partial v/\partial y \\ \partial u/\partial y + \partial v/\partial x \end{bmatrix} = -z \begin{bmatrix} \partial \theta_x/\partial x \\ \partial \theta_y/\partial y \\ \partial \theta_x/\partial y + \partial \theta_y/\partial x \end{bmatrix} = -z \begin{bmatrix} \partial^2 w/\partial x^2 \\ \partial^2 w/\partial y^2 \\ 2\partial^2 w/\partial x \partial y \end{bmatrix}, \qquad (9)$$

while transverse shear can be computed from:

$$\begin{bmatrix} \gamma_{xz} \\ \gamma_{yz} \end{bmatrix} = \begin{bmatrix} \partial w/\partial x + \partial u/\partial z \\ \partial w/\partial y + \partial v/\partial z \end{bmatrix} = \begin{bmatrix} 0 \\ 0 \end{bmatrix}. \qquad (10)$$

This assumption does not allow to calculate the transverse shear. Therefore, the Mindlin–Reissner theory should be applied, where the rotation is described by the formula:

$$\left\{ \begin{array}{c} \theta_x \\ \theta_y \end{array} \right\} = \left\{ \begin{array}{c} \partial w/\partial x + \phi_x \\ \partial w/\partial y + \phi_y \end{array} \right\}, \qquad (11)$$

where the normal rotation is obtained as the sum of two rotations: (i) The corresponding slope of the middle plane of the plate and (ii) the additional rotation ϕ, which results from the lack of orthogonality of the normal to the middle plane after deformation. Consequently we have:

$$\left\{ \begin{array}{c} \partial u/\partial z \\ \partial v/\partial z \end{array} \right\} = \left\{ \begin{array}{c} -(\partial w/\partial x + \phi_x) \\ -(\partial w/\partial y + \phi_y) \end{array} \right\}. \qquad (12)$$

Now the transverse shear reads:

$$\begin{bmatrix} \gamma_{xz} \\ \gamma_{yz} \end{bmatrix} = \begin{bmatrix} \partial w/\partial x + \partial u/\partial z \\ \partial w/\partial y + \partial v/\partial z \end{bmatrix} = \begin{bmatrix} \partial w/\partial x - \theta_x \\ \partial w/\partial y - \theta_y \end{bmatrix} = \begin{bmatrix} -\phi_x \\ -\phi_y \end{bmatrix}, \qquad (13)$$

while the curvatures are:

$$\begin{bmatrix} \kappa_x \\ \kappa_y \\ \kappa_{xy} \end{bmatrix} = - \begin{bmatrix} \partial \theta_x / \partial x \\ \partial \theta_y / \partial y \\ \partial \theta_x / \partial y + \partial \theta_y / \partial x \end{bmatrix}. \tag{14}$$

Using the Mindlin–Reissner theory the normal strains consists of membrane and bending behaviors as follow:

$$\begin{bmatrix} \varepsilon_x \\ \varepsilon_y \\ \gamma_{xy} \end{bmatrix} = \begin{bmatrix} \partial u / \partial x \\ \partial v / \partial y \\ \partial v / \partial x + \partial u / \partial y \end{bmatrix} = \begin{bmatrix} \varepsilon_x^0 \\ \varepsilon_y^0 \\ \gamma_{xy}^0 \end{bmatrix} + z \begin{bmatrix} \kappa_x \\ \kappa_y \\ \kappa_{xy} \end{bmatrix}, \tag{15}$$

that permit to calculate (from Equations (13)–(15)) by integration the in plane displacement fields along x-axis as follows:

$$u(x,y,z) = x\left(\varepsilon_x^0 + z\kappa_x\right) + \frac{y}{2}\left(\gamma_{xy}^0 + z\kappa_{xy}\right) - \frac{z}{2}\gamma_{xz}, \tag{16}$$

and along y-axis as follows:

$$v(x,y,z) = y\left(\varepsilon_y^0 + z\kappa_y\right) + \frac{x}{2}\left(\gamma_{xy}^0 + z\kappa_{xy}\right) - \frac{z}{2}\gamma_{yz}, \tag{17}$$

while out of plane displacements are:

$$w(x,y) = -\frac{x^2}{2}\kappa_x - \frac{xy}{2}\kappa_{xy} - \frac{y^2}{2}\kappa_y - \frac{x}{2}\gamma_{xz} - \frac{y}{2}\gamma_{yz}. \tag{18}$$

Recalling the definition of curvatures in Equation (14) and after a first integration of angular rotation with respect to x-axis, the following rotation with respect to y-axis is obtained:

$$\theta_x(x,y) = \phi_x + \frac{\partial w}{\partial x} = -y\kappa_y - \frac{x}{2}\kappa_{xy}, \tag{19}$$

while the rotation with respect to x-axis is:

$$\theta_y(x,y) = x\kappa_x + \frac{y}{2}\kappa_{xy}. \tag{20}$$

The originally proposed by Biancolini [30] and here extended (by taking into account also both transverse shear) relationship between generalized constant strains and the position of the external nodes can be expressed by the following transform:

$$\mathbf{u}_i = \mathbf{A}_i \, \boldsymbol{\epsilon}_i, \tag{21}$$

where for single node ($x_i = x$, $y_i = y$, $z_i = z$) we have:

$$\begin{bmatrix} u_x \\ u_y \\ u_z \\ \theta_x \\ \theta_y \end{bmatrix}_i = \begin{bmatrix} x & 0 & y/2 & z/2 & 0 & xz & 0 & yz/2 \\ 0 & y & x/2 & 0 & z/2 & 0 & yz & xz/2 \\ 0 & 0 & 0 & x/2 & y/2 & -x^2/2 & -y^2/2 & -xy/2 \\ 0 & 0 & 0 & 0 & 0 & 0 & -y & -x/2 \\ 0 & 0 & 0 & 0 & 0 & x & 0 & y/2 \end{bmatrix}_i \begin{bmatrix} \varepsilon_x \\ \varepsilon_y \\ \gamma_{xy} \\ \gamma_{xz} \\ \gamma_{yz} \\ \kappa_x \\ \kappa_y \\ \kappa_{xy} \end{bmatrix}_i. \tag{22}$$

Recalling the definition of the strain energy for the discrete model:

$$E = \frac{1}{2}\mathbf{u}_e^T \mathbf{K} \mathbf{u}_e = \frac{1}{2}\boldsymbol{\epsilon}_e^T \mathbf{A}_e^T \mathbf{K} \mathbf{A}_e \, \boldsymbol{\epsilon}_e, \tag{23}$$

and considering that for a shell subjected to bending, traction and transverse shear the internal energy is:

$$E = \frac{1}{2}\boldsymbol{\epsilon}_e^T \mathbf{A}_k \boldsymbol{\epsilon}_e \{area\}, \quad (24)$$

overall stiffness matrix for the laminate could be easily extracted from the discrete matrix as:

$$\mathbf{A}_k = \frac{\mathbf{A}_e^T \mathbf{K} \mathbf{A}_e}{area}. \quad (25)$$

3. Results

The numerical examples presented in the study are referring to the material and geometrical data used in the work of Biancolini [30]. In the Table 1, the material properties used in this paper for liners and fluting are shown, namely, E_1, E_2, v_{12}, G_{12}, G_{13}, and G_{23}, i.e., Young moduli in both directions, Poisson's ratio and shear moduli, respectively. Also, the paper thicknesses, t, are shown in Table 1. The fluting period used here equals 8 mm. Apart Section 3.1, the axial spacing between internal and externa liners equals 3.51 mm. In Section 3.1, the axial spacing between liners itself was analyzed.

Table 1. Thicknesses and material properties of liners and fluting used in this study.

Layers	t (mm)	E_1 (MPa)	E_2 (MPa)	v_{12} (-)	G_{12} (MPa)	G_{13} (MPa)	G_{23} (MPa)
liners	0.29	3326	1694	0.34	859	429.5	429.5
fluting	0.30	2614	1532	0.32	724	362	362

3.1. Stiffnesses Variation Due to Different Approach for Modelling Cross-Direction Section

In the first step of numerical part of the study, the examples presented by Biancolini [30] were used as reference and recreated. The saw tooth type geometry was considered here, see Figure 4. In the referred paper only the overall data regarding the geometry were explicitly given, there was a lack of detailed information about the modelling of the cross-section geometry. For instance, if the height of 3.8 mm used, was the overall outer thickness of the cardboard or the axial distance between the liners. Thus, in this study, we have utilized different approaches to model the cross-section geometry, see Figure 5, to verify which approach was used by the author. In Figure 5a, the axial spacing between shell liners equals 3.51 mm; the outer thickness equals 3.8 mm. In Figure 5b, the shells with offset technique were adopted; in this case the outer thickness was also 3.8 mm. In Figure 5c, the axial spacing between the shell liners equals 3.8 mm; the outer thickness equals 4.09 mm. In numerical examples of this section, the 4-node quadrilateral element with full integration scheme (labelled in Abaqus FEA as S4) was used.

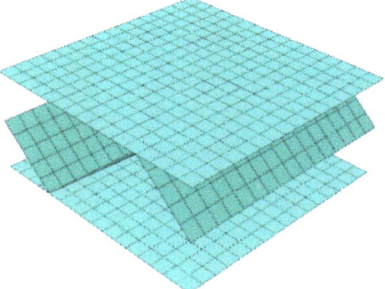

Figure 4. Representative shell elements of saw tooth geometry with quadrilateral mesh (single period).

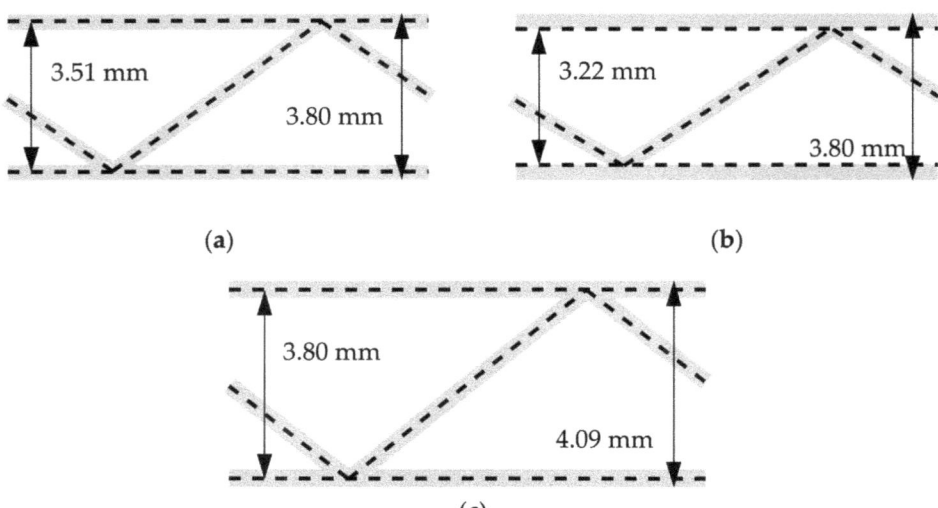

Figure 5. The different approach of modelling the cardboard cross-direction section of the saw tooth geometry: (a) 3.80 mm as the outer cardboard dimension, (b) 3.80 mm as the outer cardboard dimension with offset technique used and (c) 3.80 mm as axial spacing between liners.

Our computational results for saw tooth geometry are presented in Table 2. In the second column, the values according to [30] were demonstrated. In the third, fourth and fifth columns, the results computed using different geometry are presented, see Figure 5a–c, respectively and Materials and Methods section.

Table 2. The stiffnesses of representative shell element computed for a different approach of modelling confronted with data from ref. [30] for saw tooth geometry.

Stiffness	Ref. [30]	Axial Geometry	Inner Geometry	Outer Geometry
A_{11}, (kPa·m)	2158	2140	2154	2131
A_{22}, (kPa·m)	1660	1665	1643	1687
A_{12}, (kPa·m)	379.9	382.9	385.4	381.9
A_{33}, (kPa·m)	677.6	662.5	668.4	656.8
D_{11}, (Pa·m^3)	6.370	6.392	6.389	7.482
D_{22}, (Pa·m^3)	3.824	3.859	3.740	4.549
D_{12}, (Pa·m^3)	1.092	1.115	1.113	1.305
D_{33}, (Pa·m^3)	1.655	1.656	1.639	1.937
A_{44}, (Pa·m)	-	202.4	179.4	218.5
A_{55}, (Pa·m)	-	99.0	89.0	112.4

3.2. Stiffnesses Variation Due to Different Finite Element Type

In this section, the influence of using different element type in RVE on determination of A_k stiffnesses was verified. Here, the sine geometry of fluting was used. In Table 3, the second column represents the results from the model with the 4-node quadrilateral element with full integration scheme (labelled in Abaqus FEA as S4). The third column represents the results from the model with the 4-node quadrilateral element with a reduced integration scheme (labelled in Abaqus FEA as S4R). The fourth column represent the results from the model with the 3-node triangular element (labelled in Abaqus FEA as S3). In the fifth column, the results for quadrilateral, bilinear deflection and rotations and linear transverse shear strain fields (QLLL) element was shown, embedded in in-house finite element method code [13]. In all cases, the number of nodes is the same, however, in the mesh with triangular element type the number of elements is almost twice bigger, see Table 3.

Table 3. The stiffnesses of the representative shell element computed for different element type-sine geometry.

Stiffness	Quadrilateral Element (S4)	Reduced Quadrilateral Element (S4R)	Triangular Element (S3)	QLLL Element
A_{11}, (kPa·m)	2219	2218	2225	2128
A_{22}, (kPa·m)	1694	1694	1694	1677
A_{12}, (kPa·m)	411.8	411.5	413.4	378.9
A_{33}, (kPa·m)	659.3	659.3	659.6	659.7
D_{11}, (Pa·m^3)	6.521	6.517	6.535	6.443
D_{22}, (Pa·m^3)	4.071	4.066	4.091	4.035
D_{12}, (Pa·m^3)	1.149	1.148	1.152	1.135
D_{33}, (Pa·m^3)	1.729	1.728	1.731	1.716
A_{44}, (Pa·m)	140.5	139.8	143.8	71.1
A_{55}, (Pa·m)	132.6	132.4	135.6	102.4
nodes/element	969/896	969/896	969/1792	969/896

3.3. Stiffnesses Variation Due to Different Fluting Discretization

Next, the fluting shape discretization was analyzed to derive, how the number of segments influence the determination of $\mathbf{A}_k$ matrix. For this purpose different discretizations were considered, namely, 4, 8, 12, 16, 20, 24, 28, 32, 36, 40, 44, 48, 52, 56, 60, and 64 segments for a single fluting period. Two RVS were selected, the one with unsymmetric fluting (flute period starts from the middle), and the one with symmetric fluting (flute period starts from the liner). Three selected discretizations with 8, 16, and 32 segments on unsymmetric model are presented in the Figure 6. In the first row, the three-dimensional fluting cardboards are presented, in the second row the corresponding cross-sections are shown. In those numerical examples, the quadrilateral, bilinear deflection and rotations and linear transverse shear strain fields (QLLL) element was used.

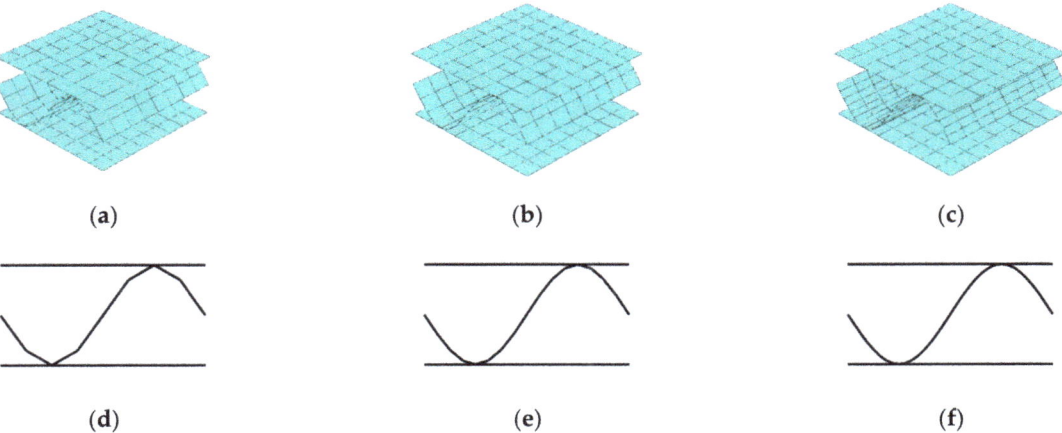

Figure 6. Different discretizations of cardboard fluting for unsymmetric RVE: (**a**) 8, (**b**) 16, and (**c**) 32 fluting segments; and corresponding cross-sections: (**d**) 8, (**e**) 16, and (**f**) 32 fluting segments.

The $\mathbf{A}_k$ stiffnesses obtained for those cases are presented in Table 4. In Figure 7, the results of A_{44} and A_{55} for all used flute segments (16 cases) are plotted separately.

Table 4. The stiffnesses of the representative shell element computed for different number of segments for one fluting period–sine geometry.

Stiffness	Unsymmetric 8 Segments	Unsymmetric 16 Segments	Unsymmetric 32 Segments	Symmetric 8 Segments	Symmetric 16 Segments	Symmetric 32 Segments
A_{11}, (kPa·m)	2128	2108	2106	2126	2114	2107
A_{22}, (kPa·m)	1677	1681	1682	1678	1681	1682
A_{12}, (kPa·m)	378.9	373.7	373.4	380.4	375.9	373.7
A_{33}, (kPa·m)	659.7	658.7	658.3	659.6	658.4	658.1
D_{11}, (Pa·m^3)	6.443	6.433	6.432	6.445	6.435	6.429
D_{22}, (Pa·m^3)	4.035	4.087	4.101	4.033	4.086	4.099
D_{12}, (Pa·m^3)	1.135	1.130	1.130	1.137	1.131	1.129
D_{33}, (Pa·m^3)	1.715	1.728	1.732	1.682	1.694	1.698
A_{44}, (Pa·m)	71.1	48.0	43.1	75.0	49.0	42.5
A_{55}, (Pa·m)	102.4	104.4	104.7	113.4	114.4	114.6

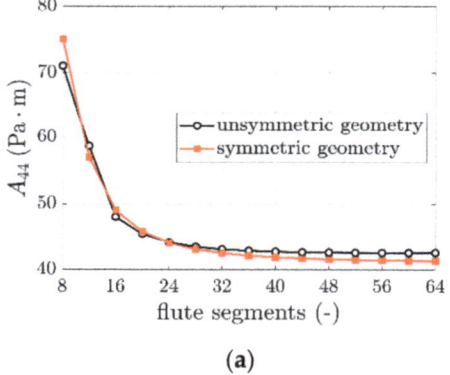 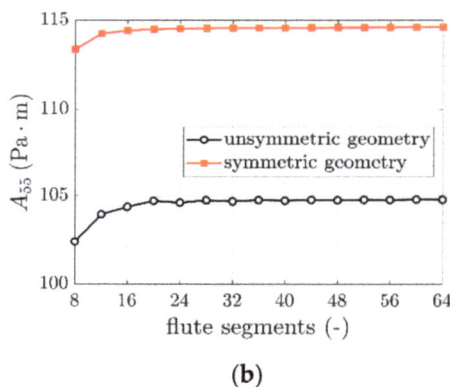

(a) (b)

Figure 7. The variation of (a) A_{44} and (b) A_{55} due to different number of fluting segments used.

3.4. Stiffnesses Variation Due to Different Numbers of Periods

Because the application of general strains (γ_{13}) at RVE edges allows free deformation of liners and fluting (see Figure 8) therefore the influence of the number of periods of the internal layer on the calculated transversal shear stiffness A_{44} was checked here. The different numbers of periods (namely 1, 2, or 3 periods) for corrugated cardboard with sine-shaped fluting was studied. Two geometries were analyzed, i.e., with the period starting from the middle of fluting–unsymmetric, see Figure 9a–c; and with the period starting from the liner–symmetric, see Figure 9d–f. In those numerical examples, the quadrilateral, bilinear deflection and rotations and linear transverse shear strain fields (QLLL) element was used. Note that in CD the length is conservatively assumed to be equal the period length, i.e., 8 mm. In Table 5, the second to fourth columns represent the results from the model with the unsymmetric periods—1, 2, or 3, respectively. The fifth to seventh columns represent the results from the symmetric periods—1, 2, or 3, respectively.

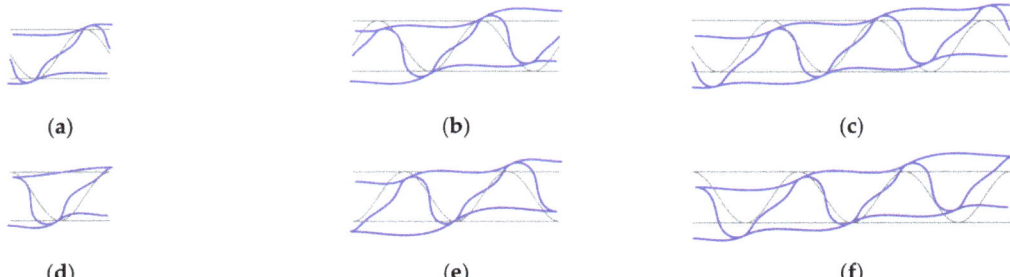

Figure 8. Deformation of RVE cross-section under transverse shear strains for different numbers of periods of corrugated cardboard for unsymmetric fluting cardboards: (**a**) 1, (**b**) 2, and (**c**) 3 periods; and symmetric fluting cardboards: (**d**) 1, (**e**) 2, and (**f**) 3 periods.

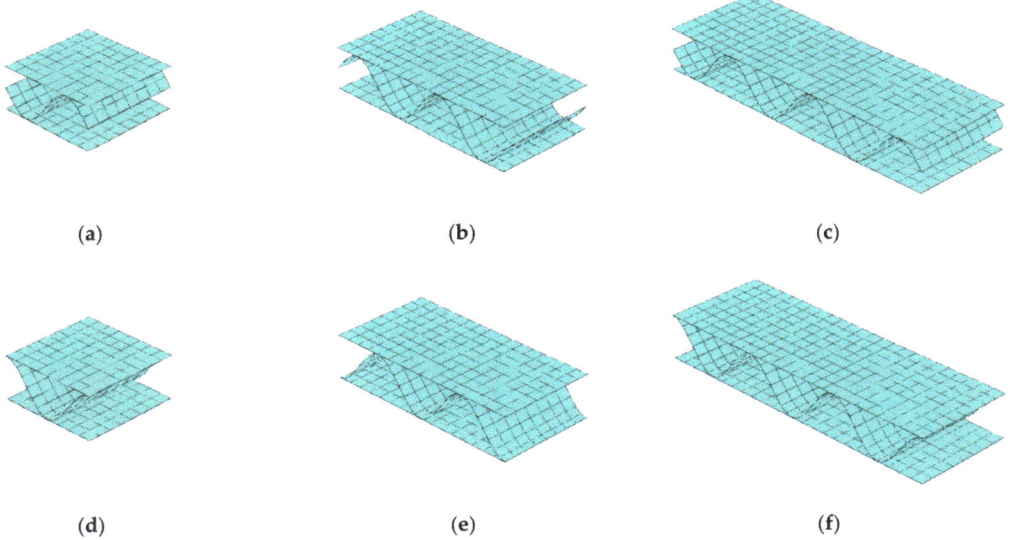

Figure 9. Different numbers of periods of corrugated cardboard for unsymmetric fluting cardboards: (**a**) 1, (**b**) 2, and (**c**) 3 periods; and symmetric fluting cardboards: (**d**) 1, (**e**) 2, and (**f**) 3 periods.

Table 5. The stiffnesses of the representative shell element computed for different numbers of periods for unsymmetric and symmetric sine geometry.

Stiffness	Unsymmetric 1 Period	Unsymmetric 2 Periods	Unsymmetric 3 Periods	Symmetric 1 Period	Symmetric 2 Periods	Symmetric 3 Periods
A_{11}, (kPa·m)	2108	2106	2106	2114	2110	2108
A_{22}, (kPa·m)	1681	1680	1680	1681	1681	1681
A_{12}, (kPa·m)	373.7	373.4	373.3	375.9	374.5	374.0
A_{33}, (kPa·m)	658.7	658.5	658.4	658.4	658.4	658.4
D_{11}, (Pa·m^3)	6.433	6.445	6.458	6.435	6.428	6.426
D_{22}, (Pa·m^3)	4.087	4.085	4.085	4.086	4.085	4.084
D_{12}, (Pa·m^3)	1.130	1.129	1.129	1.131	1.129	1.128
D_{33}, (Pa·m^3)	1.728	1.713	1.710	1.694	1.694	1.694
A_{44}, (Pa·m)	48.0	45.9	45.1	49.0	46.4	45.4
A_{55}, (Pa·m)	104.4	102.8	102.3	114.4	107.8	105.6

4. Discussion

4.1. Different Approach of Modelling Cross-Direction Section

Regarding results presented in Section 3.1 concerning modelling cross-direction section it should be noted, that the extended approach derived in this paper, in which A_{44} and A_{55} are computed from the RVE, does not influence the computed values of A_{11}, A_{22}, A_{12}, A_{33}, D_{11}, D_{22}, D_{12}, and D_{33}. Therefore, the data in the second column from Biancolini [30] may be directly compared with the third, fourth, and fifth columns. The stiffness in the second and third column are the closest to each other, thus, it may be concluded that this approach was used by author.

Notice that the inner geometry case (fourth column) is closer to the real-world geometry, but the offset technique used here is rarely available in finite element method software. Via comparing the third and the fourth columns, it may be concluded, that the inner geometry case does not give meaningful changes to the axial geometry case. Thus, the fluting simplification with the axial geometry case, without the use of the offset technique, is justified. On contrary, the outer geometry case meaningfully differs with other cases, especially in D_{11}, D_{22}, D_{12}, and D_{33}, in which distance between liners plays important role. In this case, corrugated cardboard thickness is 0.29 mm higher than in previous cases, cf. Figure 5c with Figure 5a,b.

4.2. Different Finite Element Type

Regarding results presented in Section 3.2 concerning different finite element type, while comparing results from using quadrilateral elements (second column) and results from using quadrilateral elements with reduced integration scheme (third column), it may be observed that all $\mathbf{A}_k$ corresponding stiffnesses are very similar (difference less than 0.5%). There is no significant difference between the full quadrilateral and reduced quadrilateral element in A_{44} and A_{55}.

While comparing the results from using quadrilateral elements (second column) and results from using triangular elements (fourth column), it may be observed that again $\mathbf{A}_k$ corresponding stiffnesses are very close to each other (difference less than 0.5%). Here, there are some differences between full quadrilateral and triangular element in A_{44} and A_{55}, 2.3% and 2.3%, respectively.

On the other hand, the differences obtained from QLLL and S4 elements are quite large, the most significant differences was in A_{44} and A_{55}, i.e., about 27% and 46%, respectively. Since, this element approach was proved to be exceeding the S4/S4R/S3 elements, see [13], QLLL element was used in computations in Sections 3.3 and 3.4.

4.3. Different Fluting Discretization

Regarding results presented in Section 3.3 concerning different fluting discretizations considered, while comparing unsymmetric and symmetric cases the results from using 32 segments (fourth column) with the results from using 16 and 8 segments, it may be observed that $\mathbf{A}_k$ corresponding stiffnesses are similar. The difference less is than 1.7%. However, it should be noted that, as presented in Table 4 and Figure 7 there is a meaningful difference between the values of A_{44} and A_{55} considered for different segments number; it stabilizes with increasing number of fluting segments. As presented in Figure 7 an asymptote is reached for approximately 32 segments. The same effect is shown for both cases analyzed (unsymmetric and symmetric period).

4.4. Different Numbers of Periods

Regarding results presented in Section 3.4 concerning numbers of periods used, it may be noted that between unsymmetric period and symmetric period cases the differences in $\mathbf{A}_k$ corresponding stiffnesses are negligible. The biggest differences are visible for A_{44} and A_{55}, but they are still less than 5%, while for other stiffnesses they are less than 2%, which proves that the obtained results are independent of the RVE size.

5. Conclusions

In this research study, the homogenization technique for corrugated cardboard shell structures was considered, however it may be adopted for any periodic shell structure. The strain energy equivalence with condensation technique used to determine the stiffness properties of homogenized shell was extended here to determine not only the membrane and bending stiffnesses but also the transverse shear stiffnesses of any periodic shell structure. The techniques requires computing the FE global stiffness matrix of the full 3D FE shell structure and simple algebraic operations.

Based on this study several guidelines may be defined for robust determination of membrane, bending and transverse shear stiffnesses of corrugated cardboard. If one would like to acquire only membrane and bending stiffnesses the RVE selectin, in particular the fluting segments number or unsymmetric/symmetric geometry do not play any important role. But it should be noted that in order to determine proper values of transverse shear stiffnesses of the corrugated cardboard, at least 32 segments must be used for correct reconstruction of sine-shaped fluting. Furthermore, the selected number of periods in RVE is not affecting the obtained results, assuming the RVE dimension in CD length is constant. The presented here homogenization method together with practical guidelines can be successfully used to obtain stiffness properties of any corrugated shell structures.

Author Contributions: T.G. (Tomasz Garbowski): Conceptualization, Methodology, Software, Writing—Original Draft, Writing—Review and Editing, Supervision, Project Administration, Visualization; T.G. (Tomasz Gajewski): Software, Validation, Formal analysis, Investigation, Writing—Original Draft, Writing—Review and Editing, Visualization, Funding Acquisition. All authors have read and agreed to the published version of the manuscript.

Funding: The APC was funded by the Ministry of Science and Higher Education, Poland, grant at Poznan University of Technology, grant number 0411/SBAD/0002.

Institutional Review Board Statement: Not applicable.

Informed Consent Statement: Not applicable.

Data Availability Statement: The data presented in this study are available on request from the corresponding author.

Conflicts of Interest: The authors declare no conflict of interest. The funders had no role in the design of the study; in the collection, analyses, or interpretation of data; in the writing of the manuscript, or in the decision to publish the results.

References

1. McKee, R.C.; Gander, J.W.; Wachuta, J.R. Compression strength formula for corrugated boxes. *Paperboard Packag.* **1963**, *48*, 149–159.
2. Allerby, I.M.; Laing, G.N.; Cardwell, R.D. Compressive strength—From components to corrugated containers. *Appita Conf. Notes* **1985**, 1–11.
3. Batelka, J.J.; Smith, C.N. *Package Compression Model*; Institute of Paper Science and Technology: Atlanta, GA, USA, 1993.
4. Urbanik, T.J.; Frank, B. Box compression analysis of world-wide data spanning 46 years. *Wood Fiber Sci.* **2006**, *38*, 399–416.
5. Ristinmaa, M.; Ottosen, N.S.; Korin, C. Analytical Prediction of Package Collapse Loads-Basic considerations. *Nord. Pulp Pap. Res. J.* **2012**, *27*, 806–813. [CrossRef]
6. Garbowski, T.; Gajewski, T.; Grabski, J.K. Estimation of the compressive strength of corrugated cardboard boxes with various openings. *Energies* **2021**, *14*, 155. [CrossRef]
7. Garbowski, T.; Gajewski, T.; Grabski, J.K. Estimation of the compressive strength of corrugated cardboard boxes with various perforations. *Energies* **2021**, *14*, 1095. [CrossRef]
8. Schrampfer, K.E.; Whitsitt, W.J.; Baum, G.A. *Combined Board Edge Crush (ECT) Technology*; Institute of Paper Chemistry: Appleton, WI, USA, 1987.
9. Norstrand, T. On buckling loads for edge-loaded orthotropic plates including transverse shear. *Comp. Struct.* **2004**, *65*, 1–6. [CrossRef]
10. Urbanik, T.J.; Saliklis, E.P. Finite element corroboration of buckling phenomena observed in corrugated boxes. *Wood Fiber Sci.* **2003**, *35*, 322–333.
11. Garbowski, T.; Borysiewicz, A. The Stability of Corrugated Board Packages. *Pol. Pap. Rev.* **2014**, *70*, 452–458. (In Polish)

12. Garbowski, T.; Przybyszewski, G. The Sensitivity Analysis of Critical Force in Box Compression Test. *Pol. Pap. Rev.* **2015**, *71*, 275–280. (In Polish)
13. Garbowski, T.; Gajewski, T.; Grabski, J.K. Torsional and transversal stiffness of orthotropic sandwich panels. *Materials* **2020**, *13*, 5016. [CrossRef]
14. Garbowski, T.; Gajewski, T.; Grabski, J.K. The role of buckling in the estimation of compressive strength of corrugated cardboard boxes. *Materials* **2020**, *13*, 4578. [CrossRef]
15. Fadiji, T.; Coetzee, C.J.; Opara, U.L. Compression strength of ventilated corrugated paperboard packages: Numerical modelling, experimental validation and effects of vent geometric design. *Biosyst. Eng.* **2016**, *151*, 231–247. [CrossRef]
16. Garbowski, T.; Jarmuszczak, M. Numerical strength estimate of corrugated board packages. Part 1. Theoretical assumptions in numerical modeling of paperboard packages. *Pol. Pap. Rev.* **2014**, *70*, 219–222. (In Polish)
17. Garbowski, T.; Jarmuszczak, M. Numerical Strength Estimate of Corrugated Board Packages. Part 2. Experimental tests and numerical analysis of paperboard packages. *Pol. Pap. Rev.* **2014**, *70*, 277–281. (In Polish)
18. Fadiji, T.; Ambaw, A.; Coetzee, C.J.; Berry, T.M.; Opara, U.L. Application of finite element analysis to predict the mechanical strength of ventilated corrugated paperboard packaging for handling fresh produce. *Biosyst. Eng.* **2018**, *174*, 260–281. [CrossRef]
19. Suarez, B.; Muneta, M.L.M.; Sanz-Bobi, J.D.; Romero, G. Application of homogenization approaches to the numerical analysis of seating made of multi-wall corrugated cardboard. *Compos. Struct.* **2021**, *262*, 113642. [CrossRef]
20. Simon, J.W. A Review of Recent Trends and Challenges in Computational Modeling of Paper and Paperboard at Different Scales. *Arch. Comput. Methods Eng.* **2020**. [CrossRef]
21. Zienkiewicz, O.C.; Taylor, R.L. *The Finite Element Method for Solid and Structural Mechanics*, 6th ed.; Butterworth-Heinemann: Oxford, UK, 2005.
22. Bathe, K.J.; Dvorkin, E.N. A four node plate bending element based on Mindlin-Reissner plate theory and mixed interpolation. *Int. J. Numer. Meth. Eng.* **1985**, *21*, 367–383. [CrossRef]
23. Dvorkin, E.N.; Bathe, K.J. A continuum mechanics based four node shell element for general non-linear analysis. *Eng. Comput.* **1984**, *1*, 77–88. [CrossRef]
24. MacNeal, R.H. A simple quadrilateral shell element. *Comput. Struct.* **1978**, *8*, 175–183. [CrossRef]
25. MacNeal, R.H. *Finite Elements: Their Design and Performance*; Marcel Dekker: New York, NY, USA, 1994.
26. Donea, J.; Lamain, L.G. A modified representation of transverse shear in C0 quadrilateral plate elements. *Comput. Methods Appl. Mech. Eng.* **1987**, *63*, 183–207. [CrossRef]
27. Onate, E.; Castro, J. Derivation of plate elements based on assumed shear strain fields. In *Recent Advances on Computational Structural Mechanics*; Ladeveze, P., Zienkiewicz, O.C., Eds.; Elsevier Pub: Amsterdam, The Netherlands, 1991.
28. Hohe, J. A direct homogenization approach for determination of the stiffness matrix for microheterogeneous plates with application to sandwich panels. *Compos. Part B* **2003**, *34*, 615–626. [CrossRef]
29. Buannic, N.; Cartraud, P.; Quesnel, T. Homogenization of corrugated core sandwich panels. *Comp. Struct.* **2003**, *59*, 299–312. [CrossRef]
30. Biancolini, M.E. Evaluation of equivalent stiffness properties of corrugated board. *Comp. Struct.* **2005**, *69*, 322–328. [CrossRef]
31. Garbowski, T.; Jarmuszczak, M. Homogenization of corrugated paperboard. Part 1. Analytical homogenization. *Pol. Pap. Rev.* **2014**, *70*, 345–349. (In Polish)
32. Garbowski, T.; Jarmuszczak, M. Homogenization of corrugated paperboard. Part 2. Numerical homogenization. *Pol. Pap. Rev.* **2014**, *70*, 390–394. (In Polish)
33. Marek, A.; Garbowski, T. Homogenization of sandwich panels. *Comput. Assist. Methods Eng. Sci.* **2015**, *22*, 39–50.
34. Garbowski, T.; Marek, A. Homogenization of corrugated boards through inverse analysis. In Proceedings of the 1st International Conference on Engineering and Applied Sciences Optimization, Kos Island, Greece, 4–6 June 2014; pp. 1751–1766.
35. Nordstrand, T.; Carlsson, L. Evaluation of transverse shear stiffness of structural core sandwich plates. *Comp. Struct.* **1997**, *37*, 145–153. [CrossRef]
36. Nordstrand, T. Basic Testing and Strength Design of Corrugated Board and Containers. Ph.D. Thesis, Lund University, Lund, Sweden, 2003.
37. Avilés, F.; Carlsson, L.A.; May-Pat, A. A shear-corrected formulation of the sandwich twist specimen. *Exp. Mech.* **2012**, *52*, 17–23. [CrossRef]
38. Garbowski, T.; Gajewski, T.; Grabski, J.K. Role of transverse shear modulus in the performance of corrugated materials. *Materials* **2020**, *13*, 3791. [CrossRef] [PubMed]
39. Richardson, M.O.W.; Wisheart, M.J. Review of low-velocity impact properties of composite materials. *Compos. Part A Appl. Sci. Manuf.* **1996**, *27*, 1123–1131. [CrossRef]
40. Zangana, S.; Epaarachchi, J.; Ferdous, W.; Leng, J. A novel hybridised composite sandwich core with Glass, Kevlar and Zylon fibres—Investigation under low-velocity impact. *Int. J. Impact Eng.* **2020**, *137*, 103430. [CrossRef]

MDPI
St. Alban-Anlage 66
4052 Basel
Switzerland
Tel. +41 61 683 77 34
Fax +41 61 302 89 18
www.mdpi.com

Materials Editorial Office
E-mail: materials@mdpi.com
www.mdpi.com/journal/materials

www.ingramcontent.com/pod-product-compliance
Lightning Source LLC
LaVergne TN
LVHW070205100526
838202LV00015B/2000